A HISTORY OF
Russian Literature

D. S. MIRSKY

A HISTORY OF

Russian Literature

Comprising

A HISTORY OF RUSSIAN LITERATURE

and

CONTEMPORARY RUSSIAN LITERATURE

Edited and abridged by

FRANCIS J. WHITFIELD

NEW YORK: *ALFRED A. KNOPF*

1 9 5 8

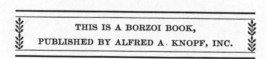

THIS IS A BORZOI BOOK,
PUBLISHED BY ALFRED A. KNOPF, INC.

THIS EDITION REVISED, RESET, AND PRINTED FROM NEW PLATES

REPRINTED SEPTEMBER, 1955
REPRINTED AUGUST, 1958

※》》》※《-《《

Editor's Preface

WHEN I was invited to prepare a new edition of Mirsky's *History of Russian Literature* and *Contemporary Russian Literature*, it was with the understanding that the text must be abridged so that the two books might be published as a single volume of moderate size. To satisfy this requirement I have omitted from the second book an interchapter on the October Revolution, the "paralipomena" on drama and literary criticism, two short sections on minor and "non-literary" novelists of the early years of this century, and those sections at the end of the book where Mirsky had to give very incomplete pictures of contemporary writers on the basis of what they had produced by 1925. Elsewhere I have been forced to gain space by reducing the number of quotations and the amount of biographical material; I have recast sentences and paragraphs, and I have introduced certain typographical changes—all in order to preserve as much as possible of Mirsky's literary criticism. Where I have discovered errors of fact, I have silently corrected them, and I have occasionally added small items of biographical and bibliographical information. I have not consciously altered the tone of the author's literary or political [1] judgments, and I have not attempted to extend or modify his interpretations of authors who continued to write after he had finished his work. At the publisher's request I have added a postscript reviewing the general development of Soviet literature. Since it was not my purpose to shorten Mirsky's text in order to make room for my own, I have kept this section within the closest possible bounds, and the reader is referred to the

[1] It is an interesting fact that Mirsky eventually returned to Russia, where for a time he took active part in Soviet literary life. He has long since disappeared from the scene, and the Soviet Embassy in Washington has been unable to give me any recent information concerning him.

v

bibliography for more extensive works on the subject. The bibliography is restricted to general studies in English and to anthologies of English translations. Our libraries are rather better provided with Russian bibliographical material than they were twenty-five years ago, and it would have been wasteful of precious space to reproduce the detailed lists that Mirsky gives. It is expected that the student will consult the *Handbook of Slavic Studies,* edited by L. I. Strakhovsky, for further information.

In the original prefaces the author expressed his gratitude to the British Museum, the London Library, Sir Bernard Pares, Jane E. Harrison, N. B. Jopson, and, for permission to reprint, to the Hogarth Press and the *Slavonic Review.* My own thanks are due to Professor George V. Bobrinskoy, to my colleagues in the Institute of Slavic Studies and the Slavic Department at the University of California—particularly Dmitry Grigorieff and Lawrence L. Thomas—and to Robert H. Glauber. For their work in the preparation of the manuscript I am indebted to Charles J. Adams, Mrs. Jay Calhoun, Mrs. Reuel N. Denney, and Maren E. Dunkel.

I have preserved Mirsky's dedications of the original two books. This edition is respectfully offered to Dr. Paul E. McGeorge.

F. J. W.

Berkeley
January 1, 1949

A Note on Transliteration

THERE is unfortunately no universally accepted system of trans-
literating the Cyrillic alphabet. The following tables will permit
the reader to compare the system used in this book with that
used by the Library of Congress and most American libraries.
Even specialists have not been able to agree on the matter, but
the third table is representative of systems used by Continental
European (and, increasingly, by American) scholars.

	USED IN THE PRESENT BOOK	USED BY THE LIBRARY OF CONGRESS	USED BY SPECIALISTS
а	a	a	a
б	b	b	b
в	v	v	v
г	g	g	g
д	d	d	d
е	e	e	e
ж	zh	zh	ž
з	z	z	z
и	i	i	i
й	y	ï	j
к	k	k	k
л	l	l	l
м	m	m	m
н	n	n	n
о	o	o	o
п	p	p	p
р	r	r	r
с	s	s	s
т	t	t	t
у	u	u	u
ф	f	f	f
х	kh	kh	ch
ц	ts	t͡s	c
ч	ch	ch	č
ш	sh	sh	š
щ	sch	shch	šč

vii

	USED IN THE PRESENT BOOK	USED BY THE LIBRARY OF CONGRESS	USED BY SPECIALISTS
ъ	omitted	″	″
ы	y	y	y
ь	omitted	′	′
э	e	é	e
ю	yu	i͡u	ju
я	ya	i͡a	ja

Final unaccented "ий" and "ый" have been transliterated as "y," and further exceptions from the general rules have been made for the following combinations:

ае	aye		ье	ie
ое	oye		ьи	yi
уе	uye		ью	iu
юе	yuye		ья	ia
яе	yaye		кс	x

The place of the accent in Russian words and names has been indicated throughout. When "e" falls under the accent, it is, in some words, pronounced (approximately) "yo." Where this occurs I have used the symbol "ë."

As in the first edition, many familiar Christian names are given in their English form (thus Peter for Pëtr, Michael for Mikhaíl, and so on).

Contents

3. *Prose Fiction after Chékhov*   374
    GÓRKY   THE *Znánie* SCHOOL OF FICTION   KÚPRIN
    BÚNIN   ANDRÉYEV   ARTSYBÁSHEV
    SERGÉYEV-TSÉNSKY   FEUILLETONISTS AND HUMORISTS

4. *The New Movements of the Nineties*   407
    THE ÆSTHETIC REVIVAL   MEREZHKÓVSKY   RÓZANOV
    SHESTÓV   OTHER "RELIGIOUS PHILOSOPHERS"
    The Landmarks AND AFTER

5. *The Symbolists*   430
    BÁLMONT   BRYÚSOV   METAPHYSICAL POETS   SOLOGÚB
    ÁNNENSKY   VYACHESLÁV IVÁNOV   VOLÓSHIN   BLOK
    BÉLY   MINOR SYMBOLISTS
    "STYLIZATORS"   KHODASÉVICH   RÉMIZOV

6. *Poetry after 1910*   485
    GUMILËV AND THE POETS' GUILD   ANNA AKHMÁTOVA
    MANDELSTAM   SEVERYÁNIN
    FEMININE POETRY
    "PEASANT POETS" AND IMAGINISTS
    THE RISE OF FUTURISM   MAYAKÓVSKY   PASTERNÁK

    Editor's Postscript   504

    Bibliography   517

    Index   *follows page 518*

Book One: to 1881

❯❯❯-❯❯❯-❯❯❯❯❮❮-❮❮❮-❮❮❮-❮❮❮

T O
Jane Ellen Harrison

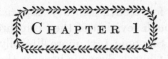

CHAPTER 1

The Literature of Old Russia

(Eleventh to Seventeenth Centuries)

FROM its beginning in the eleventh century to the end of the seventeenth, Russian literature lived entirely out of touch with contemporary developments of Latin Christendom. Like Russian art it was a branch of the Greek trunk. Its germs were brought late in the tenth century from Constantinople, together with the Orthodox faith. But as it was the practice of the Eastern Church to favor the translation of the Scriptures and liturgies into the vernacular, the clergy of the converted nations had no need to learn Greek, and the absence of Greek scholarship in Russia had as its consequence the absence of all acquaintance with secular Greek literature and pre-Christian classical tradition.

THE LITERARY LANGUAGE

The literary language of Old Russia is known as Old Church Slavonic. It is based on some Bulgarian dialect from around Salonika, elevated to the rank of a liturgic and literary language in the ninth century by the apostles of Slavdom, SS. Cyril and Methodius. It was used by the South Slavs and Romanians as well as by the Russians. It was saturated with Greek influence in vocabulary and syntax, and was very different from what we may imagine the spoken language to have been. In the course of time this artificiality increased, and while the spoken languages (in Russia as well as in the Balkans) underwent, between the eleventh and fourteenth centuries, rapid and radical changes, Church Slavonic remained stationary and even tended to approach still closer to its Greek

3

prototype. In the fourteenth century especially, South Slavic
clerks made a thorough revision of the Scriptures and liturgies in
order to make the Slavonic text more literally adequate to the
Greek. This form of Church Slavonic became the literary language
of Muscovite Russia.

Though the only literary, Church Slavonic was not the only
written language. The administrative offices of the Russian princes
and communes evolved a more vernacular form of writing, and
towards the end of the fifteenth century the language of the Muscovite chanceries became the official language of the Empire. It is
expressive and often picturesque, but it was obviously incapable
of displacing Slavonic for literary purposes. As for the literary
language, the vernacular element insinuated itself only to the
degree of the writers' illiteracy or inability to find Slavonic molds
for expressing their stronger feelings. The Russian vernacular was
first consciously used for literary purposes in the third quarter of
the seventeenth century in the writings of a great and original man
of genius—the Archpriest Avvakúm.

LITERARY CONDITIONS

Authorship was not one of the recognized activities of Old Russia.
There were no "writers," but only "bookmen" (*knízhniki*). The
"reading of books" (*knízhnoye pochitánie*) was a respectable and
edifying occupation, but new literary works were written only
when some practical necessity called for them. The humanistic
tradition, so lively in Constantinople, was not transmitted to
Russia, and traces of the acquaintance of Russian clerics with even
the names of the ancients are negligible. Imaginative literature
formed an insignificant part of the reading of the Old Russians.
When he wanted to read, the Russian bookman turned to the holy
books and other collections of edifying matter. There was no need
for fresh literary invention.

As in the mediæval West, the copying of books was regarded
as a work agreeable to God, and was, especially in pre-Muscovite
times, carried on mainly by monks. Printing was introduced into
Russia very late. The first book printed on Russian territory (in
Moscow) appeared in 1564. Even after the establishment of the
printing press the cost of printing was so great and printers so few

that only books of the greatest importance (Bibles, liturgies, statutes, and official instructions) could be printed. Till about the middle of the eighteenth century there were more manuscripts than printed books in circulation. Not until the reign of Catherine II did mediæval conditions cease to prevail in the Russian book market.

Judged exclusively by its literature, Old Russian civilization cannot fail to produce an impression of poverty. But it would be wrong to regard literature as its principal expression. The very nature of this civilization, traditional and ritual, reduced literary originality to very little. The real expression of the creative genius of Old Russia is its architecture and painting, and those who want to gauge its true value must turn to the history of Russian art rather than to that of literature.

TRANSLATED WORKS

The principal and most permanent part of the verbal impressions of the Old Russian came from the liturgies. It was by attending church services rather than by reading that his mind became saturated with the intellectual food of Orthodox Christianity. The liturgies of the Eastern Church are full of sublime and elevated poetry. The Greek hymns were translated into a beautiful prose, devoid of all metrical construction but carefully adapted to the music to which they were sung. The original hymnology of the Orthodox Slavs is negligible.

The Bible was known chiefly through the liturgy. The Psalms were the most familiar of all books to the Old Russian reader, and he usually knew them by heart. Of the other Old Testament books the favorites were those which presented a philosophy of life agreeable to the taste of the Old Russian bookman—Ecclesiastes, Proverbs, the Wisdom of Solomon, and Sirach. As the Psalms were his treasure house of poetry, so were these his mine of wisdom. Copies of the Prophets and of the Apocalypse were usually accompanied by the commentary of the Greek Fathers. The historical books of the Old Testament were little read. Expositions of the Old Testament story known as *Paléya* (Greek παλαιά) were the ordinary sources of the Old Russian's knowledge of Biblical history. The books of the Slavonic Bible were copied out and circulated separately. The first Bible printed in Russia was that of Ostróg (1581), and the first complete edition to appear in Moscow was that of 1663. The final "Authorized Version" of the Russian-Slavonic Bible appeared almost a century later, in 1751.

Next to the liturgies and the Bible, the Fathers were the most authoritative books. The most widely read was St. Chrysostom, the great moral teacher and the great examplar of eloquence. The highest theological authority was St. John Damascene. The lives of saints were extensively read. Some were the works of reputed and highly authoritative authors, and these were copied with particular care and exactitude. One of these was the story of Barlaam and Josaphat, ascribed to St. John Damascene. This Byzantine version of the life of the Buddha deeply impressed itself on the Russian religious mind. The form in which saints' lives were most frequently read was that of calendars or menologia (*minéi*) where the lives of the several saints were arranged under the dates of their respective feasts. Authoritative and official *minéi* were compiled in the sixteenth century by Macarius, Metropolitan of Moscow, and under Peter the Great by St. Demetrius, Metropolitan of Rostóv. But by the side of these official collections there were others of a more popular and arbitrary composition which were more widely read. Such, above all, was the *Prologue*, a vast collection of the most varied religious readings for every day. It had numerous redactions and contained lives of saints, pious anecdotes, and readings from the Fathers. Its contents varied, and, by the side of a prevailing majority of translations from the Greek, many of its entries were of native origin. Although highly esteemed, it never received the official sanction of the Church. Some of the matter included in it no doubt verges on the apocryphal. After the great schism of the seventeenth century it began to be looked at askance by the Church, but it remained in favor with the Old Believers and has come down in numerous manuscripts. In recent times the *Prologue* has attracted considerable literary attention, and modern writers, like Tolstóy, Leskóv, and Rémizov, have retold many of its stories.

The *Prologue* is halfway between canonical and apocryphal literature, and so is the *Paléya*, which includes much that is not found in the Bible. Numerous apocrypha, many of early Christian origin, formed a vast mass of Old Russian literature. Those which were not at variance with Orthodoxy were countenanced by the

Church and, at times of low learning, hardly distinguished from canonical books. The most popular were those dealing with the future life. One of them, the legend of the Virgin's visit to hell, particularly impressed itself on the Russian imagination: moved by the suffering of the damned, she implores God to be allowed to share it, and finally obtains from Him that all the damned be henceforth given each year a respite from their torments, from Maundy Thursday to Whitsunday.

The books whence the Old Russians drew their secular scientific information were not the residue of the scientific achievement of the ancients preserved by the Byzantines. The sounder part of the Old Russians' ideas on nature came from the Fathers that had written on the creation. The secular books they had were those current among the lower cultural strata of Byzantine Greece—such as the cosmography of Cosmas Indicopleustes and the *Physiologus*.

Of Byzantine historians, again, the more classical and "highbrow," as for instance Procopius, remained unknown, and Russian bookmen drew their historical information from the more "popular" chronicles, such as those of John Malalas and George Hamartolos. These chronicles presented the history of the world, beginning with the story of the Old and New Testaments, followed by the fall of Jerusalem and the persecutions of the primitive Church; they enumerated the early Cæsars and then gave a more or less detailed history of the Byzantine emperors.

The only author known in Old Russia that may be termed a classic was Josephus. Besides epitomes of his works in various compilations, there exists a very early Russian-Slavonic version of the *De Bello Judaico*, apparently made in Russia about 1100. For its intelligent freedom in following the text it is unique among Slavonic translations. It seems to have been very popular among the higher intellectuals of the twelfth century, and traces of the influence of its diction are evident in *The Campaign of Ígor*. But the Russian Josephus is interesting not only for its important part in Russian literature. It contains six passages on Christ and Pilate that are not found in extant Greek manuscripts, and which appear to be early Christian interpolations (first and second centuries). Other passages, expressive of strongly anti-Roman feeling, have even been explained as going back to an original version that Josephus afterwards changed to avoid offending his patrons.

In Byzantine and mediæval literature in general it is not easy to distinguish history from fiction. It is the fashion today, for instance, to include the mediæval stories of Troy and Alexander in the department of fiction, but the Old Russian scribe inserted them in his historical compilations. Neither story received any romantic development on Russian soil, for the subject of romantic love was alien to the Old Russians. The same is even more evident in the Russian prose version of the Byzantine epic *Digenis Akritas*. The original contains an appreciable element of romance, but this is entirely eliminated in the Russian version. Another kind of imported fiction was stories of wisdom, consisting of dialogues, parables, and apologues, or turning on the solution of riddles. Most of these stories were ultimately of Indian or Arabic origin, but all came to Russia via Greece.

THE KIEVAN PERIOD

From the tenth century to the invasion of the Tatars in the middle of the thirteenth, the political and cultural center of Russia was Kíev. The civilization of the period was dominated by two classes: the urban clergy and the military aristocracy. The former was largely recruited from the latter. The clergy, especially the higher monastic clergy, were the principal depositories of culture, and the art and literature of the time are mainly religious. The military class, headed by a numerous and warlike race of princes, submitted to the authority of the Church and were Christians in their moral ideals, but they retained heathen traditions and loved war, the chase, and the pleasures of the table above all things. They produced the only real literary masterpiece of the period, the prose poem of *The Campaign of Ígor*.

The most strictly Byzantine department of Kievan literature is the writings of the higher clergy. As early as between 1040 and 1050 a piece of Russian oratory was produced that is quite comparable to the highest rhetorical achievement of contemporary Greece. This is the *Oration of Law and Grace*, ascribed to Ilarion, Metropolitan of Kíev, the first Russian to occupy that seat. It is a piece of subtle theological eloquence on the opposition of the New and the Old Testament, followed by an elaborate panegyric upon St. Vladímir. The same kind of ornate and subtle rhetoric was cultivated in the second half of the twelfth century by Cyril,

Bishop of Túrov. Both Ilarion and Cyril are fully versed in the art of balancing their phrase and constructing their paragraph, and are at home in the whole Byzantine arsenal of trope, simile, and allusion. Their sermons could find evidently but a small public, and the common run of Kievan preachers used a far simpler style. Such, for instance, are the extant sermons of St. Theodosius, Abbot of the Crypt Monastery, one of the founders of Russian monasticism.

The Crypt (*Pechérsky*) Monastery in Kíev, founded in the middle of the eleventh century, was for two centuries the nursery garden of Russian abbots and bishops, and the center of ecclesiastical learning. Néstor (*c.* 1080), a monk of this monastery, was the first notable Russian hagiologist. He wrote the lives of the martyred princes Borís and Gleb and of St. Theodosius. The latter, especially in the part concerning the holy abbot's early years, gives a more intimate and familiar idea of the everyday life of Kievan Russia than any other literary work of the time. Towards the end of the present period Simon, Bishop of Vladímir (d. 1226), wrote down for the edification of the monk Polycarp the lives of some of the Crypt saints. These formed the nucleus of the *Book of the Crypt Fathers* (*Pechérsky paterík*), which, extensively added to in following centuries, became one of the most popular hagiographical writings in the language.

Another Russian monk who has left a name in the history of literature is the Abbot Daniel, who in 1106–8 went to the Holy Land and described his journey in a famous *Pilgrimage*. It is written in a simple, matter-of-fact, but by no means dry or tedious, style and is remarkable for its exact and reliable account of the Holy Land under the first Frankish king. It is also interesting for the patriotic feeling that animates it: in every holy place he visited, Daniel never omitted to pray for the Russian princes and all the land of Russia.

Ecclesiastical learning was not confined to the clerics, and two remarkable works by laymen are full of reflections of clerical knowledge. One of these is the *Testament* of Vladímir Monomákh (Great Prince of Kíev in 1113–25), the most popular and universally respected prince of the period. Written shortly before his death, it tells of his active life, full of wars against the nomads and punitive expeditions against seditious princes, of conferences, of distant voyages, and of big-game hunting. Vladímir's tone is full of dignity and the consciousness of his own achievement, but at the same time free from all pride or vanity. It is humble in a truly Christian sense. He has been called a "Slavonic Marcus Aurelius," but there is nothing of the Roman Emperor's stoical sadness in the Russian King, whose main characteristics are a simple piety, an honest sense of duty, and lucid common sense.

Very different is the other secular sermon that has come down to us—*The Supplication of Daniel the Exile.* Written probably early in the thirteenth century in the province of Súzdal, it takes the form of a petition from the disinherited son of a good serving-family to his prince that he may accept him into his service. It is primarily a show-off of reading and consists mainly of quotations from the gnomic books of the Bible, oriental wisdom tales, and other sources, including popular proverbs, all welded together with elaborate rhetoric. *The Supplication* was copied and interpolated, and finally became a sort of commonplace book, so that its original form of a petition became entirely obliterated. It is interesting for the light it throws on the taste of the average literate Old Russian and on the kind of wisdom he appreciated.

THE CHRONICLES

The largest and (except for *The Campaign of Ígor*) the most valu-able, original, and interesting monument of Kievan literature is the Chronicles or Annals (*Létopisi*). Russian annal writing began about the same time as Russian literature, and its uninterrupted tradition was continued far into the seventeenth, in the case of Siberia, even into the eighteenth, century. The Annals were the work partly of monks, partly of lay bookmen, and, in Muscovite times, of official scribes. Like by far the greater part of Old Russian literature, they are anonymous and have come down to us not in their original and individual forms, but as parts of large codices, varying greatly from manuscript to manuscript. The Annals of the Kievan period are contained chiefly in two compilations, which in one form or another appear at the head of most later codices. These are the so-called Primitive Chronicle (*Nachálnaya létopis*), cov-ering the period from "the beginning of Russia" to 1110, and the so-called Kievan Chronicle, continuing the history to 1200. The former is ascribed in certain late manuscripts to St. Néstor, the

hagiographer previously mentioned. Another name connected with
it is that of Sylvester, Abbot of St. Michael's in Kíev, who prepared a copy of it in 1116. Whether he merely copied or whether
his work was rather that of an editor we do not know, and, in
general, the problems of authorship and sources are still matters
of the widest conjecture.

The Primitive Chronicle begins with a genealogy of the Slavs
"from the generation of Japheth." This is followed by an account
of the early history of the Slavs, of their divisions and manners,
which is strangely "nineteenth century" in its Panslavist sentiment
and its ethnographical interest. Then follows the well-known story
of the "invitation of the Varangians" to Nóvgorod, which is
curiously similar to that of Hengist and Horsa. The account of
events of the later ninth and of the tenth centuries is based on a
fairly solid chronological skeleton, but the strictly annalistic
entries are very few. They are enlivened by numerous vivid and
spirited traditional tales, which form the chief attraction of this
part of the Chronicle. The earliest is entered under 882, and they
continue as far as the early years of Yaroslár (1019–54). They are
obviously founded on oral tradition, but there is no ground to
believe that this tradition was poetical. They are just anecdotes,
of the same kind as the anecdotes that are the chief charm of
Herodotus. One of the Russian annalist's anecdotes is even identical with one of the tales of the father of history (the story of the
siege of Bélgorod by the Pechenégs and that of the siege of Miletos
by the Lydians). Another, the tale of how Olég met death from his
favorite horse, is a version of a story found in the Old Norse
Qrvar-Odd Saga (Púshkin later made it the subject of a famous
ballad). Besides such stories the early Chronicle contains more
connected and generalized passages, such as the account of the
wars of the great adventurer Prince Svyatosláv, part of which is
closely paraphrased by Gibbon in *The Decline and Fall*. The account
of Vladímir's reign includes the remarkable story of how that
prince examined the various religions before deciding to adopt
Greek Christianity. Rejecting Islam because "it is the Russians'
joy to drink; we cannot do without it," he finally chose Orthodoxy,
under the impression of the account given him by his envoys of
the beauty and splendor of the service at St. Sophia in Constantinople, a motive that throws an important light on the Old Russian's essentially ritualistic and æsthetic conception of his religion.

The part of the Chronicle subsequent to *c.* 1040 appears to have been mainly the work of a monk of the Crypt Monastery, perhaps Néstor. The chronicler writes in a deeply religious spirit and regards all events as the direct action of Providence. He takes a keen interest in portents and omens, and regards all the woes of Russia as a punishment for the wicked conduct of the princes: the second half of the eleventh century was one incessant civil war between the sons and grandsons of Yarosláv. The annalist exhorts the princes to forget their feuds and turn their attention to the defense of the steppe marches against the steadily advancing nomads. He is particularly partial to Vladímir Monomákh, who alone of all Russian princes answered to his ideal of a patriotic prince. Inserted in this part of the Chronicle, under the year 1097, is a narrative of exceptional merit, the work apparently of a cleric named Vasíly. It is the story of the blinding of Vasílko, Prince of Terebóvl (in Galicia), by his cousin and neighbor David of Volynia, and of the events that followed it. The story is told in greater detail than the rest of the Chronicle and is a masterpiece of simple, direct narrative. For its straightforward and comprehensively human manner it may almost be compared with the stories of the book of Genesis.

The Kievan Chronicle of the twelfth century is, like its predecessor, a composite document. Most valuable is its account of the years 1146–54, dealing with the struggle of Prince Izyasláv II (grandson of Monomákh) for the throne of Kíev. It is evidently by a soldier, one of Prince Izyasláv's "companions," and is full of the spirit of military prowess. The ambition of the princes and their desire to win honor in the field are the main motive of their actions. The narrative is lucid, leisurely, detailed, straightforward; the style ample and free from rhetorical devices. It is altogether the masterpiece of Kievan historical literature and can rank with the best examples of mediæval history.

After the decline of Kíev the Annals were continued both in the north and in the southwest, in the Kingdom of Galicia, which flourished in the second half of the thirteenth century and which has an honorable place in literary history owing to its single extant production—the so-called Volynian Chronicle. This Chronicle is different from the others in that its form is not a succession of isolated entries under every year, but a connected account of causes and effects. It is pretty difficult reading and not infrequently obscure. The characters speak almost invariably in proverbs and aphorisms; the literary influence of the Old Testament (Kings and Isaiah) is clearly apparent; the descriptions are full of vivid and hyperbolic imagery. Though not devoid of considerable ecclesiastical culture, the spirit of the story is purely secular and military. The story is carried on till 1290. After that date the southwest of Russia becomes silent for several centuries.

THE CAMPAIGN OF ÍGOR AND ITS FAMILY

The Word of the Campaign of Ígor (*Slóvo o pŭlku Igorevĕ*) was discovered in 1795 by an enlightened nobleman, Count A. I. Músin-Púshkin, in a (sixteenth-century?) manuscript codex that contained only secular matter, including a version of *Digenis Akritas*. The manuscript was destroyed in the fire of Moscow in 1812, so that the *editio princeps* (1800) and a copy made for Catherine II are now our only authority for the text. They were made at a time when Russian palæography was in its youth, and contain numerous corrupt passages, which we do not know whether to attribute to the destroyed manuscript or to its decipherers.

The *Slóvo* was discovered at a time when the Ossianic question occupied all minds. The admirers of the poem immediately compared it to Ossian, while its detractors affirmed that it was as much a forgery as "Ossian" himself. Skepticism, however, was soon silenced, chiefly by the discovery of a verbatim quotation from the *Slóvo* in a dated manuscript of 1307, and of an early fifteenth-century prose poem on the battle of Kulikóvo, which was nothing but a rather unintelligent paraphrase of *The Campaign of Ígor*.[1]

From the first the work stood out as a startlingly isolated phenomenon, unrelated to anything of its age. One quite obvious thing was that it had been composed very soon after the events described, probably within the same year, and that its account of the campaign was substantially historical, for it squared most exactly with the account in the Kievan Chronicle, without there being any trace of verbal coincidence between the two documents. The problem of the *Slóvo* cannot yet be regarded as finally settled,

---

[1] Professor André Mazon, of the Collège de France, has recently revived the question of the *Slóvo's* authenticity, but his doubts are not generally shared.—Ed.

and there is still considerable variety of opinion on many points, but the available internal and external evidence seems to be best interpreted in the following way.

There existed in Kievan times a secular oral poetry, preserved by singers belonging to the upper military class of the prince's companions and similar to, but less professional than, the Norse scalds. This poetry flourished in the eleventh century; some of the poems were still remembered in the end of the twelfth. They were associated with the name of a great singer, Bayán, whose songs are quoted by the author of the *Slóvo*. But it is not clear that at the time of the composition of the *Slóvo* this oral poetry was still alive. *The Campaign of Ígor* itself is a purely literary work, *written*, and not sung. The author, though anonymous, has a powerful individuality. He was a layman, probably the companion of some prince. He was steeped in books and in oral tradition. The great originality of his work was that he used the methods of oral poetry in a work of written literature. There is no reason to believe that he had had any literary predecessors in this manner of writing, but he has roots in the literary tradition. The similarity of some turns of phrases and expressions with the Russian Josephus (*v. supra*) is very striking, and there are more distant associations with the style of the ecclesiastical orators and that of the Annals. The rhythmic structure of the poem is not that of verse. The rhythm of prose is different in *kind* from the rhythm of verse, for it lacks the essential element of the latter—*the line*. It must be remembered that the parts of the Slavonic liturgy that are sung are nevertheless couched in prose, and that consequently even if *The Campaign of Ígor* was actually a song (which is very unlikely) it need not necessarily have been in verse. Analysis reveals that the *Slóvo* possesses a very real and efficient rhythm, but a rhythm far more complex than that of any metrical pattern. No rhythmical prose I know of in any language can so much as approach it for infinitely varied flexibility.

It is not only the nature of its rhythmical prose that makes *The Campaign of Ígor* unique. It is altogether difficult to classify. Neither a lyric, nor an epic, nor a piece of political oratory, it is all these blended into one. Its skeleton is narrative. It relates the story of the unfortunate campaign of Prince Ígor against the Pólovtsy, his initial success, his subsequent defeat, and his captivity. This constitutes what may be regarded as the first part of the poem. This is followed by a long lyrical or oratorical digression. The Great Prince of Kíev is described dreaming a dream of ill omen, symbolic of Ígor's disaster. Then the poet apostrophizes, one after the other, the several Great Princes of the land of Russia, exhorting them to save Ígor. Then Ígor's wife is introduced, lamenting on the walls of her town of Putívl—this passage forming one of the most beautiful summits of the poem. After a rapid and abrupt transition the third part begins—the account of Ígor's escape from captivity. Like that of his advance and disaster it closely agrees in fact with, but differs strikingly in style from, the Chronicle account.

The spirit of the *Slóvo* is a blend of the warrior spirit of the military aristocracy as reflected in the Chronicle of 1146–54, with a wider patriotic outlook that is more akin to that of Monomákh and of the patriotic clerics, and which regards self-sacrifice for Russia as the noblest of virtues. It is also distinctly secular in spirit. Christianity appears only incidentally and rather as an element of contemporary life than as part of the poet's inner world. On the other hand, reminiscences of an older nature worship are part of the most intimate texture of the poem.

The style of the poem is the reverse of the primitive and barbaric. It is curiously, disconcertingly modern, all suggestion and allusion, full of splendid imagery, subtly symbolic and complex. Professor Hrushéwsky has rightly remarked that only now, after a prolonged education in the school of modern poetry, are we really able to feel and understand the poetical methods of the *Slóvo*. It is far too modern for anyone to have been able to forge it in 1795.

Nature symbolism and nature parallelism play a large part in the poem. The movements of men have their "correspondences" in the movements of the "vegetable universe." This feature has been adduced as proof of the kinship of the *Slóvo* to "popular poetry." A vague kinship there certainly may be, but no similarity of detail with later Great Russian or Ukrainian folk song. Besides, a nature parallelism of a very similar kind was a time-honored form of expression in Byzantine sacred oratory.

The Campaign of Ígor, alone of all Old Russian literature, has become a national classic, familiar to every educated Russian and often known by heart by lovers of poetry. The quality of its poetry is entirely different from the quality of the poetry of the

Classical Age of Púshkin, but it cannot be regarded as inferior. If Púshkin is Russia's greatest classical poet, the author of the *Slóvo* is the greatest master of ornate, romantic, and symbolic poetry. His work is a continuous succession of purple patches, the least of which has no counterpart in modern Russian poetry.

The language of the *Slóvo* is, of course, antiquated and unintelligible to an absolutely uncultured Russian. It is, with minor peculiarities, the usual Russo-Slavonic literary language of the twelfth century. But the modern Russian reader needs very little preparation to be able to understand it, especially if he has read his Slavonic Bible and understands his Slavonic prayers (achievements which, unfortunately, are becoming ever rarer).

However unique its quality, *The Campaign of Ígor* is not so absolutely isolated as it appeared to be at first sight. I have already alluded to some of its ancestry and direct progeny. Traces have come down to us of other fragments, not directly dependent on it but belonging, broadly speaking, to the same school. One is a small fragment in honor of Prince Román of Volynia (d. 1205) inserted in the Volynian Chronicle. Another, a fragment of little over two hundred words inscribed *Oration (Slóvo) on the Ruin of the Land of Russia,* is the beginning of what was evidently a long and elaborate lament on the destruction of Russian power by the Tatars.

More important, and different from the rest in its subject matter, is *The Appeal (Slóvo) of Adam to Lazarus in Hell.* No Greek source of it has been found; and though a priori it is dangerous to admit the absolute originality of its actual matter, there can be no doubt as to the originality of its actual form. Its date is unknown. It has certain affinities of style with *The Campaign of Ígor* and other Kievan writings of the same family. *The Appeal of Adam* is also a prose poem, but its rhythm seems to be less akin to that of the Kievan orators than to the prophetic books of the Slavonic Old Testament. The theme of the poem is Adam's appeal to Lazarus, about to leave hell on his resurrection, on behalf of all the righteous men of the Old Testament, and the oration ends with the descent into hell and the release of the righteous patriarchs. But there is in the questions of Adam a "Jobean" spirit that is rare in Old Russian writings. The powerful eloquence of the poem has deeply influenced the style of the prose poems of Rémizov, a writer saturated with the form and spirit of the Old Russian apocrypha.

BETWEEN KÍEV AND MOSCOW

In 1238–40 the Tatars, as the Mongols are always called in Russian sources, overran practically the whole of Russia, subjected all its eastern part, and destroyed Kíev. Except for the short period during which the Kievan tradition was continued in the Kingdom of Galicia, Russian civilization survived only in the north and east. Its centers there became the great merchant city of Nóvgorod and the principalities of the upper Volga, one of which, Moscow, ultimately succeeded in unifying the nation.

If we consider nothing but its literature, the period that extends from the Tatar invasion to the unification of Russia by Iván III of Moscow may be called a Dark Age. Its literature is either a more or less impoverished reminiscence of Kievan traditions or an unoriginal imitation of South Slavonic models. But here more than ever it is necessary to bear in mind that literature does not give the true measure of Old Russian culture. The fourteenth and fifteenth centuries, the Dark Age of literature, were at the same time the Golden Age of Russian religious painting.

Nowhere is the concretely æsthetic and non-intellectual character of Old Russian civilization so obviously apparent as in Nóvgorod. That wealthy city, for three hundred years the source of Europe's supply of furs and other northern commodities, was ruled by an art-loving merchant aristocracy that succeeded in making it something like a Russian Venice. But like Venice, though it produced great art, Nóvgorod has no literature to speak of. The Nóvgorod Chronicles, though admirable for their freedom from irrelevant talk and their strict matter-of-factness, are not literature. The civilization of Nóvgorod is perhaps the most characteristic expression of Old Russia, and the fact that it produced no literature is certainly significant.

The country ruled by the princely house of Súzdal (later the provinces of Moscow, Vladímir, Kostromá, Yaroslav, and Tver and the district of the White Lake), though culturally and economically inferior to Nóvgorod, produced more interesting liter-

ature. The chronicles and the "military narratives" connected
with the Tatar invasion are of considerable interest. The *Life of
St. Alexander* (d. 1263), Russia's champion against the Latin West,
is a particularly remarkable "military narrative" and has left a
lasting trace on the national memory.

Still more interesting are the "military narratives" relating to
the victory of Kulikóvo (1380). These are the *Zadónschina* ("Trans-
Doniad") written in the early fifteenth century by the priest
Sophonia of Ryazán, and *The Legend of the Rout of Mamáy* (the
vizier who commanded the Tatars), extant in several later redactions. The former is artistically the finer production. Its style is
rhetorically and poetically colored, but its construction is strictly
narrative. Its interest, apart from the importance of its subject,
lies in the author's genuine gift of poetical atmosphere and his
discrete and skillful use of reminiscences of *The Campaign of Ígor*.

Towards the end of the present period a new style of writing
was imported by the numerous Serbian and Bulgarian clerics who
came to Russia after the conquest of their countries by the Turks.
Outstanding among these ecclesiastics was Cyprian, Metropolitan
of Moscow (d. 1406). The first Russian bookman to use the new
style was Epiphanius the Wise, a monk of the Trinity Monastery
and a disciple of St. Sergius. The new style found its chief expression in hagiography. Its main characteristic was a disregard for
concrete detail and a conventionalized treatment of the subject.
The individual was so reduced to the typical that the writings of
the school have practically no value as historical evidence. In
Epiphanius's *Life of St. Sergius* this stage is not yet quite reached—
he had a too intimate knowledge of his master to let the saint's
personality be lost in a conventional pattern. But his other work,
the *Life of St. Stephen of Permia*, became the type of such writings
for the following centuries. Nor was the influence of the new style
limited to hagiography. Its conventional and impersonal rhetoric
was adopted by all writers with any literary pretension. The very
language was changed under South Slavonic influence, and a
stricter and more pedantic standard Church Slavonic replaced the
strongly vernacularized language of the thirteenth and fourteenth
centuries.

Somewhat off the main track, and probably not intended as
literature, is the *Journey beyond the Three Seas*, by Afanásy
Nikítin, a merchant of the city of Tver. It is the account of his

commercial travels and life in India in 1466–72. It is interesting
not only as an account of India a quarter of a century before the
discovery of the sea route, but also as a revelatory reflection of the
mental experience of an average Russian in unfamiliar surroundings.

THE MUSCOVITE PERIOD

Within less than a generation of the taking of Constantinople by
the Turks the Prince of Moscow became the effective monarch of
all Great Russia and threw off the last remnants of Tatar supremacy (1480). This succession of events produced a revolution in the
state of the Orthodox world, which was immediately taken into
account by the Muscovites and became the basis of their political
philosophy. Moscow became the third Rome, the sole depository
of all imperial power and the only receptacle of unsullied Orthodoxy. The marriage of Iván III to a Palæologue princess and his
assumption of the title "Autocrat" transformed the Prince of
Moscow, who had been little more than a *primus inter pares* among
other princes, into the sole successor of the Cæsars. The official
crowning and assumption of the title of "Tsar" (Cæsar) was the
work of Iván III's grandson and namesake of "Terrible" reputation.

The first century or so after the accession of the first Autocrat
(1462) was marked by violent political and religious conflicts. They
gave rise to an interesting polemical literature, which, however,
belongs to the domain of the general rather than of the literary
historian. The conflict was at first chiefly between the party of
bishops and abbots, who insisted on the worldly claims of the
Church and on taking an active part in secular government, and
the party of the "Hermits from beyond the Volga," whose headquarters were the monastery of St. Cyril on the White Lake (east
of St. Petersburg) and who favored a more mystical and ascetic
conception of the Church. The chief man of the clerical party was
Joseph, Abbot of Volokolámsk, a vigorous pamphleteer who wrote
in a correct Slavonic full of expletives. The leader of the Hermits
was Blessed Nil Sórsky, a disciple of Mount Athos and the most
remarkable mystical and ascetic writer of Old Russia. The Hermits
were supported by part of the aristocracy, who regarded the

bishops and abbots as usurpers of their political rights and desired to limit the growing power of the Tsar.

By the middle of the sixteenth century the religious controversy was over, the clerical party being victorious on all points. But the political controversy between the partisans of autocracy and the oligarchs was continued into the reign of Iván the Terrible (b. 1530, crowned Tsar 1547, d. 1584). Iván was no doubt a cruel tyrant, but he was a pamphleteer of genius. His epistles are the masterpieces of Old Russian (perhaps all Russian) political journalism. They may be too full of texts from the Scriptures and the Fathers, and their Slavonic is not always correct. But they are full of cruel irony, expressed in pointedly forcible terms. The shameless bully and the great polemist are seen together in a flash when he taunts the runaway Kúrbsky by the question: "If you are so sure of your righteousness, why did you run away and not prefer martyrdom at my hands?" Such strokes were well calculated to drive his correspondent into a rage. The part of the cruel tyrant elaborately upbraiding an escaped victim while he continues torturing those in his reach may be detestable, but Iván plays it with truly Shaksperian breadth of imagination. Besides his letters to Kúrbsky he wrote other satirical invectives to men in his power. The best is the letter to the Abbot of St. Cyril's Monastery where he pours out all the poison of his grim irony on the unascetic life of the boyars, shorn monks, and those exiled by his order. His picture of their luxurious life in the citadel of asceticism is a masterpiece of trenchant sarcasm.

Iván's principal opponent, Prince Andréy Mikháylovich Kúrbsky (c. 1528–83), was one of the most cultured and enlightened men in Muscovy. He played a prominent part in the administration and distinguished himself as a soldier at the siege of Kazán and in the Livonian war. In 1564, during the war with Lithuania, when Iván had instituted his reign of terror, Kúrbsky, fearing responsibility for a reverse of his army, deserted to the enemy. From Lithuania he wrote his famous epistles to the Tsar and a *History* of his reign. The latter work is pragmatic, not annalistic, and shows him a man of keen and constructive intellect. He deliberately exaggerates the crimes of his archenemy and is not to be trusted as impartial evidence. His style is strongly infused with West Russian, Polish, and Latin influences. It does not reveal any original literary temperament. The same with his epistles: for all their sincere violence, just indignation, and forcible argument, as literature they are inferior to those of his opponent.

The fixation of the Muscovite mentality took place in the middle of the sixteenth century. About that time was undertaken and accomplished a series of compilations that together form a sort of encyclopædia of Muscovite culture. These works cannot all be regarded as falling within the cognizance of literary history. Thus the *Stogláv* (*Book of a Hundred Chapters*), which contains the decisions on dogmatic, ritual, administrative, and disciplinary subjects of a Provincial Council of the Russian Church held in Moscow in 1551, belongs to canon law rather than to literature. Nor has the *Domostróy* (*House-Orderer*), edited by the priest Sylvester (d. 1566) substantially greater claims to be regarded as literature: it is a didactic work setting down in literary Slavonic, but without literary prentensions, the principles by which the head of the house is to rule his family.

A more literary work is the great *Menologion* or *Saints' Calendar* (*Chetyí-Minéi*) compiled by Macarius, Metropolitan of Moscow (d. 1563). It remained the official calendar of the Russian Church until the reign of Peter the Great. Macarius also gave its final form to another vast work of codification: *The Book of Degrees* (i.e., of generations, *Stepénnaya kníga*), so called because the Russian princes and tsars were grouped in the order of their generations. The collection had been started by Cyprian, the fourteenth-century Serbian Metropolitan of Moscow, but was completed only about 1563. In substance *The Book of Degrees* was a compilation from the Russian Annals, but these were recast so as to suit the literary taste and the historical philosophy of sixteenth-century Muscovy. The Annals, officially conducted throughout this period by Muscovite scribes, also reflect the all-pervading taste for rhetoric, and the political philosophy of the time.

MUSCOVITE HISTORIES

Besides these compilations and official Annals, there was no lack of historical literature in Muscovite times. Prince Kúrbsky's *History* stands somewhat apart, from the fact of having absorbed Western influences. But there was a local tradition of historical narratives of isolated, chiefly military events, with a style of their

own that goes back to the *Rout of Mamáy* and the Russian Josephus, and is thus a collateral relative of *The Campaign of Ígor*.
An early example is the *Story of the Taking of Pskov* (1510) by the
Muscovites, one of the most beautiful "short histories" of Old
Russia. The history of the Muscovites' leisurely perseverance is
told with admirable simplicity and art. An atmosphere of descending doom pervades the whole narrative: all is useless, and whatever
the Pskovites can do, the Muscovite cat will take its time and eat
the mouse when and how it pleases.

The series of events that stimulated the most intense his-
toriographical activity was the great political crisis of the early
seventeenth century (1604–13) known in Russian historical tradition as the Time of Troubles. Three works especially stand out:
that attributed to Prince Iván Katyrëv of Rostóv and those by
Avraámy Pálitsyn, Bursar of the Trinity Monastery, and by the
scribe Iván Timoféyev. Katyrëv's narrative is the most distinctly
literary of the three: it is in the traditional style of the "military
story," with very little regard for concrete details, with numerous
recurrent stock passages, at times attaining to something like
poetry. Pálitsyn's work is the most perfectly written. It is a piece
of powerful and skillful rhetoric, inspired with a definite purpose
and displaying great ability in the effective arrangement of its
climaxes. The passages describing the horrors of civil war and
foreign invasion are particularly memorable. Pálitsyn's work was
the most popular of the whole family, and up to recent times his
interpretation of the facts dominated Russian literary and historical tradition. Timoféyev's work is the greatest curio in all Muscovite literature. His amazingly quaint and elaborate style is the
reductio ad absurdum of Muscovite rhetoric. On no account will he
call a spade a spade. The rich become in his hands "those who have
large receptacles." A river is "the element of watery nature." His
grammar is complicated and contorted, and his meaning as a rule
wonderfully obscure. But he is also the shrewdest and most intelligent of all contemporary historians. His story is a real story
with a beginning and an end. Timoféyev has been given high
praise as a chronicler and as a trustworthy witness by the greatest
of our modern historians, Professor Platónov, who has singled him
out as a particular favorite.

A last fruit of the Old Russian "military story" is the *Story
of the Defense of Azóv* by the Don Cossacks against the Turks in

1641. It is really the official report of the Cossacks to the Tsar, but it is written as a story with definite literary aims, and as such became widely popular. It is a sort of epitome of all the traditions of Old Russian war narrative, with echoes of the Russian Josephus and all its progeny, of the *Rout of Mamáy*, of the *Tale of Troy*—and, on the other hand, of more modern forms of folklore, as represented now by the so-called *bylíny* and robber songs. It is full of the poetry of war and is one of the most stimulating of Old Russian writings.

The majority of saints' lives written during the Muscovite period are in the style introduced by the Serbs and by Epiphanius, and have no individual interest. An exception is the *Life of St. Juliánia Lazarévsky*, by her son Kalistrát Osóryin. St. Juliánia herself is an exception, being the only Russian female saint who was neither a nun nor a princess but merely a virtuous matron. The fact of a son's writing his mother's life is also unique. The *Life* is full of concrete detail and inspired by an intense feeling of Christian charity. It is one of the most attractive evocations of Old Russian life in the whole of literature.

BEGINNINGS OF FICTION

It is very difficult to draw a line between hagiography and biography, and fiction. There is a whole intermediate region that modern historians usually include in fiction but that the contemporary reader did not distinguish from hagiography. Such are the numerous legends standing in somewhat the same relation to the lives of saints as the Apocrypha stand to the Bible. Some were included in Macarius's compilation, and the unofficial Prologues contain even more. They were of course regarded primarily as books of edification, but the element of marvel and narrative interest is far more prominent than in the approved type of saint's life. Some have a distinctly fairy-tale appearance, as for instance the charming *Legend of Prince Peter of Múrom and of the Maiden Fevrónia*, with its battle against the dragon, and the wise maiden guessing the Prince's riddles.

A further step towards fiction is found in a remarkable seventeenth-century work, *The Story of Sávva Grúdtsyn*. It is in literary Church Slavonic and has all the appearance of a story of pure fact, with dates and place names in abundance, but it is probably a work of fiction written for purposes of edification. Sávva Grúdtsyn is a kind of Russian Dr. Faustus, who sells his soul to the Devil in return, not for knowledge, but for power and pleasure. The Devil serves him well, but finally Savva repents and saves his soul in a monastery.

Along with these first essays in edifying narrative other types of fiction began to appear. It is probable that Russian narrative folk poetry as we now know it came into existence in the middle or second half of the sixteenth century. It is certain that its first written traces appear in the early seventeenth century, when it begins to exercise an appreciable influence on written literature. We have seen its influence in the *Siege of Azóv*. It is still more unmistakable in the story of *Woe-Misfortune* (*Góre-Zloschástie*), which is an isolated instance of the use of actual folk-song *meter* in a literary work. Like *Sávva Grúdtsyn* it is a work of edification, in a style not derived from ecclesiastical Muscovite literature, but from devotional folk poetry. "Góre-Zloschástie" is a man's ill luck, personified as a kind of guardian devil who accompanies his man from cradle to grave. He leads a fine young man of respectable and wealthy family from his father's house into the wide world, brings him to tavern and highroad and thence well-nigh to the gallows. But the young man finally escapes and ends his days in a monastery, the never-failing refuge of the Russian sinner. The figure of Góre is a powerfully poetical symbol, and the whole work bears evidence of being the work of a talented and original poet. Like all Old Russian fiction it is anonymous and cannot be exactly dated. It seems to belong to the middle of the seventeenth century.

Folk-song influence is again apparent in two romances introduced into Russia from abroad by the first half of the seventeenth century—*Bová Korolévich* and *Eruslán Lázarevich*. *Bová* is of French origin, a descendant of the Carolingian romance *Bueves d'Anston* (English: *Bevis of Hampton*). It came to Russia by way of a North Italian *Bovo d'Antona* and thence through Bohemia and White Russia. In Russia it was completely assimilated and thoroughly Russianized. It is amusing to see how the French romance has been transformed into a story of purely fairy-tale adventure, with all the chivalrous and courtly element eliminated. *Bová* and *Eruslán* (a distant descendant of the Persian Rustam) were immensely popular as chapbooks. It was from them that the poets of the eighteenth and early nineteenth centuries formed their idea of Russian folklore, of which they were the principal representatives before the discovery of the *"bylíny."* Another popular chapbook was *Apollón of Tyre,* a version of the Greek romance that is the source of Shakspere's *Pericles.* It came to Russia rather late in the seventeenth century via a Latin version, but the Russian reader easily discovered its familiar Byzantine flavor and rapidly adopted it. Rémizov has made use of it in one of his most delightful legendary stories.

A curious little production connected, like *Góre-Zloschástie* and *Bová,* with folk poetry, but again in a different way, is *The Story of a Young Man and a Girl,* a dialogue between a suitor and a disdainful maiden. He praises her in imaginative language closely connected with the language of folk poetry. To every tirade of his she answers with a tirade of coarse and equally imaginative vituperation, which is also connected with popular charms and curses. She ends, however, by yielding. It is a piece of elaborate verbal art and has no parallel in Old Russian literature. It seems to have been composed in the north (where folk poetry was and is most alive) at the end of the seventeenth century.

These last-mentioned works are entirely secular and free from all intention of edifying. Still more distinctly secular and unedifying are the stories derived from, or similar to, old French fabliaux and the tales of the *Decameron.* A good example is the *Story of the Merchant Karp Sutúlov* and of his wife, who successfully defended her virtue against all the attempts of another merchant (a friend of Karp's), of her confessor, and of the bishop. The chief defect of these stories lies in their language, a rather colorless and illiterate form of Slavonic. This defect is not shared by the masterpiece of Muscovite fabliaux—the story of *Frol Skobéyev.* This interesting story is written without any literary pretenses in a pure colloquial language with a simple syntax. It is a piece of vivid and cynical realism, telling in the calmest fashion and with evident, but unobtrusive, relish the tricks by which a low scrivener contrived to seduce and marry clandestinely a nobleman's daughter, and how he succeeded in reconciling himself with her parents and becoming ultimately a man of position. The naked and matter-of-fact simplicity of the story enhances the effect of its cynical picaresqueness.

The only rival to *Frol Skobéyev's* unique position in the (unconsciously) literary use of the vernacular is the delightful story of the Gremille (*Érsh Schetínnikov*) and of the lawsuit intended against him by his neighbor fishes of the lake of Rostóv. It is also a picaresque story, for it tells of the Gremille's evading by lawful and lawless means all the rightful demands of the other fishes. The story is in the form of a lawsuit and is a delightful parody of Muscovite legal procedure and legal language.

It is impossible to date these with any precision. Some of them may have been written in the early years of the eighteenth century, but in substance they all belong to that latter half of the seventeenth when Muscovy was still Muscovite but when the foundations of its traditional, ecclesiastic civilization were being slowly undermined by a growing and disintegrating tide of secularization.

THE END OF OLD MUSCOVY: AVVAKÙM

Before it came to an end, Old Russian civilization found something like its final and definitive expression in two very dissimilar but, in a way, complementary figures—Tsar Alexis and Archpriest Avvakúm. Alexis (reigned 1645–76) wrote little. A few private letters and an instruction to his falconers are all we have of him. But it is sufficient to make him the most attractive of Russian monarchs. He acquired the surname *Tisháyshy*, which means "most quiet" or "most peaceful." Certain aspects of Russian Orthodoxy, not its most purely spiritual, but its æsthetic and worldly aspects, found in him their most complete expression. The essence of Alexis's personality is a certain spiritual epicureanism, manifested in an optimistic Christian faith, in a profound, but unfanatical, attachment to the traditions and ritual of the Church, in a desire to see everyone round him happy and at peace, and in a highly developed capacity to extract a quiet and mellow enjoyment from all things.

By an irony of fate the reign of this monarch was one of the most agitated in Russian history. Apart from wars and social unrest it was marked by the Great Schism of the Russian Church, a tragic development that split in twain the conservative core of the nation and whose influence has lasted to this day. Its origin was connected with the revision of the liturgic books. In the preceding reign the development of printing had made the fixation of the sacred texts an important matter. In the 1640's a revision of all sacred books, in agreement with the best available Slavonic texts, was carried out under the auspices of the Patriarch Joseph. It was done largely by a group of young secular priests who were full of zeal to purge the Russian Church of the spirit of sloth and laxity and who demanded from clergy and laity a stricter observance of tradition. Their reforms were conservative and intended to revive the good practice of early Muscovite times. Among other things they renewed the practice of preaching, which had been in abeyance for about a century. One of the most fervid of these reformers was the priest (later archpriest) Avvakúm. He was the son of a country parson of the district of Nízhny-Nóvgorod, where he was born about 1620. In his fervor he more than once met with ill treatment at the hand of the laity and worldly priests, who resented his rigorous preaching and his interference with the old-established usages of lazy laxity.

In 1652 the Patriarch Joseph died and was succeeded by Níkon, Archbishop of Nóvgorod. He had been a friend of the reformers. Once patriarch, he decided to go one better in the revision of books and restoration of rituals, and, instead of limiting himself to Old Russian models, he turned to the Greek. This new revision resulted in the publication of texts conforming to the Greek and in certain changes of ritual where Russian practice had differed from that of the Greeks, as, for example, in making the sign of the cross with two fingers and saying alleluia twice instead of the Greek three fingers and treble alleluia. It was such seemingly unimportant points that led to the schism. Avvakúm and his friends refused to accept them and denounced Níkon as a heretic and a tool of Satan. The main reason for their revolt was that they regarded the practice of the Russian Orthodox Church as one whole, dogma and ritual, of which not a tittle might be changed. Russia was the only repository of the faith and had nothing to learn from the Greeks, whose orthodoxy had been adulterated by dalliance with the heretic and subjection to the infidel. Níkon, who was then practically an autocrat, stood firm, and Avvakúm and his friends were exiled. Avvakúm was sent to Siberia and ordered to join the expeditionary force of Páshkov, whose task it was to conquer Dáuria (the present Transbaykália). Páshkov was a valiant "builder of empire" but had no patience with any religious nonsense. He treated Avvakúm with brutal cruelty.

For nine years Avvakúm remained in Siberia, dragged about from place to place and persecuted in every manner. In 1664 he was brought back to Moscow, where during his absence considerable changes had taken place, Níkon had fallen, and a synod was going to meet to judge both Níkon and Avvakúm. The Tsar was disposed to concessions. But Avvakúm was opposed to all compromise, and Alexis was forced to submit to the guidance of the Greek party. The Synod of 1666–7 condemned Avvakúm's ritual tenets, and thus the schism became final: the conservatives were henceforth schismatics (*raskólniki*). Avvakúm himself was shorn monk and exiled to Pustozérsk in the far northeast of Russia. There he became an even more prominent, active, and dangerous leader than he had been before. It was then he wrote his famous *Life* and his powerful epistles to his friends, in which he urged them to keep faithful to the old faith, to defy their persecutors, and to seek martyrdom. He himself, by writing a violent letter to the young Tsar Theodore, seems to have courted martyrdom. It came at last: he was burned at the stake in April 1682, together with his most faithful and trusty friends, the monk Epiphanius and the priest Lazarus.

Avvakúm's writings are not voluminous. They consist of a *Life Written by Himself* (1672–3) and of a score of epistles, hortatory and consolatory to friends, and abusive to enemies, all written during his last years at Pustozérsk. He is above all remarkable for his language, which is the first attempt to use colloquial Russian for literary purposes. Though we do not know anything of the character of his oral preaching, it is highly probable that his written work had its roots in his spoken sermons. The daring originality of Avvakúm's venture cannot be overestimated, and the use he made of his Russian places him in the very first rank of Russian writers: no one has since excelled him in vigor and raciness and in the skillful command of all the expressive means of everyday language for the most striking literary effects. The freshness of his Russian is enhanced by his use of Church Slavonic, which he employs only in quotations from the holy books or allusions to them. The sacred texts shine like hard and solid jewels in the flexible and living texture of his spontaneous Russian. Avvakúm is a great artist of words, and his example is still full of instruction to every writer of Russian.

But Avvakúm is not only the efficient master of expression. He is a firm and fiery fighter, a good hater and a good friend. Scorn and indignation are mixed in his writings with a fierce and manly tenderness that has nothing sentimental in it: the best lot he desires for his best disciples is a martyr's death. His style is constantly relieved by a delightful humor, which ranges from that Christian humor at one's own expense which is so genuinely akin to humility, to stinging and cruel sarcasm at the expense of his foes, which, however, is never far removed from a smiling pity for the torturers who know not what they do. His masterpiece is his *Life*, in which he relates his striving for the truth, and his sufferings at the hands of Páshkov and of the bishops. It has been admirably rendered into English by Jane E. Harrison and Hope Mirrlees, whose translation should be read by everyone who is at all interested in things Russian or in good literature.

Avvakúm's writings were immensely influential with his followers, the Old Believers or Raskólniks. But his manner of writing found no imitator among them, while outside their communities no one read him before the mid nineteenth century except for purposes of confutation.

CHAPTER 2

The Passing of Old Russia

THE SOUTHWESTERN REVIVAL

AFTER the Union of Lúblin (1569) all the west of Russia (White Russia, Galicia, and Ukraine) came under the direct rule of Poland. The Poles, organized by the Jesuits, started a vigorous campaign against the Orthodox faith and the Russian nationality. They easily succeeded in winning over the West Russian nobility, but met with the determined opposition of the middle and lower classes. The most active form this opposition took was the series of Cossack rebellions. Its other aspect was a religious and intellectual movement in the Church and laity. Schools were founded, and there sprung up an active polemical literature to counteract the Roman propaganda.

The early stage of the movement produced an original and talented writer, Iván Výshensky (of Výshnya, in Galicia; *flor.* 1588–1614), a sort of attenuated Ukrainian Avvakúm. He opposed his co-religionaries' tendency to adopt Latin methods in fighting the Latins, which seemed to him in itself a capitulation to the alien civilization. But the advantages of adopting the Jesuits' learning were too obvious, and by the end of the first quarter of the seventeenth century this method of fighting the enemy had finally triumphed among the West Russians. The Kíev Academy, founded in 1631 by Peter Mohíla (1596–1647), Abbot of the Crypt Monastery and afterwards Metropolitan of Kíev, became the center of all intellectual activity in West Russia.

The Latin culture adopted by West Russia was purely ecclesiastical and scholastic, and so was the literature it produced. Its principal interest lies in its attempts to assimilate Polish and Polish-Latin forms of poetry and drama, which will be discussed later. Apart from these, Kievan literature consisted mainly of polemical writings, sermons, and textbooks. The sacred oratory of the period is a conscientious effort to adopt the forms of classical rhetoric. Its principal representatives were Ioánniky Golyatóvsky, Rector of the Kíev Academy, and Lázar Baranóvich, Archbishop of Chernígov, both of whom flourished in the third quarter of the seventeenth century. More important are the writers of the following period, whose work belongs already to the reign of Peter the Great.

THE TRANSITION IN MOSCOW AND PETERSBURG

In Muscovy Western influences began to play an appreciable part about the year 1669, when the Westernizer Artamón Matvéyev became head of the administration. They came by two channels —one from the southwest, the other via the German Liberty (*Nemétskaya slobodá*) of Moscow. This was a settlement of foreigners in the military or financial service of the government and of foreign businessmen, nearly all of them from the Protestant nations, Germany, Holland, and Scotland. As literature and art were mainly an ecclesiastical business, the predominating Western influence in literature was at first that of the southwestern current.

By the time Peter the Great began his "Reforms," the progress of Westernization had advanced considerably in Moscow. But it had proceeded along familiar lines, Westernizing the fabric of the Church but leaving it the center of all civilization. Peter's reforms were far more revolutionary. They aimed at displacing the Church from its place of honor and at secularizing the whole of the Russian polity. Literature took some time before it fully felt the new state of things, and the literature of the reign of Peter is largely a continuation of the preceding period. Its outstanding men of letters were three prelates of Ukrainian origin, bred in the Latin methods of the Kíev Academy: St. Demetrius Tuptálo (1651–1709), Metropolitan of Rostóv, Stephen Yavórsky (1658–1722), locum tenens of the patriarchal chair, and Theophán Prokopóvich (1681–1736), Archbishop of Nóvgorod.

Demetrius of Rostóv is a particularly attractive character. A great scholar and lover of books and learning, he was a peace-loving, meek, and charitable prelate who won the boundless love

and gratitude of his flock. After his death he came to be venerated
as a saint and was officially canonized in 1757. He is the most exquisite fruit of the cultural revival of seventeenth-century Kíev.
His most voluminous work is his *Calendar of Saints*, which, compiled along more European and scholastic lines than Macarius's,
replaced the older work and is to this day the standard compen-
dium of Russian hagiology. He is particularly interesting as a playwright (*v. infra*).

Stephen Yavórsky is chiefly notable as a preacher. His sermons are composed in a simple and manly style, free from excessive rhetorical ornament. They are often outspoken in dealing
with current issues. Yavórsky deeply resented many of Peter's
innovations and showed sympathy with the Old Muscovite opposition. He dared to rebuke Peter for his divorce, lamented the
fate of the Church in a secularized Russia, and dared to raise his
voice against the intolerable weight of conscriptions and taxes that
ground down the lower classes.

Theophán Prokopóvich, a younger man, was animated with
a different spirit. In secularizing his own mentality he went further
than any other prelate. Very widely educated, he was the first
Russian writer to go direct to the fountainhead of European culture in Italy and not to be satisfied with Polish and Polish-Latin
learning. He was a powerful orator, and his funeral oration on
Peter the Great remained for over a century the most famous
piece of Russian solemn oratory. His sermons and orations are
secular in tone, inspired with a cult of enlightened despotism and
a hero worship of the great despot that sounds even less Protestant
than pagan.

The secular literature of the age of Peter discarded Slavonic
and made Russian the literary language. But it was a curious Russian, full of Slavonic reminiscences and saturated with undigested
words of every conceivable foreign origin—Greek, Latin, Polish,
German, Dutch, Italian, and French. The formal rupture with the
old language was symbolized by the introduction of a new alphabet, in which the Slavonic letters were modified so as to resemble
Latin characters. Henceforward Russia had two alphabets: the
Church continued using the old alphabet with the old language;
the lay society used only the new. The books printed in "civil"
characters during Peter's reign and some time afterwards were
either laws and official resolutions, or translations. As the nature

of Peter's reforms was above all practical, the books translated all referred to practical knowledge.

Of the original writings of the period those of Peter himself are easily the best. His Russian was quaintly mixed with barbarisms, but he used it with vigor, terseness, and originality. His literary originality is evident everywhere—in his journals, in his letters, even, and perhaps best of all, in his official ordinances. The vivid and realistic imagery of his style makes his ukases the most enjoyable literature of the time. He had a genius for pithy and memorable statement, and many of his sayings still live in everyone's memory.

Of the other secular writers of the period the most interesting are Iván Pososhkóv (1652–1726), a tradesman and self-educated man who wrote a book, *On Indigence and Wealth*, and Vasíly Nikítich Tatíschev (1686–1750), whose *History of Russia*, though formless from the literary point of view, is the first really scholarly attempt to tackle the vast material in the Russian Annals together with the evidence of foreign writers. It is quite on a level with contemporary European erudition. Tatíschev was one of the most cultured men of his class and time, a politician, and an administrator. His *Testament*, addressed to his son, is an interesting document, reflecting the high sense of duty and practical patriotism that is characteristic of the men of Peter's school.

THE FIRST LITERARY VERSE

Verse writing was introduced into Russia from Poland in the late sixteenth century. The oldest extant specimens are found in the rhymed preface to the Ostróg Bible (1581). In the seventeenth century much rhymed verse was written by West Russian scholars. The prosody they employed was Polish, which, like French and Italian, is based on the counting of syllables, without any obligatory position for stress accent. The matter of this West Russian poetry is panegyrical or didactic. About 1670 it was imported to Moscow by the White Russian cleric Sýmeon of Pólotsk, who flourished at the courts of Alexis and his son Theodore and who attained considerable elegance in the turning of syllabic verses. But no trace of anything that may, except by courtesy, be styled poetry is to be discovered before the age of Peter. Apart from dramatic poetry the only versifier of the school with a grain of the poet in him was Theophán Prokopóvich. His pastoral elegy on the hard times that befell the men of Peter's making after the death of the Great Monarch is one of the first genuinely poetical literary lyrics in the language.

When young Muscovite laymen became acquainted with the technique of rhyming, they began trying their hand at amatory verse. Doggerel rhymes on amatory subjects are extant from the last years of the seventeenth century (the oldest specimens, interestingly enough, occur in criminal lawsuits), and in the reign of Peter the Great this new art spread rapidly. Manuscript collections of love poems in syllabic verse have come down from the first half of the eighteenth century. They reflect the love songs that were current at the time in Germany. Altogether the Germans played a prominent part in the first developments of Russian poetry. Wilhelm Mons, a German of Moscow who was the lover of Peter's wife Catherine and was executed in 1724, wrote amatory verses in Russian but in German characters. They have a quaint intensity that makes us believe he was something of a poet. The first attempts to introduce regular feet into Russian verse were made by two Germans, the Pastor Ernst Glück (in whose house Catherine I had been a servant) and the Magister Johann Werner Pauss. They translated Lutheran hymns into a Russian that, though very incorrect, is studiously pure of foreign words. By 1730 Russian society was ready to receive a more ambitious and regular poetry on the European model.

THE DRAMA

The ritual of the Eastern Church, like that of the Western, contained the germs of drama, but in the East they never grew into dramatic representations. Russian drama is entirely an importation from the West. Like most Western things it came by two distinct routes. One leads from the Latin school drama to the Kíev Academy and thence to Moscow; the other comes direct from the strolling secular players of Germany to the German Liberty of Moscow.

School dramas on religious subjects were introduced into West Russian schools very early, before the end of the sixteenth century.

By the middle of the seventeenth they were a popular and stable institution. When not in Latin or Polish they were always translations from Latin or Polish. Their style was mediæval—they were the late-born children of the miracle and mystery play. The neo-classical theory of dramatic poetry was taught in the rhetoric class of the Kíev Academy, but before the eighteenth century these theories did not affect the practice. Kievan students continued playing, and their masters translated or adapted, plays of a purely mediæval type. There is little originality in the serious parts of these plays, but the comic interludes early received independent treatment. Native Ukrainian characters—the Cossack, the clerk, the Jew, the braggart Pole, the faithless wife and the comic husband—became traditional types, surviving the interlude and its successor the puppet play and living for ever in the early tales of Gógol. Before long the school drama left the school walls and went out into the wide world. Strolling bands of students performing miracle plays became a popular feature of Ukrainian life in the seventeenth and eighteenth centuries. A further development was the puppet theater, which finally assumed an entirely popular character and became one of the important starting points of modern Ukrainian literature.

When Kievan prelates and clerics came to Muscovy to rule the Muscovite Church, the school drama spread over Great Russia, but it failed to flourish on Great Russian soil and never became a popular institution. One reason was that here it had an important rival in the secular play of German origin. In 1672 Tsar Alexis caused Dr. Gregori, the Lutheran pastor of the German Liberty of Moscow, to form a troupe of amateur players to act before the Tsar's Majesty. Plays from the repertory of the German strolling players were translated by scribes of the Foreign Office into stilted and unidiomatic Slavonic prose (which sounds especially quaint in the comic parts), and a theater was instituted at the Royal Palace. One of the first plays produced was a distant descendant of *Tamburlaine the Great*. It was only after Gregori's first production that Sýmeon of Pólotsk ventured to introduce the Kievan school drama and wrote his *Action of the Prodigal Son* in rhymed syllabic verse. In the last years of the century, with the growth of Kievan influence in Muscovy, the rhymed school drama became predominant, but under Peter the Great the secular prose play translated from the German again took the upper hand. Public theaters were opened and the school drama was relegated to the seminaries and academies.

From the literary point of view, by far the greater part of this early drama is uninteresting and unoriginal. The secular prose drama is outside literature. The same cannot be said of the verse drama. Besides an interesting series of realistic comic interludes, it produced in the plays of Theophán Prokopóvich and Demetrius of Rostóv serious works of genuine literary value. Those of St. Demetrius are particularly attractive. They are quaintly baroque in their strangely concrete representation of the supernatural and their audacious use of humor when speaking of things solemn. The shepherds' dialogue in his *Nativity Play* and their discussion of the appearance of the approaching angels are particularly good.

Theophán Prokopóvich, who had studied in Italy and was much more modern than St. Demetrius, broke away from the mystery-play tradition, and his tragicomedy of *Saint Vladímir* (1705) is the first fruit of classical theory in Russia. Its model is the Italian renaissance drama. It is a *pièce à thèse* dealing with the introduction of Christianity into Russia by St. Vladímir despite the opposition of the heathen priests. These priests are satirically intended—they stand for the "idolatrous" Roman Catholics and conservative Orthodox ritualists, over whom triumphs the rational Christianity of the enlightened despot Vladímir-Peter. Together with his lyric poetry and with the plays of St. Demetrius, Theophán's dramatic work marks the highest poetic level reached by the Kievan school.

FICTION AND CHAPBOOKS

The evolution of Russian prose fiction owed little to the southwest, nor was it connected with the clergy. It answered to a demand of the educated or semi-educated laity. Young men of the nobility and gentry, government scribes (especially those of the Foreign Office), and open-minded young merchants of Moscow and of the commercial north were the first readers of fiction, the translators, copiers, and authors of the first Russian novels. Our principal landmark in the early history of Russian fiction is a group of works translated in Moscow in or about the year 1677. These stories are not Russianized out of recognition, as is the case with the earlier *Bová*, and they retain, in their heavy, unidiomatic Slavonic, traces of the languages from which they were translated. They include a number of romances from the Polish that go back in substance to chivalric romances of the late Middle Ages and early Renaissance. It was precisely their foreign, un-Muscovite spirit that attracted the young boyars and scribes to these stories. What they liked most was the presentation of romantic, chivalrous, and sentimental love, so conspicuously absent in Old Russian literature. Fiction became widely popular and was widely circulated in manuscript far into the eighteenth century, but no novel was printed in Russia before 1750.

Original novel writing after these new models began in the time of Peter. Several manuscript novels are extant belonging to the first half of the eighteenth century. They follow a more or less uniform pattern. The subject is always the experiences of a young Russian gentleman in foreign countries, where he meets with more or less romantic and sentimental adventures. The style sometimes inclines to rhythmical parallelism, and the characters are often made to speak in rhymed doggerel. Together with the love rhymes of the period they were the irruption into Russian civilization of the Western conception of sentimental and gallant love.

Standing apart from this main line of development is the one preserved fragment of what its modern editor has called a "novel in verse." It is unique in kind and impossible to date (except for the use of rhyme there is no formal evidence pointing to a date later than 1670–80). Its meterless doggerel is written in a simple vernacular style with constant parallelism or reduplication and with a certain kinship to popular poetry. The narrator, a woman, tells of her relations with her lover and her unloved husband. The setting is the drab and ordinary one of everyday life. Some passages are outspokenly and coarsely, but not in the least cynically, realistic. There is an unsweetened directness and sense of tragedy in the narrative, which makes one think of some nineteenth-century realist, like Písemsky or Maupassant.

Soon after the death of Peter, Russian literature finally becomes modern and Western. But the new, French-bred literature was confined to the upper classes, and the people remained more or less aloof from it. The later eighteenth century produced a popular literature distinct from both the literature of the upper classes and the unwritten folk poetry. It catered to the lower

middle and lower urban classes and was a direct continuation of
the literature of the age of Peter.

When, in the middle of the eighteenth century, the printing
press became an accessible and universal means of expression,
numerous books and inscribed woodcuts began to be published for
popular consumption. The publication of popular literature continued into the nineteenth and twentieth centuries, but its really
interesting period is the second half of the eighteenth. Many, perhaps most, of these popular publications were books of edification
—mainly lives of saints. But these are of little interest, being
nothing but more or less modernized and vulgarized reproductions
of older versions from the *Prologue* or the official *Menologion*. More
interesting are the secular stories. *Eruslán, Bová, Apollón of Tyre,*
and several translated romances of the late seventeenth century
were first printed soon after 1750 and constantly reprinted. Of
original productions that may be assigned to the second half of the
eighteenth century, the most remarkable is the story of the famous
robber, and afterwards police agent, *Vánka Káin* (Jack Cain). The
story is told in the first person. It is an original specimen of the
Russian picaresque imagination. Its style is a mixture of rhymed
doggerel, cruel jokes, crude puns, and cynically roguish paraphrase
and circumlocution. It was exceedingly popular: fifteen editions of
it appeared in the last third of the eighteenth century.

Alongside the narrative chapbooks are the explanatory
rhymed inscriptions that appear on the cheap woodcuts published
for popular circulation in the eighteenth and early nineteenth
centuries. In style they are clearly related to the showmen's cries
at the open-air shows that were a prominent feature of Russian
town life of that time, and which are themselves closely connected
with Great Russian popular theater. Like the woodcuts they ac-
company, the doggerel inscriptions employ a rude and primitive
technique. They cover a great variety of subjects. Their ultimate
source is usually some book of the late seventeenth or early
eighteenth century. Fairy-tale and novelistic subjects are particularly frequent. In the course of time the censorship learned to
keep a watchful eye on these productions, but interesting satirical
and political prints have come down to us from the earlier times.
The most interesting of these is the famous picture of *The Mice
Burying the Cat.* Though with the lapse of time its satirical mean-

ing was lost, and it continued popular merely as an amusing bit of
fun, it is in substance a savage satire on the death of Peter the
Great. It reflects the feelings of the Old Believers and other enemies
of the great tyrant, the exultation of the oppressed and martyred
mice at the end of their persecutor.

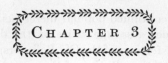

The Age of Classicism

MODERN Russian literature dates from the establishment of a continuous tradition of secular imaginative literature in the second quarter of the eighteenth century. The adoption of French classical standards by four men, all born in the reign of Peter, and their variously successful attempts to transpose these standards into Russian and to produce original work according to them are the starting point of all subsequent literary development. The four men were Kantemír, Trediakóvsky, Lomonósov, and Sumarókov.

KANTEMÍR

Prince Antioch Kantemír (1708–44), the son of a wealthy and cultured noble (his father's history of the Turks, written in Latin, remained for over a century the standard work on the subject), was himself, at the age of twenty-two, probably the most cultured man in Russia. During the crisis of 1730 he was a leader of the anti-oligarchic party, and, together with Theophán Prokopóvich and the historian Tatíschev, persuaded the Empress Anne to cancel the constitution she had sworn to observe. In the same year he was appointed Minister-Resident to London. In 1738 he was transferred to Paris, where he remained Russian Minister till his death in 1744. While in Paris he kept up close relations with many eminent French men of letters, including Fontenelle and Montesquieu.

His literary work is contained in his satires, written between 1729 and 1739. They remained in manuscript till long after his death, and when they were at last published, in 1762 (a French version had appeared in London in 1749), it was too late for them to influence the development of Russian literature, for their language and "syllabic" meter had already become antiquated as a result of Lomonósov's reforms. Kantemír's style is Latin rather than French. Despite the use of rhyme, his verse produces an effect closely similar to that of the hexameter of Horace. His language is racy and colloquial, considerably less bookish and Slavonic than that which was to triumph with Lomonósov. His painting of life is vigorous, and, though he adheres to the main lines of the classic tradition, his characters are living types, taken from the thick of contemporary Russian life. Kantemír has every right to be regarded as the first deliberate and artistically conscious realist in Russian literature. The edge of his satire is directed against the enemies of enlightenment, the unfaithful successors of Peter's work, the old prejudices of Muscovy, and the new foppishness of the semi-educated, Europeanized young nobles.

TREDIAKÓVSKY

Very different were the career and work of Vasíly Kiríllovich Trediakóvsky (1703–69), the son of a poor priest of Ástrakhan. There is an anecdote that Peter the Great, passing through that city, saw the boy and, patting him on the head, called him a "lifelong drudge," a prophecy that sums up Trediakóvsky's whole career. He was the first non-noble Russian to receive a humanistic education abroad (in Paris), and he learned to compose fugitive verses in French that were not beneath the accepted level. Soon after his return to Russia he was appointed Acting Secretary to the Academy. One of his duties in this post was to compose complimentary odes and panegyrics on various occasions and solemn orations in Russian and Latin. Innumerable pathetic anecdotes reflect his humiliating relations with the arrogant nobles of his time, who regarded the professional poet and orator as an inferior kind of domestic servant. His numerous translations are extraordinarily clumsy. His verse is devoid of all poetic merits and began to seem unreadable long before his death. His principal work, a translation in hexameters of Fénélon's *Télémaque* (1766), as soon as it appeared, became a byword for all that is pedantic and ugly.

His claim to recognition as an important figure in Russian literary history is mainly based on his work as a theoretician of poetry and prosody. His *View of the Origin of Poetry and of Verse* (1752) is the first statement in Russian of the classical theory of imitation. Still more important are his works on Russian prosody. Although he did not, as was once thought, introduce regular accentual feet into Russian verse, his theories were not only remarkable for their time, but are interesting even today.

LOMONÓSOV

Kantemír and Trediakóvsky were precursors. The real founder of modern Russian literature and of modern Russian culture was a greater man than either of them—Mikháylo Vasílievich Lomonósov. He was born in 1711, the son of a "peasant" of Kholmogóry (south of Archangel) who was a deep-sea fisherman by trade. Much of his boyhood was spent on his father's boat, in the White Sea and Arctic Ocean, where they used to go as far as the Murman coast and Nova Zembla. The boy was early taught the Slavonic alphabet, but his father did not countenance his insatiable thirst for further knowledge. In December 1730, therefore, he left home and went to Moscow, where he entered the Slavo-Græco-Latin Academy as a student. Without any support from his father he persevered and, in 1736, was sent to Germany to complete his education. At Marburg he studied philosophy, physics, and chemistry under the famous Christian Wolff; afterwards, at Freiburg in Saxony, he learned practical mining. It was from Germany that he sent to the Academy of S. Petersburg an *Ode on the Taking of Khótin* (1739), the first Russian poem written in what has since become our classical prosody. In 1741 Lomonósov returned to Russia and was appointed Assistant Professor at the Academy of Science. His connection with the Academy, of which he became virtual head in 1758, continued till his death. From the outset Lomonósov gave proof of an extraordinary working capacity and an incredible range of interest and knowledge. Chemistry, physics, mathematics, mining, the making of mosaics, grammar, rhetoric, poetry, and history were among his principal occupations, and in all except history and mosaics he produced work of lasting value. At the same time he worked at reorganizing the Academy and

actively combated the "German party," whose policy it was to
make the Russian Academy a snug home for unemployed German
Literaten. Worn out by his toils and endless strife with Germans
and unsympathetic ministers, he became addicted to drink, and
in his last years he was little better than a ruin of his former self.
He died in 1765.

Two passions reigned in Lomonósov: patriotism and the love
of science. To create a Russian science and a Russian literature
worthy to rival those of the West was his one dream. His upright,
unbending character and his firm sense of dignity won him universal esteem in an age when birth and power were as a rule the
only claim to esteem. His hostility to the Academic Germans never
prevented him from recognizing the achievement of German
scientists. When the physicist Richmann lost his life while experimenting in electricity, Lomonósov used all his influence to save
from poverty the widow and children of this martyr of science.
The letter he wrote on the occasion to the minister Shuválov is one
of the noblest expressions of his faith in the nobility of science.
Lomonósov's vocation was to be a scientist. His achievements in
physics and chemistry are important, and he is regarded today as
an advanced precursor of the methods of physical chemistry. In
his lifetime only the most advanced minds, like the great mathematician Euler, were able to gauge the full extent of his scientific
genius. To the great majority of his contemporaries he was primarily a poet and an orator. Since then the situation has been reversed, and in the later nineteenth century it became the fashion
to praise the scientist at the expense of the poet. We are in a
position to give him better justice.

In literature Lomonósov was first of all a legislator. He fixed
the standards of the literary language and introduced a new
prosody, which, despite numerous revolutionary attempts to dis-
lodge it, still rules the greater part of Russian poetry. Church
Slavonic had ceased to be the language of secular literature before
Lomonósov's time, but literary Russian was still in a state of
standardless chaos. It had freely borrowed from the older idiom,
as it had to if it were to become a literary language, but the fusion
of the Russian and Slavonic elements was incomplete and un-
settled. It was Lomonósov's task to find a *modus vivendi* for the
two and to give the new literary language a final form. His linguistic reform is contained in his practice as poet and prose writer

and in his legislative writings, which include a *Rhetoric*, a *Russian Grammar*, and a remarkable essay, *On the Use of Sacred Books in the Russian Tongue*. Without entering into details of his reform, suffice it to say that he made the best use of the great lexical and grammatical wealth of Church Slavonic, thus to a certain extent repeating the work done in the Western languages by the humanistic scholars who enriched French, Italian, and English by the infusion of Latin blood. Although Lomonósov's solution of the problem has since been modified, the essentials have survived, and his Russian is in many ways nearer to ours than to the language of his immediate predecessors. An important feature of his linguistic legislation is his—characteristically classicist—doctrine of the three styles of diction: "high," "middle," and "low." They were to be distinguished chiefly by the relative abundance of Slavonic elements. Where there were two words, Slavonic and vernacular, to denote the same thing, the Slavonic was to be preferred in the "high" style, while none but strictly colloquial expressions were to be used in the "low."

Lomonósov's language has, no doubt, become antiquated. Because of the later evolution of the colloquial language it is often his boldest colloquialisms that seem to us most antiquated. Slavonic doubtlets of many Russian words have also gradually been dropped, though they survived in poetry long after the fall of classicism. It is, however, in the syntax, which betrays an excessive influence of Latin and German periodic construction, that Lomonósov's Russian has least survived. Nevertheless his importance as the legislator and actual *founder* of the literary language of modern Russia cannot be exaggerated.

Lomonósov's metrical reform consisted in the introduction of equisyllabic and accentual feet instead of the old syllabic prosody. His system was largely an adaptation of the prosody introduced into German by Opitz and further perfected by Fleming, Gryphius, and Lomonósov's immediate model, Günther. As a theorist of prosody Lomonósov was inferior to Trediakóvsky and Sumarókov, but the force of his example, of his own poetical practice, carried all opposition before it.

In the second half of the nineteenth century it was the fashion to belittle Lomonósov's poetry and even to deny him the title of poet. But the eighteenth century regarded him as a great poet, not only as a "Russian Malherbe," but as a "Russian Pindar"—and we are not very far from reverting to this view. Like a true classicist he rigorously distinguished between the various kinds of poetry, and the style of his didactic epistles is different from that of his odes. In the former he writes a very pure Russian, and though he submits to the eighteenth-century fashion of paraphrase, he conveys his idea with almost scientific precision. The famous epistle *On the Use of Glass*, ridiculed by the nineteenth century for its prosaic subject, might easily be used as a chapter from a textbook, so exact is its language. His principal poetical works are, however, his odes, sacred and panegyrical. They are not the expression of individual experience, but the ideal voicing of the sentiments and aspirations of a nation, or at least of its intellectual elite. The panegyrical odes extol Peter the Great as Russia's "culture hero" and his daughter Elizabeth for continuing her father's work, neglected by his first successors. They sing the glory of Russian armies and the greatness of the Empire, but, above all, the praise of science, learning, and industry. They call on Russia to produce "her own Platos and quick-witted Newtons" that she may eclipse her Western teachers. But Lomonósov's highest range as a poet is attained in the sacred odes, inspired by the rationalistic conception of a legislating God who manifests Himself in the grand, immutable laws of nature. The two *Meditations on the Divine Majesty* are especially fine examples of Lomonósov's philosophic poetry—and of his power to trace in grand, broad strokes the solemn and majestic aspects of nature. But the finest example of his eloquence, his "mighty line," and his "curious felicity" of diction is the admirable *Ode, selected from Job, Chapters xxxviii–xli*, where the Jealous God of the Old Testament is with convincing vigor transformed into a Leibnitzian Legislator of the universe.

NARRATIVE AND LYRIC POETRY AFTER LOMONÓSOV

If Lomonósov was the father of modern Russian civilization, the father of the Russian literary profession was Alexánder Petróvich Sumarókov (1718–77). Born of a good family of Muscovite gentry, he was educated at the Cadet School in Petersburg, where he acquired an intimate familiarity with French polite learning. Neither an aristocratic dilettante like Kantemír nor a learned professor like Trediakóvsky or Lomonósov, he was the first *gentleman* in

Russia to choose the profession of letters. He wrote much and regularly, chiefly in those literary kinds neglected by Lomonósov. His principal importance rests in his plays, but his non-dramatic work is by no means negligible. His fables are the first attempt in a genre that was destined to flourish in Russia with particular vigor. His satires, in which he occasionally imitates the manner of popular poetry, are racy and witty attacks against the archenemies of his class—the government clerks and officers of law. His songs are, of all his writings, those which still can be expected to attract the reader of poetry. They are remarkable for a truly prodigious metrical inventiveness (not so much as imitated by his successors) and a genuine gift of melody. In subject matter they are entirely within the pale of classical, conventional love poetry.

Sumarókov also pioneered in journalism and literary criticism. His criticism is usually carping and superficial, but it did much to inculcate on the Russian public the canons of classical taste. He was a loyal follower of Voltaire, with whom he prided himself on having exchanged several letters. He used Voltaire's authority in combating the abominations of sentimental taste which, in the form of the English sentimental drama, began to insinuate themselves into Russia towards the end of his life. Vain and self-conscious, Sumarókov considered himself a Russian Racine and Voltaire in one. In personal relations he was irritable, touchy, and often petty. But this exacting touchiness contributed, almost as much as did Lomonósov's calm dignity, to raise the profession of the pen and to give it a definite place in society.

Lomonósov and Sumarókov inaugurated the reign of classicism and established the undisputable authority of "one Boileau" and of his heir on the critical throne—Voltaire. Poetry became the principal field for literary ambition. It was strictly divided into immutably established kinds, each with its prescribed forms, style, and meter. Individual poets might write in every one of these kinds, but they might not mix them. The high kinds were tragedy, epic, and the solemn ode. On a lower level stood the Horatian ode, the song, the satire, the tale in verse (as canonized by La Fontaine), the fable, and the burlesque.

The epic was regarded as the highest form of poetry, and a literature could not pretend to independent importance unless it had produced a national epic. Lomonósov had attempted an epic on Peter the Great, but left it barely begun. Michael Kheráskov

(1733–1807), a gentleman of Moldavian origin, a piettis, a Free-mason, for many years Curator of the University of Moscow, and one of the most enlightened and universally respected men of the century, renewed the attempt at a national epic. He wrote two vast narrative poems modeled on Voltaire's *Henriade: Rossiáda* (1778), on the taking of Kazán by Ivan the Terrible, and *Vladímir* (1785), on the introduction of Christianity by St. Vladímir. In the latter the author's pietistic and mystical tendencies come to the fore. Both poems, especially the patriotic *Rossiáda*, were very popular, and Kheráskov was for a time regarded as the "Russian Homer." He was one of the first poets of the eighteenth century to be rejected by the nineteenth, but readers of Aksákov will re-member with what enthusiasm he recited passages from Kheráskov when a small boy in the late 1790's.

The ode in Elizabeth's and Catherine's Russia was an impor-tant institution. There was a constant demand for odes at court, and ode writing brought more tangible results in the form of pensions and honors than any other kind of literary exercise. The average level of ode writing was naturally low. Except Derzhávin alone, all the ode writers of the time of Catherine were more or less unoriginal imitators of Lomonósov. The most famous of them was Vasíly Petróv (1736–99), who lived for two years in England and was an admirer and translator of Pope. A more pleasing and ac-complished poet was Derzhávin's brother-in-law, the Ukrainian Vasíly Kapníst (1757–1823). He was the most polished and elegant poet of his time, excelling chiefly in the Horatian ode, a "middle" kind of poetry that stands halfway between the real ode and the frankly frivolous song.

Of the narrative kinds other than the regular epic, two of the most popular, the fable and the tale in verse, had for their origin the amiable genius of La Fontaine. The fable after Sumarókov was brilliantly represented by Iván Ivánovich Khemnítser (1745–84), a friend of Derzhávin and the first Russian fabulist to sound an original note. His fables give something more than a foretaste of Krylóv and are written in an admirable, vigorous, popular lan-guage. Some of them are among the few eighteenth-century poems that have remained universally popular ever since. The verse tale is represented by Ippolít Bogdanóvich (1743–1803), a Ukrainian who took the reading public by storm with his *Dúshenka*, an adap-tation of La Fontaine's *Psyche et Cupidon*. For half a century

Dúshenka was regarded as an exquisite masterpiece of light poetry.
The "lowermost" forms of narrative poetry were the mock-
heroic poem and the burlesque. The former flourished in the hands
of Vasíly Máykov (1728–78), whose *Eliséy, or Bacchus Infuriated*
(1771) was the favorite comic reading of two generations of Russian readers. It abounds in crude but virile realism, and is, next to
Khemnítser's fables, the best piece of unsweetened, colloquial
Russian of its time. The burlesque produced several travesties of
the *Æneid*, one of which is of special interest and considerable
historical importance. This is the Little Russian *Æneid* of Ko-
tlyarévsky (1798)—the starting point of modern Ukrainian literature.

DERZHÁVIN

Towering above the respectable and derivative mediocrity of all
these verse writers stands the greatest poet of the century, one of
the greatest and most original of all Russian poets—Gavríla
Románovich Derzhávin. He was born in 1743 of a family of small
squires of the Province of Kazán, and was educated at the Kazán
high school. He acquired there a knowledge of German, but not of
French or Latin. From school Derzhávin went to Petersburg, where
he became a private in the footguards. Having no powerful protectors he rose but slowly to officer's rank. In 1773 the Pugachëv
Rebellion found him on leave of absence in Kazán, where he attracted the attention of persons in power by writing for the nobility of the province an address with expressions of loyalty to the
Empress. He became A.D.C. to General Bíbikov and, on the suppression of the rebellion, was given promotion and lands in the
newly annexed White Russia. In 1777 he returned to Petersburg
and entered the Civil Service. It was only now that he began to
devote himself seriously to poetry. By 1780 Derzhávin was enjoying a considerable reputation as a poet. The reputation soon
grew into a boom when there appeared, one after another, *Felítsa*,
a semi-humorous ode to Catherine, and the famous *Ode to God*. In
the former, Derzhávin extolled the virtues of the Empress and
satirized the vices of her principal courtiers. It brought him Catherine's particular favor. When, shortly after its publication,
Derzhávin quarreled with his superior and had to leave his office,

he was immediately given a higher post and appointed Governor
of Olonéts. But there again he quarreled with his associate governor and, on being transferred to the governorship of Tambóv,
quarreled again. In 1791 he was appointed Secretary to the Empress for the receipt of petitions, but he did not get on with her,
and when, after Catherine's death, Paul tried to employ him in a
similar capacity, he found the poet equally difficult. Alexander I
in 1802 made a last attempt to use him as an administrator and
appointed him Minister of Justice. But the liberal spirit of the
young Emperor's administration was against the grain of the old
poet, who was an outspoken reactionary, and the experiment did
not last more than a year. In 1803 Derzhávin left the Civil Service
and settled down to enjoy life in his recently acquired estate of
Zvánka, in the province of Nóvgorod. His spacious, epicurean,
and philosophically quiet life there is described with verve in one
of the most charming poems of his old age, *To Eugene, Life at
Zvánka* (1807). During his last years Derzhávin's lyric genius remained almost undiminished, and when he died, in 1816, his last
lines, the splendid opening stanza of an *Ode on Mortality*, had just
been jotted down on a slate.

Derzhávin's work is almost exclusively lyric. His tragedies,
written in his later years, are negligible. His writings in prose are
more important. The *Essay on Lyric Poetry* is a remarkable piece
of uninformed, but inspired, criticism. The commentary he wrote
to his poems is full of delightfully quaint and illuminating details.
His *Memoirs* give a convincing picture of his obstinate and contrary character. His prose is rapid and nervous—quite free from
the pedantic involutions of German-Latin rhetoric—next to
Suvórov's the most personal and virile prose of the century.

His lyric poetry is great. For sheer imaginative power he is
one of the small number of Russia's greatest poets. His philosophy
is a joyous and avid epicureanism that does not deny God but
admires Him quite disinterestedly. He accepts death and annihilation with a manful thankfulness for the joys of ephemeral life.
He combines in a curious way a high moral sentiment of justice
and duty with the resolute and conscious decision to enjoy life to
the full. He loved the sublime in all its forms: the metaphysical
majesty of a deistic God, the physical grandness of a waterfall,
the political greatness of the Empire, of its builders and warriors.
Gógol was right when he called Derzhávin "the poet of greatness."

But though all these features are essentially classical, Derzhávin was a barbarian, not only in his love of material enjoyment, but also in his use of the language. "His genius," said Púshkin, "thought in Tatar, and knew no Russian grammar for want of time." His style is a continuous violence to the Russian tongue, an unceasing, vigorous, personal, virile, but often cruel, deformation of it. Like his great contemporary Suvórov, Derzhávin was not afraid of losses when the issue was victory. His greatest odes (as the famous *Waterfall*) consist too often of isolated and giddy peaks of poetry rising over a chaotic wilderness of harsh commonplace.

Derzhávin's range is wide. He wrote sacred and panegyrical odes, Anacreontic and Horatian lyrics, dithyrambs and cantatas, and even, in his later years, ballads. He was an audacious innovator, but his innovations conformed to the spirit of classicism. In his paraphrase of Horace's *Exegi Monumentum* he adduces as his principal claim to immortality the creation of a new genre: the humorous panegyrical ode. This bold mixture of the sublime with the realistic and comic is characteristic of his most popular odes, and it was largely owing to this novelty that he struck his contemporaries with such force. But apart from this innovation Derzhávin is also the greatest Russian poet in the orthodox classical manner, the most eloquent singer of the great immemorial commonplaces of poetry and universal experience. His greatest moral odes are the magnificent ode *On the Death of Prince Meschérsky*, than where the Horatian philosophy of *carpe diem* was never worded with more Biblical majesty; the short and vigorous paraphrase of Psalm lxxxii, against bad kings, which brought to the poet considerable unpleasantness after the French Revolution (the only way he could answer accusations was that "King David was not a Jacobin, so my poem can be disagreeable to no one"); and *The Nobleman*, a powerful invective against the great favorites of the eighteenth century, where a keen sarcasm goes hand in hand with a stern moral earnestness.

But what makes Derzhávin unique is his extraordinary power of conveying impressions of light and color. He saw the world as a heap of precious stones, and metals, and fire. His greatest achievements in this line are the opening of the *Waterfall*, which is also the acme of his rhythmical power; the astounding *Peacock* (so willfully spoiled at the end by a flat moral maxim); and the middle stanzas of the ode, *On the Return of Count Zúbov from Persia* (which is, by the way, a striking example of Derzhávin's independence and contrariness: written in 1797, immediately after the accession of Paul, who notoriously hated the Zúbovs, it was addressed to the brother of the late Empress's last favorite). It is in such poems that Derzhávin's genius reaches its most triumphant pinnacles. It is very hard to give an idea of them; their effect depends so largely on the extraordinary character of the words, the syntax, and, above all, the metrical divisions. His visual flashes and rhetorical eruptions make Derzhávin the poet par excellence of "purple patches."

A very peculiar division of Derzhávin's poetical work is the Anacreontic poems of his later years (first collected in 1804). Of all Russian poets Derzhávin is alone in striking this note of joyous, sturdy, sane sensuality of a green old age. The poems are not inspired merely by sexual sensuality, but by an enormous love of life in all its forms. Such are *Life in Zvánka*, the gastronomic-moralistic *Invitation to Dinner*, and the lines to Dmítriev on the gypsies. (Derzhávin was the first in the long line of great Russian writers—Púshkin, Grivóriev, Tolstóy, Leskóv, Blok—who did homage to the intoxication of gypsy music and gypsy dancing.) But among the later Anacreontic poems, there are also other poems of wonderful sweetness and melodiousness, in which (as Derzhávin tells us in his commentary) he avoided "the letter *r*, to prove the mellifluousness of the Russian language."

Derzhávin's poetry is a universe of amazing richness; its only drawback was that the great poet was of no use either as a master or as an example. He did nothing to raise the level of literary taste or to improve the literary language, and as for his poetical flights, it was obviously impossible to follow him into those giddy spheres.

THE DRAMA

The continuous history of the Russian drama and of the Russian theater begins in the reign of Elizabeth. The first regular drama, written according to French standards, was Sumarókov's tragedy *Khorév*, acted before the Empress in 1749 by young men of the Cadet School. The first regular troupe of players was founded a

few years later in the city of Yaroslávl (on the upper Volga) by
a local merchant, Fëdor Vólkov (1729–63). Elizabeth, who was a
passionate lover of the theater, heard of the Yaroslávl players and
summoned them to Petersburg. They played before her in 1752 to
her entire satisfaction. Sumarókov was also delighted by Vólkov,
and from their contact was born the first permanent theater in
Russia (1756), with Sumarókov as its first director and Vólkov its
leading actor. As has more often than not been the case in Russia
ever since, the actors of the eighteenth century were superior to
its playwrights. The great name in the history of the Russian
classical theater is that of the tragic actor Dmítrevsky (1734–
1821), one of Vólkov's original cast. He assimilated the French
grand style of tragic acting, and heads the list of great Russian
actors.

The classical theater rapidly became a popular institution.
The educated and semi-educated, and even uneducated, classes of
the time were fascinated by the acting of classical actors in classical
tragedies and comedies. It was no doubt the good acting that
made the reputation of Sumarókov, as the literary value of his
plays is small. His tragedies are a stultification of the classical
method; their Alexandrine couplets are exceedingly harsh; their
characters are marionettes. His comedies are adaptations of
French plays, with a feeble sprinkling of Russian traits. Their
dialogue is a stilted prose that had never been spoken by anyone
and reeked of translation.

After Sumarókov, tragedy made little progress except in the
fluency and elegance of the Alexandrine couplet. The principal
tragic author of the age of Catherine was Sumarókov's son-in-law,
Yákov Knyazhnín (1742–91), an imitator of Voltaire. Some of his
most interesting tragedies (e.g., *Vadím*) breathe an almost revolutionary spirit of political freethinking. Comedy was a much liver
business and, after Sumarókov, made great strides towards a firmer
grasp of the material of Russian life.

The most remarkable playwright of the age was Denís Ivánovich Fonvízin. Born in 1745, in Moscow, of a family of gentry, he
received a good education at the University of Moscow and very
early began writing and translating. He entered the Civil Service,
became secretary to Count Pánin, one of the great noblemen of
the reign, and, about 1766, wrote the first of his two famous
comedies, *The Brigadier-General*. A man of means, he was always

a dilettante rather than a professional author, though he became prominent in literary and intellectual circles. In 1777–8 he traveled abroad, the principal aim of his journey being the medical faculty of Montpellier. He described his voyage in his *Letters from France*— one of the most elegant specimens of the prose of the period, and the most striking document of that anti-French nationalism which in the Russian elite of the time of Catherine went hand in hand with a complete dependence on French literary taste. In 1782 appeared Fonvízin's second and best comedy *The Minor*, which definitely classed him as the foremost of Russian playwrights. His last years were passed in constant suffering and traveling abroad for his health. He died in 1792.

Fonvízin's reputation rests almost entirely on his two comedies, which are beyond doubt the best Russian plays before Griboyédov. They are both in prose and adhere to the canons of classical comedy. Fonvízin's principal model, however, was not Molière, but the great Danish playwright Holberg, whom he read in German, and some of whose plays he had translated. Both comedies are plays of social satire with definite axes to grind. *The Brigadier-General* is a satire against the fashionable French semi-education of the *"petits-maîtres."* It is full of excellent fun, and though less serious than *The Minor*, it is better constructed. But *The Minor*, though imperfect in dramatic construction, is a more remarkable work and justly considered Fonvízin's masterpiece. As is the rule with Russian classical comedies, it contains a pair of virtuous lovers, who are uninteresting and conventional. All the interest is concentrated in the Prostakóv family and their surroundings. The point of the satire is directed against the brutish and selfish crudeness and barbarity of the uneducated country gentry. Mme Prostakóv is a domineering bully with only one human feeling—her love for her sixteen-year-old son Mitrophán, whom she persists in calling "the child." Her maternal affection is of a purely animal and material nature: her one desire is that Mitrophán should eat his fill, not catch cold, not be bothered by duties or obligations, and that he might marry an heiress. In addition are her brother Skotínin (Mr. Brute), who confesses to a greater family feeling for pigs than for human beings; her sheepish husband Prostakóv (Mr. Simpleton); the nurse, doting on her "baby," who only bullies her; and finally the hero himself, Mitrophán. He is the accomplished type of vulgar and brutal selfishness, unredeemed by a single human feature—even his fondly doting mother gets nothing from him for her pains. The dialogue of these vicious characters (in contrast to the stilted language of the lovers and their virtuous uncles) is wonderful—true to life and finely individualized; and they are all masterpieces of characterization— a worthy introduction to the great portrait gallery of Russian fiction.

Fonvízin is superior to all his contemporaries in the art of drawing character and writing comical dialogue, but he is surrounded by a galaxy of talented comic playwrights, whose works present a lively picture gallery of the times. The most prolific was Knyazhnín, whose comedies are better than his tragedies. They are mostly in verse, and though for character drawing and dialogue they cannot rival Fonvízin's, they are often superior from the point of view of stagecraft. One of the best is *An Accident with a Carriage* (1779), a satire on serfdom that is bolder if less serious than Fonvízin's. Another notable dramatist was Michael Matínsky, a serf by birth, whose comedy *The Bazaar* (1787) is a vigorous satire on government clerks and their thievish ways. It is in prose, and partly in dialect. But the most famous dramatic satire, next to Fonvízin's, was Kapníst's *Chicane* (1798), in which the amiable author of Horatian odes revealed himself a savage satirist. His victims are the judges and officers of law, whom he paints as an unredeemed lot of thieves and extortioners. The play is in rather harsh Alexandrines and is full of outrages against the spirit of the Russian language, but it produces a powerful effect by the force of its passionate sarcasm. The two greatest Russian comedies of the nineteenth century, Griboyédov's *Woe from Wit* and Gógol's *Inspector General*, owe not a little to the crude and primitive comedy of Kapníst.

Closely connected with comedy, but less ambitious and less serious, was the comic opera, which had a great vogue in the late eighteenth century. Its principal champion was Alexander Ablesímov (1742–83), whose *Miller, Wizard, Quack, and Matchmaker* (1779) was the greatest theatrical success of the century. It is a lively and merry play, with excellent, sprightly dialogue and delightful, genuinely popular songs. Quite free from all social or moral preoccupation, full of unrestrained and purely Russian merriment, Ablesímov's is one of the masterpieces of Russian eighteenth-century literature.

EIGHTEENTH-CENTURY PROSE [1]

The standards of the new literary prose were set up by Lomonósov and remained in force till the advent of Karamzín. Lomonósov's own practice was limited chiefly to the higher kinds—solemn eloquence and rhetorical history. Sumarókov in his periodicals was the first to cultivate the more everyday forms. The age of Catherine saw a great extension in the use of prose, together with the spread of European and modern ideas.

Catherine herself was an author. In the early years of her reign she piqued herself on being one of the most advanced minds in Europe. She was in constant correspondence with Voltaire, Diderot, and Grimm, and did her best to appear enlightened in the eyes of these leaders of European opinion. Her *Instruction* (*Nakáz*) to the Committee of Deputies convened in 1767 was based on the ideas of Montesquieu and Beccaria. It was so openly liberal that in France it was prohibited by the censorship, and a French translation of it could appear only in Neuchâtel. But before long, under the influence of the Pugachëv Rebellion, Catherine's liberalism was greatly damped. In the end of her reign, under the influence of the French Revolution, she finally discarded all liberal pretence and became an overt reactionary. As a writer she is not devoid of merits, but her best is to be found in her French writings. French critics praise her French, which, though less correct than Frederick II's, is personal and vigorous. In her letters to Grimm she is on her best intellectual behavior and tries to show off her native wit and cleverness. Her Russian writings, considering her German origin, are quite respectable. But neither her satirical papers, nor her comedies, nor her tales, nor her historical chronicles (clumsily imitative of Shakspere) are in any way above mediocrity. On the strength of her remarkable memoirs and her corre-

---

[1] Russian literary historians usually neglect all ecclesiastical literature after the age of Peter. But the eighteenth century produced an abundant harvest of sermons of a much more ambitious kind than was the rule in Old Russia. There was considerable mutual influence between secular and ecclesiastical literature, all the more so as the prelates of the age of Elizabeth and Catherine were more secular in outlook than their successors in the nineteenth century. The most celebrated preachers of the period were Gedeón Krinóvsky, Bishop of Pskov (1726–63), whose best-known sermon was preached against Voltaire on the occasion of the latter's poem on the Lisbon earthquake; and Platón Lévshin, Metropolitan of Moscow (1737–1812), the most typical representative of the Broad-Church mentality of the Age of Reason.

spondence with Grimm she has a higher place in French literature than she can be given in Russian.

It was Catherine herself who started, in 1769, the publication of satirical journals, after the model of the famous English papers. For four or five years (1769–74) this kind of journalism flourished in Russia, until it became too independent and was put an end to by the same Catherine. Its most brilliant representative was Nikoláy Ivánovich Nóvikov (1744–1818), one of the most remarkable men of his generation. He edited the *Drone* (1769–70) and the *Painter* (1772–73), both of which were, like most of the other journals, the almost exclusive work of the editor. But instead of making his papers, as his fellow journalists did, and as Catherine wanted them to do, a collection of harmless jokes at the expense of old-fashioned prejudice, he tried to make them the weapon of serious social satire. He aimed his blows at the very core of contemporary society—the system of serfdom. In his polemics with Catherine's own magazine he dared to disagree with her opinion that satire should smile at foibles rather than chastise vices. It was precisely Nóvikov's witty and earnest attacks on serfdom that made Catherine put a stop to the whole lot of satirical journals. Nóvikov transferred his activities to another sphere. He started a publishing business, which he conducted in a highly public-spirited way, aiming, not at gain, but at the extension of enlightenment. From 1775 to 1789 his press turned out a greater number of books than had been printed in Russia since the beginning of printing. He may be said to have formed the Russian reading public. About the same time Nóvikov became a Freemason—one of the most prominent and respected men of that sect. In his publications he gave occasional expression to his religious and moral views, and this was his undoing. He became one of the first victims of the reaction caused in Catherine by the French Revolution. In 1791 his printing press was closed. He himself was arrested and remained in prison till the accession of Paul, who liberated him, not so much from any liberal impulse, as from a desire to undo all his mother had done. Nóvikov never returned to active life but spent his remaining years on his country place, devoting himself to mystical meditations. As a writer he is to be remembered for his satirical papers of 1769–73 and for a few stories. The most interesting of these is *The Novgorodian Girls' Wedding Eve*—an improved version of the old picaresque story of *Frol Skobéyev*.

About 1790 there was a short-lived revival of satirical journalism, but, as had happened twenty years earlier, the journals
soon assumed an independent tone that caused the authorities to
put an end to them. The principal part in this revival was played
by the young Krylóv, who was later to become the great fabulist.

Even at their boldest the satirical journals never touched on
strictly political matters. But Catherine's own initiative in con-
vening an elected Committee of Deputies in the beginning of her
reign (1767), and the effect of the French Revolution in the end,
gave rise to some purely political literature. Of the writers connected with the first of these impulses the most remarkable was
Prince Michael Scherbátov (1733–90). He was an aristocrat and a
conservative, one of the first enlightened Russians who began to
condemn Peter the Great for introducing the corrupt morality of
the West into the solid family life of Old Russia. His most interesting pamphlet is *On the Decline of Morals*, a lurid account of
the misconduct of the eighteenth-century empresses and of their
favorites. Scherbátov also wrote a history of Russia, which is inferior from a literary point of view to his other writings, a mere
ill-digested compilation of the Chronicles. A much more intelligent
historian was I. N. Bóltin (1735–92), who has every right to be
regarded as the father of Russian history. His *Notes* (1788) on
Leclerc's history of ancient and modern Russia are the first evidence of a critical historical spirit in Russian scholarship.

The second great political stimulus of the reign—the French
Revolution—found its expression in a famous book of political
invective, *A Voyage from Petersburg to Moscow*, by Alexander
Nikoláyevich Radíschev (1749–1802). Radíschev had been sent
as a young man to complete his education at Leipzig, where he
came under the influence of the more extreme French philosophers
—Helvetius, Raynal, and Rousseau. On his return he quietly
served in the Civil Service, and nothing predicted the development
his career was to take. In 1790 he started a private press and issued
from it his famous *Voyage*. The style of the book is one of intense
and unrelieved rhetoric, and its Russian is exceptionally heavy
and clumsy. It is a furious attack against existing social and
political conditions. The brunt of it was directed against serfdom,
but it also contained expressions of anti-monarchic feeling and
materialistic opinions. The book was immediately seized, its author arrested and exiled to East Siberia. He was released by Paul

in 1797 and received back into the Civil Service with complete rehabilitation by Alexander I in 1801. But during his exile he had become a victim to nervous melancholy, and in 1802 he committed suicide. He has come to be regarded by the radical intelligentsia as its first spokesman and martyr. The sincerity of his book has been questioned both by his early advocates and by his later detractors. It would seem that he wrote it merely out of literary ambition and that it is no more than a rhetorical exercise on a subject suggested and familiarized by Raynal. However this may be, the book is devoid of literary merit. But Radíschev was also a poet of no mean talent. He held paradoxical views, preferring Trediakóvsky to Lomonósov, and tried to introduce Greek measures into Russian prosody. A short love poem of his in the Sapphic meter is among the most charming lyrics of the century, and his elegy (in distichs) on *The Eighteenth Century* has both poetical power and intellectual substance.

The eighteenth century has left us an interesting series of memoirs. First in time and, probably, in human interest came the memoirs of Princess Nathalie Dolgorúky, nee Countess Sheremétev (1714–71). She was the fiancée of one of the oligarchs of the Dolgorúky family when the *coup d'état* of Anne (1730) restored autocracy and sent the Dolgorúkys into exile. In spite of this she married the exile and followed him through all his ordeals. After his execution she became a nun and in her old age wrote her life for her children and grandchildren. Its principal attraction, apart from the high moral character of the author, resides in the great simplicity and unpretentious sincerity of the narrative and in its beautiful, undefiled Russian, such as could be written only by a gentlewoman who lived before the age of schoolmasters.

Of the later memoirists I have already spoken of Derzhávin. The memoirs of Bólotov (1738–1833) and of Danílov (1722–c. 90) are priceless historical documents and agreeable and interesting reading.

Private letters, and even official correspondence of the eighteenth century, are often of considerable literary interest. Non-literary men were as a rule more independent of grammar and rhetoric than the men of letters and wrote a more vigorous and personal Russian. Field Marshal Suvórov, one of the most cultured men of his time, gave much attention to the form of his correspondence, and especially of his orders of the day. These latter are highly original, deliberately aiming at unexpected and striking effects. Their style is a succession of nervous staccato sentences, which produce the effect of blows and flashes. Suvórov's official reports often assume a memorable and striking form.[2] His writings are as different from the common run of classical prose as his tactics were from those of Frederick or Marlborough. He was, in a sense, the first Russian romanticist—and in his old age his bedside book was Ossian, in the admirable Russian translation of Kostróv, dedicated to the great soldier.

KARAMZÍN

The last years of Catherine's reign saw the beginning of the literary movement that is connected with the name of Karamzín. It was not a violent revolution. The spirit of the eighteenth century continued alive till much later, and the new movement was even to a large extent a further assertion of that spirit. The reform of the literary language, which was its most striking and immediately apparent aspect, was a direct continuation of the Europeanizing and secularizing reforms of Peter and Lomonósov. But, as Europe itself had changed since the first half of the century, the new wave of Europeanization brought with it new ideas and new tastes—the new sensibility of Richardson and Rousseau and the first signs of the beginning revolt against classicism.

The main question at issue, however, was that of language. Karamzín's object was to make literary Russian less like the old ecclesiastical languages, Slavonic and Latin, and more like French, the new language of polite society and secular knowledge. He exchanged Lomonósov's heavy German-Latin syntax for a more elegant French style. While ejecting hundreds of Slavonic words, Karamzín introduced numerous Gallicisms—exact translations from the French of words and expressions denoting ideas connected with the new sensibility or the advance of knowledge. His reform was successful and immediately accepted by the majority of writers, but it was by no means an unmixed blessing to the lan-

[2] One of his rhymed reports is quoted, somewhat inaccurately, by Byron in a note to *Don Juan*.

guage. It only substituted one foreign model for another. It even increased the distance between the written and the spoken language, for it did away (virtually) with Lomonósov's distinction of three styles by merging them all in the "middle" style and practically abandoning the "low." It is doubtful whether the language has profited as much as has been supposed by the exclusion of so many Slavonic synonyms of Russian words: they added color and variety. By reforming the language as he did, Karamzín contributed to widen the gap between the educated classes and the people, and between new and old Russia. The reform was anti-democratic (in this a true child of the eighteenth century) and anti-national (in this still more so). But whatever we may say against it, it was victorious and facilitated the coming of an age of *classical* poetry: the ultimate justification of Karamzín's language is that it became the language of Púshkin.

Another aspect of the Karamzinian movement was the new sensibility. It had been prepared by the slow infiltration of sentimental novels and the emotional pietism of the Freemasons, but the cult of feeling, the obedient submission to emotional impulses, the conception of virtue as the outcome of man's natural goodness —all these were first explicitly preached by Karamzín.

Nikoláy Mikháylovich Karamzín was born in 1766, in Simbírsk (on the middle Volga), of a family of provincial gentry. He received a good secondary education at the private school of a German professor of the University of Moscow. After leaving school he was in danger of becoming a dissipated, pleasure-seeking young squire, when he met I. P. Turgénev, a prominent Freemason, who led him from the ways of vice and introduced him to Nóvikov. These Masonic influences had a principal part in framing Karamzín's mind. Their vaguely religious, sentimental, and cosmopolitan ideas paved the way to the understanding of Rousseau and Herder. Karamzín began to write for Nóvikov's publications. His first work to appear in book form was a translation of *Julius Cæsar* (1787). He also translated Thomson's *Seasons*. In 1789 he went abroad, where he remained for about eighteen months, traveling in Germany, Switzerland, France, and England. On his return he started a monthly review, mostly written by himself called the *Moscow Journal* (1791–2), which marks the real beginning of the new movement. The most important of his contributions was

Letters of a Russian Traveler, which were received by the public
as something of a revelation: the revelation of a new, enlightened,
and cosmopolitan sensibility, and of a delightfully new style.
Karamzín became a leader, the most important literary figure of
his generation.

In the reign of Paul (1796–1801) the growing severity of the
censorship forced him to silence, but the liberal beginning of the
reign of Alexander I prompted him into renewed activity. In 1802
he started a new monthly, the *Messenger of Europe*, largely devoted
to politics. It judged contemporary events from the point of view
of a sentimentalized Plutarchian "Virtue," condemned Napoleon,
and glorified Washington and Toussaint L'Ouverture. In 1803
Karamzín gave up the editorship of his magazine, abandoned all
literary work, and devoted himself to historical research.

The intrinsic value of Karamzín's literary work does not
today strike us as great. He was not a creative mind. He was an
interpreter, a schoolmaster, an importer of foreign wealth. Besides
being the most cultured mind, he was the most elegant writer of
his age. Never had Russian prose sought so much to enchant and
fascinate, and the sweetness of his style was what struck his
readers most of all.

All Karamzín's early work bears the stamp of the New Sensibility. It is the work of a man who has first discovered in his feelings an infinite source of interest and pleasure. He announces the
good news of Sensibility: that happiness consists in making the
best use of our spontaneous impulses, and that to be happy we
must have confidence in our feelings, for they are *natural*, and
Nature is good. But Karamzín's Rousseauism is tempered by an
innate mediocrity (in the unabusive Aristotelian sense of the
term). An elegant moderation and a cultured urbanity are the
constant characteristics of his writings. And to remind us that we
are still up to the ears in the eighteenth century, his Sensibility is
never divorced from an intellect that judges at least as keenly as
it feels.

The subject of Karamzín's first and best-known tale, *Poor
Liza* (1792), is the story of the seduced girl who is abandoned by
her lover and commits suicide—a favorite theme of the sentimental
age. The success of the story was immense. A pond in the environs
of Moscow where Karamzín located Liza's suicide became a

favorite shrine of sentimental Muscovites. Karamzín was the first Russian author to give prose fiction a degree of attention and artistic finish that raised it to the rank of literature. But apart from this the merits of his tales and novels are small. His later stories, *A Knight of Our Times* and *The Sensitive Man and the Cold Man*, are superior to the rest, for they display a genuine originality of psychological observation and sentimental analysis.

Karamzín's poetry is imitative, but important, like the rest of his work, as the indication of a new period. He was the first in Russia for whom poetry was a means of expressing his "inner life." He also left a distinct trace on the technique of Russian verse, both by refining the traditional French verse forms and by introducing new forms of Germanic origin. In all these respects, however, he was but the forerunner of Zhukóvsky, the real father of modern Russian poetry.

After his withdrawal from literature and journalism, Karamzín lived in the quietness of archives, working at *The History of the Russian State*. His historical studies produced a profound change in his ideas. Though he retained his cult of virtue and feeling, he became imbued with patriotism and State worship. He came to the conclusion, expressed in his memoir, *On Ancient and Modern Russia* (1811), that to be efficient the State must be strong, monarchic, and autocratic. The memoir (published only long after Karamzín's death) was aimed against Speránsky's liberal Francophil policy and constitutional reforms, then under discussion. It is remarkable for its outspoken criticism of the Russian monarchs of the eighteenth century, from Peter to Paul. From a literary point of view, its vigorous clarity of argument, unblurred by rhetoric and sentimentality, make it the writer's masterpiece. It produced a strong impression on Alexander and made its author a political influence to be counted with. In 1816 Karamzín came to Petersburg to supervise the printing of his *History*, the first eight volumes of which appeared in 1818. Three more volumes appeared later, while the twelfth (which brought the narrative down to 1612) remained incomplete and was published posthumously. Karamzín's residence at Petersburg brought him into closer contact with Alexander, and a warm friendship developed between them. The death of Alexander (November 1825) was a severe blow to Karamzín. He did not survive his royal friend very long, but died in 1826. His reputation as the greatest writer of Russian prose and a great historian became a principal tenet of the official creed and of all the conservative part of the literary world. Thus it was that, beginning as a reforming, almost revolutionary, force, Karamzín passed into posterity as the symbol and perfect embodiment of Imperial Russia's official ideals.

The success of *The History of the Russian State* was immediate and universal. Even the liberals, who disliked its fundamental thesis of the all-efficiency of autocracy, were carried away by its literary charm and the novelty of its facts. No one today would revive the ecstasies of the reading public of 1818. Karamzín's historical outlook is narrow and crippled by the essentially eighteenth-century character of his mind. He concentrated almost exclusively on the political actions of Russian sovereigns and practically overlooked the Russian people. His judgment of the rulers is often sentimentally moralistic, and his basic idea of the virtues of autocracy distorts his reading of individual facts.

But these defects have their redeeming points. By forcing on the reader a consistent view of Russian history as a whole, Karamzín helped to understand its essential unity. By taking a moralistic view of the behavior of sovereigns, he was able to condemn their selfish or tyrannical policies. By concentrating on the actions of princes, he added dramatic value to his work: the parts that struck the readers' imagination most powerfully were precisely those stories of individual monarchs, founded no doubt on solid fact, but arranged and unified with the consummate skill of a dramatist. The most famous of these stories is that of Borís Godunóv, which became the great tragic myth of Russian poetry and produced Púshkin's tragedy and Musórgsky's popular opera.

The style of the *History* is rhetorical and sustainedly eloquent. It is a compromise with the literary conservatives, who forgave Karamzín all his early sins for having written the *History*. But in the main it is a development of the essentially French eighteenth-century style of the younger Karamzín. Abstract and sentimental, it avoids, or rather misses, all historical and local color. The choice of words is calculated to universalize and humanize, not to individualize, Old Russia, and the monotonously rounded cadences convey an idea of the continuousness, but not of the complexity, of history. Contemporaries liked his style. A few critics found fault with its stiltedness and sentimentality, but on the whole the age was fascinated by it and recognized it as the greatest achievement of Russian prose.

CONTEMPORARIES OF KARAMZÍN

Karamzín's early work met with a strong conservative opposition, led by Admiral Alexander Semënovich Shishkóv (1753–1841), an all-round conservative and patriot, author of the stirring 1812 manifesto on the invasion of Napoleon, and champion of the Greek-Slavonic tradition in the literary language. In his campaign against the Karamzinians, Shishkóv counted among his adherents such men as Derzhávin, Krylóv, and, in the younger generation, Griboyédov, Katénin, and Küchelbecker, but the trend of the times was against him, and he lost his battle. His linguistic writings, though often rather wildly dilettantish, are interesting for his great insight into the shades of meaning of words, for his pious, if uninformed, interest in Old Russian literature and folklore, and for the excellent Russian in which they are written.

The poets that followed the colors of Shishkóv were rather a motley throng and cannot be all bracketed as one school. They are distinguished from Karamzín's followers in that they continued the eighteenth-century tradition of high poetry, for which they were ridiculed by the Karamzinian wits. But at least two poets of Shishkóv's party, Semën Bobróv (1767–1810) and Prince Sergius (Shirínsky-) Shikhmátov (1783–1837), have greater merit than any Karamzinian before Zhukóvsky. Bobróv's poetry is remarkable for its rich diction and splendid imagery, for the soaring flights of his imagination and the sublimity of his design. Shikhmátov's *Peter the Great* (1810), a "lyrical epic" in eight cantos, is devoid of narrative (or metaphysical) interest, but its style is remarkable. Such a saturated and ornate style is not to be found in Russian poetry until we come to Vyacheslav Ivánov. •

Karamzín's following was more numerous that Shishkóv's, and it occupies the highway of Russian literary tradition. But before we come to Zhukóvsky and Bátyushkov it is not strikingly rich in talent. The Karamzinian poets abandoned the great themes and "high" style of the Russian eighteenth century and devoted themselves to the cultivation of the *poésie légère* of the French eighteenth century. The most eminent of these poets, Iván Ivánovich Dmítriev (1760–1837) strove to write verse in a style as polished as that of Karamzín's prose. His songs, short odes, elegies, epigrams, fables, and verse tales are all eminently elegant, but long before his death Dmítriev's elegance had become antiquated, and his poetry the quaint rococo toy of a hopelessly irrevertible past. Other poets of the Karamzinian coterie were Vasíly Lvóvich Púshkin (1767–1830), the uncle of a greater nephew, who wrote polished sentimental trifles—and a lively, but very coarse burlesque, *A Dangerous Neighbor;* and A. F. Merzlyakóv (1778–1830), an eclectic follower of senescent classicism, who was particularly successful in his songs.

The vogue of songbooks is a prominent feature of the Karamzinian age, and several poets, including Dmítriev, Merzlyakóv, and Yúry Alexándrovich Nelédinsky-Melétsky (1752–1828), acquired a reputation with their songs, some of which have become folk songs. But only Merzlyakóv's songs are genuinely akin to those of the folk; Nelédinsky's and Dmítriev's are quite as conventional as the older songs of Sumarókov, merely substituting a new, sentimental convention for the classical convention of sensual love, and an elegantly monotonous singsong for the rhythmical variety of the older poet.

A more modern and subjective poet was Gavríla Petróvich Kámenev (1772–1803), the first to follow Karamzín in making his poetry express individual emotional experience. He cultivated the new "Germanic" and rhymeless forms of verse and was under the strong influence of Ossian and Young. But the new subjective poetry acquired only later a really sincere tone and efficient forms of expression. The elegies of the short-lived Andréy Turgénev (1781–1803) and the early work of Zhukóvsky are the first swallows of the Golden Age. But the distinctive quality of that age begins first to be felt in the maturer work of Zhukóvsky, from about 1808 onwards.

There remains to be mentioned Prince Iván Mikháylovich Dolgorúky (1764–1823), who belonged to neither Shishkóv's party nor Karamzín's. Studiously avoiding all sentiment and sentimentality, Dolgorúky tried to make common sense and the simple pleasures of domestic life the subject of his poetry. Garrulous and puerile at his worst, he is distinguished at his best by ease, raciness, and a well-bred naïveté. His prose, especially that quaint alphabetical dictionary of his friends, *The Temple of My Heart*, is a good example of pure colloquial Russian, uncontaminated by foreign influence or literary fashion.

In the drama of the period the French classical standards were giving way to a taste for the sentimental drama, or *comédie larmoyante*, which had begun to insinuate itself into Russia some twenty years earlier. The new style did not produce any original work of value, and the Russian stage had to rely chiefly on the plays of the famous German melodramatist Kotzebue. The one outstanding dramatic author of the period was Vladisláv Alexándrovich Ózerov (1769–1816), whose tragedies were produced between 1804 and 1809. Their success was tremendous, largely owing to the remarkable acting of one of the greatest of Russian tragediennes, Catherine Semënova. What the public liked in these tragedies was the atmosphere of sensibility and the polished, Karamzinian sweetness that Ózerov infused into the classical forms. One of his first successes was *Fingal*, a sentimental tragedy with choruses in an Ossianic setting. The climax was reached in *Dimítry of the Don*, first acted within a few days of the battle of Preussisch-Eylau (1807), when its patriotic tirades were received with overwhelming enthusiasm. Ózerov's last play, *Polyxene*, was less successful, but intrinsically it is his best, and no doubt the best Russian tragedy on the French classical model. The subject is handled in a broad and manly manner that makes the play genuinely evocative of the atmosphere of the *Iliad*.

KRYLÓV

At the end of the eighteenth and in the first years of the nineteenth centuries, fable writing became a veritable craze, and the fable plays an important part in Russian literary development. It was one of the principal schools for training writers in that realism which is the main feature of later Russian literature. A robust, open-eyed realism is already the outstanding feature of Khemnítser's fables. It is mellowed down, conventionalized, and gentilified in the drawing-room fables of Dmítriev. It regains all its vigor in the crude, but racy, picaresque fables of Alexander Izmáylov (1779–1831) and in the work of the greatest Russian fabulist—Krylóv.

Iván Andréyevich Krylóv was born in 1769, the son of a poor army officer who had risen from the ranks. He received a very summary education and was a small boy when he entered the Civil Service as a minor clerk. At the age of fourteen he found a post in Petersburg and in the same year began his literary career with a comic opera. Afterwards Krylóv turned to satirical journalism and edited the *Spectator* (1792) and the *St. Petersburg Mercury* (1793). Among much inferior sentimental matter these journals contained several vigorous satirical essays in a manner very different from the skeptical common sense of the fables. The best of these papers is *A Panegyric of my Grandfather* (1792)—a tremendous caricature of a rude, selfish, savage, hunting country squire, who, like Fonvízin's Skotínin, has a greater family feeling for his hounds and horses than for his serfs. The *Mercury* was short-lived, being suppressed for the dangerously violent tone of Krylóv's satire. For twelve years Krylóv practically disappeared from literature. Part of this period he lived as a secretary, a tutor, or simply a parasite in the houses of great noblemen, but for long periods he entirely escapes the eye of the biographer. At this new school of life Krylóv seems to have lost his early violence and acquired the passive and complacently ironic shrewdness of the fables. In 1805 Krylóv returned to literature; he wrote his first translation from La Fontaine and made a fresh attempt to conquer the stage: during the first wars with Napoleon he wrote two comedies satirizing the French fashions of the Russian ladies. Their success was considerable, but Krylóv did not try to improve it, for he had found his right vein in the fable. In 1809 twenty-three of his fables were published in book form and had a success unprecedented in the annals of Russian literature. Henceforward he wrote nothing but fables. In 1812 he received a peaceful and commodious post (practically a sinecure) in the Public Library of St. Petersburg, where he remained for over thirty years. He died in 1844. He was noted for laziness, untidiness, good appetite, and shrewd malicious common sense. His fat, bulky figure was a familiar feature in the drawing-rooms of Petersburg, where he used to sit for whole evenings without opening his mouth, his little eyes half shut or gazing vacantly, with an air of boredom and indifference to all around him.

Krylóv's *Fables*, most of them written between 1810 and 1820, are contained in nine books. Their enormous popularity was due to both their matter and their manner. Krylóv's outlook was representative of what is perhaps the typical outlook of a Great Russian of the lower or middle classes. It has a foundation of sound common sense. The virtues he respects above all things are efficiency and aptness. The vices he satirizes most readily are self-satisfied inaptitude and arrogant stupidity. Like the typical middle-class philosopher he is, Krylóv has no faith in big words and high ideals. Intellectual ambition finds no sympathy with him. There is a vast amount of Philistine inertness and laziness in his philosophy of life. It is eminently conservative, and some of Krylóv's most poisonous shafts were aimed at the fashionable progressive ideas of his time. But his common sense has no more patience with the absurdities and ineptitudes of the upper classes and of people in power. His satire is a smiling satire. His weapon is ridicule, not indignation, but it is keen and pointed, and can make his victim smart.

Krylóv is a great master of words, and this makes his place in the pantheon of Russian literature impregnable. He did not achieve from the outset that mastery and originality now associated with his name. The 1809 volume contains several fables that are little more than good translations from La Fontaine. But the greater part of the first book already displays his style at its best. Krylóv was no friend of the reforming Karamzinians. He was a thorough classicist, a nationalist, and not averse to archaism. The descriptive and lyrical passages of the *Fables* are quite eighteenth-century in tone. Even the raciness of his colloquial passages is different from the realism of such eighteenth-century writers as V. Máykov or Khemnítser, not so much in kind as in quality. But the quality is of the highest. Krylóv most emphatically "had language." His words are alive. The line is tightly filled with them. And they are real, living words, words from the street and the tavern, used in the true spirit of the *people's*, not of the schoolmaster's, Russian. Krylóv is at his best in condensed epigrammatic statement. The pointed conclusions and morals of his *Fables* are the legitimate descendants of the popular proverb (no language is richer than Russian in the wealth and beauty of its proverbs), and hundreds of them have themselves become proverbs without anyone's now thinking of where they came from.

Some of Krylóv's best fables are pointed against inefficiency and the pretensions of the unskilled man to do skilled work. Others are political pamphlets produced by current events, especially during the war of 1812–14. Several are satires against vain and importunate poetasters and criticasters. Others again are social satires, like the famous one of *The Geese* who protested against being sold at the market because they were descended from the geese that had saved the Capitol from the Gauls. But it is impossible to give any enumeration or classification to Krylóv's fables. Fortunately (although Krylóv would seem on the face of it to be an untranslatable author) they have been admirably rendered into English by Sir Bernard Pares, who has succeeded in finding wonderfully happy equivalents for Krylóv's raciest idioms. The reader is advised to get a copy of Sir Bernard's translations and taste for himself of Krylóv's immense variety.

THE NOVEL

Classical theory did not regard the novel on an equal footing with the drama and other forms of poetry, and no novels were printed in Russia till 1750. After that date translated fiction appeared in increasing numbers, but the first original Russian novel was published only in 1763. For many years original novels remained both exceedingly rare and considerably below the general level of literature. The Russian reader's demand for fiction was met by numerous translations from French, German, and English. The first Russian novelist was Fëdor Émin (*c.* 1735–70), who wrote didactic and philosophical romances of adventure in a florid and prolix literary prose. A more realistic style that had been popularized by translations of Marivaux and Fielding was taken up by Michael Chulkóv (*c.* 1743–92) in his novel *The Fair Cook, or the Adventures of a Debauched Woman* (1770), a sort of Russian *Moll Flanders*. This practically exhausts the list of *literary* novels before the time of Karamzín.

The example and success of Karamzín as a novelist provoked a somewhat increased output of prose fiction, but his direct imitators are negligible. Robuster work was done by men unconnected with the sentimentalist movement. Alexander Benítsky (1781–1809) wrote philosophical oriental tales in the best tradition of Voltaire. His style surpassed in elegance and lucidity everything written in Russian prose before Púshkin. The novel of manners is represented by *Eugene, or the Results of Bad Upbringing* (1799–1801), an early work of the fabulist Alexander Izmáylov, a cautionary and moral story, where the author describes vice with such realistic gusto that his critics were inclined to doubt the sincerity of his moral purpose.

The most significant, and prolific, novelist was the Ukrainian Vasíly Trofímovich Narézhny (1780–1825), a robust and conscious realist in the tradition of Smollett, Fielding, and Lesage. In his stories of Ukrainian life he was the first to present to the Russian reader a colorful, humorous, and realistic picture of Cossack and post-Cossack Ukraine, so much more memorably revived a generation later by Gógol. Narézhny's principal work is *A Russian Gil Blas*, a novel in six parts, three of which appeared in 1814, while the remaining three were held up by the censorship. It is a vast and unsweetened picture of Russian life in the provinces and the capitals, turning round the adventures of a poor squire, little more than a peasant, who by an irony of fate bears a prince's title. Narézhny had a grip on real life, which places him above all the "prehistorical" Russian novelists. But he was too little of an artist, and his books, owing to their heavy style and their diffuseness, are difficult reading. He was in fact little read, and his influence on the development of the Russian novel is almost negligible.

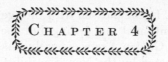

CHAPTER 4

The Golden Age of Poetry

THE Golden Age of Russian poetry is roughly contemporary with the great age of romantic poetry in western Europe. But its poetry is not romantic; it is far more *formal*, active, selective—in short, *classical*—than any other nineteenth-century school of poetry. It was, in a sense, behind the times, a posthumous child of the eighteenth century. For general tone and atmosphere Púshkin has been compared to Mozart. The western European poets nearest in tone and feeling to those of our Golden Age are poets of the later eighteenth century—Burns, Chénier, Parny. What is particularly important—the technical efficiency of the poets of the Golden Age never lags behind their inspiration. Their poetry is perfect, even when it is minor poetry; and when it is major poetry, it is great without qualification. Its technical perfection marks off the poetry of the twenties both from the primitive rudeness of the age of Derzhávin and from the degenerate laxity of the later nineteenth century.

Though creative and original where the other had been merely receptive, the poetry of the Golden Age was a direct continuation of the Karamzinian movement, its best fruit and chief justification. Being a continuation of that movement, it was "French"—and French of the eighteenth century, for it remained hostile to French romanticism. From 1820 onward the movement called itself romantic and was in open revolt against the rules of French classicism. It desired greater freedom and novelty of forms; it liked originality and picturesqueness. It admired Shakspere for the broadness of his design and for his profound understanding of the human heart, and Byron for his mighty eloquence and effective narrative methods. In comparison with the age of classicism, there was a revival of sentiment and feeling, but the sensibility of most of the poets of the Golden Age was purely classical; only a minority were at all infected by the New Sensibility, and then only by its earliest eighteenth-century forms. Nor was there any "return to Nature." Even the nature symbolism of the Ossianic school is absent from the poetry of Púshkin and his contemporaries. Romantic pantheism and romantic animism do not appear in Russian literature before the thirties.

What still more emphasizes the eighteenth-century character of the Golden Age is its distinct social coloring. It was a movement inside the gentry, a movement of *gentlemen*. Hence, in its early stages, the prevalence of light, society verse, of convivial and Anacreontic subjects: the cult of friendship, of good company, and wine. Socially the age of Púshkin marks the high-water mark of the literary hegemony of the gentry. Higher literature is completely monopolized by men of that class. At the same time the literary press is almost entirely in the hands of the non-noble class—of pedants, hacks, and hucksters. The opposition between the two classes is clearly marked. The gentry, to whatever literary party they belonged, showed a contemptuous united front to the plebeians. The plebeians had their revenge in the thirties.

The Golden Age may be said to begin at the moment when poetry emerges from the placid insipidities of the school of Dmítriev and acquires an independent and original accent in the first mature work of Zhukóvsky, about 1808. A few years later, after the end of the wars, the younger partisans of Karamzín, headed by Zhukóvsky, Bátyushkov, and Vyázemsky, founded the semi-humorous literary society "Arzamás." Its sittings were a parody of the solemn meetings of Shishkóv's conservative literary society. The Arzamasians cultivated poetical friendship, literary small talk, and the lighter forms of verse.

After 1820 the movement becomes more serious. The influence of Byron reigns for about five years after 1821. The tale in verse becomes the principal form of expression. The catchword of romanticism is defiantly accepted in the teeth of the conservatives. The works of Púshkin follow in rapid succession, and meet with loud success, which is rivaled by that of Zhukóvsky, Baratýnsky, and Kozlóv. Poetry almost monopolizes the book market. The gentlemen's party acquires control over all literary opinion. But

their day was short and early clouded. The repression of the Decembrist Revolt by Nicholas I (1825–6) was an irremediable blow
to the intellectual elite of the gentry. At the same time the clear
eighteenth-century atmosphere of the Golden Age is poisoned:
young men of a somewhat younger generation introduce the first
germs of German idealism. Lower-class journalists, more intellectually ambitious and progressive than hitherto, control the press
and rise in the public favor. French romanticism, with its unbridled license of bad taste, infects the air. After 1829 the novel,
stimulated by Scott, begins to sell better than poetry. Délvig, the
center of the friendly circle of poets, dies in 1831. Púshkin marries
in the same year and becomes the leader of a conservative literary
aristocracy. The young are no longer young, the summer of the
Golden Age is over. After 1831 the front stage of literature is occupied, in Petersburg, by a host of vulgarizers and charlatans; in
Moscow, by the Adams of the new intelligentsia, who respect in
Púshkin a venerable relic of the past but discard his traditions,
despise his friends, and refuse to read his new works. In 1834 appears Belínsky's first article—the manifesto of a new era in the
history of Russian civilization. When, in 1837, Púshkin died,
Russian literature was far advanced in its new ways. Those who
survived him, Zhukóvsky, Baratýnsky, Yazýkov, Vyázemsky,
were a small and isolated group in an alien, forgetful, and mainly
hostile world.

ZHUKÓVSKY

Vasíly Andréyevich Zhukóvsky, the first pioneer and the accepted patriarch of the Golden Age, was born in 1783, in Túla, the
natural son of a country gentleman of the name of Búnin and of a
Turkish captive girl. His education in Moscow was dominated by
pietist influences. After completing his education he lived on his
father's estate, where he gave lessons to his cousins and brought
them up in the ways of sensibility. One of them, Marie Protásov
(later Móyer) became the object of a Platonic attachment that
survived her death (1823). In 1802 Zhukóvsky sent to Karamzín's
Messenger of Europe a translation of Gray's *Elegy*. The publication
of that poem has more than once been declared to be the birthday
of Russian poetry. In 1808 appeared Zhukóvsky's first ballad, an

adaptation of Bürger's *Lenore*, which gave the signal for a general ballad craze. In 1812, on the invasion of Napoleon, Zhukóvsky joined the militia. He did no actual fighting, but a poem he wrote shortly after the battle of Borodinó, while Napoleon was still in Moscow (*The Bard in the Camp of the Russian Warriors*), made him famous outside literary circles. In 1815–17 Zhukóvsky was the most eminent, though not the most active, member of the Arzamás. About the same time he was invited to give Russian lessons to the Princess of Prussia, then affianced to the future Emperor Nicholas I. The young couple liked Zhukóvsky, and when, in 1818, the future Alexander II was born, the poet was appointed his tutor. He remained in this situation till Alexander's majority. Zhukóvsky's influence on his pupil has generally been regarded as highly beneficial and humanizing. His situation at court and his position as the eldest and, next to Púshkin, greatest poet of the time made him a prominent figure in the literary world. From the first steps of the younger poet he was intimately related with Púshkin and was always helpful when Púshkin got into trouble with the authorities. From 1831, after Púshkin's marriage, the poets exercised a sort of diarchy over what henceforward came to be known as the "literary aristocracy." Zhukóvsky also befriended Gógol, and in 1838 played a principal part in the emancipation from serfdom of the Ukrainian poet Shevchénko. In 1841 he retired from court, and in the same year he married a very young German girl and henceforward lived permanently on the Rhine, working at vast poetical enterprises and only occasionally visiting Russia. He died in 1852, at Baden-Baden.

Up to about 1820 Zhukóvsky was the leader of the advanced literary movement, and the extent of his influence may be compared with that of Spenser's or Ronsard's. He created a new poetical language on the basis of the Karamzinian reform. Both his metrical methods and his diction remained the standard for all the nineteenth century. Besides these formal innovations Zhukóvsky reformed the very conception of poetry. In his hands it became, for the first time in Russia, the direct expression of feeling. There is no trace in his poetry of raw, unmastered, merely recorded, emotion: the sentimental experience is always completely transformed. But it was a step in the direction of expressive, emotional poetry. The next step was made by Lérmontov. It was not made by Púshkin; the subjective element in Púshkin's poetry is less prominent and more subordinate to the creative design than in Zhukóvsky's.

It is one of the curios of literary history that this first, and for some time to come most, personal and subjective Russian poet was almost exclusively a translator. His original work is small in extent, consisting of a few humorous epistles, occasional elegies, and lyrics. But these last are alone sufficient to give Zhukóvsky a place in the first rank of poets. The æthereal lightness, the melodiousness of his verse and the exquisite purity of his diction reach in them their highest perfection. Romantic melancholy and the resigned hope in a better beyond have never spoken in nobler or more exquisite accents. But it is characteristic of Zhukóvsky that even these lyrics have sources in foreign poetry. Thus the wonderful lyric on the death of Marie Móyer (*19th March 1823*) closely resembles in meter and construction a poem of the German romanticist Brentano. It is the actual words, cadences, and intonation, the very texture of the verse, that make the poem what it is— and those slight touches which are at the hand of only the great poet. Zhukóvsky's poetry of 1808–21 charmed the public by its atmosphere of romantic sensibility, daydreams, optimistic religiosity, and sweet resignation, with a touch of the mildly fantastic paraphernalia of the balladry of terror. But what the initiated most admired was the poet's supreme mastery, his metrical inventiveness, and, above all, the absolutely unheard-of purity, sweetness, and melodiousness of his verse and diction, which were such a contrast to the splendidly barbaric ruggedness of Derzhávin.

The poets Zhukóvsky translated in this period were the romantic, pre-romantic, and even classical poets of Germany and England. His special favorites in Germany were Uhland and Schiller, whose Greek ballads (*Die Siegesfest* and others) are, owing to Zhukóvsky, quite as much classics in Russia as they are in Germany (if not more so). The English poets translated by him were Dryden (*Alexander's Feast*), Thomson, Gray (the *Elegy*), Southey, Scott, Moore, Campbell, and Byron (*The Prisoner of Chillon*). After what I have said of Zhukóvsky's supreme and impeccable mastery in Russian verse it will scarcely be startling if I add that certain of his translations from his English contemporaries (none of whom was really a great craftsman) are very often superior to the original. Southey's *Queen Urraca*, Campbell's *Lord Ullin's Daughter*, Moore's *Death of the Peri*, Scott's *Eve of St. John*,

and Byron's *Prisoner of Chillon* have both relatively and absolutely a higher place in Russian than they have in English poetry.

After 1830 Zhukóvsky gradually abandoned the too fluent
sweetness that had made him popular. Like Púshkin in the same
years he strove after greater objectivity, a more Doric outline and
more epic manner. Almost all his later work is either in hexameters
or blank verse. He uses both forms with the utmost freedom and
variety, placing his words in the most "unpoetical" order, using
the most destructive overflows, attaining a style that is *"beau
comme de la prose"* and (in blank verse) reminiscent of the later
Shakspere. Among the principal works of this period are the
adaptations (from the German) of *Rustam and Sohrab* and *Nala
and Damayanti*. In both he succeeded in eschewing all sentimentality. In the former, the effect is one of grand, primæval, rude
majesty; in the latter, of genuinely Indian wealth and color. Still
more remarkable is his adaptation, in very free and enjambed
hexameters, of the German romanticist Fouqué's prose romance
Undine. The atmosphere of the poem is one of optimistic religiosity and romantic fantasy, and akin to that of his early lyrics and
elegies, but the story is told with majestic leisure and has a true
epic tone. The most extensive task of his old age was the translation of the *Odyssey*, completed in 1847. Though he knew no Greek,
and translated Homer from a word-for-word German translation,
it is a masterpiece of exactness and reliability. Zhukóvsky's *Odyssey* was intended to complete the Russian Homer, and is, as it
were, a sequel to Gnédich's translation of the *Iliad* (1829).

Nikoláy Ivánovich Gnédich (1784–1833) was a poet of considerable merit who wrote a few exquisite lyrics and a much-
admired Russian idyl in the style of Theocritus. His *Iliad* is high-
sounding and magnificent, full of splendid Slavicisms, with a
Virgilian accompaniment of sonorous trumpets and with wonderfully invented composite epithets. It is the most splendid example
in Russian poetry of the grand classical style.

The *Odyssey* of Zhukóvsky is very different. He deliberately
avoids Slavicism. He makes the *Odyssey* a homely, leisurely, Biblical story of the daily life of patriarchal kings. But Zhukóvsky
does not sentimentalize Homer, and, though perhaps it is in the
Telemachos and Nausicaa cantos that he is at his best, even in the
cruelest parts of the *Mnesteroktonia* he gives a faithful reflection
of the true Homer. The two Russian Homers are in a most happy

way mutually complementary, and if Gnédich's *Iliad* is our highest achievement in the grand manner, Zhukóvsky's *Odyssey* is unsurpassed as a heroic idyl.

OTHER POETS OF THE OLDER GENERATION

Zhukóvsky was not alone, between 1810 and 1820, in his work of perfecting and refining the instrument of Russian verse. Another most important poet, for some time almost a rival to Zhukóvsky's supremacy, was Constantine Nikoláyevich Bátyushkov. Born in 1787 in Vólogda, Bátyushkov served in the army, was wounded in 1807 at Heilsberg, and took part in the campaigns of 1813 and 1814. After the end of the wars he was a prominent member of the Arzamás. His collected works appeared in 1817. Soon after that date he became a victim to a morbid melancholy. A prolonged stay in Italy failed to cure him, and in 1821 he became a permanent mental invalid. He lived for thirty-four years more in his native town, with only rare and transient luminous intervals. He died in 1855.

Like Zhukóvsky, Bátyushkov was a modernist in verse and language, a continuer of the work of Karamzín, and a resolute enemy of Church Slavonic and archaistic rudeness. But unlike Zhukóvsky, who was more romantic than most of his contemporaries and saturated with German and English influences, Bátyushkov was thoroughly "eighteenth-century" and "Latin." Though he was no stranger to the New Sensibility, the groundwork of his personality was pagan and sensual. His masters were Latin and classical: the Latin and French elegiac poets Tibullus and Parny; Tasso and Petrarch; and the Greek Anthology. Bátyushkov's ambition was to rival in Russian the sweetness and melody of Italian; this in the judgment of his contemporaries he almost achieved. His Russian is miles apart from the barbaric virility of Derzhávin. It is soft and sweet to the point of effeminacy. Bátyushkov's output was not large. It consists of a few elegies and lyrics, where the language of sentimentalism is placed at the service of a purely sensual passion; of some elegies of a more rhetorical character, such as the sometime famous *Dying Tasso* and the exquisite elegy to *The Shade of a Friend*. In 1818 appeared the (free) translations of amorous epigrams from the Greek Anthology, which for beauty of rhythm and diction are his masterpieces. In the years immediately preceding his madness (1819–21) Bátyushkov wrote some lyrical epigrams in a different manner from that of all his earlier verse. For strange beauty and haunting emotional intensity they are unique in Russian poetry. They are a rare instance of the creative influence of mental illness on poetry.

Another pioneer of form was Pável Alexándrovich Katénin (1792–1853), who began as an early champion of romanticism and, when romanticism became the slogan of the majority, turned classicist and Shishkovian and wrote *Andromache*, the last "regular" Russian tragedy. His principal contention was that poetry should be *national*, and it was this which led him away from the Karamzinians and Zhukovskyites. In his early ballads, written under the impulse of Bürger, he tried to attain nationality by the use of aggressive (and at that time objectionable) realism in diction and detail. These ballads had an appreciable influence on the Russian ballads of Púshkin, who esteemed Katénin highly and was almost alone in doing justice to his poetry. In his later work Katénin became agressively archaic, finally breaking away from the taste of the day. In all he did he was a genuine master of technique, but he lacked the fire that alone infects and attracts. After 1832 he abandoned literature and lived in the seclusion of his estate, a profoundly embittered and dissatisfied man.

Younger than these poets, but belonging to the same early stages of the movement, was Baron Antón Antónovich Délvig (1798–1831), Púshkin's schoolfellow at the Lyceum and his best friend. Noted for his indolence ("poetical laziness"), kindheartedness, and common sense, he exerted an enormous personal influence on the lives of his poet contemporaries. From 1825 to his death he edited the yearly miscellany of the poets' party, *Northern Flowers*. In 1830 he succeeded in obtaining permission to publish a *Literary Gazette*. His early death in 1831 was a cruel blow to Púshkin and to all the poets of their circle.

As a poet Délvig developed early, but he published little and late, owing chiefly to his famous laziness. He never became popular, though Púshkin and Baratýnsky ranked him very high. Like the poets of the eighteenth century he does not make his inner life the material of his poetry, but takes his subjects from outside. His Russian songs were in his time his most popular work, but his most exquisite poems are those in the classical measures. No one, before or after, ever wrote such perfect epigrams (in the Greek sense) as Délvig did. Still better are his idyls, highly valued by Púshkin: *The Bathing Women* is unquestionably the highest achievement in Russian poetry in the more purely sensuous vision of classical antiquity. Impersonal, unemotional, formal, eminently craftsmanlike, and quite singularly unmeretricious, Délvig's poetry was made to be treated with contempt by the later nineteenth century. Our time has made a great effort to revive him, and he has been restored to his lawful place in history, possibly even more than that. For, like Katénin, though a great master, Délvig lacks that human significance which after all alone makes major poetry.

The younger Karamzinians and Arzamasians cultivated with greatest zest what the French eighteenth century called "fugitive" poetry. Even Zhukóvsky's high seriousness stooped to such light verse, and Bátyushkov made his literary reputation with the epistle *My Penates*, which was considered the masterpiece of the kind. Púshkin's work before his exile to the south of Russia consists almost entirely of fugitive poems.

Two masters of fugitive poetry in the first decade of the Golden Age were Davýdov and Vyázemsky. Though lesser poets than Zhukóvsky or Bátyushkov, these two men are even more characteristic of their generation and more typical of their school. Both are high-spirited, healthy, virile, unromantic, and—ultimately—shallowish. Both were great wits and fond of fun, in life as well as in literature.

Denís Vasílievich Davýdov [1] (1784–1839) was one of the most famous and popular soldiers of his day (he was also a past master in making use of his military celebrity to advertise his literary work, and vice versa). His early and most popular verses are in a style of his own making, known as the "hussar style." In them he sings the praise of reckless valor, on the field of battle as well as before the bottle. The diction in some is rather unconventional, and occasionally his words have to be replaced by dots, but it is always full of spirit and great rhythmical go. His later poems are inspired by a late love for a very young girl. They are passionately sentimental and as vivid and alive in diction and rhythmical

[1] Though Davýdov was probably a starting point for Denísov in *War and Peace*, Tolstóy's creation is, in its final form, entirely unlike the real Davýdov.

elasticity as his hussar verses. Púshkin had a high opinion of his poetry and used to say that Davýdov showed him the way to be original.

Prince Peter Andréyevich Vyázemsky (1792–1878) was one of the most active members of the Arzamás and became an intimate friend of Púshkin. Their correspondence is a treasure house of wit, fine criticism, and good Russian. In the twenties Vyázemsky was the most combative and brilliant champion of what then went by the name of romanticism. In the thirties, like all the "literary aristocracy," he found himself out of date and out of tune with the young generation. He had the great sadness of surviving all his contemporaries. Though it was precisely in his last years that his poetical talent bore its best fruit, he was forgotten and abandoned by critics and public long before he died. He grew into an irritated reactionary who heartily detested everyone born after 1810. Though he was the journalistic leader of Russian romanticism, there can be nothing less romantic than his early poetry: it consists either of very elegant, polished, and cold exercises on the set commonplaces of poetry, or of brilliant essays in word play, where pun begets pun, and conceit begets conceit, heaping up mountains of verbal wit. His later poetry is more sober and more significant. It never became strictly personal, like Zhukóvsky's or Púshkin's. It remained universal and typical—essentially classical. But the old and embittered man found new and beautiful intonations for the great eternal commonplaces, and as he approached death, the subject drew increasingly moving notes from him. Such poems as the stanzas to the memory of Davýdov and the one on a funeral in Venice are among the purest gems of Russian poetry.

PÚSHKIN

Alexander Sergéyevich Púshkin was born in Moscow, May 26, 1799. His father's family was one of the oldest of the Russian gentry. His mother, nee Gannibal, was the granddaughter of "Peter the Great's Nigger"—more exactly Abyssinian—Engineer General, Abraham Gannibal. The poet was always proud both of his "six-hundred-year-old nobility" and of his African blood. His childhood and early boyhood were spent at home in a French eighteenth-century atmosphere of frivolous and superficial culture.

There was no mutual affection between son and parents. In 1811 Púshkin went to school at the Lyceum of Tsárskoye Seló (founded that year). The Lyceum became more of a home to him than his family, and his schoolfellows always commanded the warmest and most permanent of his affections. While still at the Lyceum, Púshkin began writing verses. In 1814 his first poems appeared in the *Messenger of Europe*, and before he left the Lyceum he was a member of the Arzamás, and was regarded as a rival, almost an equal, by Zhukóvsky and Bátyushkov. In 1817, on completing his studies, he became a clerk in the Foreign Office, but the appointment was merely nominal and he did no office work. He lived in St. Petersburg, mixing with the most advanced, brilliant, and dissipated of his contemporaries, and tasting unreservedly of the pleasures of carnal love. All the time he was working at a "romantic epic" in six cantos, *Ruslán and Lyudmíla*, which appeared in the spring of 1820, taking by storm the young generation and being violently censured by the old. Zhukóvsky, on reading the manuscript, gave Púshkin his portrait with the inscription "To a victorious pupil from a defeated master." But before its publication some of Púshkin's revolutionary epigrams had reached the knowledge of Alexander I, and the poet was ordered to leave Petersburg. He was transferred to a government office in Ekaterinosláv. Almost immediately on arriving there he fell ill and was taken to the Caucasus by General Rayévsky, a famous soldier of 1812, with whose sons he contracted a lasting friendship and for whose daughters he held a fervent admiration. The two months spent in the company of the Rayévskys in the Caucasus and the Crimea were one of the happiest periods in Púshkin's life. It was from the Rayévskys also that he got his first knowledge of Byron. From the end of 1820 to 1823 Púshkin served in Kishinëv, doing very little official work, detesting the filthy barbarity of the Moldavians, leading the same reckless life he had led in Petersburg, and having sufficient freedom to pass much of his time at Kámenka, an estate in the Province of Kíev that was one of the principal centers of the Revolutionary movement. But he worked more seriously than in Petersburg. He wrote *The Captive of the Caucasus*—which appeared in 1822 and had an even greater success than *Ruslán and Lyudmíla*—*The Fountain of Bakhchisaráy*, and numerous short poems, and began *Evgény Onégin*. In 1823 he was transferred to Odessa. He was delighted to breathe the freer and more European air of a big seaport, but his life became even more irregular and passionate. His Odessa life is marked by his love (almost simultaneous) for two women—the Dalmatian Amália Ríznich, and the wife of the Viceroy, Countess Elizabeth Vorontsóv. The former seems to have been the strongest sensual passion in his life and the object of several of his greatest love lyrics. His love for the latter led him into social entanglements, where he appears to have been most treacherously served by his Byronic friend, Alexander Rayévsky—himself a lover of the Countess. In August 1824 Púshkin was suddenly expelled from the Civil Service and ordered to live permanently on his mother's estate of Mikháylovskoye in the Province of Pskov. The pretext for this disgrace was a private letter intercepted by the police in which the poet expressed the opinion that "pure atheism," though by no means a comforting philosophy, was "the most probable." On arriving at Mikháylovskoye, Púshkin found his parents there, but a succession of scenes between the poet and his father led to the latter's leaving his scapegrace and dangerous son to himself. Púshkin remained in Mikháylovskoye, alone except for the company of his old nurse, and the neighborhood of Trigórskoye, a country place inhabited by a charming family of ladies—Mme Ósipova and her two daughters. There Púshkin met Mme Kern, who became the subject of a rather trivial love affair with him and of one of his most famous and inspired lyrics. The years spent at Mikháylovskoye were particularly productive.

Púshkin's forced seclusion at Mikháylovskoye prevented him from taking part in the December Revolt of 1825. His connections with the rebels were obvious, but the new Emperor overlooked them and, by a master stroke of clever policy, summoned the poet to Moscow (September 1826), granted him a complete pardon, and promised to be his special protector and patron. Though apparently more free, Púshkin was subjected to an even more meddling supervision than under the preceding reign. What was worse, his inner freedom was forfeited, for he was made to understand that his amnesty was such a signal display of mercy that he could never do too much to live up to it. After several abortive attempts at settling down, in 1829 Púshkin fell in love with Nathalie Goncharóva, a young girl of sixteen, a dazzling beauty, but frivolous and insignificant. He proposed but was rejected. Under the influence of this check he suddenly went off to the Caucasus,

where a war was going on with Turkey, but was severely rebuked
for doing so without permission. In the winter of 1829—30 he
made several attempts to go abroad, but was not permitted to do
so by his "protectors." In the spring of 1830 he again proposed to
Nathalie and was this time accepted. His own financial affairs
were far from brilliant—he got handsome sums for his books, but
this was a precarious and irregular income, all the more so because
Nicholas's censorship often held them up. *Borís Godunóv* had been
thus prohibited since 1826, but now as a special favor, in order
that he might meet the demand of his future family life, he was
allowed to print it. It appeared in January 1831, but was met with
faint praise and loud blame. The autumn before his marriage
Púshkin spent in the country, at Bóldino, and these two months
were the most marvelously productive in his life. He was married
in February 1831. His marriage was, at first, externally happy.
But there was no real sympathy between the pair. Nathalie was
frivolous and cold, besides being trivial and almost vulgar and
quite free from all intellectual or poetical interests. Nathalie's
beauty made her an immense success in Petersburg, in town and
at court. It was to be able to invite her to court balls that Nicholas
in 1834 made Púshkin a "gentleman of the chamber," an honor
deeply resented by the poet. No longer the leader of an advanced
school, Púshkin was now the head of the "literary aristocracy."
He was venerated by the younger generation rather as a relic of
the past than as a living force. All he wrote after 1830 met with
no success. He half abandoned poetry and devoted himself to a
history of Peter the Great, which was never to be written. In 1836
he was, after repeated refusals, allowed to start a literary quarterly,
Sovreménnik (*The Contemporary*), which, however, like all he had
done since 1831, met with no success. Meanwhile his thraldom to
the court increased—he became more and more dependent on the
royal favor, especially since he had contracted considerable debts
to the Treasury. He felt that he was suffocating in a society where
a mere poet, in spite of his "six-hundred-year-old nobility," was
looked down upon by the great courtiers descended from the
favorites of eighteenth-century empresses, and was little more than
his wife's husband. He tried to free himself from the noxious and
deteriorating atmosphere, but was given to understand that if he
left town it would be in disgrace. At last came the tragic end. His
jealousy was exasperated by the attention paid to Nathalie by

Baron Georges D'Anthès, a French Royalist in the Russian service. Púshkin called him out. D'Anthès at first succeeded in evading a duel by marrying Nathalie's sister, thus pretending to show that Púshkin was mistaken in his suspicions. But a few days after the marriage Púshkin learned that Nathalie and D'Anthès had again secretly met. He called him out a second time, in terms that made all escape impossible for D'Anthès. The duel was fought on January 27, 1837. Púshkin was mortally wounded, and died on the 29th. For fear of public demonstrations of sympathy his coffin was hurried away in the night from Petersburg to the monastery near Mikháylovskoye, which he had chosen for his burial place.

Púshkin began writing early. There is a tradition, founded on the recollection of his elder sister, that he wrote French verse before he left home for the Lyceum. His earliest datable work in Russian belongs to 1814. Only two or three immature and crude poems may be assigned, on internal evidence, to an earlier date. With the exception of these, Púshkin's verse was from the very beginning extraordinarily easy and fluent, almost on the highest level of a time when ease and fluency were the main aim of poets. If till about 1820 he remained inferior to Zhukóvsky and Bátyushkov, it was not for lack of mastery, but rather for the lack of original inspiration. Púshkin's Lyceum verses are imitative and, for a boy's verse, strikingly unemotional and unsentimental. He was a consummate technician before he really became a poet—an order of development not usual with nineteenth-century poets. Some of his Lyceum verses are exercises in the forms practiced by Zhukóvsky and Derzhávin, but by far the greater part belong to the favorite Arzamasian kinds of fugitive poetry, friendly epistles, and Anacreontic lyrics. His style grew up in the school of Zhukóvsky and Bátyushkov, but the direct influence on it of the French classical poets is also considerable, and of these Voltaire was for a long time Púshkin's favorite. Next came the influence of Parny, whose remarkable and long-neglected elegies, inspired with unsentimental, classical, but genuinely passionate, love, were the models for the first of Púshkin's poems in which we can discern the accent of serious passion. By 1818 Púshkin's verse finally acquires that accent which is his alone. The epistles and elegies of these years are already latently great poetry. Through the impersonal brilliance of their Arzamasian wit we distinctly discern a heart and nerves of exceptionally rich vitality. There is a clear and cold atmosphere in these poems—and no feeling underlying them. The same atmosphere pervades *Ruslán and Lyudmíla.* This is a semi-ironic and frivolous romance, where only a few names and the barest skeletons of motifs are taken from the chapbooks of the type of *Bová* and *Eruslán*, but where all the treatment is essentially eighteenth century. There is nothing in it that might have shocked the taste of Voltaire. There is no seriousness in *Ruslán and Lyudmíla* except the seriousness of very conscientious craftsmanship. It is pure play, like the classical ballet, which Púshkin was so fond of at the time he was writing the poem. It is the work of a confident and buoyant young man who is already a past master in the craft of poetry but not yet quite a poet in the highest sense.

By 1818–20 the essential groundwork of Púshkin's poetic style was established, and remained unchanged till the end. It is "French" and classical. Its most characteristic feature—one that is particularly disconcerting to the romantic-bred reader—is the complete avoidance of all imagery and metaphor. Púshkin's images are all dependent on the happy use of the *mot juste*, and his poetic effectiveness on the use of metonymy and similar purely verbal figures of speech.

Taken as a whole, the early verse of Púshkin and that of his later verse which is in the same style are perhaps the nearest approach outside French poetry to "that tone of mingled distinction, gaiety, and grace which," says Lytton Strachey, "is one of the unique products of the mature poetical genius of France."

The last French master of Púshkin was André Chénier, whose remains were published in 1819. This was to be the last external influence that affected the inner texture of Púshkin's style. Later influences affected only his choice of subject and his methods of construction.

The principal of these influences was Byron's, which dominates Púshkin's second period (1820–3). But the nature of this influence must be clearly understood. Púshkin had no essential kinship with the English poet. His exact and logical style is poles apart from Byron's untidy rhetoric. Byron's influence is limited to the narrative poems of this period, and in these it was the choice of subject and the disposition of the material that are due to Byron—the actual style remained as classical as before. The principal Byronic poems of Púshkin are *The Captive of the Caucasus* (written 1820–1, published 1822) and *The Fountain of Bakhchi-saráy* (written 1822, published 1824). The success of both of these poems was greater than that of any other work of Púshkin's. It was they that made Púshkin the most popular poet of the twenties. They are very far from giving the full measure of his genius. As in all that preceded them, the form is consistently greater than the content. The form (verse and diction) is perfect. In certain respects, even, it was never excelled by Púshkin himself, and certainly never approached by any other poet. The public reveled in the sheer beauty of word and sound that the poet so triumphantly upheld at the same flawless level from beginning to end. The effect is all the more marvelous as Púshkin's verse does not "sing." Its beauty and harmony are purely verbal—based on complete mutual adequacy of rhythm and syntax, and on an extraordinarily subtle and complex system of what one might call alliteration if the word might be used to denote anything so variedly and consistently unobtrusive. The perfection of this verbal harmony is reached in *The Fountain of Bakhchisaráy.* Afterwards Púshkin deliberately avoided the too fluent and caressing effects of this manner.

As I have said, the Byronic element in the two Byronic poems is limited to the subject and the narrative construction. The oriental beauty, with her fierce or devoted love, the disillusioned hero, with strong passions in the past, the oriental potentate, grim and silent, the hot atmosphere of "the clime of the East"—these are the elements taken by Púshkin from Byron. The fragmentary and dramatic manner of presentation, with its beginning *in medias res*, the abrupt transitions, and its lyrical epilogues, is the trace of Byron's narrative manner. But the Byronic spirit was only superficially assimilated by Púshkin, and the two poems must be regarded as further impersonal exercises on a borrowed theme. The most original and the most beautiful parts in both poems are the purely descriptive passages: in *The Captive*, the account of the warlike habits of the Circassians, as exact and as reliable in point of fact as those of the shrewdest eighteenth-century travelers; in *The Fountain*, the more lyrical and atmospheric, but always eminently precise and plastic, descriptions of the harem and evocations of the Crimea. Of the shorter romantic and Byronic poems belonging to this period, *The Robber Brothers* (1821), which has less verbal beauty than the two longer poems, is interesting as having attained an exceptional popularity among the people: it has even been incorporated in a folk play.

Púshkin's lyric poetry of the period is conspicuously free from every formal, and almost every emotional, trace of Byronism. It is a continuation of the poems of 1816–19. But it gradually acquires a more passionate and manly tone, becomes more personal and more perfect in form. The direct influence of Chénier is apparent in a series of descriptive and elegiac epigrams, full of beautiful restraint and plastic expressiveness. The same influence in a more transformed and digested form is present in the greatest lyrical poem of the period (and one of the greatest he ever wrote), the wonderful *Napoleon* of 1821.

The strictly French, eighteenth-century, and Voltairian element persisted in Púshkin some time after his acquaintance with Byron. It was only now that he wrote the most Voltairian of his poems, the blasphemous and lascivious *Gavriliáda* (1821), which brought him much trouble in the next reign and was printed only long after his death (London, 1861). Though quite in the style of Voltaire's and Parny's anti-religious poems, it is different from them in that it is not serious—not intended for anti-Christian propaganda, but merely the froth of an irreverent, sensuous, and unbridled youth.

Púshkin's middle period may be regarded as coextensive with the writing of *Evgény Onégin*, his longest, most popular and influential, and in certain ways most characteristic work. It is a "Novel in Verse," in eight cantos, which are called chapters. It was begun in the spring of 1823 and completed in the autumn of 1830, a few finishing touches being added in 1831. The initial impulse came from *Don Juan*, but apart from the general idea of writing a long narrative poem in stanzaed verse, with a subject taken from contemporary life, and in a tone mingled of gravity and gaiety, *Evgény Onégin* has little in common with Byron's epic. It does not have the qualities of *Don Juan*—its sea-like sweep or its satiric power. The qualities it has are of a nature entirely unlike Byron's. It is less loose and, though when Púshkin began it he had not any fixed idea how he was going to finish it, it is a story with a beginning, a middle, and an end. Its unity is not an intended and premeditated unity, but rather like the organic unity of an individual life. It reflects the stages through which the poet passed between his twenty-fourth and thirty-second years. The transition from the boisterously young high spirits of the first chapter to the resigned and muffled tragedy of the eighth is gradual, like the growth of a tree.

The first chapter, written in 1823, is the crowning glory of Púshkin's youth. It is the most brilliant of all his works. It sparkles and bubbles like champagne—a comparison long hackneyed but still inevitable. It is the description of the life of a young St. Petersburg dandy (the English word is used), the life familiar to Púshkin himself before his exile. It is the only one of the eight chapters where the gay definitely predominates over the grave. The later chapters are in the same style, but chastened and mellowed down as years proceed. The mixture of humor (not satire) and poetical sentiment and the infinite wealth and variety of the emotional shadings and transitions recall *Tristram Shandy* (whose author Púshkin esteemed highly), but with a freedom, a spontaneity, a vigorous go that was entirely beyond the reach of Sterne.

Evgény Onégin is the crowning glory of Púshkin's first maturity and the fullest expression of what may be called his "subjective" manner, as opposed to the objective and impersonal manner of his latter years. Of all his works it has the least *apparent* restraint: the poet lets himself go in digressions, lyrical, humorous, polemical. He makes no show of artistic economy. More than anywhere else he relies for his effects on atmosphere. But his sense of measure and his unerring mastery are as present in *Onégin* as elsewhere.

The actual manner of *Onégin* has been imitated by numerous Russian poets, never with more than questionable success. It demanded two qualities that are extremely rare in conjunction— a boundless, spontaneous vitality and an unerring sense of artistic measure. When I speak of the important influence of *Onégin* on later literary developments, I do not allude to the direct and metrical progeny of this "novel in verse." It is the kind of realism first introduced in it, the style of character drawing, the characters themselves, and the construction of the story that are to be regarded as the fountainheads of the later Russian novel. The realism of *Onégin* is that peculiarly Russian realism which is poetical without idealizing and without surrendering anything of reality. It is the same realism that will live again in Lérmontov's novel, in Turgénev, in Goncharóv, in *War and Peace*, and in the best of

Chékhov—though its legitimacy outside the perfect poetical form given it by Púshkin is open to doubt. The character drawing of *Onégin* is not analytical or psychological, but poetical, dependent on the lyrical and emotional atmosphere accompanying the personages—not on the anatomy of their thoughts and sentiments. This style of portraiture was inherited from Púshkin by Turgénev and other Russian novelists, but not by Tolstóy or Dostoyévsky. Of the characters themselves, Onégin and Tatiána are the ancestors of a whole race of characters in Russian fiction; Lérmontov's, Goncharóv's and Turgénev's, especially, are entirely of this family. Finally the construction of the story, so different from that of Púshkin's prose stories, became the standard for the Russian novel. The simplicity of the plot, its logical development from the essential features of the heroes, and the unhappy, suggestively muffled ending, gave the pattern to the Russian novelists—especially, again, to Turgénev. Much in the methods of *Onégin* may be termed romantic. But the spirit of the poem is not. As in all the mature works of Púshkin it is dominated by the stern moral law of the Fates. Onégin's irresponsible self-indulgence and fidelity to self subtly, inevitably, untheatrically undo him, while the calm self-command and resignation of Tatiána give her that unquestionable halo of moral greatness which is forever associated with her name. The greatness of Púshkin in the creation of Tatiána is that he avoided the almost unavoidable pit of making a prig or a puritan out of the virtuous wife who coldly rejects the man she loves. Tatiána is redeemed in her virtue by the sadness she will never conquer, by her resigned and calm resolve never to enter her only possible paradise, but to live with never a possibility of happiness. The Tatiána-Onégin relation has often been revived in Russian fiction, and the juxtaposition of a small and weak man with a strong woman became almost hackneyed in Turgénev and others. But the classical attitude of Púshkin, of sympathy without pity for the man and of respect without reward for the woman, has never been revived.

During the time Púshkin was at work at *Evgény Onégin* he wrote numerous other short and long poems, of varied initial significance but invariable perfection. The nearest kin to *Onégin* are the tales in verse of contemporary Russian life: *Count Núlin* (1825), a crisp, clever anecdote in verse in a more purely realistic

and ironic manner; and *The Little House in Kolómna* (1830), a poem
in octaves, a kind of Russian *Beppo*, his last essay in the "extensive" style of *Onégin*.

The Byronic narrative-poem form was continued in *The Gypsies* (1824, published 1827) and *Poltáva* (1828, published 1829).
These poems are immeasurably superior to the two earlier Byronic
tales. Of the influence of Byron nothing remains in them but the
merest idea of narrative in verse with a lyrical coloring and with
abrupt passages from episode to episode. *The Gypsies* is among
the greatest works of Púshkin. It is, with *Onégin*, the first in which
he reached the full measure of his genius, and the first, also, in
which begins the gradual evolution from the "extensive," mellifluous, and caressing style of his youth to the sterner beauty of his
later work. Its setting is conventional—the gypsies of Bessarabia
are not treated realistically, but merely as ideal representatives of
a natural state of human society. The subject is the tragic inability of sophisticated and civilized man to throw away his con-
vention-bred feelings and passions, especially the feeling of owner-
ship of his mate. The poem is, on the face of it, a strong affirmation
of freedom—of the freedom of the woman against the man—and a
denunciation of the unnatural wickedness of vengeance and of
punishment. It is obviously and patently a plea for anarchism, and
has been commented on in this sense by Dostoyévsky (in his famous Púshkin Address) and by Vyachesl´v Ivánov. However
strangely out of tune this anarchism may be with all the later work
of Púshkin, it cannot be explained away and must be accepted as
an essential ingredient of his philosophy. But the essentially classical religion of the Tragic Fates, of Nemesis working as an inevitable law of nature, is nowhere more fully expressed than in
The Gypsies. It was Púshkin's first attempt at tragedy, and one of
his greatest. It is too easy to philosophize about *The Gypsies*—the
most temptingly universal imaginative work in the Russian language. It is less easy to do justice to its poetical beauty, and speaking of it, one is too likely to forget the lesson of restraint that is
the best lesson to be learned from Púshkin. The verse, less fluent
and voluptuous than in *The Captive* and in *The Fountain*, is tighter,
fuller, more saturated with complex expressiveness. Such passages
as the old gypsy's tale of Ovid, the end of the poem (with the
speech of the old man on Aléko's murder), and especially the
epilogue, are unsurpassable summits of poetry. One can only be

deeply grateful to the Fates for allowing us to have such plenty.

Poltáva is a further step towards the objective and impersonal manner. In it Púshkin deliberately and studiously avoids the fluent loveliness of his southern poems. To us its stern and harsh style sounds magnificently heroic, but its first readers were disagreeably taken aback by this new departure and refused to admire it. It is not a perfect whole—the romantic love story of the old hetman Mazéppa for his godchild is imperfectly fused with the national epic of the struggle of Peter with Charles of Sweden. The epic itself, which forms the background of the first two cantos and the prevailing subject of the third (with its famous description, so exact in its condensed ornateness, of the battle of Poltáva), is Púshkin's first contribution to that impersonal, national, group poetry which had inspired Lomonósov and Derzhávin, and which had been dead since the triumph of the Karamzinists. After Púshkin it was once more to die. The great glory of *Poltáva*, apart from this voicing of national and supra-individual sentiment, is its diction, magnificent in its very baldness and terseness, so happily grand and powerful is the choice of words, never archaic, but always charged with the richest and greatest associations.

A style similar to *Poltáva*, terse and saturated, is used in several unfinished narrative fragments of this and the following period. The most important are *Cleopatra, or the Egyptian Nights* (begun 1825, resumed 1835) and *Gálub* (c. 1830). The latter is a story of the Caucasus strikingly different in style from *The Captive;* the former, one of Púshkin's most memorable conceptions, a magnificent poem of death and lust.

The period of *Evgény Onégin* is also the period of Púshkin's best and greatest lyrical output. With few exceptions (the most notable being the great Napoleon ode) none of his lyric poems written before 1824 are on the very highest level of his genius. After that date he often continued to write in the lighter, occasional style of his early years, and these poems acquire a mellower and subtler grace, even if they lose the clear, youthful vigor of the earlier ones. But his serious lyric poetry written between 1824 and 1830 is a body of lyric verse unapproached in Russian and unsurpassed in any poetry. It is impossible without quotations from the originals to prove the statement or to give an adequate idea of the nature of this poetry. Much of it is subjective, occasional, and emotional—the actual biographical occasion is frequently known.

But the occasions are idealized, sublimated, and universalized, and the poems preserve no ragged edges of extrapoetic sentiment or undistilled emotion. Though subjective and demonstrably based on individual experience, they are general in tone, as classical poetry is. They seldom contain any striking psychological observation or any revelation of the all too personal. Their appeal, like the appeal of Sappho, is to common human experience. Their style, which is a further development of Zhukóvsky's, is also of that classical quality which, says Montesquieu in speaking of Raphael, *"frappe moins d'abord pour frapper plus en suite."* The beauty of the style, which, as always in Púshkin, is free from wit, imagery, and metaphor, is a Greek beauty that depends as much on what is left unsaid as on what is said. It depends on the choice of words, on the adequacy of rhythm to intonation, and on the complex texture of sound—the wonderful *alliteratio Pushkiniana,* so elusive and so all-conditioning. It is impossible here to quote or analyze any of these lyrics. I can only enumerate some of the most beautiful: the lines on jealousy beginning: "The stormy day is spent"; the Lyceum anniversary of 1825—the greatest hymn to friendship in all poetry; the stanzas to Mme Kern ("I remember a wonderful moment," 1825) the elegy (sixteen lines) on the death of Amália Ríznich (1826); the *Foreboding* (1828); and the lyrics addressed to a dead mistress, probably Amália Ríznich, written a few months before his marriage (1830), especially, what is perhaps the most intensely perfect of all, *For the Shores of Thy Distant Fatherland* (*Dlya beregóv otchízny dálnoy*). A group apart is formed by the nature lyrics—the most classical of all—with their conception of inanimate and irresponsive nature. Among the best are *The Storm* (1827), with its famous comparison between the beauty of the storm and the beauty of "a girl on the rock," to the latter's advantage; *The Winter Morning* (1829); and *The Avalanche* (1829). On an even higher level of poetical significance are two poems that are Púshkin's grandest utterances in the grand style—the often quoted and much too often commented-on *Prophet* (1826); and the tense and terrible *Upas-tree* (*Anchár,* 1828).

To the same period belong Púshkin's best ballads, *The Bridegroom* (1825) and *The Drowned Man* (1828). The style of these ballads is the realistic style introduced by Katénin but perfected and refined with all the mastery of Púshkin.

After 1830 Púshkin's lyrical poetry tends to become impersonally universal and severely bare of all ornament. Henceforward its characteristics are restraint, reticence, and an ascetic avoidance of all that the public associates with poetic beauty—mellifluous ease, melodious tone, attractive sentiment. The most characteristic poems of the thirties are impersonal elegiac meditations, proceeding from a "thinking heart" brooding on the great commonplaces of universal experience. The most majestic of these poems is *The Captain* (1836), an elegy on the portrait of the wronged and misunderstood hero of 1812—Field Marshal Barcláy de Tólly. But by the side of this *odi profanum vulgus* sentiment Púshkin attempted to voice "group feelings," as in his famous retort to the French friends of Poland, *To the Detractors of Russia* (1831). One of the most perfect, unadorned, prosaic, and simplest poems is that noble tribute to the man in the hero—*The Feast of Peter the Great* (1835). But by the side of these high and supra-personal utterances, other sounds came from him—the fruit of his prolonged torture at the hand of Nicholas, Nathalie, and society. The noble restraint of *The Captain* is a striking contrast to the grim and weird irony of those lines on *Madness* (*Ne day mne Bog soytí s umá*, 1833), which are one of the most poignant "mad poems" ever written. The few lyrics of this latter type were published only after the poet's death.

Most of Púshkin's narrative poems written after 1830 are personative, or "stylized," as we say in Russia. The poet is masked in a borrowed form, or borrowed subject, or both, and his human personality is carefully and effectively hidden. Such is *Angelo* (1833), a paraphrase of *Measure for Measure*, where Púshkin tried to preserve Shakspere's "broad painting of character" while stripping it of the irrelevancies and excrescences of Elizabethan exuberance. Of all Púshkin's poems, *Angelo* has had the least share of praise, but it throws an important light on the workings of his creative mind. More purely impersonal are the *Songs of the Western Slavs* (1832), adaptations of Mérimée's forgeries of Serbian folklore in the style of the Russian folk epic; and, above all, the fairy tales (*Skázki*, 1831–2); the cynically witty *Parson and His Man Baldá*, an admirable revival of the manner of the popular doggerel verse of the eighteenth century; the maliciously ironical *Golden Cockerel;* and the best of all, *King Saltán*. The longer one lives, the more one is inclined to regard *King Saltán* as the masterpiece of Russian poetry. It is purest art, free from all the irrelevancies of emotion and symbol, "a thing of beauty" and "a joy for ever."

It is also the most universal art, for it has the same appeal for a child of six and for the most sophisticated poetry reader of sixty. It requires no understanding; its reception is immediate, direct, unquestionable. It is not frivolous, nor witty, nor humorous. But it is light, exhilarating, bracing. It has high seriousness, for what can be more highly serious than the creation of a world of perfect beauty and freedom, open to all?

I fully realize that the claim for *King Saltán* to be accepted as *the* masterpiece of Púshkin has little chance of getting a majority of votes. Such a majority is virtually pledged to the last great narrative poem of Púshkin—*The Bronze Horseman* (written 1833, published posthumously 1841). This poem certainly has very substantial claims to absolute pre-eminence. There is no conception of poetic greatness from the standpoint of which this pre-eminence could be challenged, except that (hypothetic) standpoint which would demand of all poetry that it be as free from human irrelevancies as is *King Saltán*. The classicist, the romanticist, the realist, the symbolist, and the expressionist must all agree in their appreciation of *The Bronze Horseman*. Its actual subject is the Petersburg inundation of 1824 and the effect it had on Evgény, a poor and insignificant clerk, by washing away into the sea his sweetheart's house with all its inhabitants. Its philosophical (or whatever the word) subject is the irreconcilable conflict of the rights of the community, as incarnate in the *genius loci* of the city, the bronze statue of Peter the Great on the Senate Square—and of those of the individual, as represented by the wretched Evgény, who is undone by the mere geographical factor of the site of Petersburg. The greatness of the poem lies particularly in the fact that Púshkin makes no attempt to reconcile the two in any superior harmony. And though the poem begins with a splendid hymn to Peter and Petersburg, and the figure of the great Emperor dominates it in semi-divine proportions, it is a strikingly different figure from the human Peter of *Poltáva* and of *The Feast of Peter the Great*—an inhuman and potent demon who knows no mercy. The poet's essential sympathy for the undone Evgény is by no means impaired by the greatness of his enemy. And the issue of the moral conflict remains in the balance—unsolved. In style *The Bronze Horseman* is a step further in the direction of *Poltáva*. The concentrated fullness and tightness of the octosyllabics; the vocabulary, strictly realistic, but saturated with the utmost expressiveness; the elemental majesty of the movement; the endless inward vistas opened by each word and by the whole—give the poem a poetic weight that fully justifies acceptance of it as the greatest example in Russian of great poetry.

Púshkin's first, and longest, play, *Borís Godunóv* (1825, published 1831), was written, like his first stories in prose, primarily as a formal experiment. In writing it he was interested not so much in the doings and destinies of his characters as in the destinies of Russian tragedy and of Russian dramatic meter. *Borís Godunóv* is a first essay in Russian romantic—Shaksperian— tragedy as opposed to the hitherto prevalent French forms. When, in 1826, Púshkin brought it to Moscow, it was acclaimed as his masterpiece by the young idealists whose idols were Shakspere (a German Shakspere) and Goethe. It is hardly possible today to share their view. *Borís Godunóv* must rather be regarded as one of the immature and preparatory works of Púshkin, less mature and less perfect than much that had preceded it—than *The Gypsies*, for instance, or the early chapters of *Onégin*. The subject of the play is taken from Karamzín. It is one of those inset dramatic stories which are the principal literary attraction of his *History*. In his interpretation of the facts Púshkin closely followed Karamzín, and this was a severe handicap. *Borís Godunóv* is a tragedy of expiation, but nowhere else does Púshkin treat the theme with less inevitable mastery. At times it is almost sentimental. The meter, a particularly monotonous form of blank verse, is not quite satisfactory. The diction is somewhat stilted and conventional. And the construction of the play is in many ways narrative rather than dramatic. For a dialogued chronicle, however, to be read, not acted, it is masterly, and one of Púshkin's first triumphs in economy. The characters, especially the False Demetrius, are admirably drawn. The prose scenes, with their fine irony, are the best in the play and have nothing to compare with them in all previous Russian literature. In two or three places the tragedy attains real dramatic beauty—as in the scene of Borís's death and in the grandly condensed final scene, with the massacre of the Godunóvs (*behind* the scenes—a French touch) and the proclamation of the imposter as tsar. *Borís Godunóv* remained a closet play. Púshkin's dream of seeing it revolutionize the Russian stage never came true.

Its influence, both immediate and posthumous, was extensive but not intrinsically significant—Russia never succeeded in producing really original "Shaksperian" tragedy.

On a much higher level of perfection and originality stand Púshkin's later plays—the four so-called "Little Tragedies" and *Rusálka*. The former were written mainly in the wonderful Bóldino autumn of 1830. Two of them, *Mozart and Salieri* and *The Feast during the Plague*, were published shortly afterwards; the third, *The Covetous Knight* (the English title is Púshkin's own), in 1836 (anonymously). *The Stone Guest*, finally revised only in that year, remained unpublished till after the poet's death (1840). Unlike *Borís Godunóv*, the Little Tragedies were not planned as experiments in form. They were rather essays in understanding of character and of dramatic situation. One of the titles proposed and rejected by Púshkin for the whole group was "Dramatical Investigations." The form of the diminutive tragedy was suggested by the similar productions of Barry Cornwall (whom Púshkin, like many of his contemporaries, even in England, valued higher than we do). *The Covetous Knight* bears the subheading "Scenes from the tragicomedy by Chenstone." [2] *The Feast during the Plague* is a fairly accurate translation of a scene of John Wilson's *City of the Plague*. Thus the Little Tragedies may be regarded as largely due to English suggestion.

They are among the most original, characteristic, and perfect work of the poet. In them Púshkin reached his greatest degree of concentration. With the exception of *The Stone Guest* they can hardly be called plays. They are rather isolated situations, dramatic "points," but points charged with such significance that they do not demand any further development. They are the application to drama of the lyrical method of concentration. Their length varies from one scene and a little over two hundred lines (*The Feast*) to four acts and about five hundred lines (*The Stone Guest*). The least complex is *The Feast*. Púshkin's creative work in it was reduced to choosing where to begin and where to end, to translating Wilson's indifferent English verse into his own supreme Russian, and to adding two songs, both of which are among his

---

[2] It is possible that Púshkin had the English poet William Shenstone (1714–63) in mind when he made this acknowledgment. As far as is known, Shenstone wrote nothing called *The Covetous Knight*. Púshkin was probably merely coining a name to avoid any tie-up between his authorship of this work and his own father, a notorious miser.—Ed.

best; one of them, *The Hymn in Honor of the Plague*, is the most terrible and weird he ever wrote—one of his rare revelations of the dark side of things. *Mozart and Salieri* is a study of the passion of envy, and of the Divine Injustice that endows with genius whom it will and rewards not the lifelong labor of the devotee. *The Covetous Knight* is one of the greatest and grandest studies of the miser—the second scene, in which the miserly baron soliloquizes in his treasure vault, is the grandest dramatic monologue in Russian and perhaps Púshkin's most sustained piece of poetic magnificence. As for *The Stone Guest*, it shares with *The Bronze Horseman* the right to be regarded as Púshkin's masterpiece. It is less ornate and less apparently saturated than *The Horseman*. From beginning to end it never once abandons the diction of prose, but it even outdoes *The Horseman* in the limitless psychological and poetic suggestiveness of its severely unornamented verse. It is the story of Don Juan's last love affair—with the widow of the man he had murdered—and of his tragic end. It is Púshkin's highest achievement on the subject of Nemesis—his greatest subject. For the flexibility of the blank verse (so different from that of *Borís Godunóv*), for the infinitely subtle marriage of colloquial with metrical rhythm, for the boundless pregnancy of the dialogue, for the subtly distilled atmosphere of the south—and of atonement—it has no equal. In spite of its Spanish subject, it is also of all Púshkin's works the most characteristically Russian—not in any metaphysical meaning of that much abused word, but because it achieves what can be achieved only in Russian, in being at once classical, colloquial, and poetical, and because it embodies in their perfection all the best aspirations of Russian poetry—its striving towards selective, unornamental, realistic, and lyrical perfection. It is also of Púshkin's works the one that most defies translation—for in it the poetical and emotional value of every word is put to the fullest use and fully exhausted, and the natural possibilities of Russian rhythm (*at the same time* colloquial and metrical) are made to yield all they can. The mere skeleton of the play will give an idea of Púshkin's sober economy and restraint but not of the infinite wealth behind them.

The last of Púshkin's dramatic essays, *Rusálka* (*The River Nymph*), remains a fragment. Were it not for that, it would be third, with *The Bronze Horseman* and *The Stone Guest*, in claiming the first place in Russian poetry. What has been said of the verse and diction of *The Stone Guest* has to be repeated of *Rusálka*. The difference is that the subject and atmosphere are Russian. It was also to be a tragedy of expiation—the revenge of the seduced girl, who throws herself into the river and becomes "a powerful and cold water-nymph," on her faithless wooer, the prince.

Púshkin's greatest contemporary successes (with the general public) were *The Captive of the Caucasus* and *The Fountain of Bakhchisaráy* and (with the critical elite of his generation) *Borís Godunóv*—all of them works of immature youth. His later works, beginning with *Poltáva*, met with increasingly cool receptions, and on the eve of his death he was regarded by the young generation as a venerable, but obsolete classic, who had outlived his time and was ossified alive. His death was a signal for his recognition as a national glory. But the men of the forties were far from giving him his due—they regarded him as an admirable artist who had formed the language and established the originality of Russian literature but who was going to be, or actually had been, superseded by more national and modern writers. For the Slavophils he was not Russian; for the radical Westernizers, not modern enough. Both preferred Gógol. Only a minority of men, like Turgénev on the one hand and Grigóriev and Dostoyévsky on the other, laid the foundation of that uncompromising Púshkin cult which is now the common inheritance of every educated Russian. But if Turgénev was to a certain extent the genuine heir to the less vigorous and vital, more "feminine," sides of Púshkin, Grigóriev and Dostoyévsky were men of an entirely alien spirit, and their cult of Púshkin was precisely due to their awareness of the presence in him of supreme values that were unaccessible to them. Their cult of Púshkin was the religion of a paradise lost. The main mass of the intelligentsia in the second half of the nineteenth century was either indifferent or hostile to Púshkin. For many years the rule of utilitarianism prevented them from seeing his greatness. But among the elect the cult grew steadily. There can be no doubt that Dostoyévsky's Address in 1880, for all its fantastic un-Pushkinity, was powerfully effective in promoting it. A further date was the lapse of the copyright in the poet's works in 1887, which inaugurated an era of cheap and numerous editions. The consciousness of Púshkin's supremacy and centralness in Russian literature and civilization grew apace, unostentatiously, but irrevocably. The twentieth century received it full-grown. By the

time of the Revolution it was so ubiquitous and unconquerable
that even the Bolshevíks, who are in spirit as alien to Púshkin as
Dostoyévsky was, excluded his name almost alone from their
general oblivious condemnation of pre-Revolutionary Russia.

MINOR POETS

Poetry was more universally popular in the twenties than it has
ever been in Russia, either before or since. The principal form it
took was the Byronic tale in verse, whose vogue was started in
1822 by Púshkin's *The Captive* and Zhukóvsky's translation of
The Prisoner of Chillon, and lasted till the end of the decade. Before the sudden outburst of novel writing in 1829, tales in verse
were even best sellers. The greatest successes were Púshkin's two
"Southern poems" (*The Captive* and *The Fountain*). Almost, if not
quite, equal to Púshkin's was the success of Kozlóv.

Iván Ivánovich Kozlóv (1779–1840) was a man of an older
generation, but he began writing poetry only after 1820, when he
became blind. He stands out among the poets of the Golden Age
for the comparative inadequacy of his technique. His poetry appealed to the easily awakened emotions of the sentimental rather
than to the higher poetic receptivity. His popularity with contemporaries was based chiefly on *The Monk* (1825)—a verse tale in
which the darkness of a Byronic hero is sentimentalized and redeemed by ultimate repentance. *The Monk* produced as large a
family of imitations as either of Púshkin's Byronic poems. Kozlóv's
two other narrative poems, *Princess Nathalie Dolgorúky* (1828), a
sentimental variation on the theme of that noblewoman's misfortunes, and *The Mad Girl* (1830), met with a somewhat diminished success. Today the only poems of his still universally remembered are his translations of Moore's *Evening Bells* and of
Charles Wolfe's *Burial of Sir John Moore at Corunna*. The latter
in particular is both an exceptionally faithful translation and a
beautiful piece of Russian verse.

Another poet who won general recognition in the Byronic
narrative poem was Kondráty Fëdorovich Ryléyev (1795–1826),
who was hanged after the suppression of the Decembrist Revolt,
of which he was one of the principal leaders. His life belongs to
political more than to literary history. Suffice it to say that he was

one of the sincerest, noblest, and purest of the revolutionaries.
His literary career began in 1820. In 1823, together with his fellow
conspirator, the novelist and poet Alexander Bestúzhev, he started
publishing a yearly "almanac," the *Polar Star*, which was the first
publication to be entirely controlled by the "gentlemen." His
patriotic and historical *Meditations*, suggested by the similar poems
of the Polish poet Niemcéwicz, proceed from a Plutarchian conception of Russian history as a collection of exemplars of civic
virtue. With few exceptions the poems are stilted and conventional.
Much superior is the narrative poem *Voynaróvsky* (1825), about
Mazéppa's nephew, a champion of Ukrainian liberty, pining away
in his Siberian exile. Though not a perfect work of art, and somewhat monotonous in its rhythmical movement, it is a noble and
manly poem, inspired by the love of freedom. It was highly valued
by Púshkin, who even imitated some passages of it in *Poltáva*. But
Ryléyev's best poems are those inspired by his revolutionary
eagerness, written in the year of the Revolt: the narrative fragment
The Confession of Nalivávko and, especially, *The Citizen*, written
a few days before the Revolt. This last poem is one of the finest
pieces of revolutionary eloquence in the language.

The other kind of verse that was most popular in the twenties
was the elegy and the short, semi-society lyric of sentiment. Its
greatest (and most popular) masters were Zhukóvsky, Púshkin,
and Baratýnsky. But other poets of far less genius wrote short
elegies and stanzaed poems of elegiac sentiment that are almost
as good as the average of the great masters. These minor poets
need not detain us, and I will only just mention, as one of the most
pleasantly representative, Peter Alexándrovich Pletnëv (1792–
1865)—Púshkin's friend and literary agent, and, after the latter's
death, editor of his magazine *Sovreménnik*.

BARATÝNSKY

Púshkin's worthiest rival among his contemporaries, and the only
other poet of the twenties who may claim the adjective "great,"
was Evgény Abrámovich Baratýnsky (or Boratýnsky). He was
born in 1800, and, at the age of twelve, was sent to the "Corps of
Pages," an aristocratic military school. Being shortly thereafter
expelled for theft, he was reduced to becoming a private soldier,

at first in a regiment of the footguards in Petersburg. It was then he made his acquaintance with Délvig, who encouraged him, rallied his falling spirits, and introduced him to the literary press. In 1820 Baratýnsky was transferred to Finland, where he remained six years. The poetry written during this period established his reputation. In 1825 he at last received a commission, and the next year left the service and settled in Moscow. He married, and his family life was happy, but a profound melancholy remained the background of his mind and of his poetry. During this period he published several books of verse that were highly valued by the best critics of the "poets' party," including Púshkin and Kiréyev-sky, but met with the comparatively cool reception of the public, and violent ridicule on the part of the young "plebeian" journalists, like Nadézhdin. In 1843 Baratýnsky left Moscow for a journey to France and Italy. He died in Naples, of a sudden illness, on June 29, 1844.

Baratýnsky's tales in verse would never have been written without the example of Púshkin, but they are not so much imitations of the greater poet as conscious efforts to write differently. The first, *Éda*, is the simple story of the seduction of a Finnish farmer's daughter by a hussar officer billeted in her father's house—a subject old-fashioned already in the twenties, and reminiscent of the eighteenth century. It is treated with careful and consistent avoidance of rhetoric in a realistic and homely style, with a touch of sentimental pathos but not a trace of romanticism. It is written, like all that Baratýnsky wrote, in a wonderfully precise style, next to which Púshkin's seems hazy. The descriptive passages are among the best—the stern nature of Finland was particularly dear to Baratýnsky. But what is especially pleasing is the delicate psychological drawing of the heroine—as mere psychology no doubt superior to everything in Russian literature before it.

His second narrative poem, *The Ball* (1828), is more romantic. It is the story of the suicide of a fatal and romantic society lioness, abandoned by her lover for "an affected little minx, with dulcet silliness in her eyes, all in fluffy curls, like a King Charlie, with a sleepy smile on her lips"—the favorite romantic contrast of the dark and the fair beauty. The setting is realistic, but the attempts at humor are unhappy: Baratýnsky conspicuously lacked that natural ease without which humor is so hard to stand. The third tale in verse, and the longest, is *The Concubine* (1829–30; a later version, *The Gypsy Girl*, appeared in 1842). It is in the same style as *The Ball* and on a similar subject; only the dark lady is a gypsy, and instead of committing suicide she inadvertently kills her faithless lover, believing she is giving him a love drink.

In his earlier lyric verse, which belongs to the Arzamás school, Baratýnsky is the most brilliant and representative poet of the twenties. The principal influences are the young Púshkin, the French poets of the later eighteenth century (Parny, Millevoye), and Bátyushkov. What it has in common with the later period is the exceedingly clear and dry atmosphere—dryer and clearer than anything in the whole of Russian poetry—and the cold, metallic brilliance and sonority of the verse. For anything like the effect in English poetry one can go only to Pope. It consists of fugitive, light pieces in the Anacreontic and Horatian manner, some of which are decidedly the masterpieces of the kind; of love elegies, where a delicate, but impersonalized, sentiment is clothed in brilliant wit; of epistles to friends, where his wit is made still better use of; of meditative elegies in (roughly) the style of Gray. The longest and perhaps the best of all these early poems is *Feasts*, where an epicurean praise of the joys of the table is delicately mingled with a wistful melancholy. This background of melancholy gradually found more original forms of expression and was ultimately transformed into the philosophical pessimism of the mature Baratýnsky.

In his mature work (which includes all his short poems written after 1829) Baratýnsky is a poet of thought, perhaps of all the poets of the "stupid nineteenth century" the one who made the best use of thought as a material for poetry. This made him alien to his younger contemporaries and to all the later part of the century, which identified poetry with sentiment. His poetry is, as it were, a short cut from the wit of the eighteenth-century poets to the metaphysical ambitions of the twentieth (in terms of English poetry, from Pope to T. S. Eliot). As in his earlier work he excelled in the lighter forms of (serious) wit, his later work is saturated with wit in the higher sense, which in his case would not be exactly the sense given to the word either by Donne or by Pope, but would be necessarily included in any definition of poetic wit broad enough to include both Pope and Donne. Baratýnsky's poetry is intellectual in content, but the intellectual content is really transformed into poetry. His style is classical. It always remained fundamentally eighteenth-century, much more so than Púshkin's. But in his effort to give his thought the tersest and most concentrated statement, he sometimes becomes obscure by sheer dint of compression. He had not that divine, Mozartian lightness which produces the (false) impression that Púshkin's work cost him no labor—Baratýnsky's obvious labor gives his verse a certain air of brittleness which is at poles' ends from Púshkin's elasticity. But this is for the real lover of poetry precisely the special charm of Baratýnsky, for one assists all the time at the hardly won, but always complete, victory of the master over the resistant material. Among other things, Baratýnsky is one of the few Russian poets who were, in verse, masters of the complicated sentence, expanded by subordinate clauses and parentheses.

Baratýnsky was a classicist in his manner, but his outlook was, if not romantic, at least semi-romantic. A great intellectualist, he was the victim of intellect, of analytic knowledge. He aspired after a fuller union with nature, after a more primitive spontaneity of mental life. He saw the steady, inexorable movement of mankind away from nature. The aspiration after a more organic and natural past is one of the main motives of Baratýnsky's poetry. He symbolized it in the growing discord between nature's child—the poet —and the human herd, which were growing, with every generation, more absorbed by industrial cares. Hence the growing isolation of the poet in the modern world, where he is deprived of the popular response that met his highest inspirations in "the market places of the Greek towns." The only response in the modern world that greets the modern poet is that of his own rhymes (*Rhyme*, 1841). He turns away from poetry and seeks for a response from nature by planting trees (*On the Plantation of a Forest*, 1843). The future of industrialized and mechanized mankind will be brilliant and glorious in the nearest future, but universal happiness and peace will be bought at the cost of the loss of all higher values of poetry (*The Last Poet*). And inevitably, after an age of intellectual refinement, humanity will lose its vital sap and die from sexual impotence. Then earth will be restored to her primæval majesty (*The Last Death*, 1827). This philosophy, allying itself to his profound temperamental melancholy, produced poems of extraordinary majesty, which can compare with nothing in the poetry of pessimism, except Leopardi. Such is the crushing majesty of that long ode to dejection, *Autumn* (1838). Here and in other poems (as in the famous *Death*, 1833) Baratýnsky is splendidly rhetorical in the grandest manner of classicism, though with a pronouncedly personal accent. But always he is intellectual, and the imaginative wit of these great odes never allows them to be trite or commonplace. In other poems he displays an almost Spinozan power of reasoning, as in *On the Death of Goethe* (1832), which is constructed like a syllogism but is so rich in poetry that even the nineteenth century could not miss it, and it went through all the anthologies.

YAZÝKOV

Nikoláy Mikháylovich Yazýkov (1803–46) was the third major poet of the twenties. Like Baratýnsky he was sponsored in literature by Délvig. His first verses appeared in print in 1822. The same year he went to the (then German) University of Dorpat, where he made himself famous with his riotously anacreontic verse in praise of the student's merry life. For his summer vacations he went to Trigórskoye, where he met Púshkin. After leaving Dorpat, without a degree, he lived between Moscow and his Simbírsk estate. He became intimate with the nationalist and Slavophil circles of Moscow, and as he was of a distinctly unintellectual turn of mind, their nationalism was reflected in him in the form of a very crude jingoism. His poetry was highly esteemed by the Slavophils and by the "poets' party"—but the young idealists dismissed it as contemptibly lacking in ideas. This embittered Yazýkov, and in his later years he wrote some rather tasteless attacks on his enemies. His health, undermined by the Dorpat excesses, began to fail very early, and from about 1835 he was a permanent sufferer from gout and dyspepsia, and a restless wanderer from one health resort to another. The Genoese Riviera, Nice, Gastein, and other German *Kurorte* are the frequent background of his later verse.

Gógol, whose favorite poet Yazýkov was, said of him, playing on his name (*yazýk*—tongue, language): "Not in vain was he given such a name; he is master of his language as an Arab is of his fiery steed." Púshkin protested that the Castalian fount of which Yazýkov drank ran not with water, but with champagne. The almost physical intoxication produced by the verse of Yazýkov is

an experience familiar to his readers. His poetry is cold and seeth-
ing like champagne or like a mineral spring. There is no human
significance in it. Its force lies not in what it means, but in what it
is. The tremendous—physical or nervous—momentum of his verse
is a thing that can hardly be paralleled elsewhere. It must not be
imagined, however, that he was a fountain of word torrents like
Hugo or Swinburne. In all this verbal rush there is a restraint and
a master's grip that prove Yazýkov the true contemporary of
Púshkin and Baratýnsky. His early poetry is devoted to the praise
of wine and merrymaking, and was particularly appreciated by his
contemporaries. But the intoxication of his rhythms is perhaps
even more potent where the subject is less obviously Bacchic. It
may easily be imagined what he could make of such a subject as
A Waterfall (1828), but his more peaceful nature poems (*Trigórskoye*, and the one on Lake Peipus) are as vivid and impulsive in
their cold crystalline splendor. Of course Yazýkov had no sympathy with nature. It was purely a dazzling vision on his retina
transformed into a dazzling rush of words. In his power of seeing
nature as an orgy of light and color he approaches Derzhávin, but
he had neither the barbaric ruggedness nor the spontaneous and
naïve humanity of the older bard. His later poems are on the whole
superior to his earlier ones. His Slavophil and reactionary effusions
are rather second-rate, but some of the elegies, written in a state
of dejection during his sufferings, have genuine human feeling in
them without losing any of his verbal splendor. But his best and
greatest poems must be accepted as purely verbal magnificences.
Perhaps best of all are the lines *To the Rhine* (1840), where he
greets the German stream in the name of the Volga and all her
tributaries: the enumeration of these tributaries, an uninterrupted
catalogue of about fifty lines, is one of the greatest triumphs of
Russian verbal art, and an unsurpassed record of long breath—the
recitation of the poem is the most difficult, and, if successful, should
be the most glorious achievement of the poetry reciter.

METAPHYSICAL POETS

The poets of the twenties formed a real and, for all its diversity,
united movement. They are usually referred to as "the Púshkin
Pleiad." But there were also poets who stood outside the movement

and consequently remained more or less unrecognized by their contemporaries. Such were Fëdor Glínka and Wilhelm Küchelbecker, of whom the former was almost a major, and the latter, if an imperfect, a very individual poet.

Fëdor Nikoláyevich Glínka (1786–1880), a cousin of the composer, was one of the very few Russian poets who devoted themselves almost exclusively to religious poetry. His originality and independence from contemporary example is startlingly great. Like the other poets of his time, Glínka was a careful and conscientious craftsman. But his poetry is mystical, and, though his religion was strictly Orthodox, his mysticism was in substance of a Protestant type. His style, at once realistic and sublime, is distinctly akin to that of the great Anglican mystics Herbert and Vaughan. His metaphors are sometimes disconcertingly martial. There is a great swing and go in his verse when he speaks of the last judgment or when he paraphrases the prophets. He was never appreciated at his right value and has not yet been entirely rediscovered, but such a rediscovery is one of the maturest possibilities of Russian literary judgment.

Another poet who was out of joint with the times was Púshkin's schoolfellow Wilhelm Küchelbecker (1797–1846). Though of German blood, he was the most ardent of Russian patriots, and though in reality the most advanced of the romanticists, he insisted on calling himself an extreme literary conservative and a supporter of Admiral Shishkóv. He was an enthusiastic idealist, joined in the December conspiracy, and spent the last twenty years of his life in prison and in Siberia. He was a quixotic figure, ridiculous in appearance and behavior, but all who knew him had a warm affection for him, and Púshkin, who was one of his principal teasers, dedicated to him one of the best and sincerest stanzas of the *Lyceum Anniversary* of 1825.[3] In spite of his ridiculous appearance and comic enthusiasm Küchelbecker was a man of no small brains, and his short career as a literary critic (1824–5) gives him, together with Kiréyevsky, the first place among the critics of the Golden Age. It was courageous in 1825 to write long and enthusiastic articles on Shikhmátov, and it was proof of a singular force of judgment to give equal praise to Shakspere and Racine

---

[3] Küchelbecker is the hero of Yúry Tynyánov's biographical novel *Kyúkhlya* (1925), one of the best historical novels in the Russian language.

while denying Byron a footing of equality with them. As a poet, Küchelbecker had a fine, pantheistic vision of the world but did not succeed in giving it a definite expression—like so much of the poetry of the later part of the century, his poetry is an inchoate world awaiting a builder. Only occasionally did he hit on an adequate form, and then he would produce a poem of real beauty. Such is the noble elegy on the death of Púshkin (*October 19*), which is curiously near in time, if not in tone, to Wordsworth's *Extempore Effusion*. It is a *Lament of the Makaris*, closing the Golden Age of Russian poetry.

Küchelbecker's miscellany *Mnemosyne* (1824–5) was the first publication to give place to the young Idealists, who were to introduce into Russia the cult of Goethe and Schelling's metaphysics. These young men, for the most part of good family and exceptionally good education, lived in Moscow and formed a sort of friendly society, calling themselves the Wisdom-lovers (*lyubomúdry*—Slavonic translation of *philosophoi*). They included Prince Vladímir Odóyevsky, Pogódin, Shevyrëv, Khomyakóv, Iván Kiréyevsky, all of them names we shall meet with again in the following chapter, but their leader was a man whose short-lived career necessarily belongs to the twenties. This was Dmítry Vladímirovich Venevítinov, a distant cousin of Púshkin. Born in 1805, he died in his twenty-second year, carrying away with him one of the greatest hopes of Russian literature. His death was accidental—he caught a chill when driving home from a ball in the winter. It is impossible to predict what might not have come of him. He was a man of dazzling abundance of gifts—a strong brain, a born metaphysician, a mature and lofty poet—at twenty-one. His thirst for knowledge was truly Faustian, and his capacity of acquiring it reminiscent of Pico. At the same time he was a virile, attractive young man who loved all the pleasures of life. There was also in him an essential sanity and balance of all the functions of soul and body that remind one of Goethe. His literary remains are not extensive. His few philosophical and critical articles introduce us for the first time to a Russian mentality modified by the grafting on it of German idealism. But in these propylæa of a new learning there is a sane coolness and broadness of grasp for which we shall look in vain in his successors, the Idealists of the thirties. His poetry is almost perfect. Its style is based on Púshkin's and

Zhukóvsky's, but with an individual mastery of his own. His diction is very pure, and his rhythms pure and majestic. His most characteristic poems are philosophical.

THE THEATER

The classical tragedy in Alexandrines died out after Ózerov, but classical comedy survived, and even had a revival. However, with the single exception of the great but isolated comedy of Griboyédov, it produced nothing to compare with the better plays of the eighteenth century. The playwrights worked for the theater and for their own day—not for literature and time. Some of their plays are amusing, especially those where the dramatists (all of them conservatives and classicists) satirized the Karamzinians and the romanticists (e.g. Shakhovskóy's *Lípetsk Spa* and Griboyédov's *Student*), but all are insignificant, frankly and unambitiously so. The futility and absence of serious literary interests in all this world of comedy are admirably pictured in Aksákov's *Literary and Theatrical Reminiscences*. The chief figures of this theater were the versatile and prolific Prince Alexander Shakhovskóy (1777–1846); Michael Nikoláyevich Zagóskin (1789–1852), who afterwards became more famous as a "Waverley" novelist; Nikoláy Ivánovich Khmelnítsky (1789–1846); and Alexander Ivánovich Písarev (1803–1828), the greatest master of stagecraft among them, and a particular friend of Aksákov's. Khmelnítsky and Písarev excelled chiefly in the vaudeville, a dramatic form the craze for which in Russia began about 1820 and reached its maximum about 1840. Griboyédov in his early comedies was nothing but a furnisher of stageable plays: they have curiously little in common with the one great comedy that makes him a classic almost comparable with Púshkin.

GRIBOYÉDOV

Alexander Sergéyevich Griboyédov (1795–1829) was born in Moscow. By the age of seventeen he had taken degrees at the University of Moscow in science and in law, and was preparing for a doctorate when his studies were interrupted by Napoleon's invasion. He enlisted in a cavalry regiment but saw no fighting. In 1816 he went to Petersburg, where he became a clerk in the Foreign Office. Griboyédov plunged eagerly into the animated and excited postwar life of the capital. The theater became (as it was to so many of his contemporaries) the center of his interests. He wrote and staged indifferent comedies and courted actresses. He mixed in the revolutionary circles and was received a Freemason. In the literary quarrels he sided with the Shishkovists. He easily acquired the reputation of being one of the cleverest men and greatest wits in Russia. All the time he did serious work at the Foreign Office; so that when a particularly reliable official was wanted to go as secretary to a mission in Persia, the post was offered to Griboyédov.

Griboyédov passed the years 1818–25 partly in Tiflís, partly in Persia. He made friends with the famous "Proconsul" of the Caucasus, General Ermólov, the most popular officeholder of the day and one of the most remarkable, who liked in Griboyédov a kindred spirit and made him his secretary. It was in 1822–3 that Griboyédov wrote his great comedy *Woe from Wit*. Only the final touches were added during his two years' leave of absence in Moscow and Petersburg (1823–5). *Woe from Wit* was not passed by the censorship for the stage, and only portions of it were allowed to appear in an almanac for 1825. But it was read out by the author to "all Moscow" and to "all Petersburg" and circulated in innumerable copies, so it was as good as published in 1825.

In the end of that year Griboyédov had to return to Ermólov's headquarters in the Caucasus. But he did not remain there long. Immediately after the Revolt of December 14th a courier was sent to arrest him. It is reported that Ermólov (who was popular with the Decembrists) warned Griboyédov of the impending arrest and gave him time to destroy compromising papers. Griboyédov was brought to Petersburg and placed under custody. He was highly incensed by the arrest and wrote to Nicholas a vehement letter couched in such language that the Emperor's A.D.C. did not dare present it to him. At the inquiry Griboyédov behaved with consistent firmness. In spite of his close connections with many of the rebels he succeeded in exculpating himself. He was set free, and, as a compensation for the trouble he had undergone, he was given promotion and a year's salary. The affair, however, remains somewhat mysterious, for it is practically certain that Griboyédov was not innocent in the matter.

He now returned to the Caucasus, where in the meantime hostilities had begun with Persia. Ermólov, disliked and distrusted by Nicholas, had had to resign, but the new Viceroy, the Emperor's particular favorite and intimate friend, Paskévich, was Griboyédov's cousin by marriage, and the relations of the two were most cordial. He joined Paskévich's headquarters at the front and accompanied him throughout the war. He negotiated the Peace of Turkmenchai (February 10, 1828) and took the treaty to Petersburg for ratification. His arrival at the capital was met with salvos from the fortress; he was given high rewards and appointed Russian Minister to Persia. On his way back, in Tiflís, he fell in love with a sixteen-year-old Georgian girl, Princess Nina Chavchavádze, and married her. At the height of happiness he set off with his young bride to Tabriz, whence he was to supervise the fulfillment of the treaty by the Persians.

This was no easy and no agreeable task. The treaty provided for the payment of a large contribution and for the repatriation of all Christian prisoners, principally Armenian women in Persian harems. The former clause was impracticable, as Persia was insolvent; the latter was felt by the Persians as a profound insult to the sanctity of the harem, a principal foundation of their religious polity. In December 1828 Griboyédov went to Teheran to negotiate more directly with the Shah, leaving his wife in Tabriz. He at once realized (and wrote in his dispatches) that the Russian demands were excessive, but he enforced them with conscientious energy and without respect for oriental susceptibilities. Before long a popular movement was fomented against him, and on January 30 a crowd attacked the legation and massacred all the inmates except one. Griboyédov fell fighting. His stripped and mangled body, it is reported, could be recognized only by his crooked finger, which had been mutilated in a duel some years before. His widow, on hearing of his death, gave premature birth to a child, who died a few hours later. She lived another thirty years after her husband's death, rejecting all suitors and winning universal admiration by her fidelity to his memory.

Griboyédov is a *homo unius libri*. This book is the great comedy *Woe from Wit* (*Góre ot umá*). His other comedies, one of which was written after *Góre ot umá*, are negligible and curiously unlike it. The fragments left us of *Georgian Night*, a social tragedy of Georgian history he was working at in his last years, are also very disappointing. Of his few lyrics, some are quite good, but they are only intimations of unrealized possibilities. More important are his letters, which are among the best in the language. It is they that reveal to us the man, but the great imaginative writer is revealed only in *Góre ot umá*.

Góre ot umá belongs to the classical school of comedy—its principal antecedents are in Molière. Like Fonvízin before him and like the founders of the Russian realistic tradition after him, Griboyédov lays far greater stress on the characters and his dialogue than on his plot. The comedy is loosely constructed, but in the dialogue and in the character drawing Griboyédov is supreme and unique. The dialogue is in rhymed verse, in iambic lines of variable length—a meter that was introduced into Russia by the fabulists as the equivalent of La Fontaine's *vers libre* and that had reached a high degree of perfection in the hands of Krylóv. Griboyédov's dialogue is a continuous tour de force. It always attempts and achieves the impossible: the squeezing of everyday conversation into a rebellious metrical form. Griboyédov seemed to multiply difficulties on purpose. He was, for instance, alone in his age to use unexpected, sonorous, punning rhymes. There are just enough toughness and angularity in his verse to constantly remind the reader of the pains undergone and the difficulties triumphantly overcome by the poet. Despite the fetters of the metrical form, Griboyédov's dialogue has the natural rhythm of conversation and is more easily colloquial than any prose. It is full of wit, variety, and character, and is a veritable store book of the best spoken Russian of a period when the speech of the upper classes had not yet been disfigured and emasculated by schoolmastery and grammar. Almost every other line of the comedy has become part of the language, and proverbs from Griboyédov are as numerous as proverbs from Krylóv. For epigram, repartee, terse and concise wit, Griboyédov has no rivals in Russian and is superior even to Krylóv.

In the art of character drawing Griboyédov is also unique. He had a quality that he inherited from the classicists and that was not possessed by any other Russian realist. He shares it with the great masters of the seventeenth and eighteenth centuries—with Molière and Fielding—and of all nineteenth-century writers, I think, with Thackeray alone. It is a certain universality that makes Tartuffe and Squire Western and Miss Crawley something more than mere individualities. They are persons, but they are also *types*—archetypes or quintessences of humanity, endowed with all we have of life and individuality, but endowed also with a super-individual existence, like that of the Platonic ideas, or of the *universalia* of the schoolmen. This is a rare art—perhaps the rarest of all; and of all Russian writers Griboyédov possessed it in the highest degree. This is not to say that his characters are not alive; they are, and very lively too, but they have a life more durable and universal than our own. They are stamped in the really common clay of humanity. Fámusov, the father, the head of an important department, the born conservative of all time, the cynical and placid philosopher of good digestion, the pillar of stable society; Molchálin, the secretary, the sneak who plays whist with old ladies, pets their dogs, and acts the lover to his patron's daughter; Repetílov, the orator of the coffee room and of the club, burning for freedom and stinking of liquor, the witless admirer of wit, and the bosom friend of all his acquaintances—all, down to the most episodic characters, have the same perfection of finish and clearness of outline. The only exceptions are the two protagonists, Sophia and Chátsky. Unlike the rest they are not meant satirically, and as characters they may be underdone. And yet the play owes much of its unique charm to them. Sophia is not a type, but she is a person. She is a rare phenomenon in classical comedy: a heroine that is neither idealized nor caricatured. There is a strange, drily romantic flavor in her, with her fixity of purpose, her ready wit, and her deep, but reticent, passionateness. She is the principal *active* force in the play, and the plot is advanced mainly by her actions.

Chátsky has often been criticized as irrelevantly eloquent. There is no sense of fitness in his harangues to Fámusov and his set, and there may be mistakes of proportion in Griboyédov's conception of him. But in spite of this, Chátsky is the principal thing in the play. He is its imaginative and emotional focus, its yeast and its zest. Not only is all the best wit put into his mouth, but he gives the tone to the whole performance. His generous, if vague, revolt against the vegetably selfish world of Fámusovs and Molchálins is its real spirit. His exhilarating, youthful idealism, his go, his *élan*, infect and brace you. He is of the family of Romeo; and it is significant that, in spite of all his apparent lack of clear-cut personality, his part is the traditional touchstone for a Russian actor. Great Chátskys are as rare and as highly valued in Russia as are great Hamlets.

THE POETS' PROSE

The high-water mark of French linguistic influence in Russia was reached in the reign of Alexander I. All the members of the educated gentry who were brought up during that reign knew French as well as, or better than, Russian. The same conditions obtained for the middle and provincial gentry: Púshkin is careful to record that Tatiána wrote her famous letter to Onégin in French, for, as he says, "to this day our proud language has not been broken to postal prose." To break it was one of the principal tasks of the poets and wits of the Arzamás, and of the other men of the Poets' and Gentlemen's party. Letter writing between 1815 and 1830 was, for the poets, an important branch of their literary activity, and the Golden Age of poetry is also the Golden Age of letter writing.

Púshkin is as much the greatest Russian letter writer as he is the greatest poet. His "postal prose" is an ever fresh source of delight to all who love good Russian. It is the language of everyday conversation, only refined in the laboratory of a great artistic mind. For flexibility, grace, and freshness Púshkin's epistolary Russian has no equals. Moreover, his letters are a mine of keen wit, sound judgment, and good criticism. But Púshkin *never* speaks in them of his feelings, neither to his nearest friends nor to his wife. The only emotions he ever gives vent to are impatience and indignation. This gives his letters a particularly healthy and bracing atmosphere.

Griboyédov stands next to Púshkin as a letter writer. His Russian is terse and more nervous than Púshkin's. It is full of the dry, pungent wit of *Góre ot umá*, and of a canalized and disciplined passionateness. Griboyédov always knows his mind and says what he thinks in a direct and straight manner. If Púshkin's letters have no equal for flexibility and freshness, Griboyédov is first among Russian writers for pointed and vigorous statement.

Another remarkable body of epistolary Russian is contained in the correspondence of Vyázemsky with Alexander Ivánovich Turgénev (1785–1846)—a friend of all the Arzamasians and one of the most intelligent men of the period. The correspondence forms a sort of running commentary on the Russian literature and life of the time.

In their published prose the poets of the Golden Age continued the work of Karamzín, who, though his reform had been accepted, had not succeeded in creating a universally applicable style of literary prose. The formation of such a style was one of the most difficult tasks before the poets, and here again French was in the way. Púshkin confessed that it was easier for him to express himself in French than in Russian where he had anything to say in prose that was not merely descriptive of fact. The poets applied themselves to their task with painstaking industry. But they failed to establish a canon of Russian prose for the succeeding ages, and all their work was undone by the journalists of the thirties, who are the real founders of modern Russian prose.

The elder generation of poets followed closely Karamzín's example. Zhukóvsky, both in his early stories and in his later moral essays, wrote fluent, agreeable, but somewhat emasculated and placid prose. Bátyushkov in his essays tried to Italianize Russian prose as he had Russian verse. Davýdov and Vyázemsky introduced into literature the manner of their epistolary prose. Davýdov's works include an *Essay towards a Theory of Guerrilla Welfare* (1821), an autobiography prefixed to the 1832 edition of his poems, and a series of recollections of military life. In his autobiography he indulges in a veritable orgy of puns and jokes not always in the best taste. His military writings are fresh, vigorous, and racy, and his memoirs contain some of the best military reading in the language. Vyázemsky is also sometimes exaggeratedly witty, but vigor and raciness are as ubiquitous in his prose as in Davýdov's. His best is contained in the admirable anecdotes of his *Old Notebook*, an inexhaustible mine of sparkling and often wonderful information on the great and small men of the early nineteenth century.

The anecdote was a favorite form in the times of Púshkin, and the great poet himself was a devotee to the art. The anecdotes contained in his (naturally posthumous) *Table Talk* (the title is in English) are masterpieces of the kind, and in a Russian more closely akin to that of his letters than that of his literary prose.

Of the other poets, Baratýnsky wrote very little prose, but this little contains a quite disproportionate amount of the best things ever said in Russian on the subject of poetry. Two of his utterances should be especially remembered: his definition of lyrical poetry as "the fullest awareness of a given moment," and his remark that good poetry is rare because two qualities, as a rule mutually exclusive, are necessary to the making of a poet—"the fire of creative imagination and the coldness of controlling reason."

THE RISE OF THE NOVEL

The Russian novel continued vegetating rather halfheartedly until in 1829 there was a sudden outburst of novel writing. In that year the notorious Tadéusz Bulháryn published his moralizing picaresque novel *Iván Výzhigin*, which had a record sale; and the same year Michael Nikoláyevich Zagóskin (1789–1852), who had already won a reputation as a comedy writer, published the first Russian novel in the style of Scott, *Yúry Miloslávsky, or the Russians in 1612*. It is a story of the Time of Troubles, when the Poles occupied Moscow, and of the victory of the national forces. In spite of its conventionality, crude nationalism, cardboard psychology, and lack of real historical color, it is a very good romance of its kind. Its immediate success was enormous, and it set the fashion for "Waverley" novels, a great number of which were turned out in Russia within the next ten or fifteen years. The best of the Russian Scottists is Iván Ivánovich Lazhéchnikov (1792–1869). His knowledge of the past is greater than Zagóskin's. His characters are more complex and more alive, and his moral sense, as clear-cut as Zagóskin's, is less conventional and more generous.

Another kind of romanticism is discernible in the works of Alexéy Peróvsky (1787–1836), who wrote under the pseudonym of Antón Pogorélsky, and was the only man of the Poets' and Gentlemen's party who made a reputation solely by his fiction. His principal work, *The Convent Girl* (1828), is a charmingly humorous picture of the manners of the provincial Ukrainian gentry. The novel is obviously influenced by Fielding, but there is also an admixture of a mild and domestic romanticism. In his shorter stories Pogorélsky is more romantic and fantastic. The best of them, *The Black Hen*, is a really delightful story. It is plainly as dependent on Hoffmann's *Nutcracker* as *The Convent Girl* is on *Tom Jones*. Tolstóy mentions it as the book that produced the strongest impression on him in his childhood.

The most brilliant of these early novelists was Alexander Alexándrovich Bestúzhev (1797–1837), co-editor with Ryléyev of the early miscellany the *Polar Star*. An officer in the dragoon guards, he took part in the Decembrist Revolt and was exiled to the farthest parts of Siberia. In 1829 he was transferred to the Caucasus as a private soldier. There he was able to resume his literary activity, and his best and best-known novels were published in the early thirties over the signature of A. Marlínsky. As a soldier he soon became noted for exceptional bravery. He was recommended for promotion and for the St. George's Cross, but the same year he was charged with the murder of his mistress, and, though the inquest failed to prove his guilt, the promotion and the cross were withheld. This incident left a profound mark on his mind. He ceased writing and lost all interest in life. In 1837 at the storming of Adler (on the Black Sea coast) he was, literally, hewn to pieces by the Circassians.

Bestúzhev was a poet of no mean talent. But it was his novels and stories that fascinated the public of the thirties. His manner, though showy and superficial, is certainly brilliant. His sparkling verbal imagination makes him show very brightly on the somewhat drab background of Zagóskin or Pogorélsky. His dialogue is especially brilliant, a constant battledore and shuttlecock of pithy epigram and witty repartee. His superficially passionate heroes, with their Byronic pose, are rather cheap. But the stories are thrilling, and the style keeps the reader in constant excitement. His best novel is *Ammalat Bek* (1832), a story of the Caucasian war. It contains the splendid *Songs of Death* of the mountaineers, a thing unequaled of its kind in the language.

THE PROSE OF PÚSHKIN

Púshkin was the first in Russia to write *permanent* fiction, the first really original Russian novelist. But his place in the history of the Russian novel is not comparable to his place in the history of Russian literature as a whole, and his prose, however perfect some of his stories and however unique his total achievement, is not of the same order of greatness as his poetry. A principal difference between his poetry and his prose is that he was primarily a poet, and that in verse he spoke his natural language, of which he him-

self was the supreme standard and judge, while prose was to him
a foreign tongue, acquired by more or less laborious learning. He
succeeded in mastering the idiom and the intonation of this foreign tongue, and his Parnassian accent can be discerned only by a
trained ear. But there is always in his prose a sense of constraint,
a lack of freedom, a harking back to some outer rule, which is
never the case with his poetry.

It was only after 1830 that Púshkin turned most of his attention to prose. But from the very beginning he had fixed his mind
on what it was to be like. In 1822 he wrote in a notebook: "Voltaire
may be regarded as an excellent example of sensible style. . . .
Precision, tidiness, these are the prime merits of prose. It demands
matter and matter, brilliant expressions are of no use to it; poetry
is another business." Púshkin's literary prose is rational, analytical,
intentionally bald, pruned of all irrelevant ornament, and almost
affected in its simplicity. One is most tempted to compare it to
Cæsar's prose, for, however comparable to Voltaire's in elegance
and purity, it lacks the free, impulsive vivacity and unfettered
swiftness of the great Frenchman's. On the whole the eighteenth-
century atmosphere common to the whole of Púshkin's work is
nowhere more apparent than in his stories, even in those where,
like others of his generation, he was influenced by the example of
Scott and Hoffmann.

His first attempt at fiction was the unfinished historical novel
The Nigger of Peter the Great (1828). It was to be the story of his
grandsire Gannibal. It remained unfinished, and only two fragments from it were published during his lifetime.

In the autumn of 1830, during his seclusion at Bóldino, Púshkin wrote the five *Tales of Bélkin*, which were published the following year without his name. If not the best, they are in many
ways his most characteristic stories. Nowhere did he carry further
the principles of detachment, restraint, and self-limitation. The
tales are told by a simple, provincial squire: a device to justify the
storyteller's impersonality. There is no human, no psychological
or descriptive, interest in the stories. They are pure, unadulterated
narrative, anecdotes raised to the rank of serious art by the
seriousness of the artistic process. As pure narrative they are unsurpassed in Russian literature except by Púshkin's own *Queen of
Spades*. They were met by contemporaries with amazed disappointment, and only very gradually have they become acknowl-

edged as masterpieces. The figure of the supposed author, Bélkin himself, barely outlined in the preface of the *Tales*, was more fully developed in the posthumous *History of the Manor of Goryúkhino*, one of Púshkin's most remarkable prose works. It is also one of the most complex—it is at once a parody of Polevóy's sciolistic and pretentious *History of the Russian People*, a Swiftian satire of the whole social order based on serfdom, and the portrait of one of the most charming characters in the whole of Russian fiction, the simple-minded, naïvely and shyly ambitious Iván Petróvich Bélkin.

After 1831 Púshkin wrote more prose than verse. Only three stories (including *The Captain's Daughter* and *The Queen of Spades*) were completed and printed. But numerous fragments in various states of completion were preserved and published posthumously. They include several alternative beginnings for the story that was to introduce the poem of *Cleopatra* (one of these contains the highly interesting character sketch of Chársky, the poet who, from motives of social vanity and reserve, does not want to be considered a poet) and *Dubróvsky*, an almost completed robber novel with a social background. Had it been finished, it would have been the best Russian novel of action. It is refreshingly (and very consciously) melodramatic, with a virtuous gentleman Robin Hood and an ideal heroine. Like *Goryúkhino* it is full of satire. The figures of the two great noblemen, Troyekúrov and Veréysky—one a rude, old-world bully, the other a Frenchified and refined egoist—are among the glories of the portrait gallery of Russian fiction.

The only full-sized novel Púshkin completed and published during his lifetime is *The Captain's Daughter* (1836), a story of the Pugachëv Rebellion (the great rising of the lower classes in East Russia in 1773). It belongs to the school of Scott in its treatment of the past, but it is curiously unlike any Waverley novel. It is about a fifth of the size of an average Scott novel. The manner is terse, precise, economical, though somewhat more spacious and leisurely than in any other of Púshkin's stories. There is in it, as in *Dubróvsky*, a zest of orthodox melodrama—in the figure of the rebel leader himself and in the frankly conventional character of the villain (the only villain in Púshkin), Shvábrin. It is full of delightful humor, as in the scene of the hero's duel with Shvábrin and the refusal of the old garrison officer risen from the ranks to understand the use of a duel. But the best thing in the novel is the characters: Captain Mirónov and his wife, charming figures of idyllic comedy in time of peace, who, when the rebels come, suddenly reveal an unpretending, modest, as it were casual, courage and die as heroes. Then there is Savélyich, the hero's old manservant, sincerely servile and unbendingly despotic. Besides *Evgény Onégin*, *The Captain's Daughter* was the only work of Púshkin's that had a powerful influence on the next age—it contains all the essence of what Russian realism was to become—though it is still a story told in the orthodox manner, as a story should be. Its understated, economical, discreetly humorous realism is a striking contrast to another great historical novel that appeared within two years of it—the rhetorical, swollen, magnificent *Tarás Búlba* of Gógol.

The Captain's Daughter is Púshkin's most influential, but it is not his greatest or most characteristic, story—this distinction belongs to *The Queen of Spades* (1834). The story cannot be summarized. Like *The Tales of Bélkin* it is pure art and possesses no human interest except as a whole. For imaginative power it stands above everything else in Púshkin's prose. It is as tense as a compressed spring. There is a fierce romanticism in it—akin to that which inspired *The Hymn in Honor of the Plague* and *God Forbid That I Should Go Mad*. But the fantastically romantic subject has been canalized into a perfect, classical form, so economic and terse in its noble baldness that even Prosper Mérimée, that most fastidiously economical of French writers, had not the courage to translate it as it was, and introduced various embellishments and amplifications into his French version.

Púshkin was a first-class critic, and his serious critiques and reviews are admirable for the considered soundness of his judgments and for the precise lucidity of his statement. His polemical journalism (in the *Literary Gazette*) is also, in its kind, unsurpassed. His neat, up-to-the-point, closely aimed irony possessed a sting his enemies never forgot. His attacks against Bulháryn, the "reptile" journalist in the pay of the secret police, are admirably and calmly cruel. They contributed to the speedy suppression of the *Literary Gazette* by exasperating its sneakingly influential rival.

After 1832 Púshkin's principal occupation was, at least officially, history. His plan of writing a history of Peter the Great never matured, but in 1834 he published a *History of the Pugachëv Rebellion*. It is a masterpiece of narrative literature, comparable to

Caesar's *Gallic War*. Its defect is one of information: it was impossible for Púshkin to know much that was essential to his subject. He was too much of an eighteenth-century classicist to treat history in terms of "mass movement" and "class struggles," but he admirably exposed the social mainsprings of the great Rebellion. In 1836 he published *A Voyage to Arzrum*, an account of his journey to the Caucasus front in 1829, in which he reached the limits of noble and bare terseness.

THE GROWTH OF JOURNALISM

Besides its other claims to literary distinction, the decade 1825–34 is important as the period beginning the uninterrupted history of Russian journalism. Despite severe pressure from the censorship, the journalists of this decade and the two following made a plucky stand for independence, if not in political, at least in general cultural questions. And it was owing to their efforts that a public opinion began to take shape.

The Poets' and Gentlemen's party were not very successful in their journalistic ventures. Délvig's *Literary Gazette* (1830–1) and Iván Kiréyevsky's *European* (1832) were suppressed by the censorship. When in 1836 Púshkin started the *Contemporary*, it was out of date and could not command a paying audience. The journalists proper were despised and disliked by the "Gentlemen," who scarcely distinguished between the different varieties of those plebeians. But the difference was very substantial between the servile Petersburg press and the sometimes unkempt, but independent and enthusiastic, Moscow magazines. In Petersburg a monopoly of political information belonged to the daily *Northern Bee*, founded in 1825 by Tadéusz Bulháryn (in Russian spelling, Bulgárin, 1789–1859). Bulháryn, a Polish deserter from Napoleon's army, had ingratiated himself to the secret police by giving evidence against Decembrist friends of his, and during the reign of Nicholas I he acquired the reputation of a vile sycophant whom all honest men abhorred. He was a clever, but essentially vulgar, journalist. His paper had a far larger sale than any other. His influence was used to combat all that was young, talented, and independent. Púshkin, Gógol, Belínsky, Lérmontov, and the natural school of the forties were in turn the enemies against whom he used all means, public and clandestine.

Very different was the Muscovite journalist Nicholas Polevóy (1796–1846). He was a self-made man, the son of a tradesman. He could never "become a gentleman," and the Gentlemen always despised him. But his enthusiasm (often misguided) did much to spread the new literature and to intensify Russian literary life. His magazine, the *Moscow Telegraph* (1825–34), was an enthusiastic, if undiscriminating, pioneer of romanticism. In 1834 the *Telegraph* was suppressed for printing an unfavorable review of a patriotic play by Kúkolnik. Polevóy was ruined. In his misfortunes he did not show himself a hero—he entered on a compromise with the Bulháryn party, and thus ceased to count in literature. But his memory after his death was deservedly reverenced by the new intelligentsia as that of a pioneer and, in a sense, a martyr.

Another pioneer of the intelligentsia was Nicholas Nadézhdin (1804–56). Also a plebeian by birth, he began his career by publishing a series of scurrilous, though at times witty, articles against the Poets, where he confounded Púshkin and Baratýnsky with their second-rate imitators in a sweeping condemnation. He attacked Russian romanticism from the point of view of Schelling's German romantic idealism, denying all ideological significance to the Russian pseudo romanticism (as he rightly called it). In a thesis on romantic poetry submitted to the University of Moscow in 1830 he advocated a synthesis of classicism and romanticism. In 1831 he started a monthly magazine, the *Telescope*, where he continued his policy of belittling in the light of philosophical standards the achievement of Russian literature. In 1836 the magazine was suppressed for publishing Chaadáyev's *Philosophical Letter*. Nadézhdin himself was exiled to the north and not till some time afterwards allowed to return to Moscow. After that he renounced literature and devoted himself exclusively to his archæological and geographical studies.

The successor of Polevóy and Nadézhdin was Belínsky, the dictator of literary opinion from 1834 to 1848, and the father of the Russian intelligentsia.

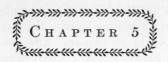

CHAPTER 5

The Age of Gógol

THE DECLINE OF POETRY

POETRY early began to decline from the high standards set up by the Golden Age. The harmony, distinction, restraint, and unerring mastery of the great poets from Zhukóvsky to Venevítinov was soon lost. The art of verse degenerated either into an empty and undistinguished tidiness, or into an equally hollow wit unsupported by inspiration, or into a formless rush of untransformed emotion. A veneer of polished versification, covering a void of imagination and substituted for the delicate mastery of the older generation, is the characteristic of all the younger poets who claimed to belong to the older "Poets' party." The Petersburg journalists encouraged poetry of a more meretricious type. Its laureate was Vladímir Grigórievich Benedíktov (1807–73), a clerk in the Ministry of Finance and for ten years the idol of all the romantically inclined officials of every rank throughout Russia. His method consisted in squeezing out of a striking metaphor or simile all it could give. A typical poem of his, *The Belle of Battles*, makes the most of the parallel between the unsheathed saber and the naked woman. Later on, Benedíktov gave up his conceits and developed into a polished versifier of the ordinary type.

Another group of poets had in common with Benedíktov a love for external brilliancy in rhymes, images, and vocabulary, but differed from him by their higher seriousness. The most notable of them were Khomyakóv (whose poetry I shall discuss later) and Caroline Pávlova, nee Jaenisch (1807–93), the most interesting of the Russian "blues." When a young girl, she had been loved by the great Polish poet Mickiéwicz, for whom she retained a lifelong romantic attachment. Afterward she was unhappily married to the novelist Nicholas Pávlov. Her literary *salon* was one of the most frequented in Moscow; but her talent was never appreciated by her friends, and she contrived to make herself a bore and a common laughing-stock. Her poetry is deeply attractive, both for the somewhat harsh, but unquestionable, excellence of her technique and for its profound and reticent pathos. The main subject of her poetry is the courage of suppressed suffering. "Grin and bear it" is the pith of her best poems.

The most progressive and modern poets of the thirties rejected the formal discipline of the school of Zhukóvsky and Púshkin and aimed at developing the emotional and expressionist character of poetry. Lérmontov in his early work must be reckoned as one of them. Of the minor poets who may be regarded as first proofs of Lérmontov, the most notable were Prince Alexander Odóyevsky (1802–39) and Alexander Ivánovich Polezháyev (1805–38). Alexander Odóyevsky, a first cousin of Griboyédov and of the novelist Vladímir Odóyevsky, took part in the Decembrist Revolt, was deported to Siberia and afterward sent as a private soldier to the Caucasus. He is chiefly remembered today for the elegy written on his death by Lérmontov, the most beautiful dirge in the Russian language. His own poems were first published long after his death. Most of them are concerned with the sorrows of the exile, but one of them, the well-known answer to Púshkin's famous *Epistle into Siberia* (1827), in which the great poet exhorted the exiled rebels not to lose their spirits, is an animated assertion of the undaunted spirit of revolt.

Polezháyev was the natural son of a squire of the name of Strúysky—and thus a *déclassé*. As a student of Moscow University he led a riotous life of drunkenness and debauchery, and described it in the burlesque poem *Sáshka* (1825–6). The poem contained some passages expressive of liberal sentiment, and these, much rather than its obscenity, attracted the attention of the police. The matter reached Nicholas I, who was then in Moscow fresh from the trial and execution of the Decembrists. Polezháyev was summoned into the Emperor's presence. Nicholas, with his usual consummate stagecraft, played the part of the kind chastising father—Polezháyev was to serve as a private soldier, but he was allowed to write direct to the Emperor if he had any grievances.

This Polezháyev did very soon, for he had plenty of grievances, but the letters had no effect. He attempted to desert, was arrested for more than a year, narrowly escaped corporal punishment, and was told off to the Caucasus. Gradually Polezháyev sank into degradation—drank heavily and in his relations with the kind of people who tried to lighten up his hopeless lot behaved with shameless cynicism. At the front, however, he gave proof of courage and was at last recommended for a commission, but the promotion arrived only after his death. Polezháyev was strongly influenced by Hugo and Byron, and romantic grandiloquence and gaudiness had a too great attraction for him. Looseness, turgidity, and garrulity are his besetting sins. Only a dozen or so of his shorter poems preserve his name in the treasury of Russian verse. There are in them a passionate force, a rhythmic rush, and a romantic fire that are his alone. He was particularly a master of rapid, staccato meters. All his best poems are concerned either with the lurid romance of oriental warfare or with the grim despair of his ruined life. His most famous poem is the remarkably effective *Song of the Sailor Doomed to Wreck* (or rather, "in the process of being wrecked"), in vigorous, three-syllabled lines, and *The Song of the Captive Iroquois*—bound to the stake and calmly awaiting the protracted death his captors are preparing for him.

KOLTSÓV

One of the most interesting developments of the thirties was the culmination of the school of literary folk song in the work of Koltsóv. The tradition of the artificial folk song goes back to the eighteenth century. In the twenties it was brought to further perfection by the versatile Délvig, whose exquisitely artificial "Russian songs" (as the genre was called) were the most popular part of his work. Less artificial and more spontaneous are the beautiful songs of Nicholas Grigórievich Tsygánov (1797–1831), a wandering actor and the son of a serf. He had no contact with literary circles, and, though the form of his "Russian songs" is dependent on the literary, not on the oral tradition, their spirit is genuinely popular and "folklore." They are personative, most of them placed in the mouth of a woman. Their symbolism, their imagery, their unsentimental sentiment, are all thoroughly popular and Russian. They were published posthumously in 1834, only a year before the publication of the first book of Koltsóv.

Alexéy Vasílievich Koltsóv was born in 1809 in Vorónezh (South Central Russia). His father was a wholesale cattle dealer, and Koltsóv spent much of his boyhood and youth in the Don steppes, accompanying his father's herds to distant markets. His education was desultory. His early verses attracted the attention of Stankévich, the famous head of the idealist circle, who introduced Koltsóv to his Moscow friends. This resulted in a lasting friendship between Koltsóv and Belínsky. In 1835 a first book of songs by Koltsóv was published, which was universally greeted with great warmth. After that, Koltsóv continued living in Vorónezh, managing his father's business and coming to Moscow and Petersburg only in connection with his father's lawsuits. Koltsóv was a man of tact and dignity, and his educated and noble friends highly admired his character. These qualities are always present in his attractive letters, which are also remarkable for the solid common sense displayed in them. He shared the generous aspirations of his idealist friends, though he never quite lost the practical sense and efficiency of the Russian tradesman. But he felt lonely and miserable in Vorónezh. His relations with his father, a selfish, despotic, and unimaginative bourgeois, went from bad to worse, and gradually his family life became a hell to him. He was saved from it by sudden death in 1842. He had almost ceased to write after 1840.

Koltsóv's poetry falls into three distinct sections: his attempts, chiefly belonging to the period before 1835, to write in the accepted literary style of the Púshkin and pre-Púshkin school; his "Russian Songs"; and the philosophical meditations (*dúmy*) of his last years. Of these three classes, only the second secures for Koltsóv a permanent place as a classic. Koltsóv has been called a Russian Burns. If the title implies anything like equality of genius with the great Scotsman, it is simply nonsense. In *size* of talent Koltsóv comes nearer Hogg than Burns. But in *kind* there is no doubt a certain kinship, not altogether superficial. Like Burns, Koltsóv depended on a literary tradition of quasi folk song. Like Burns, he was in direct touch with the realities of peasant life, though, unlike Burns, he was not himself a peasant. Like Burns,

he had a certain freshness and freedom of outlook his more educated and blue-blooded contemporaries were incapable of. Like
Burns, lastly, he was a realist, and, like Burns, he had genuine
passion. But he is more feminine and sentimental than Burns.
Characteristically some of Koltsóv's best songs are placed in the
mouth of women. His purely lyrical songs are perhaps the best and
have become the most popular among the people; there is in them
a typically Russian longing for freedom, adventure, and elbow
room. Though they are usually in rhyme and thus more obviously
literary in form, they have much more genuine popular feeling in
them than the nature and peasant-life songs. As in real folk songs,
nature appears as a sympathetic source of symbols for the singer's
feelings. In the more elaborate nature songs it becomes rather in-
volvedly personified and philosophized. But there is no more
beautiful evocation of the wide steppe than *The Mower*, who goes
out to sell his strength to the rich Cossacks of the Lower Don.
Prostór and *privólye*, two untranslatable Russian words meaning,
roughly, space and elbow room, but with an inexpressible poetical
overtone, are the keynotes of some of Koltsóv's best songs. His
love songs, with all their range of slightly sentimentalized and
romancified, but genuine and strong, passion, are equally exquisite.
The beautiful song of the *mal mariée*, beginning "Ah, why did
they marry me against my will to an old, unloved husband?" is
one of the purest gems of Russian emotional lyric poetry. The
least genuinely popular part of Koltsóv's songs is those in which
he idealizes peasant life and agricultural labor—a theme entirely
alien to actual folk song. But this does not make them less good.
Some of them, such as *A Peasants' Carouse*, are almost Homeric in
the simple, unsentimentalized stateliness with which he endows
simple life.

TYÚTCHEV

The literary history of Tyútchev is rather curious. His first verse
was published only three years after Púshkin's first appearance in
print; most of the poems on which his reputation rests appeared
in Púshkin's quarterly in 1836–8, but his poetry had to wait for a
first critical appreciation till 1850, when he was "discovered" by
Nekrásov and it was suddenly realized that he was a very important poet. This recognition came on the eve of the general

decline of all interest in poetry, and only the few preserved his cult till the end of the century, when he was again taken up by Vladímir Soloviëv and by the symbolists. Today he is unquestionably recognized as one of the three greatest Russian poets, and the majority, probably, of poetry readers place Tyútchev, not Lérmontov, to the right of Púshkin. Outside Russia, however, though he is much more accessible to the modern romantic taste than is Púshkin, few people have realized his importance. I know from personal experience that when English poetry readers do discover him they almost invariably prefer him to all other Russian poets. This is only natural, for of all Russian poets Tyútchev abounds in those qualities which the English poetry reader has learned to value in nineteenth-century poetry.

Fëdor Ivánovich Tyútchev was born in 1803 of a family of ancient nobility. He received a good education at home and at the University of Moscow. His tutor was the poet Ráich, who afterwards remained his friend and tried to be his literary sponsor. In 1822 Tyútchev entered the diplomatic service and, except for several short visits to Russia, remained abroad twenty-two years. Most of the time he was in Munich, where he met Heine and Schelling, both of whom corresponded with him. He married a Bavarian noblewoman and came to regard Munich as his home. He wrote much; the infrequency of his appearances in print has been explained by his indifference to his poetic work, but the true reason seems to have been his supersensitive shyness of criticism. But in 1836 he was persuaded to send some verses to Púshkin's *Sovreménnik*. From 1836 to 1838 about forty lyrics, all of which (quite literally) are known by heart today by everyone who cares for Russian poetry, appeared over the signature of "F. T." They drew no attention from the critics, and Tyútchev ceased to publish. Meanwhile Tyútchev lost his first wife and married a second time, again a Bavarian. He was transferred to Turin. He did not like this change and was homesick for Munich. While chargé d'affaires of the legation, he left Turin and the Sardinian States without permission, and for this breach of discipline was expelled from the diplomatic service. He settled in Munich, but in 1844 he came to Russia and a little later received a post in the Censorship. His political articles and memoranda written in the revolutionary year 1848 attracted official attention. He began to play a political role as a convinced reactionary and an ardent Panslavist. He began

also to cut a very prominent figure in the drawing-rooms, and acquired the reputation of the greatest wit and most brilliant con-
versationalist in Russia. In 1854 his verse at last appeared in book
form, and he became famous as a poet. About the same time his
liaison with Mlle Denísieva began, his daughter's governess. Their
love was profound and passionate on both sides, and an infinite
source of torture to both. The young woman's reputation was
ruined and Tyútchev's own gravely tainted, as well as his family
happiness. When, in 1864, Mlle Denísieva died, gloom and despair took possession of Tyútchev. The wonderful tact and for-
bearance of his wife in the whole affair only increased his suffering
by a profound feeling of guilt. But his social and political activities
never slackened. His slight, shriveled figure continued appearing
in ballrooms, his witticisms continued to enchant society, and he
developed a more than usual pugnacity in politics—becoming one
of the pillars of an unbending nationalist policy. Most of his
political verse belongs to the last ten years of his life. He died in
1873, after a stroke that left him in a state of paralysis with only
his brain unimpaired.

From the linguistic point of view Tyútchev is a curious phenomenon. In private and public life he spoke and wrote nothing
but French. All his letters, all his political writings, are in that
language, as well as all his reported witticisms. Neither his first
nor his second wife spoke Russian. He does not seem to have used
Russian except for poetical purposes. His few French poems, on
the other hand, though interesting, are for the most part trifles
and give no hint of the great poet he was in Russian.

Tyútchev's style always remained more archaic than Púshkin's or Zhukóvsky's, and, except his tutor, Ráich, the only Russian poets who influenced him were the classics of the eighteenth
century, Derzhávin and Lomonósov, whose oratorical movement
is easily recognizable in many of his poems. His style attained its
maturity rather early, and the few poems printed in 1829 already
display all its essential features. From about that date Tyútchev's
poetry is all of a piece (except for the political poems and the love
lyrics of his "last love") and may be considered apart from all
chronological limits. The greatest number of his best poems belongs to the decade 1830–40.

Tyútchev's poetry is metaphysical and based on a pantheistic
conception of the universe. As is the case with every metaphysical

poet, Tyútchev's philosophy cannot be stripped of its poetic form without loss of meaning. But the main lines of it must be briefly stated. Its chief difference from that of the great English poets is that it is profoundly pessimistic and dualistic—Manichæan in fact. There are two worlds—Chaos and Cosmos. Cosmos is the living organism of nature, a throbbing and personal being, but it has a secondary and lesser reality as compared to Chaos, the real reality, in which Cosmos is but a slight and precarious spark of ordered beauty. This opposition is one of Tyútchev's fundamental themes. But Cosmos, the vegetable universe, though leading a precarious existence in the womb of Chaos, is opposed as a higher and greater being to the smallness and weakness of the individual consciousness. This theme finds a rhetorical expression (strongly reminiscent of Derzhávin's famous paraphrase of Psalm lxxxi) in the wonderful poem beginning: "Nature is not what you imagine" ("*Ne to chto mníte vy priróda*," (1836), one of the most grandly eloquent and closely reasoned sermons ever written in verse. It finds another kind of expression in numerous "nature fragments," most of them not over a dozen lines in length.

The two elements of Tyútchev's style—the rhetorical-classical and the visual-romantic—are mixed in his poems in varying proportions. In certain cases the romantic style, saturated with bold, visionary imagery, is given almost free play. Such for instance is the marvelous *Dream at Sea* (1836), the most wildly beautiful poem in the language, for richness and purity of romantic vision comparable to Coleridge's best. But even here the precision of the weird and feverish images is reminiscent of Tyútchev's classical training.

In other poems the classical, oratorical, intellectual element predominates as in the one already mentioned (*Nature is not what you imagine*) and perhaps the most famous of all, *Silentium!* (1833), which contains the famous line: "An uttered thought is a lie." In such poems the romantic vision is recognizable only in the wealth and glow of certain expressions and in the cunning arrangement of the sounds.

Tyútchev's love poetry written at the time of his liaison with Mlle Denísieva has all the unique beauty of his philosophical and nature lyrics but is more passionate and poignant. It is the most profound, subtle, and moving, tragic love poetry in the language. Its main motive is a racking compassion for the woman who has been destroyed and ruined by her overwhelming love for him. The later lyrics, written after her death, are simpler and more direct than anything he ever wrote before. They are cries of anguish and despair, as simple as poetry can be.

Tyútchev's political and occasional poems do not display the highest qualities of his genius, but some of them are splendid pieces of poetical eloquence, and others exquisite examples of poetical wit. Most of his later political poetry (after 1848) is crudely nationalistic and reactionary in sentiment, and much of it (especially after 1863, when he began to write more often than before) is little more than rhymed journalism. But even in this cruder order of ideas he produced such a masterpiece as the lines *On the Arrival of the Austrian Archduke for the Funeral of Nicholas I*, a splendid lyrical invective, one of the most powerful poems ever inspired by indignation.

Tyútchev was famous for his wit, but he made his prose epigrams in French, and he was rarely capable of making his wit collaborate with his art of Russian verse. But he has left several masterpieces in a more serious style of wit, such as the following poem on the Lutheran service (written in 1834):

> *I like the church-service of the Lutherans,*
> *Their severe, solemn, and simple rite.*
> *Of these bare walls, of this empty nave,*
> *I can understand the sublime teaching.*
> *But don't you see? Ready to leave,*
> *Faith is for the last time with us;*
> *She has not yet crossed the threshold,*
> *But her house is already empty and bare.*
> *She has not yet crossed the threshold;*
> *The door has not yet closed behind her.*
> *But the hour has come, has struck. . . . Pray to God:*
> *It is the last time you will pray.*

LÉRMONTOV

The fact that Tyútchev's poetry passed so completely unnoticed in 1836 was only one of the symptoms of a growing general feeling that the day of poetry was done. It was to have only one more

moment of instant and general success in the short, flashlike career
of Lérmontov. His early death was accepted as the final closure of
the age of verse, but the school of poetry had closed before that
date. There is an all-important difference between the conditions
in which Púshkin and his contemporaries worked and those in
which Tyútchev and Lérmontov were placed. The latter poets
lacked the invigorating environment of a literary movement and
the sympathetic proximity of fellow craftsmen working at the
same task. They were alone in a wasteland. The fact that Lérmontov found an innumerable audience and Tyútchev practically none
should not obscure the essential similarity of their situation. Both
were cut off from all creative support from the "cultural ambient."

Michael Yúrievich Lérmontov was born October 2, 1814, in
Moscow. His father, an army officer and small squire, was a
descendant of Captain George Learmont, a Scottish adventurer
who in the early seventeenth century entered the Russian service.
Learmont, it will be remembered, was the surname of Thomas the
Rhymer, and the Learmonts are traditionally descended from him.
Lérmontov, however, seems to have been ignorant of this poetic
ancestry. His mother was an Arséniev, and her mother, nee Stolýpin, was a wealthy landowner and an important figure in Moscow
society. There was a considerable social inequality between the
two parents of the poet. When he was three his mother died, and
this led to a breach between his father and Mme Arséniev, who
appropriated her little grandson and brought him up as a spoiled
child. At nine he was taken to the Caucasian waters—where the
mountains and the new environment left a lasting impression on
him. He was thirteen when he began reading and writing verse and
developed a cult of Byron. He also developed, in a society of
numerous, chiefly female, cousins and acquaintances, a morbid
self-consciousness and highly sensitive vanity. He began taking
himself Byronically and learned to magnify his feelings (such as
his adolescent loves) and his circumstances (such as his separation
from his father) on the grand romantic scale. In 1830 he entered the
University, but studied little and kept aloof from the Idealists who
were there at the same time as he. As a penalty for some riotous
conduct he was not allowed to take an intermediate examination,
and in 1832 he left the University of Moscow and went to Petersburg with the intention of matriculating at the University there.
But instead of the University he entered the School of Ensigns of

the Guards and of Cavalry Cadets. Lérmontov did not like either
Petersburg or the school. But he soon adapted himself to his new
surroundings and became, on the face of it at least, a typical
cavalry cadet. His self-consciousness was suppressed and became
less apparent. His Byronic pose was transformed into that of a
smart and cynical bully. Romantic love, the dominant sentiment
of his Moscow days, was suppressed and driven in, and the surface
was occupied by easy and venal amours, and after school by callous
and calculated Don Juanry. The school brought Lérmontov in
touch with reality, and it was there that his poetry turned from
the magniloquent introspections of his earlier youth to frankly
coarse, unprintable cadet poems—which, however, are the first
germ of his later realism. In 1834 Lérmontov was given a commission in the Hussars of the Guard. He was introduced to the best
Petersburg society, but his Muscovite connections were not sufficient to give him a prominent place in it. His vanity suffered from
constant pinpricks and was only partly soothed by his victories
over female hearts. But under this surface Lérmontov lived his
life of a poet and gradually attained his maturity. His poetic and
romantic nature burst out at the death of Púshkin. In a memorable
poem (which may sound today like rhetoric rather than poetry but
is in any case rhetoric of the finest quality) he voiced the feelings
of the better side of society—despair at the death of the nation's
greatest glory, indignation at the alien murderer, who "could not
understand whose life he attempted," and scorn and hatred for the
base and unworthy courtiers that had allowed the foreigner to kill
the poet. The poem hit its mark—and Nicholas reacted accordingly. Lérmontov was arrested, tried by court-martial, expelled
from the Guards, and transferred to a regiment of the line stationed
in the Caucasus.

The first disgrace was not of long duration. Before he had
been a year in the Caucasus he was pardoned and restored to the
Guards. But the short time spent in the Caucasus revived his old
romantic attachment for that domestic orient of the Russians and
is abundantly reflected in his work. By the beginning of 1838 he
was back in Petersburg, this time a famous poet and a lion.

Though a tale in verse by Lérmontov, *Hajjî Abrék*, had appeared in a magazine in 1835, his literary career may be considered
to begin with the poem on the death of Púshkin, which (though of
course it could not be printed) was widely circulated. In 1837 and

1838 several poems of his appeared in various periodicals, each time attracting considerable attention. In 1839 his friend Krayévsky founded a big magazine, *Otéchestvennye zapíski* (*Notes of the Fatherland*), and only then Lérmontov's work began to appear regularly and frequently. In 1840 a selection of his poems and the novel *A Hero of Our Times* appeared in book form. But like Púshkin, only with more real grounds and more effectively, Lérmontov disliked being regarded as a man of letters. He mixed little with literary circles, and Krayévsky was the only man of letters he ever became intimate with. On the other hand he took a keen interest in political questions, and in 1836–7 belonged to a secret debating society—the Sixteen.

Society life, in spite of all the satisfactions it provided for his vanity, galled and goaded Lérmontov. He had several real and sincere friends in society, but his general feeling towards it was an indignant and bored contempt. His life at Petersburg came to an abrupt end. On a most trivial pretext he fought a duel with M. de Barante, the son of the French Ambassador. No blood was spilled, but all the same the poet was arrested and once again transferred to a line regiment in the Caucasus (1840). This time he took part in several military expeditions against the Chechens and proved himself a brilliantly brave officer. He was mentioned in dispatches and twice recommended for rewards, but these were not approved in Petersburg. In the summer of 1841 he went to Pyatigórsk, the Caucasian watering-place, where he found many acquaintances from Petersburg and Moscow, among them his old schoolfellow, Major Martýnov. Lérmontov and Martýnov paid court to the same lady, and Lérmontov poisoned Martýnov's life by teasing his rival in the presence of the lady. Martýnov bore it for some time but at last called Lérmontov out. Lérmontov was always glad of a duel. They met on July 15, 1841, in the plain near Pyatigórsk. Martýnov was the first to fire, and Lérmontov was killed on the spot.

During his life Lérmontov published very little, and only such of his later work as he considered to be mature. But almost immediately after his death the publication was begun of his early work, strikingly different in quality from what he himself had considered worth publishing. The proportion of this inferior work grew with every new edition and ultimately resulted in swamping the small quantity of his perfect poetry in an ocean of childish effusions. In dealing with Lérmontov it is necessary to distinguish clearly between the immature and the mature, and not to be misled by the (unfortunately, always) *first* volumes of his collected works.

His early poetry is voluminous and formless. To the biographer who is capable of discounting the attitude of the young poet it is valuable, but to the reader of poetry by far the greater part of it is of no use. There occur in it from time to time flashes of genius, bits of song displaying a hitherto unguessed-of power of direct lyrical cry, and piercing passages of self-expression. There is no mastery in this work, no "finer touch," no command of technique—but the raw material of lyric poetry in abundance. Apart from all the rest of the verse of these years stands *The Angel*, written in 1832, which remains one of Lérmontov's highest flights, perhaps the most wonderful *romantic* lyric in the Russian language. It is perfect—though its perfection is not that of maturity. Never has the unconquerable homesickness of the earth-bound soul for its heavenly fatherland been expressed with purer musical truth than in the sixteen lines of this poem by a boy of seventeen.

The following period (1832–6) was less productive than the first. The lyrical output especially is insignificant. At school Lérmontov wrote little more than the obscene cadet poems. They are the antithesis of his early poetry, and it was in a synthesis of the two elements, realistic and romantic, that Lérmontov's true personality was to find its expression. The cadet poems lead on to *Sáshka*, where this synthesis is already half achieved. *Sáshka* is a genuine and lawful son of Byron's *Don Juan*—perhaps the only one of all his progeny who really looks like his father, though he is certainly both more romantic and less polite. Much of the poem is unprintable and goes back, not to Byron, but to the domestic tradition of coarse verse. All the same the general impression is distinctly romantic. *Sáshka* remained unfinished and was published only long after Lérmontov's death. The same realistic vein, but without either the romanticism or the obscenity of *Sáshka*, is apparent in *The Treasurer's Wife* (published 1838), a comic story of provincial life, in the *Onégin* stanza, and directly derived from Púshkin's *Count Núlin*. Lérmontov's first published poem, *Hajjí Abrék* (1835), is a Caucasian tale of revenge, free from Byronic darkness and prolixity, written in a rapid tempo, with a somewhat crude but vigorous martial beat.

With the single exception of *The Angel*, all that constitutes the absolutely valuable part of Lérmontov's poetry belongs to the last four or five years of his life. In Lérmontov's way of working there was a peculiarity that, as far as I am aware, he shared with nobody: numerous themes and passages of various lengths that appear for the first time in his early verses are taken up again and again, in various settings and with various compositional functions, till at last they find an adequate place in some definitive poem of 1838–40. This migration is characteristic of the general abstract character of Lérmontov's poetry. It is not occasional. Reality is an accident. There are permanent visions, permanent knots of emotion, by which he is obsessed; he cannot be at rest until he has freed himself of them. Even in the most deeply felt of his occasional poems, *On the Death of Alexander Odóyevsky* (1839), the central passage is bodily transferred from *Sáshka*. And the two largest poems of his mature period—*The Demon* and *Mtsýri*— are only fulfillments of conceptions that originated as early as 1829 and 1830.

The Demon, at which he worked from 1829–33, was resumed in 1837 during his stay in Georgia and completed in 1839. The theme is the love of a demon for a mortal. In the early drafts the setting is vague, but in the final form it is Georgia, and the famous descriptive passages of the first part belong to the last period of its creation. The poem could not appear in the reign of Nicholas, as the censorship considered its subject anti-religious, but it was circulated in innumerable copies. In the second half of the nineteenth century it was probably the most universally popular single poem in Russia. It attracted the poetry reader by the same quality that had attracted him in Púshkin's southern poems—its exquisite mellifluousness. Lérmontov's mellifluousness is more purely musical than Púshkin's. It is not tempered by the precise classical training of the elder poet. Our time has greatly reduced its estimate of *The Demon*. The content of the poem is on a level with the Angel-and-Peri poems of Moore. The Demon himself is merely operatic, and the fact that *The Demon* became the libretto of the most operatic of Russian operas (by Anton Rubinstein) is significant. For most Russian poetry readers *The Demon* is a serious drawback in the general appreciation of Lérmontov. But there is in it, after all, a wonderful verbal music, and a haunting magic that had the power of conquering such a man as the great visionary painter

Vrúbel and inspiring him to his most memorable imaginings. It is still a source of inspiration to great poets, like Blok and Pasternák, who are able to find more in it than the fastidious uncreative poetry reader can. For behind its obvious puerility and apparent tinsel there is what can hardly be described otherwise than the real presence of demons.

Mtsýri (a Georgian word meaning "novice") has a somewhat similar history. Its theme is the confession at the hour of death of a rebellious young man to his spiritual father—a defiance of the rule and a declaration of unbroken spirit. It is closely related in meter and diction to Zhukóvsky's *Prisoner of Chillon*. Its first draft— *The Confession* (1830)—like the first draft of *The Demon*, is only vaguely localized. Its second draft—*The Boyár Órsha* (1835)—has an operatic "Old Russia" setting and a complicated but incoherent plot. In the final version, as in that of *The Demon*, the scene is laid in Georgia. *Mtsýri* is a poem of great power and may be regarded as the most sustained piece of poetic rhetoric (in the best and highest sense of the word) in Russian. But it is more than that. All that part of the poem which is about nature belongs to the central, small, but priceless, visionary core of Lérmontov—the only Russian poet who knew the "distant land" of the English and German romanticists.

This vision of a "distant land" of eternity shimmering through the visions of this world had already found a definitive expression in *The Angel*. It is the positive side of Lérmontov's romanticism. Its negative side is his passionate contempt for the human herd. Indignation against "empty society" is a dominant note in much of the poetry of his last years. Such poems as *The Death of the Poet*, *The Poet*, the bitter *Meditation* on his contemporaries, or the invective against the French nation on the occasion of the burial of Napoleon at the Invalides (*The Last Housewarming*) are splendidly effective eloquence, and poetry in so far as they are eloquence in verse. But there is one poem in which *both* the romantic aspects of Lérmontov, the visionary and the rhetorical, are blended in one supreme and matchless unity. That is *New Year's Night:* surrounded by the gay, aristocratic crowd at a ball in town, the poet remembers the pure, transcendent visions of his early years—"the creation of my dream, with eyes full of an azure fire, with a rosy smile like the first brilliancy of the young dawn behind the grove"

—and, brought back to reality, ends in a cry of indignant scorn at the mob round him.

But Lérmontov was not only a romanticist. The older he grew, the more he realized that reality was not merely an ugly veil thrown over eternity, not merely a thralldom of his heaven-born spirit, but a world to live in and to act in. The realistic element makes its first appearance in the cadet poems and in *Sáshka*. It continues asserting itself in the work of his maturity, when, parallel to the ridding himself of his romantic obsessions, he gradually developed a new manner, in which he proved himself a greater *master* than in his romantic poetry. For the romantic poems are either a splendid display of effective, rather than refined, rhetoric, which is saved from being bombast and prose merely by the force of the poetic breath that fills it, or gusts of heavenly music overheard from the spheres rather than consciously created. In his realistic poetry Lérmontov is a genuine master, a disciple of Púshkin. By sheer intuition he was able to guess many of the secrets of the poet from whom he was severed not so much by years as by a breach of tradition. For Lérmontov grew up in a world already unfamiliar with French and classical culture and never had the benefit of knowing men who might have taught him. His style was at first strikingly unlike Púshkin's. It was as vague as Púshkin's was precise, as swollen as Púshkin's was terse—it seemed to consist, not of individual words with distinct meanings, but of verbal masses molten into indistinguishable concrete. It was precisely his vagueness, so compatible with music and "heavenly song," that allowed him to achieve his highest romantic effects; but outside these purple patches, his poetry, in his romantic poems, is merely the rush of verbal torrents. In his realistic poems he worked at making himself a new style that would bear no traces either of a heaven-born origin or of romantic untidiness. Beginning with the Russian poems of 1837—the stirring and simple war ballad of *Borodinó*, written in the language and expressing the ideas of an old veteran, and the wonderful *Song of the Merchant Kaláshnikov*, a narrative of Old Russia in a meter and a style taken with admirable intuition from the epic folk songs (though the subject and spirit are frankly romantic)—he achieved style and measure, creating these masterpieces without the elusive aid of heavenly tunes and purple patches. He now became able to treat a romantic theme (like that of *The Fugitive*, 1841) with a concise clarity worthy of Púshkin and with a martial go that was his alone. In a few poems of his last two years he attempted a purely realistic poetry, in the language and diction of prose but on the big themes and with the high seriousness of great poetry. Together with *The Angel* and its kin the poems of this group are his greatest achievement in verse. They bear out his claim to stand in the national esteem by the side of Púshkin. The most remarkable are *The Testament* of a dying officer of the Caucasian Army (admirably translated by Maurice Baring in his *Outline of Russian Literature*), and *Valérik*, a "letter in verse" describing in a style of simple but pregnant realism, a battle against the mountaineers. It is a link between *The Bronze Horseman* and the military scenes of *War and Peace*.

What Lérmontov might have grown into as a poet is a matter of wide speculation. Even as it is, he is one of the small number of great poets, and, though today his star is under an eclipse, it is probable that posterity will once again confirm the judgment of the nineteenth century and place him immediately next to Púshkin. As a romantic poet he has (with the conceivable exception of Blok) no rival in Russia, and he had in him everything to become also a great realist (in the Russian sense). But it is highly probable also that the main line of his further development would have been in prose, which is regarded today as his least questionable title to a first rank.

THE POETRY OF REFLECTION

The poetry of the Golden Age had been, above all and first of all, "poietic"—in the etymological sense of the word ποιητής (maker). The poets of that age were "makers." Their poetry was not a transcript of their experience, but a creation out of the material of experience. The poetry of Lérmontov was (like all real poetry) also a creation and a transformation, but the element of raw experience and the will to express it play a much larger part in it than in that of his elders. In his later work he certainly turned towards a more "poietic" method of working. But to the reader poetry ceased to be the making of "things of beauty," whose very beauty resided in the fact that they were new and transcended this

experience, and became a direct response to his actual—psychological—emotions, "a beautiful language of emotion"—in short,
the beautiful statement of feelings he had actually experienced.
When once poetry reaches this stage it ceases to have an independent existence.

Feeling—inner experience—formed the chief interest in life
of the better class of Russians in the thirties and forties. Hamlet
was their hero, and introspection their principal occupation. The
cult of feeling, with the conviction that great feelings are a man's
only claim to superiority, was shared by all. But almost invariably
introspection failed to detect feelings of sufficient greatness in the
introspected subject. Dissatisfaction with one's own self at not
finding there the great, ennobling feelings of romantic tradition is
the common theme of the literature of the time. In Lérmontov this
kind of feeling and this kind of writing were only one side of his
weaker—human, not "poietic"—self. But in the minor poets of his
generation, the so-called poets of reflection (which in Russian
means critical introspection), a similar feeling is practically the
only note, while their style is merely a versified transcript of such
feelings. The most characteristic of these poets were Iván Pávlovich Klyúshnikov (1811–95) and, especially, Nicholas Platónovich
Ogarëv (1813–77), the childhood friend, and for many years the
political ally, of Herzen. A man of great but undisciplined nobility
of soul, Ogarëv was unhappy in his family life. He emigrated in
1856 and was co-editor with Herzen of the *Bell*. He was to a great
extent Herzen's evil angel, not on account of any evilness of his
intentions, but because he was entirely devoid of that genius of
political tact which was so prominent in his great associate. His
poetry (which he began publishing in 1840 and which first appeared in book form in 1856) is typical of the idealistic forties.
Melancholy, disillusionment, impotent longing, wistful recollections of missed happiness, are his principal themes. The poetry of
Ogarëv is the poetry that might have been expected from a hero
of Turgénev's novels.

Turgénev himself began his career by writing verse. His poetic
activity lasted from 1838 to 1845. He is far more artistic than Klyúshnikov and Ogarëv, for through the intermediation of Pletnëv he
had a direct contact with the Golden Age. But the theme of his
poetry is the same as theirs—melancholy, disillusionment, idealistic irony on the falling off and fading of "great feelings." His

most memorable (and longest) poem is *Parásha*, which was enthusiastically greeted in 1843 by Belínsky. It is a poem of idealistic irony—the subject is the degeneration of the ideal love of youth into the humdrum realities of middle age. The style is a descendant of that of *Don Juan*, of *Evgény Onégin*, and of Lérmontov (whose prosody is admirably aped). Without being a great poem, or comparable to the best of Turgénev's stories, it is not by any means a contemptible production.

THE DRAMA

The Russian theater in the thirties and forties continued to be adorned by great actors and a high level of acting—but not by great playwrights. The one exception emphasizes the rule—the comedies of Gógol are as isolated and alone in the thirties as the comedy of Griboyédov was in the twenties. The common run of playwriting was by no means superior to that of the preceding period. In tragedy romanticism had triumphed, but its triumph was no benefit to the Russian stage. The plays of Nestor Kúkolnik (1809–68), in blank verse, on romantic themes, and cast in a mold borrowed from Schiller, held the stage with tremendous success, especially in Petersburg, where a public of government clerks found just what it required of romanticism in the cheap and showy tinsel of Kúkolnik. Less obviously meretricious, but in other respects no better than Kúkolnik's, were the romantic and patriotic plays of the unfortunate Polevóy. Nor can anything better be said of Baron George Rosen (1800–66), the author of the libretto for Glinka's great opera *Life for the Tsar* (1836), though, for some reasons that entirely escape us, he was at one time patronized by Púshkin.

The real tragic poet of the thirties was neither Kúkolnik nor Polevóy—but Shakspere. This is true especially of Moscow, where the audiences were more intellectual and more democratic than in Petersburg and consisted of students of the University and of young merchants and city clerks avid for culture and beauty. *Hamlet* especially was the play of the moment. The Idealists found in Hamlet a fellow spirit, while the rest of the audience were carried away by the romantic beauty of the dialogue, and still more by the inspired acting of Paul Mochálov (1800–48), Russia's great romantic tragedian.

At the same time, there was steady progress towards a new, Russian, conception of realism. The growth of realism on the Russian stage is much more regular and logical than in literature, owing to the great personality of Michael Schépkin (1787–1863), who in the second quarter of the century revolutionized comic acting and laid the foundations of the purely Russian realistic style. The comic repertory, especially in Petersburg, was almost entirely dominated by the vaudeville. Though the later vaudevillists chose Russian subjects for their plays and invented Russian plots, the genre was eminently unoriginal and French. It was full of a gay and lighthearted *Scribisme*, and its literary significance is small. But from the theatrical point of view it was an exceedingly grateful kind of play, for it was full of action and gave ample opportunity to the actors to individualize their parts. It has been said that from the point of view of stagecraft the vaudevillists of the thirties and forties have never been surpassed in Russian dramatic literature.

THE NOVELISTS OF THE THIRTIES

The imaginative prose of the thirties and early forties was a chaos, but a fertile chaos. Romanticism and realism, fantasy and everyday life, idealism and satire, construction and style, are all in a state of fertile fermentation, all mixed and jumbled together. The chaos was to take a form only in the second half of the forties, when the Russian realistic school was born.

The main tendencies of the fiction of the period may be classified under three heads: German romanticism, French romanticism, and Russian naturalism. The first is represented by Alexéy Fomích Weltmann (1800–60) and Prince Vladímir Odóyevsky (1803–69); the second by Nicholas Pávlov (1805–64) and Eléna Hahn, nee Fadéyev (1814–43; pseudonym "Zinaída R-va"). The third group, represented by Pogódin and Dahl, cannot be considered before we have spoken of Gógol. In Gógol all three tendencies are present, but he transcends them all by the sheer greatness of his originality.

Weltmann's delightfully readable style is based on Sterne, Jean-Paul, and the German romanticists. A blend of imagination and playfully irresponsible humor is the groundwork of his loosely constructed stories. The idealists of the thirties and early forties appreciated Weltmann's romantic humor and his whimsical methods of construction as the expression of "romantic irony"—the irony of the superior poet for the imperfection of the finite world. Prince Vladímir Odóyevsky's best stories are all strongly marked by the influence of E. T. A. Hoffmann. The contrast between the inferior and dubious reality of common life and the higher reality of ideal life is the main subject. All his stories are inspired by a contempt for the low and fleshly life of the Philistine herd. His most ambitious work is *The Russian Nights* (1844), a series of philosophical conversations on the inadequacy of philosophical science when unguided by the higher knowledge to solve the riddles of the universe.

The "French" romanticists cultivated ideas of a simpler and more immediately practical kind—liberty and the cult of passion—and the more forcible forms of rhetoric. The most successful was Pávlov, the disreputable husband of Caroline Pávlova. His *Three Tales* (1835), carelessly passed by the censorship, were one of the greatest literary sensations of the period. Their principal interest lay in a note of strong social protest, a note that had never sounded so strongly in Russian fiction. The most striking of the three tales was the tragic story of a musician of talent who was a serf. Pávlov did not fulfill the promise of his first book. His second book (*New Tales*, 1839) was inferior to it, and after that he devoted himself entirely to gambling and dinner speeches. The influence, shortly to become so powerful, of George Sand made its first appearance in the work of Eléna Hahn. Her husband was an artillery officer, and she spent her life wandering from one God-forsaken billet to another. All her stories are a protest against the sickening boredom, vulgarity, and emptiness of provincial and garrison life. Her sweet, silent, but passionate, heroines are pathetically naïve and helpless, and invariably fall victims to the envy and slander of provincial gossip. The male characters are either cads who seduce women by a pretense of love, or cowards whose passions are too weak to make them act honorably with the women who love them.

Apart from the main line of development, and parallel to, rather than in any way dependent on, Gógol, are the novels of Ukrainian life of Gregory Kvítka (1779–1843), who wrote under the name of Osnovyánenko. Most of his work is in Ukrainian and falls outside the scope of the present volume, but his novel *Pan Khalyávsky*, a heavily realistic and heavily humorous picture of the uninspired and purely materialistic life of the Ukrainian squires, is a notable landmark in the evolution towards pure physiological naturalism.

GÓGOL

Nikoláy Vasílievich Gógol was born on March 19, 1809, in the market town of Sorochíntsy, in the Province of Poltáva. He came of a family of Ukrainian Cossack gentry. His father was a small squire and an amateur Ukrainian playwright. In 1820 Gógol went to a provincial grammar school and remained there till 1828. It was there he began writing. He was not very popular among his schoolfellows, but with two or three of them he formed lasting friendships. Very early he developed a dark and secretive disposition, mingled of painful self-consciousness and boundless ambition. Equally early he developed an extraordinary mimic talent, which later on made him a matchless reader of his own works. In 1828, on leaving school, Gógol came to Petersburg, full of vague but glowingly ambitious hopes. They were at once cruelly frustrated. He had hoped for literary fame and brought with him a poem, very weak and puerile, of German idyllic life—*Hanz (sic) Küchelgarten.* He had it published, at his own expense of course, and under the name of "V. Alov." It was met by the magazines with deserved derision. He bought up all the copies and destroyed them. In this state of disillusionment he suddenly went off abroad, with the intention, as he said, of going to America. But he went only as far as Lübeck. After a few days' stay there he returned to Petersburg and once more tried his fortune, this time with better patience. He entered the Civil Service, still hoping to become a great administrator, and he began writing prose stories. He came in touch with the "literary aristocracy," had a story published in Délvig's *Northern Flowers*, was taken up by Zhukóvsky and Pletněv, and, in 1831, was introduced to Púshkin. He was well received in this most select of literary sets and, with his usual vanity, became enormously proud of his success and very self-confident. Thanks to Pletněv's good offices, he was appointed teacher of history at a young ladies' institute and at once began to imagine that the way he was to become great was by writing history. In the meantime (1831) he brought out the first volume of his Ukrainian stories (*Evenings on a Farm near Dikánka*), which met with immediate success. It was followed in 1832 by a second volume, and in 1835 by two volumes of stories entitled *Mírgorod* (containing *Viy*, *Tarás Búlba*, *Old-World Landowners*, and *Iván Ivánovich and Iván Nikíforovich*), as well as by two volumes of miscellaneous prose entitled *Arabesques* (containing, besides a variety of essays, *The Névsky Prospect*, *The Memoirs of a Madman*, and the first draft of *The Portrait*). In 1834 Gógol was made Professor of History of the University of St. Petersburg, though, except an unlimited self-confidence, he had absolutely no qualifications for the chair. This academic venture proved a signal failure. His first lecture, an introduction to mediæval history, was a brilliant piece of showy rhetoric, but those which followed it were poor and empty. Turgénev, who happened to be one of Gógol's audience, has left a record of the painful impression they produced. Gógol soon realized his failure (though he does not seem to have acknowledged his inadequacy) and resigned his chair in 1835. His good relations with the "literary aristocracy" continued, and Púshkin and Zhukóvsky continued encouraging him. But there was never any real intimacy between either Púshkin or Zhukóvsky and Gógol. They liked him and appreciated his talent, and refused to idolize him. It is probable, after all, that they undervalued him. But while the "aristocracy" gave him qualified admiration, in Moscow Gógol met with the adulation and entire recognition sufficient to satisfy him. The young Idealists, with Belínsky at their head, carried him to the skies, but it was not with them he made friends. The set that became his principal sanctuary were the Slavophils, especially the Aksákov family, in which he could taste of absolute and unconditioned admiration.

Though between 1832 and 1836 Gógol worked at his imaginative creations with great energy, and though almost all his work has in one way or another its sources in these four years of contact with Púshkin, he had not yet decided that his ambitions were to be fulfilled by success in literature. It was only after the presentation, on April 19, 1836, of his comedy *Revizór* that he finally believed in his literary vocation. The comedy, a violent satire of Russian provincial bureaucracy, saw the stage owing only to the personal interference of Nicholas I. It was met by enthusiastic praise and virulent obloquy. The Petersburg journalists, the spokesmen of the official classes, raised the hue and cry against

Gógol, while the "aristocrats" and the Moscow Idealists of every shade of opinion were equally emphatic in admiring it. They received it as more than a work of art—as a great moral and social event. Though hurt by the attacks of the Philistines, Gógol was in much greater degree elated by the praise of his admirers. When, two months after the first night, he left Petersburg for abroad, he was finally convinced that his vocation was to "be useful" to his country by the power of his imaginative genius. Henceforward for twelve years (1836–48) he lived abroad, coming to Russia for short periods only. He chose Rome for his headquarters. He became enamored with the Eternal City, which answered to his highly developed sense of the magnificent, and where even the visions that always obsessed him of vulgar and animal humanity assumed picturesque and poetical appearances that filled harmoniously into the beautiful whole. The death of Púshkin produced a strong impression on Gógol, especially by emphasizing his conviction that *he* was now the head of Russian literature and that great things were expected of him. His principal work during these years was the great satirical epic (*poéma*, as its Russian subheading goes) *Dead Souls*. At the same time he worked at other tasks—recast *Tarás Búlba* and *The Portrait*, completed his second comedy, *Marriage*, wrote the fragment *Rome* and the famous tale *The Greatcoat*. In 1841 the first part of *Dead Souls* was ready, and Gógol took it to Russia to supervise its printing. It appeared in Moscow in 1842, under the title, imposed by the censorship, of *The Adventures of Chíchikov, or Dead Souls*. Simultaneously a collected edition of his earlier work was brought out in four volumes. The reception of the new book by all those who counted was enthusiastic. This was the summit of Gógol's literary career and, practically, the end of his work as an imaginative writer. The subsequent developments were unexpected and disappointing, and still form one of the strangest and most disconcerting passages in the history of the Russian mind.

Gógol's imaginative creation, especially his most ambitious and influential works, *Revizór* and *Dead Souls*, was satirical. It seemed satire pure and simple, leveled at the dark and animal forces of stagnant Russia. It was accepted as such both by the interested side—the bureaucrats and their journalistic mouthpieces—and by the dissatisfied elite. To the latter the author of these satires appeared as a teacher, a man with a great message of moral and social regeneration, an enemy of dark social forces, and a friend of progress and enlightenment. There was in this attitude a great misunderstanding. Gógol's work was satirical, but not in the ordinary sense. It was not objective, but subjective, satire. His characters were not realistic caricatures of the world without, but introspective caricatures of the fauna of his own mind. They were exteriorizations of his own "ugliness" and "vices": *Revizór* and *Dead Souls* were satires of self, and of Russia and mankind only in so far as Russia and mankind reflected that self. On the other hand, while he was endowed with a superhuman power of creative imagination (in which in the world's literature he has had equals but certainly no superior), his understanding was strikingly inadequate to his genius. His ideas were those of his provincial home, of his simple, childish mother, modified only by an equally primitive romantic cult of beauty and of art, imbibed during the first years of his literary career. But his limitless ambition, stimulated by the homage paid him by his Moscow friends, urged him to become more than a mere comic writer, to be a prophet and a teacher. He worked himself into a faith in his divine mission, which was to lead sin-bound Russia to moral regeneration.

After the publication of the first part of *Dead Souls*, Gógol, it would seem, intended to continue it on the plan of Dante's *Divine Comedy*. The first part, which contained none but caricatures, was to be the *Inferno*. The second part was to be the gradual purification and transformation of the rogue Chíchikov under the influence of virtuous publicans and governors—*Purgatory*. Gógol began working at the second part immediately, but it proceeded haltingly and was put aside. Instead he decided to write a book of direct moral preaching that would reveal his message to the world. But he had no message to reveal, apart from the weird mask exteriorized by his subconscious self, or the glowing heroic and romantic images of his creative imagination. The "message" that was embodied in the new book was nothing but a hotchpotch of provincial, very earthly and uninspired, religious flatness, sprinkled by a little æsthetic romanticism and served up to justify the existing order of things (including serfdom, corporal punishment, and so on) and to impress on every man the duty of *conforming* conscientiously and to the best of his might with the present God-ordained order of things. The book, entitled *Selected Passages from a*

Correspondence with Friends (though it contained practically no
passages from actual letters), appeared in 1847. Gógol expected
it to be received with awe and gratitude, like a message from
Sinai. He actually believed that it would be a signal for the immediate regeneration of Russians from sin. He was cruelly disappointed before long. His best friends, the Slavophils, were painfully and unmistakably disgusted. Aksákov, the very archpriest
of the Gógol cult, wrote to him a letter of bitterly wounded friendship, accusing him of Satanic pride masquerading in the guise of
humility. After this and similar rebukes from people whom he regarded as his own, the violent, vehement, and outspoken letter of
Belínsky, which accused him of falsifying Christianity for the
profit of those in power and of adoring reaction and barbarity,
though it hurt Gógol deeply, contributed little to increase his self-
disillusionment. His inferiority complex rose in a wave of self-
disgust, and Gógol threw himself on the mercy of religion. But he
was not made for a religious life, and however despairingly he
forced himself to it, he could not succeed. His tragedy entered on
a new stage. Instead of trying to proclaim a message he had not
got, he now tried to acquire an experience of which he was incapable. His early education made him view Christianity in its
simplest form: as the fear of death and hell. But he had no inner
impulse towards Christ. His despair of himself was enhanced by
the pilgrimage he undertook (in 1848) to the Holy Land. His in-
capacity to warm himself up to genuine religious experience in the
presence of the Lord's footsteps increased his conviction that he
was irrevocably lost and damned. From Palestine he returned to
Russia and passed his last years in restless movement from one
part of the country to another. He met Father Matthew Kon-
stantínovsky, a fierce and narrow ascetic, who seems to have had a
great influence on him and strengthened in him his fear of perdition
by insisting on the sinfulness of all his imaginative work. However,
Gógol continued working at the second part of *Dead Souls*, a first
draft of which he had destroyed in 1846 as unsatisfactory. His
health gradually gave way. He undermined it by exaggerated
ascetic practices, all the time trying to compel himself to a Christian inner life. In an access of self-mortification he destroyed some
of his manuscripts, which contained most of the second part of
Dead Souls. He explained this as a mistake—a practical joke

played on him by the Devil. It is not clear whether he really meant
to do it or not. After that he fell into a state of black melancholy,
and died on February 21, 1852.

The significance of Gógol is twofold—he is not only a great
imaginative writer; he is a supremely interesting individuality, a
psychological phenomenon of exceptional curiosity. This psychological side still remains, and will probably always remain, very
largely a mystery. I am not here concerned with it, except in so
far as it is directly connected with the nature of his creative work.
But as a writer Gógol is not twofold in the sense Tolstóy or
Dostoyévsky is. There is no common *literary* measure between his
imaginative work and his miscellaneous and moralistic writings.
The latter are remarkable only as they throw light on the psychological, human personality of Gógol. The early essays contained in
Arabesques are rhetoric pure and simple, of a kind that is but the
manure for the really magnificent rhetoric of such early stories as
The Terrible Vengeance or *Tarás Búlba.* The *Correspondence with
Friends* is painful, almost humiliating, reading, in spite of the
occasional flashes of imagination that break through its heavy and
poisonous mist. The critical pages, with their sometimes genuinely
and sublimely imaginative appreciation and impressionistic portraits of Russian poets (especially of his favorites Yazýkov and
Derzhávin), may be alone singled out for praise. Of the writings
of his last years, the commentary on the liturgy is derivative and
irresponsible. While *The Author's Confession* is notable as a human
document of considerable importance, it has no claim to comparison with the *Confession* of Tolstóy. Still, even in these writings
the unique, unrepeatable personality of Gógol is always present in
the labored, consciously original style, with its constant suggestion
of the presence of unconquered chaos and disorder.

His imaginative work is a very different business. It is one
of the most marvelous, unexpected—in the strictest sense, original
—worlds ever created by an artist of words. If mere creative force
is to be the standard of valuation, Gógol is the greatest of Russian
writers. In this respect he need hardly fear comparison with
Shakspere, and can boldly stand by the side of Rabelais. Neither
Púshkin nor Tolstóy possessed anything like that volcano of
imaginative creativeness. The enormous potency of his imagination stands as a strange contrast (or complement) to his physical
sterility. He seems sexually never to have emerged from an in-

fantile (or rather, early adolescent) stage. Woman was to him a terrible, fascinating, but unapproachable obsession, and he is known never to have loved. This makes the women of his imagination either strange, inhuman visions of form and color that are redeemed from melodramatic banality only by the elemental force of the rhetoric they are enshrined in, or entirely unsexed, even dehumanized, caricatures.

The main and most persistent characteristic of Gógol's style is its verbal expressiveness. He wrote with a view not so much to the acoustic effect on the ears of the listener as to the sensuous effect on the vocal apparatus of the reciter. This makes his prose intense and saturated. It is composed of two elements, romantically contrasted and romantically extreme—high-pitched, poetic rhetoric, and grotesque farce. Gógol never wrote simply—he is always either elaborately rhythmical or quite as elaborately mimetic. It is not only in his dialogue that the intonations of spoken speech are reproduced. His prose is never empty. It is all alive with the vibration of actual speech. This makes it hopelessly untranslatable —more untranslatable than any other Russian prose.

The other main characteristic of Gógol's genius is the extraordinary intensity and vividness of his *sight*. He saw the outer world romantically transformed; and even when he saw the same details as we do, they acquired such proportions in his vision as to become entirely different in meaning and measure. Gógol's pictures of nature are either romantically fantastic transformations (like the famous description of the Dnepr in *The Terrible Vengeance*) or strange mounds of detail heaped on detail, resulting in an unconnected chaos of things. Where he is absolutely supreme and definitive is in his vision of the human figure. His people are caricatures, drawn with the method of the caricaturist—which is to exaggerate salient features and to reduce them to geometrical pattern. But these caricatures have a convincingness, a truthfulness, an inevitability—attained as a rule by slight but definitive strokes of unexpected reality—that seems to beggar the visible world itself.

I have alluded to the great and exceptional originality of Gógol. This does not mean that numerous influences cannot be discerned in his work. The principal of these are: the tradition of the Ukrainian folk and puppet theater, with which the plays of Gógol's father were closely linked; the heroic poetry of the Ukrain-

ian *dumy*, or Cossack ballads; the *Iliad* in the Russian version of
Gnédich; the numerous and mixed traditions of comic writing
from Molière to the vaudevillists of the twenties; the novel of
manners from Le Sage to Narézhny; Sterne, chiefly through the
medium of German romanticism; the German romanticists themselves, especially Tieck and E. T. A. Hoffmann; the "furious school"
of French romanticism, with, at its head, Hugo and Jules Janin,
and their common master, Maturin—a long and yet incomplete
list. Many of the elements of Gógol's art may be traced back to
these sources. And they are not merely borrowings and reminiscences of motives; most of them had a profound effect on his very
manner and technique. Yet they are only constituent details in a
whole of more than expectable originality.

The first part of *Evenings* (containing *Sorochinsky Fair, St.
John's Eve, The May Night, or The Drowned Girl,* and *The Lost
Charter*) together with two of the four stories of the second part
(*Christmas Night* and *The Charmed Spot*) are the early Gógol. They
are much simpler, less sophisticated and tense, than anything he
wrote later. Their fun, which was what attracted the reader above
all, is simple and unadulterated. Their romance is somewhat
youthfully operatic but free from sophistication. Their devilry is
gay and lighthearted. The picture they give of Ukraine is of
course quite fantastic, but it was so attractive, at once so prettily
romantic and so hugely funny, that not even the Ukrainians themselves (except till much later) remarked all the absurdities, all the
supreme disregard for (and ignorance of) reality displayed by
Gógol. The prefaces to each of the two volumes, placed in the
mouth of the suppositious narrator, the beekeeper Red Pánko,
are already masterpieces of Gógol's mimetic art. The stories themselves depend for the humor on the stock characters of the Ukrainian puppet theater; for the spook and romance on the various
fictions of chiefly German romanticists. Gógol is present in the
blend of the two elements, in the verbal intensity of the style, in
the vivid convincingness of the largely fantastical dialogue of the
comic figures, in the unique, physical infectiousness of the laughter.

Of the remaining two stories in the second part of *Evenings*,
The Terrible Vengeance is a creation of the purest romantic imagination. Strongly redolent of foreign romanticism and full of reminiscences of the Cossack songs, *The Terrible Vengeance* is, in a
certain sense, a masterpiece. It is Gógol's greatest effort at purely

ornate prose. The beautiful rhythmical movement is sustained
without breach or flaw from beginning to end. The story is grue-
some and creepy, and at a first reading almost intolerably impressive. It is one of his very few stories where humor is entirely
absent.

Of the stories contained in the *Mírgorod* volumes, the romantic
element is present in *Tarás Búlba* and in *Viy*.[1] The former is a
historical romance of Cossack Ukraine. Though suggested by, it
is very unlike, the romances of Scott. It is supremely free from
considerations of historical exactitude but nevertheless full of the
spirit of the old Cossack warriors and echoes of their poetry. It is
almost as full, in the battle scenes, of reminiscences of the *Iliad*.
Its place in Russian literature is unique—it has had no imitators
or followers (except, perhaps, Bábel in his stories of the Red Army).
It is heroic, frankly and openly heroic, but it is also broadly humorous and realistic. It is perhaps the only Russian imaginative
work that has that many-sided exuberance which might claim the
epithet Shaksperian. *Viy* is also a wonderful blend of romantic
weirdness with realistic and homely humor. The construction of the
story, the absence from it of questionable rhetoric, and, especially,
the perfect fusion of the two discordant elements of terror and
humor, all make *Viy* one of the fullest and richest of Gógol's
stories.

Gógol's stories of everyday life of contemporary Russia are
introspective—not in the sense that he analyzed and described his
psychic experience as Tolstóy, Dostoyévsky, or Proust did, but
because his characters are exteriorized and objectivated symbols
of his experience. His inferiority complex and his deep roots in the
animal, or rather vegetable, life of a rural squiredom gave these
symbols the form of caricatures of grotesque vulgarity. The aspect
under which he sees reality is expressed by the untranslatable
Russian word *póshlost*, which is perhaps best rendered as "self-
satisfied inferiority," moral and spiritual. But other subjective
aspects may be discovered in his realistic stories—in particular
what we might call a "sterility complex," which makes its appearance in the very first of these stories, in *Iván Fëdorovich
Shpónka and His Aunt*, the fourth story of the second volume of
Evenings.

Until after the publication of the first part of *Dead Souls*,

[1] The Ukranian name for a terrifying gnome whose eyelids reach to the ground.

Gógol took scant interest in reality as such but relied for the creation of his characters entirely on his unaided imagination. But he was a realist in the sense that he introduced (as details and as material) innumerable elements and aspects of reality that had hitherto not possessed the freedom of literature. He was (like Tolstóy, Górky, and Andréyev, after him) a great lifter of taboos, a great destroyer of prohibitions. He made vulgarity reign where only the sublime and the beautiful had reigned. This was *historically* the most important aspect of his work. Nor was the younger generation's general concept of him as a social satirist entirely unjustified. He did not paint (and scarcely knew) the social evils of Russia. But the caricatures he drew were, weirdly and terribly, *like* the reality about him; and the sheer vividness and convincingness of his paintings simply eclipsed the paler truth and irrevocably held the fascinated eye of the reader.

In his attitude towards "vegetable life" Gógol oscillated between sympathetic complacency and scornful irony. The sentimental and sympathetic attitude is most fully expressed in the *Old-World Landowners* (in *Mírgorod*), where the vegetable humors of the old pair, their sloth, their gluttony, their selfishness, are idealized and sentimentalized. The purely ironic attitude is expressed with equal purity in the other realistic story of *Mírgorod*— *The Story of How Iván Ivánovich Quarreled with Iván Nikíforovich*. It is one of the greatest of Gógol's masterpieces. His comic gift (always verging on impossible caricature and impossible farce) appears in its absolute purity. But like almost all his later stories it results ultimately in a vision of depressingly hopeless gloom. The story, begun as a merry farce, grows, towards the end, uncannily symbolical, and ends with the famous words: "It is gloomy in this world, gentlemen" (*"Skúchno na étom svéte, gospodá"*).

Of the five short stories whose scene is set in Petersburg, *The Portrait* is purely romantic, devoid of humor, and curiously reminiscent of Poe. *The Memoirs of a Madman* (1835) and *Névsky Prospect* (1835), one of Gógol's masterpieces, are romantic in the Hoffmannesque sense, for their subject is the juxtaposition of dream life and real life. *The Nose* (1836) is a piece of sheer play, almost sheer nonsense. In it more than anywhere else Gógol displays his extraordinary magic power of making great comic art out of nothing.

The last in time of the Petersburg stories is *The Greatcoat*

(1842), which, together with *Revizór* and *Dead Souls*, turned out
to be Gógol's most influential work. It is the story of a poor clerk
who lives on four hundred rubles a year and whose only dream in
life is to have a new greatcoat. When at last he has the money
and the greatcoat is ready, the first time he goes out he is waylaid
by thieves and robbed of the greatcoat. He is represented as a
pathetically humble and inferior figure, and the story passes
through all the gamut of attitudes towards him, from sheer fun to
poignant pity. It is this poignancy of pity for the poor and insignificant man that so strongly impressed the contemporary
reader. *The Greatcoat* gave rise to a whole literature of philanthropic
stories about the poor clerk, of which the most significant is
Dostoyévsky's *Poor Folk.*

The plot of *Dead Souls* revolves around Chíchikov and his
roguish plan of buying up "dead souls" (that is, serfs who had
died since the last census and for whom their owners continued to
pay the poll-tax) for nothing and then getting money by pawning
them. The construction is loose, and the narrative spacious. The
verbal and visual wealth of the style is as intense as in *The Greatcoat*. The characters are, together with those of *Revizór*, the most
memorable and permanent of Gógol's legacy to the Russian mind.
Chíchikov is the greatest of Gógol's subjective caricatures—he is
the incarnation of *póshlost*. His psychological leitmotiv is complacency, and his geometrical expression roundness. He is the golden
mean. The other characters—the squires Chíchikov visits on his
shady business—are typical "humors" (for Gógol's method of
comic character drawing, with its exaggerations and geometrical
simplification, is strongly reminiscent of Ben Jonson's). Sobakévich,
the strong, silent, economical man, square and bearlike; Manílov,
the silly sentimentalist with pursed lips; Mme Koróbochka, the
stupid widow; Nozdrëv, the cheat and bully, with the manners of a
hearty good fellow—all are types of eternal solidity. Plyúshkin, the
miser, stands apart, for in him Gógol sounds a note of tragedy—
he is the man ruined by his "humor"; he transcends *póshlost*, for
in the depth of his degradation he is not complacent but miserable;
he has a tragic greatness. Among other things the first part of
Dead Souls contains "The Story of Captain Kopéykin," in which
Gógol transcended himself in the wealth of verbal expressiveness.

The second part of the great epic, to judge by what has been
left us of it, was a distinct decline. In it Gógol tried to overcome

the natural tendencies of his style and to become more objective and realistic. He succeeded only in forfeiting his strength. It contains first-class work in the style of the first part (especially the "humor" of the glutton, Petúkh), but the new manner was a complete failure. The objectively drawn, good-and-bad-mixed characters are comparatively lifeless, and the ideal characters of the good publican and the virtuous governor quite unconvincing and hollow.

Gógol's greatness as a dramatist rests chiefly on the *Revizór*, doubtless the greatest play in the Russian language. It is not only supreme in character drawing and dialogue—it is one of the few Russian plays that is a play constructed with unerring art from beginning to end. The great originality of its plan consisted in the absence of all love interest and of sympathetic characters. The latter feature was deeply resented by Gógol's enemies, and as a satire the play gained immensely from it. *Revizór* was intended as a *moral* satire against bad officials, not a social satire against the *system* of corruption and irresponsible despotism. But quite apart from the author's intention, it was received as a social satire, and in the great oppositional movement against the despotism of Nicholas I and the system of bureaucratic irresponsibility, its influence was greater than that of any other single literary work. In their great symbolic and comprehensive popularity the characters of *Revizór* stand by the side of those of *Dead Souls*. They are less obviously geometrical, and, the characterization depending entirely on the dialogue, more supple and human. They are less markedly "humorous," more ordinary, more average, than Sobakévich and his like. The head of the local administration, the *Gorodníchy*, is a satirical figure of immense symbolism and pregnancy. As for the central character, Khlestakóv, the supposed inspector general himself, he is as subjective and introspective as Chíchikov. If in Chíchikov Gógol exteriorized all the vegetable elements of his self, in Khlestakóv he symbolized the irresponsibility, the light-mindedness, the absence of measure, that was such a salient trait of his own personality. But, like Chíchikov, Khlestakóv is entirely "transposed," entirely alive—the most alive of all the characters of Russian fiction—meaningless movement and meaningless fermentation incarnate, on a foundation of placidly ambitious inferiority. As for the dialogue of *Revizór*, it is above admiration. There is not a wrong word or intonation from beginning to end, and the comic tensity is of a quality that even in Gógol was not always at his beck and call.

Of Gógol's other plays, *The Vladímir Order*, planned in 1833 as a satire of the Petersburg bureaucracy, remained unfinished, apparently because Gógol despaired of seeing it through the censorship. *Marriage*, begun in 1832 and completed in 1842, is very different from *Revizór*. It is not satirical, and it is loosely built, with dialogue greatly dominating over action. It is pure fun, though undoubtedly on a Freudian foundation (the same sterility complex as in *Shpónka*.) The characters and the dialogue are marvelous. For here, unfettered by any message, Gógol gave free reign to his grotesque, mimetic imagination and surpassed himself in the exuberance of his comic creation. The remaining play, *The Gamblers*, is inferior to the two great comedies. It is an unpleasant play, inhabited by scoundrels that are not funny, and, though the construction is neat, it is dry and lacks the richness of the true Gógol.

On the stage, as in fiction, Gógol's action, historically, was in the direction of realism. Here as elsewhere he was an opener of doors, an introducer of hitherto forbidden material. *Marriage* especially, with its broad and original treatment of merchant manners, had an appreciable influence on Ostróvsky. And it was in these two comedies (and in *Góre ot umá*) that Schépkin achieved the greatest triumphs of his realistic acting.

LÉRMONTOV'S PROSE

Between the ages of fifteen and eighteen Lérmontov wrote three plays in prose that are on the same low level as his early verse. With a rhetorical style descended from Schiller's *Robbers*, they deal in high-strung passions and melodramatic situations. The most notable thing in them is several strong and realistic scenes describing the serf owners' abuse of despotic power. In 1835 Lérmontov returned to the dramatic form with *Masquerade*, written in the measure of *Góre ot umá*. Like the early plays, to which it is superior only in its forcible, rhetorical verse, it is a swollen melodrama with unreal personages. Lérmontov's first attempt at fiction—also from his pre-cavalry days—is an unfinished romance of the Pugachëv Rebellion, with a dark Byronic revenger

for hero and in the style of the French "furious school," its shrill
rhetoric relieved at times by scenes of brutal realism. His second
attempt was an unfinished novel of Petersburg society, *Princess
Lígovsky*, at which he worked in 1835–6 in collaboration with his
friend Svyatosláv Rayévsky. It possesses already many of the
qualities of *A Hero of Our Times*, and its principal character is a
first draft of Pechórin.

In 1837–9 Lérmontov's creative evolution was in two directions—on the one hand he was ridding himself of the subjective
obsessions of his early years, on the other he was evolving a new,
impersonal, objective, and realistic manner. Thus it was that the
same Caucasian impressions of 1839 found their way both into
The Demon and *Mtsýri* and into their opposite, *A Hero of Our
Times*.

A Hero of Our Times (1840) had an immediate success, and a
second edition (preceded by a remarkable preface, in which
Lérmontov made fun of his readers for believing that in his hero,
Pechórin, he had portrayed himself) appeared before his death,
in 1841. The novel is one of those works in the valuation of which
Russians and foreigners differ most. Russian critical opinion is
unanimous in assigning an exceedingly high place to *A Hero of
Our Times*, and almost unanimous in considering it of greater
importance than Lérmontov's poetical work. Abroad it has failed
to kindle enthusiasm, for reasons similar to those which have kept
Western people from appreciating Púshkin at his true worth:
Lérmontov is too European, too human, too insufficiently Russian,
to please the spice-craving palates of Latin and Anglo-Saxon
Russopaths. On the other hand the perfection, negative rather
than positive, of his style and narrative manner can be appreciated
only by those who really know Russian, who feel the fine impon-
derable shades of words and know what has been left out as well
as what has been put in. Lérmontov's prose is the best Russian
prose ever written, if we judge by the standards of perfection and
not by those of wealth. It is transparent, for it is absolutely adequate to the content and neither overlaps it nor is overlapped by
it. It is different from Púshkin's in its complete freedom and in the
absence of that constraint which is always present in the greater
poet's prose.

The novel consists of five stories. The first (*Béla*) relates the
narrator's meeting on the road from Tiflís to Vladikavkáz with

the Caucasian veteran Captain Maxím Maxímych. Maxím Maxímych tells the story of Pechórin, who was his subaltern for a time
in a fort on the mountain frontier, and of Pechórin's love affair
with a Caucasian girl. In the second, the narrator meets Pechórin
himself and comes by his journal. The remaining three stories are
extracts from the journal of Pechórin. The first, *Tamán*, relating
an incident he had with some smugglers in the town of that name,
is perhaps the masterpiece of Russian fiction. At least it was so
considered by Chékhov, who owed much of his method to its
atmospheric construction. Next comes *Princess Mary*, which itself
may be regarded as a complete short novel. It is the diary of
Pechórin, describing his stay at the Caucasian waters. It is analytic, and a large part of Pechórin's entries are a direct dissection
of his mind in an aphoristic style closely connected with that of
the French moralists and is first cousin to Stendhal's. The construction of the story is delicately suggestive of a parody of *Evgény
Onégin*. The last story is *The Fatalist*, in which Pechórin is nothing
but a narrator and plays no part. It is an intensified anecdote, akin
to the tales of Púshkin.

Pechórin, the hero, is a strong, silent man with a poetic soul
who, from noble shyness and high contempt for the herd, especially
for the aristocratic herd, assumes the mask of a snob and a bully.
He is capable of noble and generous passions, but life has robbed
him of all opportunity to experience them, and his devastated
heart is like an extinct volcano. Pechórin was not only a great
literary influence—he was imitated in life as well as in fiction. To
us Pechórin is redeemed from operatic cheapness by the magical
atmosphere of the novel, which lifts him above the possibility of
ridicule or second-rateness. It is an atmosphere difficult to define.
It has a particular fine, refined quality, at once ironic, tragic, and
visionary. Goethe would have called it "daimonic." The vision
behind the novel is never so much as hinted at, but it is unmistakably present and gives it that air of nobility which (in spite of its
complete freedom from the vice of poeticality) raises it above the
level of mere prose fiction. This atmosphere, together with the
perfection of the verbal and narrative form, is what has induced
people by no means extravagant or paradoxical to call *A Hero of
Our Times* the greatest Russian novel, thus placing it above *War
and Peace*.

Another notable feature of the novel, and one that had the

greatest effect on the immediate future, is the figure of Maxím
Maxímych, the veteran captain of the line, the simple, humble,
and casual hero of duty, kindness, and common sense, who is one
of the greatest creations of Russian realism. It is a connecting link
between Púshkin's Captain Mirónov and Tolstóy's humble heroes
of army officers, and in this line it is, unquestionably, the fullest
and most comprehensive expression of the type.

After *A Hero of Our Times* Lérmontov wrote little prose, nor
had he much time to write more. *Ashík-Keríb*, a Tatar tale, shows
how genuine and sympathetic was his understanding of the East.
He also left the beginning of a novel of Petersburg—full of a cold
and condensed romanticism that has its roots in *The Queen of
Spades*, which makes us lament all the more the untimely death of
one who, had he lived, might have shown the Russian novel a
manlier and stronger way than it actually took.

THE FIRST NATURALISTS

Under the influence of Gógol's taboo-lifting and boundary-re-
moving work there arose towards 1840 what called itself the
"Natural School." The movement ultimately culminated in the
birth of the national school of realism in the memorable years
1846–7. Before that date its pioneers, apart from Gógol, were
Dahl, Sollohúb, and Butkóv.

Vladímir Ivánovich Dahl (1801–72), who was of Danish origin, is remembered chiefly for his *Reasoned Dictionary of the Living
Great-Russian Language* (four volumes, 1864–8), which still forms
the basis of our knowledge of Russian as it was spoken by the
people before the spread of standard schoolmastery. In literature
Dahl desired to free Russian from its Græco-Latin-German-French
fetters, but he had no real sense of style, and his stories and anecdotes, written (in the thirties and forties) in illustration of his
linguistic aspirations, are not remarkable. His stories of contemporary life in the "natural style" were historically more important.
He was the first to introduce the form of the "physiological
sketch"; that is, of short, descriptive stories illustrating the peculiarities of this or that particular social milieu, a form that had a
great vogue in the forties.

Count Vladímir Alexándrovich Sollohúb (1814–82) was an

aristocratic dilettante. His best known work, *Tarantás* (1844), is a satirical journey from Moscow to Kazán in a tumble-down traveling cart. The satire, superficial and uninspired, is directed against the ideas of the Slavophils and the unpractical dreaminess of the romantic idealists. There are a greater intensity and seriousness in the work of Yákov Butkóv (*c.* 1815–56), whose *Summits* (i.e. attics) *of Petersburg* (1844–5) is the most important landmark of philanthropic literature between Gógol's *Greatcoat* and Dostoyévsky's *Poor Folk*. Himself a penniless proletarian and the sweated drudge of the publisher Krayévsky, Butkóv's stories are devoted to the sentimental and humorous evocation of the life of the poor government clerks of the capital.

THE PETERSBURG JOURNALISTS

Journalism flourished and its importance increased in the course of the present period. In spite of the censorship, whose rigor was never for a moment abated during the whole reign of Nicholas I, it was precisely now that the Russian magazines finally became the leaders of public opinion and acquired the peculiar form and coloring they retained till the great Revolution. Petersburg journalism was at first dominated by the notorious triumvirate— Bulháryn, Grech, and Senkówski, of whom the most talented was Joseph-Julian Senkówski (1800–59). An Arabic scholar of considerable achievement and, like Bulháryn, a Pole by birth, from 1834 he edited the *Library for Reading* and wrote in it under the pseudonym of Baron Brambeus. Fundamentally cynical, he had no respect for genius, sincerity, or generous emotion. His smart and witty reviews and critical surveys poured out contempt and obloquy on all the best authors of the time. His style, flippant, facile, tasteless, and cheaply humorous, had an immense influence on the formation of Russian journalese. Senkówski and Belínsky, so unlike in their spiritual content, were equally operative in putting an end to the elegant and distinguished "French" prose of the Karamzín-Púshkin tradition.

THE MOSCOW "CIRCLES"

The contrast, in the thirties, between bureaucratic, cynical, pleasure-seeking, meretricious Petersburg and young, idealistic, inspired, philosophical Moscow was striking. While the papers of the Petersburg triumvirate, servile and subservient, flourished, brought in big incomes, and were never so much as frowned at by the authorities, the history of the Moscow magazines is a succession of martyrdoms at the hands of the censorship, and of financial failures in the hands of dilettante publishers. The history of Muscovite idealism is much less connected with its journals than with the famous "circles."

These "circles" were invariably connected with the University. In the twenties the Wisdom-lovers had been already a typical "circle" of the kind. They were one of the germs out of which, in the thirties, grew up the Slavophil group. In the early thirties the University of Moscow contained among its undergraduates a remarkable group of young men who formed the two famous "circles" of Stankévich and of Herzen. The former devoted themselves to the enthusiastic study of German idealistic philosophy—Schelling, Fichte, and Hegel. Herzen's circle concentrated on political and social questions, and were the first to introduce the doctrines of the idealistic socialism of Saint-Simon and Fourier. The University of Moscow was a crucible wherein all classes were melted into a non-class intelligentsia. The *raznochíntsy* [2] were an increasingly important element in the mixture, and though Stankévich and others were great landowners, the principal leader of the Westernizers was Belínsky, a plebeian, with a strong plebeian pride.

In spite of this growing plebeian element, the Moscow "circles" retained a semi-aristocratic character and maintained a close connection with the intellectual part of Moscow society. The debates on philosophical, historical, and literary subjects that were such a prominent and famous feature of intellectual Moscow in the later thirties and forties took place at the *salons* of the Elágins, of the Sverbéyevs, at the Khomyakóvs', at Chaadáyev's, at Caroline Pávlova's. It was in these *salons* that a new Russian culture was forged. Though many of the great intellectuals of the thirties and forties, partly owing to the rigors of the censorship, partly owing to a deeply embedded aristocratic dilettantism, have left few traces in literature, it has become the tradition to include

[2] *Raznochíntsy* (singular *raznochínets*) means literally "men of various classes." They included all those who, having received an education, had ceased to be members of the lower classes but had not become nobles.

at least a mention of the principal leaders of intellectual Moscow in every history of literature.

The oldest of them was Peter Yákovlevich Chaadáyev (1793–1856), who in his early years had been a Hussar of the Guards, a Liberal, and a friend of Púshkin's. In the twenties he underwent a conversion to mystical Christianity, with a strong leaning to Rome. About 1830 he wrote his *Philosophical Letters* (in French) on the meaning of history. They contained a ruthless criticism of Russian history from the point of view of Roman Catholicism. They were not originally intended for publication, but Chaadáyev was persuaded to have them printed in Nadézhdin's *Telescope*. The first letter appeared in 1836. It passed the censorship, but when it was out, it produced the effect of a bombshell. The *Telescope* was suppressed, and Chaadáyev was officially declared a lunatic and placed under medical supervision. He continued to live in Moscow, surrounded by a halo of martyrdom and courage in the eyes of the young Westernizers, who, in spite of his Romanism, looked up to him as a leader and a patriarch. His striking figure, with his high and bald forehead, was a principal ornament of the intellectual *salons*, where to the last he waged his war of words with the nationalists. His writings, though so exiguous in extent, give him an important place in the history of Russian thought, for, whatever we think of his conclusions, he stated some of the most essential problems of Russian history and Russian civilization with unique historical grasp and ruthless courage.

The most remarkable of the Moscow journalists was Michael Petróvich Pogódin (1800–75). The son of a serf and of a self-made made man, he was at the University of Moscow with the future Wisdom-lovers and became their friend. He was later made Professor of Russian History, and in his untiring researches accumulated an exceptionally valuable collection of old Russian documents. Being by birth more businesslike than his aristocratic friends, he became their publisher and the editor of their magazines, the most important of which was the *Moskvityánin* (1841–56).

Pogódin is one of the most curious and comprehensive characters of modern Russian history, a strange blend of the most contrasting characteristics: morbidly close, but disinterested in his love of Old Russia; highly cultured, but essentially retaining the mentality of a provincial merchant; naturally a coward, yet capable of such real civic courage as the remarkable memoranda

that he addressed, during the Crimean War, to Nicholas I with
an outspoken criticism of his whole reign. All people who knew
him were more or less disgusted by him; and yet there were in him
a power and a message that made that great and erratic genius
Apollón Grigóriev look up to him as his only master and guide.

For fifty years Pogódin was the center of literary Moscow, and
his biography (in twenty-four volumes!) by N. P. Barsukóv is
practically a history of Russian literary life from 1825 to 1875.
But his literary work need not detain us long. As an historian he
had no constructive genius. As a publicist he was handicapped by
lack of sincerity and courage (except in the memoranda). Nor does
his early imaginative work give him a high place as a writer,
though in his tales he was one of the first swallows of national
realism.

Pogódin's associate, Stepán Petróvich Shevyrëv (1806–64),
Professor of Literature at the University of Moscow, was one of
the most cultured and European men of his generation and a
critic of great merit. His essays on Púshkin (*Moskvityánin*, 1841)
are one of the most illuminating criticisms of the great poet.

THE SLAVOPHILS

Slavophilism in the strict sense was a creation of Khomyakóv and
the Kiréyevskys in the thirties, but Slavophil feelings had long
been alive in many Russian minds. I have spoken already of the
naïve nationalism of Admiral Shishkóv. S. T. Aksákov was a living
link between these older forms and the developed creed of the
thirties and forties. The latter included liberal and semi-anarchistic
elements, and may be perhaps best defined as conservative anarchism. The primacy of the moral and religious law, of ancestral
tradition, and of the spontaneous sense of the right and just over
the written laws and regulations of the state, and the primacy of
the whole unreflecting reason over the lower logical and dissecting
reason were the principal tenets of the Slavophils. This they found
in Old Russia and in the Orthodox Church, but not in western
Europe and in the Roman Church, where logical reason and formal
law had from time immemorial got the upper hand of whole
reason. Peter the Great and the Petersburg monarchy had abjured
the national ideals and gone to the school of the godless absolutism

of the West. They had enslaved and humiliated the Church, which only in its secret heart had preserved its true light and was on the surface Europeanized and secularized.

The greatest of the Slavophils was Alexéy Stepánovich Khomyakóv (1804–60), who belongs to literary history as a poet, a philosopher of history, and a theologian.

His early poetry is coldly brilliant and full of conceits. Later he abandoned this manner and made his verse the mouthpiece of his political and religious feelings. He is not a great poet, but in what is perhaps poetic eloquence rather than poetry he has few rivals in Russia. His religious poems, especially that wonderful poem *The Laborer* (1858), are (with the possible exception of some of Fëdor Glínka's) the best in the language for profound sincerity of the (unmystical) feeling and the noble simplicity of the expression. His political verse is on Slavophil themes. The best of it is inspired by indignation at Russia's unworthiness of her great historical and religious mission. The poems written during the Crimean War have a particularly high place in the anthology of Russian political verse.

Khomyakóv's great work was to be a treatise on the philosophy of history. It remained unfinished and is little more than a curious monument of constructive imagination. He is far more important as a theologian. His central idea was the idea of liberty, of the spontaneous, unforced love of man for God, and of the spontaneous acceptance of the law of God, not as law, but as freedom. In theory Khomyakóv was equally opposed to Roman Catholicism and Protestantism, but the edge of his criticism is much more often directed against the former. Like all the Slavophils, he greatly preferred the Protestant to the Catholic nations of Europe. He had a particular liking for England and the Anglicans. But the England he liked was only the traditional England of the Tories and not the progressive England of the Whigs. He recognized in the former, in its neglect of written law, in its fidelity to custom and to unwritten understanding, his favorite ideals of conservative anarchism.

Khomyakóv's theology did not receive the sanction of the official Church, and his theological works were even not allowed to be published till 1879. But all Orthodox thinking in Russia has ever since followed his lead, and today he is practically (though not explicitly) regarded as a Doctor of the Church.

As a writer of prose Khomyakóv is remarkable for the clearness, fullness, and beautiful ease of his Russian, which is free both from the Gallicisms of the Karamzín-Púshkin school and from the untidiness and vulgarity of later nineteenth-century journalism. In non-narrative prose Khomyakóv has a place similar to Aksákov's in narrative prose.

Next to Khomyakóv the two most remarkable older Slavophils were the two brothers Kiréyevsky, Iván (1806–56) and Peter (1808–56). Their mother, remarried to a Mr. Elágin, was the hostess of one of the most famous intellectual *salons* in Moscow. Peter hardly belongs to the history of literature, for his few articles are not particularly important. But he was, as it were, a keeper of the sacred fire of the Slavophil religion. He spent much of his life wandering over Russia collecting the songs of the people.

Iván's literary career was misshapen and thwarted. His criticisms published in the late twenties marked him out as the best critic hitherto born in Russia. In 1832 he started editing a big literary review, the *European*, which was almost immediately suppressed. After this venture he ceased writing for many years. Partly under the influence of his brother and of Khomyakóv, from a follower of Schelling he became a Slavophil and an Orthodox churchman. In 1845 he took over the editorship of Pogódin's *Moskvityánin*, but failed to get on with him and retired before the end of the year. In 1852 he once more published an article in a purely Slavophil miscellany, for which the miscellany was suppressed.

Kiréyevsky was the master of a beautiful style, which, unlike Khomyakóv's, is closely akin to Karamzín's and Púshkin's. He was the first Russian intellectual layman to resume the long-lost contact with the profoundest and most alive mystical currents inside the Orthodox Church, and in this respect he is, with Khomyakóv, the fountainhead of all modern Orthodox culture.

BELÍNSKY

The movement of the Westernizers took form about 1840, when the philosophical idealists of Stankévich's circle and the socialist idealists of Herzen's circle became united in one movement, equally opposed to official Russia and to Slavophilism. They were anti-clerical, and in politics liberal or socialist.

Of the two circles of the thirties, the principal leaders were Timothy Granóvsky (1813–55), a brilliant lecturer and an elegant writer, but not an original scholar; Herzen, whose work belongs mainly to a later period; and, most important of all, Belínsky.

Vissarión Grigórievich Belínsky was born in 1811, the son of a poor army doctor. In 1829 he entered the University of Moscow and there soon became intimate with Stankévich and other young idealists. After three years at the University he was dismissed and never received a degree. His education was acquired, much more than by regular study, by omnivorous reading and personal contact with fellow students. Of all foreign languages, he knew only French, and that imperfectly. German and English books he could read only in translations. For his philosophical information (the great thing in the Moscow circles of the time) he depended on his better-educated friends. On leaving the University, Belínsky engaged in journalism and soon joined Nadézhdin's *Telescope*. In 1834 he published the famous *Literary Musings*, which may be regarded as the beginning of Russian intelligentsia journalism. In it and in his subsequent articles Belínsky displayed from the outset that eminently pugnacious and enthusiastic temperament which earned him the nickname of the "furious Vissarión." His articles were inspired with a youthful irreverance for all that was old and respected in Russian letters, and an equally youthful enthusiasm for the new ideas of idealism and for the creative forces of the young generation. He rapidly became the bogy of the conservative and the leader of the young.

In 1836 the *Telescope* was suppressed, and Belínsky left without a regular job. At first he engaged in tutorial work and wrote a Russian grammar. Then for some time he was editor of *Moskóvsky nablyudátel* (*Moscow Observer*), which his friend and (then) philosophical authority Bakúnin had acquired from Pogódin. Neither Bakúnin nor Belínsky was businesslike, and the venture was a failure. At last, in 1839, Belínsky was invited by Krayévsky to be principal critic of *Otéchestvennye zapíski* (*Notes of the Fatherland*). He went to Petersburg and settled there. Though grossly underpaid and sweated by Krayévsky, he was at least saved from all danger of absolute destitution.

During his work with Nadézhdin, Belínsky had been inspired by the romantic idealism of Schelling, with its high idea of poetic and artistic creation. Afterward he was led away by Bakúnin towards the moral idealism of Fichte and thence to Hegel. He came to Petersburg full of the latter philosopher. His first articles in Krayévsky's review caused considerable consternation among his readers by their unexpectedly enthusiastic conservatism and "official nationalism." The public was not aware of the hidden logic of the critic's philosophical evolution, and that he was now living up to Hegel's famous proposition: "All that is, is rational." The proposition led Belínsky (who did not like stopping halfway) to the conclusion that the existing social and political regime was rational. This "conservative Hegelism," however, was only a transient stage in Belínsky, and by 1841 his ideas assumed their final form, historically the most important. This last change was owing partly to the influence of the way Hegel's thesis was interpreted by the "Left Hegelians"; partly to that of Herzen and his socialism; but above all it was a natural reaction of the "furious" critic's temperament, which was that of a fighter and a revolutionary. Henceforward Belínsky became the moving spirit of the progressive Westernizers and the herald of the new literature, which was to be neither classical nor romantic, but modern. That literature should be true to life and, at the same time, inspired by socially significant ideas, became his principal demand, and Gógol and George Sand its fullest incarnations. In 1846–7 Belínsky had the gratification of seeing the birth of a school of realistic literature that precisely answered to the ideals he had heralded.

In 1846 Nekrásov and Panáyev, men of Belínsky's party and partly of his making, purchased Púshkin's *Sovreménnik* from Pletnëv, and Belínsky left Krayévsky to become the critic of the *Sovreménnik*. In 1847, owing to his failing health, he went abroad, and there, once free from the censorship and from the inquisitiveness of the Russian post, wrote his famous letter to Gógol on the occasion of the latter's *Correspondence with Friends*. The letter is full of passionate and wounded indignation at the "lost leader" (Gógol had never really been a leader), and is perhaps the most characteristic statement of the faith that animated the progressive intelligentsia from 1840 to 1905. Soon after his return to Russia, Belínsky died (May 26, 1848). He had remained unmolested by the police and suffered comparatively little from the censorship, for he had learned the art of adapting his words to its exigencies. But had he lived a little longer, there is small doubt that, terrorized as the government was by the events of 1848, he would have in one way or another become a martyr and perhaps shared the fate of Dostoyévsky.

Belínsky's historical importance can scarcely be exaggerated. Socially he marks the end of the rule of the gentry and the advent of the *raznochíntsy* to cultural leadership. He was the first in a dynasty of journalists who exercised an unlimited influence on Russian progressive opinion. He was the true father of the intelligentsia, the embodiment of what remained its spirit for more than two generations—of social idealism, of the passion for improving the world, of disrespect for all tradition, and of highly strung, disinterested enthusiasm.

There is much to be said both for and against Belínsky. It remains to his lasting credit that he was the most genuine, the most thoroughgoing, the most consistent of literary revolutionaries. He was inspired by a love of the immediate future, which he foresaw with wonderful intuition. Perhaps never was a critic so genuinely in sympathy with the true trend of his times. And, what is more, he discerned almost unerringly what was genuine and what meretricious among his contemporaries. His judgments on writers who began their work between 1830 and 1848 may be accepted almost without qualification. This is high praise for a critic, and one that few deserve. In his judgments of the literature of the preceding age and generation, he was handicapped by party feeling, or rather by certain too definite standards of taste which, to our best understanding, were wrong. He understood only a certain kind of literary excellence (it happened to be practically the only kind practiced by men of his generation) and was blind to other kinds. He judged the writers of the eighteenth century and of the Golden Age from the point of view of his own idealistic realism. The selection he made of them imposed itself on Russian literary opinion for two thirds of a century. We have emancipated ourselves from it. But from his point of view it was admirably judicious and consistent. His judgments of foreign literature were on the whole much less happy, which is hardly astonishing considering his linguistic limitations. All said and done, he cannot be denied the name of an exceptionally sensitive and prophetic critic.

His faults, however, are also serious. First of all comes his style, which is responsible for the dreadful diffuseness and untidiness (as Senkówski's is for the disgusting vulgarity) of Russian journalese (I mean high journalese) in the second half of the nineteenth century. Certainly no writer of anything like Belínsky's importance ever wrote such an execrable lingo.

Secondly, the message of Belínsky as a critic is hardly capable of kindling any enthusiasm today. Not that the civic note he introduced in the forties was avoidable or harmful. It was necessary, and it was in tune with the times. The civic attitude to literature in the later years of Nicholas I's reign was shared by all who were of any value, and was merely an expression of civic conscience. It is his *literary* doctrine that is difficult not to quarrel with. He was not entirely responsible for it, but he was, more than anyone, effective in so widely propagating it. It was Belínsky, more than anyone else, who poisoned Russian literature by the itch for expressing ideas, which has survived so woefully long. It was he also who was instrumental in spreading all the commonplaces of romantic criticism—inspiration, sincerity, genius, and talent, contempt for work and technique, and the strange aberration of identifying imaginative literature with what he called "thinking in images." Belínsky (not as the civic, but as the romantic, critic) is largely responsible for the contempt of form and workmanship which just missed killing Russian literature in the sixties and seventies. It is, however, only fair to say that, if the most influential, Belínsky was not the only man who contributed to the infection. The weight of the sin rests on the whole generation.

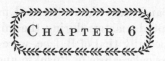

CHAPTER 6

The Age of Realism: The Novelists (I)

ORIGIN AND CHARACTER OF THE RUSSIAN REALISTIC NOVEL

THE realistic novel (a term that must be made to include shorter and less definite narrative forms as well as the full-sized novel) dominated Russian literature (roughly) from 1845 to 1905, almost to the exclusion of other forms of imaginative writing. To most foreign readers it is the most interesting thing in the whole language. It is Russia's principal contribution to *European* literature, if we take that term as denoting, not the sum total of the national literatures of Europe, but the international literature belonging in an equal degree to all European mankind.

From Aksákov and Turgénev to Chékhov, and even to Górky, Búnin, and other writers of their generation, the Russian realistic novel may and must be regarded as one literary growth, with a unity even greater than, for instance, that of the Elizabethan drama. Of course there were movement and change inside the school. Chékhov's and Búnin's work is in many ways different from Aksákov's and Goncharóv's, but, taken all in all, it answers to the same standards of taste and to the same conceptions of the function of art; while the work of Púshkin and Gógol in the earlier period, of Rémizov and Bély in later days, proceeds from different conceptions and has to be judged by different standards.

Russian realism [1] was born in the second half of the forties, more exactly in the years 1846–7. Its genealogy is mixed. In substance it is a cross between the satirical naturalism of Gógol and an older sentimental realism revived and represented in the thirties and forties chiefly by the then enormously influential George Sand.

[1] It will be noted in the course of the following that the term "realism" is used in Russia with a different shade of meaning from what it has in English.

Gógol and George Sand were the father and mother of Russian realism and its accepted masters during the initial stages. Other foreign examples, especially that of Balzac, were not without their importance. The classical realism of Púshkin and Lérmontov presided over the fusion of the heterogenous elements, and *Evgény Onégin* and *A Hero of Our Times* influenced Russian realistic fiction very powerfully. Finally a factor of considerable importance in giving the Russian novel its idealistic and civic character was the evolution of the intellectual Moscow circles of the thirties and forties and the definite form their idealism took in the latter decade. Belínsky especially played a part that can hardly be exaggerated. His critical writings of 1841–5 practically foretold the whole movement. Never did a literary development so exactly answer to the expectations entertained by a leading critic.

In the preceding chapter I have analyzed the "naturalism" of Gógol and spoken of his first followers. The fully developed Russian realism is different from the school of Gógol in that while Gógol's naturalism is suited only for the representation of the baser sides of humanity in their most vulgar and grotesque aspects, the realists emancipated themselves from this one-sidedness and took possession of the whole of life, not only of its ugly aspects. The task before them was to find satisfactory realistic forms for the painting of the higher and middle levels of humanity, of mixed good and evil, of the ordinary man, considered, not as a caricature of mankind, but as a human being. Gógol himself had given hints in this direction by his sentimental treatment of vegetable life in *Old-World Landowners*, and by the "philanthropic" (as the phrase went) attitude to the small and ridiculous man in *The Greatcoat*. The "philanthropic" attitude was strengthened by George Sand (and to a less extent by Dickens), but the main influences that emancipated Russian realism from pure satire were Púshkin and Lérmontov. Not that there was any "philanthropic" sentimentality in their works, but they gave the example of an equal, level, human treatment of all humanity. The "philanthropic" attitude in its more sentimental forms did not much survive the forties, but its substance, a sympathetic attitude to human beings, without distinction (not only of class but) of intrinsic moral significance, became a principal characteristic of Russian realism. People are not good or bad; they are only more or less unhappy and deserving of sympathy—this may be taken as the formula of all the Russian novelists from Turgénev to Chékhov. This was what Europe accepted as their message to mankind when they were first revealed to the West.

Taken as a whole, Russian realism has little in common with Gógol, its professed master. What it inherited from him may be reduced to the following: In the first place, it retained his great attention to detail, vivifying and enlivening—not only the detail of outer things, but, above all, the detail of a person's appearance and movements. In this respect the continuer of Gógol was Tolstóy, otherwise so unlike him, who in his later work (after 1880) was the first to react against the method of "superfluous detail." In the second place, the realists endorsed Gógol's taboo-lifting work—the admission to the freedom of fiction of the vulgar, base, unprepossessing, and unedifying aspects of life. But no further taboos were lifted by them—the physical side of sex, as well as of disease and death, continued to be concealed, and though the rules of reticence in Russian realistic fiction were not the same as in Victorian England, it was as reticent in substance as the Victorian novel. A new taboo-lifting period was begun only half a century later by Tolstóy, in his later work, and by Górky. In the third place, the realists inherited from Gógol his satirical attitude to the existing forms of life. This is not quite so true of all the school as the preceding generalization, but on the whole a satirical attitude towards vegetable life and social routine pervades the Russian novel of the later nineteenth century.

Another characteristic that, though not common to all the realists, is typical of them as a school is their relative neglect of narrative construction and narrative interest, and the concentration on extra-narrative interest, on character and introspection. In this respect the Russian novel, especially Tolstóy, was far ahead of the European novel of the times and was outdone by Western novelists only in the later work of Henry James, in that of Proust and of James Joyce.

Another important and general characteristic of the Russian realistic novel is quite opposed to the example of Gógol—this is its artistic simplicity, a consistent effort to make its style as unobtrusive and as unstriking as possible. The realists avoided all fine writing. What they regarded as good prose was prose adequate to the thing described, prose that answered to the reality it spoke of, transparent prose that should not be noticed by the reader. This is the antithesis of Gógol's method, and was very largely because of the example of Púshkin and of Lérmontov, especially of the latter.

Another obligation generally recognized by the realists was the duty of choosing their subjects exclusively from contemporary or almost contemporary Russian life. This was owing not only to their honest desire to speak of nothing but what they actually knew, but also the social position of fiction in mid- and late-nineteenth-century Russia. The novelists were expected to react, sensitively and significantly, to the current life of the nation. Partly owing to the severity of the censorship for other branches of literature, fiction, from the forties onward, became an important and widely listened-to mouthpiece of social thinking, and the critics demanded that every time a novelist gave his work to the world, it should contain things worth meditating on and worth analyzing from the point of view of the social issues of the day. As a rule, the novelists took the obligation very seriously and never ignored it, at least in their more ambitious work. This "social" (*obschéstvenny*) or "civic" (*grazhdánsky*) coloring is a general characteristic of the European novel of the mid nineteenth century, but it is nowhere more apparent than in Russia. It gives it an almost journalistic character and makes it tempting as an actual source of information on Russian social history. It has been used in that way more than once by Russian and foreign authors, but of course this is bad method. Only persons ignorant alike of the nature of imaginative literature and of that of historical evidence will attempt to use Russian fiction as a historical source unless its evidence is corroborated by extra-literary sources, in which case it becomes superfluous.

DOSTOYÉVSKY'S EARLY WORK

The first great success of the new school was Dostoyévsky's maiden novel, *Poor Folk*. In it and in the other early novels and tales of Dostoyévsky the connection of the new realism with Gógol is particularly apparent. This consideration makes it profitable to begin the survey of the individual realists with Dostoyévsky. On the other hand, Dostoyévsky's later work is so in advance of its time, so closely connected with later developments, and went

home to the reading public so much later, that it is advisable, in a
general history of Russian literature, to divide Dostoyévsky in
two, an operation facilitated by the long break in his literary career
caused by his conviction and deportation in 1849. His writings
after his release from prison will be reserved for a following chapter.

Fëdor Mikháylovich Dostoyévsky was born October 30, 1821,
in Moscow, where his father was a doctor at a big public hospital.
The Dostoyévskys were a family of southwestern (Volynian)
origin, while Dostoyévsky's mother was the daughter of a Moscow
merchant; so he united Ukrainian and Muscovite blood. Very
early Fëdor and his elder brother Michael (afterwards his associate
in journalism) developed a passion for reading, and Dostoyévsky's
cult of Púshkin dates also from very early. The brothers studied
at a private school in Moscow, whence in 1837 Fëdor went to
Petersburg, to the Military Engineers' School. He remained there
for four years, not very deeply interested in engineering but much
more in literature and reading. In 1841 he obtained a commission
but continued his studies at the school for another year, after
which he received a post in the engineering department. In return
for his five years at school he was obliged to serve two years in the
army. He did not remain in the service any longer than was obligatory but resigned his commission in 1844. Dostoyévsky was not
penniless, his father having left a small fortune, but he was im-
practical and improvident and thus often in financial difficulties.
On leaving the service he decided to devote himself to literature
and in the winter of 1844–5 wrote *Poor Folk*. Grigoróvich, a beginning novelist of the new school, advised him to take the novel
to Nekrásov, who was then planning the publication of a literary
miscellany. On reading it Nekrásov was overwhelmed with admiration and took it to Belínsky. "A new Gógol has arisen!" he
exclaimed, breaking into the critic's room. "Gógols grow like
mushrooms in your imagination," Belínsky replied, but took and
read the novel and was impressed with it as Nekrásov had been.
A meeting was arranged between Dostoyévsky and Belínsky, and
the latter poured out to the young novelist all his enthusiasm, ex-
claiming: "Do you yourself understand *what* you have written?"
Dostoyévsky, remembering the whole business thirty years later,
said that this was the happiest day of his life. *Poor Folk* appeared
in January 1846 in Nekrásov's *Petersburg Miscellany*. It was
rapturously reviewed by Belínsky and by other critics friendly to

the new school and received with great favor by the public. Dostoyévsky did not take his success lightly—he was puffed with pride; and curious anecdotes are recorded of his overbearing vanity. His second novel, *The Double*, (1846), had a much cooler reception. Dostoyévsky's relations with Belínsky and his friends began to spoil. The vanity he had shown on the occasion of his first novel was intensified by their disillusionment in his subsequent work. He was teased and ridiculed by Turgénev and he ceased to frequent their company. His works continued appearing but met with little approval. Though his friendship with the advanced literary coterie did not last, Dostoyévsky continued a radical and a Westernizer. He was a member of the socialist circle of Petrashévsky, who gathered to read Fourier, to talk of socialism, and to criticize the existing conditions. The reaction that followed the Revolution of 1848 was fatal to the Petrashevskians: in April 1849 they were arrested. Dostoyévsky was confined in the Peter and Paul Fortress for eight months while a court-martial was deciding on the fate of the "conspirators." Dostoyévsky was found guilty of "having taken part in criminal plans, of having circulated the letter of the journalist Belínsky (to Gógol) full of insolent expressions against the Orthodox Church and the Supreme Power, and of having attempted, together with others, to circulate anti-Government writings with the aid of a private press." He was sentenced to eight years' penal servitude. The sentence was commuted by the Emperor to four years, after which he was to serve as a private soldier. But instead of simply communicating the sentence to the prisoners, the authorities enacted a wantonly cruel tragicomedy: a sentence of death was read out to them, and preparations were made for shooting them. Only when the first batch of prisoners had already been tied to the posts, were the real sentences read. All the prisoners naturally took the death sentence quite seriously. One of them went mad. Dostoyévsky never forgot the day: he remembers it twice in his writings—in *The Idiot* and in *An Author's Diary for 1873*. This took place December 22, 1849. Two days later Dostoyévsky was taken off to Siberia, where he was to serve his term. For nine years he drops out of literature.

For his own sake it is convenient to regard the young Dostoyévsky as a different writer from the author of his later novels; a lesser writer, no doubt, but not a minor one, a writer with a marked originality and an important place among his contemporaries. The principal feature that distinguishes him is his particularly close connection with Gógol. Like Gógol, he concentrated on style. His is as tense and saturated as Gógol's, if not always as unerringly right. Like the other realists, he seeks, in *Poor Folk*, to transcend Gógol's purely satirical naturalism by infusing it with elements of sympathy and human emotion. But while the others sought to solve the problem by adopting a middle way between the extremes of the grotesque and of the sentimental, Dostoyévsky in a much more truly Gogolian spirit, and continuing, as it were, the tradition of *The Greatcoat*, sought to combine extreme grotesque naturalism with intense sentiment; without losing their individuality in a golden mean, the two elements are fused together. But the message of *Poor Folk* is not Gógol's. It is not disgust at the vulgarity of life, but pity, intense sympathy for the downtrodden, half-dehumanized, ridiculous, and still noble human being. *Poor Folk* is the acme of the "philanthropic" literature of the forties, and has a foretaste of the wracking visions of pity that are such a lurid feature of the Dostoyévsky of the great novels. It is a novel of letters between a young girl who ends by going wrong and her elder friend the government clerk Makár Dévushkin. It is long, and the concentration on style tends to lengthen it. But it is a carefully and cleverly constructed work of art in which all the details are made to contribute to the complex effect of the whole.

His second story, *The Double*, is also rooted in Gógol and still more original. It is the story, told in great detail and in a style intensely saturated with phonetic and rhythmical expressiveness, of a government clerk who goes mad, obsessed by the idea that a fellow clerk has usurped his identity. It is painful, almost intolerable reading. With the cruelty later on marked out by Mikhaylóvsky as his characteristic feature, Dostoyévsky dwells with convincing power on the sufferings of the humiliated human dignity of Mr. Golyádkin. In its own, perhaps illegitimate, kind of cruel literature (cruel although, or rather because, intended to be humorous) *The Double* is a perfect work of art. Closely connected with it is the still stranger and madder *Mr. Prokhárchin* (1846), the story, in places deliberately obscure and unintelligible, of the death of a miser who had accumulated a fortune while living in abject filth in a wretched slum.

The Landlady (1847) is unexpectedly romantic. The dialogue is in an elevated, rhetorical style, imitative of the diction of folk poetry and strongly reminiscent of Gógol's *Terrible Vengeance*. The story is far less consistent and perfect than the first three, but there is in it a more definite foretaste of the later Dostoyévsky. The heroine seems to be a foreboding of the demon-ridden women of the great novels. But in style and composition it is derivative—too deeply dependent on Gógol, Hoffmann, and Balzac. *Nétochka Nezvánova* (1849) was planned on a vaster scale than any one of the preceding novels. Its completion was interrupted by Dostoyévsky's arrest and conviction. It remains a powerful and somewhat mysterious fragment, full of that heavy and overstrung tension familiar to readers of *The Idiot* and *The Brothers Karamázov*. The heroine, a poor musician's stepdaughter brought up in a rich house, is the first of those proud women of Dostoyévsky's, a predecessor of Dúnya (*Crime and Punishment*), of Agláya (*The Idiot*), and of Katerína Ivánovna (*The Brothers Karamázov*).

AKSÁKOV

Dostoyévsky's method of evolving a new style by the *fusion* of extremes was not followed by any of his contemporaries, who preferred to arrive at a golden mean by the avoidance of extremes. This triumph of a *middle* style is the characteristic feature of Russian realism from the forties to Chékhov. It was first achieved in the work of three writers, all of them belonging to the settled and propertied class of gentlemen and not to the rootless plebeian intelligentsia: Aksákov, Goncharóv and Turgénev.

The oldest of them was Sergéy Timoféyevich Aksákov (1791–1859). He was a man of a much older generation, older even than either Púshkin or Griboyédov, and has consequently many features to distinguish him from the strictly realistic generation. But he was born to literature through the influence (exercised to a rather unexpected result) of Gógol, and all his work belongs to the period of the realistic triumph.

Aksákov had dabbled in literature ever since boyhood. But the nationalists and conservatives, with whom he principally associated, had nothing to show him in the way of literary forms but those of French classicism; and classicism, especially in its higher *genres*, was profoundly uncongenial to the rural mind of Aksákov. In 1832 Aksákov met Gógol and recognized in him what he had failed to see in Púshkin or any other man—a purely Russian genius. Aksákov's house, a stronghold of pure Russianism in Moscow society, became the temple of the cult of Gógol, and Aksákov its high priest. Gógol's genius was in essence as profoundly uncongenial to Aksákov's as Racine's or Kheráskov's, but it was Gógol who revealed to Aksákov the possibility of a new attitude towards reality, an attitude that had not been foreseen by the classicists—the possibility of taking life as it comes, of making use of the whole material of life, without necessarily forcing it into the molds of classical form. Of course this truth might have been revealed to Aksákov in some other way besides the evidently more-than-that route of Gógol, but it so happened that it was Gógol's art that removed the film of obligatory stylization from Aksákov's eyes. His first attempt in a new, realistic manner was a short descriptive story, *The Blizzard*, printed in 1834. It is distinctly experimental and immature. Towards 1840, urged by Gógol, Aksákov began writing *A Family Chronicle*, substantial fragments of which were published anonymously in 1846 in a Slavophil miscellany. In the following years Aksákov published a series of books on sport in his native Orenbúrg country. They were enthusiastically reviewed by Turgénev, and Gógol wrote to the author: "Your birds and fishes are more alive than my men and women." When in 1856 *A Family Chronicle* (together with *Recollections*) appeared, Aksákov saw himself recognized by the most influential critics as the foremost living writer. He increased his literary output. In 1858 he published *Years of Childhood of Bagróv-Grandson*, and wrote the greater part of the contents of his collected works in his last remaining years.

The principal characteristic of Aksákov's work is its objectivity. His art is purely receptive. Even when he is introspective, as he is in the greater part of *Years of Childhood*, he is objectively introspective. He remains unmoved by any active desire except to find once again the time that has been lost—*"retrouver le temps perdu."* The Proustian phrase is not out of place, for Aksákov's sensibility is curiously and strikingly akin to that of the French novelist; only he was as sane and normal as Proust was perverse and morbid, and instead of the close and stuffy atmosphere of the never aired flat of the boulevard Haussmann, there breathes in Aksákov's books the air of the open steppe. Like Proust, Aksákov is all senses. His style is transparent. One does not notice it, for it is entirely adequate to *what* it expresses. It possesses, moreover, a beautiful Russian purity and an air of distinction and unaffected grace that gives it a fair chance of being recognized as the best, the standard, Russian prose. If it has a defect, it is the defect of its merit—a certain placidity, a certain excessive "creaminess," a lack of the thin, "daimonic," mountain air of poetry. It is of the earth earthy: the air one breathes in it is a fresh and open air, but it is the air of the lowermost atmospheric layers of a country without mountains. This is why, all said and done, it must be regarded as second in quality when compared with Lérmontov's.

The most characteristic and Aksakovian of Aksákov's books is unquestionably *Years of Childhood of Bagróv-Grandson*.[2] It is the story of a peaceful and uneventful childhood, exceptional only for the exceptional sensibility of a child encouraged by an exceptionally sympathetic education. The most memorable passages in it are perhaps those which refer to nature, for instance the wonderful account of the coming of spring in the steppe. Many readers who prefer incident to the everyday, and the exceptional to the humdrum, find *Years of Childhood* tedious. But if ordinary life, unruffled by unusual incident, is a legitimate subject of literature, Aksákov, in *Years of Childhood*, wrote a masterpiece of realistic narrative. In it he came nearer than any other Russian writer, even than Tolstóy in *War and Peace*, to a modern, evolutionary, continuous presentation of human life, as distinct from the dramatic and incidental presentation customary to the older novelists.

A Family Chronicle is less exclusively personal and more entertaining. It is fuller of incident, and, being the story of the author's grandparents and parents before his own birth, it is necessarily free from introspection. It is also strikingly and unusually objective. The story of a great pioneering serf owner is told, and the picture of the golden age of the serf owners under Catherine is drawn without wrath or love. It is so dispassionate that it could be used by socialists as a weapon to strike at the Russian gentry, and by the conservatives to defend it. Russian rural life, especially on the thinly peopled borderlands (Aksákov's grandfather had been among the first to plant a colony of Russian serfs in the

[2] Here and in *A Family Chronicle* Aksákov uses fictitious names for real places and people. Bagróv and Bagróvo are Aksákov and Aksákovo. In *Recollections* the real names are used.

Bashkirian steppe), was strongly reminiscent of mediæval, or rather even of patriarchal, conditions. The landlord had nothing above him except God, with whom he felt himself in essential understanding, and the Tsar, who sanctioned his power and had practically no way of reaching him. These conditions bred men of Biblical dimensions. Stepán Mikháylovich Bagróv is a patriarch, strong, righteous, kind, generous, fearless, but strongly conscious of his rights and with no sentimental scruples as to using them. Another aspect of a great serf owner is drawn in the wicked Kuralésov, who marries Bagróv's cousin and is ultimately brought back to the ways of lawfulness by Bagróv. The latter part of the book narrates the story of the wooing of Sophie Zúbova by Aksákov's father. Here also there is a monumental, Biblical, Homeric simplicity that gives the figure of Sophie Zúbova something like heroic proportions. Aksákov's father is treated much less heroically —he is one of the most remarkable figures of the *ordinary* man in Russian fiction. The whole episode is perfect from beginning to end and is quite unique in modern literature for its tone at once so primævally magnifying and so scrupulously objective.

The other works of Aksákov are of less universal appeal. *Recollections*, the story of his life from eight to sixteen, is interesting rather as a picture of Russian provincial culture about 1805 than as a revelation of a great literary temperament. The same may be said of his *Literary and Theatrical Reminiscences*, in which he tells of his relations with the actors and playwrights of 1810–30. They are delightful and at times amusing, but the portraits he paints are visual impressions left on a sensitive retina, not profound intuitions into other people's souls. The same applies to his delightful sketch of Admiral Shishkóv (who had been an early patron of Aksákov's) but not to the remarkable *Recollections of Gógol*. These have a place apart. Aksákov was not as a rule a student of other people's minds. He took people as they came, as parts of his world, and gave them a sensual, rather than a mental, reality. But in the case of Gógol the elusive and evasive personality of the great writer caused him such bitter disappointment and disillusionment that he was forced to make an exceptional effort to understand the workings of the strange man's mind, where genius and baseness were so strangely mingled. The effort was painful but extraordinarily successful, and Aksákov's memoir is to this day our principal approach to the problem of Gógol.

Aksákov's objectivity and impartiality are enough to mark him off from the rest of the Russian novelists of the mid nineteenth century. The latter, all of them, either were, or seemed to be, or tried to be, novelists with a purpose; and their work may almost invariably be described as problem stories. Two of the greatest successes of the literary spring of 1846–7 were the two problem novels, *Whose Fault?* by Herzen, and *Pólinka Sachs*, by Druzhínin. But the greatest of the problem novelists are of course Turgénev and Goncharóv.

GONCHARÓV

Iván Alexándrovich Goncharóv (1812–91), born in Simbírsk of a wealthy merchant family, grew up in the conditions typical of the provincial gentry. He studied at the University of Moscow at the same time as Lérmontov and Belínsky but mixed with neither. On taking his degree he entered the Civil Service, where he remained all his life, at first in the Ministry of Finance, later, when in 1856 it was decided to liberalize the censorship, as a censor. The only events of his life are his literary activities and his voyage to the Far East. His first novel, *A Common Story*, appeared in 1847 and was greeted by Belínsky as, next to *Poor Folk*, the masterpiece of the incipient realistic school. It was followed in 1849 by *The Dream of Oblómov*, which was the first germ of his most famous novel. Having casually expressed the wish to go to the Far East as secretary to a mission to Japan, he was taken at his word, and only when it was too late, he realized that he was obliged to go, at the risk of appearing ridiculous. He did not enjoy the long sea voyage—he found the ocean shockingly devoid of orderliness. But he avidly absorbed every kind of new visual and human impression and kept a diary. During the voyage war broke out with England, and Goncharóv had to return to Petersburg by the exceedingly long and inconvenient way of Okhótsk, Yakútsk, and Irkútsk. He was happy to be back in his comfortable flat in Petersburg and, now it was over, to remember his heroic journey. His travel notes appeared in 1855–7 under the title of *The Frigate "Palláda."* In 1859 he completed and published *Oblómov*, begun more than ten years earlier. It success was immense and definitely made him a national classic. He had begun working at a third novel, *The*

Precipice, almost simultaneously with *Oblómov* and continued working at it after the publication of the latter. It took him almost twenty years to complete it. It appeared in 1869 and met with much less success, partly owing to its lesser merits, partly owing to the hostility of the radicals, who resented the caricature he made of them in one of the characters. *The Precipice* is connected with a curious development in Goncharóv's life that borders on insanity. At an early stage of the novel's progress he had read fragments of it to Turgénev, and ever since then he was obsessed by the notion that Turgénev had stolen all the ideas contained in them, and was not only making use of them in his own work, but communicating them to all his Russian and foreign friends. Not only *Fathers and Sons,* but novels by Auerbach and Flaubert's *Éducation Sentimentale* were recognized by Goncharóv as plagiarized from *The Precipice.* He ascribed his novel's lack of success to its thus having been robbed before its publication. He wrote an account of his wrongs as they appeared to him in a curious document entitled *An Uncommon Story.* This psychopathic document, published only in 1924, revealed an unexpected side of a writer who had always been regarded as the incarnation of staid respectability.

After *The Precipice* Goncharóv wrote little—some recollections of his early years; an essay on Griboyédov, which has had the good, or ill, fortune of being singled out by schoolmasters and professors of literature for special admiration; and a series of sketches on *Old Servants,* which have had the equally doubtful advantage of being used in England as texts for beginners in Russian. Goncharóv's place as a Russian classic is almost entirely based on the second of his three novels—*Oblómov.* The other two are on a distinctly inferior level. *A Common Story* is a neatly constructed *roman à thèse,* showing in an almost mathematically elegant succession of episodes the disillusionment of a young idealist in his generous, but unpractical ideals. The success of *A Common Story* rested chiefly on its thesis and was a sign of the times, which were shifting their allegiance from the generous ideals of the thirties to the positive and practical progressiveness of the reign of Alexander II. Nor is *The Precipice,* the third of Goncharóv's novels, a masterpiece. It displays all his shortcomings: an absence of imagination; an extreme subjectivity in psychological painting, and the consequent lifelessness of all the characters that

are not founded on introspection; an absence of poetry and of real
inspiration; and an unsurmountable *smallness* of soul. It may be
said that all is unsatisfactory in *The Precipice* except the picture,
based on his reminiscences of childhood, of the patriarchal, despotic, and kindly grandmamma, and of her life, at once spacious
and economical, in her vast, almost rural estate in the city over-
hanging "the precipice" above the Volga. The ineffective hero,
Ráysky, is a pale and generalized reflection of the author's self.
The proud and passionate heroine, Vera, is badly drawn, and the
nihilist, Mark Vólokhov, is simply flat and absurd.

Oblómov is a different business. It is a great book. The current
schoolmaster and professor-of-literature view of Goncharóv is
that he was a great stylist and a great *objective* painter of reality.
This view is ludicrously wrong: in both cases almost the contrary
is true. Goncharóv's prose is, like Aksákov's and Turgénev's, a
golden mean, but while Aksákov's and Turgénev's has all the
beauty of measure, Goncharóv's has all the flatness of mediocrity.
It lacks both the beautiful plenitude and abundance of Aksákov's
and the grace and sweetness of Turgénev's. As to his objectivity,
Goncharóv was as incapable of seeing into another human being
as Gógol had been. He was capable of seeing and recording external
things, and he was capable of evolving out of his inner self more
or less sublimated reflections. The greatest of these reflections is
Oblómov. Oblómov is more than a character; he is a symbol. The
fact that he is drawn with the aid of none but purely and modestly
realistic methods only enhances the force of the symbolism. He
obviously was, and was immediately recognized to be, the embodiment of a whole side of the Russian soul, or rather of a side of the
soul of the Russian gentry—its sloth and ineffectiveness. He has a
high sense of values. He is open to generous aspirations but incapable of effort or discipline. The fragment of *Oblómov* that first
appeared in print—*Oblómov's Dream*—is a vast, synthetically intended picture of the life of the Russian rural gentry, the soil of
vegetable comfort, easy wealth, and irresponsibility, that produced
the flower of Oblómov. *Oblómov's Dream* is contained in the first
part of the novel, the best-known and the most frequently commented on. We are shown Oblómov in his Petersburg flat—the
way he spends his day between his bed and his dressing gown. The
slow and leisurely narrative is calculated to enhance the impression
of being hopelessly and irremediably stuck in slimy sloth. It takes

Oblómov a whole chapter to get out of bed. His spacious dressing gown, to quote Miss Harrison, dominates the whole story, as "an Ibsenian symbol of the impossibility of being well groomed, physically or mentally." Oblómov's manservant, Zakhár, is in complete harmony with his master. Then the contrast to Oblómov is introduced, the practical and energetic Stolz, characteristically represented as half German, a devotee to work and efficiency. It is here that Goncharóv's intellectual and moral insufficiency comes out: Stolz is hopelessly uninteresting and flat. Of course the whole of the author's subconscious and imaginative sympathy is with Oblómov, but Goncharóv, the bureaucrat and the littérateur, in trying to endow the hero of work, Stolz, with all he could imagine of efficient virtue, only revealed his own smallness. In the second part Oblómov is shown in a love affair that falls flat because he cannot tear himself away from the torpor of his slovenly habits, and finally disgusts the long-patient lady. Like all Goncharóv's love stories (and in spite of its autobiographical foundation), it is very inadequate, and the heroine as unconvincing as Vera in *The Precipice.* The third and fourth parts are less often quoted and read in schools, but they are unquestionably the highest achievement of Goncharóv.[3] Oblómov, yielding more and more to his slovenly indolence, which always remains poisoned by a sting of dissatisfaction, drops out of society. His landlady, an uneducated young woman, Agáfia Mikháylovna, loves him and becomes his mistress. She loves him sincerely and pathetically, but she is dominated by her people, unscrupulous rascals who exploit Oblómov's love for her to cajole and blackmail him out of all his possessions. In spite of the energetic intervention of the ever energetic and efficient Stolz, Oblómov sinks lower and lower into the ooze of his new surroundings and dies in the arms of Agáfia Mikháylovna, to her despair and to the rejoicing of her people. The atmosphere of inevitable doom gradually descending on Oblómov—the irrevertible action of the slime sucking him in—is conveyed with truly wonderful power. Russian realistic fiction is rich in stories of overpowering gloom, but none of them (with the exception of Saltykóv's great novel) excels in this respect the high achievement of Goncharóv in the third and fourth parts of *Oblómov.*

Goncharóv, like Aksákov, and more than Turgénev, is char-

[3] In the English translation they are abridged out of all recognition.

acteristic of the tendency of the Russian novel to do without all narrative interest. There are no events or happenings in *Oblómov;* there are in *The Precipice*, but dealt with in so flat and puerile a manner that the less said the better. There is nothing but the continuous, evolutionary unfolding of an inevitable development. This is what Miss Harrison has called the "imperfective" tendency of the Russian novel—the "imperfective" being that form of the Russian verb which views the action *in the process* of happening. The tendency dominates all Russian fiction after the times of Lérmontov, except the plebeian novelists—Leskóv and Písemsky. But nowhere is it so all-prevailing and so justified as in *Oblómov*, for here the evolutionary determinism of the manner (which is in fact the negation of the efficacy of human will) is in complete harmony with the indolent and impotent determinism of the hero.

TURGÉNEV

Iván Sergéyevich Turgénev was born on October 28, 1818, in Orël. His father, a handsome but impoverished squire who had served in the cavalry, was married to an heiress older than himself. She had had a very unhappy childhood and girlhood and adored her husband, who never loved her. This combined with the control of a large fortune to make of Mme Turgénev an embittered and intolerable domestic tyrant. Though she was attached to her son, she treated him with exasperating despotism, and with her serfs and servants she was plainly cruel. It was in his mother's house that the future author of *A Sportsman's Sketches* saw serfdom in its least attractive form.

In 1833 Turgénev entered the University of Moscow, but remained there only one year, for in 1834 his mother moved to Petersburg and he went over to the other university. He studied under Púshkin's friend, Professor Pletnëv, and had occasion to meet the great poet himself. His first verses were published in Pletnëv's, formerly Púshkin's, *Sovreménnik* (1838). This connection with the "literary aristocracy" is of importance: alone of all his contemporaries, Turgénev had a living link with the age of poetry. After taking his degree he went to Berlin to complete his philosophical education at the university that had been the abode and was still the temple of Hegel—the divinity of the young generation of Russian idealists. Several of them, including Stankévich and Granóvsky, Turgénev met at Berlin, and henceforward he became the friend and ally of the Westernizers. His three years at Berlin (1838–41) imbued him with a lifelong love for Western civilization and for Germany. When in 1841 he returned to Russia he at first intended to devote himself to a university career. As this did not come off, he entered the Civil Service, but there also he remained only two years, and after 1845 abandoned all pursuits except literature. His work at first was chiefly in verse, and in the mid forties he was regarded, chiefly on the strength of the narrative poem *Parásha* (1843), as one of the principal hopes of the young generation in poetry.

In 1845 Turgénev fell out with his mother, who ceased to give him money, and for the following years, till her death, he had to live the life of a literary Bohemian. The reason for Mme Turgénev's displeasure was partly that she resented her son's leaving the Civil Service and becoming a scribbler of a dangerous, revolutionary kind, but especially that she strongly disapproved of his infatuation for the famous singer Pauline García (Mme Viardot). This infatuation proved to be the love of his life. Mme Viardot tolerated it and liked Turgénev's company, and so he was able most of his life to live near her. In 1847 he went abroad, following her, and returned only in 1850, at the news of his mother's dangerous illness. On her death he found himself the possessor of a large fortune.

Meanwhile Turgénev had abandoned verse for prose. In 1847 Nekrásov's *Sovreménnik* started the publication of the short stories that were to form *A Sportsman's Sketches*. They appeared in book form in 1852, and this, together with the publication, about the same time, of other stories, gave Turgénev one of the first places, if not the first, among Russian writers. *A Sportsman's Sketches* was a great social as well as literary event. On the background of the complete silence of those years of reaction, the *Sketches*, seemingly harmless if taken one by one, produced a cumulative effect of considerable power. Their consistent presentation of the serf as a being, not only human, but superior in humanity to his masters, made the book a loud protest against the system of serfdom. It is said to have produced a strong impression on the future Emperor Alexander II and caused in him the decision to do away with the system. Meanwhile the authorities were alarmed. The censor who had passed the book was ordered to leave the service. Shortly after that an obituary notice of Gógol by Turgénev, written in what seemed to the police a too enthusiastic tone, led to his arrest and banishment to his estate, where he remained eighteen months (1852–3). When he was released he came to Petersburg already in the full glory of success. For several years he was the *de facto* head of Petersburg literature, and his judgment and decisions had the force of law.

The first years of Alexander II's reign were the summer of Turgénev's popularity. No one profited more than he from the unanimity of the progressive and reforming enthusiasm that had taken hold of Russian society. He was accepted as its spokesman. In his early sketches and stories he had denounced serfdom; in *Rúdin* (1856) he paid homage to the idealism of the elder generation while exposing its inefficiency; in *A Nest of Gentlefolk* (1859) he glorified all that was noble in the old Orthodox ideals of the old gentry; in *On the Eve* (1860) he attempted to paint the heroic figure of a young girl of the new generation. Dobrolyúbov and Chernyshévsky, the leaders of advanced opinion, chose his works for the texts of their journalistic sermons. His art answered to the demands of everyone. It was civic but not "tendentious." It painted life as it was, and chose for its subjects the most burning problems of the day. It was full of truth and, at the same time, of poetry and beauty. It satisfied Left and Right. It was the mean term, the middle style for which the forties had groped in vain. It avoided in an equal measure the pitfalls of grotesque caricature and of sentimental "philanthropy." It was perfect. Turgénev was very sensitive to his success, and particularly sensitive to the praise of the young generation and of advanced opinion, whose spokesman he appeared, and aspired, to be.

The only thing he had been censured for (or rather, as everyone believed in the photographic veracity of Turgénev's representation of Russia, it was not he, but Russian life, that was found fault with) was that while he had given such a beautiful succession of heroines, he had failed to give a Russian hero; it was noticed that when he had wanted a man of action, he had chosen a Bulgarian (Insárov in *On the Eve*). This led the critics to surmise that he believed a Russian hero an impossibility. Now Turgénev decided to make up for this shortcoming and give a real Russian man of action—a hero of the young generation. This he did in

Bazárov, the nihilist hero of *Fathers and Sons* (1862). He created
him with love and admiration, but the result was unexpected. The
radicals were indignant. This, they said, was a caricature and no
hero. This nihilist, with his militant materialism, with his negation
of all religious and æsthetic values and his faith in nothing but
frogs (the dissection of frogs was the mystical rite of Darwinian
naturalism and anti-spiritualism), was a caricature of the young
generation drawn to please the reactionaries. The radicals raised
a hue and cry against Turgénev, who was proclaimed to have
"written himself out." A little later, it is true, a still younger and
more extreme section of radicals, in the person of the brilliant
young critic Písarev, reversed the older radicals' verdict, accepted
the name of nihilist, and recognized in Bazárov the ideal to be
followed. But this belated recognition from the extreme Left did
not console Turgénev for the profound wound inflicted on him by
the first reception given to Bazárov. He decided to abandon
Russia and Russian literature. He was abroad when *Fathers and
Sons* appeared and the campaign against him began. He remained
abroad in the shade of Mme Viardot, at first in Baden-Baden and
after 1871 in Paris, and never returned to Russia except for short
periods. His decision to abandon literature found expression in the
fragment of lyrical prose *Enough*, where he gave full play to his
pessimism and disillusionment. He did not, however, abandon
literature, and continued writing to his death. But in by far
the greater part of his later work he turned away from contemporary Russia, so distasteful and unresponsive to him, towards the
times of his childhood, the old Russia of before the reforms. Most
of his work after 1862 is either frankly memoirs, or fiction built
out of the material of early experience. He was loath, however, to
resign himself to the fate of a writer who had outlived his times.
Twice again he attempted to tackle the problems of the day in big
works of fiction. In *Smoke* (1867) he gave full vent to his bitterness
against all classes of Russian society; and in *Virgin Soil* (1877) he
attempted to give a picture of the revolutionary movement of the
seventies. But the two novels only emphasized his growing estrangement from living Russia, the former by its impotent bitterness, the latter by its lack of information and of all sense of
reality in the treatment of the powerful movement of the seventies.
Gradually, however, as party feeling, at least in literature, sank,
Turgénev returned into his own (the popularity of his *early* work

had never diminished). The revival of "æsthetics" in the later seventies contributed to a revival of his popularity, and his last visit to Russia in 1880 was a triumphant progress.

In the meantime, especially after he settled in Paris, Turgénev became intimate with French literary circles—with Mérimée, Flaubert, and the young naturalists. His works began to be translated into French and German, and before long his fame became international. He was the first Russian author to win a European reputation. In the literary world of Paris he became an important personality. He was one of the first to discern the talent of the young Maupassant, and Henry James (who included an essay on Turgénev in a volume on *French* novelists) and other beginning writers looked up to him as to a master. When he died, Renan, with pardonable lack of information, proclaimed that it was through Turgénev that Russia, so long mute,[4] had at last become vocal. Turgénev felt much more at home among his French confreres than among his Russian equals (with most of whom, including Tolstóy, Dostoyévsky, and Nekrásov, he sooner or later quarreled), and there is a striking difference between the impressions he produced on foreigners and on Russians. Foreigners were always impressed by the grace, charm, and sincerity of his manner. With Russians he was arrogant and vain, and no amount of hero worship could make his Russian visitors blind to these disagreeable characteristics.

Soon after his last visit to Russia Turgénev fell ill. He died on August 22, 1883, in the small commune of Bougival, on the Seine below Paris.

Turgénev's first attempt at prose fiction [5] was in the wake of Lérmontov, from whom he derived the romantic halo round his first Pechórin-like heroes (*Andréy Kólosov, The Duelist, Three Portraits*) and the method of the intensified anecdote (*The Jew*). In *A Sportsman's Sketches*, begun in 1847, he was to free himself from the romantic conventions of these early stories by abandoning all narrative skeleton and limiting himself to "slices of life." But even for some time after that date he remained unable in his more distinctly narrative work to hit on what was to become his true manner. Thus, for instance, *Three Meetings* (1852) is a story of

[4] One will remember the words of Carlyle on "mute Russia" written in 1840, three years after the death of Púshkin.
[5] For the poetic work of Turgénev see Chapter V; for his dramatic work, Chapter VII.

pure atmosphere woven round a very slender theme, saturated in its descriptions of moonlit nights, with an excess of romantic and "poetical" poetry. *The Diary of a Superfluous Man* (1850) is reminiscent of Gógol and of the young Dostoyévsky, developing as it does the Dostoyevskian theme of humiliated human dignity and of morbid delight in humiliation, but aspiring to a Gógol-like and very un-Turgenevian verbal intensity. (The phrase "a superfluous man" had an extraordinary fortune and is still applied by literary and social historians to the type of ineffective idealist portrayed so often by Turgénev and his contemporaries.) At last *Mumú* (1854), the well-known story of the deaf serf and his favorite dog, and of how his mistress ordered it to be destroyed, is a "philanthropic" story in the tradition of *The Greatcoat* and of *Poor Folk*, where an intense sensation of pity is arrived at by methods that strike the modern reader as illegitimate, working on the nerves rather than on the imagination.

A Sportsman's Sketches, on the other hand, written in 1847–51, belongs to the highest, most lasting, and least questionable achievement of Turgénev and of Russian realism. The book describes the casual and various meetings of the narrator during his wanderings with a gun and a dog in his native district of Bólkhov and in the surrounding country. The sketches are arranged in a random order and have no narrative skeleton, containing nothing but accounts of what the narrator saw and heard. Some of them are purely descriptive, of scenery or character; others consist of conversation, addressed to the narrator or overheard. At times there is a dramatic *motive*, but the development is only hinted at by the successive glimpses the narrator gets of his personages. This absolute matter-of-factness and studious avoidance of everything artificial and made-up were the most prominent characteristics of the book when it appeared—it was a new genre. The peasants are described from the outside, as seen (or overseen) by the narrator, not in their intimate, unoverlooked life. As I have said, they are drawn with obviously greater sympathy than the upper classes. The squires are represented as either vulgar, or cruel, or ineffective. In the peasants, Turgénev emphasized their humanity, their imaginativeness, their poetical and artistic giftedness, their sense of dignity, their intelligence. It was in this quiet and unobtrusive way that the book struck the readers with the injustice and ineptitude of serfdom. Now, when the issue of serfdom is a thing of the past, the *Sketches* seem once more as harmless and as innocent as a book can be, and it requires a certain degree of historical imagination to reconstruct the atmosphere in which they had the effect of a mild bombshell.

Judged as literature, the *Sketches* are frequently, if not always, above praise. In the representation of rural scenery and peasant character, Turgénev never surpassed such masterpieces as *The Singers* and *Bézhin Meadow*.⁶ *The Singers* especially, even after *First Love* and *Fathers and Sons*, may claim to be his crowning achievement and the quintessence of all the most characteristic qualities of his art. It is the description of a singing-match at a village pub between the peasant Yáshka Túrok and a tradesman from Zhízdra. The story is representative of Turgénev's manner of painting his peasants; he does not one-sidedly idealize them; the impression produced by the match, with its revelation of the singers' high sense of artistic values, is qualified by the drunken orgy the artists lapse into after the match is over and the publican treats Yáshka to the fruit of his victory. *The Singers* may also be taken as giving Turgénev's prose at its highest and most characteristic. It is careful and in a sense artificial, but the impression of absolute ease and simplicity is exhaled from every word and turn of phrase. It is a carefully *selected* language, rich, but curiously avoiding words and phrases, crude or journalese, that might jar on the reader. The beauty of the landscape painting is due chiefly to the choice of exact and delicately suggestive and descriptive words. There is no ornamental imagery after the manner of Gógol, no rhetorical rhythm, no splendid cadences. But the sometime poet's and poets' disciple's hand is evident in the careful, varied, and unobtrusively perfect balance of the phrases.

The first thing Turgénev wrote after the *Sketches* and *Mumú* was *The Inn*. Like *Mumú* it turns on the unjust and callous treatment of serfs by their masters, but the sentimental, "philanthropic" element is replaced for the first time in his work by the characteristic Turgenevian atmosphere of tragic necessity. *The Inn* was followed in 1853–61 by a succession of masterpieces. They were divided by the author himself into two categories: novels and *nouvelles* (in Russian, *romány* and *póvesti*). The difference between the two forms in the case of Turgénev is not so much one of size

⁶ It is interesting to note that these two pieces are precisely those Henry James singles out for particular praise.

or scope as that the novels aim at social significance and at the statement of social problems, while the *nouvelles* are pure and simple stories of emotional incident, free from civic preoccupations. Each novel includes a narrative kernel similar in subject and bulk to that of a *nouvelle*, but it is expanded into an answer to some burning problem of the day. The novels of this period are *Rúdin* (1856), *A Nest of Gentlefolk* (1859), *On the Eve* (1860), and *Fathers and Sons* (1862); the *nouvelles*, *Two Friends* (1854), *A Quiet Spot* (1854), *Yákov Pásynkov* (1855), *A Correspondence* (1856), *Faust* (1856), *Ásya* (1858), and *First Love* (1860). It will be noticed that the civic novels belong chiefly to the age of reform (1856–61), while the purely private *nouvelles* predominate in the reactionary years that precede it. But even "on the eve" of the Emancipation, Turgénev could be sufficiently detached from civic issues to write the perfectly uncivic *First Love*.

The novels of Turgénev are, thus, those of his stories in which he, voluntarily, submitted to the obligation of writing works of social significance. This significance is arrived at in the first place by the nature of the characters, who are made to be representative of phases successively traversed by the Russian intellectual. Rúdin is the progressive idealist of the forties; Lavrétsky, the more Slavophil idealist of the same generation; Eléna, in *On the Eve*, personifies the vaguely generous and active fermentation of the generation immediately preceding the reforms; Bazárov, the militant materialism of the generation of 1860. Secondly, the social significance is served by the insertion of numerous *conversations* between the characters on topics of current interest (Slavophilism and Westernism, the ability of the educated Russian to act, the place in life of art and science, and so on). These conversations are what especially distinguished Turgénev's novels from his *nouvelles*. They have little relation to the action, and not always much more to the character of the representative hero. They were what the civic critics seized upon for comment, but they are certainly the least permanent and most dating part of the novels. There frequently occur characters who are introduced with no other motive but to do the talking, and whom one would have rather wished away. But the central, representative characters—the heroes—are in most cases not only representative, but alive. Rúdin, the first in date, is one of the masterpieces of nineteenth-century character drawing. An eminent French novelist (who is old-fashioned enough still to prefer Turgénev to Tolstóy, Dostoyévsky, and Chékhov) has pointed out to me the wonderfully delicate mastery with which the impression produced by Rúdin on the other characters and on the reader is made gradually to change from the first appearance in the glamour of superiority to the bankruptcy of his pusillanimous breach with Natália, then to the gloomy glimpse of the undone and degenerate man, and to the redeeming flash of his heroic and ineffective death on the barricades of the faubourg St. Antoine. The French writer thought this delicate change of attitude unique in fiction. Had he known more Russian, he would have realized that Turgénev had merely been a highly intelligent and creative pupil of Púshkin's. Like Púshkin in *Evgény Onégin*, Turgénev does not analyze and dissect his heroes, as Tolstóy and Dostoyévsky would have done; he does not uncover their souls; he only conveys their atmosphere, partly by showing how they are reflected in others, partly by an exceedingly delicate and thinly woven aura of suggestive accompaniment—a method that at once betrays its origin in a *poetic* novel. Where Turgénev attempts to show us the *inner* life of his heroes by other methods, he always fails—the description of Eléna's feelings for Insárov in *On the Eve* is distinctly painful reading. Turgénev had to use all the power of self-criticism and self-restraint to avoid the pitfall of false poetry and false beauty.

Still, the characters, constructed though they are by means of suggestion, not dissection, are the vivifying principle of Turgénev's stories. Like most Russian novelists he makes character predominate over plot, and it is the characters that we remember. The population of Turgénev's novels (apart from the peasant stories) may be classified under several heads. First comes the division into the Philistines and the elect. The Philistines are the direct descendants of Gógol's characters—heroes of *póshlost*, self-satisfied inferiority. Of course there is not a trace in them of Gógol's exuberant and grotesque caricature; the irony of Turgénev is fine, delicate, unobtrusive, hardly at all aided by any obvious comical devices. On the other side are the elect, the men and women with a sense of values, superior to those of vegetable enjoyment and social position. The men, again, are very different from the women. The fair sex comes out distinctly more advantageously from the hands of Turgénev. The strong, pure, passionate, and virtuous woman, opposed to the weak, potentially generous, but ineffective and ultimately shallow man, was introduced into literature by Púshkin, and recurs again and again in the work of the realists, but nowhere more insistently than in Turgénev's. His heroines are famous all the world over and have done much to spread a high reputation of Russian womanhood. Moral force and courage are the keynote to Turgénev's heroine—the power to sacrifice all worldly considerations to passion (Natália in *Rúdin*), or all happiness to duty (Líza in *A Nest of Gentlefolk*). But what goes home to the general reader in these women is not so much the height of their moral beauty as the extraordinary *poetical* beauty woven round them by the delicate and perfect art of their begetter. Turgénev reaches his highest perfection in this, his own and unique art, in two of the shorter stories, *A Quiet Spot* and *First Love*. In the first, the purely Turgenevian, tragic, poetic, and rural atmosphere reaches its maximum of concentration, and the richness of suggestion that conditions the characters surpasses all he ever wrote. It transcends mere fiction and rises into poetry, not by the beauty of the single words and parts, but by sheer force of suggestion and saturated significance. *First Love* stands somewhat apart from the rest of Turgénev's work. Its atmosphere is cooler and clearer, more reminiscent of the rarefied air of Lérmontov. The heroes—Zinaída and the narrator's father (who is traditionally supposed to portray the author's own father)—are more *animal* and vital than Turgénev usually allows his heroes to be. Their passions are tense and clear-cut, free from vagueness and idealistic haze, selfish, but with a selfishness that is redeemed by self-justifying vitality. Unique in the whole of his work, *First Love* is the least relaxing of Turgénev's stories. But, characteristically, the story is told from the point of view of the boy admirer of Zinaída and of his pangs of adolescent jealousy for his rival and father.

At the height of his popularity, in 1860, Turgénev wrote a famous essay on *Hamlet and Don Quixote*. He considered these characters as the two prototypes of the elect intellectual portion of mankind, which was divided into self-conscious, introspective, and consequently ineffective, Hamlets, and enthusiastic, single-minded, courageous at the risk of seeming ridiculous, Quixotes. He himself and the great majority of his heroes were Hamlets. But he had always wanted to create Quixotes, whose freedom from reflection and questioning would make them efficient, while their

possession of higher values would raise them above the Philistines.
In the later forties the critics, who had taken note of the consistent
inefficiency of Turgénev's heroes, clamored for him to produce a
more active and effective hero. This he attempted in *On the Eve*.
But the attempt was a failure. He made his hero a Bulgarian
patriot, Insárov. But he failed to breathe into him the spirit of
life. Insárov is merely a strong, silent puppet, at times almost
ludicrous. In conjunction with the stilted and vapid Eléna, Insárov
makes *On the Eve* distinctly the worst of all Turgénev's mature
work.

The best of the novels and ultimately the most important of
Turgénev's works is *Fathers and Sons*, one of the greatest novels of
the nineteenth century. Here Turgénev triumphantly solved two
tasks that he had been attempting to solve: to create a living
masculine character not based on introspection, and to overcome
the contradiction between the imaginative and the social theme.
Fathers and Sons is Turgenev's only novel where the social problem
is distilled without residue into art, and leaves no bits of undigested
journalism sticking out. Here the delicate and poetic narrative art
of Turgénev reaches its perfection, and Bazárov is the only one of
Turgénev's men who is worthy to stand by the side of his women.
But nowhere perhaps does the essential debility and feminineness
of his genius come out more clearly than in this, the best of his
novels. Bazárov is a strong man, but he is painted with admiration
and wonder by one to whom a strong man is something abnormal.
Turgénev is incapable of making his hero triumph, and to spare
him the inadequate treatment that would have been his lot in the
case of success, he lets him die, not from any natural development
of the nature of the subject, but by the blind decree of fate. For
fate, blind chance, crass casualty, presides over Turgénev's universe as it does over Hardy's, but Turgénev's people submit to it
with passive resignation. Even the heroic Bazárov dies as resigned
as a flower in the field, with silent courage but without protest.

It would be wrong to affirm that after *Fathers and Sons*
Turgénev's genius began to decline, but at any rate it ceased to
grow. What was more important for his contemporaries, he lost
touch with Russian life and thus ceased to count as a *contemporary*
writer, though he remained a permanent classic. His attempts
again to tackle the problems of the day in *Smoke* (1867) and in
Virgin Soil (1877) only emphasized his loss of touch with the new

age. *Smoke* is the worst-constructed of his novels: it contains a beautiful love story, which is interrupted and interlarded with conversations that have no relation to its characters and are just dialogued journalism on the thesis that all intellectual and educated Russia was nothing but smoke. *Virgin Soil* is a complete failure, and was immediately recognized as such. Though it contains much that is in the best manner of Turgénev (the characters of the bureaucratic-aristocratic Sipyágin family are among his best satirical drawings), the whole novel is disqualified by an entirely uninformed and necessarily false conception of what he was writing about. His presentation of the revolutionaries of the seventies is like an account of a foreign country by one who had never seen it.

But while Turgénev had lost the power of writing for the times, he had not lost the genius of creating those wonderful love stories which are his most personal contribution to the world's literature. Pruned of its conversations, *Smoke* is a beautiful *nouvelle*, comparable to the best he wrote in the fifties, and so is *The Torrents of Spring* (1872). Both are on the same subject: a young man loves a pure and sweet young girl but forsakes her for a mature and lascivious woman of thirty, who is loved by many and for whom he is the plaything of a fleeting passion. The characters of Irína, the older woman in *Smoke*, and of Gemma, the Italian girl in *The Torrents of Spring*, are among the most beautiful in the whole of his gallery. *The Torrents of Spring* is given a retrospective setting, and in most of the other stories of this last period the scene is set in the old times of pre-Reform Russia. Some of these stories are purely objective little tragedies (one of the best is *A Lear of the Steppes*, 1870); others are non-narrative fragments from reminiscences, partly continuing the manner and theme of *A Sportsman's Sketches*. There are also the purely biographical reminiscences, including interesting accounts of the author's acquaintance with Púshkin and Belínsky and the remarkable account of *The Execution of Troppmann* (1870), which in its fascinated objectivity is one of the most terrible descriptions ever made of an execution.

There had always been in Turgénev a poetic or romantic vein, as opposed to the prevailing realistic atmosphere of his principal work. His attitude to nature had always been lyrical, and he had always had a lurking desire to transcend the limits imposed on the

Russian novelist by the dogma of realism. Not only did he begin
his career as a lyrical poet and end it with his *Poems in Prose*, but
even in his most realistic and civic novels the construction and
atmosphere are mainly lyrical. *A Sportsman's Sketches* includes
many purely lyrical pages of natural description, and to the period
of his highest maturity belongs that remarkable piece *A Tour in
the Forest* (1857), where for the first time Turgénev's conception of
indifferent and eternal nature opposed to transient man found expression in a sober and simple prose that attains poetry by the
simplest means of unaided suggestion. His last period begins with
the purely lyrical prose poem *Enough* and culminates in the *Poems
in Prose*. At the same time the fantastic element asserts itself. In
some stories (*The Dog, Knock! Knock! Knock!* and *The Story of
Father Alexis*) it appears only in the form of a suggestion of mysterious presences in an ordinary realistic setting. The most important of these stories is his last, *Clara Mílich* (1883), written
under the influence of spiritualistic readings and musings. It is as
good as most of his stories of purely human love, but the mysterious
element is somewhat difficult to appreciate quite whole-heartedly
today. It has all the inevitable flatness of Victorian spiritualism.
In a few stories Turgénev freed himself from the conventions of
realistic form and wrote such things as the purely visionary *Phan-
toms* (1864) and *The Song of Triumphant Love* (1881), written in
the style of an Italian *novella* of the sixteenth century. There can
be no greater contrast than between these and such stories of
Dostoyévsky as *The Double* or *Mr. Prokhárchin*. Dostoyévsky,
with the material of sordid reality, succeeds in building fabrics of
weird fantasy. Turgénev, in spite of all the paraphernalia introduced, never succeeded in freeing himself from the second-rate
atmosphere of the medium's consulting room. *The Song of Triumphant Love* shows up his limitation of another kind—the
inadequacy of his language for treating subjects of insufficient
reality. This limitation Turgénev shared with all his contemporaries (except Tolstóy and Leskóv). They did not have a sufficient
feeling of words, of language as language (as Púshkin and Gógol
had had), to make it serve them in unfamiliar fields. Words for
them were only signs of familiar things and familiar feelings. Language had entered with them on a strictly limited engagement—
it would serve only in so far as it had not to leave the everyday
realities of the nineteenth century.

The same stylistic limitation is apparent in Turgénev's last and most purely lyrical work, *Poems in Prose* (1879–83). (Turgénev originally entitled them *Senilia;* the present title was given them with the author's silent approval by the editor of the *Messenger of Europe*, where they first appeared.) They are a series of short prose fragments, most of them gathered round some more or less narrative kernel. They are comparable in construction to the objectivated lyrics of the French Parnassians, who used visual symbols to express their subjective experience. Sometimes they verge on the fable and the apologue. In these "poems" is to be found the final and most hopeless expression of Turgénev's agnostic pessimism, of his awe of unresponsive nature and necessity, and of his pitying contempt for human futility. The best of the "poems" are those where these feelings are given an ironic garb. The more purely poetical ones have suffered from time, and date too distinctly from about 1880—a date that can hardly add beauty to anything connected with it. The one that closes the series, *The Russian Language*, has suffered particularly—not from time only, but from excessive handling. It displays in a condensed form all the weakness and ineffectiveness of Turgénev's style when it was divorced from concrete and familiar *things*. The art of eloquence had been lost.

Turgénev was the first Russian writer to charm the Western reader. There are still retarded Victorians who consider him the only Russian writer who is not disgusting. But for most lovers of Russian he has been replaced by spicier food. Turgénev was very nineteenth century, perhaps the most representative man of its latter part, whether in Russia or west of it. He was a Victorian, a man of compromise, more Victorian than any one of his Russian contemporaries. This made him so acceptable to Europe, and this has now made him lose so much of his reputation there. Turgénev struck the West at first as something new, something typically Russian. But it is hardly necessary to insist today on the fact that he is not in any sense representative of Russia as a whole. He was representative only of his class—the idealistically educated middle gentry, tending already to become a non-class intelligentsia—and of his generation, which failed to gain real touch with Russian realities,[7] which failed to find itself a place in life and which, in-

[7] What Turgénev was in touch with were not the raw realities of Russian life, but only their reflection in the minds of his generation of intellectuals.

effective in the sphere of action, produced one of the most beautiful literary growths of the nineteenth century. In his day Turgénev was regarded as a leader of opinion on social problems; now this seems strange and unintelligible. Long since, the issues that he fought out have ceased to be of any actual interest. Unlike Tolstóy or Dostoyévsky, unlike Griboyédov, Púshkin, Lérmontov, and Gógol, unlike Chaadáyev, Grigóriev, and Herzen—Turgénev is no longer a teacher or even a ferment. His work has become pure art— and perhaps it has won more from this transformation than it has lost. It has taken a permanent place in the Russian tradition, a place that stands above the changes of taste or the revolutions of time. We do not seek for wisdom or guidance in it, but it is impossible to imagine a time when *The Singers, A Quiet Spot, First Love,* or *Fathers and Sons* will cease to be among the most cherished of joys to Russian readers.

THE SENTIMENTAL PHILANTHROPISTS

Turgénev in *A Sportsman's Sketches* was not the first of the realists to take his subjects from peasant life. He had been preceded by Dmítry Vasílievich Grigoróvich (1822–99), whose stories of peasant life, *The Village* and *Antón Goremýka,* published respectively in 1846 and 1847, were among the principal events of those eventful two years. They produced a strong impression on the partisans of the new literature by a deliberate effort to paint peasant life from the point of view of the characters themselves. But the intention was better than the execution, and the stories can hardly be regarded as satisfactory or intrinsically significant. Grigoróvich has a more important place in literary biography than in literature, for it was he who, in 1845, introduced Dostoyévsky to Nekrásov and Belínsky and, more than forty years later, played a principal part in the discovery of Chékhov.

After *The Village* and *A Sportsman's Sketches* the sentimental, "philanthropic" presentation of peasant life became one of the set subjects of the novelists of the realistic school. Only one writer, however, made a name on it. This was Marie Alexándrovna Márkovich, *née* Velínsky (1834–1907), who wrote in both Ukrainian and Russian under the name of Márko-Vovchók. Her stories are folk tales, with clear-cut characters, which leave no doubt as to their moral value, and a good deal of healthy and orthodox melodrama. The peasants are all painted white; their oppressors, the landlords, black. In spite of this somewhat naïve monochromy the narrative merit of her stories is so great that they quite justify her place as a classic in the Ukrainian tradition.

PÍSEMSKY

Alexéy Theofiláktovich Písemsky (1820–81) came of a noble, but very poor family and may in many ways be regarded as a plebeian. At twenty he went to the University of Moscow, but was not infected by the metaphysical and social idealism prevalent there. A sort of skeptical common sense remained forever the foundation of his mentality, coupled with an intense Russian feeling, which took no interest in foreign things, but neither idealized Russia and the Russians nor shared the nationalist idealism of the Slavophils. After taking his degree he entered the Civil Service and, with several intervals, remained most of his life a civil servant. In 1847 he presented to the censorship his novel *Boyárschina*, but it was not passed, the censor finding too gloomy the picture it presented of Russian life. So the first novel by Písemsky to appear was *The Muff* (1850). Soon after its publication Písemsky became a member of the so-called "young editorial staff of the *Moskvityánin*," a group of highly gifted young men (the leaders were Ostróvsky and Grigóriev). They were inspired by a love of Russia that was more democratic and less dogmatic than Slavophilism. Písemsky was attracted by their enthusiasm for originality and raciness. But his independence and distrust of all theories and ideas prevented him from identifying himself with them altogether. Their spirit is easily recognized in the popular stories he wrote in the early fifties. Throughout the fifties Písemsky continued producing masterpieces that met with increasing recognition. He attained the height of his popularity after the publication of the novel *A Thousand Souls* (1858) and the realistic tragedy *A Hard Lot* (1859). But in spite of his success he was out of tune with the times: he lacked the reforming zeal, the enthusiasm for rational progress, the faith in social theories that inspired the Russia of his day. In 1858 he rashly ventured into journalism, and when, after 1861, the atmosphere changed and violent party feeling took the place of the

unanimous enthusiasm of the preceding years, Písemsky was one
of the first to suffer. He conducted his review in a spirit of skepticism and of disbelief in progress and in the young generation.
Some rather harmless skeptical remarks on Sunday schools (one
of the pet toys of the time) were enough to provoke a storm of
indignation that forced Písemsky to close his review, to retire to
Moscow, and to seek readmission to the Civil Service. In 1863 he
published a new novel, *Troubled Seas*, which contained a satirical
presentation of the young generation. This naturally increased the
hostility of the radicals. Písemsky became a profoundly embittered
man. He began to loathe not only the radicals but everything
around him. In particular he was moved to wrath by the orgy of
unbridled money-making that was such a feature of the years
following the Emancipation. His gloom was aggravated by the
suicide of his son. He became a victim to hypochondria, which
poisoned his last years. He courageously fought against it, forcing
himself to write a certain number of hours each day, but his talent
steadily declined and his popularity still more. By the time of his
death he had long ceased to be regarded as a living literary force.

Písemsky is different in many ways from his contemporaries.
Most of the essential features I have spoken of as common to the
Russian realists are absent from his work. To begin with, he is
free from all idealism, and this in two senses—he has no use for
ideas and theories, and he does not take an optimistic view of
mankind. In the painting of human baseness, meanness, and
smallness he has no rivals and he is the true successor of Gógol.
But he is infinitely more objective than either Gógol or any of the
realists. He painted life as he saw it, without breaking it to any
preconceived idea. The people who inhabit his stories are not
subjective creations, ultimately based on the exteriorization of
personal experience, like Gógol's and like those of most of the
realists, but really *other* people, seen with the eyes and understood
by the sense of kind. Another feature of Písemsky is the predominance in his work of outline over atmosphere. His people do not
move about in a mellow autumnal haze like Turgénev's, but stand
out in the fierce glare of sunlight. Closely connected with this
feature is a far greater element of narrative interest than is usual
in Russian fiction. Like others among the Russian realists Písemsky
is gloomy rather than otherwise, but again in a different way—his
gloom is not, like Turgénev's, a hopeless surrender to the mysteri-

ous forces of the universe, but a hearty and virile disgust at the vileness of the majority of mankind and at the futility in particular of the Russian educated classes. All these characteristics, together with his somewhat cynical attitude to life, make Písemsky unlike the main current of Russian realism and much more like the French naturalists. He has points in common with Balzac and is anticipatory of Zola and of Maupassant. But the Russian characteristics of Russian realism that we do not find in Písemsky are not so much typical of the Russian mind as of a very particular phase of it—the mind of the idealist of the forties. Písemsky, who kept himself uncontaminated by idealism, was in his own time regarded as much more characteristically Russian than his more cultured contemporaries. And this is true, Písemsky was in much closer touch with Russian life, in particular with the life of the uneducated middle and lower classes, than were the more genteel novelists. He was, together with Ostróvsky, and before Leskóv, the first to open that wonderful gallery of Russian characters of *non-noble* birth which is one of the greatest things in Russian literature yet to be discovered by the West. Písemsky's great narrative gift and exceptionally strong grip on reality make him one of the best Russian novelists, and if this is not sufficiently realized, it is (apart from considerations of fashion) because of his regrettable lack of culture. It was lack of culture that made Písemsky too weak to hold out against the ravages of age and permitted him to degenerate so sadly in his later work. It was lack of culture also that made him so unsatisfactory a stylist, for he had a command of language (his peasant dialogue is infinitely superior to anything before of its kind), but he was undone by his lack of respect for the individual work—which is after all the beginning and end of the craft of letters. It is chiefly for this reason that he has to be placed below Leskóv.

Písemsky's first novel, *Boyárschina* (written, 1845; published, 1858), already possessed most of his best qualities. It has even more narrative tensity than his later stories, and a substantial element of melodrama, which is absent from his maturer work but reappears in the dramas he wrote in the sixties. The painting of provincial society is powerfully scornful, and Písemsky already displays an art in which he was to excel—the art of relating with wonderfully vivid convincingness the growth and spread of scandal and calumny. Here also appears the first of these strong men of the people, the peasant squire Savély, said to be a reminiscence of the writer's father.

The Muff is free from the melodramatic and idealistic residue of *Boyárschina*. It is a distinctly unpleasant story. It has no sympathetic characters and, at the same time, no villains. All are equally mean and small; but nothing is to blame except everyone's insincerity in pretending to be something better than he really is. The story of the unhappy marriage of two equally mediocre and despicable people is told with extraordinary power, which in spite of the triviality of the souls involved rises to the level of tragedy. *The Muff* was followed by a succession of stories and by the wonderful *Sketches of Peasant Life*, which introduced an entirely new attitude to the people, poles away from the superior compassion of Grigoróvich and Turgénev. The peasant (it must be remembered that the peasants of Písemsky's native province are not agriculturists but traders and craftsmen, who make their money in the towns) is represented not as a poor creature to be sympathized with for his humanity and pitied for his sufferings, but as a strong and shrewd man, the superior, in moral strength and will power, of his social superior—a man untainted by the vulgarity of provincial gentility, unpoisoned by the weakness of emasculated feelings, who knows what he wants, can yield to his passions, and can control them. The greatest of Písemsky's popular creations is the drama *A Hard Lot*, but the *Sketches* also contain masterpieces of character drawing, vigorous narrative, and racy Russian.

A Thousand Souls (1858) was Písemsky's most ambitious work. It is the story of Kalínovich, a young man of talent and promise, whose one desire is to *parvenir*, to become somebody. He fails in literature, but he succeeds in marrying an heiress (the owner of "a thousand souls") with powerful family connections but with a doubtful past. Thanks to her connections, and especially to her lover and cousin, Prince Iván, Kalínovich reaches a degree of importance in the official world, where he feels himself independent enough to get rid of his steppingstones. He casts aside his wife. He is made a provincial governor and shows himself a fierce champion of honesty and integrity. He prosecutes the dishonest and powerful Prince Iván but, in his zeal to undo his enemy, goes beyond the limits of legality and has to leave the service. The story is as unsweetened and ruthless in its unidealized view of mankind as any story of Písemsky's, but its gloom and squalor are redeemed by the person of Kalínovich's first fiancée, and later mistress, Nástya, in her courageous womanhood one of the most charming figures in Russian fiction.

Troubled Seas, which sealed Písemsky's quarrel with the radicals, is not so good as *A Thousand Souls*. The first three parts are quite on his best level, but the last three are a scurrilous and unfair satire on the young generation, too profoundly distorted by the personal embitterment of the author.

The novels he wrote after that date are on a still lower level. Though he always retained his power of narrative development, it glided down into the cheaply melodramatic. His characters lose their vitality, his Russian becomes intolerable journalese, and his values are hopelessly distorted by bitterness and hypochondria.[8]

NOVELISTS OF PROVINCIAL CHARACTER

Písemsky's stories of popular life were part of a movement. Other young writers belonging to the "young staff of the *Moskvityánin*" cultivated what we may call the literature of popular *character*, as opposed to the "philanthropic" peasant fiction of the Westernizers. They approached the lower and uneducated classes of Russian society not as objects of pity, but as the purest and finest expression of Russian national originality. Except for Písemsky and Ostróvsky none of the writers of this school are of the first rank, and all are more or less forgotten.

After the general awakening of 1856 numerous writers devoted themselves to the study of the various forms of the people's life. The literature produced by the ethnographers takes every intermediate form between pure fiction and pure journalistic or scientific description.

Pável Ivánovich Mélnikov (pseudonym "Andréy Pechérsky," 1819–83) described the life of the Old Believers in the backwoods beyond the middle Vólga (opposite Nízhny-Nóvgorod). His works are not really first-class literature and are disfigured by a meretricious pseudo-poetical style, imitative of folklore. But the interest of the milieu described and the author's knowledge of it are so great that they make absorbingly interesting reading. The life of that stubborn and conservative community of Old Believers is

[8] For Písemsky's dramatic work see Chapter VII.

strikingly unlike the life of the genteel intelligentsia. Rising on a foundation of imperfectly subdued, exuberant, and lusty heathenism, and held in check by the powerful discipline of ascetic and fanatical religion, it offers a powerfully picturesque picture.

Here is probably the best place to introduce Nadézhda Stepánovna Sokhánsky (1825–84, "Kokhanóvskaya"). Although she took the subject matter of her stories from the life of the provincial gentry, she resembles the novelists of popular character in bringing out the peculiarities and the old-fashioned originality of the class she describes, the small, uneducated squires of her native province of Khárkov. She was herself the daughter of such a squire, and her work is inspired by a love for the simple and backwater provincial life of her class of people and a devotion to the Slavophil ideals of family unity and paternal authority. Her stories of contemporary life may be regarded as a continuation of the tradition of Gógol's *Old-World Landowners*. In the use of language, racy, picturesque, and varied, she is also a more worthy disciple of the great novelist than most of her contemporaries. Better even than her stories of contemporary manners are those which revive the more spacious life of the great provincial squires of the age of Catherine. Her pictures of that life need not fear comparison with Aksákov's *Family Chronicle*. They are in a different key—more romantic—and the characters, drawn, like Aksákov's, bigger than nature, are heroic in a different way— heroes of romance rather than of epic.

CHAPTER 7

The Age of Realism:
Journalists, Poets, and Playwrights

CRITICISM AFTER BELÍNSKY

W HEN, in 1846, Belínsky left Krayévsky's review for Nekrásov's *Sovreménnik*, his part of chief critic in the former was
taken by a young man of unusual promise, Valérian Nikoláyevich
Máykov (1823–47), brother of the poet Apollón Máykov. He
possessed an amount of common sense, a breadth of understanding,
and a sense of literary values that it would be vain to look for in
any other Russian critic of the "intelligentsia" age. His early
death was a real calamity: like Venevítinov before him and
Pomyalóvsky after him, he was one of those who, had they been
granted a longer life, might have turned the course of Russian
civilization into more creative and less Chekhovian ways. Máykov
was a civic critic and a socialist. But he was a *critic*, one of the
small number of genuine critics in Russian literature. His criticism
of Dostoyévsky's early work can even now be accepted almost
without qualifications, and he was the first to give public appreciation to the poetry of Tyútchev.

After the deaths of Máykov and Belínsky the critical leadership of the Westernizing press passed to the right-wing Westernizers, the non-civic, æsthetic critics for whom art was an ultimate
expression of ideas that were above the problems of today and a
matter of enjoyment, not of values.

The most notable were Alexander Vasílievich Druzhínin
(1824–64), already mentioned as the author of the problem novel
Pólinka Sachs, and Pável Vasílievich Ánnenkov (1813–87). Ánnenkov was at one time Gógol's secretary and afterward became

the intimate friend of Turgénev. In 1853–6 the two together and Nekrásov formed a sort of triumvirate that practically controlled Russian (at least Petersburg) literature. Ánnenkov's book on *Púshkin in the Reign of Alexander I* (1875) is a masterpiece of social history, indispensable to any student of Russian civilization. Equally shrewd and suggestive are his numerous memoirs and biographical sketches of his contemporaries. Together they form a richly suggestive picture of those crucial years in the life of the Russian intellectual mentality.

Apollón Alexándrovich Grigóriev (1822–64) was born in Moscow, in the heart of the merchants' quarter—a part of the town where the superficial veneer of international and genteel civilization was scarcely apparent, and where Russian character survived and throve in more or less unfettered forms. In due course Grigóriev went to the University, and there before long he was thoroughly soaked in the romantic and idealistic spirit of his age. Schiller, Byron, Lérmontov, and, above all, the theater—with Shakspere, and Mochálov to interpret him—became the air he breathed.

In 1847 he came in contact with a group of gifted young men whose center was Ostróvsky. They were united by a bubbling and boundless enthusiasm for Russian originality and for the Russian people. Under their action Grigóriev's early, vaguely generous romanticism took the form of a cult of the Russian character and Russian spirit. Ostróvsky, especially, produced an enormous impression by his wholeness and common sense, and at the same time by the new and purely Russian spirit of his dramatic work. Henceforward Grigóriev became the herald and prophet of Ostróvsky.

In 1850 Grigóriev persuaded Pogódin to hand over to him the editorship of the *Moskvityánin*. Grigóriev, Ostróvsky, and their friends became known as "the young staff of the *Moskvityánin*." The shortsighted miserliness of Pogódin gradually forced the best writers of the "young staff" to desert to the Westernizing reviews of Petersburg. In 1856, at last, the *Moskvityánin* came to an end, and Grigóriev moved to Petersburg in search of employment. But as a journalist he was unacceptable to the majority of editors, who disapproved of his enthusiastic nationalism. He fell on evil times and had to look for non-literary employment. At one time he got an excellent situation as tutor to a young aristocrat abroad, but

his connection with the family ended in one of the most notorious
scandals of his generally scandalous life. In 1861 he came in touch
with the Dostoyévsky brothers and Strákhov and took part in
their publication *Vrémya*. He found in them a kindred spirit and
a sympathetic understanding, but he was too far gone to be redeemed from his irregular life. A great part of his last years was
spent in a debtor's prison. In 1864, when the *Vrémya* (suppressed
in 1863) was revived as the *Epoch*, Grigóriev was invited by the
Dostoyévskys to be chief critic. In the few months left him Grigóriev wrote what is probably his most significant prose work, *My
Literary and Moral Wanderings* and *Paradoxes of Organic Criticism*.
The *Wanderings* may be described as a cultural autobiography. It
is not the complete history of his soul, but the history of his experience as related to the cultural milieu that produced him and to
the cultural life of the nation during his early years. Grigóriev was
extraordinarily sensitive to the movement of history, and no one
was more capable than he of reviving the smell and taste of a
particular phase of time. The book is almost unique in kind—the
only other book that in any sense approaches it is Herzen's *My
Past and Thoughts*, different in tone but similar in the power of
historical intuition.

As a poet he is typical of the post-Lérmontov period, when all
technical effort was practically discarded and poetry relied on
inspiration pure and simple. Grigóriev's narrative poems are un-
readably diffuse. His best verse belongs to the days of his carousals
with the "young staff." Published some years later in second-rate
newspapers, it remained uncollected until Blok's edition of 1915.
The best of these poems were inspired by his intimacy with the
gypsy choruses. His address to his guitar and the wonderful lyric
fugue beginning *Two Guitars* can rank with the most purely and
beautifully inspired lyrics in the language. The latter poem,
though uneven, crude, and excessively long, is certainly a wonderful flight of lyrical genius, forestalling in a certain sense Blok's
famous *The Twelve*.

As a critic Grigóriev is chiefly remembered for the theory of
"organic criticism," which insisted on the necessity of art and
literature's being an organic growth of the national *soil* (*póchva;*
hence the name of *póchvenniki* for his followers.*)* This *organic*
quality he found in Púshkin and in his contemporary Ostróvsky,
whose herald he prided himself on being. Grigóriev loved all that

was Russian for being Russian, and apart from all other considerations. "Meekness" was to him the characteristic of the Russian
character, as opposed to the "predatory" quality of European man.
The "new word" that he hoped would be uttered by Russia was
the creation of "meek types"; the first indication of it he discerned
in Púshkin's Bélkin and in Lérmontov's Maxím Maxímych. He
did not live to see what he might have accepted as its final expression, Dostoyévsky's *Idiot*.

But the "predatory" type incarnate in Lérmontov (and his
Pechórin) and, above all, in Byron had an unconquerable fascination for Grigóriev. In fact nothing that was romantic was alien
to him, and for all his love of the classical and balanced geniuses
of Púshkin and Ostróvsky, his innermost sympathy went to the
most exuberant of the romanticists and to the sublimest of the
idealists. Byron, Victor Hugo, and Schiller were his most intimate
preferences. He was also a great admirer of Carlyle, of Emerson,
and of Michelet. With Michelet his affinities are particularly great.
What is perhaps the most valuable part of all the critical theories
of Grigóriev, his intuition of life as an organic, complex, self-
conditioned unity, is strongly reminiscent of the great French
historian. Of course he does not come near to Michelet as an artist
of words—Grigóriev's writings are all more or less unkempt and
slovenly journalism where flashes of genius and intuition are
stifled by the overgrown weeds of verbosity. Only in *My Literary
and Moral Wanderings* and in *Paradoxes of Organic Criticism* does
he really reach something like adequate expression. The latter was
written in answer to an invitation from Dostoyévsky to give a
definite statement of his *Weltanschauung*. It contains these words,
the quintessence of his intuition: "Life is something mysterious
and inexhaustible, an abyss that engulfs all finite reason, an un-
spannable ocean, the logical conclusion of the wisest brain—something even ironical, and at the same time full of love, procreating
one world after another. . . ."

HERZEN

Alexander Ivánovich Herzen (1812–70), although an illegitimate
child, grew up in every respect as the son of a rich nobleman. He
received the usual, French and unpractical, education and was

much less of a *déclassé* than Turgénev or Nekrásov. His lifelong friendship with N. P. Ogarëv began very early. The two boys were strongly impressed by the Decembrist Revolt and vowed themselves to the completion of the work of the defeated rebels. In the University (where Herzen was in the early thirties) the two friends became the center of a circle that concentrated on political ideas and on socialism. In 1834 the members of the circle were arrested, and Herzen was exiled to the provinces, not as a prisoner, but as a clerk in the Civil Service. In 1840 Herzen was allowed to return, and he immediately became a prominent figure. He had a decisive influence on Belínsky, and it was from the contact of the two men that Russian Westernism arose in its definite form. In literature he began making a name by a series of articles on progress and natural science (over the signature of Iskander) that were the first symptoms of the general turn of the Russian mind from romantic idealism to scientific positivism. In 1846–7 he also published several stories, including the novel *Whose Fault?* In 1847, after the death of his father, he came into a large fortune. Not without difficulty he succeeded in obtaining a foreign passport and left Russia for Paris. From Paris he sent to Nekrásov's *Sovreménnik* four remarkable *Letters from the Avenue Marigny*, which were a rather open assertion of socialist ideas in the teeth of the censorship. Soon after Herzen's arrival in Paris there broke out the February Revolution. He greeted it enthusiastically and openly, thus destroying for himself all possibility of returning to Russia. Henceforward he identified himself with the revolutionary movement of Europe. Expelled from France after the victory of Cavaignac, he went to Rome; and, after the failure of the Roman Revolution, to Switzerland, where he was naturalized a Swiss citizen; to Nice; and ultimately to England. The failure of the Revolution was a profound wound to Herzen. Under its immediate influence he wrote that series of essays and dialogues *From the Other Shore* (first published in German, as *Vom andern Ufer*) which is probably his masterpiece and his greatest claim to immortality. In 1852 Herzen settled in England and there founded the first Russian free press abroad. After the Crimean War, when the general awakening of Russia gave new hopes to Herzen, he turned his interest from European revolution to Russian reform. In 1857 he founded the *Bell* (*Kólokol*), a weekly paper that at once acquired an enormous influence and, though officially prohibited, poured into Russia in numerous copies. It was read by everyone, and not least by those in power. Its revelations of abuses and misgovernment often led to immediate official action in removing the most objectionable culprits. In the years 1857–61 the *Bell* was the principal political force in Russia. This was owing very largely to Herzen's gift of political tact: without surrendering a tittle of his extreme socialistic and federalistic theories, in practice he was ready to give his support to a reforming monarchy as long as he believed in the sincerity of its good intentions. This made it possible for him actively to influence the solution of the peasant problem. But after 1861 his influence declined. His openly pro-Polish position in 1862–3 repelled from him all that section of opinion which was not openly revolutionary, while on the other hand his theories were beginning to seem backward and his mentality antiquated to the young radicals. In 1864 he left London for Geneva, where he continued sporadically publishing numbers of the *Bell*, but with nothing like the former success. He died in 1870 in Paris and was buried in Nice.

Herzen has an equally important place in political history, in the history of ideas, and in purely literary history. A more detailed account of his political activities than I have already given in the foregoing paragraphs would be out of place in a history of literature. Nor can I here give his ideas the detailed treatment they would claim in any history of Russian thought. Herzen was the pioneer in Russia of the positivist and scientific mentality of nineteenth-century Europe and of socialism. But he was deeply rooted in the romantic and aristocratic past, and though the content of his ideas was materialistic and scientific, their tone and flavor always remained romantic. The first stimulant of his thought was the French socialist Saint-Simon, and his gospel of the "emancipation of the flesh" from the traditional fetters of religion always remained one of Herzen's fundamental watchwords.

Socialism to Herzen was not so much a positive program as an incentive and a ferment that was to destroy the outworn civilization of the West and to rejuvenate the senescent tissues of European humanity. He was the first to lay the foundations of Russian agrarian socialism, which hoped to build a socialistic Russia not so much on a Europeanized proletariat as on the communistic tradition of the Russian peasant and the revolutionary initiative of an enlightened and generous minority. But he was always more political than social, and the inspiration of his thought was always liberty rather than equality. Few Russians have felt individual freedom and the rights of man as keenly as Herzen.

Herzen's socialism has a distinctly national coloring. He believed in Russia's vitality as he did not believe in that of the West, and he loved Russia with a passionate love. He hated the government of Nicholas I and the forces of reaction, but he loved not only the people, but also all that was sincere and generous in the intellectual classes; he had a warm feeling for the Slavophils, with whose Christianity he was in no sort of sympathy but from whom he derived much of his faith in the Russian people. In the West, though at one time he gave himself entirely to the European revolution, he had sympathy with the workman only, especially the French workman, in whom he saw a force that was to destroy the selfish bourgeois civilization he loathed.

What makes Herzen, however, much more than a mere teacher of revolutionary doctrines, and conciliates with him even those who are at least inclined to share his aspirations, is his intellectual fairness and capacity for detachment. In spite of the extremeness of his views, he could understand his enemies and judge them by *their* standards. His historical intuition, his ability to see history in broad outline, to understand the significance of details and to *relate* them to the main lines, is marvelous. His thought is mainly historical, and the way he understood history as a spontaneous, unpredestined, incalculable force continuing the equally spontaneous and unpredestined evolution of nature makes him, like Grigóriev, akin to Bergson. He saw the "creativeness" of the process of becoming, the novelty of every future in relation to every past, and the pages he devotes to the confutation of all idea of predestination, all notion of an extrinsic *idea* guiding human history, are among the most eloquent he wrote.

As a writer Herzen lives chiefly by what he wrote between his departure from Russia and the foundation of the *Bell* (1857). His writings after that date are of much greater importance for the political than for the literary historian, and his early work written before he left Russia gives only a foretaste of the essential Herzen. His stories and his novel do not give him a place among the greater novelists, in spite of their considerable psychological interest and delicacy of observation.

But the works written during his first ten years abroad (1847–

57) secure for Herzen a permanent place among the national classics. They include *Letters from France and Italy* (1847–50), *From the Other Shore* (1847–50), a series of propaganda pamphlets written in the early fifties, and *My Past and Thoughts*, an autobiography written mainly in 1852–5 but continued fragmentarily after that date and to which he was still adding in the sixties.

By far the most important of Herzen's political writings are his eight articles (three of them are in dialogue form) that compose *From the Other Shore*. The book was called forth by the failure of what Herzen had hoped would be the dawn of a revolutionary and socialist Europe. Although distinctly dated in most of the details, it still reads as one of the most significant things ever written on human history and is perhaps particularly suggestive and appropriate reading in our own days, even though we find it often impossible to endorse Herzen's reading of historical facts. Alone of all Herzen's political writings, it was not written for propaganda purposes, and the edge of its irony is directed not against the old Europe, but against the idealistic optimism of revolutionaries, who expected too much and too early and were either too soon disillusioned or held too firmly to their errors and superstitions. To destroy the *religion* of revolution and socialism, with its rhetoric and its official optimism, and to replace it by a clear and sober *will* for revolution were Herzen's aim. It is here that his intuition of life receives full expression—a hopeful and active acceptance of the "stream of history" viewed as a *creative* process, not as preordained necessity, is the keynote of the book.

His other political writings are different in being primarily propaganda and written not in the disinterested pursuit of truth for itself, but with the aim of influencing other men's actions and opinions. It is in them, however, that Herzen's eloquence comes out especially well. It is a French and romantic type of eloquence— loosely built, spacious, varied, abundantly availing itself of repetition and purely emotional effects, never losing an opportunity to make a side stroke or score a point in a parenthesis or subordinate clause. The best example of this kind of writing is his letter to Michelet, on *The Russian People and Socialism*, an eloquent assertion of the difference between the people and the state and a defense of the former from all responsibility for the crimes of the latter, in particular in relation to Poland.

The same characteristics of his style, but in an even more unfettered and spontaneous form, still more like conversation and relatively free from rhetoric, recur in his autobiography, *My Past and Thoughts*. To the majority of readers it will ever remain his principal work. Its attraction lies above all in its freedom and obvious sincerity. Not that there is no pose in it—Herzen was too French and too romantic to do without a pose. He was, in fact, a rare example of a Russian not afraid of an obvious pose. The absence of self-conscious and excessive sincerity, the superficiality, the somewhat matter-of-course theatricality of *My Past and Thoughts*, are its essential charm to the open-minded reader. Apart from the tone of the voice, there is little self in Herzen's memoirs and less introspection. The relative conventionality of his psychology makes it all the simpler and truer, for he speaks of himself in universal and accepted terms. The best part of the book from this point of view is the wonderful account of his wife's love affair with the German revolutionary poet Herwegh. Here the impression of absolute human sincerity is attained precisely because Herzen openly and sincerely speaks of the relations in terms of current fiction; and this relating the true emotions of two real people to the accepted clichés of current psychological thinking produces that impression of universal humanity which no one who reads those pages can fail to have.

But the greater part of the book is not subjective, and its most frequently memorable pages are those in which he speaks of the outer world. Herzen is a great portrait painter, an impressionist— and the impressions he left of his father and other relations, of the Moscow idealists, and of the leaders of the European revolution are unforgettably vivid. His lightness of touch, which never insists and always moves on, gives them a wonderfully convincing mobility. Not the least remarkable passages of the book are those in which he gives a wider historical background to the narrative: the first parts devoted to his life before his exile contain the broadest, truest, and most penetrating view of Russian social and cultural history in the first half of the nineteenth century. They are a great historical classic.

THE RADICAL LEADERS

The influence of Herzen as a begetter of ideas and a ferment of thought and also as a purely political journalist was very great, but he was too individual and too complex a personality to be a representative man or to become the adequate mouthpiece of a movement, and no group of Russian radicals ever adhered to him as a teacher or recognized him for a leader. The leadership of the radical intelligentsia, vacant since the death of Belínsky, was from 1856 onward exercised by a succession of truly representative men —Chernyshévsky, Dobrolyúbov, Písarev, Lavróv, and Mikhaylóvsky.

The first two had much in common. Both were the sons of comparatively prosperous and highly venerated priests. While rejecting all the traditional ideas of their homes, they retained much of the moral atmosphere they had been brought up in: they were puritans—almost ascetics—and fanatics. Herzen called them the "bilious set," and Turgénev said to Chernyshévsky on one occasion: "You are a snake, but Dobrolyúbov is a rattlesnake." They were plebeians, uncontaminated by the artistic and æsthetic culture of the educated gentry, and they simply had no use for any non-utilitarian cultural values. To them Russian literature before their time was concentrated in Belínsky and in Gógol, interpreted as a purely social satirist. The literature of their time they regarded as a collection of texts for utilitarian sermons or as a map of contemporary life, of which the only merit lay in its handiness and accuracy. All that was traditional and romantic they rejected. Their faith was in only two gods—in Western science as the principle of progress, and in the Russian peasant as the depository of socialistic ideals. A new plebeian intelligentsia, risen from the people and imbued with scientific rationalism, was to build a new Russia in place of the corrupt land of serfdom.

The older of the two, Nikoláy Gavrílovich Chernyshévsky, (1828–89) published a doctoral thesis in 1855 on *The Æsthetic Relations of Art to Reality*, in which he contended that art, being nothing but a more or less adequate imitation of reality, is always inferior to the reality it represents. In the following years he published *Studies of the Age of Gógol*, which laid the foundation of the utilitarian, civic criticism of literature and revived the cult of Belínsky, whose name had been taboo in the years of extreme reaction. After 1857 he concentrated on economic and social questions. He became the recognized leader of the radical young generation. After 1861, dissatisfied by the Emancipation, he passed to more active revolutionary action, and round him grew up the first nucleuses of Revolutionary Socialism. They did not go further than the printing of proclamations, but in 1862 Chernyshévsky was arrested. For two years he was confined in the Fortress of Petersburg and there wrote his famous novel *What to Do?* the first and most influential of a long succession of tendentious radical novels. In the person of the hero, Rakhmétov, he represented the ideal radical, pure and strong—a populist and an ascetic. In 1864 Chernyshévsky was deported to Siberia, where he remained at first in a convict prison, then in the isolated northeastern town of Vilyúysk. In 1883 he was allowed to live in Astrakhan, and afterward in his native Sarátov. He died in 1889.

Nikoláy Alexándrovich Dobrolyúbov (1836–61) began contributing to the *Soveménnik* in 1856, and from 1857 to his early death was its chief critic. Like Chernyshévsky he came to be regarded as a saint by the radical intelligentsia. He was the most famous and influential of the critics after Belínsky: all the radical intelligentsia from 1860 to 1905 were brought up on him. Although all his criticism is about works of imaginative literature, it would be grossly unjust to call it literary criticism. Dobrolyúbov had, it is true, a certain sense of literary values, and the choice of works he consented to use as texts for his sermons was, on the whole, happy, but he never so much as attempted to discuss their literary aspects. All his most famous articles—*What Is Oblomovism?* (Goncharóv's *Oblómov*), *A Kingdom of Darkness* (Ostróvsky's early plays), *A Ray of Light in the Kingdom of Darkness* (Ostróvsky's *Thunderstorm*), *When Will There Be Really Day?* (Turgénev's *On the Eve*)—are criticisms of Russian life as reflected in those works. His task was to create a democratic intelligentsia that would be inspired by faith in progress and a desire to serve the people and that might take the place of the romantic and æsthetic, lazy and ineffective, educated gentry—of which he regarded Oblómov as the true incarnation. All Old Russia—the gentry, the merchants, the traditions of Church and State—he hated with equal violence, and to tear the intelligentsia and the people away from everything connected with old times was his one aim.

Dobrolyúbov died the year of the Emancipation, and about the same time a new generation of radicals came to the forefront, concentrating on the propaganda of materialism. Natural science became the order of the day and the principal enemy, not so much of the government, as of the old superstitions of idealism, art, and everything romantic. The descent of man from apes became the first article of the new creed, and the dissection of frogs a symbolic rite of their religion. The new radicals called themselves "thinking realists" but did not resent the appellation of "nihilists" given them by their enemies. Their leader was Dmítry Ivánovich Písarev (1840–68), a squire by birth, but thoroughly imbued with the new anti-romantic and materialistic ideas. Like Chernyshévsky and Dobrolyúbov, he was a man of high moral character and, though an apostle of the emancipation of the flesh, a puritan in life. In 1862 he was involved in the printing of proclamations and sentenced to four years' imprisonment in the Fortress. There it was he wrote most of his articles. After his release, in 1866, he almost ceased writing. Two years later he was drowned while bathing. Písarev was unquestionably a man of brilliant gifts. Though diffuse, like all Russian journalists, and truculent, like all those of the sixties, he was a born polemist and a past master in the art of killing his enemies. In the domain of literary criticism he rejected all art, admitting "art with a purpose" only in so far as it was immediately useful for the purposes of educating a scientific intelligentsia. His famous uncrowning of Púshkin, for all its naïveté, may still be read with pleasure. It is healthily sincere and outspoken. At any rate Písarev shows very well in it the entire wrongness of Belínsky's idealistic interpretation of the great poet.

After Písarev's death the spirit of nihilism begins to degenerate; socialism and revolution once more come to the fore. The seventies are the age of the populists (*naródniki*), the successors of Herzen and Chernyshévsky.

Their most influential journalistic leaders were Lavróv and Mikhaylóvsky. Peter Lávrovich Lavróv (1823–1900) was a man of the older, pre-Reform generation. At the end of the sixties he emigrated, and after the death of Herzen he became the principal figure of the Russian political emigration. His principal work was the *Historical Letters* (1870), in which he explains all progress as the effect of the action of "critically thinking individualities." The book is a powerful assertion of the role of the individual in history and became the gospel of revolutionary action. It was made particularly wide use of to justify political terror.

Nikoláy Konstantínovich Mikhaylóvsky (1842–1904) was one of that generation of the young gentry whom it is customary to call "conscience-stricken nobles"—nobles who were dominated by a peculiar complex of social guilt: to wipe out the guilt of their serf-owning ancestors by sacrificing their lives to the people was their one aim in life. Mikhaylóvsky took no part in revolutionary or illegal propagandist activities, considering it his duty to preserve as far as possible an open tribune for the propaganda of radical views. His influence in the seventies was enormous and, together with Lavróv's, practically all-powerful among the young generation of radicals. The starting point of Mikhaylóvsky's socialism was the idea of right and justice, and its moral and idealistic tone colored the whole of Russian socialism till the advent of Marxism. Mikhaylóvsky was primarily a sociologist, and his most important work is *What is Progress?* (1873) directed against the mechanical struggle-for-life conception of the English evolutionists. In literary criticism Mikhaylóvsky was a man of strong party feeling and made his criticism quite subservient to civic ends. But he was not devoid of genuine critical insight, and his articles on Tolstóy (1873) and Dostoyévsky (1882) will ever give him a place among genuine critics. In the former he foresaw with wonderful acumen the essentially anarchistic foundation of Tolstóy's thought, which was to lead him to his later social doctrines. The latter is still one of the most forceful statements of the case against Dostoyévsky.

SLAVOPHILS AND NATIONALISTS

The Slavophil movement, started by Khomyakóv and the Kiréyevskys, was continued by men of the next generation—Yúry Samárin (1819–76) and the two Aksákovs, the sons of S. T. Aksákov, Constantine (1817–61) and Iván (1823–86).

The latter is the greatest literary name among the younger Slavophils. He carried the initial idealistic impulse of Slavophilism undiminished and undiluted into the gloomy days of Alexander III, and in a time of violent party hatred he was one of the few public men respected by his opponents. He began his literary career as a poet (*v. infra*), but it was as a political publicist that he became famous. He was exceptionally outspoken and (unlike most of the radicals) refused to learn the art of evading the censorship by circumlocution. He was always particularly courageous in insisting on the rights of free speech. The height of his influence was reached in 1876–8, when he was the mouthpiece of the general enthusiasm for the liberation of the Balkan Slavs. Next to Herzen, Aksákov is the greatest of Russian political journalists. His style is vigorous and straightforward, less rhetorical than Herzen's. His Russian, like Khomyakóv's, retains the distinction of the preceding age without its Gallicisms. Aksákov was married to a daughter of Tyútchev, and, after his father-in-law's death, wrote the latter's *Life*, which, though it dwells chiefly on the political aspects of Tyútchev's activities, contains pages that are among the best in all Russian literary criticism.

The pure Slavophilism of the older generation, idealistic and (not so much in doctrine as in tone) aristocratic, came to an end with Iván Aksákov. Only minor men of the younger generation carried on its traditions. But new types of Slavophilism arose in the fifties and sixties. These were the democratic Slavophilism of Grigóriev and Dostoyévsky, and the biological nationalism of N. Danilévsky. Of the former I have already spoken in connection with Grigóriev and shall speak again in connection with Dostoyévsky. Besides these two great men its most eminent partisan was Nikoláy Nikoláyevich Strákhov (1828–95), the friend of Tolstóy, a philosopher and a critic of considerable eminence. The doctrine of "biological nationalism" was first voiced by Nikoláy Yákovlevich Danilévsky (1822–85), whose *Russia and Europe* (1869) is still a living influence.

The reign of Alexander II was an age not only of reform and revolution, but also of wars and of rapid military expansion. The heroes of this expansion, Generals Chernyáyev and Skóbelev, were immensely popular, particularly among the Slavophils. There grew up a sort of Slavophil doctrine of strategy and tactics that insisted on the existence of a Russian school of warfare and on the great tradition of Suvórev. The principal exponent of this was General M. I. Dragomírov (1830–1908), a man of considerable literary gifts, famous in his later years for his cutting epigrams and witticisms, and General Rostisláv Fadéyev (1824–83), the brother of "Zinaída R-va" and the uncle of Count Witte, a brilliant writer on military subjects as well as a remarkable political journalist.

The growth of the revolutionary movement and the Polish rebellion of 1863 brought into existence a new reactionary movement. Its principal mouthpiece was Michael Nikíforovich Katkóv (1818–87), next to Herzen and Iván Aksákov the most influential political journalist of his time. Never in the course of Russian history was a journalist so attentively listened to by the government or so often responsible for the government's policy. But he was in no sense a creator of ideas, and besides mere security of the State he had really no superior principles to lean against. As a writer he is distinctly inferior to Herzen and to Aksákov.

THE ECLECTIC POETS

After the death of Lérmontov it became the general conviction that the age of poetry was over. In the fifties there was a certain revival of interest in poets and poetry. But in the sixties the school of Písarev launched a systematic campaign against all verse, and some of the most prominent poets were actually hooted into silence. With few exceptions the poets of this Silver Age lack vitality, and with hardly an exception their technique is lax and insufficiently conscious. A feature common to the poets of the period, which they do not share with the novelists, is their *eclecticism*, their submission to a compromise. They did not believe in the rights of the poetical imagination and sought to reconcile it with the modern spirit of science and positive knowledge. Only two poets remained free from this eclecticism: Fet, who had a genuinely transcendent poetic vision, and Nekrásov, who was truly in tune with the stream of history. But Fet was appreciated only by the extreme literary right, and Nekrásov only by the left —the middle poets met with much more universal and unquestionable approbation.

The characteristic feature of a central group of poets of the generation of the forties might be defined as their "imagism," which was partly due to the German-born theory of Belínsky that poetry was by definition "thinking in images." It was a parallel development to French Parnassianism and the poetry of the English Keatsians. It expressed itself in a predilection for visual subjects, among which nature and classical antiquity were particularly popular.

The most famous in his own day of these "imagists," and altogether the most representative poet of the age, was Apollón Nikoláyevich Máykov (1821–97). Máykov's verse answered admirably to the taste of an age which had forgotten that poetry was the art of words. It had lost all interest in romantic feeling but did not want to go without all poetical enjoyment. It could not conceive that poetry might and ought to cease being "poetical," and so its one resource was images. Máykov was mildly "poetical" and mildly realistic; mildly tendentious, and never emotional. Images are always the principal thing in his poems. Some of them (always subject to the restriction that he had no style and no diction) are happy discoveries, like the short and very well-known poems on spring and rain. But his more realistic poems are spoiled by sentimentality, and his more "poetic" poems hopelessly inadequate—their beauty is mere mid-Victorian tinsel. Few of his more ambitious attempts are successful. The best is the delightful idyl on *Fishing* (1855), where for once he recovered the relative sense of style he had displayed in his early poems. Máykov always aspired to express ideas. His *opus magnum* was to be a large tragedy on the subject of the struggle between Imperial Rome and the early Christians. Published in final form in 1882, under the title of *Two Worlds*, it contains numerous passages that prove Máykov had a strong brain, but the verse is flat and the conception of the whole is a failure, chiefly owing to his entire lack of sympathy with early Christianity. There is reason to think that Máykov the poet did not come up to the caliber of Máykov the man. At any rate Dostoyévsky had more respect for him than for any of his contemporaries and found in him the most stimulating and responsive of correspondents.

Of the other "imagists" of the mid nineteenth century I shall mention only Nikoláy Fëdorovich Scherbína (1821–69) and Leo Alexándrovich Mey (1822–62). The former had in him the stuff of a true poet; he had something to say and a personal vision of the world. His mother was a Greek, and his vision of antiquity has something homely and intimate in it that can be explained only by racial affinity.

The "imagists" imagined themselves to be continuers of the "objective" tradition of Púshkin. But the romantic "subjective" tradition of Lérmontov also survived. The most romantic of the mid-nineteenth-century eclecticists was Yákov Petróvich Polónsky (1819–98), for sheer gift of song one of the greatest poets of his generation. He is the most typical instance of that conflict between the rights of poetry and of modern thought of which I have spoken. His poetical experience was purely romantic, but he was afraid to give himself away to it and considered it his duty to write well-meaning verse on the light of progress, on freedom of speech, and other modern subjects. But the really valuable part of his poetry is quite uncivic and quite free from the expression of ideas. He is the only Russian poet capable of evoking the delicate, forest effects of the German romanticists, and next to Lérmontov the only one who had a vision of a distant land beyond the clouds of sunset. He has also Lérmontov's power of making the most delicate and poignant poetry out of the common stuff of everyday life and words. His romanticism is very Russian, genuinely akin to the spirit of Russian folk song and folk tales. Of all Russian poets, Polónsky, in his best lyrics, is the one who is surest to captivate the English reader of Russian poetry, for he has both the qualities that the English romanticist regards as synonymic with all poetry, and a simplicity and modest, realistic grace that are peculiarly, and obviously, Russian. It is no wonder that he was a special favorite of Maurice Baring.

A. K. TOLSTÓY

The most popular, the most versatile, and ultimately the most personally significant of the eclectic poets was Count Alexéy Konstantínovich Tolstóy (1817–75), a distant cousin of the great novelist. He began his literary career in 1841 with a fantastic story (*The Vampire*) in the style of the German romanticists, but it was only by 1854 that his poetic individuality assumed a mature form and he began regularly publishing his verse. A little earlier, together with his two cousins Zhemchúzhnikov, he had begun publishing satirical, humorous, and nonsense verse and prose under the joint pseudonym of Kuzmá Prutkóv. "Kuzmá Prutkóv" flourished from 1853 to 1863. Besides two volumes of lyrical narrative verse, A. Tolstóy is the author of a historical novel, *Prince Serébryany* (1862), and a dramatic trilogy (1866–70) (*v. infra*).

Like Máykov and Polónsky, A. Tolstóy was an eclectic, but his eclecticism was the natural expression of an internal harmony and a balance of adjusted forces. A many-sided and versatile serenity firmly grounded in an idealistic (Platonic) philosophy is the main characteristic of his poetry. He is the least tragic, the least disharmonious of Russian poets, but his harmony is free from complacency and placidity. It is very clean and noble. From top to toe, in poetry as in life, Alexéy Tolstóy was a gentleman.

Not being a sufficiently great and original poet to transcend the limitations of his degenerate age, Tolstóy shared with his contemporaries a certain technical inefficiency, an occasional flabbiness and indistinction of rhythm, and an uncertainty of diction. But he had a sense of the value of words, which ultimately muddled him through into style. His command of expression ranged over a great variety of manner and subject matter. He is by far the greatest of Russian humorous and nonsense poets, and at the same time he was, in his generation, without rivals in the grand manner. There is nothing after Derzhávin to compare with the solemn beauty of his paraphrase of St. John Damascene's prayer for the dead, used in the requiem of the Orthodox Church. His lyrics are sometimes the worse for wear and show too much banality and sentimentality, but many of them have preserved all their freshness and still produce the impression of exquisitely clear dewdrops. One of the chief charms is that poetical realism which seems to be an almost exclusive monopoly of the Russian nineteenth century. A charming example is the one translated by Maurice Baring in the preface to *The Oxford Book of Russian Verse*.

Alexéy Tolstóy's ballads are often operatic and date too distinctly from about 1860. But in some of them his sense of language and his unique power of making use of proper names are displayed at their best. Of his longer narrative poems, *The Dragon* (1875) contains long passages of grandly sonorous verse, really evocative of Dantesque majesty—as, for instance, the splendid invective of the Guelph narrator against the traitorous Ghibelline cities of Upper Italy, where the mere enumeration of the names of the Lombard cities produces an effect of thundering beauty. The most original and exquisite of the longer poems is *The Portrait* (1874), a romantic, humorous poem in octaves in a style descended, through Lérmontov, from Byron's *Don Juan*, relating the love of the adolescent poet for an eighteenth-century portrait of a lady. The blend of humor and semi-mystical romance is perfectly successful, and the feeling of ironical and wistful homesickness for a distant land is expressed with exquisite delicacy.

The Portrait is first cousin to the purely humorous poems of

Alexéy Tolstóy, of which *The Dream of Councilor Popóv* is likewise in octaves. It is the purest glory of Russian humorous poetry—a mixture of keen and pointed satire (aimed at the popularity-seeking minister Valúyev and at the Secret Police) with sheer delight in preposterous fun. It is today probably the least questionable of Tolstóy's claims to immortality. Another delightful humorous poem is the *Mutiny in the Vatican*, where a risqué subject (the revolt of the papal *castrati*) is treated with delightful ambiguity and playfulness.

But the most famous of Alexéy Tolstóy's humorous creations is Kuzmá Prutkóv, which he shares with the two Zhemchúzhnikovs. Kuzmá Prutkóv is a sort of Russian Prudhomme. He is a clerk in the Ministry of Finance (a side hit at the poet Benedíktov) and the incarnation of self-centered and arrogantly naïve complacency. The character of Prutkóv is chiefly given in his biography and in his proudly platitudinous fables. But he is also made the pretext for witty parodies of contemporary poets, while his father and grandfather are made to contribute plays and anecdotes that are a mixture of excellent parody of old styles with sheer absurdity and nonsense. Kuzmá Prutkóv became the founder of a whole school of nonsense poetry. Its most eminent members in the later nineteenth century were Vladímir Soloviëv and his friend, the gifted dilettante designer, Count Theodore Sollohúb.

FET

Afanásy Afanásievich Fet (1820–92) was the son of a squire named Shenshín and a German lady, whose marriage, contracted abroad, was invalid in Russia. It was not until 1876 that he was authorized by an imperial decree to assume the name of Shenshín. He retained his former name in literature until his death.

In 1840 Fet published, at his own expense, a first volume of very immature verse, which contains hardly any promise of a future poet. But already in 1842 he published in the *Moskvityánin* some of his most lasting and perfect lyrics. On leaving the University he entered the military service and for fifteen years served in various cavalry regiments, firmly intent on obtaining the grade that gave nobility. His ill luck was such that during his service this grade was twice raised, and only in 1856, on being promoted to Captain of the Guards, could he leave the service with the satisfaction of being at last a Russian noble. After a short journey abroad he married (very practically and unsentimentally) and settled down on a small estate to make a fortune. Meanwhile his poems had made him a reputation, and in the later fifties he was one of the most prominent figures in the literary world. He contracted lasting friendships with Turgénev and Tolstóy, who appreciated his common sense and did not dislike his extreme reserve. It is from Fet that we know the details of the famous quarrel of the two great novelists. It was he also who afterward brought them together once more. Meanwhile the young generation of anti-æsthetic radicals, provoked by the overtly uncivic character of his poetry and by his notoriously reactionary sympathies, started a systematic campaign against him. They eventually succeeded in hooting him into silence; after the publication in 1863 of a third edition of his poems Fet disappeared from the printed page for twenty years. His poetic genius continued maturing during these years of apparent silence. In 1883 at last he once more appeared before the public and from that date onward published a succession of small volumes under the title of *Evening Lights*. He was never prolific as a poet, and he gave his spare time to vast enterprises of a more mechanical nature: he wrote three volumes of memoirs and translated his favorite Roman poets and his favorite philosopher, Schopenhauer.

Fet is a typical example of a poet with a double life. In his student years he was, like all his contemporaries, expansive and naïvely open to generous and ideal feelings, but later on he disciplined himself into a guarded reserve that had all the appearance (and a good deal of the substance) of callousness. Hence that strange inadequacy which struck his contemporaries between the staid and ordered life of his old age and the saturated passionateness of his late lyrics, built of the complete and disinterested *poetic* exploitation of repressed and sublimated emotions. The self of real life is present in some of his odes, in some second-rate epigrams, and above all in his remarkable, unusually reticent, and yet fascinating memoirs.

In poetry Fet was first and foremost the uncompromising champion of the rights of pure poetry. He was no eclecticist, but entirely devoted himself to the true expression of his poetic experience, which was in sympathy with many of his best contemporaries but was much against the grain of the leaders of critical opinion.

His early verse includes purely "imagist" poems of classical subjects, which are better than Máykov's or Scherbína's but would not be sufficient to single out Fet as the greatest "art-for-art" poet of his age. The real early Fet is contained in the wonderful nature lyrics and "melodies," the art of which he seems to have learned from no one. They have much in common with Verlaine, except that Fet's robust pantheism is very unlike the morbid sensibility of the French poet. Such poems, deliberately excluding all but the music of emotion and associations, do not strike us today as very exceptional. But to the mid-nineteenth-century Russian critics (*not* to a creative artist, like Turgénev, Tolstóy, or Nekrásov, all of whom were fervent admirers of Fet) they seemed little better than downright moonshine.

After 1863, and especially in the eighties, Fet became more metaphysical. He more frequently tackled philosophical subjects and brooded on the eternal problems of artistic perception and expression. His syntax becomes more difficult and condensed, at times obscure, sometimes not unlike that of the sonnets of Shakspere. The highest summits of Fet's later poetry are reached in his love poems, certainly the most extraordinary and concentratedly passionate love poems ever written by a man of seventy (not excepting Goethe). In them Fet's method of utilizing nothing but his repressed emotions for his poetry wins its most brilliant victories. They have a saturation that makes them look as if they were the quintessence of a life of passion, and they are among the most precious diamonds of our poetry.

REALISTIC POETS

All the preceding poets were bracketed by their contemporaries as the party of "pure art" or "art for art's sake." This was not quite correct, as almost all of them used their verse to grind some ax or other. But they were united by a common traditional conception of poetical beauty, a beauty of subject matter, that was above and apart from current life. They were contrasted to the civic poets, who were the conscious mouthpieces of contemporary political and social feeling, and who, like the novelists, used the material of contemporary life for their poetry. The strength of the traditional conception of poetry as a thing unrelated to life may be gauged by the fact that while in the novel no subject matter was made use of that was not directly taken from contemporary Russian life, only a minority of the poets had the courage to introduce into their verse details of Russian reality. Poetry for the majority continued to be romantically conceived as a land of escape.

Civic poetry, in the hands of its more significant representatives, did become realistic, but the rank and file of civic bards were often as eclectic as, and more conventional than, the "pure art" poets. Such, for instance, is the flat and tiresome poetry of the very amiable and respectable A. N. Pleschéyev (1825–93), a member of the Petrashévsky circle. Most of the civic poets were radicals of some kind or other, but one of the first and best was the Slavophil Iván Aksákov, whose publicistic poems written in the forties and fifties, in which he calls the Russian intellectual to work and discipline, and inveighs against his Oblómov-and-Rúdin ineffectiveness and sloth, are admirable for their unadorned and straightforward strength. His narrative, realistic poem, *The Tramp* (1852) was the first Russian *poem* of peasant life and in many ways forestalls Nekrásov. There is much in common with Iván Aksákov's in the poetry of Alexéy Mikháylovich Zhemchúzhnikov (1821–1908), a first cousin of Alexéy Tolstóy's, and a co-creator with him of "Kuzmá Prutkóv." His serious poetry belongs chiefly to his old age and is inspired by indignation at the abandonment by the generation of the eighties of the high ideals of the age of reform.

Somewhat less civic and more eclectic is the poetry of Iván Sávvich Nikítin (1824–61), whose principal claim to attention lies in his realistic poems of the life of the poor. He was inclined sometimes to idealize and sentimentalize them, but his best things are free from this sin. There is an almost epic calm in the long, uneventful, and powerful *Night Rest of the Drivers*, and an unsweetened realism in such poems of tragic misery as *The Tailor*. In *Kulak*, his *opus magnum*, Nikítin introduced into poetry the methods of realistic prose. He succeeds in evoking pity and terror by the simple account of sordid and trivial misery. But he was not strong enough to create a really new art or a really new attitude to poetry. And Russian poetical and civic realism would have to be regarded as a rather second-rate growth were it not for the great name of Nekrásov.

NEKRÁSOV

Nikoláy Alexéyevich Nekrásov (1821–78) published his first volume of verse in 1840. It contained very little promise and was severely criticized by Belínsky. Unsupported by his father, a rude hunting squire and a brutal bully, Nekrásov had to give up his studies at the University of Petersburg and engage in literary and theatrical hack work and in publishing enterprises, where he gave proof of considerable business ability. By 1845 he stood on his own legs and had become virtually the principal publisher of the young literary school. A series of literary miscellanies published by him had a considerable financial success. One of them was the famous *Peterbúrgsky sbórnik*, which contained Dostoyévsky's *Poor Folk* and the first mature poems of Nekrásov himself. He became an intimate friend of Belínsky, who was as enthusiastic about his new verse as he had been severe to the 1840 volume. In 1846 Nekrásov acquired from Pletněv what had been Púshkin's *Sovreménnik*, and, from the valetudinarian antique that it had become in the hands of the remnants of the "aristocracy," it became a splendidly paying concern and the best and most living literary review in Russia. It weathered the bad times of reaction and in 1856 became the rallying ground of the extreme left. It was suppressed in 1866 during the official panic that followed on the first attempt on Alexander II's life. But two years later Nekrásov, together with Saltykóv, took over the *Otéchestvennye zapíski* and remained the publisher and editor of that principal radical review until his death. Nekrásov was an editor of genius: his ability to get the best literature and to find the right man to write on current subjects was marvelous. As a publisher, however, he was a businessman, unscrupulous, some said, and, all agreed, harsh and grasping. Nor was his personal life up to the standards of radical puritanism. He gambled heavily and regularly. He spent much money on his table and on his mistresses. He was not free from snobbery and liked the company of his social superiors. All this, in the opinion of many contemporaries, was not in harmony with the "philanthropic" and democratic character of his poetry. But what especially served against him was his cowardly behavior on the eve of the suppression of the *Sovreménnik*, when, to save himself and his review, he composed and recited in public a poem in praise of the dictator Count Muraviëv, the most ruthless and determined of reactionaries. But, though Turgénev, Herzen, and most of his contemporaries hated Nekrásov, the radicals who had to work with him admired and loved him unreservedly and pardoned as venial his private and even his public sins. His funeral was one of the most striking demonstrations of popularity ever accorded to a Russian writer.

In spite of his enormous popularity among the radicals, in spite of the tribute given to him as a poet by enemies like Grigóriev and Dostoyévsky, Nekrásov can hardly be said to have had his due during his lifetime. Even his admirers admired the matter of his poetry rather than its manner, and many of them believed that Nekrásov was a great poet only because matter mattered more than form, and in spite of his having written inartistically. To the æsthetes he was frankly unpalatable. According to Turgénev, "Poetry never so much as spent a night in his verse." Perhaps Grigóriev, with his profound intuition of values, was alone capable of really gauging the greatness of Nekrásov. After Nekrásov's death his poetry continued to be judged along party lines, rejected en bloc by the right wing and praised in spite of its inadequate form by the left. Only in relatively recent times has he come into his own, and his great originality and newness been fully appreciated. This has been owing, first of all, to our increased ability to understand "non-poetic" poetry. It is also owing to the displacement of Nekrásov the legendary radical saint (which he most certainly was not, in the sense in which Belínsky, Chernyshévsky, Dobrolyúbov, Gleb Uspénsky were) by a better-known and more real Nekrásov, a complex, not always edifying, but profoundly human and original, personality.

So different in most respects from his contemporaries, Nekrásov shared with them a lack of conscious craftsmanship and of artistic culture. He only dimly and subconsciously knew what he was after, and, though an excellent critic of other people's verse, he had no judgment of his own. He wasted much of his creative energy on ungrateful subjects that were not really congenial to him. He had a dangerous verse-writing facility that he had developed during his years of hack work in writing vaudevilles and rhymed *feuilletons*. He was essentially a rebel against all the stock in trade of "poetic" poetry, and the essence of his best work is precisely the bold creation of a new poetry unfettered by traditional standards of taste. But his own creative taste was not always unerring, and though he came very near creating a new and self-justified style (especially in his great satiric poem *Who Is Happy?*), he never obtained a secure command of it. But the inspiration, the sheer poetic energy of many of even his most questionable poems, is so great that one has to accept the occasional bathos as an ingredient of the whole. For originality and for energy Nekrásov holds one of the very first places among Russian poets and need not fear a comparison with Derzhávin.

The main subject of Nekrásov's poetry was, in his own phrase, "the sufferings of the people." But his inspiration is subjective and individual rather than social. Except in those of his poems in which he approaches nearest to the spirit of folk song and thus frees himself from the all too personal, his poetry is always personal, never group poetry. The social wrongs of contemporary Russia are for Nekrásov not so much an objective fact as a torturing subjective experience. One can speak of a "social compassion" complex in Nekrásov. It is precisely compassion (suffering with the other), not pity (condescending to the other's suffering), that animates the poetry of Nekrásov. For all the political seriousness and sincerity of Nekrásov's democratic feelings, psychologically speaking, "the sufferings of the people" were to him an emanation, a symbol of his own sufferings—from poverty, from illness, from gloom, from the pangs of conscience. He had an unusual power of idealization, and the need to create gods was the most profound of his needs. The Russian people was the principal of these gods; next to it stood the equally idealized and subjectively conditioned myths of his mother and of Belínsky. His idealized conception of the people of course tended towards sentimentality, and he did not always avoid this pitfall, but at his (frequent) best all suspicion of sentimentality is purged by the red heat of his poetic energy and poetic sincerity. Questions of taste and good form are supremely idle and irrelevant in the presence of such elemental creative processes as produced, for instance, the realistic myth poem of *Frost the Red-Nosed*. But Nekrásov's people were not only an object of compassion and worship. He could sympathize with their humor and their laughter as well as their sufferings, and of all Russian poets of the nineteenth century, he was the only one who was genuinely and creatively akin to the spirit of popular songs; he did not imitate it—he simply had in him the soul of a popular singer.

All Nekrásov's work may be divided into two sections: that in which he uses forms conditioned (though often only negatively conditioned) by the preceding development of literary poetry, and that in which he worked in a spirit of folk song. It may be generally said that in the former he is subjective; in the latter, objective and impersonal. The two aspects of Nekrásov are very different, but it is the combination of the two that makes his unique personality. On the whole the traditionally literary part of his work is much the more uneven of the two. Its lower strata merge in the absolutely inartistic and mechanical verse mongery in which he engaged in the early forties and which he never abandoned. Much of that which was particularly highly praised by his contemporaries for its civic and humanistic contents today seems rather a negative item in the legacy of Nekrásov. On the other hand, his ironic and satirical poems probably find more response in us than they did in our fathers and grandfathers. The biting and bilious, tersely concentrated sarcasm of such a condensed masterpiece as *The Thief* is enough to place Nekrásov in the front rank of the world's greatest satirists. And in most cases his poems of rhetorical invective have won from the action of time more than the lesser Nekrásov has lost. Personally I think that such a poem as the elegy *Home* is one the highest pinnacles of Russian poetry, and leaves most of the poetical invective of Lérmontov simply nowhere. Another group of Nekrásov's poems that have won by the lapse of time are his love lyrics—remarkably original in their unsweetened, unsentimental, poignantly passionate, and tragic accounts of a love that brings more pain than joy to both parties. Lastly, among his very earliest poems (1846) there is that veritably immortal poem which so many people (Grigóriev, among others, and Rózanov) have felt and experienced as something more than poetry, that poem of tragic love on the brink of starvation and moral degradation which begins: "Whether I am driving in the night down a dark street" (*"Édu li nóchiu po úlitse tëmnoy"*). The same intensity is often present in the poems written during his last illness (*Last Songs*).

Of his objective and narrative poems, *Sásha* (1856), which he was accused of plagarizing from Turgénev's *Rúdin*, is an attempt at a problem story in verse and, though it contains some beautiful passages, compares very poorly with the novels of Turgénev. Much more interesting are the numerous chiefly short and dramatic narrative poems of peasant life. Among the most famous is *Vlas* (1854), one of those poems in which Nekrásov gave proof of his sympathy, not only with the people's sufferings, but also with their religious ideals. The most ambitious of his poems not in folk-song style is the majestic and statuesque *Frost the Red-Nosed* (1863), with its almost mythological idealization of the Russian peasant woman and the grand pictures of the silent and frozen forest.

In his folk-song poetry Nekrásov transcends his *moi haïssable*, frees himself from his torturing obsessions of suffering, and becomes the poet of more than individual expression. This is already noticeable in the poems for children, especially in the delightful *General Toptýgin* (where a performing bear is taken by a terrorized postmaster for an angry general). But it is especially apparent in the most singing of all Nekrásov's poems, *The Pedlars* (1861) a story ultimately of tragic content but told in a lusty and vigorous major key. The opening of the poem in particular has been appropriated by the people as a folk song. It is perhaps the most genuinely popular snatch of song in the whole range of Russian literary poetry. A very different note is struck in the same poem by the weirdly effective *Song of the Wanderer*, one of the most powerful and purely original ever written by Nekrásov. It is one of those poems which are human because (in Synge's phrase, so often applicable to Nekrásov) they are brutal.

Nekrásov's greatest achievement in the folk-song style, and perhaps his greatest achievement altogether, is the vast, realistic satire *Who Is Happy in Russia?* at which he worked in the seventies. The poem relates how seven peasants, to settle the question as to who lives happily in Russia, set out on foot to walk the round of the country. They meet representatives of various classes of society, the Squire, the Parson, the Peasant Woman, and so on. They are told tales of extraordinary moral achievements, heroism, and crime, and the poem ends on a note of joyful confidence in the future of the people with the help of the new democratic intelligentsia. The style is full of originality, wonderfully racy and vigorous. The poet never lets himself fall into his usual subjective lamentations, but conducts the story in a tone of keen and often good-humored, shrewd satire, in a popular style, with frequent scenes of strong and simple realism, and occasionally a heroic note when speaking of the virtues of the strong Russian peasant. Full of remarkable verbal expressiveness, vigor, and inventiveness, the poem is one of the most original productions of nineteenth-century Russian poetry.

THE UTTER DECLINE OF POETRY

From 1860 to the end of the seventies there appeared no new poet of even tolerable mediocrity. Both parties—the civic poets and the partisans of "pure art"—were equally poor. The latter, it is true, produced in Constantine Sluchévsky (1837–1904) a poet of real significance. But after a short first appearance in 1857–60, he, like Fet, disappeared from the scene for almost twenty years, not to reappear before the end of the seventies. He had a genuinely original vision of the world, the foundation of real genius, and he seemed the man to create a really new, really modern poetry, but his ill luck in falling on times of exceptionally low technical culture never allowed him to develop into anything better than a stammerer.

The only other poet of the period worth mentioning is Dmítry Nikoláyevich Sadóvnikov (1843–83), a native of Simbírsk, who attempted to create a sort of local Volga poetry, of which the most famous example is the well-known, but now anonymous (for no one remembers the authorship) ballad of *Sténka Rázin and the Persian Princess.*

In the absence of original poetry there developed in the sixties and seventies an enormous translating activity. Very severe to native poets, the extreme anti-æstheticians retained a degree of reverence for certain foreign reputations, especially for those which were in some way or other connected with revolution—Byron, Béranger, and Heine. Byron retained much of his old reputation— and was given lip service even by Písarev. And it is hardly an exaggeration to say that Béranger and Heine, in translation, were more popular with the wide mass of the intelligentsia than any Russian poet.

THE DRAMA

Realism had a simpler and more unilinear development on the Russian stage than it had in the Russian novel. Its history may be summed up in a few representative names in a way the parallel periods of fiction cannot. Its three phases are dominated, the first (roughly 1830–50) by a great actor, the second (1850–95) by a great playwright, the third by a great producer. They are respectively Schépkin, Ostróvsky, and Stanislávsky. Schépkin was the pioneer of realistic acting. But his roots were deep in the classical tradition of universal human truths, and the realism he sought was not that of the particular, but of general human nature. His art was an art of psychological, not of social, types. The second phase of Russian scenic realism concentrated on social realism, on the least universal, and most individual, aspects of a given social milieu. It became "ethnographical" realism—or, to use the technical Russian term, the realism of *byt*, which means life considered in its local and temporal aspects.

This phase found its complete expression in the plays of Ostróvsky and in the acting of Prov Sadóvsky (1818–72), the personal friend of the dramatist. The first representation of a play by Ostróvsky (1853) inaugurated the new theatrical era, which lasted for half a century.

Ostróvsky gives his name and impress to the period. Like the contemporary novel, the drama in his hands tended to become a selected arrangement of slices of life, with the minimum of adaptation to scenic demands. The same tendency is apparent in the dramatic work of Turgénev, who at the beginning of his career hesitated for some time between devoting himself to drama and devoting himself to fiction. With the exception of Písemsky, Turgénev, of all the novelists, is the most important as a playwright.[1] His plays belong to the years 1843–52. They are largely experimental gropings after an adequate personal form of expression. The most stageable is the *Provincial Lady*, a delicately characterized light comedy (1851). The most interesting historically is *A Month in the Country* (1850), a psychological play on the time-

---

[1] Of the other great novelists, Saltykóv wrote the comedy *The Death of Pazúkhin*, which was staged by Stanislávsky in 1914. Most of Tolstóy's plays belong to the period after 1880.

honored theme of the rivalry in love between a mature woman and a young girl, which in style and construction (absence of apparent action and complexity of inner psychological and atmospheric pattern) has an obvious foretaste of Chékhov.

OSTRÓVSKY

Alexander Nikoláyevich Ostróvsky (1823–86) was born in Moscow, on the south side of the river, in the center of the merchant residential quarter. His father was a government clerk and afterward a sort of lawyer whose practice was among the merchants of the South Side. The dramatist went to the University, but in 1843, after a row with the University authorities, left and entered the government service as a clerk of the Commercial Court. The eight years he spent at the court were an important addition to his early experiences at home in the Moscow merchant community and served him well in his later knowledge of its *byt*. His first work was published in 1847. This was a fragment of a comedy, *The Bankrupt*, which was completed in 1849. The first of his plays to be produced on the stage was *The Poor Bride*, in 1853. After that, and till his death, no year passed without a new, original play of his appearing on the stage of the imperial theaters. The height of his popularity was reached simultaneously with that of Turgénev, Goncharóv, and Písemsky in the years 1856–60. After the latter date Ostróvsky's popularity, though it did not decline, came to a standstill, and critics and public began to insist on the superiority of his earlier to his new plays.

Between 1847 and 1886 Ostróvsky wrote about forty plays in prose [2] besides eight in blank verse. They are of unequal merit, but taken as a whole, doubtless the most remarkable body of dramatic work in Russian. Griboyédov and Gógol had written great and original plays, and each of them is a man of greater genius than Ostróvsky, but it was left to Ostróvsky to create a school of Russian drama, a Russian theater that may be put by the side of the national theaters of the West, if not on equal, at least on comparable terms. The limitations of Ostróvsky's art are obvious. His plays (with few exceptions) are neither tragedies nor

[2] Among other things, he translated *The Taming of the Shrew* and the interludes of Cervantes.

comedies, but belong to the middle and bastard kind of drama.
The dramatic skeleton in most of them, sacrificed to the exigencies
of the slice-of-life method, lacks the firm consistency of classical
art. With few exceptions his plays are devoid of poetry, and even
where poetry is present, as it is in *The Thunderstorm*, it is a poetry
of atmosphere, not of words and texture. Though an admirable
master of individualized and typical dialogue, Ostróvsky is not a
master of language in the sense Gógol, Leskóv, or (to use an English instance) Synge was. His language is purely representational;
he uses it truthfully, but uncreatively. His very raciness of the
Russian soil is in a certain sense a limitation, for his plays are
always narrowly native and do not have universal significance.
Were it not for this limitation, and had he been universal in his
nationality, Ostróvsky's place would have been among the greatest. The breadth, the grasp, the variety of Ostróvsky's vision of
Russian life are almost infinite. He is the least subjective of Russian
writers. His would be a hopeless case for the psychoanalyst. His
characters are not in any sense emanations of himself. They are
genuine reflections of "the other." He is no psychologist; his characters are not, as Tolstóy's are, inner worlds to which we are
introduced by a supreme power of intuition; they are just people
as seen by other people. But this superficial realism is not the
external, pictorial realism of Gógol and Goncharóv, but a truly
dramatic realism, for it gives the characters in their relations to
the other characters, which is the simplest and oldest way of
narrative and dramatic characterization by speech and action,
enriched only by an enormous wealth of social, ethnographic detail. And in spite of this superficiality, they have the individuality
and the uniqueness we recognize in our fellow creatures, even
without getting inside their skull.

These general remarks on the art of Ostróvsky refer chiefly
to his early and most characteristic work, up to about 1861. The
subject matter of these plays is taken for the most part from the
life of Moscow and provincial merchants and of the lower strata
of the official world. The vast and varied picture of the conservative and un-Europeanized life of the Russian merchants was what
struck his contemporaries most strongly in the work of Ostróvsky,
for the reality underlying literary creation interested them more
than the art that transformed it. The critics of the fifties spilled
endless ink over the elucidation of Ostróvsky's attitude towards

the conservative mainstays of the merchant class. He himself gave disconcertingly abundant food for such discussions and for every kind of interpretation, for his artistic sympathy is distributed in different ways in different plays. Every interpretation, from the most enthusiastic idealization of stolid conservatism and patriarchal despotism to the fierce denunciation of the merchants as an unredeemed kingdom of darkness, could find a peg to hang on in the text of the plays. As for Ostróvsky's own attitude, it was simply unstable, or, to be more exact, the moral and social attitude was a secondary thing to him. His task was to build plays out of the elements of reality as he saw it. An attitude of sympathy or antipathy was to him entirely a matter of dramatic expediency, of pure technique, for, though an "anti-artificial" realist, he felt very keenly the inner laws along which, and not along those of life, he had to construct each play. So his moral judgment over the tyrannical merchant paterfamilias depended on his dramatic function in the particular play. Apart from this it is extraordinarily difficult to extract a social and political *Weltanschauung* out of Ostróvsky.

Technically speaking, the most interesting of all Ostróvsky's plays are the first two, *The Bankrupt* (written 1847–9, published in 1850 under the title *Among Friends One Always Comes to Terms*) and *The Poor Bride* (published 1852, acted 1853). The former was as striking and sensational a beginning for a young author as there is on record in Russian literary history. Gógol in *Marriage* had given an example of a characteristic painting of the merchant milieu. In particular the character of the professional matchmaker practicing among the merchants was already abundantly exploited. In the inclusion of none but unsympathetic characters Ostróvsky also followed the example of Gógol in *Revizór*. But here he went one better and discarded the most time-honored of all traditions of comedy—the poetic justice that punishes vice. The triumph of vice, and precisely of the most unredeemed of all the characters, gives Ostróvsky's play its particular note of bold originality. It was this which incensed even such an old realist as Schépkin, who thought the play cynical and dirty. The realism of Ostróvsky, in spite of the obvious influence of Gógol, is in substance of an opposite nature to Gógol's. It is free from all expressiveness for the sake of expressiveness; it keeps clear of caricature and farce; it is based on a solid, intimate, first-hand knowledge of the life described. The dialogue aims at truthfulness to life, not at verbal richness. The art of using realistic speech without producing the effect of grotesqueness and without obtruding it is a characteristic art of the Russian realists, but it reaches its perfection in Ostróv- sky. Finally the untheatrical construction is entirely un-Gogolian, and in the deliberate discarding of all tricks and contrivances at scenic effect Ostróvsky from the outset attains his best. The mainstay of the play is the characters, and the plot is entirely a result of the characters. But the characters are taken in their social aspect. They are not men and women in general, but Mos- cow merchants and assistants, and cannot be torn away from the social setting.

The Poor Bride is entirely different in tone and atmosphere from *The Bankrupt*. The milieu is not merchants but minor offi- cials. The unpleasantness of it is redeemed by the character of the heroine, a strong girl, in no way inferior to and more actively alive than the heroines of Turgénev. She ends characteristically, after being let down by her romantic, ideal admirer, in submitting to her fate and marrying the successful brute Benevolénsky, who can alone save her mother from imminent ruin. All the characters are masterpieces, and Ostróvsky's skill at building the action en- tirely on the characters is at its best. But what is especially re- markable is the last act—a bold technical novelty. The play ends on a mass scene, where the crowd discusses the marriage of Benevolénsky and where a wonderfully new note is introduced by the appearance in the crowd of his former mistress. The delicacy and pregnancy of these last scenes, in which the heroes hardly appear, were really a new word in dramatic art. Ostróvsky's power of creating atmospheric poetry is revealed for the first time in this fifth act of *The Poor Bride*. In *Poverty Is No Crime* (1854) Ostróvsky went still further in de-theatricalizing the theater, but with less intrinsic success. The immediate success of the play was great, owing to the original and Slavophil character of the noble drunkard, the ruined merchant Lyubím Tortsóv, who has re- mained one of the most popular roles in the Russian repertory. But as a play it is much less satisfactory, and the "sliciness" of the technique inclines to mere looseness.

Of the plays written in 1856–61, *The Ward* (1859) attains to almost intolerable power in the painting of a character that often reappears in his later work—the selfish, rich, and self-righteous

old woman. The three short comedies united by the character of
the silly and conceited young clerk Balzamínov (1858–61) are his
masterpieces in the comic vein for the characters of Balzamínov
and of his mother, fondly doting and yet fully conscious of her
son's extreme silliness, and for the saturated painting of their social
environment. In another comedy of the same period *Your Drink—
My Hangover* (*V chuzhóm pirú pokhmélie,* 1856), Ostróvsky concentrated into the character of the merchant Kit Kítych all the
essence of the *samodúr*—the willful domestic tyrant who is decided
to make everyone do "what my left toe wishes," but who is easily
bulliable.

By far the most significant work of this period, and ultimately the masterpiece of Ostróvsky, is *The Thunderstorm* (1860).
It is the most famous of his plays and has been most abundantly
written about. Dobrolyúbov took it as the text for one of his most
effective and influential sermons against the dark forces of conservatism and tradition, and Grigóriev saw in it the highest expression of Ostróvsky's love for the traditional life and character
of the undefiled Russian middle classes. In reality it is a purely
poetical work, a purely atmospheric creation, a great poem of love
and death, of freedom and thralldom. It is intensely local and
Russian, and the saturation of the atmosphere with the very essence of Russian *byt* and Russian poetical feeling makes it hardly
understandable to a foreigner. For every detail of it is intensified
by the background of a whole emotional tradition (expressed perhaps best of all in the lyrical songs of the Russian people), and
without this background it loses most of its appeal. *The Thunderstorm* is a rare example of a supreme masterpiece built of exclusively national material.

After 1861 Ostróvsky sought new ways. He devoted himself
at one time to historical plays (*v. infra*), and in his prose plays he
departed from much of his original novelty. He almost abandoned
the merchant milieu, which under the influence of the Reforms
and of the spread of education was rapidly transforming into a
drabber middle class, and he more and more submitted to the
traditional method of playmaking, never, however, condescending
to use the mere artificial and improbable tricks of the French
school. Owing to his example, Russia, unlike most other countries,
succeeded in keeping clear from the all-pervading school of Scribe
and Sardou. Still there are more intrigue and plot in most of his

later than in his early plays, and though the critics as a rule disapproved of them, some later plays of Ostróvsky (*Enough Simplicity in Every Wise Man*, 1868; *The Forest*, 1871; *Wolves and Sheep*, 1875) proved even greater favorites with the public than his more characteristic early masterpieces. The first two are distinctly among his best work, and *The Forest* shares with *The Thunderstorm* the honor of being regarded as his masterpiece. Less exclusively original, the comedy is extraordinarily rich in its character drawing. Of all Ostróvsky's plays, it is the one in which the essential nobility of man is most triumphantly asserted. But it also contains the most unsweetened types of cynical and complacent meanness and selfishness in the whole of Russian literature.

Ostróvsky never stood still, but always sought for new ways and methods. In his later plays (*The Dowerless Girl*, 1879) he attempted a more psychological method of character drawing. But on the whole his later plays mark a certain drying-up of his creative sources. At the time of his death he dominated the Russian stage by the mass of his work. But the successors he left were minor and uncreative men, who were capable only of writing plays with "grateful parts" for the excellent actors and actresses brought up in the school of Schépkin and of Ostróvsky, but not of carrying on a vital tradition of literary drama.

SUKHOVÓ-KOBÝLIN, PÍSEMSKY, AND MINOR DRAMATISTS

The only two contemporary dramatists who come at all near to Ostróvsky, if not for the quantity, at least from the quality of their work, were Sukhovó-Kobýlin and Písemsky, both of whom are more traditional, more "artificial," and more theatrical than he.

Alexander Vasílievich Sukhovó-Kobýlin (1817–1903) was a typical educated nobleman of his generation, soaked in Hegel and in German idealism. He considered metaphysics his true vocation, and playwriting was only a short episode in his life. The wonderful thing is that neither his metaphysical bent nor the unprofessionality of his playwriting has left any impress on his plays. They are curiously free from ideas, and as for sheer stagecraft they have no rivals in Russian literary drama. The one important event in Sukhovó-Kobýlin's life was the murder of his mistress in 1850.

He was suspected of being guilty of the crime, and for seven years he was under trial (at one time in prison); only in 1857 was he finally acquitted. The episode, which brought him face to face with the horror and ineptitude of the pre-Reform law courts, left a profound trace in him and filled him with that bitter hatred for all the official class which informs his two later plays. All his work consists of only three comedies: *The Wedding of Krechínsky* (acted 1855), *The Affair*, and *The Death of Tarélkin*. The latter two appeared in print in 1869, but were prohibited for the stage till much later. *The Wedding of Krechínsky* is a pure comedy of picaresque intrigue in which the rogue triumphs over the stupidity of the virtuous characters. The critics found it lacking in ideas and too dependent in plot, too French in style. But the public made it a tremendous success, and it became one of the favorite and securest plays of the Russian repertory. For general familiarity with the text it rivals *Góre ot umá* and *Revizór*.

The Affair and *The Death of Tarélkin* are very different in tone. They are satires that, in the author's own phrase, are calculated, not to make the audience laugh, but shudder. The savage bitterness of the satire is such that by their side Saltykóv seems harmless. They were too much even for the radicals of the sixties. Sukhovó-Kobýlin used in them methods of grotesque exaggeration and improbable caricature in the way Gógol had used them, but much more fearlessly and savagely—methods that were profoundly alien to the spirit of Russian realism. *The Death of Tarélkin* is a thing unique in its way, combining, as it were, the wisely calculated cruelty of Ben Jonson with the passionately serious rage of Swift.

Písemsky began his dramatic career with comedies (*The Hypochondriac*, 1852), in which he abundantly availed himself of the Gogolian tradition of farce and obvious incongruity. But his greatest achievement was in realistic tragedy. This genre is represented in Russian literature by practically only two plays—Písemsky's *A Hard Lot* (1859) and Tolstóy's *Power of Darkness*. For all the intensity and power of the latter, an unprejudiced critical judgment can hardly fail to conclude that, if the two are equal in human and tragic significance, Písemsky's is the greater play, the completer artistic success. It has the tensity and inevitability of the classical drama, and while *Power of Darkness* is best of all defined as a morality play, *A Hard Lot* is a genuine tragedy with that supreme logical unity which is the great characteristic of the plays of Racine. The subject, like those of Racine, is simple, almost geometrical. A squire, a weakling of the Hamlet, idealist type, has seduced, in the absence of her husband, the wife of one of his serfs. The husband is a strong character of the type that occurs in Písemsky's and Leskóv's popular stories. Though a serf, he is a prosperous tradesman and has made money in Petersburg. He returns home (this is the initial situation) and by degrees discovers the guilt of his wife and reacts accordingly. The squire is the master of the husband, while the husband is the master of his wife—so it is a conflict between, on the one hand, the squire's rights as a serf owner and the dignity of his serf; on the other, between the rights of free love (an essential point is that the squire and the serf's wife do love each other) and the rights of the master of the house over his wife. The double conflict is unfolded with supreme mastery, and the spectator's sympathy is held in balance between the rights of human dignity and the rights of free love. The tragedy ends in the husband's killing the lovers' child and then (a trait particularly praised by Russian critics but suggested to Písemsky by the actor Martýnov) delivering himself into the hand of the law.

Písemsky's later plays do not come up to the high standard of *A Hard Lot*. They consist of two cycles—a series of historical melodramas of the eighteenth century and a series of dramas satirizing the money-making frenzy of the sixties and seventies. The former are tantalizing and strange creations. Their dramatic manner is terse, almost sketchy. They are full of rapid and melodramatic incident. The dramatist seems willfully to avoid the finer touch, and gives an almost puppet-theater psychology. Yet these plays have a strange fascination and, if revived on the stage, should prove extraordinarily effective. The satirical plays of contemporary life are akin to Sukhovó-Kobýlin's in the savageness of their satire. But they are long and technically imperfect and show a distinct decline of the writer's creative forces.

The numerous minor dramatists of the period partly endeavored to assimilate Ostróvsky's methods in the portrayal of Russian *byt*, partly wrote what were called "plays of exposure," that is to say, denunciations of various official and social vices, especially of pre-Reform conditions. Here also the lead had been given by Ostróvsky in *A Profitable Post*. The real rival, in the public favor, of the literary realistic drama of Ostróvsky was the operetta of Offenbach, which in the latter half of the sixties flooded the Russian stage and relegated into a comparative unpopularity all other forms of dramatic art. But it remained a purely imported commodity, and no attempt was made by Russian authors to imitate it.

THE COSTUME PLAY

By the end of the forties the pseudo-romantic drama of Kúkolnik and his like had lost all credit. It was not till some ten years later that there began a new movement to revive the verse drama. Its starting point was the example of Púshkin's *Borís Godunóv*. The first to begin the movement was the poet Mey, whose *Maid of Pskov* (1860), a conventionally pretty drama of the times of Iván the Terrible, started a continuous series of plays on subjects from Old Russian history before the time of Peter the Great, chiefly from the Moscow period. In spite of the solid historical knowledge at the basis of most of these plays, they are, as a whole, remarkably lacking in Old Russian flavor. Old Russia was to the authors, and still more to the public, above all a land of picturesque and luxurious "boyar costumes." Its life was seen through the prism of the European romantic drama, and the motive of romantic love, so alien to the spirit of real Muscovy, was almost inevitably introduced into every play. The great drawback of all these plays is their language (which is the conventional language of contemporary poetry larded with idioms from old documents and from folklore), and especially their meter—blank verse. Besides the technical laxity common to the verse writers of the period, Russian blank verse, even in Púshkin's hand, has always been the least Russian of meters, and is always suggestive of translation; the only really effective romantic blank verse in the language is Púshkin's in the Little Tragedies, which all deal with subjects from foreign life.[3] The use of it in dramas of Muscovite life is particularly inappropriate. Lastly, the example of *Borís Godunóv* and of

[3] And, it is true, in *Rusálka*, but *Rusálka* is, in the exact sense of the word, unique, a miracle and no example; besides, the Russian element in *Rusálka* is not Muscovite, and is, as it were, universalized.

the common model, the histories of Shakspere, is responsible for the excess detail and the overcrowding of the stage with secondary personages. Altogether the school as a whole must be regarded as unsatisfactory and one of the least original and least significant of Russian literary developments.

This is not to say that the plays of its best representatives are devoid of merit. Ostróvsky's chronicles (1862–8) are distinctly the poorest part of all his work, though *historically* they are often interesting and suggestive. Infinitely better is *The Snow Maiden* (*Snegúrochka*), which is the only really poetical romantic comedy in the language. Based on somewhat naïvely interpreted mythological material, it is full of that atmospheric poetry of which Ostróvsky gave such a masterpiece in *The Thunderstorm*. But in *The Snow Maiden* the nature poetry is all transfused with a delicate humor, owing to which even the ineffective blank verse of Ostróvsky loses much of its inadequacy. And in the songs he finally transcended all his limitations and unexpectedly created genuinely folklore-like poetry that can almost be compared with Nekrásov's.

Alexéy Tolstóy is superior to Ostróvsky as an historical dramatist. Though all the strictures on the school in general apply to him as well, his famous historical trilogy (*The Death of Iván the Terrible*, 1866; *Tsar Theodore*, 1868; and *Tsar Borís*, 1870) deserves to a certain extent its high reputation. The plays are intellectually *interesting* and suggestive. They are full of excellent character drawing. In most cases it is, perhaps, intelligent and shrewd rather than genuinely imaginative. But in the character of Tsar Theodore, Alexéy Tolstóy succeeded in creating one of the most interesting figures in Russian literature—the good and weak sovereign, with an unerring sense of values and a complete inability to impose his good will on his crafty councilor.

The principal interest of all this drama is its connection with the far more vigorous growth of the Russian opera; Rímsky-Kórsakov's librettist, Bélsky, was one of its best writers, and above all it can claim kinship with the greatest Russian tragic poet of the period, Modést Musórgsky. Musórgsky himself wrote the libretto of *Khovánschina* and adapted with great skill Púshkin's *Borís Godunóv* to make his popular opera. That he had dramatic as well as musical genius cannot be denied, but the literary his-

torian unfortunately has no right to appropriate him or to sever
the dramatic from the musical texture of his dramas. The *spirit*
of Musórgsky was very different from that of his contemporary
dramatists, and his real spiritual kin in literature were Nekrásov
and Dostoyévsky.

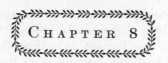

CHAPTER 8

The Age of Realism: The Novelists (II)

TOLSTÓY (BEFORE 1880)

TWENTY years ago [1] there was no difference of opinion outside Russia as to who was the greatest of Russian writers— Tolstóy dominated Russian literature in a way that no writer had dominated a national literature in the eyes of the world since the death of Goethe, or even, if we think of the enormous extraliterary prestige of Tolstóy, since the days of Voltaire. Since then the wheel of fashion, or the laws of growth of the occidental mind, has displaced Tolstóy from his place of ascendancy and substituted for his the idols of Dostoyévsky and, in these last years (strangest of occidental whims), of Chékhov. It is left to the future to show whether the wheel will turn again, or whether the advanced elite of the Western world has definitely reached a stage of mental senility that can be satisfied only by the autumnal genius of Chékhov.

For his own compatriots Tolstóy, though often preferred to all other writers, never was the center or the symbol of Russian literature as a whole—a part irrevertibly belonging to Púshkin. The enormous moral and personal prestige he enjoyed in the last twenty-five years of his life was not inevitably linked with a recognition of his absolute literary supremacy. But the permanence of Tolstóy has never been put to question, and, as far as we can see ahead, never will be. To compare him to Chékhov is as impossible to a level-headed Russian as it is to say that Brussels is a bigger city than London. The actuality, the influence of Tolstóy may have its ebb and flow; we may (as we happen to do today)

[1] This passage (with a few others in similar tone) has been preserved for its special interest for the English-speaking reader, who should remember that it was first published in 1927.—Editor

find nothing we should like ourselves to imitate in *War and Peace;* but the star of Tolstóy will never be eclipsed by any other body. Humanly speaking, it is impossible to deny that he was the biggest man (not the best, nor perhaps even the greatest, but just morally the bulkiest) that trod the Russian soil within the last few lifetimes; the biggest man, if not the greatest artist, in all Russian literary history.

The bigness of Tolstóy has seemed to me sufficient to justify a procedure that would have been disastrously unfair to anyone of lesser bulk: I have cut him in two between this and its companion volume, and the reader will find an account of his work after 1880 in my *Contemporary Russian Literature.*[2] If I were mainly concerned with Tolstóy the man, this halving him between two volumes would be unjustifiable—the essential unity of the young and the old Tolstóy is an all-important point to every student of his personality and, especially, of his ideas. But literary history is concerned with literature, which is a supra-personal growth, and in which biography and psychology are matters of secondary importance as compared to the supra-personal evolution of a nation's literature as a whole and of its component parts, the evolutions of the individual genres. It so happens that Tolstóy's conversion, about 1880, to the religion of his later years coincided with a profound change in his artistic views and aims that was partly conditioned by that conversion but was also an independent literary development with a definite place of its own in the general evolution of Russian literature, and was almost a negation of the whole achievement of the realistic school. In this chapter I am concerned only with that of Tolstóy's work in which he is a typical, even an extreme (if in certain points eccentric), representative of the main tendencies of the Russian realistic school, its finest flower and highest æsthetic justification.

Count Leo Nikoláyevich Tolstóy was born on August 28, 1828, on his father's estate of Yásnaya Polyána, in the Province of Túla. The Tolstóys are a family of old Russian nobility, and the writer's mother was born a Princess Volkónsky. His father and mother are respectively the starting points for the characters of Nicholas Rostóv and Princess Márya in *War and Peace.* They belonged to the best Russian nobility, and this fact of belonging by birth to the upper layer of the ruling class marks off Tolstóy very

[2] Published as Book II of this edition.—Editor

distinctly from the other writers of his time. He always remained
a class-conscious nobleman (even when this class consciousness
became purely negative) and kept aloof from the intelligentsia.

Tolstóy's childhood and boyhood were passed between Moscow and Yásnaya Polyána, in a large family of several brothers.
He has left us an extraordinarily vivid record of his early human
environment in the wonderful notes he wrote for his biographer
P. I. Biryukóv. He lost his mother when he was two, and his
father when he was nine. His subsequent education was in the
hands of his aunt, Mlle Érgolsky, who is supposed to be the starting point for Sónya in *War and Peace*. In 1844 Tolstóy matriculated
at the University of Kazán, where he studied first oriental languages and afterward law, but which he left in 1847 without re-
ceiving a degree. In 1849 he settled down at Yásnaya Polyána,
where he attempted to be useful to his peasants but soon discovered the ineffectiveness of his uninformed zeal. Much of the
life he led at the University and after leaving it was of a kind
usual with young men of his class, irregular and full of pleasure
seeking—wine, cards, and women—not entirely unlike the life
led by Púshkin before his exile to the south. But Tolstóy was incapable of that lighthearted acceptance of life as it came. From
the very beginning, his diary (which is extant from 1847) reveals
an insatiate thirst for a rational and moral justification of life, a
thirst that forever remained the ruling force of his mind. The same
diary was his first experiment in forging that technique of psychological analysis which was to become his principal literary weapon.
To the year 1851 belongs his first attempt at a more ambitious and
more definitely creative kind of writing.

In the same year, sick of his empty and useless life in Moscow,
he went off to the Caucasus, where he joined an artillery unit
garrisoned in the Cossack country on the Térek, as a *junker*—that
is to say, a volunteer of private rank, but of noble birth. In 1852
he completed his first story (*Childhood*) and sent it to Nekrásov
for publication in the *Sovreménnik*. The story had a considerable
and immediate success and gave Tolstóy a definite place in literature.

In his battery Tolstóy lived, in agreeable billets, the rather
easy and unoccupied life of a *junker* of means. He had much spare
time, and most of it was spent in hunting. In the little fighting he
saw, he did very well. In 1854 he received his commission and was,

at his request, transferred to the army operating against the Turks in Wallachia, where he took part in the siege of Silistria. In November of the same year he joined the garrison of Sevastópol. There he saw very serious fighting. He took part in the defense of the famous Fourth Bastion and in the battle of Chërnaya Réchka, the bad management of which he satirized in a humorous song, the only piece of verse he is known to have written.[3] In Sevastópol he wrote his famous *Sevastópol Stories*, which, appearing as they did in the *Sovreménnik* while the siege was still on, greatly increased the general interest in their author. Soon after the abandonment of the fortress, Tolstóy went on leave of absence to Petersburg and Moscow, and the following year he left the army.

These years after the Crimean War were the only time in Tolstóy's life when he mixed with the literary world. He was welcomed by the littérateurs of Petersburg and Moscow as one of their most eminent fellow craftsmen. As he confessed afterwards, his vanity and pride were greatly flattered by his success. But he did not get on with them. He was too much of an aristocrat to like this semi-Bohemian intelligentsia. They were too self-consciously plebeian for him, while they resented the way he obviously preferred "society" to their company. Cutting epigrams on this subject passed between him and Turgénev. On the other hand, all the structure of his mind was against the grain of the progressive Westernizers. The way they stated their problems was uninteresting to him. He did not believe in progress or culture. His lack of sympathy with the literary world was increased by their disappointment in his new work. All he had written since *Childhood* had shown no advance from the point of view of artistic perfection, and his critics failed to realize the experimental value of this imperfect work. All this made his connection with the literary world short-lived. It culminated in a resounding quarrel with Turgénev (1861), whom he challenged and afterward apologized to for so doing. The whole story is very characteristic and revelatory of his character, with its profound and sensitive self-consciousness and impatience of other people's assumed superiority. The only writers with whom he remained friends were the reactionary and "landlordist" Fet and the democratic Slavophil

---

[3] Professor George R. Noyes has pointed out to me that this statement is not quite correct. There is also a letter in verse, written to Fet on November 12, 1872.— Editor

Strákhov, both of them men entirely out of tune with the main current of contemporary progressive thought.

The years 1856–61 were passed between Petersburg, Moscow, and Yásnaya, and foreign countries. In 1857 (and again in 1860–1) he traveled abroad, and returned disgusted by the selfishness and materialism of European bourgeois civilization. In 1859 he started a school for peasant children at Yásnaya, and in 1862 published a pedagogical magazine, *Yásnaya Polyána*, in which he astonished the progressive world by contending that it was not the intellectuals who should teach the peasants, but rather the peasants the intellectuals. In 1861 he accepted the post of Arbiter of the Peace, a magistrature that had been introduced to supervise the carrying into life of the Emancipation Act. Meanwhile his insatiate quest for moral stability continued to torment him. He had now abandoned the wild living of his youth, and thought of marrying. In 1856 he made his first unsuccessful attempt to marry (Mlle Arséniev). In 1860 he was profoundly affected by the death of his brother Nicholas, which was for him the first encounter with the inevitable reality of death. In 1862, at last, after long hesitations (he was convinced that since he was old—thirty-four!—and ugly, no woman could love him) he proposed to Sophie Andréyevna Behrs and was accepted. They were married in the September of the same year.

His marriage is one of the two most important landmarks in the life of Tolstóy, the other being his conversion. He was always dominated by one preoccupation—how to justify his life before his conscience and thus attain a stable moral welfare. In his bachelor years he oscillated between two opposite desires. One was a passionate and hopeless aspiration after that whole and unreflecting "natural" state which he found among the peasants, and especially among the Cossacks in whose villages he had lived in the Caucasus—a state that has no need to justify life because it is free from the consciousness that demands such a justification. He tried to find such an unquestioning state in a deliberate surrender to the animal impulses—in living the life of his friends and (here he was nearest to attaining it) in his favorite occupation of hunting. But he seemed incapable of finding it for good, and the other equally passionate desire—to find a rational justification of life—tore him away every time he hoped he had attained the goal of self-satisfaction. His marriage was for him the gate towards a

more stable and lasting "natural state." Family life, and an un-
reasoning acceptance of and submission to the life to which he
was born, now became his religion.

For the first fifteen years of his married life he lived in this
blissful state of confidently satisfied vegetable life, whose philosophy is expressed with supreme creative power in *War and Peace.*
In his family life he was exceptionally and shamelessly happy.
Sophie Andréyevna, almost a girl when he married her, was easily
molded into the form he desired, and informed with his new philosophy, of which, to the later undoing of the household, she became the impregnable rock and unalterable depository. She proved
an ideal wife and mother and mistress of the house. She was, moreover, a devoted help to her husband in his literary work, and the
story is well known how she copied out *War and Peace* seven
times from beginning to end. The family fortune, owing to Tolstóy's efficient management of his estates and to the sales of his
works, was prosperous, making it possible to provide adequately
for the increasing family. But Tolstóy, though absorbed and
largely satisfied by his self-justified life, though glorifying it with
unsurpassed imaginative power in his greatest novel, was not
capable of being merged in family life as his wife had become
merged. Nor could his "life in art" absorb him as it did his fellow
craftsmen. The worm of moral thirst, reduced at one time to
negligible proportions, could never die. Tolstóy was constantly
agitated by moral problems and moral urges. In 1866 he was
counsel (unsuccessfully) before a court-martial for a soldier accused of striking an officer. In 1873 he published articles on
popular education which enabled that shrewd critic Mikhaylóvsky
practically to predict the later developments of his ideas. *Anna
Karénina,* written in 1873–7, is appreciably less "vegetable" and
more moralistic than *War and Peace.* While he was writing that
second novel, the crisis overcame him that led to his conversion,
described with Biblical power in *A Confession.* It was caused by a
growing obsession of the reality of death, which again brought
forward the unquenchable thirst and need for ultimate justification. At first it led Tolstóy to the Orthodox Church. But his all-
pervading rationalism led him on to a purely rational religion that
accepted only the moral without the theological and mystical
doctrines of Christianity, and that became at last the final justification for which his spirit had yearned. In 1879 the process was

at an end, and in 1880 he began *A Confession*. Only in 1884, largely under the influence of Chertkóv, Tolstóy began an active propaganda for his new religion. In his personal life his conversion led to an estrangement from his wife, whom he was this time unable to mold nearer to his heart's changed desire. The story of his later years, up to his death in 1910, is outlined in the second part of this volume.

Tolstóy's conversion coincided with an important change in the style and manner of his imaginative writings. He discarded the methods he had used in his earlier work, the dissecting analysis of the subconscious and semiconscious workings of the human mind, and all that he later on (in *What Is Art?*) condemned as "superfluous detail." In his early work he was a representative man of the Russian realistic school, which relied entirely on the method of "superfluous detail" that had been introduced by Gógol. It was "superfluous" detail that gave the particular and individual convincingness that is the very essence of the realistic novel. The general effect of such detail is to bring out the particular, the individual, the local, and the temporary at the expense of the general and the universal. At its logical term it produced the purely ethnographical *byt* realism of Ostróvsky. This particularity which excludes a universal appeal and emphasizes social and national differences was what the old Tolstóy condemned in the methods of realistic fiction. In his early work he had entirely adopted them and carried them farther than his predecessors. In physical description of character he outdid Gógol and has never been surpassed. But he is different from his compeers in that he never inclined towards *byt*. The interest of his work is always psychological, never ethnographical. The essence of Tolstóy's early art was to push analysis to its furthest limit; hence it is that the details he offers are not complex cultural facts, but, as it were, *atoms* of experience—the indivisible units of immediate perception. An important form of this dissecting and atomizing method (and one that survived all the changes of his style) is what Victor Shklóvsky has called "making it strange." It consists in never calling complex things by their accepted name, but always disintegrating a complex action or object into its indivisible components. The method strips the world of the labels attached to it by habit and by social convention, and gives it a "dis-civilized" appearance, as it might have appeared to Adam on the day of creation. It is easy to see that the method, while it gives unusual freshness to imaginative representation, is in essence hostile to all culture and all social form, and is psychologically akin to anarchism. This method is the principal feature that distinguishes the work of Tolstóy from that of other realists. The universality of Tolstóy's realism is increased by his concentration on the inner life, and especially on its more elusive experiences. When arrested and expressed in words, they give a particularly keen feeling of unexpected familiarity, for it seems that the author is aware of the reader's most intimate, secret, and inexpressible feelings. This mastering of the elusive is irresistible and overwhelming, at least to people who have grown up in a roughly similar emotional ambient. How far this particular side of Tolstóy strengthens his appeals to a Chinese or to an Arab I cannot say. Tolstóy himself in his old age believed it did not, and in his later work intended for the world, irrespective of race and civilization, he avoided this method of what Constantine Leóntiev called "psychological eavesdropping." But within certain limits the "eavesdropping" only enhances the human and universal as against the local and social appeal of the early Tolstóy.

Again the subject matter of Tolstóy and his way of approaching it increase the universal as much as they diminish the ethnographical appeal of his work. The issues of his stories are not the public issues of contemporary Russia. Except for certain parts of *Anna Karénina* (and for the posthumous comedy, *A Contaminated Family*), contemporary issues are absent from Tolstóy's work. This disqualified it for being used as texts for the civic sermons of Chernyshévsky and Dobrolyúbov, but has also prevented it from dating. The issues and the conflicts are moral and psychological, not social, a considerable asset in winning the unqualified understanding of the foreign reader. In his later work this feature is only further developed. His universality gives Tolstóy a somewhat eccentric standing among the Russian novelists of his time. But in another respect he is again eminently representative of the movement. He carried further than anyone (except Aksákov) the deliberate neglect of narrative interest and the deliberate avoidance of artificial construction. He also carried to the furthest the purity of his prose from all extra-representational elements. His style is deliberately prosaic—purged to chemical purity of all "poetry" and rhetoric—sternly puritanical prose His syntax, especially in the earliest work, is sometimes clumsy and exaggeratedly involved. But at its best it is beautifully adequate and transparent—a prose admirably adapted to its task and perfectly obedient to what it is made to express. The *language* of Tolstóy also deserves special notice for the pains he took to avoid the bookish vocabulary of literature and to use with consistent purity the spoken vocabulary of his class. It is the best example (after Griboyédov and after Púshkin's epistolary prose) of the spoken Russian of the nobility. But his syntax is based on the example of the French analysts and uses all the means at its disposal for complicated logical subordination. This combination of a very pure colloquial vocabulary with a very complicated and logical syntax makes the peculiar individuality of Tolstóy's Russian. In his dialogue, on the other hand, especially from *War and Peace* (and *A Contaminated Family*) onward, he achieved a purity and convincingness of colloquial idiom and intonation that have not been surpassed. The highest achievement of his art of dialogue, however, belongs to his last period and is to be found in his last plays, *The Light Shines in the Darkness* and *The Living Corpse*.

The roots of Tolstóy's art are to be found in his diary, which we know from 1847 onward. Like Stendhal, with whom as a psychologist he has much in common, and whom he recognized as one of his masters, Tolstóy is particularly interested in discovering the semiconscious suppressed motives of his actions, in exposing the insincerity of the superficial, as it were, official, ego. A detail that cannot fail to strike the reader of Tolstóy's diaries (as well as of certain of his stories written in the fifties) is his inordinate love for classifications, which he marshals under numbered headings. It is a minor, but significant, detail. It has often been affirmed that Tolstóy was an eminently natural, subconscious, elemental man, and that in this he was akin to primitive man, as yet imperfectly differentiated from nature. Nothing can be more misleading. He was on the contrary a rationalist to the marrow, one of the greatest that ever lived. Nothing was safe from the lancet of his analysis. His art is not the spontaneous revelation of the subconscious but the conquest of the subconscious by lucid understanding. Tolstóy was a predecessor of Freud, but the striking difference between the artist and the scientist is that the artist is incomparably less imaginative, more matter-of-fact and levelheaded than the scientist.

From the beginnings of his diary to the time he wrote *War and Peace*, writing was to Tolstóy above all a struggle to master reality, to found a method and a technique of reducing it to words. To this, from 1851, he added the problem of transforming notation of fact into literature. Tolstóy did not achieve it at a single stroke. His first attempt at imaginative writing, a fragment entitled *An Account of Yesterday*, is apparently the beginning of an account of an actual twenty-four hours spent by him, with no invention, nothing but notation. It was only to be fuller and less selective than the diaries and subordinated to a general design. In point of detail the *Account* is almost on a Proustian if not a Joycean scale. The author revels, as it were, in his analysis. He is a young man in possession of a new instrument, who has unbounded confidence in his command of it. The same impression is never again given in any of his later work. This exuberance wanted repression and disciplining before it was ready to be shown to the public. It wanted a more literary, a less immediately "recording" appearance. It wanted the discipline of convention. For all his pioneering courage, Tolstóy did not have the audacity to continue in this line of extensive notation. It is almost a pity he did not. The sheer originality of *An Account of Yesterday* remains unsurpassed. If he had continued in that line, he would probably have met with less immediate recognition, but he might have ultimately produced an even more astounding body of work.

In the light of *An Account of Yesterday*, *Childhood* seems almost a surrender to all the conventions of literature. Of all Tolstóy's writings it is the one where extraneous literary influences (Sterne, Rousseau, Töpfer) are most clearly apparent. But even now, in the light of *War and Peace*, *Childhood* retains its unique and unfading charm. It has already that wonderful poetry of reality which is attained without the slightest aid of poetical device, without the aid of language (the few sentimental, rhetorical passages rather tend to destroy it), by the sole help of the choice of significant psychological and real detail. What struck the world as a new thing, hitherto done by no one, was this gift of evoking memories and associations, recognized by everyone as his own intimate and unique memories, by the choice of details memorable to everyone, but rejected by everyone as insignificant and not worth while. It needed the avid rationalism of Tolstóy to fix for ever these

moments which *were* but had remained unrecorded since the beginning of time.

In *Childhood* Tolstóy succeeded for the first time in transpos-
ing the raw material of recorded experience into art. For a moment
Tolstóy abandoned his pioneering energy and was content to draw
up a balance of what he had already acquired, in a form not too
unlike the accepted conventions of literature. In all he wrote after
Childhood and up to *War and Peace* he continued his forward
movement, experimenting, forging his instrument, never condescending to sacrifice his interest in the process of production to the
artistic effect of the finished product. This is apparent in the
sequels of *Childhood—Boyhood* (1854) and *Youth* (1857)—when
the poetic, evocative atmosphere of *Childhood* becomes thinner
and thinner and the element of sheer untransformed analysis pro-
trudes more and more. It is still more apparent in his stories of war
and of the Caucasus: *A Raid* (1853), *Sevastópol in December, Sevastópol in May* (1855), *Sevastópol in August* (1856), *A Wood Felling*
(1855). In them he set out to destroy the existing romantic conceptions of those two arch-romantic themes. To be understood in
their genesis, these stories have to be felt against their background
of romantic literature, against the romances of Bestúzhev and the
Byronic poems of Púshkin and Lérmontov. The unromanticizing
of Caucasus and war is achieved by Tolstóy's usual method of ever
advancing analysis and of "making it strange." Battles and skir-
mishes are not described in terms of military history, with its
grand nomenclature, nor in terms of battle painting, but in the
ordinary and unprepossessing details that strike the actual observer and are only afterward transformed by a name-ridden
memory into heroic battle scenes. Here more than anywhere
Tolstóy followed in the steps of Stendhal, whose account of Water-
loo he recognized as a perfect example of military realism. The
same process of destroying the heroic convention was further promoted by the ruthless analysis of the psychological workings that
result in the display of courage, which are composed of vanity,
lack of imagination, and stereotyped thinking. But in spite of this
exposure of war and military virtues, the general effect of Tolstóy's
military stories is not unheroic or anti-militarist. It results much
rather in the glorification of the unconscious and unambitious at
the expense of conscious and ambitious heroism, of the private

soldier and professional army officer at the expense of the smart young officer from Petersburg who has come to the front to taste of the poetry of war and to win his St. George's Cross. The casual, matter-of-fact courage of the plain soldier and officer is what strikes the reader most of all in these stories. These humble heroes of Tolstóy's early war stories are descendants of Púshkin's Captain Mirónov and of Lérmontov's Maxím Maxímych, and landmarks on the way to the soldiers and army officers of *War and Peace*.

In the stories written in the second half of the fifties and early sixties Tolstóy's center of interest is shifted from analysis to morality. These stories—*The Memoirs of a Billiard Marker, Two Hussars, Albert, Lucerne, Three Deaths, Family Happiness, Poli-kúshka,* and *Kholstomér, the Story of a Horse*—are frankly didactic and moralistic, much more so than any of the stories of his last, dogmatic period. The main moral of these stories is the fallacy of civilization and the inferiority of the civilized, conscious, sophisti- cated man, with his artificially multiplied needs, to natural man. On the whole they mark an advance neither, as the war stories did, in Tolstóy's method of annexing and digesting reality, nor in his skill in transferring the raw experience of life into art (as in *Child- hood* and *War and Peace*). Most of them are crude, and some (as, for instance, *Three Deaths*) did not need a Tolstóy to write them. Contemporary criticism was right in regarding them, if not as a decline, at least as a standstill in the development of his genius. But they are important as an expression of that moral urge which was finally to bring Tolstóy to *A Confession* and to all his later work and teaching. *Lucerne,* for its earnest and bitter indignation against the selfishness of the rich (which, it is true, he was inclined at that time to regard, semi-Slavophilwise, as a peculiarity of the materialistic civilization of the West) is particularly suggestive of the spirit of his later work. As a sermon in fiction it is certainly one of the most powerful things of its kind. The nearest approach to complete artistic success is *Two Hussars,* a charming story that betrays its purpose only in the excessively neat parallelism be- tween the characters of the two Hussars, father and son. The father is an "unconscious," "natural" man who lives a rather unedifying life, but who, precisely on account of his unconscious- ness and proximity to nature, is noble even in his vices and reveals the essential nobility of man. The son in circumstances similar to those of his father shows himself a coward and a cad precisely be-

cause he is contaminated by the evil influences of civilization, and
what he does, he does self-consciously. Lastly, *Kholstomér, the
Story of a Horse* is certainly one of the most characteristic and
curious of all Tolstóy's writings. It is a satire upon civilized mankind from the point of view of a horse. The method of "making it
strange" is pushed to its furthest limits. It is essentially a descendant of the Persian, Chinese, and suchlike letters of the eighteenth
century, where oriental observers were introduced just to expose
the absurdities of contemporary life by making it strange. Here
more than elsewhere Tolstóy is the faithful disciple of French
rationalism. It is interesting, however, that the keenest point of
the satire is turned against the institution of property, and it is
characteristic that the story, written just before his marriage, was
published only after his conversion.

Apart from the rest of his earliest work stands *The Cossacks*.
It was written during his life in the Caucasus, but Tolstóy remained unsatisfied with it, returned to it again, and, still unsatisfied, would not have published it were it not for the necessity
he found himself in of paying a debt at cards. It appeared in 1863
in a form Tolstóy regarded as unsatisfactory. What he would have
done with it ultimately we do not know, but as it is, it is probably
his masterpiece before *War and Peace*. It is the story of the life
of Olénin, a young volunteer of noble birth and university education, in a Cossack village on the Térek. The main idea is the
contrast of his sophisticated and self-conscious personality to the
"natural men" that are the Cossacks. Unlike the "natural man"
of Rousseau (and of Tolstóy's own later teaching), "natural man"
in *The Cossacks* is not an incarnation of good. But the very fact of
his being natural places him above the distinction of good and
evil. The Cossacks kill, fornicate, steal, and still are beautiful in
their naturalness, and hopelessly superior to the much more moral,
but civilized and consequently contaminated, Olénin. The young
Cossack Lukáshka, the Cossack girl Mariánka, and especially the
old huntsman Eróshka are among the most memorable and lasting creations of Tolstóy. They are his first great successes in the
objective painting of the human figure. But the objective painting
of the human soul he was to achieve only in *War and Peace*, for in
his early work his analyzed and dissected heroes are either emanations of his own self or else only more or less abstract and generalized human material for dissection, like the "other" officers in

the Sevastópol stories, who are not more psychologically alive
than the horse Kholstomér. The processes that go on in them are
convincing, but the details of this psychological mechanism are
not welded into a whole to form an individuality.

Tolstóy's first literary work after his marriage was the (posthumously published) comedy *A Contaminated Family*. It shows
already the conservative trend of his married mind. It is a satire
of the nihilist, ending in the triumph of the meek, but fundamentally sensible, father over his rebellious children. It is a masterpiece of delicate character drawing and dialogue. It contains more
genuine and good-humored humor than any other of his works.
At one time Tolstóy was very keen on having it acted. But it
was rejected by the Imperial Theater, probably for fear of offending the younger generation.

Soon after his marriage Tolstóy began to be attracted by the
recent past of the Russian society, and planned a novel on the
subject of the Decembrists. Some fragments of this novel were
written and published, but before long he found himself unable to
understand the Decembrists without a study of the preceding
generation, and this led to the writing of *War and Peace*. It took
him over four years. A first fragment under the title *1805* appeared
in 1865. The whole novel was completed and published in 1869.

War and Peace is, not only in size, but in perfection, the
masterpiece of the early Tolstóy. It is also the most important
work in the whole of Russian realistic fiction. If in the whole range
of the European novel of the nineteenth century it has equals, it
has no superiors, and the peculiarities of the modern, as opposed
to the pre-nineteenth-century, novel are more clearly seen in it than
in such rivals as *Madame Bovary* or *Le Rouge et le Noir*. It was an
advanced pioneering work, a work that widened, as few novels
have done, the province and the horizon of fiction. In a textbook,
where space is limited, it is impossible to speak at all adequately
of the great novel. Besides, more than anything else in Russian
literature, it belongs to Europe as much as it does to Russia. A
history of the European novel would have to place it, not so much
in its Russian, as in its international, setting, on the line of development that leads from the novels of Stendhal to those of
Henry James and Proust. In many respects *War and Peace* is a
direct continuation of the preceding works of Tolstóy. The methods of analysis and of "making it strange" are the same, only

carried to a greater perfection. The use of apparently elusive, but emotionally significant detail for the creation of poetic atmosphere is a direct development of the methods of *Childhood*. The presentation of war as an unromantic and sordid reality, but one that is nevertheless pregnant with heroical beauty in the courage of its unconscious heroes, is a direct continuation of the Sevastópol stories. The glorification of "natural man," of Natásha and Nicholas Rostóv at the expense of the sophisticated Prince Andrew, and of the peasant Platón Karatáyev at the expense of all the civilized heroes, continues the line of thought of *Two Hussars* and of *The Cossacks*. The satirical representation of society and of diplomacy is completely in line with Tolstóy's disgust at European civilization. However, in other respects it is different from the earlier work. First of all it is more objective. Here for the first time Tolstóy becomes capable of stepping out of himself and of seeing into the other. Unlike *The Cossacks* and *Childhood* the novel is not egocentrical. There are several heroes with equal rights, none of whom is Tolstóy, though the two principal ones, Prince Andrew and Pierre Bezúkhov, are no doubt transpositions of Tolstóy. But the most wonderful difference of *War and Peace* from the earlier stories are the women, Princess Maria and especially Natásha. There can be no doubt that it was his increased knowledge of feminine nature, due to marriage, that enabled Tolstóy to annex this new province of psychological experience. The art of individualization also attains to unsurpassable perfection. The little details that made the unique and unprecedented charm of *Childhood* are used here with a supreme and elusive perfection that transcends art and gives the book (and *Anna Karénina*)—alone, perhaps, among all books—the appearance of actual life. To many of Tolstóy's readers his personages are not classified with other characters of fiction, but with men and women of actual experience. The roundness, the completeness, the liveness of the characters, even of the most episodic, are perfect and absolute. This is attained, of course, by the extraordinary subtlety, delicacy, and variety of the analysis (we are far removed from the crudish and schematic methods of *Sevastópol*), but it is also attained by the means of more elusive detail, of "accompaniment," and especially of language. The speech Tolstóy lends his characters is something that surpasses perfection. In *War and Peace* he attains for the first time to a complete mastery of this medium. It gives the reader the impression of actually hearing the different individual voices of the characters. You recognize the voice of Natásha, or Vera, or Borís Drubetskóy as you recognize the voice of a friend. In this art of individualized intonation Tolstóy has only one rival—Dostoyévsky. There is no need to dwell on the individual characters. But it is impossible not to insist once more on the supreme creation of Natásha, certainly the most wonderfully made character in any novel. Natásha is also the center of the novel, for she is the symbol of "natural man," the ideal.

The transformation of reality into art is also more perfect in *War and Peace* than in anything that preceded it. It is almost complete.[4] The novel is built along its own laws (Tolstóy has let escape him some interesting hints as to these laws) and contains few undigested bits of raw material. The narrative is a miracle. The vast proportions, the numerous personages, the frequent changes of scene, and the close and necessary interconnection of all give the impression of being really a record of a society, not only of so many individuals.

The philosophy of the novel is the glorification of nature and life at the expense of the sophistications of reason and civilization. It is the surrender of the rationalist Tolstóy to the irrational forces of existence. It is emphasized in the theoretical chapters and it is symbolized in the last volume in the figure of Karatáyev. The philosophy is profoundly optimistic, for it is confidence in the blind forces of life, a profound belief that the best one can do is not to choose, but to trust in the goodness of things. The passive and determinist Kutúzov embodies the philosophy of wise passivity as against the ambitious smallness of Napoleon. The optimistic nature of the philosophy is reflected in the idyllic tone of the narrative. In spite of the horror—by no means veiled—of war, and the ineptitude—assiduously unmasked—of sophisticated and futile civilization, the general message of *War and Peace* is one of beauty and satisfaction that the world should be so beautiful. It is only the sophistication of conscious reason that contrives to spoil it. The general tone may be properly described as idyllic. The inclination towards the idyllic was from first to last an ever

---

[4] Not so complete as in certain works of other great realists; not for instance so complete as in *Madame Bovary*. But then neither Flaubert nor anyone else absorbed so much of reality in the transforming process. The quantity of transforming energy utilized in *War and Peace* is greater than in any other work of realistic fiction.

present possibility in Tolstóy. It is the opposite pole to his unceasing moral uneasiness. Before the time of *War and Peace* it
pervades *Childhood*, and it strangely and unexpectedly crops up
in his autobiographical notes written in his last years for Biryukóv.
Its roots are in a sense of unity with his class, with the happy and
prosperous *byt* of the Russian nobility. And it is, after all, no
exaggeration to say that, all said and done, *War and Peace* is a
tremendous "heroic idyl" of the Russian nobility.

There are two conceivable strictures on *War and Peace*, the
figure of Karatáyev, and the theoretical chapters on history and
warfare. Personally I do not admit the validity of the latter drawback. It is an essential of Tolstóy's art to be not only art, but
knowledge. And to the vast canvas of the great novel the theoretical chapters add a perspective and an intellectual atmosphere one
cannot wish away.[5] I feel it more difficult to put up with Karatáyev. In spite of his quintessential importance for the idea of the
novel, he jars. He is not a human being among human beings, as
the other two ideally natural characters, Natásha and Kutúzov,
are. He is an abstraction, a myth, a being with different dimensions
and laws from those of the rest of the novel. He does not fit in.

After *War and Peace* Tolstóy, pursuing his historical studies,
ascended the stream of Russian history to the age of Peter the
Great. The period appeared to him as critical in bringing about
the cleft between the people and the educated classes and in
poisoning the latter with European civilization. He tried several
plans and wrote several beginnings of a novel of those times, but
in the course of his studies Tolstóy became so disgusted with the
person of the great Emperor—the embodiment of all he hated—
that he gave it up. Instead he began in 1873 to write a novel of
contemporary life—*Anna Karénina*. The first instalments appeared in 1875, and the publication of the novel was completed in
1877.

Anna Karénina is in all essentials a continuation of *War and
Peace*. The methods of Tolstóy are the same in both, and the two
novels are justly named together. What has been said of the personages of *War and Peace* may be repeated of those of *Anna*

[5] It may be remarked that as an historian of war Tolstóy gave proof of remarkable
insight. His reading of the battle of Borodinó, which he arrived at by sheer intuition, has been since corroborated by documental evidence and accepted by
military historians.

Karénina. The figures of Anna, of Dolly, of Kitty, of Stíva Oblónsky, of Vrónsky, of all the episodic and secondary personages, are as memorable as those of Natásha and of Nicholas Rostóv. Perhaps there is even a greater variety and a more varied sympathy in the characters of *Anna Karénina.* Vrónsky particularly is a genuine and fundamental addition to the world of Tolstóy; more than any other of Tolstóy's characters, he is fundamentally different from the author and in no way based on subjective vision. He and Anna are perhaps Tolstóy's greatest achievements in the understanding of "the other." But Lëvin is a much less happily transformed Tolstóy than are his emanations in *War and Peace*, Prince Andrew and Pierre. Lëvin is a return to the subjective, diaristic Nekhlyúdovs and Olénins of the early stories, and he jars in the story as much as does Platón Karatáyev in *War and Peace*, though in an exactly opposite way. Another difference between the two novels is that *Anna Karénina* contains no separate philosophical chapters, but a more obtrusive and insidious moral philosophy is diffused throughout the story. The philosophy is less irrational and optimistic, more puritan, and is everywhere felt as distinct from and alien to the main groundwork of the novel. The groundwork has the idyllic flavor of *War and Peace*. But in the philosophy of the novel there is an ominous suggestion of the approach of a more tragic God than the blind and good life-God of *War and Peace*. The tragic atmosphere thickens as the story advances towards the end. The romance of Anna and Vrónsky, who had transgressed the moral and social law, culminates in blood and horror to which there is no counterpart in the earlier novel. Even the idyllic romance of the good and obedient-to-nature Lëvin and Kitty ends on a note of confused perplexity. The novel dies like a cry of anguish in the desert air. Both the great novels have an indefinite ending, but while in *War and Peace* it suggests only the infinite continuity of life, of which the given narrative has been only a detached fragment, in *Anna Karénina* it definitely suggests a no-thoroughfare, a path gradually losing itself before the steps of the wayfarer. And in fact before Tolstóy had finished *Anna Karénina*, he had already entered on the crisis that was to bring him to his conversion. The perplexed ending of the novel is only a reflection of the tragic perplexity he was himself experiencing. He was never again to write a novel like these two. After finishing

Anna Karénina he attempted to resume his work on Peter and the Decembrists, but it was soon forsaken, and instead, two years after the completion of his last idyl, he wrote *A Confession.*

Anna Karénina leads up to the moral and religious crisis that was so profoundly to revolutionize Tolstóy. Before he began it he had already begun to cast his eyes on new artistic methods— abandoning the psychological and analytical manner of super-fluous detail and discovering a simpler narrative style that could be applied not only to the sophisticated and corrupt educated classes, but to the undeveloped mind of the people. The stories he wrote for the people in 1872 (*God Sees the Truth* and *The Captive in the Caucasus,* which by the way, is merely a translation into unromantic terms, a sort of parody, of the poem of Púshkin) already announce the popular tales of 1885–6. They are not yet so pointedly moral, but they are all concentrated on narrative and action and are entirely free from all "eavesdropping."

DOSTOYÉVSKY (AFTER 1849)

From January 1850 to January 1854 Dostoyévsky [6] served his term of penal servitude at Omsk convict prison. During the whole term he had no books to read but a Bible and he was never for a moment alone. During these years he underwent a profound re-ligious crisis: he rejected the social and progressive ideas of his youth and became converted to the religion of the Russian people, in the sense that he began not only to believe in what the people believed, but to believe in it *because* the people believed. On the other hand his four years of hard labor greatly injured his health, and his epilepsy became more marked and more frequent.

On completing his term he was transferred as a private soldier to an infantry battalion garrisoned at Semipalátinsk. In October 1856 his commission was restored to him. He was now free to write and receive letters and to resume his literary work. In 1857, while staying at Kuznétsk, he married the widow Isáyeva. This first marriage was not a happy one. He remained in Siberia till 1859. During these five years he wrote, besides some shorter stories, the novel *The Manor of Stepánchikovo,* which appeared in

[6] For the early life and work of Dostoyévsky see Chapter VI.

1859, and began *Memoirs from the House of Death*. In 1859 he was allowed to return to European Russia. Later in the same year he was finally amnestied and came to Petersburg.

He arrived in the midst of the great reform movement and was immediately sucked into the journalistic whirlpool. Together with his brother Michael he started the review *Vrémya* (*The Time*), which began appearing in January 1861. In the first two years he contributed to the review a novel, *The Humiliated and Insulted*, and *The House of Death*, besides a great number of articles. Though the position that the Dostoyévskys took up fitted in with no party, their review was a success. What they stood for was a sort of mystical populism that did not want to make the people happy along Western and progressive lines, but to assimilate the ideals of the people. They found a valuable ally in Strákhov. Their other ally, Grigóriev, was of little use at the time, as he was traversing the most chaotic and anarchic period of his life. Dostoyévsky himself worked furiously, and often succumbed to the overstrain. But he was exhilarated by success and by the atmosphere of struggle. In 1862–3 he traveled for the first time abroad, visiting England, France, and Germany, and recorded his impressions of the West in *Winter Notes on Summer Impressions*, which appeared in 1863. In them he attacked and condemned the impious bourgeois civilization of the West from a point of view that is connected at once with Herzen's and with that of the Slavophils. In 1863, like a bolt from the blue, came the suppression of *Vrémya* for an article on the Polish question by Strákhov, which had been, quite literally, misread by the censorship. The misunderstanding was cleared up before long, and the Dostoyévskys were allowed to resume their review in January 1864 under a new name (*The Epoch*), but the financial damages caused them by the suppression were incalculable. For eight years Dostoyévsky was unable to free himself from them. Meanwhile he was undergoing a crisis of greater significance than his conversion in Siberia. To the years 1862–3 belongs his liaison with Apollinária Súslova, the most important love affair of his life. After the suppression of *Vrémya* he traveled with her abroad. It was on this journey that for the first time he lost heavily at roulette. Mlle Súslova (who afterwards married the great writer Rózanov) was a proud and (to use a Dostoyevskian epithet) "infernal" woman, with unknown depths of cruelty and of evil. She seems to have been to Dostoyévsky an important revelation of the dark side of things.

The Epoch began under the worst auspices. The action of the authorities prevented it from being advertised in due time, and it never succeeded in recovering the good will of the subscribers of *Vrémya*. Soon after it was started, Dostoyévsky's wife and, almost simultaneously, Michael Dostoyévsky both died. The death of Grigóriev in the autumn of the same year was a further blow to the review. Dostoyévsky found himself alone, and with the whole family of his brother to provide for. After fifteen months of heroical and hectic labor he gave in, recognizing that *The Epoch* could not be saved. The review was closed. Dostoyévsky was bankrupt. It was in the terrible year 1864 that Dostoyévsky wrote the most unique of all his works, *Memoirs from Underground*.

To meet his enormous liabilities he set down to work at his great novels. In 1865–6 he wrote *Crime and Punishment*. He sold the copyright of all his works for the ludicrous sum of three thousand roubles ($1,500) to the publisher Stellóvsky. The contract stipulated that besides all previously published work Dostoyévsky was to deliver to Stellóvsky by November 1866 a full-length unpublished novel. To meet this obligation he began writing *The Gambler*, and, to be able to finish in time, he engaged a shorthand secretary, Anna Grigórievna Snítkin. Owing to her efficient help, *The Gambler* was delivered in time. A few months later he married his secretary (February 1867).

Anne Grigórievna proved the best of wives, and in the long run it was owing to her devotion and practical sense (as much as to his own enormous working capacity) that Dostoyévsky freed himself from his debts and was able to spend the last ten years of his life in comparatively easy circumstances. But the first years after their marriage were beset with the most cruel ordeals. Very soon after the wedding Dostoyévsky had to leave Russia, and for four years remained abroad for fear of falling into the hands of his creditors if he returned to Russia. His difficulties were aggravated by a new access of gambling frenzy in the summer of 1867. Only gradually, by dint of hard and hurried labor at his great novels, and with the aid of Anna Grigórievna, he once more stood on his feet and in 1871 could return to Russia. The years between the suppression of *Vrémya* and his return to Russia after four years' life abroad were, both in quantity and in significance, the most productive of his whole life. *Memoirs from Underground, Crime and Punishment, The Gambler, The Idiot* (1868), *The Eternal Husband* (1870), and *The Possessed* (1871–2), all belong to this period, while the plan of *The Life of a Great Sinner*, planned in the same year, contains the germ of *The Brothers Karamázov*.

When they returned to Petersburg, the Dostoyévskys, though not at first free from all difficulties, began to have better luck. The publication in book form, at their own expense, of *The Possessed* (Russian title *Bésy* "Devils" 1873) was a success. In the same year Dostoyévsky became editor of Prince V. Meschérsky's weekly *The Citizen*. This gave him a settled income. In 1876 he himself began publishing *An Author's Diary*, which had a considerable sale. The political ideas of Dostoyévsky were now more in tune with the times, and his influence grew. He felt a more sympathetic atmosphere round him. The high-water mark of his popularity was reached in the year preceding his death, when *The Brothers Karamázov* appeared. The culmination was his famous address on the occasion of the unveiling of the Púshkin memorial in Moscow, delivered on June 8, 1880. The address evoked an enthusiasm that had no precedents in Russian literary history. The following winter he fell seriously ill, and, on January 28, 1881, he died.

Both psychologically and historically Dostoyévsky is a very complex figure, and it is necessary to distinguish not only between the various periods of his life and the various currents of his mind, but between the different *levels* of his personality. The higher—or rather, deeper—level is present only in the imaginative work of his last seventeen years, beginning with *Memoirs from Underground*. The lower—or rather, more superficial—level is apparent in all his work, but more particularly in his journalistic writings and in the imaginative work of before 1864. The deeper, the essential, Dostoyévsky is one of the most significant and ominous figures in the whole history of the human mind, one of its boldest and most disastrous adventures in the sphere of ultimate spiritual quest. The superficial Dostoyévsky is a man of his time, comparable—and not always favorably comparable—to many other Russian novelists and publicists of the age of Alexander II, a mind that had many rivals and that cannot be placed in any way apart from, or above, Herzen, Grigóriev, or Leóntiev. The other one, the essential

Dostoyévsky, for the profundity, complexity, and significance of his spiritual experience, has only two possible rivals in the whole range of Russian literature—Rózanov and of course Tolstóy, who, however, seems to have been given to the world for the special purpose of being contrasted with Dostoyévsky.

The comparison between Tolstóy and Dostoyévsky has for many years been, with Russian and foreign critics, a favorite subject of discussion. Much has been said of the aristocratic nature of the former and the plebeian nature of the latter; of the one's Luciferian pride and the other's Christian humility; of the naturalism of the one and the spiritualism of the other. Apart from the difference of social position and education, a main difference between the two is that Tolstóy was a puritan, and Dostoyévsky a symbolist. That is to say that for Dostoyévsky all relative values were related to absolute values and received their significance, positive or negative, from the way they reflected the higher values. For Tolstóy the absolute and the relative are two disconnected worlds, and the relative is in itself evil. Hence Tolstóy's contempt for the meaningless diversity of human history, and Dostoyévsky's eminently historical mode of thinking, which relates to all the main line of higher Russian thought—to Chaadáyev, the Slavophils, Herzen, Grigóriev, Leóntiev, and Soloviëv. Dostoyévsky is one of them: his thought is always historically related. Even in their most purely spiritual form, his problems are not concerned with an eternal, static, and immutable law, but with the drama that is being played out in human history by the supreme forces of the universe. Hence the great complexity, fluidity, and many-sidedness of his thought as compared to the rigidly geometrical and rectilinear thinking of Tolstóy. Tolstóy (in spite of his sensitiveness to the infinitesimals of life) was in his moral philosophy, both on the high level of *A Confession* and on the much lower level of his anti-alcoholic and vegetarian tracts, a Euclid of moral quantities. Dostoyévsky deals in the elusive calculus of fluid values. Hence also what Strákhov so happily called the "purity" of Tolstóy and what may be called the obvious "impurity" of Dostoyévsky. He was never dealing with stable entities, but with fluid processes; and not seldom the process was one of dissolution and putrefaction.

On a more social and historical plane it is also important to note that while Tolstóy was an aristocrat and (alone of his literary contemporaries) culturally had his roots in the old French and

eighteenth-century civilization of the Russian gentry, Dostoyévsky
was, to the core, a plebeian and a democrat. He belonged to the
same historical and social formation that produced Belínsky,
Nekrásov, and Grigóriev, and to this is due, among other things,
that absence of all grace and elegance, whether internal or external,
which characterizes all his work, together with an absence of reserve, discipline, and dignity, and an excess of abnormal self-
consciousness.

The great, later novels of Dostoyévsky are ideological novels.
The idea of the novel is inseparable from the imaginative conception, and neither can it be abstracted from the story nor the story
stripped of the idea. But this does not apply to the novels of his
middle period, 1857–63, which are in many ways a continuation of
his early work (1845–9) rather than an anticipation of what was
to follow. The work of 1857–63 belongs to the same superficial
level as Dostoyévsky's earlier work. The deeper abysses of his
consciousness are not yet revealed in it. It is different, however,
from the work of the forties in that it is free from the immediate
influence of Gógol and from the intense stylistic preoccupation
that marks *Poor Folk* and *The Double.* The principal works of this
period are *The Manor of Stepánchikovo and its Inhabitants* (1859;
in Mrs. Garnett's translation, *The Friend of the Family*), *The Humiliated and Insulted* (1861), and *Memoirs from the House of Death*
(1861–2). Of these, *The Humiliated and Insulted* is a novel closely
connected in style and tone with the French romantic novel of
social compassion and with the later and less humorous novels of
Dickens. The religion of compassion, verging often on melodramatic sentimentality, finds there its purest expression, as yet un-
complicated by the deeper problems of the next period.

Stepánchikovo also lacks the intellectual passionateness and
richness of the essential Dostoyévsky, but in other respects it is
one of the most characteristic of his works. All his great novels
have a construction that is dramatic rather than narrative.
Stepánchikovo is the most dramatic of all (it was originally planned
as a play)—only, of course, it is far too long for the theater. It is
also interesting for the way it displays what Mikhaylóvsky called
the "cruelty" of Dostoyévsky. Its subject is the intolerable psychological bullying inflicted by the hypocrite and parasite, Fomá
Opískin, on his host, Colonel Rostánev. The imbecile meekness
with which the colonel consents to be bullied and allows all around

him—his friends, and servants—to be bullied by Opískin, and the perverse inventiveness of Fomá in devising various psychological humiliations for his victims, produce an impression of intolerable, almost physical pain. Fomá Opískin is a weird figure of grotesque, gratuitous, irresponsible, petty, and ultimately joyless evil that together with Saltykóv's Porfíry Golovlëv and Sologúb's Peredónov form a trinity to which probably no foreign literature has anything to compare. *Stepánchikovo* was intended for a comical and humorous story with a touch of satire (aimed, it would seem, at Gógol, as revealed by *A Correspondence with Friends*), but it must be confessed that though the element of humor is unmistakably present, it is a kind of humor that requires a rather peculiar constitution to enjoy.

The same "cruelty" in an even more elaborate form is to be found in the most characteristic of the shorter stories of this period—*A Bad Predicament* (1862), in which, with a detail on the scale of *The Double*, Dostoyévsky describes the sufferings of humiliated self-consciousness experienced by a superior civil servant at a wedding of a minor clerk of his, where he comes uninvited, behaves himself ridiculously, gets drunk, and involves the poor clerk in heavy expenses.

Apart from these stories stand *Memoirs from the House of Death* (1861–2), during the lifetime of Dostoyévsky his most famous and most universally recognized book. It is the account of a term of penal servitude spent by a convict of the educated classes in a Siberian prison, based mainly on autobiographical material. Like the other works of Dostoyévsky before 1864, it is free from his later complex and deeper experience. Its ultimate message is one of human and optimistic sympathy. Even the moral degradation of the most hardened criminals is not represented so as to make one lose faith in human nature. It is rather a protest against the inefficiency of punishment. In spite of the dreadful, sordid, and degrading details of crime and cruelty, *The House of Death* is, after all, a bright and glad book, full of "uplift," and well made to fit in with an age of optimistic social idealism. The main motif of the book was the tragic estrangement between the educated convict and the people: even at the end of his term the narrator feels himself an outcast in a world of outcasts. Stripped of all external social privilege and placed in equal conditions with several hundreds of simple Russian people, he discovers that he is rejected by

them and will ever remain an outcast from their midst for the
mere fact of belonging to the educated class that had torn itself
away from the people's ideals. This idea closely relates *The House
of Death* to the journalistic writings of Dostoyévsky.

Dostoyévsky's non-imaginative writings belong to two principal periods: the articles he contributed in 1861–5 to *Vrémya* and
The Epoch, and *An Author's Diary* of 1873–81. On the whole his
political philosophy may be defined as a democratic Slavophilism
or a mystical populism. It has points of contact with Grigóriev
and the Slavophils, but also with Herzen and the populists. Its
main idea is that Russian educated society must be redeemed by a
renewal of contact with the people, and by an acceptance of the
people's religious ideals—that is to say, of Orthodoxy. On the
whole it may be said that the democratic and populist element
predominates in the writings of the sixties, while in the seventies,
under the influence of the growth of revolutionary socialism, the
nationalist and conservative element tends to get the upper hand.
But on the whole Dostoyévsky's journalism is more or less of a
piece from beginning to end. His religion is Orthodoxy *because* it
is the religion of the Russian people, whose mission it is to redeem
the world by a reassertion of the Christian faith. Christianity is to
him the religion not so much of purity and salvation, as of charity
and compassion. All this is obviously connected with the ideas of
Grigóriev and his teaching of meekness as the essential message of
Russia to the world. Dostoyévsky's enemies were the atheistic
radicals and socialists, and all the impious forces of Western,
atheistic civilization. The victory of Christian Russia over the
godless West was his political and historical faith. The taking of
Constantinople is a necessary symbolic item of his program as the
sanction of the universal mission of the Russian nation.

Somewhat apart, and once more strongly inclining to the left,
stands the Púshkin address, the most famous and concentratedly
significant of his unimaginative writings. Here he praises Púshkin
for the virtue of "pan-humanity," which is the gift of understanding all peoples and civilizations. It is the main feature of the
Russian people. The union of all humanity is the message and
mission of Russia to the world—a strange prophecy of the Third
International. In the same address, largely retracting from his
previous writings, he extolled the "Russian wanderer," by which
term he covertly designated the Revolutionaries and their pred-

ecessors. He discerned in them a yearning after religious truth that was only temporarily obscured by the lure of atheistic socialism. In commenting on the *Gypsies*, moreover, he expounded something like a theory of mystical anarchism and proclaimed the wickedness of all violence and punishment, thus unexpectedly forestalling Tolstóy's doctrine of non-opposition. The Púshkin address did much to reconcile the radicals with Dostoyévsky.

It also displays one of the most attractive features of Dostoyévsky the publicist—his boundless faculty of enthusiasm and admiration. The greatest portion of it went to Púshkin. But he speaks with equal enthusiasm of Racine, and there have been few nobler tributes to the memory of a literary and political enemy than Dostoyévsky's obituary of Nekrásov.

Dostoyévsky's style in his journalistic writings is of course unmistakably personal. But like all the journalistic press of the time, it is diffuse and formless. The individual vices of Dostoyévsky as a prose writer are a certain nervous shrillness and uneasiness of tone, which reappear in his novels wherever he has to speak in his own person.

The dialogue of the novels and the monologue of those of his writings that are written in the person of some fictitious character are also marked by a nervous tension and an exasperated (and perhaps exasperating) "on-end-ness" that was their creator's own. They are all agitated, as it were, by a wind of desperate spiritual passion and anxiety, rising from the innermost recesses of his subconsciousness. In spite of the *air de famille* of all his characters, Dostoyévsky's dialogue and personative monologue are incomparable for his wonderful art of individualization. There is an enormous variety of individuality in the comparatively limited and narrow compass of Dostoyévsky's mankind.

In all the later imaginative work of Dostoyévsky (from *Memoirs from Underground* to *The Brothers Karamázov*) it is impossible to separate the ideological from the artistic conception. These are novels of ideas, in which the characters, for all their enormous vitality and individuality, are after all only atoms charged with the electricity of ideas. It has been said of Dostoyévsky that he "felt ideas," as others feel cold and heat and pain. This distinguishes him from all other imaginative writers—the same faculty of "feeling ideas" is to be discovered only in certain great religious thinkers, in St. Paul, St. Augustine, Pascal, and Nietzsche.

Dostoyévsky is a psychological novelist, and his principal means of expression is analysis. In this he is the twin and counterpart of Tolstóy. But both the object and the method of his analysis are quite different from Tolstóy's. Tolstóy dissects the soul in its vital aspects; he studies the physiological basis of the mind, the subconscious workings of the will, the anatomy of the individual act. The higher spiritual states, when he comes to them, are discovered to be *outside* and on a different plane from life. They have no dimensions; they are entirely irrational to the ordinary stream of experience. Dostoyévsky, on the contrary, deals in those psychic strata where the mind and will are in constant contact with higher spiritual entities, where the ordinary stream of experience is constantly deflected by ultimate and absolute values and agitated by a never subsiding wind of the spirit. It is interesting to compare the treatment of the same feeling—the feeling of self-consciousness—by Tolstóy and by Dostoyévsky. Both were painfully self-conscious. But in Tolstóy it is purely social sensitiveness, the consciousness of the unfavorable impression produced by one's own personal appearance and conduct on persons one would like to impress favorably. Hence, with the growth of his social independence and the extinction of his social ambitions, the theme ceases to occupy Tolstóy. In Dostoyévsky the torture of self-consciousness is the torture of the ultimate and absolute value of a human personality, wounded, unrecognized, and humiliated by other human personalities. Dostoyévsky's "cruelty" finds a particularly rich field to feed on in the analysis of wounded and suffering human dignity. Either Tolstóy's self-consciousness is social or it ceases to operate; Dostoyévsky's is metaphysical and religious and can never disappear. This again brings forward the "purity" of Tolstóy and the "impurity" of Dostoyévsky: Tolstóy could overcome all his human failures and become a "naked man" before eternity. In Dostoyévsky his very spirit was inextricably entagled in the symbolical meshes of "relative reality." Hence also Tolstóy's later condemnation of the superfluous details of realism, with their absence of bearing on essential things, and Dostoyévsky's inability ever to transcend the limit of the temporal.

Dostoyévsky's method of analysis is also different from Tolstóy's. He does not dissect, but reconstructs. Tolstóy's question is always *why?* Dostoyévsky's *what?* This enables Dostoyévsky in many of his novels to do without all direct analysis of feelings and to reveal the inner life of his characters by their acts and speeches. For what they are is inevitable reflected in what they do and say. This is the symbolist attitude, with its faith in the necessary and real interconnection of the relative (behavior) and the absolute (personality); while for the "puritan" mentality of Tolstóy, behavior is only a veil cast over the non-dimensional core of the soul.

Memoirs from Underground, the work that introduces us, chronologically, to the "mature" Dostoyévsky, contains at once the essence of his essential self. It cannot be regarded as imaginative literature pure and simple. There is in it quite as much philosophy as literature. It would have to be connected with his journalistic writings were it not that it proceeded from a deeper and more significant spiritual level of his personality. The work occupies a central place in the creation of Dostoyévsky. Here his essential tragical intuition is expressed in the most unadulterated and ruthless form. It transcends art and literature, and its place is among the great mystical revelations of mankind. The faith in the supreme value of the human personality and its freedom, and in the irrational religious and tragic foundation of the spiritual universe, which is above reason, above the distinction of good and evil (the faith, ultimately, of all mystical religion), is expressed in a paradoxical, unexpected, and entirely spontaneous form. The central position of *Memoirs from Underground* in the work of Dostoyévsky was first discerned by Nietzsche and Rózanov. It stands in the center of the writings of Shestóv, the greatest of Dostoyévsky's commentators. Viewed as literature, it is also the most original of Dostoyévsky's works, although also the most unpleasant and the most "cruel." It cannot be recommended to those who are not either sufficiently strong to overcome it or sufficiently innocent to remain unpoisoned. It is a strong poison, which is most safely left untouched.

Of the novels, *The Gambler*, *The Eternal Husband*, *The Adolescent* are not philosophical in the same sense as the four great novels are. *The Gambler* is interesting as being demonstrably self-revelatory in its description of the gambling fever, and as giving in the figure of Pauline one of the most remarkable expressions of Dostoyévsky's favorite type of the proud and demoniac woman, which seems to be connected with the real person of Apollinária Súslova. *The Eternal Husband* belongs to the most "cruel" of his writings. It turns round the irreparable spiritual injury inflicted on the wronged human dignity of a husband by the lover of his wife, and his subtle and slow revenge (a torture to himself as to the other) on his wronger. *The Adolescent* (1875) of all Dostoyévsky's writings is most closely connected with the journalistic *Author's Diary*, and is ideologically on a lower plane than the four great novels.

Crime and Punishment (1866), *The Idiot* (1868), *The Possessed* (1871–2), and *The Brothers Karamázov* (1880), the four great novels, form, as it were, a connected cycle. They are all dramatic in construction, tragical in conception, and philosophical in significance. They are very complex wholes: not only is the plot inextricably woven into the philosophy—in the philosophy itself the essential Dostoyévsky, whom we have in a pure form in *Memoirs from Underground*, is inseparably mixed with the more journalistic Dostoyévsky of *An Author's Diary*. Hence the possibility of reading these novels in at least three different ways. The first, the way their contemporaries read them, relates them to the current issues of Russian public and social life of 1865–80. The second views them as the progressive disclosure of a "new Christianity," which found its final expression in the figures of Zosíma and Alësha Karamázov in the last of the four novels. The third connects them with *Memoirs from Underground* and the central tragic core of Dostoyévsky's spiritual experience. At last our contemporaries have discovered a fourth way of reading them, which pays no attention to their philosophy and takes them as pure stories of melodramatic incident.

His contemporaries, who kept to the first set of readings, regarded Dostoyévsky as a writer of great natural gifts but questionable taste and insufficient artistic discipline, who had original views on matters of general interest and a considerable power to make his characters live. They deplored his lack of taste, his grotesque misrepresentation of real life, his weakness for crudely sensational effects, but admired his great knowledge of morbid human types and the power of his psychopathic analysis. If they were conservatives, they recognized truth in the picture he drew of the nihilists; if they were radicals, they lamented that a man who had been ennobled by political martyrdom should stoop to be the ally of dirty reactionaries.

The Dostoyevskians of the following generation accepted the

novels as a revelation of a new Christianity in which ultimate
problems of good and evil were discussed and played out with
ultimate decisiveness, and which, taken as a whole, gave a new
doctrine, complete in all points, of spiritual Christianity. The tragic
failure of Raskólnikov to assert his individuality "without God";
the saintly idiocy of Prince Mýshkin; the dreadful picture of godless socialism in *The Possessed;* above all, the figure of the "pure"
Alësha Karamázov and the preachings of the holy Zosíma; these
were accepted as dogmatic revelations of a new ultimate form of
religion. This attitude towards Dostoyévsky, dominant in the
early years of this century, has still numerous partisans among the
older generation. To them Dostoyévsky is the prophet of a new
and supreme "universal harmony," which will transcend and
pacify all the discords and tragedies of mankind.

But the truth is (and here lies the exceptional significance of
Dostoyévsky as a spiritual case) that the tragedies of Dostoyévsky
are irreducible tragedies that cannot be solved or pacified. His
harmonies and his solutions are all on a lower or shallower level
than his conflicts and his tragedies. To understand Dostoyévsky
is to accept his tragedies as irreducible and not to try to shirk them
by the contrivances of his smaller self. His Christianity in particular is of a very doubtful kind. It is impossible to overlook the
fact that it was no ultimate solution to him, that it did not reach
into the ultimate depths of his soul, that it was a more or less
superficial spiritual formation which it is dangerous to identify
with real Christianity. But these issues are too complicated, too
important, and too debatable to be more than pointed at in a book
of the present kind.

The ideological character of Dostoyévsky's novels is in itself
sufficient to mark him off from the rest of the Russian realistic
school. It is obviously different in kind from the social messages of
the novels of Turgénev or Goncharóv. The interests at stake are of
a different order. The fusion of the philosophical and imaginative
fabric is complete; the conversations are never irrelevant, because
they *are* the novel (as the analysis can never be irrelevant in
Tolstóy's, or the atmosphere in Turgénev's, novels). Novels of the
same kind have been written only under the direct influence of
Dostoyévsky by novelists of the symbolist school, but of them
only Andréy Bély has succeeded in being original and creative.

Another feature that distinguishes Dostoyévsky from the other realists is his partiality for sensationalism and elaborate intrigue. In this he is a true disciple of Balzac, of the French sensational school, and of Dickens. His novels, however charged they may be with ideas and philosophy, are in substance novels of mystery and suspense. He was in complete control of the technique of this kind of novel. The devices he uses to lengthen the suspense and mystery of his novels are numerous. Everyone remembers the ultimately unsolved mystery of the murder of old Karamázov and the cat-and-mouse game of Porfíry, the examining magistrate, with Raskólnikov. A characteristic device is also the omission in *The Idiot* of all account of the life of Prince Mýshkin, Rogózhin, and Nastásia Filípovna in Moscow in the period between the first and second parts, to which allusion is often mysteriously made in an offhand manner as if to explain their subsequent relations. The atmosphere of tension to bursting point is arrived at by a series of minor devices, familiar to every reader of every novel of Dostoyévsky, that are easily reducible to a common principle. This combination of the ideological and sensational elements is, from the literary point of view, the most striking feature of Dostoyévsky's "developed manner."

In his interestedness in current social issues, in his "philanthropic" sympathy for the suffering, insignificant man, above all in his choice of milieu, and in the elaboration of concrete, realistic detail, especially in the speech of his characters, Dostoyévsky belongs to the realistic school. It would, however, be a mistake to regard his novels as *representations* of Russian life under Alexander II—not only because it is in general dangerous to regard even realistic fiction as a representation of life, but because Dostoyévsky is in substance less true to life than any other writer. Aksákov, Turgénev, Goncharóv, Tolstóy, did at least honestly try to represent Russian life as they saw it. Dostoyévsky did not. He dealt in spiritual essences, in emanations of his own infinitely fertile spiritual experience. He only gave them the externally realistic garbs of current life and attached them to current facts of Russian life. But *The Possessed* is no more a true picture of the terrorists of the sixties than Gógol's Plyúshkin is the true picture of a typical miser. They are exteriorizations of the author's self. Hence their latent "prophetic" and universal significance. They are distinctly on a different scale from the Russian life of the time. *The Possessed*, though a novel of terroristic conspiracy, is about something quite different from what the actual terroristic movement was about. Dostoyévsky's Russia is no more the real Russia of Alexander II than the characters of *Wuthering Heights* are the real West Riding of the early nineteenth century. They are related to it and symbolical of it, but they belong to another order of existence.

The essential units of Dostoyévsky's novels are the characters, and in this respect he is in the true tradition of Russian novel writing, which regards the novelist as primarily a maker of characters. His characters are at once saturated with metaphysical significance and symbolism, and intensely individual. Dostoyévsky is as great a master as Tolstóy in giving individuality to the people of his creation. But the nature of this individuality is different: Tolstóy's characters are faces, flesh and blood, men and women of our acquaintance, ordinary and unique, like people in real life. Dostoyévsky's are souls, spirits. Even in his lewd and sensual sinners, their carnal self is not so much their body and their nerves as the spiritual essence of their body, of their carnality. Flesh— real, material flesh—is absent from the world of Dostoyévsky, but the idea, the spirit of flesh, is very present, and this is why in that world the spirit can be assailed by the flesh on its own spiritual ground. These spiritual extracts of the flesh are among the most terrible and tremendous creations of Dostoyévsky—and no one has ever created anything approaching the impure grandeur of old Karamázov.

The portrait gallery of Dostoyévsky is enormous and varied. It is impossible to enumerate the portraits or to give briefly characteristics of them: their vitality, reality, and complexity, and their quantity are too great. They live in every one of the great novels (and in the minor novels too) a strange, morbid, dematerialized life, of terribly human demons or terribly live ghosts— with their "cracks" (*nadrýv*, a word used in a sense not unlike Freud's "complex") and wounds, their spiritual intensity and intense personality, their self-consciousness, their pride (the "proud women" especially), and their knowledge of good and evil—a suffering, tormented, and never-to-be-pacified race. Of the individual novels, the most rich in persons is perhaps *The Possessed*, which contains at least three creations that come at the top of the list—the terrible and weirdly empty figure of the hero, Stavrógin; the "pure" atheist, Kirílov, perhaps next to *Memoirs from Underground*, the most ultimately profound creation of Dostoyévsky; and the no less terrible "little demon," the mean and strong plotter, flatterer, idolater, and murderer, Peter Verkhovénsky. These three figures are enough to indicate in their maker a creative force in which he has had no human rivals.

Though influential as a publicist, and always recognized (chiefly, however, on the strength of *Poor Folk* and *The House of Death*) as a very eminent novelist, Dostoyévsky during his lifetime did not get anything like adequate recognition. This is only natural: his mentality was "prophetic" and belonged historically, not to his own time, but to that preceding the great Revolution. He was the first and the greatest symptom of the spiritual decomposition of the Russain soul in its highest levels which preceded the final break-up of Imperial Russia.

His literary influence during his lifetime and in the eighties was insignificant and limited to a certain revival of the theme of pity and compassion, and to a certain vogue of morbid psychology among a few second-rate novelists. Nor was his influence in the strictly literary sense important even afterwards. Very few writers can in any strict sense be called his literary progeny. But the influence of Dostoyévsky as a whole and complete phenomenon cannot be exaggerated. The pre-Revolutionary generation, especially that born between 1865 and 1880 (that is to say, by a curious coincidence, between the dates of the first and last of his great novels), was literally soaked with his ideas and his mentality. Since then the younger generation has become more indifferent to him. Not that his greatness is put to question, not even that he is less read or less written about. But our organism has grown immune to his poisons, which we have assimilated and ejected. The most typical attitude of our contemporaries towards Dostoyévsky is to accept him as an absorbingly interesting novelist of adventure. The young men of today are not very far from putting him on a level with Dumas, an attitude that testifies of course to a very limited sensitiveness to his essential individuality. But it would be wrong to lament this attitude; for the real Dostoyévsky is food that is easily assimilated only by a profoundly diseased spiritual organism.

SALTYKÓV-SCHEDRÍN

The civic and social element already so prominent in the work of Turgénev and of the other novelists of the forties was further emphasized by the writers of the reign of Alexander II. The antiæsthetic movement on the one hand, and the increased possibility of exposing and satirizing existing social and administrative conditions on the other, led to the formation of a literary genre that stood halfway between fiction and journalism. The first and the most remarkable of these semi-novelists and semi-journalists, as well as the only one who was to win more or less general recognition and to be included in the number of classics, was Michael Evgráfovich Saltykóv (1826–89), better known in his own time under the pseudonym of N. Schedrín.

Born of a family of country squires, Saltykóv was educated at the same Lyceum where Púshkin had studied. In 1844, on the completion of his studies, he entered the Civil Service. At the same time he came in touch with the progressive circles of the young generation and began writing for the Westernizing press. Two stories by him, in the style of the "natural school," appeared in 1847–8, over pseudonyms. Their appearance coincided with the turn towards extreme reaction, and Saltykóv, for having written them, was suddenly transferred to the northeastern city of Vyátka (where Herzen had been transferred fourteen years earlier). In Vyátka, Saltykóv remained in the Civil Service and, in spite of his disgrace, even rose to a rather important and responsible post in the administrative board controlling the provincial police. After the accession of Alexander II he was transferred back to Petersburg and in 1858 appointed vice-governor of a province. In 1856 he resumed his literary work. *Provincial Sketches*, a series of satirical sketches of provincial officialdom, appeared in Nekrásov's *Sovreménnik* over the pseudonym of N. Schedrín. In the reforming atmosphere of 1856–61 his writings were received with general approval, and he soon became one of the most universally recognized authors. In 1868 he left the Civil Service to consecrate himself entirely to literature, and, together with Nekrásov, became the editor of *Otéchestvennye zapíski*, which was to replace the *Sovreménnik*, suppressed by the authorities in 1866. Henceforward

Saltykóv became one of the leaders of the radical intelligentsia and retained this position till his death. His review was the most advanced of all the left organs of the home press. The reaction that followed the assassination of Alexander II was fatal to it; it was suppressed in 1884. In the eighties Saltykóv remained a last remnant of the heroic age of reform and progress, universally venerated by all the advanced intelligentsia.

The greater part of Saltykóv's work is a rather nondescript kind of satirical journalism, for the most part with no narrative skeleton, and intermediate in form between the classical "character" and the modern *feuilleton*. Enormously and universally popular though it was in its own time, it has since lost much of its attraction simply because it satirizes conditions that have long ceased to exist and much of it has become unintelligible without comment.

His early works (*Provincial Sketches*, 1856–7; *Pompadours and Pompadouresses*, 1863–73, and others) are a "smiling" satire, more humorous than scornful, of the vices of the pre-Reform provincial officials. There are little earnestness and positive value in these early satires, and the extreme nihilist Písarev was not quite in the wrong when he condemned them as irresponsible and uninspired joking in a famous article entitled *Flowers of Innocent Humor* that scandalized the other radicals.

In 1869–70 appeared *The History of a Town*, which sums up the achievement of Saltykóv's first period. It is a sort of parody of Russian history, concentrated in the microcosm of a provincial town, whose successive governors are transparent caricatures of Russian sovereigns and ministers, and whose very name is representative of its qualities—Glúpov (Sillytown).

Saltykóv's later work is inspired by a keener sense of indignation and higher feeling for moral values. The satire is directed against the new post-Reform men: the "enlightened," but essentially unchanged, official; the unrooted, but unregenerate, squire; the grasping and shameless capitalist risen from the people. The intrinsic value of these books (*Gentlemen of Tashként*, 1869–72; *In the Realm of the Moderate and of the Exact*, 1874–7; *The Sanctuary Mon-Repos*, 1878–79; *Letters to Auntie*, 1881–2, and others) is greater than that of the earlier ones, but the excessive topicality of the satire makes them date very distinctly. Besides, they are written in a language that Saltykóv himself called Æsopic. It is

one continuous circumlocution in view of the censorship and demands a constant running commentary. The style, moreover, is
deeply rooted in the bad journalese of the period, which goes back
to Senkówski's and which today invariably produces an impression
of painfully elaborate vulgarity.

On a higher level of literary achievement stand the *Fables*,
written in 1880–5, in which Saltykóv achieved a greater degree of
artistic tightness, and occasionally (as in the admirable *Konyága*,
in which the destinies of the Russian peasant are symbolized in the
figure of an old downridden jade) a concentration that almost
attains to poetry.

But, after all, Saltykóv's place in Russian literature would be
only that of an eminent journalist were it not for his masterpiece—
his only genuine novel—*The Golovlëv Family* (1872–6). This one
book places him in the very front line of Russian realistic novelists
and secures him a permanent place among the national classics.
It is a social novel—the natural history of a family of provincial
squires, intended to show up the poverty and bestiality of the
civilization of the serf-owning class. The reign of brute matter
over human lives has never been portrayed with greater force.
Spiteful, greedy, selfish, without even any family feeling for each
other, without even any satisfaction or any possibility of happiness
in their dull and dark souls, the Golovlëvs are an unrelieved
wilderness of animal humanity. The book is certainly the gloomiest
in all Russian literature—all the more gloomy because the effect
is attained by the simplest means without any theatrical, melodramatic, or atmospheric effects. Together with Goncharóv's
Oblómov before, and Búnin's *Sukhodól* after it, it is the greatest
monumentum odiosum erected to the memory of the Russian provincial gentry. The most remarkable single figure in the novel is
Porfíry Golovlëv, nicknamed Iúdushka (little Judas), the empty
and mechanical hypocrite who cannot stop talking unctuous and
meaningless humbug, not for any inner need or outer profit, but
because his tongue is in need of constant exercise. It is one of the
most terrible visions of ultimately dehumanized humanity ever
conceived by an imaginative writer.

In his last years Saltykóv undertook a large work of retrospective painting—*Old Years in Poshekhónie* (1887–9)—a chronicle of the life and surroundings of a family of the middle provincial
gentry shortly before the abolition of serfdom. It contains numer-

ous reminiscences of his own childhood. "Tendentious" and un-relievedly gloomy, it abounds in powerful painting but lacks that concentration and inevitability which *The Golovlëv Family* has, and which alone would have raised it above the level of mere "literature with a purpose."

THE DECLINE OF THE NOVEL IN THE SIXTIES AND SEVENTIES

By about 1860 the rank of universally approved authors was filled in, and no new novelist who appeared after that date was able to command general recognition. This was owing to two co-operative causes: the growing intensity of party feeling, which was breaking Russian opinion into more exclusive compartments and categories; and the very evident and distinct decline of creative force among the writers of the younger generation. The only novelist after 1860 who had nothing to fear from a comparison with the men of the forties was Nicholas Leskóv (1831–95). But the exasperated state of party feeling and his inability to fit in with any party precluded his general recognition—he was hooted down by the radical press and even placed under boycott. The late recognition of Leskóv, as well as the fact that his work has features that mark it off distinctly from that of all his contemporaries, has made me decide to discuss him in a later chapter.

In his early work, however—the reactionary novels *No Way Out* (1864) and *At Daggers Drawn* (1870)—Leskóv is little more than a typical "tendentious" anti-radical whose novels are scarcely superior to the common run of reactionary novels that were written in great quantities in the sixties and seventies to satirize the new movement and the young generation. This kind of fiction includes, it is true, such superior—and different—works as Písemsky's *Troubled Seas* (1863, the first of the lot), Turgénev's *Smoke*, Goncharóv's *The Precipice*, and even Dostoyévsky's *The Possessed*. But the typical reactionary novel is on a much lower level of literary significance. It is usually the story of an aristocratic and patriotic hero who fights single-handed, in spite of the insufficient support of the authorities, against Polish intrigue and nihilism. The most typical and popular purveyor of such novels was Bole-sław Markiéwicz. Other practitioners in the kind were Victor Klyúshnikov, V. G. Avséyenko, and Vsévolod Krestóvsky.

The reactionary novel had its counterpart in the "tendentious" radical novel, which early became equally conventionalized. The most notable of these novels was the first of them, Chernyshévsky's *What to Do?* (1864), which had a considerable influence on the formation of the radical youth. Other famous and influential novels were *Signs of the Times*, by Daniel Mordóvtsev, and *Step by Step*, by Innocent Omulévsky. The most prolific of the radical novelists was A. K. Scheller-Mikháylov. All these novels are about ideal radical young men and girls victoriously struggling against hostile social conditions. From a literary point of view they are all quite worthless. But they contributed to the formation of the idealistic intelligentsia of the seventies.

In the seventies a third kind of "tendentious" novel was added to these two: the populist (*naródnik*) novel. It did not represent the individual virtues of the heroes of the educated classes, but the collective virtues of the peasant commune in its struggle against the dark faces of big and small capitalists. The most notable of these populist novelists were N. N. Zlatovrátsky (1845–1911) and P. V. Zasodímsky (1843–1912).

Other novelists continued the traditions of Turgénev and the men of the forties without exaggerating the "tendentious" element, but emphasized the social at the expense of the artistic element of their realism. Peter Dmítrievich Boborýkin (1836–1921) tried to rival Turgénev in his sensitiveness to the changes of mood of the Russian intelligentsia, and his innumerable novels form a sort of chronicle of Russian society from the sixties to the twentieth century. A more genuine spirit of the school of Turgénev will be found in the rural novels of Eugene Márkov. Another rural novelist of some importance was Sergéy Terpigórev, whose *Impoverishment* (1880) was intended as a vast picture of the social decay of the middle gentry of central Russia after the abolition of serfdom.

Somewhat apart from the other fiction of his time stand the unpretentious and quite enjoyable stories of naval life by Constantine Stanyukóvich, the only Russian novelist of the sea in the nineteenth century. Still more apart stand the fairy tales by N. P. Wagner ("Kot-Murlýka"), Professor of Zoology at the University of Petersburg, the only writer of the time who attempted to write in a style that was not dominated by the canons of the "natural school."

These canons invaded the historical novel as well as the novel of contemporary life. The romantic and moderately realistic historical novel in the style of Scott breathed its last breath in the operatic *Prince Serébryany* (1863) of Alexéy Tolstóy, a work that is considerably below the level of his poetical, and even of his dramatic, achievement. The new historical novel was a sort of vulgarization of the method used by the other Tolstóy in *War and Peace*. Its principal practitioner was Count Eugène Salias de Tournemir. Other historical novelists, greatly in vogue in the last quarter of the century among the less sophisticated, but as a rule looked down upon by the advanced and the literate, were G. P. Danilévsky and Vsévolod Soloviëv, son of the historian and brother of the famous philosopher.

All this novel writing was frankly and obviously derivative and second-rate. In so far as the younger generation (apart from Leskóv) produced anything, if not quite first-class, at least genuine, it all came from a group of young men of plebeian origin and radical convictions, who are somewhat loosely grouped by literary historians as the "plebeian novelists of the sixties" (*belletrísty raznochíntsy*).

THE "PLEBEIAN" NOVELISTS

The most notable of the plebeian novelists was Nikoláy Gerásimovich Pomyalóvsky (1835–63). He was the son of a deacon of a Petersburg suburb and was educated at a clerical seminary, which left in him, as was usual, none but the gloomiest impressions. His subsequent life was one continuous struggle for existence, which led him, as it did so many others of his time and class, to an early surrender to drink. He died at the age of twenty-eight after a particularly acute access of delirium tremens. All his work was done in the last three years of his life. His most famous book, and the one that made his reputation, was *Seminary Sketches* (1862–3), in which by the mere sober and matter-of-fact accumulation of realistic detail he succeeded in producing an impression of almost infernal horror. In *Bourgeois Happiness* and in its sequel, *Mólotov* (1861), Pomyalóvsky drew the character of a man of the young generation. He did not idealize his hero, nor did he even represent him as an idealist, but as a strong man intent on finding for himself a place in life. When Pomyalóvsky died he was working at a vast social novel, *Brother and Sister*, picturing the life of a family of small Petersburg townspeople. The fragments that remain make us bitterly regret the loss of a novelist of vast outlook, original imagination, and powerful grasp of reality. His unsweetened and unidealized, but by no means flat, realism; his careful avoidance of everything poetical and rhetorical; and his strong sense of the grim poetry of ugliness—all were an individual and new note in the orchestra of Russian realism. There was also in Pomyalóvsky a cement of practical sense that is unusual in a Russian intellectual and only transiently a feature of the first generation of plebeian intellectuals that came after the generation of the forties.

The same anti-romanticism and anti-æstheticism, a natural reaction against the idealism of the forties, produced in the sixties an attitude towards the Russian peasant that was opposed to the sentimental philanthropism of the preceding age. It did not emphasize the human values that can be discovered in the peasant, but the brutishness to which he had been reduced by centuries of oppression and ignorance. This attitude, with a touch of cynical flippancy, is apparent in the witty sketches and dialogues of Nicholas Uspénsky (1837–89; a first cousin of the more important Gleb Uspénsky, of whom presently), which appeared in 1861 and were greeted by Chernyshévsky as the dawn of a new and more sensible attitude to the people than that of the sentimental "philanthropists." The same attitude is apparent in a less trivial form in the work of Vasíly Alexéyevich Sleptsóv (1836–78), one of the most characteristic figures of the sixties. A nobleman and an exceedingly handsome man, Sleptsóv had a powerful attraction for the other sex. He put into practice the ideals of free love to which his generation was devoted. To the indignation of the radicals, he was transparently lampooned by Leskóv in the reactionary novel *No Way Out*. As a writer Sleptsóv is particularly remarkable for his brilliant command of realistic dialogue. The dialogue of his peasants, often intensely comical, preserves all the spoken intonations and all dialectal peculiarities, and has the merit of a phonographic record without forfeiting the workmanlike tensity of genuine art. Sleptsóv's most ambitious work, *Hard Times* (1865), is a satirical picture of the liberal society of the sixties.

The same unsentimental attitude to the peasants, but raised to a more earnestly tragic power, inspires the work of Fëdor Mikháylovich Reshétnikov (1841–71), whose life story is almost

identical with Pomyalóvsky's except that he was born in the
far-off Province of Perm and had to surmount still greater difficulties in his struggle for a place in life. His story, portraying the
life of the Finnish Permyaks of his native province, *The People of
Podlípnoye* (1864), produced a tremendous impression by its ruthless representation of the peasants (the critics overlooked the fact
that they were not Russian) as unmitigated, hopeless, downtrodden, and miserable brutes. The story was one of those which
most powerfully promoted the movement of the "conscience-
stricken nobles" by rousing in them a sense of social guilt for the
state to which the people had been reduced.

The biography of Alexander Ivánovich Lévitov (1835–77) is
again almost the same story over again as those of Pomyalóvsky
and Reshétnikov. He spent most of his life in wandering over the
vast expanses of Russia, and his work is concerned chiefly with
the homeless life of tramps and pilgrims. Lévitov stands out among
his contemporaries for the romantic character of his work, which
combines a poignantly lyrical note with a bitter irony in a way
that is reminiscent of Heine's.

A very notable figure in the history of the Russian intelligentsia is Gleb Ivánovich Uspénsky (1843–1902). He began his
literary career in 1866, with a series of sketches of life in the sub-
urbs of his native city of Túla, *Manners of Rasteryáyeva Street*, in
which he displayed an unmistakable gift of humor and human
sympathy as well as a sober and unbiased vision of life. But his
most characteristic and influential writings belong to the end of
the seventies and to the early eighties, when after several years in
the country he gave a series of semi-journalistic, semi-imaginative
sketches of peasant life, the most important of which is *The Power
of the Soil* (1882). They are marked by the same gifts of humor and
intense humanity, of sober, unobscured vision. They reflected his
disillusionment in the populist conception of the Russian peasant
as an ideal communist. Appearing as they did in Saltykóv's radical
review side by side with Zlatovrátsky's idealizations of the peasant
commune, they contributed powerfully to the breakdown of dogmatic populism. But Gleb Uspénsky is interesting not only as a
student of peasant life. He is in general one of the most representative and characteristic figures of the best type of Russian intellectual. Possessed of a morbidly developed moral sensitiveness,

he lived the conflicts and the tragedies of the Russian radical mind with extraordinary intensity. The tragic romance of the Russian intellectual with the Russian people was played out in his soul as in a microcosm. Unfortunately his writings, diffuse and intensely topical, are obsolete even more than Saltykóv's, and few except students of the history of the Russian intelligentsia read them nowadays. In the early nineties Gleb Uspénsky became a victim to mental illness, which lasted till his death. It took the form of a morbid disintegration of personality. He felt himself divided into two beings, one of which he designated by his Christian name, Gleb; the other by his patronymic, Ivánovich. Gleb was the embodiment of all that was good; Ivánovich of all that was evil in Uspénsky—an identification characteristic of the eminently anti-traditional and rootless nature of the Russian radical intelligentsia.

At the end of the seventies another remarkable semi-journalist was Andrew Novodvórsky (1853–82), who wrote under the pseudonym of A. Ósipovich. He took part in the revolutionary movement, and his stories are, as it were, fragments from the diary of an intellectual who was unable to identify himself wholeheartedly with what he thought the one important thing—revolutionary propaganda. The style of Novodvórsky is personal and full of a fine irony and incisive humor. He, alone in his generation, played with the plot and with the narrative illusion in the manner of Sterne. The obscurities and innuendoes impressed on him by the presence of the censorship contributed to enhance the whimsical and capricious character of his delightfully personal prose.

It is particularly agreeable for me to end this book with the name of Nicholas Afanásievich Kuschévsky, one of the most delightful and least recognized of Russian writers. His biography is similar to those of numerous plebeian writers. Born in 1847 in Siberia, he came to Petersburg at the end of the sixties in search of literary employment but met with unsurmountable difficulties and succumbed to disease, destitution, and drink. While he lay convalescent in a municipal hospital, he succeeded in writing his one important work, the novel *Nicholas Negórev, or The Happy Russian.* It appeared in Saltykóv's and Nekrásov's magazine in 1871 and in book form in 1872, and had a considerable success among the radical public. But his later work did not bear out the promise of that book and is hardly above the level of average journalism. After five more years of hopeless struggle against starvation, undermined by drink and consumption, Kuschévsky died in 1876.

Nicholas Negórev assumes the more or less orthodox form of a chronicled life, the greater part of which is occupied by the childhood and boyhood of the hero. This hero, in whose person the narrative is conducted, is a remarkable type of moderately ambitious, moderately clever, moderately cowardly, moderately priggish boy who grows up to be a successful, satisfied, and selfish bureaucrat. But it is not the central figure, however finely drawn, that makes the unique charm of the book. The other characters— Nicholas's reckless, foolish, and generous brother Andrew; their sister Liza; the extraordinary crank and fanatic Ovérin; the hero's *fiancée* Sophie Vasílievna—are all figures endowed with a convincing liveliness that challenges comparison with *War and Peace.* Kuschévsky's delicacy of touch is unique in Russian literature. For liveliness and lightness of humor the book has no equals. On a higher level of seriousness, the character of the fanatic Ovérin, with his succession of dead-serious and dangerously earnest fads while a schoolboy and his propagandist activities when grown up, and the scene of the death of Sophie Vasílievna belong to the greatest achievement of Russian fiction. From the historical point of view the novel offers an unsurpassed picture of the change that transformed the Russia of Nicholas I into the almost anarchic Russia of the sixties.

Book Two: After 1881

T O

Maurice Baring

CHAPTER 1

The End of a Great Age

THE reign of Alexander II (1855–81) was an age of great literary achievement, the Golden Age of the Russian novel. It saw the making of almost every one of the great works of Russian fiction, from Turgénev's *Rúdin* and Aksákov's *Family Chronicle* to *Anna Karénina* and *The Brothers Karamázov*. The best forces were attracted to the novel, but by its side other forms of imaginative literature continued to flourish and helped to produce the impression of a Golden Age. But there was a worm in the flower: all this great achievement was by men of an older generation, and they had no successors. Not one of the younger men who had entered the literary career since 1856 was felt worthy to stand beside them, and as one by one the old men disappeared, there was no one to take their place. The turning point came soon after 1880: Dostoyévsky died in 1881, Turgénev in 1883. Tolstóy announced his withdrawal from literature. The great age was over.

The generation born between 1830 and 1850 was by no means poor in talents, but these talents were directed into other channels than literature. It was a generation of great composers—Musórgsky, Tchaikóvsky, Rímsky-Kórsakov; of great scientists, like Mendeléyev; of eminent painters, journalists, lawyers, and historians. But its poets and novelists were recruited from among the second-rate. It was as if the nation had expended too much of its forces on literature and was now making up by giving all the genius it had to the other arts and sciences.

But apart from this mysterious process of restoring the balance between various spheres of intellectual activity, there were good reasons why literature should decline. The first is connected with certain essential features of Russian literature itself, and of Russian literary criticism in particular. The great Russian novelists were superb masters of their craft, even those of them who, like Tolstóy, most tried to hide it and affected to despise "form." But they *did* try to hide it and *did* affect to despise "form." At any rate, before the public they seemed to countenance the view that it was their message that signified, and not their art. The critics went further and crudely identified the value of literary work with the moral or social utility of its message. They "declared war on æsthetics," and proscribed all interest in "pure art." New beginners in literature became easily imbued with the doctrine that form was naught, and matter everything. This made impossible the transmission of those traditions of the craft which alone permit the normal development of literary art. The young were prevented from profiting by the example of their elders and betters by a taboo laid on all questions of form. They could only ape them, unconsciously and unintelligently, but not learn from them in any creative sense. The generation of 1860 made an attempt to break away from the established forms of the novel. This attempt promised to develop into a creative quest for new ways of expression, something like a premature futurist movement. But the atmosphere was unpropitious for such a development, and it ended in nothing. The most significant of the young innovators, Pomyalóvsky, died very young, and under the general pressure of utilitarianism the movement, instead of leading to a rejuvenation of old forms, resulted in a complete emancipation from all form. This stage is reached in the work of the most gifted democratic novelist of the period—Gleb Uspénsky. As for the more traditional and conservative writers, they were able only to repeat the processes and methods of the great realists, vulgarizing and cheapening them. Whether they applied the realistic manner to give a fresh appearance to the historical novel, or used it to make propaganda for or against radical ideas, or to describe the virtues of the peasant commune and the vices of capitalistic civilization, they are all equally unoriginal, uninteresting and, unreadable. They can only be classified, like M. P.'s, according to their political allegiance.

A second reason that accentuated the break of literary tradition was the great social upheaval produced by the Emancipation of the serfs and the other liberal reforms of the first half of Alexander II's reign. The Emancipation dealt a mortal blow to the economic welfare of the class that had up to then monopolized all literary culture—the landed gentry. Its middle strata, which were intellectually the most active, suffered most from the blow. A new class arose to replace them—the intelligentsia. The origin of this class was composite. It absorbed many members of the ruined gentry, but the groundwork consisted of men risen from the lower, or rather *outer*, classes that had not previously taken part in modern civilization. Sons of the clergy were especially numerous and prominent among the new men of the sixties. One feature is common to all these new intellectuals—complete apostasy from all parental tradition. If he was the son of a priest, he would of necessity be an atheist; if the son of a squire, an agrarian socialist. Revolt against all tradition was the only watchword of the class. To preserve a literary tradition under these circumstances was doubly difficult—and it was not preserved. Only that was retained from the older writers which was considered to be directly useful for the purposes of revolution and progress.

The Reforms produced an enormous change in Russian life and opened many new channels to ambitious and vigorous men, who under the preceding regime would most probably have turned to writing verse or fiction. The new law courts demanded large numbers of educated and civilized workers. The rapid growth of capitalistic enterprises attracted numerous workers, and the number of engineers was many times multiplied. The rise of evolutionary theories made science fashionable and attractive. The whole atmosphere became freer and more propitious for every kind of intellectual activity. Political journalism became possible and lucrative, and direct revolutionary action absorbed much of the best forces of the younger generation. It would be an error to believe that under freer conditions literature and the arts must necessarily prosper more than under despotism. The contrary is more often the case. When all other activity becomes difficult, they attract all that is ambitious and wants to express itself in intellectual work. Literature, like everything else, requires time and work, and when other work is attractive and easily found, fewer persons can give their time to the muses. When new fields of intellectual activity are suddenly thrown open, as was the case in Russia about 1860, the conditions are particularly unfavorable for the progress of literary art. When they are again closed, literature again attracts the intellectual unemployed. Milton was a political

pamphleteer and an administrator when his party were in power—
and wrote *Paradise Lost* after the triumph of his enemies. The
immediate effect on literature of the great liberal Reforms of
Alexander II was a shortage of new hands. The sixties and seventies
in the history of Russian literature were a period when work of the
first order was done by men of a preceding generation, and the
young generation, absorbed by other activities, could give to literature only its second best.

When, with the approach of the eighties, the atmosphere
began to change, the younger generation had still nothing to show
to compare with the work of their fathers. The few survivors of
the great generation were looked up to as the solitary remnants
of a better age, and the greatest of them, Tolstóy, was for many
years after his "conversion" without comparison the greatest and
most significant figure in Russian literature, a solitary giant in-
commensurable with the pygmies at his feet.

TOLSTÓY AFTER 1880

Tolstóy's writings after 1880 are divided by a deep cleft from all
his earlier work. But they belong to the same man, and much of
what appeared at first new and startling in the later Tolstóy
existed in a less developed form in the early Tolstóy. From the very
beginning we cannot fail to discern in him an obstinate search for
a rational meaning to life; a confidence in the powers of common
sense and his own reason; contempt for modern civilization with
its "artificial" multiplication of needs; a deeply rooted irreverence
for all the functions and conventions of State and Society; a sovereign disregard for accepted opinions and scientific and literary
"good form"; and a pronounced tendency to teach. But what was
disseminated and disconnected in his early writings was welded
after his conversion into a solid consistent doctrine, dogmatically
settled in every detail. And the doctrine was such as to surprise
and repel most of his old admirers. Before 1880 he had belonged,
if anywhere, to the conservative camp, and only an exceptionally
acute critic like Mikhaylóvsky could as early as 1873 discern the
essentially revolutionary foundation of Tolstóy's mentality.

Tolstóy had always been fundamentally a rationalist. But at
the time he wrote his great novels his rationalism was suffering an

eclipse. The philosophy of *War and Peace* and *Anna Karénina* (which he formulates in *A Confession* as "that one should live so as to have the best for oneself and one's family") was a surrender of his rationalism to the inherent irrationalism of life. The search for the meaning of life was abandoned. The meaning of life was Life itself. The greatest wisdom consisted in accepting without sophistication one's place in Life and making the best of it. But already in the last part of *Anna Karénina* a growing disquietude becomes very apparent. When he was writing it the crisis had already begun that is so memorably recorded in *A Confession* and from which he was to emerge the prophet of a new religious and ethical teaching.

The teaching of Tolstóy is a rationalized "Christianity," stripped of all tradition and all positive mysticism. He rejected personal immortality and concentrated exclusively on the moral teaching of the Gospels. Of the moral teaching of Christ the words, "Resist not evil," were taken to be the principle out of which all the rest follows. He rejected the authority of the Church, which sanctioned the State, and he condemned the State, which sanctioned violence and compulsion. Both were immoral, like every form of organized compulsion. His condemnation of every form of compulsion authorizes us to classify Tolstóy's teaching, in its political aspect, as anarchism. This condemnation extended to every state as such, and he had no more respect for the democratic states of the West than for Russian autocracy. But in practice the edge of his anarchism was directed against the existing regime in Russia. He allowed that a constitution might be a lesser evil than autocracy (he recommended it in *The Young Tsar*, written after Nicholas II's accession in 1894), and his attacks were often directed against the same institutions as those of the radicals and revolutionaries. His attitude towards the active revolutionaries was ambiguous. He disapproved on principle of violent methods and consequently of political murder. But there was a difference in his attitude towards revolutionary terrorism and governmental suppression. As early as 1881 he remained unmoved by the assassination of Alexander II but wrote a letter of protest against the execution of the assassins. To all intents and purposes, Tolstóy became one of the greatest forces on the side of revolution, and the revolutionaries recognized this and paid homage to the "grand old man," though they did not accept his doctrine of "non-resistance" and though they treated his followers with contempt. Tolstóy's agreement with the Socialists was further accentuated by his own communism and condemnation of private property, especially in land. The methods he proposed for the abolition of the evil were different (they included the voluntary abdication of all money and land), but the negative part of his doctrine was in this point identical with Socialism.

Tolstóy's conversion was, largely, the reaction of his fundamental rationalism against the irrationalism into which he had allowed himself to drift in the sixties and seventies. His metaphysics may be summed up as the identification of the principle of life with reason. Like Socrates, he boldly identifies absolute good with absolute knowledge. "Reason, that is, good" is a favorite phrase of his, and occupies as central a place in his doctrine as *Deus sive Natura* does in Spinoza's. Knowledge is the necessary foundation of good, and this knowledge is inherent in every man. But it is obscured and stifled by the evil fogs of civilization and sophistry. It is necessary only to listen to the inner voice of one's conscience (which he was inclined to identify with the practical reason of Kant) and not to be misled by the false lights of human sophistry, which includes the whole of civilization—art, science, social tradition, law, as well as the historical dogmas of theological religion. But for all its rationalism, Tolstóy's religion is in a sense mystical. It is true that he rejected all the accepted mysticism of the churches, declined to recognize God as a Person, and spoke with satirical scorn (which to every believer will appear as the wildest blasphemy) of the sacraments. And yet his final authority (as in fact all the final authority of every metaphysical rationalism) is the irrational human "conscience." He did his utmost to identify it in theory with reason. But the mystical *daimonion* constantly reappeared, and in all his more remarkable later works "conversion" is described as an essentially mystical experience. It is mystical in that it is personal and unique. It is the result of an intimate revelation, which may or may not be prepared by previous intellectual development, but is essentially, like every mystical experience, incommunicable. In Tolstóy's own case, as described in *A Confession*, it is led up to by his whole previous intellectual life. But all purely intellectual solutions to the essential question were unsatisfactory, and the final solution is represented as a series of mystical experiences, repeated flashes of inner light. The civilized man lives in a state of unquestioning sin. The questions of meaning and justification arise against his will—as the effect of fear of death—and the answer comes as a ray of inner light—the process described thus more than once by Tolstóy—in *A Confession*, in *The Death of Iván Ilýich*, in the *Memoirs of a Madman*, in *Master and Man*. The necessary consequence of this fact is that the truth cannot be preached, but may only be discovered for oneself. This is the doctrine of *A Confession*, which does not attempt to demonstrate, but only to narrate and to "infect." Later on, however, when the original impulse had widened, he attempted to preach it in logical form. He really always disbelieved in the efficacy of preaching. It was his disciples, men of a very different cast, who made Tolstoyism a preaching doctrine and encouraged Tolstóy to preach. In its final form the mystical element of Tolstóy's teaching is practically eliminated, and his religion becomes an essentially eudæmonistic doctrine—a doctrine founded on the search after happiness. Man must be good because it is the only way for him to be happy. In a typical work of the period when his teaching became crystallized and dogmatic—*Resurrection*—the mystical motive is absent and Nekhlyúdov's regeneration is no more than an adaptation of his life to the moral law, in order to free himself from the disagreeable reactions of conscience. In Tolstóy's final conception the moral law, which acts through the medium of conscience, is a law in the strict scientific sense, in the same sense as gravitation or any other natural law. This is powerfully expressed in the idea—borrowed from Buddhism—of Karma, a conception profoundly different from the Christian in that Karma operates mechanically, without any intervention of Divine Grace, and is a necessary consequence of sin. Morality in the finally crystallized form of Tolstoyism is the art of avoiding Karma or of adapting oneself to it. Tolstóy's morality, being a morality of happiness, is also a morality of purity, not of sympathy. Love of God, that is, of the moral law inside oneself, is the primary and only virtue, and charity—love for one's fellow creatures—is only a consequence. Charity—the actual feeling of love—is not a necessity for the Tolstoyan saint. He must act as if he loves his fellow men, and that will mean that he loves God and he will be happy. Tolstoyism is thus at the opposite pole to the teaching of Dostoyévsky. For Dostoyévsky, charity—love of men, pity—is the one supreme virtue, and God is revealed only through pity and charity. Tolstóy's religion is entirely egotistic. There is no God except the moral law inside man. The end of good actions is inner peace. This makes us understand the charge of Epicureanism that has been brought against Tolstóy, and also that of Luciferism and measureless pride, for there is nothing *outside* Tolstóy to which he bows.

Tolstóy was ever a great rationalist, and his rationalism found satisfaction in the admirably constructed system of his religion. But the irrational Tolstóy remained alive beneath the hardened crust of crystallized dogma. Tolstóy's diaries reveal how difficult it was for him to inwardly live up to his ideal of moral happiness. Except during the first years when he was carried on by the initial mystical impulse of his conversion, he was never happy in the sense he wanted to be. This was partly owing to the impossibility he found himself in of practicing what he preached, and to the constant and obstinate opposition of his family to his new ideas. But, apart from this, the old Adam was always alive. The desires of the flesh were active in him till an unusually advanced age; and the desire for expansion, the desire that gave life to *War and Peace*, the desire for the fullness of life with all its pleasure and beauty, never died in him. We catch few glimpses of all this in his writings, for he subjected them to a strict and narrow discipline. But we have a picture of Tolstóy in his old age in which the irrational, the complete man stands before us in all the relief of life—this is Maxím Górky's *Recollections of Tolstóy*, a work of genius worthy of its subject.

When the news of Tolstóy's conversion spread, it became known that Tolstóy had condemned as sinful all the writings that had made him famous, and decided to abandon all further literary work in the sense of pure and disinterested art. When this news reached Turgénev, who was on his deathbed, he wrote Tolstóy a letter that has been quoted to satiety and that contains a phrase which has become hackneyed to such a nauseous extent that it is impossible to reproduce it. The dying novelist adjured Tolstóy not to abandon literature, but to think of the duty that lay on him as the greatest of Russian writers. Turgénev greatly exaggerated his influence if he hoped that a letter from him might change the decision of a man who had always been noted for obstinacy and who had just emerged from a crisis of immeasurable gravity. But Turgénev saw a danger where there was none; though Tolstóy

condemned as sinful (and artistically wrong) *War and Peace* and
Anna Karénina and subjected all his work henceforth to the
exigencies of his moral philosophy, it is ridiculous to think that
Tolstóy ever abandoned "art." He soon returned to the narrative form, but apart from this, even in his polemical writings,
he never ceased being supremely artistic. In the most trivial of his
tracts against tobacco he never ceased being, *as a craftsman*, head
and shoulders above even the best writers of the "æsthetic" revival
of the eighties. *A Confession* itself may without exaggeration be
called in some ways his greatest artistic work. It is not a disinterested, self-contained "representation of life" like *War and Peace*
or *Anna Karénina;* it is "utilitarian," it is "propaganda work," and
in this sense it is less "pure art." But it possesses "æsthetic" qualities that are not present in the great novels. It is *constructed*, and
constructed with supreme skill and precision. It has an oratorical
movement difficult to expect from the author of *War and Peace*.
It is more synthetic and universal, and does not rely for its action
on little homely and familiar effects of realism, so abundant in the
novels. Its analysis is simple, deep, courageous—and there is nothing in it of that "psychological eavesdropping" (the phrase is
Leóntiev's) which repels many readers in his earlier works. *War
and Peace* and *Anna Karénina* have been compared, somewhat
farfetchedly, with the poems of Homer. *A Confession* might with
more appropriateness be placed by the side of no less supreme
"world's books"—Ecclesiastes and the book of Job. So it is quite
wrong to affirm that in any literary sense the change that overcame
Tolstóy about 1880 was a fall. He remained forever, not only the
supreme writer, but the supreme craftsman of Russian letters.
Even the most dryly dogmatic of his treatises is a masterpiece of
literary ability and of the best Russian. For all that, the fact remains that henceforward Tolstóy ceased to be a "writer," in the
sense of a man who writes for the sake of producing good literary
work, and became a preacher. And when he turned, as he did very
soon, towards imaginative narrative, he wrote stories that, like
everything else, were strictly subordinate to his dogmatic teaching
and intended to illustrate and to popularize it.

The first of Tolstóy's works in which he preached his new
teaching was *A Confession* (begun in 1880 and completed in 1882).[1]

[1] It was not at the time passed by the Russian censorship. It was printed in Geneva
and circulated in manuscript in Russia.

A Confession is altogether on a higher level than the rest—it is one of the world's masterpieces. It is a work of art, and Tolstóy's biographer would give proof of too much simple-mindedness if he used it as biographical material in the strict sense of the word. But the work is more important to us than the facts that led up to it. The facts have been, and are no more. Their history in *A Confession* remains as a κτῆμα ἐς ἀεί, a perfect work, a living entity. It is one of the greatest and most lasting expressions of the human soul in the presence of the eternal mysteries of life and death. To give the argument in one's own words would be presumption, to quote passages would be to destroy. For it is a wonderful whole, built with marvelous precision and effectiveness. Every detail, every turn of thought, every oratorical cadence, is in its right place to contribute to the one supreme effect. It is the greatest piece of oratory in Russian literature. But it is not conventional eloquence. Its rhythm is a logical, mathematical rhythm—a rhythm of ideas— and Tolstóy scorns all the devices of traditional rhetoric. It is sustained in the simplest of languages, in that wonderful language of Tolstóy, whose secret has not yet been caught, and which is naturally lost in a translation. A good translation (like Aylmer Maude's) will preserve the oratorical movement of the original, for this is based on the succession of ideas and large syntactical units, not on the sound and quantity of words. But the effect of Tolstóy's Russian cannot be reproduced in any of the literary languages of the West, for all of them are too far divorced from their spoken forms, and the spoken languages too full of slang. Russian alone has this felicity—that it can use everyday speech to produce effects of Biblical majesty. And Tolstóy's favorite device in *A Confession*, of illustrating his idea by a parable, is in complete keeping with the general tone of the work. Tolstóy's language was largely his own creation. He achieved in *A Confession*, for the language of abstract thought, what he had attempted in his pedagogical articles and achieved for narrative prose in his novels—the creation of a new literary language free from the bookish traditions of contemporary literature and based entirely on the language actually spoken. The language thus evolved is beyond doubt the best vehicle yet used in Russian for the expression of abstract thought. The extent of Tolstóy's innovation in the literary language is singularly great— it is almost a different language from that of his contemporaries. Many of the principal terms of his teaching are words that had not been used before Tolstóy in literary Russian, and were borrowed by him from the colloquial speech of his class. Such, for instance, is one of his most frequent words—*dúrno*—bad.

Tolstóy's other moral and religious writings are not on a level with *A Confession*, though they are written in the same admirable Russian, sometimes with even greater elegance and precision. In *A Confession* he speaks with the utmost tragical earnestness of a unique and overwhelming experience. In the later tracts he lays down the "articles" of a hard and narrow creed. They have all the best qualities of Tolstóy the rationalist, the arguer, and the logician, but it would be quite out of place to compare them, as one can compare *A Confession*, with the books of the Bible. *What Are We to Do?* is a kind of continuation of *A Confession*, but on a less mystical and more social plane. It is the story of Tolstóy's experience in the slums and night refuges of Moscow soon after his conversion. His religious views were systematized in a series of works, of which the first, *What I Believe*, was written in 1883–4. This was followed by a *Critique of Dogmatic Theology*, *The Kingdom of Heaven Is Within Us*, *An Exposition of the Gospels*, and *The Christian Doctrine*. *What I Believe* is the most comprehensive of his dogmatic writings. What he gave in *A Confession* in the form of a personal experience, in its process of becoming, is here crystallized and stabilized into a settled doctrine. *The Christian Doctrine* (1897) is an exposition of the same doctrine in a still more logical and fixed form, after the manner of a catechism. It is a source of infinite pleasure to those who admire most in Tolstóy his lucidity and his skill at definition and precise statement. *The Exposition of the Gospels* has less of this quality and more of a very farfetched and not always bona fide interpretation. In *The Critique of Dogmatic Theology* he is a polemist well versed in all the little tricks of argumentative tactics, a cunning fencer, and consummate ironist. Ridicule and an appeal to common sense are his favorite polemical methods. "This is unintelligible nonsense," is his knock-out argument. His minor tracts are numerous and touch on a great variety of points of detail, or on topics of current interest. Such is *Why Do People Intoxicate Themselves?* denouncing drink and tobacco. Such is *I Cannot Be Silent*, a violent invective against the Russian government and the numerous executions during the suppression of the First Revolution.

But of all Tolstóy's non-narrative writings, that which is of

greatest interest for the literary historian is *What Is Art?* (1897).
Tolstóy's taste in literature and art always drew him towards the
classical, the rational, and the primitive. He disliked everything
romantic, everything ornate or exuberant. He had no understanding for "pure poetry." He liked the classic theater of Racine, the
analytical novel of Stendhal, the stories of Genesis, and the songs
of the Russian people. He disliked the Elizabethan exuberance of
Shakspere. In his famous attack on Shakspere, Tolstóy charged
him with being not only an immoral writer, but a bad poet. He
preferred the pre-Shaksperian *King Leir* to Shakspere's tragedy
because it was more primitive, less exuberant, less baroque. Voltaire would have agreed with much in Tolstóy's criticism of *King
Lear.* He had many faults to find in other great writers. Homer
was an immoral poet because he idealized wrath and cruelty;
Racine and Púshkin were inferior writers because they appealed to
a restricted aristocratic audience and were unintelligible to the
people. But Shakspere was a bad writer because he wrote badly,
and Tolstóy remained unmoved by his poetry. Now art, according
to Tolstóy, is that which "infects" with sympathetic feelings. "If
a man is infected by the author's condition of soul, if he feels this
emotion and this union with others, then the object which has
effected this is art; but if there be no such infection, if there be not
this union with the author and with others who are moved by the
same work, then it is not art." Shakspere and Wagner were not
art. Tolstóy opposes to them the creations of primitive popular
art—the story of Joseph, the Hungarian *csárdás*, the theater of a
primitive Siberian tribe, the Voguls. He quotes, as an example of
genuine art, a description of a Vogul drama representing in a very
simple and naïve way a reindeer hunt and the anxiety of the doe
for her calf; "from the mere description, I felt that this was a true
work of art," because he was infected by the feelings of the doe.
Everything that does not *infect* is not art and only obscures art.
Too much technique, too much magnificence in producing a play,
too much realism, obscure and diminish the artistic value of a
picture, a play, a book. The simpler, the barer, the better. "The
author of the story of Joseph did not need to describe in detail, as
would be done nowadays, the bloodstained coat of Joseph, the
dwelling and dress of Jacob, the pose and attire of Potiphar's wife,
and how, adjusting the bracelet on her arm, she said: 'Come to
me,' and so on, because the subject matter of feelings in this novel

is so strong that all details, except the most essential—such as that Joseph went out into the other room to weep—are superfluous and would only hinder the transmission of feelings. And therefore this story is accessible to all men, touches people of all nations and classes, young and old, and has lasted to our times, and will yet last for thousands of years to come. But strip the best novels of our times of their details, and what will remain?" (*What Is Art?*) Genuine art may be moral or immoral, according to the moral value of the feelings with which it infects. *The Iliad*, for instance, is *art*, but it is morally bad art because the feelings with which it infects are bad feelings. Much of modern literature, though genuine art, is morally bad because it is class art, intelligible only to the rich and cultivated, and tends to disunite, instead of uniting. Tolstóy excepts very little of modern literature from this general condemnation. He quotes only a few works—Schiller (*The Robbers*), Hugo (*Les Misérables*), Dickens (*A Tale of Two Cities*, *A Christmas Carol*, and *The Chimes*), George Eliot (*Adam Bede*), Dostoyévsky (*Memoirs from the House of Death*), and Harriet Beecher Stowe (*Uncle Tom's Cabin*)—as "examples of the highest art flowing from the love of God and man"—of (as he calls it) "religious art." As examples of an inferior but still good kind of art, of "art transmitting the simplest feelings of common life, but such always as are accessible to all men of the world," he quotes with great reservations *Don Quixote*, Molière, *David Copperfield*, the *Pickwick Papers*, and the tales of Gógol, Púshkin, and Maupassant. But "the exceptional nature of the feelings they transmit, and the superfluity of special detail of time and locality, and, above all, the poverty of their subject matter, make them comprehensible only to people of their own circle." Tolstóy condemned his own earlier works on grounds both moral (class exclusiveness and bad feelings) and æsthetic (superfluity of detail, all the paraphernalia of realism). But long before he had completed *What Is Art?* he had already made an effort to produce new works of fiction that would be in harmony with his new ideals. The novelty of Tolstóy's later stories is not only that they are all written with and strongly subordinate to the purpose (many of his early stories, especially those written in 1856–61 are quite as much "with a purpose"), but that he abandoned in them his early realistic and detailed manner and endeavored to approach the chastity and simplicity of outline of his favorite masterpiece—the story of Joseph.

The first stories he wrote after *A Confession* were a series of edifying short stories for the people. They were published in 1885 and the following years by the firm Posrédnik, founded for the special purpose of popularizing Tolstóy's teaching. They were written with regard to the existing conditions in Russia, that is, they were meant to satisfy the censor. Consequently they contain no violent and overt satire of the Church and State. The moral is always plainly present, often in the title—*Evil Allures, but Good Endures, God Sees the Truth but Waits*—but is not always peculiarly Tolstoyan. About the time he was writing *Anna Karénina*, Tolstóy had made an attempt at a popular story—this is the only story he excluded from the general condemnation of his earlier work—*The Captive in the Caucasus* (1873), which he recognized as belonging to the inferior but still commendable category of "good universal art" (not religious art). The new stories aspired to be religious art. According to Tolstóy's new taste, the narrative in these stories is reduced to the essential subject matter and stripped of all the superfluous embellishments of "realism." But they remain realistic in that they all have for a setting the life familiar to the prospective reader—it is Russian peasant life, with sufficient local color to individualize it as Russian. All these stories are admirably told, and every one of them is a little masterpiece of construction, economy, and adaptation of means to ends. Manner and matter are one organic whole, and the moral tendency does not stand out as something external. One of the best is *Two Old Men*, the story of two peasants who set out on a pilgrimage to Jerusalem in fulfillment of a vow. One reached his goal and saw the Holy Land, but the other was detained on his way by meeting a starving family, and, in his efforts to save them, he spent all his money, lost all his time, was late for the boat, and returned home without seeing Jerusalem. The other, on his return journey, comes on the family saved from death by his companion, and is brought to understand that "the best way to keep one's vows to God and to do His will is for each man, while he lives, to show love and do good to others."

Later on, as his fame grew and he began to have a public all over the world, he wrote popular stories of a new kind, more universal and generalized. They approach still nearer to his ideal of being comprehensible to all men. Such are his adaptations from the French—*Françoise* (Maupassant's *La Vierge-des-Vents* pruned of realistic excrescences), *The Coffee-House of Surat*, and *Too Dear,* and his still later stories, *King Essarhadon, Work, Death, and Sickness*, and *Three Questions*. In these he approaches the style of the parable, which he had used with such powerful effect in *A Confession*, and of the oriental apologue.

The stories written with a view to the educated reader are different in manner: they are much longer, much fuller of detail, more "psychological," altogether nearer in style to his earlier work. There are problem stories, written not so much to teach as to communicate his own experience. They may be grouped into two categories, stories of conversion and stories on the sexual problem. The first group consists of *The Memoirs of a Madman* (unfinished, posthumous, written in 1884), *The Death of Iván Ilýich* (1886), and *Master and Man* (1895). In all these stories the subject is the conversion of the dark and unregenerated educated or rich man before the face of death or madness. *The Memoirs of a Madman* is very much akin to *A Confession*. It conveys with dreadful force the feeling of elemental metaphysical joylessness and despair before the abysmal meaninglessness of life, the feeling Tolstóy himself must have experienced at the height of his great crisis, and which seems to have returned to him at intervals after his conversion. It is the most genuinely mystical of his writings. He left it unfinished; yet it cannot be refused a central place in his work, next to, and as a "piece of evidence" even above, *A Confession*. For it is more directly sincere, more of a document, less of a work of art. In *The Death of Iván Ilýich* the hero is not a thinking and seeking man like Tolstóy of the *Confession* or like the madman. He is an ordinary, vulgar, average man of the educated classes, a judge (the class Tolstóy detested most of all). The revelation comes to him as the direct consequence of his mortal illness. When he realizes that he is dying, he loses all taste for existence and is plunged into that elemental joylessness which comes from realizing the meaninglessness and emptiness of life. But joy comes back to him in the simple and cheerful charity of his servant Gerásim, the only person who gives him help in his mortal despair. And before he dies he sees the inner light of faith, renunciation, and love. *Master and Man* is again the story of a birth to new life in the face of death. It is one of Tolstóy's masterpieces, comparable to *A Confession* in the sustained beauty of its construction and to *The Memoirs of a Madman* in the genuineness of its mystical light. It stands halfway in style between his old realistic and new popular manner, and answers more to his ideal of religious art than any of his other works not especially intended for the people.

The "sexual" stories are *The Kreutzer Sonata* (1889) and *The Devil* (written the same year, published posthumously). The first, a study of jealousy and a diatribe against the sexual education of young men and women in modern society, is a powerful production but hardly a perfect work of art. It is not sufficiently concentrated; its preaching is not always artistically "necessary"; its manner strangely enough reminds one of the untidy and excited manner of Dostoyévsky. *The Devil* is more satisfactory. It is an extraordinary analysis of that obsession by the desires of the flesh which was so peculiar to Tolstóy and of which such shrewd things have been said by Maxím Górky. It is the story of a man who loves his young and charming wife but is impelled against his will by a purely carnal desire for a peasant woman with whom he has had relations before his marriage. He is powerless to combat it, and, to save himself from succumbing, in a state of exasperation he kills the woman. Tolstóy was not completely satisfied by this ending and wrote an alternative ending, in which the hero, instead of killing the object of his desire, kills himself. In spite of this ambiguous ending, *The Devil* is one of Tolstóy's greatest masterpieces, for both the fierce sincerity and the masterly construction; the terrible inevitableness of the hero's fall, his helplessness before his carnal instinct, grow like a terrible doom and are developed with supreme mastery.

Of all Tolstóy's late narrative works, the one that attracted the greatest attention and became most widely known, and is consequently, more often than not, taken as typical of his last period, was *Resurrection* (completed and published in 1899). It is a novel in three parts—by far the longest of all his stories since 1880, almost comparable in length with *Anna Karénina* and *War and Peace*. This is the sole reason why it has usurped a principal position among his later work and is so often quoted by the side of the two earlier novels. It has often been used to prove that Tolstóy's genius declined after he became a preacher. If the imaginative work of his last thirty years is to stand or fall according to the merit of *Resurrection*, it will be in somewhat bad case, for it is quite obvious that *Resurrection* is very much inferior to *War and Peace* and *Anna Karénina*. But it is also much inferior to *Master and Man*, to *Hajjí Murád*, and to *The Living Corpse*. In

spite of its size it is by no means the work into which Tolstóy put
the most work and care. It was written, strange to say, for money,
and would probably not have seen the press before his death were
it not for the desire to find funds for the Dukhobórs. The Dukhobórs, a peasant sect of "Christian communists," were persecuted
by the government for their "conscientious objection" to military
service. Canada had offered hospitality to them, and the only
drawback to their emigration was lack of funds. Tolstóy decided
to meet the emergency by finishing in a hurry, and publishing in
one of the best-selling Russian papers, a novel he had been working
on. He was working then on *Hajjí Murád* and *Resurrection*, and he
chose the latter because he liked it less and had fewer objections to
seeing it published in an unsatisfactory form. *Resurrection* is not a
perfect work of art: the moral idea, profusely supported by texts
from the Gospels, is not organically fused into the fabric. The story
of Nekhlyúdov's conversion is on an inferior plane to that of
Tolstóy's own in *A Confession*, or of Iván Ilyích's, or of the merchant in *Master and Man*. It is not a revelation of inner light, but
a cold decision to adapt himself to the moral law so as to escape
the stings of conscience and acquire inner peace. *Resurrection*
presents Tolstóy and his teaching from the most unattractive side.
For all that, it is a book by Tolstóy. But its best qualities are not
characteristic of the later Tolstóy: they are rather, in a minor degree, those of *Anna Karónina* and *War and Peace*. The best thing
in the novel is the minor realistic details he condemned so severely
in *What Is Art?* The early story of Máslova is the best part of the
book. It is full of that elusive poetry which reminds one of the
subtle poetic atmosphere that accompanies Natásha in *War and
Peace*. The account of the trial is excellent—sustained, concentrated, unexaggerated satire. It has not been surpassed by Tolstóy,
except perhaps in the second part of the same novel, where he
satirizes the bureaucratic society of Petersburg. But his satirically
blasphemous account of an Orthodox Church service, prohibited
by the censorship and absent in pre-Revolutionary editions printed
in Russia, can scarcely be qualified otherwise than as a grave
lapse from good taste. It is quite gratuitous and unnecessary for
the mechanism of the novel.

If in *Resurrection* Tolstóy is at his worst, in its twin novel he
is at his best. *Hajjí Murád* was begun in 1896 and completed in
1904. It was published after his death. In it he tried to give a story

that would answer to his ideal of "good universal," not religious, art. *Hajjí Murád* is a masterpiece of the highest order. It is a story of the extended war that the Caucasian mountaineers, under their military and religious leader Shamíl, waged against Russia. Hajjí Murád, a prominent mountaineer chief, from motives of personal ambition and vengeance, deserts Shamíl and goes over to the Russians, who receive him with apparent friendliness but with concealed distrust. Hajjí Murád's family has remained with Shamíl, who keeps them as hostages. The desire of once more seeing his son grows on Hajjí Murád, and he decides to escape into the mountains but is killed in the attempt. Hajjí Murád is a savage. His feelings are those of a shrewd, brave, and treacherous warrior with all the virtues and all the vices of a warlike barbarian. The story is told in what Tolstóy called the "peep-show manner"—the scene is constantly shifted, and the chapters are like a succession of slides. This method brings forward with great vividness the tragic irony of mutual misunderstanding between men of various classes and nationalities. The story is stirring tragedy conveyed by the simplest means. The final scene—the death of Hajjí Murád and his four followers surrounded by hundreds of pursuers—is one of the grandest and most tragical in all literature.

Hajjí Murád, as well as *The Memoirs of a Madman* and *The Devil*, was published only in 1911, in the collected edition of Tolstóy's posthumous works.[2] This collection also includes several plays and many other stories and fragments. One of these is *Father Sergius* (1890–8), the story of an aristocrat who became a monk and a hermit—a powerful study of spiritual pride and, once again, carnal desires. It is also an excellent example of Tolstóy's later rapid and "essential" narrative manner. Still better in this respect is *The False Coupon* (1903–5), the admirably constructed story of a succession of evils diverging from one initial evil action to converge by a contrasting succession of good actions towards the common salvation of all concerned. It is impossible to list all the numerous minor stories and fragments of these wonderful three volumes. But one at least must be mentioned: one of the shortest—*Alësha Gorshók* (1905). It is a masterpiece of rare perfection. It is the apotheosis of the "holy fool," who does not himself realize his

---

[2] They were not published during his life, to avoid making the question of their copyright fresh fuel for the war waged by Chertkóv and the Countess Tolstóy over the person of their author.

goodness. It is the story, told in five or six pages, of a peasant boy who was all his life everyone's drudge but, in his simplicity of soul and meek, unquestioning submission (non-resistance), knew that inner light and purity of conscience, that perfect peace which was never attained by the conscious, rational, restless soul of Tolstóy. Concentrated into its six pages, *Alësha Gorshók* is one of his most perfect creations, and one of the very few that make one forget the bedrock Luciferism and pride of the author.

Tolstóy's plays all belong to the period after 1880. He had not the essential qualities that go to the making of a dramatist, and the merits of his plays are not of the strictly dramatic order. In spite of his French education and classical tastes, his plays are constructed in a very un-French and unclassical manner. With the exception of *The Fruits of Enlightenment*, a comedy—or rather, a farce—of intrigue, all his plays are built according to the same scheme—which is the "peep-show" scheme of *Hajjí Murád*. The action is not a continuous development, but scenes are cut out so as to present the principal moments of a story, which usually extends over a period of many years. This concentration may in some cases approach the form of a mediæval morality. It may also be easily adapted to make a movie drama. The first in date of Tolstóy's plays is the *First Distiller*, a humorous anti-liquor morality play "for the people," published originally in 1886 in the same series as the popular tales. The *First Distiller* is of course the devil. He has plenty of victims from all the rich and idle classes, but he cannot succeed in catching a single peasant into his net, for work is the peasant's safeguard from sin. He succeeds in corrupting him only by showing him the way to make spirits. It is a very amusing little play, and, as an English reviewer has remarked, would raise grave anxiety among the liquor trade if it were acted in England. This was followed by *The Power of Darkness*, the best-known and most highly esteemed of Tolstóy's plays (1887). It is also in essence a morality—but treated in a very different manner. It is a tragedy—and a realistic tragedy. It represents the life of peasants but is intended for the educated public. There is a profound inner contradiction in the play. Planned as a morality, it is executed as a realistic drama, with all the condemned paraphernalia of "superfluous details," including phonographically exact reproduction of peasant dialect, a thing the peasant spectator resents above all things. This disharmony of plan and execution, and this abundant presence of the abominations of gratuitous realism, made Tolstóy dislike this play and condemn it as belonging to the "bad manner." Like *Resurrection*, it is one of Tolstóy's least perfect works, and its great success proves only how little the Russian and the foreign public were really in tune with the genius of Tolstóy. The Russian public liked it because it was in the familiar realistic "superfluous detail" style, and because the Russian actors, trained to the style, acted it well. Abroad it was received enthusiastically because its ruthless realism was a new and piquant thing to the Western palate. All this is not to say that it has no trace of genius in it; on the contrary, the scheme of the play is one of Tolstóy's most powerful inventions. It is the best expression he ever gave to his favorite conception of Karma—the mechanical atonement of sin—and of another favorite idea of his—the great evil-begetting power of every evil action, which is expressed in the subtitle, *If a Claw Is Caught, the Bird Is Lost*. The tragical atmosphere is thick and dark, and there are few more impressive things in Tolstóy than the third act, where we see Nikíta enjoying the first joyless fruit of his initial crime. But for all its merits, *The Power of Darkness* cannot take away from a much older play, Písemsky's *Hard Lot*, the honor of being the best Russian realistic tragedy. The same realistic tendency that mars the dialogue of *The Power of Darkness* is one of the chief attractions of Tolstóy's society plays. For in the peasant play he tried to ape a dialect that was not his; in *The Fruits of Enlightenment* and in the posthumous plays he made his characters talk his own everyday language. *The Fruits of Enlightenment* (1889) is, after all, only a trifle, but the dialogue of the society people is admirable and the satire very pointed. *The Light Shines in the Darkness* (begun in the early eighties and continued in 1900–2) remained unfinished. It has the appearance of autobiography—for it is the story of a Tolstoyan moralist who is surrounded by an unsympathizing family and whose followers are sent to prison for practicing what he preaches. But it must be said in all fairness that Tolstóy does much less than justice to himself in the character of Saryntsov. Saryntsov is not the giant of Yásnaya Polyána, but a narrow, cold, hard, pedantic fanatic— perhaps more like some inferior Tolstoyan—Chertkóv, for instance. A very different thing is *The Living Corpse*, one of Tolstóy's most attractive and lovable works. There is in it something we meet in very few of his works: a distinct note of human sympathy, free from all moralizing dogmatism. There is also something one could hardly suspect in Tolstóy: a vast mellow pity for the misformed and erring human race, a respect for the sufferings of man— even of the abandoned drunkard, even of the proud society mother. It is at the opposite pole to *Resurrection*. It is, even more than *Hajjí Murád*, the most *disinterested* of all Tolstóy's later works. It is rather loosely constructed, after the familiar "peep-show" plan, and it can hardly be called a drama in any strict sense of the word. But it has been produced; and in the hands of a cast like Stanislávsky's Moscow Art Theater it acts very well. *The Living Corpse* may be taken as the last expression of Tolstóy's genius. It is distinctly a very old man's work, with that broadness and mellowness of outlook which, if it comes, is the best ornament of old age.

The life of Tolstóy after his conversion can be given here only in the briefest outline. Soon after *A Confession* became known, he began, at first against his will, to recruit disciples. The first of these was the notorious and sinister V. G. Chertkóv, an ex-officer of the Horse Guards, a narrow fanatic and a hard despotic man, who exercised an enormous practical influence on Tolstóy and became a sort of grand vizier of the new community. Other disciples came, among whom P. I. Biryukóv may be mentioned, the author of a *Life of Tolstoy*, the official life, written throughout in a tone of panegyrical admiration like the life of a saint, but valuable for its wealth of information. Tolstóy also established contact with certain sects of Christian communists and anarchists, like the Dukhobórs. The external action of Tolstóy's new doctrine found its principal expression in cases of conscientious objection to military service, which sent many men to prison and Siberia. But Tolstóy himself was unmolested by the government. Only in 1901 the Synod excommunicated him. This act, widely but very unjudiciously resented both at home and abroad, merely registered a matter of common knowledge—that Tolstóy had ceased to be an Orthodox Churchman.

The dogmatic followers of Tolstóy were never numerous, but his reputation among people of all classes grew immensely. It spread all over the world, and by the last two decades of his life Tolstóy enjoyed a place in the world's esteem that had not been held by any man of letters since the death of Voltaire. Yásnaya Polyána became a new Ferney—or even more than that, almost a new Jerusalem. Pilgrims from all parts flocked there to see the great old man. But Tolstóy's own family remained hostile to his teaching, with the exception of his youngest daughter, Alexandra. Countess Sophie Andréyevna especially took up a position of decided opposition to his new ideas. She refused to give up her possessions and asserted her duty to provide for her large family. Tolstóy renounced the copyright of his new works but had to surrender his landed property and the copyright of his earlier works to his wife. This produced an external contradiction between Tolstóy's preaching of communism and contempt of material riches, and the easy and even luxurious life he led under the regime of his wife—for Sophie Andréyevna was the embodiment of Tolstóy's earlier philosophy of *War and Peace*—"that one should live so as to have the best for oneself and one's family." This contradiction weighed heavily on him, and the consciousness of it was carefully fostered by Chertkóv. This man and Countess Tolstóy became the heads of two hostile parties who disputed the possession of Tolstóy. Tolstóy was remarkably healthy for his age, but he fell seriously ill in 1901 and had to live for a long time in the Crimea. Still he continued working to the last and never showed the slightest sign of any weakening of brain power. The story of his "escape" and death is familiar to all. Ever more oppressed by the contradiction of his private life, urged on by Chertkóv, full of a growing irritation against his wife, he left Yásnaya, in the company of his daughter Alexandra and his doctor, for an unknown destination. After some restless and aimless wandering he had to stop at Astápovo Junction (Province of Ryazán). There he was laid up in the stationmaster's house and died on November 7, 1910.

LESKÓV

Nikoláy Semënovich Leskóv (1831–95) was only three years younger than Tolstóy, but he was past thirty when he first appeared before the public, and the times were no longer the same as had given such a wholehearted and generous reception to the great generation of novelists. It was a time of intense party strife, when no writer could hope to be well received by all the critics, and only those who identified themselves with a definite party could hope for even a partial recognition. Leskóv never identified himself with any party and had to take the consequences. His success with the reading public was considerable, but the critics continued to neglect him. Leskóv's case is a striking instance of the failure of Russian criticism to do its duty.

Leskóv's father was a civil servant and the son of a priest. His mother was of a family of gentry, and his early life was that of an average squire's son. One of the lasting influences of his early life was his Aunt Polly, who had married an Englishman and followed the Quaker way of life. When he was sixteen his parents died and he had to leave school and enter the civil service. He served as a copying clerk in various provincial government offices. In this service he acquired an extensive first-hand acquaintance with various aspects of Russian reality. This knowledge of life was still more widened when he left the civil service and was employed by an Englishman, a Mr. Scott, a Nonconformist like Aunt Polly and chief steward of the estates of a rich nobleman. In this employment Leskóv acquired a far wider outlook on Russian life, and one very different from that of the typical educated gentleman of the day. Owing to this training, Leskóv is one of those Russian writers whose knowledge of life was not founded on the possession of serfs, to be later modified by university theories of French or German origin, like Turgénev's and Tolstóy's, but on practical and independent experience. This is why his view of Russian life is so unconventional and so free from that attitude of condescending and sentimental pity for the peasant which is typical of the liberal and educated serf owner. His first literary work consisted of business reports to Scott, who was quick to appreciate the wealth of common sense, the power of observation, and the knowledge of people displayed in them. Leskóv was twenty-nine when, in 1860, he first engaged in part-time journalism. Two years later he abandoned his other work, came to Petersburg, and became a professional journalist. It was a time of intense public excitement. Leskóv was absorbed by public interests as much as anyone, but his eminently practical mind and training made it impossible for him to join unreservedly any of the very unpractical and hot-headed parties of the day. Hence his isolation when the incident occurred that left such a lasting trace in his career. He wrote an article on the great fires that had in 1862 destroyed a large part of Petersburg and that popular rumor was inclined to impute to the "nihilists" and radical-minded university students. Leskóv did not support this rumor, but he mentioned it in an article and demanded that a

thorough investigation should be carried out by the police in order
that it might be either confirmed or confuted. This demand produced in the radical press the effect of a bombshell. Leskóv was
accused of inciting the populace against the students and of "in-
forming" to the police. Leskóv was put under boycott and expelled
from the progressive papers. Meanwhile he passed from journalism
to fiction. His first short story (*The Ovibos*, 1863) was followed by
a long novel (*No Way Out*, 1864) that led to further misunder-
standings. The radicals affected to recognize in some of its characters slanderous caricatures of their friends, and this sufficed to
stamp Leskóv as a vile and libelous reactionary, though the principal Socialist characters in the book were represented as little
short of saints. In his next "political" novel, *At Daggers Drawn*
(1870–1), Leskóv went much further in the representation of the
"nihilists" as a set of blackguards and scoundrels. These "political" novels are not among Leskóv's masterpieces, and they had no
part in the great reputation he enjoys today. But they were sufficient to make Leskóv the nightmare of all the radical literature
and to make it impossible for the most influential critics to treat
him with any amount of fairness. The great Slavophil critic
Apollón Grigóriev, a man of extraordinary but erratic genius, was
the only critic to welcome Leskóv, to appreciate and to encourage
him. But Grigóriev died in 1864, and all Leskóv's subsequent
popularity was entirely owing to the unguided good taste of the
public.

This popularity began especially after the publication of his
"chronicle" *Soboryáne* in 1872 and the series of stories, largely of
ecclesiastical life, that followed it in remarkable succession till the
end of the seventies. In these stories Leskóv appeared as a champion of Orthodoxy and conservative ideals, and they attracted
towards him the good will of many high-placed persons, in particular the Empress Marie Alexándrovna, the wife of Alexander
II. It was through her interest that Leskóv got an official appointment in an advising board of education, practically a sinecure. In
the later seventies he joined in a campaign in favor of Orthodoxy
against the pietist propaganda of Lord Radstock. But Leskóv
never became a thorough conservative, and even in his support of
Orthodoxy against Protestantism, his principal arguments were the
democratic humility of the first and the aristocratic individualism
of the "Society schism," as he called Radstock's sect. His attitude

towards the official government of the Church was never quite
docile, and gradually his Christianity became less traditional and
more critical. His stories of clerical life written in the early eighties
were largely satirical, and for one of these he was asked to leave
his government post. He came under the growing influence of
Tolstóy and towards the end of his life became a devoted Tolstoyan. This change of attitude towards the conservative principles pushed him back towards the left wing of journalism, and in
his later years he contributed mainly to moderate radical magazines. But the dictators of literary opinion still reserved their
judgment and were more than cold to him. When he died, he had
many readers all over Russia but few friends in the literary press.
Not long before his death he is reported to have said: "Now I am
read for the beauty of my imaginative work, but in fifty years
hence this beauty will have faded, and my books will be read only
for the ideas contained in them." This was a singularly bad
prophecy. More than ever Leskóv is read today for his qualities
of form, style, and narrative, and less than ever for his ideas. In
fact very few of his admirers realize what his ideas were. Not that
his ideas are at all obscure or concealed, but simply that the attention is concentrated on something different.

Leskóv's most striking originality lies in his Russian. His
contemporaries wrote in a level and even style, avoiding anything
too striking or questionable. Leskóv avidly absorbed every unexpected and picturesque idiom. All the various forms of professional and class language, every variety of slang, were welcome to
his pages. But his special favorites were the comic effects of colloquial Church Slavonic and the puns of "popular etymology."
These effects are of course untranslatable. Like O. Henry, he allowed himself great liberties in this direction and was the inventor
of many successful and unexpected deformations of familiar sense
or familiar sound. Another striking peculiarity that Leskóv alone
of all his contemporaries possesses is a superlative narrative gift.
His stories are mere anecdotes, told with enormous zest and ability,
and even in his longer works his favorite way of characterizing his
characters is by a series of anecdotes. This was quite contrary to
the traditions of "serious" Russian fiction and induced the critics
to regard Leskóv as a mere jester. His most original stories are
packed with incident and adventure to an extent that appeared
ludicrous to the critics, who regarded ideas and messages as the

principal thing. Tolstóy liked Leskóv's stories and enjoyed his verbal gambols, but he censured him for his exuberance. His chief fault, Tolstóy thought, was that he could not keep his talent in bounds and that there were too many good things in his stories. This taste for verbal picturesqueness and rapid and complicated narrative is in striking contrast to the habits of almost every other Russian novelist. There are no haze, no atmosphere, no mellowness in Leskóv's vision of the world: he chooses the most crying colors, the boldest relief, and the sharpest outline. If Turgénev's or Chékhov's world may be compared to a landscape by Corot, Leskóv's is a picture by Breughel the Elder, full of gay and bright colors and grotesque forms. Great virtue, extraordinary originality, strong vices, powerful passions, and grotesque humors are his favorite matter. He is at once a hero worshipper and a humorist. It can almost be said that the more heroic his heroes, the more humorously he treats them. This humorous hero worship is Leskóv's most original feature.

Leskóv's political novels are now deservedly forgotten, but the short stories he wrote at the same time are very good. They are not so rich in verbal felicity as the stories of his mature period, but they present in an eminent degree his qualities as a storyteller. Unlike his later work, they are pictures of almost unrelieved wickedness and passion. A typical instance is *A Lady Macbeth of the Mtsensk District* [3] (1865), a powerful study of the criminal passion of a woman and of the gay and cynical callousness of her lover. It is bathed in a cold and crude light and written with sustained, "naturalistic" objectivity. Another remarkable story of this period is *The Amazon*, the racy study of a Petersburg procuress who regards her profession with a deliciously naïve cynicism and is sincerely and deeply hurt by the black "thanklessness" of one of the victims whom she had first pushed into the ways of shame.

These early stories were followed by a series of "Chronicles" of the imaginary town of Stárgorod, which may be called a Russian Barchester. They form a trilogy—*Old Years in Plodomásovo* (1869), *Soboryáne* (*Cathedral*, or rather *Minster*, *Folk* (1872), and *A Decayed Family* (1874). The second of these chronicles is the most widely popular of all Leskóv's works. It deals with the Stárgorod clergy. Its head, the Archpriest Tuberózov, is one of Leskóv's most

---

[3] Used as the basis for Dmítry Shostakóvich's controversial opera of the same name.—Editor

successful and noble portraits of a "just man." The Deacon Akhíla
is his greatest character creation. It is one of the most wonderful
of the whole portrait gallery of Russian literature. The comic es-
capades and unconscious mischief-making of this enormous, exuberant, very unspiritual, and quite childlike deacon, and the constant reprimands his behavior draws from Father Tuberózov, are
familiar to every Russian reader; and Akhíla himself is a universal
favorite. But *Soboryáne* is not at all points representative of its
author—it is too leisurely, too uneventful, too placid, to be really
quite Leskovian. The very idea of a comparison with Trollope
would be ridiculous in reference to one of his more typical tales.

Such a typical tale is *The Enchanted Wanderer* (1874). Here
his narrative power reaches the high-water mark. In a little over a
hundred pages are told the eventful life and extraordinary adventures of an unwilling adventurer, who comes under a spell and
all his life, willy-nilly, is tossed from adventure to adventure. The
adventures follow in breathless succession, and each of them is
told in extraordinarily rapid tempo and saturated with expressive
and picturesque detail. The story is told in the first person—and
this is Leskóv's favorite way of giving free play to all his power
of verbal invention. *The Enchanted Wanderer* was followed in the
same year by *The Sealed Angel*, another breathless story of adventure told in the racy language of an Old Believer—the thrilling
story of the recovery of a holy image confiscated by the authorities. In these stories, as in so many others, Leskóv has for his
subject the religious life of the Russian people. His ideal, at first
very close to that of Orthodox Churchmen, in his later stories becomes more purely ethical and less Orthodox. Such already is *On
the Edge of the World* (1876), the story of how a Russian missionary
bishop was saved from death in the Siberian wilderness by a
heathen native, and how he came to the conclusion that mission
work, as it was conducted, worked only ill to the natives. Next
came *The Just Men*, a series depicting extraordinary puritan and
Christian virtue among most various classes of Russian society. In
them, as well as in the humorous and satirical *Details of Episcopal
Life*, Leskóv tends to approach pure journalism. There is no invention in these stories. The limits of the narrative form become
less distinct, and the narrative is often interrupted by discussions.
Soon after this, Leskóv came under the influence of Tolstóy, but
he never abandoned his own idiosyncrasies, and it was in the

eighties that his most exuberantly original stories were written. In such stories as *The Left-handed Smith and the Steel Flea* (1882), *A Robbery* (1887), or in most stories from the collection of *Christmas Stories* (1886) and *Appropriate Stories* (1887), there is nothing except a sheer delight in storytelling. *The Left-handed Smith* is the most extraordinary of these productions. It tells of how a steel flea of life size was made by an English smith and presented to the Emperor Alexander I. The Emperor challenges the smiths of Túla to go one better. This they do by shoeing every one of the English flea's feet in gold. The left-handed smith is taken to England but, on returning to Russia, gets into the lock-up for drunkenness. The story is told in the most wonderful language, where almost every other word is an extraordinary funny invention of Leskóv's. It stands next to *Soboryáne* in the favor of the general reader.

Still most of his later works are profoundly impregnated with his "new Christianity," which he himself identified with Tolstóy's teaching. Leskóv's Christianity, like Tolstóy's, is anti-clerical, undenominational, and purely ethical. But here the identity ends: the dominant ethical note is different. It is the cult, not of moral purity and of reason, but of humility and charity. "Spiritual pride," self-conscious righteousness, is for Leskóv the greatest of crimes, and it is doubtful whether he would have liked the hero of *The Light Shines in the Darkness.* Active charity is to him the principal virtue, and he attaches very little value to moral purity, still less to physical purity. The charity of his harlots is often pointedly contrasted with the proud and cold virtue of matrons. This feeling of sin as the necessary soil for sanctity, and the condemnation of self-righteous pride as the sin against the Holy Ghost, is intimately akin to the moral sense of the Russian people and of the Eastern Church, and very different from Tolstóy's proud Protestant and Luciferian ideal of perfection. Many of Leskóv's stories of his last years written in his early manner are among his best, and one of these is his last, bearing the title so characteristic of his cult of humility—*The Lady and the Slut.*

But the most characteristic work of his last few years, his stories of early Christian life [4] (*The Mountain, The Brigand of Ascalon, The Beautiful Áza*), are written in a new manner. The subject matter and setting prevented Leskóv from giving rein in

[4] These are for the most part borrowed from the *Prologue* (see Book I, Chapter I).

these stories to his usual verbal liberties and eccentricities. But his exuberance did not forsake him, and for all his admiration of Tolstóy, Leskóv did not seek to imitate the "classical" manner of his popular tales. He conjures up a vivid and splendidly colored pageant of life under the late pagan or early Byzantine emperors. He has very little exact knowledge of the period, commits glaring anachronisms, and is rather at sea in ancient geography. The world he evokes owes much to the Lives of the Saints, something to Flaubert, and much to his own imagination. There is a charming, ever present undercurrent of humor and finesse. The result is altogether queer and baroque. What was particularly new in them to the Russian reader was a boldly outspoken treatment of sensual episodes. The prudish Russian critics of the time cried out against this license, which seemed strange in a Tolstoyan. They charged Leskóv with insincerity, with treating his moral subjects as nothing but pretexts for the display of voluptuous and sensuous scenes. Leskóv, however, was quite sincere, and the morals of his stories were the most important thing in them to his conscious self. But there was more complexity in the marvelous storyteller than in his simple-minded critics, and his subconscious artistic self took quite as much pleasure in the descriptions of the doings of the Alexandrian flower girls as in the sublime humility of his chief characters. He had seen Russian life as a violent, crude, parti-colored pageant of crime, horseplay, and heroism. And now he had created for himself an equally magnificent and indecent Roman orient. For if there was one thing he hated in the world, it was self-centered and self-satisfied respectability.

To his last years belongs also *The Hare Park*, which was published only posthumously in 1917. It is one of his most remarkable works and his greatest achievement in concentrated satire. It is the story, told for the greater part in his own words, of Onópry Opanásovich Peregúd, an inmate of a lunatic asylum. In his former life he was the son of a petty Little Russian squire and was made police inspector through the influence of the bishop, who happened to be a schoolfellow of his father's. Onópry Opanásovich, who is a quite unusually weak-minded and imbecile creature, got on all right with his responsible post until the beginning of the revolutionary movement of the sixties, when he succumbed to the ambitious desire of catching a nihilist. He gets hold of several nihilists, who turn out to be law-abiding citizens (and one of them even a detective who is himself hunting for nihilists), and is ultimately hoodwinked by his own coachman, who turns out to be a genuine nihilist. The unexpected result unhinges him and so he comes to the lunatic asylum. The story contains all the best features of Leskóv's manner: wonderful racy diction, boisterous farce, extraordinary anecdotes; but it is subordinated to a unifying idea, and the figure of the hapless police inspector grows into a symbol of vast historical and moral significance.

Leskóv, in spite of the admiration for him of some English critics, like Maurice Baring, has not yet come into his own with the English-speaking reader. The Anglo-Saxon public have made up their mind as to what they want from a Russian writer, and Leskóv does not fit in to this idea. But those who really want to know more about Russia must sooner or later recognize that Russia is not all contained in Dostoyévsky and Chékhov, and that if you want to know a thing, you must first be free of prejudice and on your guard against hasty generalizations. Then they will perhaps come nearer to Leskóv, who is generally recognized by Russians as the most Russian of Russian writers and the one who had the deepest and widest knowledge of the Russian people as it actually is.

POETRY: SLUCHÉVSKY

Poetry, in the reign of Alexander II, suffered from the same causes as prose but to a much greater degree. Russian "Victorian" poetry was not in itself a very vigorous growth. It was eclectic; it had degenerated from the high standard of the age of Púshkin; it did not believe in its own right to be and tried to discover a compromise between pure art and public utility. The typical Russian "Victorians"—Polónsky, Máykov, Alexéy Tolstóy—wrote some very good verse, but they were distinctly minor men in comparison with their great prose-writing contemporaries—and not only minor in genius, but minor in craftsmanship. Poetry, as it existed in their hands, was incapable of further development. There were, beside them, other poets, who, breaking away in exactly opposite directions from the "Victorian compromise," produced poetry of a more vigorous, less decadent, and more fruitful kind. These were Nekrásov and Fet.[5] But "civic" poetry in the hands of Nekrásov's suc-

[5] See Book I, Chapter VIII.

cessors sank to absolute insignificance, and "art for art" poetry fell just as low.

Even if compared with the novelists of the time, the poets born between 1830 and 1850 are utterly contemptible. The chief reason was again the consistent neglect of craftsmanship. This is best seen in the work of Constantine Sluchévsky (1837–1904), who had in him the germs of genius but was incapable of expressing himself otherwise than in a stammer. He began publishing verse very early, but, like Fet, he was hissed into silence by the nihilist critics and, like Fet, ceased publishing. When the atmosphere became more propitious for poetry, he reappeared before the public and in 1880 published a collected edition of his poems. The radicals did not give him a better reception than that of twenty years earlier, but there was now a larger public who could appreciate him apart from utilitarian considerations. He even became a sort of head of a school, but, being what he was—a stammerer innocent of the principles of his craft—he was incapable of becoming a fruitful influence.

In spite of the low level of his poetical workmanship, Sluchévsky is a true poet and a poet of outstanding interest. Like Nekrásov, though in another way, he tried to spring the fetters of romantic convention and annex to poetry provinces that had hitherto been considered foreign. He had a philosophical mind and was deeply read in modern science. He had a wonderful vision of the world and delighted in the boundless multiplicity of beings and things. His "geographical" poems, especially those inspired by the north of Russia and the Murmán coast, are among his best. But he was still more powerfully attracted by the eternal problems of good and evil, and of life and death. He brooded over the problem of personal immortality, and some of his poems on the subject are most striking. Flashes of genius are frequent in his work, but on the whole it is ineffective and irritating, for one feels all the time that all this might have been expressed much better if Sluchévsky had not lived in such a degenerate age.

THE LEADERS OF THE INTELLIGENTSIA: MIKHAYLÓVSKY

The word "intelligentsia" has two meanings. In the broader sense, it includes all the educated and professional classes, irrespective of their political feelings and degree of political activity. In a narrower sense, it is used to denote a special section of these classes—that which is intensely and actively interested in political and social issues. By a still narrower application, it came to be applied in pre-Revolutionary Russia to only those groups which were more or less radically inclined. Slavophils and conservatives were not "intelligentsia." The intelligentsia in this sense is an inner circle, a sect, almost an order of knighthood. The Russian intelligentsia assumed this form in the sixties, and it subsisted till the Bolshevík Revolution. It never included the whole, and probably even never the majority of the intelligentsia in the wider sense. But it was a center, a sort of magnetic pole towards which the majority were attracted. Its influence was large. University students formed the main army of radicalism, but it was led by the literary press. There was inside this "Church" a great variety of opinion in detail, but all were united in several essential tenets. These were: hostility to the existing regime; faith in progress and democracy; a feeling of duty towards what was called in the sixties "the younger brother" —the uneducated working classes. Most of the radicals were socialists, but they regarded the more advanced liberals as "theirs" if they were sufficiently anti-government. The history of the ideas that dominated the intelligentsia has been many times written, and intelligentsia historians have often tried to identify the history of these ideas with the history of Russian literature. This is a gross falsification. But no literary history can overlook the main lines of the development.

In the sixties and seventies there were two main shades of radical opinion—the nihilists (or "thinking realists," as they called themselves) and the populists (*naródniki*). The nihilists laid stress on materialism and agnosticism. Science, especially natural science (Darwin), was their chief weapon. They carried furthest the anti-æsthetic movement. They were socialists, but their socialism stood in the background. Their first duty was to enlighten the people with practical knowledge and evolutionary science. Their influence was paramount in the sixties, when they had a gifted leader in the brilliant pamphleteer Písarev (1840–68), but it declined after his death and had almost disappeared towards the beginning of our period. The populists were more pronounced socialists. Their name came from their cult of the people—identified with the working classes, and more especially with the peasants. Many of them were "conscience-stricken noblemen," that is, members of the gentry who were obsessed by the idea of sacrificing all their lives to the people in expiation of the wrongs of serfdom. At first they were largely non-political and hoped to achieve social revolution by some internal process in the existing peasant land commune. But towards the end of the seventies they gave birth to the "People's Will" Party, which adopted more active revolutionary methods and organized the assassination of Alexander II. The reaction of the eighties put an end for a time to all active revolutionism, but the *naródniki* remained the most influential and numerous group of the intelligentsia till the advent of Marxism in the nineties. Some of them, after the defeat of the terrorists, shifted towards a more non-political attitude, and many populists of the eighties approached Tolstóy in his passive anarchism, or even the more conservative and Slavophil anarchism of Dostoyévsky. But all of them retained the cult of the virtues of the Russian people and the motto "Everything for the People." Populism was, after all, the form taken in Russia by the teaching of Jean Jacques Rousseau.

The leaders of populism in the sixties and seventies were the poet Nekrásov and the novelist Saltykóv. They gave the tone to the great majority of the young generation, but as they were imaginative writers and not theoreticians, they could play but a small part in settling the detail of the populist dogma. The great "doctor" of the populist "Church" was a younger man—Nicholas Konstantínovich Mikhaylóvsky (1842–1904), the all-authoritative expounder of its doctrine, and in his last years, the grand old man of Russian radicalism. He was a sociologist, and his book on *What Is Progress?* was considered by the successors of the populists as the *Summa Theologiae* of their doctrine. Mikhaylóvsky called his method in sociology the "subjective" method, which meant that social science was to be studied, not disinterestedly like natural science, but in terms of human progress. Progress for him meant the greatest happiness, not of the greatest number, but of all men, for human individuality was the supreme and only value and could not be sacrificed to society. Socialism was precisely the only order that allowed for the happiness of all and for the full expansion of every individuality. The means of achieving progress was the conscious action of individual persons inspired with faith and with a sense of duty towards the people. Populism, as expounded by

Mikhaylóvsky, differs from Marxian socialism principally in two things—in its ethical foundation and in its faith in human individuality. It knows nothing either of the class morality or of the superstitious faith in the laws of evolution of Marxism.

Besides his sociological writings, Mikhaylóvsky was a great journalist; his polemical writings (though, as is the case with most polemical writings, they are often not fair play) are always brilliant and full of point. He was also a critic, and though, like all the critics of his time, he considered in the writers he criticized only their "message" and their degree of public utility, he had a wonderfully acute critical insight. He was able, as early as 1873, from certain pedagogical articles by Tolstóy, to discern the essentially destructive and anarchical nature of Tolstóy's doctrine, and largely to predict the development taken by him after 1880 (*The Left and Right Hand of Count Leo Tolstóy*). Mikhaylóvsky's critical masterpiece is his essay on Dostoyévsky (*A Cruel Talent*, 1882). It is full of suppressed but unmistakable hostility to the ideas and person of Dostoyévsky, but with wonderful precision he lays his finger on the writer's love of suffering and connects it with his morbid "sadism." He was the first to bring out the importance of *The Memoirs from Underground* and recognize the central position they occupied in Dostoyévsky's work.

THE CONSERVATIVES

In political life the radicals were the opposition. But in literature they were the majority, and the supporters of the existing order were, in their turn, the opposition. Conservative writers had a considerable influence on the government, but they had fewer readers than the radicals. The Polish Revolt of 1863, and still more the assassination of Alexander II in 1881, had turned the bulk of the upper and middle classes away from radicalism in practical politics, and the reactionary policy of Alexander III's government found substantial support in the country. But this conservatism (as conservatism so often is) was merely the outcome of fear and inertness. It was not interested in conservative *ideas*. The intellectually active part of the nation remained largely radical and atheistic. Only a small minority of thinking people—but among them perhaps the most independent, original, and sincere minds

of the day—showed a critical attitude towards the dogma of agnosticism and democracy, and strove towards a creative revival
of Christian and national ideas. But the public had little use for
independent thought—they preferred either radicalism or radi-
calism-and-water, and independent conservative writers—like
Grigóriev, Dostoyévsky, Leóntiev, Rózanov—had to struggle
against general indifference and its consequences, unemployment
and poverty. Dostoyévsky was alone successful in this struggle.
Only the big men of the political press—the spokesman of one of
the two large sections of conservative opinion—could command a
hearing.

These two sections were Slavophils, represented by Aksákov,
and practical government nationalists, headed by Katkóv. Iván
Aksákov (1823–86), the son of the great memoirist, was the last
remnant of the old idealistic Slavophilism of the forties. He was
a brilliant and outspoken publicist and orator, and his political
influence, especially during the Turkish crisis of 1876–8, was enormous. But he was not a creator of ideas. Katkóv (1818–87) was
still less creative. He was an eloquent and determined journalist,
and his force of will and fixity of purpose often compelled the
government to be firmer in its policy than it would have been
without his support. But he was only the watchdog, not the philosopher of reaction. This title might rather be assigned to the
famous Pobedonóstsev (1827–1907), *"Ober-prokurór"* of the Synod
for thirty years and an enormous political influence under Alexander III and especially in the first years of Nicholas II. But his
conservatism was merely negative; it arose out of a profound disbelief in every reform; it was the outcome of a skepticism that did
not believe in the possibility of any rational betterment. He was at
bottom a nihilist who thought that the existing order was as good
as any other, and that it was better to support it by all possible
means than to launch out on any uncertain experiment.

But among those less closely connected with the government
and with politics, there were men who had better and more positive
reasons for defending the traditional groundwork of Russian State
and Church. Of the old Slavophils, romantic idealists who believed
in the inherent, God-ordained superiority of the Russian nation
and in the great responsibility of Russia for this dangerous gift of
Providence, Aksákov was the last. A later phase of Slavophilism—
more democratic and less exclusive—had lost its greatest leaders

in Grigóriev and Dostoyévsky. It was still represented by Strákhov (1828–95), a philosopher and critic, who had been the journalistic ally of Dostoyévsky but had retained little enthusiasm for his great associate—of all those who knew Dostoyévsky, Strákhov had had the most illuminating and terrible glimpses of the dark, "infernal, underground" soul of the creator of Stavrógin. Strákhov's philosophical work does not belong here, and as a critic he was not strikingly great. But he was the center of anti-radical idealism in the eighties, the principal link between the Slavophils and the mystical revival of the nineties. His place is greater in literary biography than in literary history. Besides his association with Dostoyévsky, he was an intimate friend of Tolstóy, and he became the literary godfather of the greatest writer of the mystical revival —Rózanov.

Another interesting figure was Nicholas Danilévsky (1822–85), the creator of scientific Slavophilism. He was a naturalist by training and gave his nationalism a biological foundation. His book on *Russia and Europe* (1869) develops the theory of individual, mutually watertight civilizations. In Russia and Slavdom he saw the germs of a new civilization that was to displace that of the West. He did not consider Russia in any way superior to, but merely different from, the West; and Russia's duty was to be herself, not because by being herself she would be better and holier than the West, but because as she was not of the West she could never by imitating the West become anything but an imperfect ape, not a real member of Western civilization.[6]

LEÓNTIEV

Constantine Nikoláyevich Leóntiev (1831–91) studied medicine at the University of Moscow, where he came under the influence of the "philanthropic" literature of the time and became an ardent admirer of Turgénev. In 1851, under this influence, he wrote a play full of morbid self-analysis. He took it to Turgénev, who received him, liked it, and used his influence to place it in a magazine. But it was not passed by the censor. Turgénev continued patronizing

[6] There can be no doubt that Danilévsky's book is the principal source of the ideas of Oswald Spengler.

Leóntiev and at one time considered him, next to Tolstóy, the most promising young writer of the time. In 1854, when Leóntiev was in his last year at school, the Crimean War broke out, and Leóntiev volunteered for the Crimean army as a military surgeon. He worked for the most part in hospitals—and worked hard, for he was passionately interested in his work. About this time he developed a paradoxical theory of æsthetic immoralism that took strange forms at times—thus on two occasions, as he tells us in his wonderful memoirs, he encouraged marauding in the Cossacks of a regiment he was attached to. But he remained himself scrupulously honest. He was one of the few non-combatants connected with the Crimean army who had the opportunity of enriching themselves and did not.

So when the war was over he returned to Moscow penniless. He continued practicing as a doctor, and published, in 1861–2, a series of novels that had no success. They are not great novels, but they are remarkable for the fierce intensity with which he expressed in them, always in the most striking and provoking manner, his æsthetic immoralism. This strange immoralistic pathos is best of all seen in *A Husband's Confession*, in which a middle-aged husband encourages the misconduct of his young wife, not from any idea of the "rights of woman," but because he wants her to live a full and beautiful life of passion, ecstasy, and suffering. At this period of his life he began to be attracted by the Slavophils' respect for and love of the originality of Russian life, but their moral idealism remained quite alien to him.

In 1863 he was admitted to the consular service and was appointed secretary and dragoman to the Russian consulate at Candia. He did not stay long at Candia, for he soon had to be transferred for horsewhipping the French vice-consul. This, however, did not impede his career. He moved up the ladder of consular service with great rapidity, and in 1869 he was appointed to the important and independent post of consul at Yanina, in Epirus. All this time his behavior was far from exemplary. His hero was Alcibiades, and he tried to live up to his standard of a "full" and beautiful life. He lived passionately and expensively. He was always in some love affair—and confided them to his wife. She did not like it, and it would seem that these confidences were the cause of her mental illness, for after 1869 she became, with intervals, a permanent mental invalid. This was the first shadow on the wall. In 1871 came the next—the death of his mother, for whom he had a deep affection.

In the same year he was transferred to Salonika and almost immediately had a very severe attack of local malaria. He was in imminent danger, and on his bed of sickness he made a vow to go to Mount Athos to expiate his sins. As soon as he was well enough, he fulfilled his vow and spent about a year at Athos submitting to the severe rule of the monastery and to the strict spiritual guidance of an "elder." From this time he recognized as sinful his life of the previous years and all his immoralistic writings and became converted to the most ascetic form of Byzantine and monastic orthodoxy. But his æsthetic immoralism remained in substance unchanged—it only bowed down before the rule of dogmatic Christianity. In 1873, finding himself in disagreement with Ambassador Ignátiev about the Græco-Bulgarian Church schism, he left the consular service. Ignátiev, like the Slavophil he was, and like all official Russia, took the side of the Bulgarians because they were Slavs. To Leóntiev, the Bulgarians—Slavs or no Slavs—were democrats and rebels to their lawful spiritual lord, the Œcumenical Patriarch. This was characteristic of Leóntiev—he had no interest in mere Slavdom. What he wanted was a firm conservatism in the matter of national originality and tradition, and of this he found more in the Greeks than in the Bulgarians, whom, with complete justice, he suspected of being easily Europeanized and reduced to the common level of Western democratic civilization. But the Greeks—the conservative Greek peasants, rural tradesmen, and monks—he loved passionately. They were to him the bulwark of what was to him the greatest of values—Byzantine civilization.

About the same time he became acquainted with Danilévsky's *Russia and Europe*, which produced on him a strong impression by its scientific-biological treatment of the history of civilizations. The idea of the individual civilization as a complete and self-contained organism became his own, and he gave it a brilliant development in his remarkable essay on *Byzantinism and Slavdom*. In it he confuted Danilévsky's idea of the Slavs' being an independent cultural entity and saw the originality of Russia in her being the pupil and heir of Byzantium. Unlike the Slavophils, Leóntiev did not condemn Western civilization as a whole, but only in its last stage. Civilizations were like living beings and passed, with the necessity of a natural law, three inevitable phases of development. The first phase was initial or primitive simplicity; the second, exuberant growth and complexity of creative and beautiful inequality. This was the only valuable stage. It had lasted in Europe from the eleventh to the eighteenth century. The third phase was the "secondary simplification" of dissolution and putrefaction. These phases in the life of a nation were equivalent in the life of an individual to those of embryonic life, of life, and of dissolution after death, when the complexity of a living organism is again reduced to its constituent elements.[7] Europe, since the eighteenth century, had been in the third stage, and there was reason to believe that Russia was already infected by this putrefaction.

The essay passed unnoticed, and altogether, after leaving the consular service, Leóntiev fell on evil times. His income was insignificant, and in 1881 he had to sell his estate. He passed much of his time in monasteries. At one time he was sub-editor of a provincial official paper. Then he was appointed censor. But up to his death he was in constant difficulties. During his life in Greece he had worked at a series of stories of modern Greek life. In 1876 he published them in book form (*From the Life of Christians in Turkey*, three volumes). He placed great hopes on the success of this work, but it fell flat, and the few people who noticed it admired it only as good descriptive journalism. In the eighties, with the growth of reaction, Leóntiev felt himself a little less out of tune and less alone. But though the reactionaries respected him and opened their columns to him, they did not gauge the originality of his genius, but regarded him as rather a doubtful and dangerous ally. Still, in the last years of his life he found more sympathy than before. And before he died he was surrounded by a small number of devoted followers and admirers. This brought some consolation to his last years. He spent more and more time in Óptina, the most famous of Russian ascetic monasteries, and in 1891, with the permission of his spiritual father, the "elder" Father Ambrose, he took monastic vows with the name of Clement. He settled in the ancient Trinity Monastery near Moscow, where he died in the same year.

Leóntiev's political writings (including *Byzantinism and Slavdom*) were published in two volumes under the title of *Russia*,

[7] Leóntiev's three phases are Spengler's *Vorkultur*, *Kultur*, and *Zivilisation*.

the East, and the Slavs (1885–6). They are written in a vehement, nervous, hurried, disrupted, but vigorous and pointed style. The nervous uneasiness reflected in it reminds one of Dostoyévsky. But, unlike Dostoyévsky, Leóntiev is a logician, and the outline of his argument through the agitated nervousness of his style is almost as clear as Tolstóy's. Three elements form the philosophy (if it may be called a philosophy) of Leóntiev. First came a biological foundation, owing to his medical training and strengthened by Danilévsky's influence, which made him look for and believe in natural laws in the social and moral world. Next came his temperamental æsthetic immoralism, which made him passionately enjoy the multiplicity and varied beauty of life. And at last came his unconditional submission to the guidance of monastic orthodoxy that dominated his later years; it was more a passionate desire than the actual presence of faith, but this only made it more vehement and uncompromising. These three influences resulted in his final political doctrine of extreme reaction and nationalism. He hated the modern West, both for its atheism and for its democratic, leveling tendencies that destroyed the complex and varied beauty of social life. The chief thing for Russia was to stop the process of dissolution and putrefaction coming from the West. This is expressed in the words (attributed to Leóntiev, though they do not occur in his works): "We must freeze Russia, to prevent her from rotting." But in his biological heart of hearts he did not believe in the possibility of stopping the natural process. He was a profound anti-optimist. He did not want the world to be better. He thought pessimism *here* an essential part of religion. His political "platform" is stated in his characteristically agitated and broken style in the following formulas:

(1) The State must be many-colored, complex, strong, based on class privileges, and change with circumspection; on the whole, harsh, even to fierceness. (2) The Church must be more *independent* than at present. The Episcopate must be bolder, more authoritative, more concentrated. The Church must act as a moderating influence in the State, not the contrary. (3) Life must be poetical, multiform in its national—as opposed to the West—unity (for instance, either not dance at all, but pray to God, or

else dance, but in our own way; invent or develop our
national dances to a beautiful refinement). (4) The law,
the principles of government, must be severer; individuals
must try to be personally kinder; one will counterbalance
the other. (5) Science must develop in a spirit of profound
contempt for its own utility.

In all Leóntiev did and wrote there was such a profound contempt for mere morality, such a passionate hatred of the democratic herd, such a violent assertion of the aristocratic ideal, that
he has been more than once called the Russian Nietzsche. But
Nietzsche's impulse was religious, and Leóntiev's was not. He
was a rare instance in modern times (the thing was a rule in the
Middle Ages) of an essentially unreligious man submitting consciously and obediently to the hard rule of dogmatic and exclusive
religion. But he was not a seeker after God or after the absolute.
Leóntiev's world is a finite world, a world whose very essence and
beauty lie in its finiteness and in its imperfection, *Die Liebe zum
Fernen* was quite unknown to him. He accepted and loved Orthodox Christianity, not for the perfection it promised in heaven and
announced in the Person of God, but for the stress it laid on the
imperfection of earthly life. Those who believed in progress and
wanted to introduce their paltry and inferior perfection into this
splendidly imperfect world were his worst enemies. He treats them
with splendid scorn, quite worthy of Nietzsche, in his brilliant
satire *The Average European as the Means and End of Universal
Progress.*
    Though Leóntiev preferred life to art and liked literature in
the measure it reflected beautiful, that is, organic and varied, life,
he was perhaps the only genuine literary critic of his time. For,
alone of all his contemporaries, he was capable of going to the
essential facts of literary art apart from the *message* of the author.
His book on the novels of Tolstóy (*Analysis, Style, and Atmosphere
in the Novels of Count L. N. Tolstóy,* 1890) is, for its penetrating
analysis of the novelist's means of expression, the masterpiece of
Russian criticism. In it he condemns (as Tolstóy did himself a few
years later in *What Is Art?*) the superfluous-detail manner of the
realists and praises Tolstóy for abandoning it in his then recently
published stories for the people. This is characteristic of Leóntiev's

critical fairness: he censures the style of *War and Peace* though he likes its philosophy, and praises the style of the popular stories though he hates their "new Christianity."

During the last years of his life Leóntiev published some fragments of his personal recollections, which for the general reader are his most interesting work. Their nervous style, their unlimited sincerity, and the great vividness of the story give them a unique place among Russian memoirs. The best fragments are those which were to contain a complete history of his religious life and conversion (but stop short with the first two chapters describing his childhood and his mother, and his literary relations with Turgénev) and the wonderfully vivid account of his part in the Crimean War and of the descent of the Allies on Kerch in 1855. It is truly "infectious." The reader himself becomes part of the agitated, passionate, impulsive soul of Leóntiev.

In his lifetime Leóntiev was judged exclusively on party lines, and as he was nothing if not paradoxical, he earned little else than ridicule from his opponents and qualified praise from his friends. The first man who recognized his genius without sympathizing with his ideas was Vladímir Soloviëv, who was struck by the powerful originality of his personality and, after his death, did much to keep his memory green by writing a sympathetic and detailed notice of him for the standard Russian *Encyclopædia*. Since then he has been revived. In 1912 and following years there appeared a collected edition of his works (in nine volumes); in 1911, a collection of memoirs dedicated to him, preceded by an excellent *Life of Leóntiev*, by his disciple Konoplyántsev. He has become generally (though sometimes tacitly) recognized as a classic.

CHAPTER 2

The Eighties and Early Nineties

THE reign of Alexander III (1881–94) was a period of reaction in political life. The assassination of Alexander II marked the crest of the great revolutionary wave and was followed by a collapse of the whole movement. The government opened an energetic campaign of suppression and found substantial support in the opinion of the upper and middle classes. In two or three years it succeeded in making a clean sweep of all revolutionary organizations. By 1884 all active revolutionaries were either in Schlüsselburg [1] and Siberia or abroad. For almost ten years there was no revolutionary activity to speak of. The more law-abiding radicals also suffered from the reaction. Their leading magazines were suppressed, and they lost most of their hold on the masses of the intelligentsia. Peaceful and passive non-political aspirations were the order of the day. Tolstoyism became popular, not so much for its sweeping condemnation of State and Church, as for its doctrine of non-resistance—precisely the point in which it differed from revolutionary socialism. The great majority of the middle class subsided into a life of humdrum boredom and impotent aspirations —a life familiarized to the English reader by the stories of Chékhov. But the end of the reign also saw the beginning of a new upheaval of capitalistic enterprise.

In literature, the eighties were a period of "æsthetic" reaction against the utilitarian practice of the sixties and seventies. This reaction began before 1881, so it cannot have been the result of political disillusionment. It was merely the natural and essentially healthy protest of the literary spirit against the all-pervading

[1] A prison, primarily for political offenders, near St. Petersburg.—Editor

utilitarianism of the preceding age. The movement, as a whole, did
not proclaim the doctrine of "art for art's sake," but writers began
to show a greater interest in things other than immediate public
utility—a greater interest in form, and for the "eternal" problems
of life and death, of good and evil apart from their social implica-
tions. Even those writers of the eighties who were most "with a
purpose" were at pains not to let it be seen too crudely. Poetry
was revived. In prose, the new writers tried to avoid the formless-
ness and untidiness of the "tendentious" novelists and the journalistic tendencies of Saltykóv and Uspénsky. They reverted to
the examples of Turgénev and Tolstóy, and tried to be what is
called in Russian *khudózhestvenny*. This word really means "artistic," but owing to the use to which it was put by the idealist
critics of the fortics (Belínsky), it has a very different emotional
"overtone" from its English equivalent. Among other things, it
conveyed to the late-nineteenth-century Russian *"intelligént"* a
certain mellowness and lack of crudeness, an absence of too-ap-
parent "purpose," and also an absence of intellectual elements—of
logic and "reflection." It was also colored by Belínsky's doctrine
that the essence of "art" was "thinking in images," not in concepts.
This idea is partly responsible for the great honor in which descriptions of visible things were held—especially emotionally
colored descriptions of nature in the style of Turgénev.

For all this reversal to "form" and to "eternal ideas" this
movement was very little of a renascence. It lacked force and
originality. It was conservative and placid, eclectic and timid. It
strove rather after the absence of great ugliness than after the
presence of great beauty. The revival of both a really active feeling
for form and really daring metaphysical speculation came only
later, in the nineties and in the early years of this century.

GÁRSHIN

Vsévolod Mikháylovich Gárshin (1855–88) was the first in date
and, in many ways, the most representative of the novelists of the
eighties. Of gentry origin, he was a man of extraordinarily acute
moral sensitiveness, and, brought up as he was in the period immediately following the Emancipation of the serfs, he naturally
enough acquired the mentality of a "conscience-stricken noble-

man." It did not take the direction of political work for the people, but when war broke out with Turkey (1877) he enlisted as a private soldier. He did not do this from motives of patriotism or for the love of adventure, but under the intense conviction that if the people were suffering at the front, it was his duty to suffer with them. Gárshin did well as a soldier. He was mentioned in dispatches and promoted to the grade of sergeant. In August 1877 he was wounded in the leg and invalided to Khárkov. There he wrote *Four Days*, a short story about a wounded soldier who remained four days on the battlefield unable to move and next to the putrefying corpse of a dead Turk. The story appeared in October 1877 and created a sensation. It established Gárshin's reputation once for all. He became a professional writer. Gradually his delicate moral constitution took a morbid turn and developed into a permanent and agonizing dissatisfaction with the whole of the world order. He was constantly on the brink of a mental breakdown. His conduct became eccentric. One of his first eccentricities was his visit to the Prime Minister Lóris-Mélikov, whom he endeavored to convince of the necessity of "making peace" with the revolutionaries. His personal acquaintance with the morbid states of mind helped him to write *The Red Flower* (1883), the most remarkable of all his stories. As time went on, his nervous state grew worse. He began to feel the imminent approach of madness. This aggravated his melancholy and brought him to suicide. After a particularly bad access of despair he threw himself down a staircase and broke his leg. He did not recover, but, after an agony of five days, died on March 24, 1888. All those who knew him testify to the extraordinary purity and charm of his person. His eyes especially are said to have been unique and unforgettable.

The essence of Gárshin's personality is a "genius" for pity and compassion, as intense as Dostoyévsky's but free from all the "Nietzschean," "underground," and "Karamázov" ingredients of the greater writer. This spirit of compassion and pity prevades all his writing. His work is not voluminous: it consists of some twenty stories, all of them contained in a single volume. In most of them he is an intelligent pupil of Turgénev and the early Tolstóy. In a few (*The Signal, The Legend of Proud Aggéy*) he follows the lead given by Tolstóy's "popular" stories. *That Which Was Not* and *Attalea Princeps* are fables with animals and plants in human situations. The second of these two stories is one of his best—it is saturated with a spirit of tragic irony. In *Officer and Servant* he is a forerunner of Chékhov—it is an excellently constructed story of "atmosphere," an atmosphere of drab gloom and meaningless boredom. In *A Very Short Novel* he treats, with greater felicity, the subject of Artsybáshev's *War*, the infidelity of the woman to the crippled hero. It is a little masterpiece of concentration and lyrical irony. His best-known and most characteristic story is *The Red Flower*, the first in a long row of lunatic-asylum stories (the next in time was Chékhov's *Ward No. 6*). In it Gárshin's morbid and high-strung moral sensitiveness reaches its highest pitch. It is the history of a madman who is obsessed by the desire to challenge and defeat the evil of the world. He discovers that all evil is contained in three poppies growing in the middle of the hospital garden, and with infinite astuteness and cunning he succeeds in defeating the vigilance of his warders and picking the flowers. He dies from nervous exhaustion, but dies happy and certain of having attained his end. The story is gloomy and powerful. The oppressive atmosphere of the asylum is conveyed with effective skill. The end comes as a relief, like death to a martyr, but there is in it also a pang of bitter irony.

Gárshin is hardly a great writer. His manner is too much that of a degenerate age. His technique is insufficient, and even in *The Red Flower* there are irritating lapses into the inadequate. But his style is sober and sincere, and even his occasional clumsiness seems preferable to the fluent rhetoric and cardboard dramatism of the school of Andréyev.

MINOR NOVELISTS

In the eighties and nineties there was a considerable output of Russian fiction. It was not of a very high quality, and even at the time no one thought that a great literary revival was going on. But some of it is not altogether insignificant. There is no need to give much attention to the novelists of the eighties—a brief survey will suffice. The oldest of them (for many years the dean of Russian letters), P. D. Boborýkin (1836–1921), was a journalist rather than a novelist; his novels are snapshots of the various states of mind through which the typical *"intelligént"* passed, and of various new social phenomena, such as the "cultured merchant." They are written in an "objective" style derived from the French naturalists. A journalist of another sort was Vasíly Nemiróvich-Dánchenko (1848–1936, to be distinguished from his brother Vladímir, founder of the Moscow Art Theater), who led the Russian reader on tours around the world, with just a touch of primitively mild sensationalism. He was read by the unsophisticated, who also enjoyed the historical novels of Vsévolod Soloviëv (1849–1903), the brother of the famous philosopher. But to indulge in this sort of literature was "bad form" for the self-respecting intellectual.

The influence of Dostoyévsky is discernible in the work of M. N. Álbov (1851–1911), who described at great length the morbid states of mind experienced by priests and clerics; and in that of Prince D. P. Golítsyn-Murávlin, who, starting with the character of Prince Mýshkin, attempted to portray pathological types of the aristocracy. Another side of Dostoyévsky is reflected in the work of K. S. Barantsévich, who wrote stories in the respectable tradition of *Poor Folk*, describing the sufferings of the poor and the oppressed. A sterner note sounded in the stories of D. N. Mámin-Sibiryák, who drew unsweetened pictures of the hand and joyless life of the miners in the Ural. Ieroním Yasínsky was a naturalist of the French type who early proclaimed the rights of art for art's sake. He was the first Russian writer to approach sexual subjects, and in 1917 the first non-party intellectual to join the Bolshevíks. The humorous South Russian nature found expression in the unpretending stories of I. N. Potápenko. Another popular humorist of the time was Chékhov's friend Scheglóv (pseudonym of I. L. Leóntiev). His *Suburban Husband*, an amusing picture of Russian suburbia, became a favorite catchword, almost a new word. Another famous humorous type was created by Mme Mikúlich (pseudonym of Lydia I. Veselítsky). Her *Mímochka* is a witty picture of the average *jeune fille* of Petersburg bureaucratic society—the incarnation of placid futility.

More important than any of these writers was Alexander Ivánovich Értel (1855–1908). He was a populist, but in his later years he abandoned the usual agnosticism of the Russian *"intelligént"* and tried to evolve a more spiritualist philosophy. This caused a considerable revival of interest in him about 1910 when the revival of religion was the watchword—his collected works and his letters were published then and had a considerable success. His first stories appeared in 1880, but his best and best-known novel is *The Gardénins, Their Retainers, Their Friends, and Their Enemies*, in two volumes (1898). It had the honor, when reprinted in 1908, of a preface by Tolstóy, who gave especial praise to Értel's art of dialogue. "Such good Russian," said Tolstóy, "is not to be found in any writer, old or new. He uses the people's speech, not only with accuracy, force, and beauty, but with infinite variety. . . . Who wants to know the language of the Russian people . . . must not only read but study Értel's Russian." Apart from this, *The Gardénins* is one of the best Russian novels written since the great age. It is a vast panorama of life on a big estate in south central Russia. The hero is the son of an estate agent (like Értel himself). The characters of the peasants are infinitely varied and splendidly individualized. So are those of the rural middle class and of the rural police, which of course is presented in a satirical light. But the Gardénins themselves, one of whom is a "conscience-stricken" aristocrat, are much less happily portrayed. The novel is transfused with a very keen poetical sense of nature. One of the most memorable episodes is the account of a trotting match at Khrenóvaya, which holds its own even by the side of the race scene in *Anna Karénina*.

Another writer whose work has not lost its charm was Nicholas Geórgievich Mikhaylóvsky, who wrote under the pseudonym of N. Gárin (1852–1906). He was a railway engineer by profession and took to literature rather late in life. His principal work is a trilogy describing the early life of Tëma Kartashóv—*Tëma's Childhood* (1892), *Schoolboys* (*Gimnazísty*, 1893), and *Students* (1895). The series has great charm, is written in a simple and sincere style, and was immensely popular in its day. The characters that go through the three books are drawn with great warmth, and the reader soon feels towards them as if they were boys he knew in real life. Apart from the literary qualities of the trilogy, it is an important historical document, for it is the "natural history" of a typical intelligentsia education, a school of morally inefficient and nervously unstable men.

This enumeration of minor writers may be completed by the name of Peter Filípovich Yakubóvich (1860–1911), the only active revolutionary among them. He joined the People's Will Party (after March 1st), was arrested in 1884, and spent three years in the Sts. Peter and Paul Fortress and eight years (1887–95) as a convict in Siberia. This record did not allow him to appear in literature under his own name, which has remained comparatively unknown, though his two pseudonyms, P. Ya. and L. Mélshin, became very popular. He used the first to sign his poetry, which is "civic" and very poor. Under the second he published in 1896 a remarkable book of stories of convict life, *A World of Outcasts*, the first book of its kind since Dostoyévsky's *House of Death*. Though, of course, on a much inferior level to Dostoyévsky's, Mélshin's book has considerable merit. Its attitude is characteristic of the Russian revolutionary idealist. He paints, with uncompromising objectivity, the most repulsive criminals as they are, with all their crimes and cynical heartlessness, but he descries in them flashes of humanity, and the message of the book is a firm belief in human nature and a firm respect for human individuality even in the deepest degradation.

Émigrés

Those revolutionaries who did not go to Siberia or to Schlüsselburg found refuge abroad. Their place in literary history is not great. Their political press between 1881 and 1900 was not very active, and even afterward it produced nothing to compare with Herzen's *Bell*. But this period of calm produced an interesting series of memoirs. Now at rest, the active fighters of yesterday sat down to record their experiences of the great struggle. Their memoirs were intended largely for a foreign audience (before 1905 they could not be imported into Russia), and much of it was even written in some foreign language. The idea Western people gained of the revolutionary movement (in so far as it was not quite fantastic) was derived from the works of Sergéy M. Kravchínsky, who wrote under the pseudonym of S. Stepnyák (1852–95). He was a terrorist: he had taken part in 1878 in the assassination of General Mezentsóv, chief of the political police. In 1882 he published in Italian *La Russia sotteranea* (*Underground Russia*), which he himself translated into Russian. Later on he settled down in England and wrote *The Career of a Nihilist* (1889) in English. His stories were well suited to the taste of the Western reader—they were vivid and thrilling. But they have very little value as documentary evidence. From this last point of view the memoirs of Vladímir Debogóry-Mokriévich are much more valuable. Nor are they without purely literary merits; their narrative is easy, straightforward, and full of humor, the almost inevitable virtue of all Southern Russians.

The most eminent of the Russian *émigrés* of this period was Prince Peter Kropótkin (1842–1921). He was the descendant of a very ancient family and received his education at the Corps des Pages. He served in a Cossack regiment in Siberia and made himself a name as a geographer. In the seventies he joined the revolutionary movement, was arrested, and finally escaped over the frontier. At first he lived in Switzerland and in France, but was expelled from the former and sentenced to imprisonment in the latter, in both cases for anarchist propaganda. For he had become the leader and theoretician of anarchism. In 1886 he came to London, where he lived till 1917. He was a man of aristocratic manners and great personal charm and found many friends in various classes of English society. During the first World War his attitude was patriotic. In 1917 he returned to Russia. He remained hostile to the Bolshevíks and rejected all Lénin's approaches. He died in 1921 near Moscow. His work is voluminous; it includes, besides geographical works: propaganda tracts and more elaborate expositions of his anarchism, an optimistic philosophy based on evolutionary theories, a history of the French Revolution, and a history of Russian literature. Practically all of it is in French or English. The most interesting of his books (also originally in English) is *The Memoirs of a Revolutionary* (1899), a first-class autobiography, the most remarkable work of its kind since Herzen's *My Past and Thoughts*.

Here perhaps would also be the place to mention Marie Bashkírtseva (Baschkirtseff, 1860–84). Though she was not a political *émigrée*, she lived and wrote in France and in French. Her *Journal*, published posthumously in 1887, produced a sensation in Europe and was translated into many languages (into Russian later than into English and German). It is certainly a remarkable human document and gives proof of more than ordinary power of self-observation. But its importance has probably been overrated, and in any case it stands entirely outside the line of development of Russian literature.

KOROLÉNKO

Vladímir Galaktiónovich Korolénko (1853–1921) is undoubtedly the most attractive representative of idealist radicalism in Russian literature. If Chékhov had never lived, Korolénko would also have been *facile princeps* among the novelists and poets of his time. He was born in Zhitomír, the capital of Volynia, then a semi-Polish city, and his mother was a Polish gentlewoman. In his childhood Korolénko did not very well know to which nationality he belonged, and learned to read Polish before he did Russian. Only after the Revolt of 1863 did the family have definitely to "choose" its nationality, and they became Russians. In 1870 Korolénko went to Petersburg and became a student of the Institute of Technology, and afterward of the Moscow School of Agriculture, but he did not complete his studies at either: he was expelled for belonging to a secret political organization. In 1879 he was arrested and deported to northeastern Siberia, and spent several years in a far-off part of the Yakút region. In 1885 he was allowed to come to Russia and settled in Nízhny-Nóvgorod. The same year he reappeared in literature,[2] with *Makár's Dream*, the story of a Yakút. The next ten years he spent in Nízhny, where he wrote almost all his best stories. During the famine of 1891–2 he took part in the relief work and published a volume of impressions. In 1895 he was allowed to come to Petersburg. In 1900 he was elected a member of the Academy, but resigned the title, after the incident with Górky's election (*v. infra*). In 1900 he settled in Poltáva, where he lived until his death. After the death of Mikhaylóvsky he became the most prominent figure in the populist camp. From 1895 on, he almost abandoned literature and devoted himself to the disclosure and exposition of injustices committed by the law courts and the police. After 1906 he headed the campaign against military law and capital punishment. The only work of his last period (and perhaps his best) was a sort of autobiography, *The History of My Contemporary*, the first part of which appeared in 1910, and the other parts posthumously in 1922. In 1917 and after, he remained hostile to the Bolshevíks, and his last published work was a series of letters to Lunachársky denouncing the Bolshevíks as the enemies

[2] He had begun publishing before his exile, but he never allowed this early work of his to be reprinted.

of civilization. He died in December 1921 in Poltáva, which during the last few years of his life had more than once been taken and retaken by the various parties in the civil war.

Korolénko's work is very typical of what the eighties and nineties called "artistic" in the peculiar sense explained above. It is full of emotional poetry and of nature introduced in Turgénev's manner. This lyrical element seems today a little stale and uninteresting, and most of us will prefer to all his earlier work his last book, in which he has almost freed himself of this facile poetry. But it was this poetry which appealed so strongly to the tastes of the Russian reading public thirty and forty years ago. The age that made the reputation of Korolénko also revived the cult of Turgénev. Though everyone knew that Korolénko was a radical and a revolutionary, he was received with equal enthusiasm by all parties. This non-party reception given to writers in the eighties was a sign of the times. Gárshin and Korolénko became recognized as (minor) classics before Leskóv, a much greater man, but born in worse times, was given anything like justice. Korolénko's poetry may on the whole have faded, but his best early work still retains much of its charm. For even his poetry rises above the level of mere prettiness when he has to do with the more majestic aspects of nature. The northeast of Siberia, with its vast and empty spaces, its short sub-polar days, and its dazzling wilderness of snow, lives in his early stories with impressive grandeur. But what gives Korolénko his unique flavor is the wonderful blend of poetry with a delicate humor and with his undying faith in the human soul. Sympathy and faith in human goodness are characteristic of the Russian populist. Korolénko's world is a fundamentally optimistic world, for man is good by nature, and only the evil conditions created by despotism and the brutal selfishness of capitalism make him what he is—a poor, helpless, absurd, pitiful, and irritating creature. There is a mighty poetry in Korolénko's first story, *Makár's Dream*, not only because of the suggestive painting of the Yakút landscape, but still more because of the author's profound, indestructible sympathy with the dark and unenlightened savage, whose mind is so naïvely selfish and who yet has in him a ray of the divine light. Korolénko's humor is especially delightful. It is free from all satirical intent and sophistication. It is wonderfully easy and natural—it has a lightness of touch that is rare in Russian authors, and in which he is surpassed only by that wonderful and

still unappreciated author Kuschévsky. In Korolénko this humor
is often subtly interwoven with poetry—as in the delightful story
At Night, in which a family of children discuss in their bedroom
the absorbing question of how babies are made. *The Day of Atonement*, with its funny old Jewish devil, has that blend of humor and
phantasy which is so delightful in Gógol's early stories, but
Korolénko's colors are mellower and quieter, and though he has
not an ounce of the creative exuberance of his great countryman,
he has much more human sympathy and warmth. The most purely
humorous of his stories is *Tongueless* (1895), the story of three
Ukrainian peasants who emigrated to America without knowing a
word of any language but their own. Russian critics have called it
Dickensian, and this is true in the sense that in Korolénko, as in
Dickens, the absurdity of his characters does not make them less
lovable.

Korolénko's last work is an autobiography, which seems to be
even a singularly exact and truthful account of his life but which
for some supersensitive scruple he called the history, not of himself, but of his contemporary. It is less poetical and barer than his
early work, but his two principal qualities—humor and sympathy
—are very much present. He gives a delightful picture of life in
yet semi-Polish Volynia—of his scrupulously honest but willful
father. He records his early impressions of country life, of school,
of the great events he had to witness—the Emancipation and the
Polish Revolt. It is full of wonderfully vivid, grotesque figures of
cranks and originals, perhaps the best in his whole portrait gallery.
It is certainly not thrilling, but it is a deliciously quiet story told
by an old man (he was only fifty-five when he began it, but there
always was something of the grandfather in Korolénko) who has
ample leisure and good will and who finds pleasure in reviving the
vivid memories of fifty years ago.

THE LITERARY LAWYERS

One of the most important changes introduced into Russian life in
the reign of Alexander II was the reform of the law courts. It substituted for the old secret process a public procedure after European models. It made the judges independent of the executive and
introduced a corporation of the bar. The independence of the judges

was practically done away with under Alexander III, but the bar flourished from the very beginning and turned out an important nursery of general culture. The most brilliant men of the generation adopted this profession, and many advocates soon won an all-Russian reputation by their eloquence. Contrary to what was going on elsewhere, they did not neglect to work at the form of their utterances, and more workmanship was displayed in this field than in any department of imaginative literature. The names of the advocates W. D. Spasóvich, Prince A. I. Urúsov, and the crown prosecutor (later on, Minister of Justice) N. V. Muraviëv may be mentioned as those of the most brilliant speakers of the time. Nor did the lawyers neglect more strictly literary work. Spasóvich wrote notable essays on Púshkin and Byron; Anatóly F. Kóni made a name by his life of Dr. Haas, the philanthropist, and still more by several volumes of recollections. They are written in an easy and limpid style, agreeably reminiscent of the fragmentary memoirs of Turgénev. The æsthetic revival of the eighties and nineties owes much to Prince Urúsov (1843–1900). He introduced into Russia the cult of Flaubert and of Baudelaire, and was one of the best critics of literature of his time, though all his criticism was contained in conversation and private letters.

But the most remarkable of all these literary lawyers was Sergéy Arkádievich Andreyévsky (1847–1920). He was one of the most successful advocates of his day, but his name will be remembered rather for his literary work. His verse, like practically all the verse of his time, is insignificant. But his critical essays were an important event in their day—he was the first critic to give Dostoyévsky his due place (essay on *The Brothers Karamázov*, 1888) and to begin the revival of the older poetical tradition—he "discovered" Baratýnsky. But his most important work is *The Book of Death*, which was published only posthumously, abroad. It reveals him as a delicate and refined prose writer, a diligent and intelligent pupil of Lérmontov, Turgénev, and Flaubert. The first part, written about 1891, is the most remarkable. It is the history of his first experiences of death. It contains passages of singular force and sustained beauty. Such is the wonderful chapter about his elder sister Másha, his morbid affection for her, her strange mental malady and early death. This chapter deserves a high place in Russian literature. It is wonderful for the sincere analysis of his own feelings, for the vividness of the narrative, and for the

sustained rhythm, for which there is no precedent in Lérmontov or
Turgénev. The whole chapter (some fifty pages) is one rhythmical
whole. The rhythm is all the more perfect for being quite unobtrusive—the turn of phrase is so colloquial that an untrained ear
might not suspect, or a deliberately unrhythmical delivery might
not convey to the listener, that there was anything peculiar about
it. It is one of the finest achievements of Russian prose.

POETS

Andreyévsky was typical of his time when in one of his essays he
said that the only legitimate subject matter for poetry was "beauty
and melancholy." These two words effectively sum up the poetical
work of the eighties and early nineties. The revival of poetry
began a few years before 1881 and affected both the civic and the
"art-for-art's sake" school. But there is very little difference between these two "schools." Their style is indistinguishable. The
"civic" poets concentrated on melancholy caused by the evils of
despotism and social injustice, but they had nothing of the vigorous, daring realism of Nekrásov, whom they affected to recognize
as master. The "art-for-art's sake" poets preferred to dwell on
beauty and on melancholy arising from sentimental causes, but
they had neither the high craftsmanship of Fet nor the range of
interest of Sluchévsky.

Among the "civic" poets, the most famous was Semën Yákovlevich Nádson (1862–87), a young man of partly Jewish descent
who died of consumption at a very early age. His poetry is inspired by the impotent desire to make the world better and by the
burning consciousness of his own impotence. This makes him akin
to Gárshin, but he had neither Gárshin's imaginative power nor
his great spiritual intensity. Nádson's verse is smooth and skeleton-
less, it avoids ugliness, but it is quite devoid of all life and strength.
It marks the low-water mark of Russian poetical technique; and
his great popularity, the low-water mark of Russian poetical taste.
His only rival was Mínsky (pseudonym of N. M. Vilénkin, 1855–
1937), the first full-blooded Jew to win a reputation in Russian
letters. He began before Nádson but could not compete with him—
his poetry seemed cold and intellectual. We shall meet him once
again in a later chapter. In the late eighties he abandoned "civic"

poetry and became the first swallow of the modernist movement, together with Merezhkóvsky, who also began under the auspices of Nádson as a civic poet. But Merezhkóvsky from the very first gave proof of a poetical culture superior to that of his contemporaries.

The most popular of the non-civic poets was A. N. Apúkhtin (1841–93), the friend and schoolfellow of Tchaikóvsky and a popular figure in Petersburg society, where he was noted for his abnormal stoutness. He was a sort of aristocratic counterpart of Nádson—what Nádson's poetry was to the radical intelligentsia, Apúkhtin's was to the gentry and official classes. It is also a poetry of impotent regret, but his regret is for the days of his youth when he could better enjoy the love of women and the taste of wine. It is the poetry of a man who has ruined his health by too much indulgence. It is less colorless and jelly-like than Nádson's, for he does not so studiously shun all realism and all concrete detail. Some of his lyrics have become very popular as songs, as the well-known *Sleepless Nights*, one of the most popular in the "gypsy" repertoire. A more dignified poet was Count A. A. Goleníschev-Kutúzov (1848–1912). He has been called the poet of Nirvana. He tried to revive a severe and "classical" style, but it is merely still and lifeless in his hands. He is at his best when he speaks of death and destruction. The description of a snowstorm in one of his poems is not without merit. But his principal title to glory is that some of his poems were put to music by Musórgsky, who had a peculiar weakness for his poetry. Another aristocrat who wrote poetry was Count P. D. Buturlín (1859–95). He was more than half a foreigner, with Italian and Portuguese blood in him, as well as an English education. His first work was a book of English verse printed in Florence. He contributed to the *Academy* and other English papers. He never really learned to speak the language of his country. This makes his poetry inadequate, but it is interesting as an isolated instance of English influence—Buturlín was a devoted follower of Keats and of the pre-Raphaelites.

In the later eighties the anti-radical critics tried to create a boom around the poetry of Constantine Mikháylovich Fófanov (1862–1911). Quite uncultured and uneducated (he was the son of a small shopkeeper in a Petersburg suburb), he possessed what none of his contemporaries possessed—a genuine gift of song. His poetry is all about stars, and flowers, and birds—it is sometimes quite genuine, but on the whole rather uninteresting; and as he was a very poor craftsman, it is singularly unequal. The next poetical boom was around Myrrha Lókhvitsky (1869–1905), who appeared in 1895 with a volume of passionate and exotic feminine poetry. Her poetry and Fófanov's seemed the last word of beauty in the nineties, when the real revival of poetry began with the rise of the symbolist movement.

VLADÍMIR SOLOVIËV

The eighties were a period of (mild) reaction against the utilitarian positivism of the preceding age. This reaction found expression in the anæmic revival of poetry and in a somewhat more vigorous revival of religious idealism. The radicals were by temperament idealists, but their idealism was based (to quote a joke of Soloviëv's) on the rather unjustifiable syllogism, "Man is descended from monkeys: consequently we must love each other." The eighties attempted to give this piece of reasoning a more plausible foundation. Their religious idealism found its most popular expression in the teaching of Tolstóy, which influenced contemporaries precisely in so far as it was religious and a reaction against radical materialism. Another and more orthodox expression of the same tendency is the work of Vladímir Soloviëv. The influence of Soloviëv's religious philosophy, at first insignificant, in the long run proved more important than that of Tolstoyism. Soloviëv's place in the history of Russian thought is defined by the fact that he was the first Russian thinker to divorce mystical and Orthodox Christianity from the doctrines of Slavophilism. He was to a certain extent the continuer of the less exclusive and more "occidentalist" wing of Slavophilism, which found its most complete expression in the ideas of the publicist Dostoyévsky. But there is between the two a substantial difference: to Dostoyévsky the supreme sanction of Orthodox Christianity was that it expressed the religious intuition of the *Russian people*. He was a nationalist in religion, a mystical populist: Orthodoxy was true *because* it was the faith of the Russian people. Soloviëv was quite free from this mystical nationalism, and whether he based his religion on the deductions of idealist philosophy or on the authority of the Œcumenical Church, the religious opinion of the Russian people is to him a matter completely irrelevant. His Orthodoxy had a strong leaning towards Rome, as the symbol of Christian unity, and in politics he was a Westernizing liberal. This was the chief element in his early success, for the liberals found him a valuable ally in their campaign against the government and the Slavophils, all the more valuable because in his indictment of the existing political order he appealed, not to Darwin or Marx, but to the Bible and to the fathers. His help came from an unexpected quarter, and for that reason was especially welcome.

Vladímir Sergéyevich Soloviëv (1853–1900) was born in Moscow, one of a numerous family. His father was the eminent historian S. M. Soloviëv, and he grew up in the atmosphere of the Moscow University. He belonged to that class of Moscow society which included the elite of the cultured nobility and the pick of the higher intelligentsia. He early joined a highly gifted set of humorists, who called themselves the Shakspere Society and indulged in writing nonsense verse and staging parody plays. The most brilliant of this set was Count Theodore Sologúb, the best Russian nonsense poet since "Kuzmá Prutkóv." Soloviëv himself was all his life an adept in this art. At the same time his scholarship was brilliant and precocious. As early as 1875 he published his Ph.D. thesis on *The Crisis of Western Philosophy*, directed against positivism. In the same year he went to London, where he spent most of his time in the British Museum studying the mystical doctrine of Sophia the Divine Wisdom. There, in the reading room, he had a vision and received the mystical command to go immediately to Egypt. In the desert near Cairo he had his most important and completest vision, which revealed to him the Person of Sophia. This voyage into the desert was accompanied by amusing incidents with the Arabs. It is highly characteristic of Soloviëv that twenty years later he described these visions (including an earlier one of 1862) in a humorous poem, *Three Meetings*, in which the highly lyrical and esoteric description of the visions is surrounded by verse in the style of *Beppo* and *Don Juan*. On his return to Russia, Soloviëv was appointed Reader of Philosophy at Moscow, and soon afterward at Petersburg. His university career was a short one: in March 1881 he made a speech against capital punishment in which he tried to persuade the new emperor not to execute the assassins of his father. His motive was that by going "counter to the natural inclination of

his heart and to every consideration of earthly wisdom, the Tsar
would rise to a superhuman level and in the very fact demonstrate the divine source of his royal power." In spite of this
motive, he found himself compelled to leave the university. During the eighties he worked at the idea of a universal theocracy,
which brought him nearer and nearer to Rome. He went to Zagreb
and became intimate with Bishop Strosmayer, the opponent in
1870 of papal infallibility but by now a docile servant of the
Vatican. The work of this period is summed up in his French book
La Russie et l'Eglise Universelle (1889), in which he took up an
extremely pro-Roman position, defending both the infallibility and
the Immaculate Conception, describing the Popes as the only rock
of orthodoxy throughout the ages, and denouncing the Russian
Church as State-governed. The book could not appear in Russia,
but produced a certain sensation abroad. However, Soloviëv never
actually became a Roman Catholic, and the appellation of a
"Russian Newman" given him by the French Jesuit d'Herbigny
(in his book *Un Newman russe*) is grossly misleading. *La Russie
et l'Eglise Universelle* marks the high-water mark of his Rom-
ish tendencies. They soon began to decline, and in his last
work he represented the final Union of Christian Churches as a
union between three *equal* Churches—Orthodox, Catholic, and
Protestant, with the Pope as only *primus inter pares*. In the late
eighties and nineties he conducted an energetic campaign against
the nationalist policy of Alexander III's government. These articles brought him a high reputation in liberal spheres. His mystical
life, however, continued, though his visions of Sophia ceased with
the Egyptian one. In the nineties his mysticism became less orthodox and took the form of a strange "mystical love affair" with the
Finnish Lake Saima, which found abundant expression in his poetry. He also had diabolical visitations. In the last year of his life
he entered on a correspondence with Anna Schmidt, a provincial
newspaper hack who believed herself to be the incarnation of
Sophia, and Soloviëv of the person of Christ. (There is a striking
chapter on Anna Schmidt in Górky's *Fragments from a Diary*.)
Soloviëv's answers to her were humorous in form but sympathetic
in substance, and he lent himself to her singular adoration. But
his mystical life remained little known to his contemporaries. They
knew him as an idealist philosopher and an outspoken liberal
polemist. This last capacity placed him high in the eyes of the

intelligentsia, and he was invited by the radical editors of the standard *Encyclopædia* to be editor of the philosophical department, which was consequently conducted in a spirit strongly opposed to agnosticism and materialism. He also found more devoted followers who took up and developed his philosophical doctrines. First among them were the brothers Prince Sergéy and Prince Eugene Troubetzkóy. In 1900 he published his last and, from the literary point of view, most important work, *Three Conversations on War, Progress, and the End of Human History, to Which Is Added a Short History of Antichrist*. The conversations were at once recognized as masterpieces, but the *History of Antichrist* produced a certain consternation by its strangely concrete faith in that personage. Soloviëv was by this time worn out by a too-intense intellectual, spiritual, and mystical life. He went to seek repose in Úzkoye, the Troubetzkóys' estate near Moscow. There he died on July 31, 1900, of general exhaustion.

Soloviëv's personality was extraordinarily complex, and its variations and contrasts are greater than we usually find in a single man. It is difficult to include in one formula this strange and inseparable blend of high-strung religious and moral earnestness with an invincible turn for the most nonsensical humor; his extraordinarily acute sense of orthodoxy with curious proclivities towards Gnosticism and undisciplined mysticism; his equally acute sense of social justice with the lack of fair play in his polemical writings; his profound faith in personal immortality with utterances of gaily cynical nihilism; his earthly asceticism with a morbidly developed erotic mysticism. This complexity and multiplicity of his person seem to have found their expression in his weird, uncanny laugh—which was what all who knew him considered most striking and unforgettable.

Soloviëv was a most brilliant writer, brilliant in everything he undertook. In prose he commanded a trenchant and coldly splendid style, especially suited for polemics. His more serious prose works are perhaps his least characteristic, for in them he had to suppress both his merriment and his mysticism. But they are important for their ideas, and of course it was on them that his reputation grew and is still largely based. His early works are devoted to the enunciation of the first principles of his philosophy; those written in the eighties deal chiefly with questions of Church policy *sub specie æternitatis*. *The Justification of Good* (1898) is a treatise on moral theology, mainly directed against the "non-resistance" teaching of Tolstóy. Soloviëv is considered Russia's most important philosopher in the "professional" sense of the word. He was a great scholar in philosophy, and his knowledge of ancient and modern philosophy was enormous, but he cannot in any sense be put on a level with the world's greatest philosophers, and in a universal history of philosophy he may be overlooked. His philosophy was Neoplatonic, and the Gnostics had always a great attraction for him. But I am in no way competent, and it is in the present connection irrelevant, to give any epitome of his metaphysics. As for his theology, his relations with Roman Catholicism have already been mentioned. He is studied in Roman Catholic schools, though of course he is not recognized as a Doctor. In the Orthodox Church his position is ambiguous—it is recognized that he gave the best existing definitions of Orthodoxy as opposed to every individual heresy, but his leanings towards Rome and visible Unity, as well as the undisciplined and dubious character of his mystical life, make him suspect.

The cold brilliancy of his manner is nowhere more apparent than in his polemical writings. They are splendid examples of the higher journalism, but, as has already been pointed out, when disputing with opponents who had no support in public opinion (for example, Strákhov, Rózanov, the Decadents), he preferred to use arguments that were most likely to give him easy victory in the eyes of the reader rather than to go out of his way to be intellectually fair. Far more remarkable from the literary point of view than his other prose writings are the *Three Conversations*, a true masterpiece in a difficult field. In them he gave free rein to his exuberant humor and to his sparkling wit, and succeeded in creating a work that is at once as amusing as Mark Twain and as earnest as William James. And this he achieves without the aid of paradox, that favorite weapon of all "laughing philosophers." He revels in puns and anecdotes and quotations from nonsense verse, and each of the personages in the dialogue is delightfully individualized. But each (except the purely ridiculous Lady "to whom nothing human is alien") supports his thesis with admirable logic and consistency, and uses his best arguments. The *dialogi personæ* are (besides the Lady): the General, who maintains the rights of force as the just chastiser of brute evil; the Politician, who supports modern civilization as an advance against savagery;

the Prince, who is a Tolstoyan and preaches non-resistance, and who is the villain of the play; and Mr. Z., who is Soloviëv's mouthpiece and recognizes the General and the Politician as the exponents respectively of a *partial* truth that must be merged in the higher synthesis of active Christianity. The *Conversations* are followed by the *History of Antichrist*. This is a curiously vivid and detailed story of the end of the world and of the events immediately preceding the day of judgment. Soloviëv saw in the rise of China and Japan (he wrote in 1900) a great danger for Christendom, and considered it one of the precursors of Antichrist. But Antichrist himself is a European, a philologist and a Roman bishop *in partibus* who is also a magician and a Superman according to Nietzsche.

Those admirers of Soloviëv who think his mysticism the principal aspect of his work place a particular value on his poetry. In this art he was a follower of Fet, with whom he was on intimate terms and whose militant atheism he deplored as precluding any chance of their meeting in the next world. But, like all his contemporaries, he was incapable of acquiring (perhaps even of distinguishing) Fet's superior technique, and, like all of them, he suffered from a slackness and thinness of form. Still he was a true poet—certainly the best poet of his generation. He used the usual romantic vocabulary, but in his hands it received a new significance, for its hackneyed stock words were used to denote concrete mystical facts. His poetry is mystical throughout, and for a complete understanding of it, the fundamental conceptions of his mystic experience must be constantly kept in mind. His most productive period was in the early nineties, when he wrote the beautiful series of lyrics addressed to Lake Saima, of which he speaks as of a living being. Those who want to understand anything in Soloviëv must realize that it is no poetical metaphor, but the actual feeling of a mystical person, when he addresses the lake as "gentle lady" and speaks of its eyes, its moods, and its dreams. His longest poem, *Three Meetings*, though not the best, is in many ways the most characteristic, for in it his mysticism is closely elbowed by his humorous irreverence. Soloviëv was prolific in the purest nonsense verse. It includes witty parodies, biting satire, "cautionary tales," and the Russian equivalent of limericks, but the element of pure nonsense and reckless absurdity is always very apparent. By a procedure opposite to that of *Three Meetings*, he introduced into one of his most nonsensical plays (*The White Lily*) passages of intense mystical significance and gave the whole play a mystical "second meaning." His love of nonsense is also apparent in his letters, which seethe with puns and delightfully irrelevant quotations. When they are published, most people's letters written with the view of amusing the addressee fail to amuse the reader, who has the disagreeable feeling that he is required to laugh and does not feel inclined to. Soloviëv's fun is always as amusing to the general reader—unless he feels an aversion to all forms of non-sense—as it was to the person who first read it. Only in writing to such particularly important and respectable people as Bishop Strosmayer does Soloviëv refrain from his jokes. But even apart from their nonsense his letters are full of wit and humor and are delightful reading. Next to Púshkin (who has no rivals), Soloviëv is no doubt the best of Russian letter writers, with Chékhov as a good third.

CHÉKHOV

Antón Pávlovich Chékhov (1860–1904) was born at Taganróg, on the sea of Azóv. His grandfather had been a serf on the estate of V. G. Chertkóv's grandfather but had acquired considerable wealth by trade and was able to purchase his freedom and that of all his family. Chékhov's parents were simple, half-educated, very religious people, with a strong family feeling. The family consisted of several sons and a daughter. They were all given a liberal education. Antón, who was the youngest but one, was sent to the gymnasium (secondary school) of Taganróg. But while he was there the prosperity of the Chékhovs came to an end. The building of a railway through the neighboring Rostóv was a severe blow to the commerce of Taganróg, and Paul Chékhov soon saw himself forced to close his business. In 1876 he left Taganróg and went to seek employment in Moscow. Antón remained alone in Taganróg. In 1879 he finished his time at the gymnasium and went to Moscow to join his family. He was matriculated as a student of the Faculty of Medicine. After the normal course of five years, he took his degree in 1884. From his arrival in Moscow to his death he never parted from his parents and sister, and as his literary income soon became important, he early became the mainstay of his family. The Chékhovs were an exceptionally united family—a case exceedingly rare among the intelligentsia, and owing, of course, to their peasant and merchant origins.

Chékhov began working in the comic papers the year he came to Moscow, and before he left the university he had become one of their most welcome contributors. So on taking his degree, he did not settle down to practice as a doctor, but fell back on his literary work for subsistence. In 1886 some of his comic stories were collected in book form. The book had an immediate success with the public and was soon followed by another volume of comic stories. The critics, especially the radical critics, took little notice of the book, but it attracted the attention of two influential men of letters—the veteran novelist Grigoróvich and Suvórin, editor of the pro-government *Nóvoye vrémya*, the largest daily paper of the day. The shrewd and clever Suvórin at once saw the great possibilities of Chékhov and invited him to contribute to his paper, where he even started a special weekly literary supplement for Chékhov. They became close friends, and in Chékhov's correspondence his letters to Suvórin form undoubtedly the most interesting part. Chékhov had now gained a firm footing in "big literature" and was free from the tyranny of the comic papers. This change in his social position was followed by a change in his work—he abandoned comic writing and developed the style that is most characteristically his. This change is apparent in the stories written by him in 1886–7. At the same time Chékhov wrote his first play, *Ivánov*, which was produced in Moscow in December 1887 and in Petersburg a year later. It is characteristic of this period of transition that Chékhov continued working at these pieces after their first publication; The *Steppe* and *Ivánov* that are now reproduced in his *Works* are very different from what first appeared in 1887. Henceforward Chékhov's life was rather uneventful, and what events there were, are closely connected with his writings. An isolated episode was his journey to Sakhalín, the Russian Botany Bay. He went there in 1890, traveling through Siberia (before the days of the Trans-Siberian) and returning by sea via Ceylon. He made a very thorough investigation of convict life and published the result of it in a separate book (*Sakhalín Island*, 1891). It is remarkable for its thoroughness, objectivity, and impartiality, and is an important historical document. It is supposed to have influ-

enced certain reforms in prison life introduced in 1892. This journey
was Chékhov's greatest practical contribution to the humani-
tarianism that was so near to his heart. In private life he was also
very kindhearted and generous. He gave away much of his money.
His native town of Taganróg was the recipient of a library and a
museum from him.

In 1891 Chékhov was rich enough to buy a piece of land at
Melíkhovo, some fifty miles south of Moscow. There he settled
down with his parents, sister, and younger brother, and lived for
six years. He took part in local life and spent much money on
local improvements. In 1892–3, during the cholera epidemic, he
worked as the head of a sanitary district. Here it was he wrote
many of his best and most mature stories. He remained at Melíkhovo till 1897, when the state of his health forced him to move.
Consumption had set in, and he had to spend the rest of his life
mainly between the south coast of the Crimea and foreign—
French and German—health resorts. This was not the only change
in his life. All his surroundings changed, owing to his new connection with the Moscow Art Theater and his more decided political
orientation towards the left. This latter led to his breach with
Suvórin, to whom he wrote a very angry letter in connection with
the Dreyfus affair (even in Russia the *Affaire* was a hotbed of
quarrel!) and to his friendship with the younger generation of
writers, headed by Górky and distinctly revolutionary. During
these last years (especially after 1900, when he settled down in
Yálta) he saw much of Tolstóy. In the popular opinion of that
time, Chékhov, Górky, and Tolstóy formed a sort of sacred trinity
symbolizing all that was best in independent Russia as opposed to
the dark forces of Tsarism. Chékhov lived up to his liberal reputation, and when the Academy, following a hint of the government,
excluded Górky from its membership almost immediately after
electing him, Chékhov, like the veteran socialist Korolénko, resigned his membership. But from the literary point of view this
phase is hardly of much importance—it introduced no new elements into his work. Far more important is his connection with
the Art Theater. After *Ivánov*, Chékhov had written several light
one-act comedies that had a considerable success with the public
but added little to his intrinsic achievement. In 1895 he turned
once more to serious drama and wrote *The Seagull* (as it is called
in the English translation, rather absurdly—the Russian *Cháyka*

means just *Gull*). It was produced at the State Theater of Petersburg in 1896. It was badly understood by the actors and badly
acted. The first night was a smashing failure. The play was hissed
down, and the author, confounded by his defeat, left the theater
after the second act and escaped to Melíkhovo, vowing never again
to write a play. Meanwhile K. S. Stanislávsky (Alekséyev), a
wealthy merchant of Moscow, and the dramatist Vladímir Nemiróvich-Dánchenko founded the Art Theater, which was to be
such an important landmark in the history of the Russian stage.
They succeeded in getting *The Seagull* for one of their first productions. The cast worked at it with energy and understanding,
and when the play was acted by them in 1898, it proved a triumphant success. Chékhov turned with new energy towards dramatic
writing, and wrote his most famous plays with a direct view to
Stanislávsky's casts. *Uncle Ványa* (which had been planned as
early as 1888) was produced in 1900, *The Three Sisters* in 1901, and
The Cherry Orchard in January 1904. Each play was a greater
triumph than the preceding one. There was complete harmony
among playwright, actors, and public. Chékhov's fame was at its
height. However, he did not become so rich as to compare with
Kipling, or D'Annunzio, or even with Górky. For like his favorite
heroes, he was eminently unpractical: in 1899 he sold all the works
he had hitherto written to the publisher Marx for 75,000 rubles
($37,500). It turned out after the transaction that Marx was not
aware of the extent of his writings—he had reckoned on four
volumes of short stories, and he had unconsciously bought nine!
In 1901 Chékhov married an actress of the Art Theater, Olga L.
Knípper; so his life became further changed. These last years he
lived mostly at Yálta, where he had built a villa. He was constantly besieged by importunate admirers, with whom he was very
patient and kind. In June 1904 his illness had so advanced that he
was sent by the doctors to Badenweiler, a small health resort in
the Black Forest, where he died. His body was brought to Moscow
and buried by the side of his father, who had preceded him in
1899.

Chékhov's literary career falls into two distinct periods: before and after 1886.[3] The English reader and the more "literary"
Russian public know him by his later work, but it may be safely

---

[3] A great inconvenience of the English edition of Chékhov is that it entirely disregards dates and arranges the tales in an arbitrary order.

asserted that a much greater number of Russians know him rather
as the author of his early comic stories than as the author of *My
Life* and *Three Sisters*. It is a characteristic fact that many of his
most popular and typical comic stories, precisely those which are
sure to be known to every middle-class or semi-educated Russian
(for example, *A Horse Name*, *Vint*, *The Complaint Ledger*, *Surgery*),
were not translated into English. It is true that some of these
stories are very difficult to translate, so topical and national are
the jokes. But it is also evident that the English-speaking admirer
of Chékhov has no taste for this buffoonery but looks to Chékhov
for commodities of a very different description. The level of the
comic papers in which Chékhov wrote was by no means a high
one. They were a sanctuary of every kind of vulgarity and bad
taste. Their buffoonery was vulgar and meaningless. They lacked
the noble gift of nonsense, which of all things elevates man nearest
the gods; they lacked wit, restraint, and grace. It was mere trivial
buffoonery, and Chékhov's stories stand in no striking contrast to
their general background. Except for a higher degree of craftsmanship, they are of a piece with the rest. Their dominant note is an
uninspired sneer at the weaknesses and follies of mankind, and it
would need a more than lynx-eyed critic to discern in them the
note of human sympathy and of the higher humor that is so familiar to the reader of Chékhov's mature work. The great majority
of these stories were never reprinted by Chékhov, but still the first
and second volumes of his collected edition contain several dozen
of the kind. Only a few—and all of them of a less crude variety—
have had the honor of an English translation. But even in the
crudest, Chékhov stands out as a superior craftsman, and in the
economy of his means there is a promise of *Sleepy* and *At Christmas-
time*. Before long, Chékhov began to deviate from the straight line
imposed on him by the comic papers, and as early as 1884 he could
write such a story as *The Chorus Girl*, which may yet be a little
primitive and clumsy in its lyrical construction but on the whole
stands almost on a level with the best of his mature work. *Parti-
colored Stories*, which appeared in 1886 and laid the foundation of
Chékhov's reputation in the literary circles, contained, besides
many exercises in crude buffoonery, stories of a different kind that
presented a gay appearance but were sad in substance—and that
answered admirably to the hackneyed phrase of Russian critics,
"tears through laughter." Such, for instance, is *Misery:* on a wet

winter night a cabman who has just lost his son tries to tell his
story to one after another of his fares and does not succeed in
kindling their sympathy.

In 1886, as has been said, Chékhov was able to free himself
from the comic papers and could now develop a new style that had
begun to assert itself somewhat earlier. This style was (and remained) essentially poetical, but it was some time before he
finally settled the main lines of what was to be the characteristic
Chekhovian story. In his stories of 1886–8 there are many elements
that have been yet imperfectly blended—a strain of descriptive
journalism (in its most unadulterated form in *Uprooted*); pure
anecdote, sometimes just ironical (*The First-Class Passenger*),
sometimes poignantly tragi-comical (*Vánka*); the lyrical expression
of atmosphere (*The Steppe, Happiness*); psychological studies of
morbid experience (*Typhus*); parables and moralities laid out in a
conventional, un-Russian surrounding (*The Bet, A Story without
a Title*). But already one of the favorite and most characteristic
themes asserts its domination—the mutual lack of understanding
between human beings, the impossibility for one person to feel in
tune with another. *The Privy Councilor, The Post, The Party, The
Princess*, are all based on this idea—which becomes something like
the leitmotiv of all Chékhov's later work. The most typical stories
of this period are all located in the country of his early life, the
steppe between the Sea of Azóv and the Donéts. These are *The
Steppe, Happiness, The Horse-Stealers*. They are planned as lyrical
symphonies (though the last one is also an anecdote). Their dominant note is superstition, the vague terror (Chékhov makes it
poetical) before the presences that haunt the dark and empty
steppe, the profound uninterestingness and poverty of the steppe
peasant's life, a vague hope of a happiness that may be discovered,
with the help of dark powers, in some ancient treasure mound. *The
Steppe*, at which Chékhov worked much and to which he returned
again after its publication, is the central thing in this period. It
lacks the wonderful architecture of his short stories—it is a lyrical
poem, but a poem made out of the substance of trivial, dull, and
dusky life. The long, monotonous, uneventful journey of a little
boy over the endless steppe from his native village to a distant
town is drawn out in a hundred pages to form a languid, melodious,
and tedious lullaby. A brighter aspect of Chékhov's lyrical art is
in *Easter Eve*. The monk on night duty on the ferryboat tells a

passenger about his dead fellow monk, who had the rare gift of writing lauds to the saints. He describes with loving detail the technique of this art, and one discerns Chékhov's sincere sympathy for this unnoticed, unwanted, quiet, and unambitious fellow crafts-man. To the same period belongs *Kashtánka*, the delightful history of a dog that was kidnaped by a circus clown to form part of a troupe of performing animals and escaped to her old master in the middle of a performance. The story is a wonderful blend of humor and poetry, and though it certainly sentimentalizes and humanizes its animals, one cannot help recognizing it as a masterpiece. An-other little gem is *Sleepy*, a real masterpiece of concentration, economy, and powerful effectiveness.[4]

In some stories of this period we find already the manner that is pre-eminently Chekhovian. The earliest story where it is quite distinctly discernible is *The Party* (1887), on which Chékhov him-self laid a great value, but which is not yet perfect; he confesses in a letter to Suvórin that he "would gladly have spent six months over *The Party*. . . . But what am I to do? I begin a story on September 10th with the thought that I must finish it by October 5th at the latest; if I don't, I shall fail the editor and be left with-out money. I let myself go at the beginning and write with an easy mind; but by the time I get to the middle, I begin to grow timid and fear that my story will be too long. . . . This is why the be-ginning of my stories is always very promising . . . the middle is huddled and timid, and the end is, as in a short sketch, like fire-works." [5] But the essential of Chékhov's mature style is unmis-takably present. It is the "biography" of a mood developing under the trivial pinpricks of life, but owing in substance to a deeply-lying, physiological or psychological cause (in this case the woman's pregnancy). *A Dreary Story*, published in 1889, may be considered the starting point of the mature period. The leitmotiv of mutual isolation is brought out with great power. We may date the mean-ing that has come to be associated in Russia with the words "Chekhovian state of mind" (*Chékhovskoye nastroyénie*) from *A Dreary Story*. The atmosphere of the story is produced by the pro-fessor's deep and growing disillusionment as to himself and the life

---

[4] Tolstóy is said to have held this story in high esteem, and one cannot help noticing a certain similarity it bears to his own masterpiece *Alësha Gorshók*, written eighteen years later.
[5] *Letters of Anton Tchehov*, translated by Constance Garnett, p. 101, Chatto & Windus, London.

around him, the gradual loss of faith in his vocation, the gradual
drifting apart of people linked together by life. The professor
realizes the meaninglessness of his life—and the "giftlessness"
(*bezdárnost*, a characteristically Chekhovian word) and dullness of
all that surrounds him. His only remaining friend, his former ward
Kátya, an unsuccessful disillusioned actress, breaks down under
an intenser experience of the same feelings. And though his affection for her is sincere and genuine, and though he is suffering from
the same causes as she is, he fails to find the necessary language to
approach her. An unconquerable inhibition keeps him closed to
her, and all he can say to her is:

"Let us have lunch, Kátya."

"No, thank you," she answers coldly.

Another minute passes in silence.

"I don't like Khárkov," I say; "it is so grey here—
such a grey town."

"Yes, perhaps. . . . It's ugly. . . . I am here not
for long, passing through. I am going on to-day."

"Where?"

"To the Crimea . . . that is, to the Caucasus."

"Oh! For long?"

"I don't know."

"Kátya gets up and, with a cold smile, holds out her
hand, looking at me. I want to ask her: 'Then you won't
be at my funeral?' but she does not look at me; her hand
is cold and, as it were, strange. I escort her to the door in
silence. She goes out, walks down the long corridor, without looking back. She knows that I am looking after her,
and she will look back at the turn. No, she did not look
round. I've seen her black dress for the last time; her steps
have died away! . . . Farewell, my treasure!" [6]

This ending on a minor note is repeated in all Chékhov's subsequent stories and gives the keynote to his work.

A Dreary Story opens the succession of Chékhov's mature
masterpieces. Besides the natural growth of his genius, he was
now free to work longer over them than he could when he was

[6] *The Wife and Other Stories*, translated by Constance Garnett, pp. 218–19. (N.Y.
1916–22)

writing *The Party*. So his stories written in the nineties are almost without exception perfect works of art. It is mainly on the work of this period that Chékhov's reputation now rests. The principal stories written after 1889 are, in chronological order, *The Duel*, *Ward No. 6* (1892), *An Anonymous Story* (1893), *The Black Monk*, *The Teacher of Literature* (1894), *Three Years*, *Ariadne*, *Anna on the Neck*, *An Artist's Story* (in Russian: *The House with the Maisonette*), *My Life* (1895), *Peasants* (1897), *The Darling*, *Iónych*, *The Lady with the Dog* (1898), *The New Villa* (1899), *At Christmas-time*, *In the Ravine* (1900). After this date (it was the period of *Three Sisters* and *The Cherry Orchard*) he wrote only two stories, *The Bishop* (1902) and *Betrothed* (1903).

Chékhov's art has been called psychological, but it is psychological in a very different sense from Tolstóy's, Dostoyévsky's, or Marcel Proust's. No writer excels him in conveying the mutual unsurpassable isolation of human beings and the impossibility of understanding each other. This idea forms the core of almost every one of his stories, but, in spite of this, Chékhov's characters are singularly lacking in individual personality. Personality is absent from his stories. His characters all speak (within class limits and apart from the little tricks of catchwords he lends them from time to time) the same language, which is Chékhov's own. They cannot be recognized, as Tolstóy's and Dostoyévsky's can, by the mere *sound of their voices*. They are all alike, all made of the same material—"the common stuff of humanity"—and in this sense Chékhov is the most "democratic," the most "unanimist," of all writers. For of course the similarity of all his men and women is not a sign of weakness—it is the expression of his fundamental intuition of life as a homogeneous matter but cut out into water-tight compartments by the phenomenon of individuality. Like Stendhal and the French classicists, and unlike Tolstóy, Dostoyévsky, and Proust, Chékhov is a student of "man in general." But unlike the classicists, and like Proust, he fixes his attention on the infinitesimals, the "pinpricks" and "straws" of the soul. Stendhal deals in psychological "whole numbers." He traces the major, conscious, creative lines of psychical life. Chékhov concentrates on the "differentials" of mind, its minor, unconscious, involuntary, destructive, and dissolvent forces. As art, Chékhov's method is active—more active than, for instance, Proust's, for it is based on a stricter and more conscious *choice* of material and a more complicated and elaborate disposition of it. But as "outlook," as "philosophy," it is profoundly passive and "non-resistant," for it is a surrender to the "micro-organisms," of the soul, to its destructive microbes. Hence the general impressions produced by the whole of Chékhov's work that he had a cult for inefficiency and weakness. For Chékhov has no other way of displaying his sympathy with his characters than to show in detail the process of their submission to their microbes. The strong man who does not succumb in this struggle, or who does not experience it, is always treated by Chékhov with less sympathy and comes out as the "villain of the play"—in so far as the word "villain" is at all applicable to the world Chékhov moves in. The strong man in this world of his is merely the insensate brute, with a skin thick enough not to feel the "pinpricks," which are the only important thing in life. Chékhov's art is constructive. But the construction he uses is not a narrative construction—it might rather be called musical; not, however, in the sense that his prose is melodious, for it is not. But his method of constructing a story is akin to the method used in music. His stories are at once fluid and precise. The lines along which he builds them are very complicated curves, but they have been calculated with the utmost precision. A story by him is a series of points marking out with precision the lines discerned by him in the tangled web of consciousness. Chékhov excels in the art of tracing the first stages of an emotional process; in indicating those first symptoms of a deviation when to the general eye, and to the conscious eye of the subject in question, the nascent curve still seems to coincide with a straight line. An infinitesimal touch, which at first hardly arrests the reader's attention, gives a hint at the direction the story is going to take. It is then repeated as a leit-motiv, and at each repetition the true equation of the curve becomes more apparent, and it ends by shooting away in a direction very different from that of the original straight line. Such stories as *The Teacher of Literature, Iónych,* and *The Lady with the Dog* are perfect examples of such emotional curves. The straight line, for instance, in *Iónych* is the doctor's love for Mlle Túrkin; the curve, his subsidence into the egoistical complacency of a successful provincial career. In *The Teacher of Literature* the straight line is again the hero's love; the curve, his dormant dissatisfaction with selfish happiness and his intellectual ambition. In *The Lady with the Dog* the straight line is the hero's attitude towards his affair with the lady as a trivial and passing intrigue; the curve, his overwhelming and all-pervading love for her. In most of Chékhov's stories these constructive lines are complicated by a rich and mellow atmosphere, which he produces by the abundance of emotionally significant detail. The effect is poetical, even lyrical: as in a lyric, it is not interest in the development that the reader feels, but "infection" by the poet's mood. Chékhov's stories are lyrical monoliths; they cannot be dissected into episodes, for every episode is strictly conditioned by the whole and is without significance apart from it. In architectural unity Chékhov surpasses all Russian writers of the realistic age. Only in Púshkin and Lérmontov do we find an equal or superior gift of design. Chékhov thought Lérmontov's *Tamán* was the best short story ever written, and this partiality was well founded. *Tamán* forestalled Chékhov's method of lyrical construction. Only its air is colder and clearer than the mild and mellow "autumnal" atmosphere of Chékhov's world.

Two of his best stories, *My Life* and *In the Ravine*, stand somewhat apart from the rest of his mature work. *My Life* is the story of a Tolstoyan, and one cannot help thinking that in it Chékhov tried to approach the clearer and more intellectual style of Tolstóy. There are a directness of narrative and a thinness of atmosphere that are otherwise rare in Chékhov. In spite of this relative absence of atmosphere, it is perhaps his most poetically pregnant story. It is convincingly symbolical. The hero, his father, his sister, the Azhógins, and Anyúta Blagóvo stand out with the distinctness of morality characters. The very vagueness and generality of its title helps to make it something like an *Everyman*. For poetical grasp and significance *My Life* may be recognized as the masterpiece of Chékhov—unless it is surpassed by *In the Ravine*. This, one of his last stories, is an amazing piece of work. The scene is the Moscow industrial area—it is the history of a shopkeeper's family. It is remarkably free from all excess of detail, and the atmosphere is produced, with the help of only a few descriptive touches, by the movement of the story. It is infinitely rich in emotional and symbolical significance. What is rare in Chékhov—in both these stories there is an earnestness, a keenness of moral judgment that raises them above the average of his work. All Chékhov's work is symbolical, but in most of his stories the symbolism is less concrete and more vaguely suggestive. It is akin to Maeterlinck's, in spite of the vast difference of style between the Russian realist and the Belgian mystic. *Ward No. 6*, the darkest and most terrible of all Chékhov's stories, is an especially notable example of this suggestive symbolism. It is all the more suggestive for being strictly realistic. (The only time Chékhov attempted to step out of the limits of strict realism was when he wrote the only story that is quite certainly a failure—*The Black Monk*.) But this symbolism reached its full development in his plays, beginning with *The Seagull*.

Chékhov's first attempt to use the dramatic form was *On the High Road* (1885). This is an adaptation of an earlier story of his. It did not see the stage; it was suppressed by the dramatic censorship as too "gloomy and filthy." It was published only after his death. In 1886 Chékhov wrote his first full-size play, *Ivánov*. Like *The Party* and other stories of the period, *Ivánov* is a transitional work and betrays a somewhat wavering hand that has not yet acquired a complete command of its material. *Ivánov* was successful on the stage, and, stimulated by success, Chékhov almost immediately began writing a new play, *The Forest Spirit*. But the cold reception given it by the few friends he showed it to made him put it aside and abandon serious dramatic work. Instead he wrote a series of one-act comedies (*The Bear, The Wedding,* and others) in a style closely connected with his early comic stories. These comedies were well received by the admirers of Chékhov's comic writings and became widely popular. They are still a favorite item in every provincial repertoire, and are especially often staged in private theatricals. In 1896 Chékhov returned to serious drama —and produced *The Seagull*. I have already told the story of its original failure and subsequent success. After that, Chékhov returned to *The Forest Spirit*, which became *Uncle Ványa*, to be followed by *Three Sisters* and *The Cherry Orchard*. These four famous plays form Chékhov's theater. They have received, especially the two last ones, even extravagant praise from English critics, who seem to lose the famous English virtue of "understatement" the moment they have to do with Chékhov. *The Cherry Orchard* has been described as the best play since Shakspere, and *Three Sisters* as the best play in the world. Tolstóy thought differently, and though he had an intense dislike for Shakspere, he preferred his plays to Chékhov's. Tolstóy, who considered subject matter the chief thing in plays and novels, could not have thought otherwise: there is no subject matter in Chékhov's plays, no plot, no action. They consist of nothing but "superficial detail." They are, in fact, the most undramatic plays in the world (if, however, they are not surpassed in this respect by the plays of Chékhov's bad—they were all bad—imitators). This undramatic character is a natural outcome of the Russian realistic drama. The plays of Ostróvsky, and especially of Turgénev, contain the germs of much that reached its full development in Chékhov. The Russian realistic drama is essentially static. But Chékhov carried to the extreme limit this static tendency and gave his name to a new type in drama—the undramatic drama. On the whole, his plays are constructed in the same way as his stories. The differences are owing to the differences of material and are imposed by the use of dialogue. As a general rule, it may be said that the principal difference is that the plays have less backbone, less skeleton, than the stories, and are more purely atmospheric creations. In his stories there is always one central figure that is the main element of unity—the story is conducted from the standpoint of this central figure. But the use of dialogue excludes this monocentric construction and makes all the characters equal. Chékhov amply avails himself of this fact and distributes the spectator's attention among all his people with wonderful fairness. His *dramatis personæ* live in a state of ideal democracy—where equality is no sham. This method was admirably adapted to the principles of the Moscow Art Theater, which aimed at creating a cast in which there would be no stars but all actors of equal excellence. The dialogue form is also admirably suited to the expression of one of Chékhov's favorite ideas: the mutual unintelligibility and strangeness of human beings, who cannot and do not want to understand each other. Each character speaks only of what interests him or her, and pays no attention to what the other people in the room are saying. Thus the dialogue becomes a patchwork of disconnected remarks, dominated by a poetic "atmosphere" but by no logical unity. Of course this system is entirely an artistic convention. No one in real life ever spoke as Chékhov's people do. Again it reminds one of Maeterlinck, whose plays (as Chesterton has remarked) have a meaning only if one is quite in tune with the poet's very exclusive mood; otherwise they are mere nonsense. Chékhov's plays are "infectious," as Tolstóy wanted all art to be—in fact nothing if not infectious. But, though the moods are perhaps less exclusive and more universal than Maeterlinck's, unless one has a sympathy with his moods, the dialogue is meaningless. Like his stories, Chékhov's plays are always saturated with emotional symbolism, and in his research for suggestive poetry he sometimes oversteps the limits of good taste—such lapses are, for instance, the bursting of a string in *The Cherry Orchard*, and the last scene in the same play, when Firs, the old servant, is left alone in the deserted house, where he has been locked in and forgotten. Even more consistently than in his stories, the dominant note of Chékhov's plays is one of gloom, depression, and hopelessness. The end of every one of them is managed in the same way as the end of *A Dreary Story*. They are all in the minor key and leave the spectator in a state of impotent—perhaps deliciously impotent—depression. Judged by their own standards (which can hardly be accepted as the normal standards of dramatic art), Chékhov's plays are perfect works of art, but are they really as perfect as his best stories? At any rate, his method is dangerous and has been imitated only at the imitator's imminent peril. No play written by an imitator of Chékhov is above contempt.

Chékhov's English admirers think that everything is perfect in Chékhov. To find spots in him will seem blasphemy to them. Still it is only fair to point out these spots. I have already referred to the complete lack of individuality in his characters and in their way of speaking. This is not in itself a fault, for it belongs to his fundamental intuition of life, which recognizes no personality. But it is not a virtue. It is especially noticeable when he makes his characters speak at length on abstract subjects. How different from Dostoyévsky, who "felt ideas" and who made them so splendidly individual! Chékhov did not "feel ideas," and when his characters give expression to theirs, they speak a colorless and monotonous journalese. *The Duel* is especially disfigured by such harangues. This is perhaps Chékhov's tribute to a deep-rooted tradition of Russian intelligentsia literature. Their speeches may have had some emotional significance in their time but certainly have none today. Another serious shortcoming is Chékhov's Russian. It is colorless and lacks individuality. He had no feeling for words. No Russian writer of anything like his significance used a language so devoid of all raciness and nerve. This makes Chékhov (except for topical allusions, technical terms, and occasional catchwords) so easy to translate. Of all Russian writers, he has the least to fear from the treachery of translators.

Chékhov's direct influence on Russian literature was not important. The success of his short stories contributed to the great popularity of that form, which became the predominant form in Russian fiction. But Górky, Kúprin, and Búnin, to name but the foremost of those who regarded him as their master, can hardly be recognized as his pupils. Certainly no one learned from him the art of constructing his stories. His dramas, which looked so easy to imitate, were imitated, but the style proved a pitfall. Today Russian fiction is quite free from any trace of Chékhov's influence. Some of the younger writers began, before the Revolution, as his more or less unintelligent imitators, but none of them remained true to him. In Russia, Chékhov has become a thing of the past— of a past remoter than even Turgénev, not to speak of Gógol or Leskóv. Abroad, things stand differently. If Chékhov has had a genuine heir to the secrets of his art, it is in England, where Katherine Mansfield did what no Russian has done—learned from Chékhov without imitating him. In England, and to a lesser degree in France, the cult of Chékhov has become the hallmark of the highbrow intellectual. Curiously enough, in Russia, Chékhov was always regarded as a distinctly "lowbrow" writer; the self-conscious intellectual elite was always conspicuously cool to him. The highbrows of the beginning of the century even affected to (or sincerely did) despise him. His real stronghold was in the heart of the honest Philistine in the street. Nowadays Chékhov has of course become the common property of the nation. His place as a classic—a major classic, one of the "ten best"—is not challenged. But he is a classic who has been temporarily shelved.

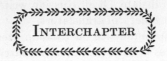

The First Revolution

THE history of Russia since the beginning of the nineteenth century may be represented as a succession of revolutionary waves and interrevolutionary troughs. Each of these waves rose higher than the one that preceded it. The first wave broke in 1825, in the entirely unsupported and unsuccessful mutiny of the Decembrists. It was followed by the long reaction of the reign of Nicholas I, during which the second wave rose. Gradually and slowly developing, it was at once held back and powerfully seconded by the liberal reforms of the sixties, reached its climax in the activity of the People's Will Party, and broke in 1881 in the assassination of Alexander II. The succeeding calm was neither so long nor so complete as that which preceded it. The Revolution regained strength by the nineties (largely owing to the effect of the hunger year 1891–2), rose to an unprecedented height, and broke with a terrible crash in 1905. The movement was again suppressed, only to reappear during the first World War and finally to triumph in 1917. The third of these waves was the first to be supported by a widespread *popular* movement, and its crest is known by the name of the First Revolution.

This Revolution of 1905, in so far as it was a conscious effort to attain definite ends, was entirely the result of the development of the revolutionary ideas of the intelligentsia, supported at a critical moment by a refusal of the propertied classes to defend autocracy. But it would have remained ineffective had it not found an army in the recently developed class of industrial workmen. This class, in its turn, was the direct outcome of the rise of capitalism in the second half of the nineteenth century. Russian

capitalism was born in the age of reform under Alexander II, but
it grew by leaps and bounds in the eighties and nineties, largely
owing to the protectionist policy of the government, embodied in
the person of Count Witte. The rise and growth of Russian capitalism out of the conservative forms of pre-Reform trade and
commerce is a matter of absorbing, but here irrelevant, interest. It
is not lacking in traits of considerable picturesque and literary
value, and has more than once been treated in literature—perhaps
by no one with more effect than by Górky (who, for all his Marxian
allegiance, had a distinct sympathy with the creative impulse of
capitalism) in *Fomá Gordéyev*, and in a chapter of *Fragments from
a Diary* dealing with the millionaire Old Believer Bugróv, of
Nízhny Nóvgorod. The merchant princes of Moscow played an important part in the nineties and after as patrons of art and literature—the æsthetic revival was largely financed by them.

One of the earliest effects of capitalism in literature was the
rise of the big daily press. The first journalist of this period was
Alekséy Sergéyevich Suvórin (1833–1911), the founder of the
Nóvoye vrémya—for many years the best-equipped of Russian
papers and the only one that had a certain influence on the government. Suvórin's *Diary* (published by the Soviet Government) is a
document of first-class importance, but on the whole he is interesting chiefly as a figure in life, and his place as a writer is insignificant. Only his connection with Chékhov and with Rózanov
gives him an honorable place in Russian literature. The greatest
literary exponent of Russian capitalism and industrialism was no
lesser man than the great chemist Dmítry Ivánovich Mendeléyev.
It may be said that he was passionately in love with the productive
forces of his country and was their champion and troubadour.
Though there can be no question of comparing his literary to his
scientific importance, he was a writer of powerful temperament
and genuine originality. His daughter was married to Alexander
Blok, and though the poet was inspired by very different ideas,
once at least he struck a note that would have pleased his father-
in-law in his grave—in his poem *The New America*, in which he
sings the praise of the Donéts coal, "the black coal, our subter-
ranean Messiah." Count Witte, the good genius of Russian industrialism, wrote three very remarkable volumes of memoirs.
Though clumsily composed and almost illiterate, they also reveal
a very personal temperament, which makes them an interesting

book quite apart from their documentary value. Unfortunately, in the English translation they have been outrageously "amended" and "adapted"—all the most racy and unconventional passages having been mercilessly cut out.

The reverse of the capitalistic medal was the rise of Russian Marxism, which became a strong movement about 1894. It is not necessary to impress the reader with the importance of this movement in Russian history—it is sufficient to say that Lénin was one of the original Marxists of the nineties. But apart from its role in 1905 and 1917 and since that date, it was an important stage in the intellectual history of the intelligentsia. In the nineties Marxism was a progressive and a liberating force because it brought with it an emancipation from the routine of populism. It appealed to the Russian intellectual, *rerum novarum cupidum*, as a fundamentally scientific doctrine. What impressed him most in it was its "dialectical method" and the conception of history as a process that obeyed fixed and immutable laws. It divorced politics from ethics, and if this had its bad side in the development of an exclusive class morality (the results of which are apparent in the U.S.S.R.), it had, at first, also a good effect, for it freed the student of political science from the blinkers of a too-narrow idealism. The chief exponent of Russian Marxism, its prophet and doctor, was a man of an older generation, Geórgy Valentínovich Plekhánov (1857–1918), during the first World War the leader of the patriotic socialists. He is universally accepted as one of the biggest brains of the Russian intelligentsia. Lénin himself began his journalistic career in the mid nineties. But from the literary point of view the most interesting Marxist writers were a group of young men known by the name of "legal Marxists" (for they worked in the "legal," that is, the home press). Their brilliant spokesman was Peter Strúve, whose influence as a Marxist in the nineties was second only to that of Plekhánov. But early in the twentieth century he abandoned socialism, and his writings after 1905 will have to be mentioned in a very different connection, for he became the leader of the national liberalism that opposed the old agnostic idealism of the radical intelligentsia. This shows how important Marxism was as an emancipation from the conventions of populist idealism, and what a powerful leaven of independent thought it could be.

By the end of the nineties the Marxists succeeded in laying

the foundations of a successful propaganda among the working
classes, and organized themselves into the Social Democratic
Party of Russia. The populists imitated them, and became the
Party of Socialist Revolutionaries. These two parties became
known respectively as the S.D.'s and the S.R.'s and played a
principal part in the events of 1905–6. The S.D.'s, as Marxists, did
not believe in the efficacy of individual action and consequently
condemned terrorism. They laid their hopes on mass action, especially on strikes. In 1903 they became divided (on points the
details of which would be irrelevant) into two factions, the Men-
shevíks (minority men) and the Bolshevíks (majority men, *not*
maximalists, the names referring merely to the number of votes
given respectively to the two shades of opinion at a particular
party congress). But the Bolshevíks did not become widely influential or strongly individualized till much later, during the first
World War, and the S.D.'s remained in substance one party. The
S.R.'s, who, following the older populists, believed in the importance of the "critically thinking individual," organized from 1900
to 1906 a series of political assassinations. They were the romantic
party that attracted all the hot-headed and adventurous youth.

A few years before 1905, Russian liberalism, which had always
had a rather valetudinarian existence, rallied its forces and for a
few years rivaled socialism in active opposition to the government.
A revolutionary organization of liberals was formed—the Union
for Liberation (*Soyúz osvobozhdéniya*)—and Peter Strúve, a valuable and recent recruit to liberalism from Marxism, left Russia and
founded in Stuttgart an uncensored liberal paper, *Liberation*,
which for a moment almost rivaled the popularity of Herzen's
Bell of forty-five years earlier. The unsuccessful war with Japan
(1904–5) very powerfully seconded the growth of opposition, and
a pact for co-operation against the government was formed among
the three parties—S.D., S.R., and Union for Liberation. During
the first period of Revolution the three parties went hand in hand,
and the great strike of October 1905, which was the immediate
cause of the granting of the Charter of October 17, was materially
helped by the Union of Unions, an organization of the professional
classes headed by the liberal leader Paul Milyukóv. But after
October 17 the ways of liberalism and socialism began to diverge.
The liberals took no part in the armed uprising of December 1905,
and the socialists boycotted the Dúma elections in the spring of

1906. The liberals formed a party that took the name of Constitutional Democrats and became known by its Russian initials, K.D., or Cadets. The most influential figure of Russian liberalism from the nineties to 1917 was Professor Paul Milyukóv, a positivist and a confirmed Westernizer. He began by making a name as a historian (*Sketches from the History of Russian Civilization* has become a standard work), and after 1905 directed all the activities, parliamentary and journalistic, of the Cadet Party. He had a decided genius for organization, but also a certain unconquerable stolidity that won him the name of "a genius of tactlessness." Milyukóv is typical of the traditional positivism and agnosticism of the older Russian liberals; but already before 1905 a new movement began, which proceeded from Soloviëv and tended to identify liberalism with Christian idealism, and, by a strange, if natural, association, with patriotism and imperialism. This movement found its most gifted expression in the work of Peter Strúve. the ex-Marxist, and of his associates, the authors of *Landmarks*, of whom I shall have more to say in discussing the movements of the nineties.

The First Revolution was a deep-reaching and infectious movement. For a moment it dominated the whole of Russian intellectual life, and even the symbolists, who had made a point of being non-political, became revolutionaries and "mystical anarchists." But this momentary excitement was followed by a depression of political, especially of radical, feeling. The years following the suppression of the Revolution were a period of anti-political individualism, which found its expression in the growth of æstheticism and sexual freedom on the one hand, and of the productive forces of capitalism on the other. There was a profound disillusionment in radicalism and in all the traditional ideas of the intelligentsia. This feeling was strongly supported by the revelations of Búrtsev, who denounced Ázev (a prominent and influential member of the S.R. party who had organized several political assassinations) as an agent of the Secret Police—a revelation that was followed by a thorough-going disintegration of the revolutionary parties. By 1914 they had lost most of their prestige and influence, and the intelligentsia was well on its way towards patriotism and imperialism.

An important result of the Revolution was the relative (in 1905–6, much more than relative) freedom of the press. The censorship disappeared, and though the government always found means of coercing the opposition papers, it became possible to treat practically all political issues in the press. This naturally raised the importance of the daily papers and relatively diminished that of the monthly papers, the bulwark of intelligentsia idealism. Politics and literature became more easily divorced. Politics became more practical, and literature was largely emancipated from the obligation of serving party ends.

The most important result of the Revolution was the establishment of a parliament, with limited functions—the Dúma. But the Dúma has little to do with literature. Unlike the opening of the new law courts forty years earlier, it did not become the starting point for a revival of public eloquence. There is little to be said of the Dúma orators from the literary point of view. The Cadets were the best. But their most famous orator, V. A. Maklakóv, was a lawyer with a settled reputation before he was returned to the Dúma. And according to many who attended the Dúma sittings, the best orator there was not a member, but the Prime Minister, P. A. Stolýpin.

CHAPTER 3

Prose Fiction after Chékhov

BEFORE Chékhov died, it seemed as if his example had brought into life a new golden age of realism, of which he was to be but the precursor. Between 1895 and 1905 there appeared one after the other a succession of young writers (born between 1868 and 1878) who attracted all the literary limelight, won world-wide reputations, and sold better than Turgénev or Dostoyévsky had ever sold. The most prominent were Górky and Andréyev—and the whole movement may be called the Górky-Andréyev school. It may be called a school without unduly straining the facts, for all the writers who constituted it have sufficient features in common to mark them off from the older pre-Chékhov school of fiction, whose last considerable representative was Korolénko, as well as from the symbolists and the modern movement in prose that was more or less affected by symbolist influences.

Górky is the earliest in date and the most significant writer of the school we are speaking of, and to a certain extent his influence is traceable in most of its other members. This influence is largely owing to the fact that he was the first to free Russian realism from its former "genteel" and "puritan" characteristics. Russian realism had always been morally delicate and avoided the crudity and outspokenness of French novelists. Ugliness and filth and the physical side of sexual relations were, on the whole, taboo to the old Russian novelist. The convention was broken by Tolstóy, who was the first to speak of the physical horrors of disease and death in *The Death of Iván Ilyích*, and of the physical foundation of love in *The Kreutzer Sonata*. He thus contributed very substantially to the destruction of nineteenth-century taboos and conventions, and his influence on Russian fiction was not entirely different from the parallel influence of Zola, whom he hated. This is one of the "little ironies" of history: the "classical" and "religious" art of Tolstóy's last years was a step in the direction of *Sánin*. The taboo-lifting work begun by Tolstóy was continued by Górky, Andréyev, and Artsybáshev. Beside this, Tolstóy's influence was also considerable as the founder of a new genre—the metaphysical and moral problem story that flourished especially in the hands of Andréyev and Artsybáshev. The influence of Chékhov was of a different kind—more technical and formal. It was partly owing to him that the short story became a favorite form with the young writers. They also tried to imitate his artistic economy—his avoidance of empty places in a story, and his care to charge every portion of it with equal significance and expressiveness. In this respect he remained an unattainable ideal, and though his turns of phrase and idiosyncrasies of expression abound in the work of the young novelists, the secret of Chékhov's narrative art was never discovered by them.

Between 1900 and 1910 Russian literature was divided into two distinct and mutually watertight parts—the Górky-Andréyev school on the one side, and the symbolists with their following on the other. At first the Górky-Andréyev group obscured the symbolists almost completely; but with time the situation was reversed, and today the first decade of this century appears to us as the age of symbolism. It is possible that some future age will again reverse the judgment and find more attractions in Kúprin and Sergéyev-Tsénsky than in Balmónt and Bryúsov. But the main issue between the two schools has nothing to do with the talents of the two parties—it is a matter of cultural level: the Górky-Andréyev school are the successors of the old intelligentsia who had lost much of the ethical education of the old radicals and acquired nothing in return beyond a "craving void" of pessimism and unbelief. The symbolists were the pioneers of a new culture that, though one-sided and imperfect, infinitely widened and enriched the Russian mind and made the intelligentsia at once more European and more national.

By 1910 the work of the Górky-Andréyev school was done. After that time it ceased to be a living movement and a literary influence. This, however, does not mean that individual members have not since produced works of permanent value, but they are works of isolated and disinterested maturity.

MAXÍM GÓRKY

Maxím Górky (pseudonym of A. M. Péshkov, 1868–1936) had a truly wonderful career. Risen from the lowest depths of the provincial proletariat, he was not yet thirty when he became the most popular writer and the most discussed man in Russia. After a period of dazzling celebrity, during which he was currently placed by the side of Tolstóy and unquestionably above Chékhov, his fame suffered an eclipse, and he was almost forgotten by the Russian educated classes. But his fame survived abroad and among the lower classes at home, and after 1917 his universal reputation and his connection with the new rulers of Russia made him the obvious champion of Russian literature.

Maxím Górky's father was an upholsterer, who by dint of hard work rose to be a shipping agent at Ástrakhan. He was married to the daughter of Vasíly Kashírin, a dyer of Nízhny-Nóvgorod (now Górky), where the writer was born. He was taken to Ástrakhan, but there, when he was five, his father died, and his mother brought him back to Nízhny to the house of his grandparents. Górky has told us the story of his *Childhood* and drawn unforgettable portraits of his close and harsh grandfather and of his charming, beauty-loving, and kind grandmother. The Kashírins were on the decline when the Péshkovs came to live with them, and as the boy grew up, the atmosphere of increasing poverty and squalid selfishness grew denser round him. His mother married again—a "semi-*intelligént*" for whom Górky has little good to say. She died before long. His grandfather sent him out into the world to earn his bread, and for more than ten years he made the acquaintance of every conceivable kind of drudgery. He began as a boy at a bootmaker's shop. Then he was, at one time, pantry boy on a Volga steamer, on which the cook, a drunken old ex-corporal of the Guards, taught him to read and write and laid the foundations of his literary education. One of the first books he read was *The Mysteries of Udolpho*, and for a long time his reading was very largely of the blood-and-thunder popular romance type—a fact that did not remain without its influence on his early work. At fifteen Górky tried to get into a school at Kazán, "but as," he says, "it was not the fashion to give education for nothing," he did not succeed in the attempt, and instead, to save himself from starving, he had to work in an underground bakery, so memorably described in *Twenty-six Men and a Girl*. In Kazán he came into contact with students who sowed in him the seeds of his future revolutionism, and he also became familiar with the life of those "ex-people" who were to become his steppingstone to celebrity. Leaving Kazán, he moved from place to place over the whole of southeastern and southern Russia, taking up odd jobs, working hard, and often remaining without work. In 1889 he came to Nízhny and became clerk to the advocate A. I. Lánin, who did much for his education and whom he always remembered as his greatest benefactor. In the same year he presented himself for conscription but was released on grounds of illness. He soon left his work and again went wandering over Russia. During these wanderings he began to write. In 1892, when he was working at the railway depot in Tiflís, his first story, the intensely romantic *Makár Chúdra*, was printed in a local daily paper over the signature that has since become so famous.[1] In the following years he continued writing for the provincial press and was soon able to rely on his literary work for a livelihood. But it was not till 1895 that he definitely entered into the "big literature," when Korolénko had one of his stories (*Chelkásh*) printed in the influential monthly *Rússkoye bogátstvo* (*Russian Riches*). Though he continued working for the provincial press, he was now a welcome guest in the Petersburg magazines. In 1898 his stories came out in book form (two volumes).

Their success was tremendous and, for a Russian author, unprecedented in the strict sense of the word. From a promising provincial journalist, Górky became the most famous writer of his country. From this date to the First Revolution, Górky was, next to Tolstóy, the figure in Russia that aroused the greatest public interest. Interviews and portraits of him flooded the press, and everyone thought it his duty to have a look at his person. International fame was not slow to follow. Germany especially went mad over him—in 1903–4 his famous play *The Lower Depths* had an uninterrupted run of over five hundred nights in Berlin.

[1] "*Górky*" means bitter or miserable.

In Petersburg, Górky came in contact with the Marxists and became himself a Marxist and a Social Democrat. His works became the *pièce de résistance* of the Marxist review *Zhizn*, to which he gave *Fomá Gordéyev* and *Three of Them* (1899–1901). It was also for a poem by Górky that the review was suppressed. This poem was the *Song of the Petrel:* the Russian name for "petrel" means storm messenger, and the *Song* was a very transparent allegory of the coming Revolutionary storm. Górky was now one of the foremost figures in the Russian radical world. He was also one of the financial powers behind the movement: his very considerable literary income was systematically drawn on by his political friends for the promotion of revolution. This state of things continued till 1917, so that Górky, in spite of the enormous financial success of his books, never enjoyed the wealth of his successful Western confreres. It was easy to become a martyr in Russia about 1900, and Górky was very soon arrested and banished to Nízhny. In 1902 he was elected an honorary member of the Imperial Academy of Science. This was an unprecedented act in regard to a writer of thirty-three. But before Górky could avail himself of his new rights, his election was annulled by the government, the new Academician being under "the supervision of the police." Following this incident, Chékhov and Korolénko renounced their membership in the Academy. Górky played a prominent part in the First Revolution. In January 1905 he was arrested for taking part in a protest against the "9th of January," and this arrest became the cause for world-wide demonstrations in his favor. After his release he edited a daily newspaper that supported the Bolshevíks and in which he published a series of articles denouncing all the Russian writers of the nineteenth century, including Dostoyévsky and Tolstóy, as "petty bourgeois" (*mescháne*). He took a prominent part in the campaign against the Russian foreign loans, and in December he gave active help to the armed rebellion in Moscow.

In 1906 he left Russia for the United States. His journey through Finland and Scandinavia was a triumphal procession. His arrival in New York was equally triumphant. But before long it transpired that the woman Górky was living with and whom he called his wife had not been wedded to him, and American opinion turned with sudden fury against the writer. He was asked to leave his hotel, and Mark Twain refused to take the chair at a banquet in his honor. It was rather natural that Górky should be deeply hurt

by this sudden outburst of puritanism, so entirely unintelligible
to a Russian, and he gave vent to his resentment in a series of
American stories, which appeared under the suggestive title of
The City of the Yellow Devil (1906). On his return to Europe he
settled in Capri, where he remained till shortly before the first
World War, and where he became immensely popular with the
natives. His Italian popularity was increased by the active part
he took in the relief work after the terrible Messina catastrophe.
In Russia, meanwhile, his popularity among the higher intellectual
classes began to sink. All his works after *The Lower Depths* (1902)
were received with comparative indifference, and from being the
great national favorite he was in 1900, he sank to the position of
the party pet of the Bolshevíks, who were almost alone in praising
his new works. But, on the other hand, his works began to penetrate into the masses of the working class and contributed largely
to forming that mentality of the Russian workman which manifested itself after 1917. On his return to Russia, Górky founded a
monthly review (*Létopis*), which did not increase his prestige.
Even *Childhood* and its sequel, which appeared in 1913 and 1915,
caused little change in the public's attitude, and have come into
their own only in the light of Górky's post-Revolutionary work.

When the first World War broke out, Górky took up a distinctly internationalist and *défaitiste* position, and in 1917 he gave
his support to his old friends the Bolshevíks. But this support was
not quite unconditional, and though the balance of Górky's influence was in favor of Lénin and his policy, he did not this time
identify himself with the party, but rather tried to assume the
role of a non-party umpire and a champion of peace and culture.
This attitude of fastidious superiority and sympathetic, but critical, aloofness lasted for a long time. The Bolshevíks were not over-
enthusiastic about it, but Górky's personal relations with their
leaders on the one hand, and the great weight of his reputation
abroad on the other, gave him a unique position: he was in 1918–21
practically the only independent public force outside the government in the whole of Soviet Russia. Górky's attitude of fastidious
superiority and "hand washing" may not arouse much sympathy,
but his activity in those dreadful years was extraordinarily useful
and salutary. He played the part to which he pretended, of de-
fender of culture and civilization, as well as he could have done.
The debt of Russian culture to him is very great. Everything that

was done between 1918 and 1921 to save the writers and other higher intellectuals from starvation was due to Górky. This was chiefly arrived at by a whole system of centralized literary establishments where poets and novelists were set to work at translations. The contrivance was by no means a perfect one, but under the circumstances it was probably the only one possible. It is also true, however, that these "circumstances" had been brought about with the active help of Górky and by his nearest political friends. Though in 1919 Górky published his *Recollections of Tolstóy,* which once more made everyone realize that he was, after all, a great writer, his literary influence remained insignificant. In 1921 Górky left Russia and settled in Germany. In 1924 he moved to Sorrento, in Italy, returning to the Soviet Union in 1928 for the celebration of his sixtieth birthday. The following year he returned for good as the unquestioned dean of Soviet letters, laboring indefatigably for the improvement of literary standards and the encouragement and training of younger writers. He also became an ardent apologist for the Stalinist regime, and his death in 1936 was, according to the allegations of Prosecutor Vyshínsky two years later, the result of a Trotskyite plot.

In all Górky's early work his realism is strongly modified by romanticism, and it was this romanticism which made for his success in Russia, although it was his realism that carried it over the frontier. To the Russian reader, the novelty of his early stories consisted in their bracing and daredevil youthfulness; to the foreign public, it was the ruthless crudeness with which he described his nether world. Hence the enormous difference between Russian and foreign appreciations of the early Górky—it comes from a difference of background. Russians saw him against the gloom and depression of Chékhov and the other novelists of the eighties; foreigners, against a screen of conventional and reticent realism of Victorian times. His very first stories are purely romantic. Such are his first published story, *Makár Chúdra, The Old Woman Izergíl* (1895), and his early poetry. This romanticism is very theatrical and tawdry, but it was genuinely infectious and did more to endear Górky to the Chékhov-fed Russian reader than all the rest of his work. It crystallized in a philosophy that is expressed most crudely and simply in the very early parable of *The Siskin Who Lied and the Truth-loving Woodpecker,* and that may be formulated as a preference for a lie that elevates the soul to a depressing and ignoble truth.

By 1895 Górky abandons the conventional stock in trade of his early gypsy-and-robber stories and develops a manner that combines realistic form and romantic inspiration. His first story to appear in the "big" press, *Chelkásh* (1895), is also one of the best. His subject is the contrast between the gay, cynical, and careless smuggler Chelkásh and the lad he employs to help him in his dangerous business, a typical peasant, timid and greedy. The story is well constructed, and though the romantic glamour round Chelkásh is anything but "realistic," his figure is drawn with convincing vividness. Other stories of the same kind are *Malvá* (1897), who is a female Chelkásh, and *My Fellow-Traveler* (1894), which, from the point of view of character drawing, is perhaps the best of the lot. One of the features of the early Górky that won him most admirers was his way of "describing nature," but it must be confessed that the brightness of his descriptions has greatly faded and fails today to take us by storm. About 1897 realism begins to outweigh romanticism, and in *Ex-People* (*Bývshie Lyúdi*, 1897; in the English version, *Creatures That Once Were Men*, an arbitrary mistranslation) realism is dominant, and the heroic gestures of Captain Kuválda fail to relieve the drab gloom of the setting. In this story and in all other stories of these years a feature appears that was to be the undoing of Górky: an immoderate love for "philosophical" conversations. As long as he kept free from it, he gave proof of a great power of construction, a power that is rare in Russian writers and that gives some of his early stories a solidness and cohesion almost comparable to Chékhov's. But he did not have Chékhov's sense of artistic economy, and though in such stories as *Her Lover* (*Bóles*, 1897) and *To Kill Time* the skeleton is firm and strong, the actual texture of the story does not have that inevitableness which is the hallmark of Chékhov. Besides (and in this respect Chékhov was no better), Górky's Russian is "neutral," the words are mere signs and have no individual life. If it were not for certain catchwords, they might have been a translation from any language. The only one of Górky's early stories that makes one forget all his shortcomings (except the mediocrity of his style) is the one that may be considered as closing the period, *Twenty-six Men and a Girl* (1899).

The scene is an underground bakery in which twenty-six men work in a dreadful airless atmosphere for sixteen hours a day for a beggar's wages. A young girl comes every day to them to take some loaves; her fresh and innocent beauty is the only ray of light in their hopeless life. A soldier who has some much easier work in the same yard bets he will seduce her, and wins his bet. When the girl appears after her fall, she is savagely hooted out by the bakers. The story is cruelly realistic. But it is traversed by such a powerful current of poetry, by such a convincing faith in beauty and freedom and in the essential nobility of man, and at the same time it is told with such precision and necessity, that it can hardly be refused the name of a masterpiece. It places Górky—the young Górky—among the true classics of our literature. But *Twenty-six Men and a Girl* is alone in its supreme beauty—and it is the last of Górky's early good work; for fourteen years he was to be a wanderer in tedious and fruitless mazes.

Górky early attempted to transcend the social limits imposed on him by his youthful experience. As early as 1897 he wrote *Várenka Olësova* (the English translation bears the title *A Naughty Girl*), in which he tried to paint the educated classes, and which is curiously anticipatory of many stories written a few years later by Artsybáshev and others. We know from his memoirs that Górky disliked being merely a writer risen from the people and wanted to become a leader and a teacher. This ambition found expression in the series of novels and plays written by him between 1899 and 1912. They are the least valuable part of his work. Two features are common to the whole series: an entire disappearance of that constructive skill which was so promising in his early work, and an immoderate prolixity in conversations on "the meaning of life" and similar subjects. Górky never wrote either a good drama or a good novel, and in so far as his works of this period have any merit, they possess it in spite of being dramas or novels. The principal novels of this period are *Fomá Gordéyev* (1899), *Three of Them* (*Tróye*) (1900–1), *The Mother* (1907), *A Confession* (1908), *Okúrov City* (1909), and *Matvéy Kozhemyákin* (1910). All of them purport to be vast synthetic pictures of Russian provincial life, shown in all its meaningless barbarity, filth, and darkness, relieved only by the efforts of isolated individuals to grasp "the meaning of life," to escape the slough of provincial stagnation, and to show the ignorant and oppressed masses the way. The first two novels are less tendentious and less distinct in their social message. The post-Revolutionary series is more definitely connected with the ideas of the Bolshevíks, though these ideas are reflected in a strangely mystical interpretation. By far the best of the whole series is the first—*Fomá Gordéyev*. Though like the rest it is disfigured by lack of architecture and by immoderate talking, it has many merits of the first order. The first chapters, containing the story of Ignát Gordéyev, Fomá's father, the maker of a great fortune, are among the best Górky ever wrote. Its constructive and masculine spirit gives it a flavor rare in Russian literature. The story of Fomá, the son, the "superfluous" man who does not know what to do with his life and wealth, contains pages of excellent, vivid painting, but as a whole it belongs to the ineffective "conversational" style. Górky's novels almost invariably begin very well, and the first few pages of *Three of Them* and *A Confession* keep the reader spellbound by the straightforward and direct development of the narrative. But then begins that interminable and tiresome "quest," which becomes even more tiresome as it approaches its goal and the hero thinks he finds the social panacea. Of the later novels, *Okúrov City* and *A Confession* are better than the others, first of all because they are shorter. Besides, *Okúrov City* contains comparatively little of the "quest for truth" element and more in the way of vivid action and incident. As for *A Confession*, it is certainly a remarkable work, for in it Górky gives the most quintessential expression to that strange religion of the people which he professed about 1908 and which is so unlike the real Górky—the Górky of both the early and the later works. This "religion" became known as *bogostroítelstvo* (the building of God), as opposed to *bogoiskátelstvo* (the quest after God). God, according to Górky, was to be "built" by the people's faith. One of the closing scenes of *A Confession* gives a very realistic, though hardly convincing, illustration of how the thing might be done—a sick person is healed by a miracle, which is wrought apparently by a miraculous image but in reality by the fervent and realistic faith of the assembled crowd. Apart from its religion, *A Confession* is, as far as about the middle, a good story of the adventures of the tramp after truth, with a rapid development of narrative on which there lies a pale and distant (very distant, but unmistakable) reflex of Leskóv's narrative masterpiece, *The Enchanted Wanderer*. Górky's plays are numerous, but most of them are unknown, even by name, to the professional reader. The fact that *The Lower Depths* (1902) was an outstanding success does not mean that it is intrinsically much better than the rest: its success was entirely due to irrelevant and unliterary causes, and there is no ground to single it out from the rest for solitary praise. As a dramatist, Górky (in spite of Chékhov's censure of his first play for its "conservatism of form") is nothing but a bad disciple of Chékhov (the word "bad," however, is superfluous, for it is impossible to be a good disciple of that dramatist). His dramatic system is exactly the same—with the same inevitable four acts undivided into scenes; the same absence of all apparent action; the same standardized suicide in the last act. The only thing Górky did not notice in Chékhov's dramatic art was the only thing that justifies it: its hidden dynamic structure. The only thing he added to it (or rather gave more room to, for Chékhov did not quite abstain from it) were "conversations on the meaning of life," which would be capable of killing even the greatest drama of Shakspere and the tensest tragedy of Racine. However it may be, Górky's first two plays met with success. In the case of *Meschâne* (*The Petty Bourgeois*, 1901), this was largely a *succès d'estime*. But his second play, *The Lower Depths*, was a triumph. At home the wonderful acting of the Stanislávsky cast was the deciding factor. Abroad it must be explained by the extreme novelty of this sort of thing: the sensational realism of the setting and the novel pleasure of listening to the profound conversations of philosophical thieves, tramps, and prostitutes—"so Russian!" *The Lower Depths* contributed more than anything else to the silly idea the average European and American *"intelligént"* formed for himself of Russia as a country of talkative philosophers occupied with finding their way to what they call "God." Górky's next two plays—*Suburbans* (1904) and *The Children of the Sun* (1905)—failed to bear out the promise of *The Lower Depths:* they lacked the sensational setting of that play, and proved signal failures. As for those that followed—*The Barbarians* (1906), *Enemies* (1906), *Vássa Zheléznova* (1910; revised, 1935), and so on—they remained quite unnoticed.

Concurrently with his plays and novels, Górky wrote a great many minor works—poems like *The Song of the Petrel* (1901) and the one-time famous *Man* (1903); political satires, for which he had no talent, lacking as he did both the necessary gifts, humor and moral earnestness; journalistic sketches (including the American series, *The City of the Yellow Devil* and *One of the Kings of the Republic*). Towards the end of this period he began publishing short sketches founded on his early recollections (*The Notes of a Passer-by*), which introduce us to his autobiographical period.

The works of this period include the three volumes of the autobiographical series, *Childhood* (1913), a volume of *Recollections* (of Tolstóy, Korolénko, Chékhov, Andréyev, and so on) and *Notes from a Diary* (1924). In these works Górky abandons the form of fiction and all (apparent) literary invention; he also hides himself and gives up taking any part in his characters' "quest for truth." He is a realist—a great realist finally freed from all the scales of romance, tendency, or dogma. He has finally become an objective writer. This makes his autobiographical series one of the strangest autobiographies ever written. It is about everyone except himself. His person is only the pretext round which to gather a wonderful gallery of portraits. Górky's most salient feature in these books is his wonderful visual convincingness. The man seems to be all eyes, and the reader sees, as if they were painted, the wonderfully live and vivid figures of the characters. We can never forget such figures as those of the old Kashírins, his grandfather and grandmother; or of the good Bishop Chrysanthus; or of that strange heathen and barbaric orgy of the inhabitants of the little station (*My Universities*). The series invariably produces an impression of hopeless gloom and pessimism on the foreign, and even on the older Russian, reader, but we who have been trained to a less conventional and reticent realism than George Eliot's fail to share that feeling. Górky is not a pessimist, and if he is, his pessimism has nothing to do with his representation of Russian life, but rather with the chaotic state of his philosophical views, which he has never succeeded in making serve his optimism, in spite of all his efforts in that direction. As it is, Górky's autobiographical series represents the world as ugly but not unrelieved—the redeeming points, which may and must save humanity, are enlightenment, beauty, and sympathy. The other two books reveal Górky as an even greater writer than does this autobiography. In speaking of Tolstóy I have already mentioned the wonderful *Recollections of Tolstóy* as the most worthwhile pages ever written about that great man. And this in spite of the fact that Górky is most certainly nothing like Tolstóy's intellectual equal. It is his eyes that see through, rather than his mind that understands. The

wonderful thing is that he saw and noted down things other people
were incapable of seeing or, if they saw, powerless to record.
Górky's image of Tolstóy is rather destructive than constructive:
it sacrifices the unity of legend to the complexity of life. It deals a
deathblow to the hagiographical image of "St. Leo." Equally remarkable are his *Recollections of Andréyev*, which contain one of
his best chapters—the one that describes the heavy and joyless
drunkenness of the younger writer. *Notes from a Diary* is a book
of characters. Nowhere more than here does Górky reveal his
artist's love for his country, which is after all to him the best
country in the world in spite of all his internationalism, of all his
scientific dreams, and of all the dirty things he has seen in her.
"Russia is a wonderful country, where even fools are original," is
the burden of the book. It is a collection of portraits, striking
characters, and glimpses of strange minds. Originality is the keynote. Some of the characters are those of very eminent men: two
fragments are devoted to Alexander Blok. Memorable portraits
are drawn of the well-known Old Believer millionaire Bugróv, who
himself used to cultivate Górky as an original; and of Anna
Schmidt, the mystical correspondent of Vladímir Soloviëv. Other
interesting chapters are those on the morbid attraction exercised
on human beings by fires, and the uncanny things people sometimes do when they are alone and don't expect to be observed.
With the exception of *Recollections of Tolstóy*, this last book is
perhaps the best Górky ever wrote.[2]

[2] In concluding this section, the author wrote in 1925: "Górky's last books have
met with universal and immediate appreciation. And yet he has not become a
living literary influence. His books are read as freshly discovered classics, not as
novelties. In spite of his great personal part in the literature of today (innumerable
young writers look up to him as their sponsor in the literary world), his work is
profoundly unlike all the work of the younger generation; first of all, for his complete lack of interest in style, and, secondly, for his very unmodern interest in
human psychology. The retrospective character of all his recent work seems to
emphasize the impression that it belongs to a world that is no more ours." In the
light of later developments in Soviet literature, notably the campaigns against
"Formalism" and the establishment of "Socialist Realism," the author would perhaps have wished to revise in some respects his estimate of Górky's influence on the
younger generation. In his last period Górky returned to fiction with *The Arta-
mánovs' Business* (1925; English title *Decadence*) and *The Life of Klim Samgín*
(1927–36; English titles of separate parts *Bystander, The Magnet, Other Fires, The
Specter*). The latter, conceived as an epic review of Russian events from the eighties
of the last century, was intended to illustrate the development of the average Russian *intelligént*. It remained unfinished, as did his projected dramatic trilogy (*Egór
Bulychëv and Others*, 1932; *Dostigáyev and Others*, 1933) about the decay of the
Russian bourgeoisie.—Editor

THE *Znánie* SCHOOL OF FICTION

Soon after his first great success Górky founded a publishing business, which received the name—characteristic of its founder—of *Znánie* (Knowledge). All the most prominent young novelists joined Górky's group and had their works published by *Znánie*. Three of them grew to be original and significant writers—Kúprin, Búnin, and Andréyev. The majority remained minor figures and may be conveniently grouped as the school of Górky—or the *Znánie* school of novelists. The common characteristic of the school is its open and emphatic tendentiousness—they are the Revolutionary school of fiction. Though kept in check by the censorship, they were more outspoken than the old radical writers, especially in and after 1905. They were also more outspoken in their realism, richly availing themselves of that emancipation from conventions which had been inaugurated by Tolstóy and confirmed by Górky. The influence of Chékhov and Górky is usually apparent, but Chékhov's is seldom more than superficial, and on the whole the writings of the school are seldom much more than glorified journalism.

There is no need to give more than a short enumeration of these writers. Their *doyen* was Evgény Nikoláyevich Chírikov, a mild and moderate representative of the school. V. Veresáyev (pseudonym of V. V. Smidówicz, 1867–1945), a doctor by profession, produced a sensation in 1901 by a book of "revelations," *The Notebook of a Doctor*, but most of his stories and novels are devoted to the description of the various moods and developments of the Marxist intelligentsia. He stayed in Russia after the October Revolution, gradually turning his attention to the field of literary biography. A. Serafimóvich (pseudonym of A. S. Popóv, 1863–1949), is also a "political" writer, and his *Iron Flood* (1924), a novel about the Civil War, has become a Soviet classic. A typical disciple of Górky is Skitálets (pseudonym of S. G. Petróv, 1868–1934), whose simple and crudely naïve stories describe the Revolutionary idealism and thirst for enlightenment of the class of men discovered by Górky. A somewhat more interesting figure is S. S. Yushkévich (1868–1927), a Jew, who concentrated on the life and manners of his people. He wrote plays as well as novels, and his *Miserere* was produced by Stanislávsky with some success. The

younger writers who came into literature after 1902–3 were less
obsessed by Revolution, and their work bears the impress of other
influences. Only one of them, V. V. Múyzhel, a clumsy, gloomy,
and scarcely readable naturalist, can be counted with the *Znánie*
school.

KÚPRIN

Alexander Ivánovich Kúprin (1870–1938) also began as a writer
of the *Znánie* school, but his literary personality is sufficiently
original for him to be treated separately. He was educated in Moscow in a cadet school and was for several years an officer in the
army. Army life is the principal subject of his early stories. He
treats it in the orthodox "oppositional" manner, representing the
wretched soldier oppressed by stupid and mechanical sergeant-
majors and brutal officers. The central figure is always a young
officer who is himself oppressed by the gloomy reality round him
and broods on the meaning of his life and life in general.

These stories culminated in a novel, *The Duel*, which appeared
in 1905, immediately after the great disasters of Mukden and
Tsushima, when all radical Russia was united in exulting over the
defeats of the Imperial Army. *The Duel* had an enormous success
and was freely quoted in attacks against the Army. For all that,
The Duel is not really a Revolutionary work. Its point of view is
rather that of the typical "Chekhovian *intelligént*." The hero is a
very sensitive young man (and a very bad officer) who is constantly wounded by the coarse reality of life. *The Duel* is very
"passive" and "morbid," but within its limitations it is a good
novel. The character drawing is excellent, and the gallery of types
of infantry officers is convincing and varied.

The Duel made Kúprin famous, and he became a prominent
and much discussed figure of literary Petersburg, largely in connection with his visits to the favorite haunt of the old (pre-poeti-
cal) literary Bohemia—the Vienna Restaurant. Between 1905 and
the beginning of the first World War, Kúprin wrote much, but he
failed to create an unforgettable and inevitable expression of himself. He was torn between various tendencies. Being essentially a
man of no culture, he could not really profit from any literary
example; and, possessing very little of artistic tact, he could not

distinguish between what was good in his writings and what was bad. He emulated Tolstóy in trying to describe the psychology of animals (a race horse in *Izumrúd*); he fell into incredible bad taste in a would-be Flaubert-like evocation of Solomon's Jerusalem (*Sulamith*), and gained doubtful popularity by a journalistically realistic, crude, and sentimental novel from the life of prostitutes (*Yáma*).

Kúprin had in him a valuable germ that remained almost undeveloped: he was attracted towards the "Western" type of story, which, unlike the Russian story, is a story of action and strong situations, which loves intrigue and does not shun sensationalism. He was attracted by Kipling and Jack London (in whose praise he wrote with great eloquence), and by that somewhat conventional idea Russians have of England as a land of pipe-smoking, strong and silent, drunken, rowdy, and sentimental sailors. He never succeeded in casting aside his intelligentsia-ism and in setting out to write *à la* Jack London. But two or three times he attained something that was not attained by any one of his contemporaries in Russian literature: he wrote several good stories of vigorous and sensational situation with a romantic and heroical keynote. One of the best is *Lieutenant-Captain Rýbnikov* (1906), the story of a Japanese spy in Petersburg who with wonderful skill succeeds in aping the appearance and mentality of an average Russian infantry officer and then betrays himself by crying *Banzai* when asleep in the arms of a harlot (this detail is the hallmark of the "Górky" school). Another good story (and this time free from "Gorkyisms") is *The Bracelet of Garnets* (1911), the romantic and melodramatic story of the love of a poor clerk for a society lady. For sheer narrative construction it is one of the best stories of its time. His works written in emigration (he returned to the Soviet Union only shortly before his death) are of minor interest.

BÚNIN

Iván Alexéyevich Búnin is rather difficult to pigeonhole. For many years he was a faithful member of the *Známie* group, but intrinsically he has little in common with that school of Revolutionary fiction. The subjects of some of his most important masterpieces are distinctly social, but his way of approaching these subjects has

nothing to do with the distinction of "right" and "left." He is
obviously a greater *artist* than either Górky or Andréyev, or any
other writer of his generation outside the symbolist school. His
literary ancestors are pretty clear—they are Chékhov, Tolstóy,
Turgénev, and Goncharóv. His obvious relationship with the two
last gives him that "classical" appearance which distinguishes him
from his contemporaries. To emphasize this difference, Búnin
comes of a class that has long lost its leadership in Russian culture
and that he was at one time alone to represent in literature. He
was born in 1870, in Vorónezh, of an ancient family of country
gentry. The great poet Zhukóvsky, the natural son of a squire
named Búnin, belonged to the same family. Búnin grew up in his
country home and in the district town of Élets—and Élets and its
neighborhood are the almost invariable setting of his most characteristic stories. While still a student at the University of Moscow
he began publishing verse in the literary press. Gradually the
anti-modernist party began to regard him as the most promising
of young poets. In 1903 the Academy assigned to him the Púshkin
Prize for literature and in 1909 elected him an honorary member.
In the late nineties he joined the Górky group, and for more than
ten years all his works were published by the *Znánie* publishing
house, but he never identified himself with the political extremists.
His stories had begun to appear as early as 1892, but he was
thought of as primarily a poet, especially since his early "stories"
are essentially "lyrical." In 1910 his "novel" (the Russian subtitle
is *poéma*, which means "a big poem," "an epic") *The Village* appeared, which placed him in the very front row of Russian novelists. *The Village* was followed by the four books that contain most
of his masterpieces: *Sukhodól* (1912), *Ioánn the Weeper* (1913), *The
Cup of Life* (1914), and *The Gentleman from San Francisco* (1916).
In the years preceding the first World War, Búnin traveled much
in Mediterranean and tropical countries. Many of his works are
dated from Capri; and Algeria, Palestine, the Red Sea, and Ceylon
are the frequent background of his stories and poems. In 1917
Búnin took a very definite anti-Bolshevík position. In 1918 he
left Soviet Russia and became, in the course of ensuing years, one
of the leading literary figures of the Emigration.

In the early years of his literary career Búnin did much translation from English, and we owe to him complete Russian versions
of the *Song of Hiawatha* and of the mystery plays of Byron. As a

poet, Búnin belongs to the old, pre-symbolist school. His technique has remained that of the eighties, but it attains a higher level, and his verse is less "empty" than Nádson's or Mínsky's. His poetry is mainly objective, and impressions of nature, Russian and exotic, are its principal subject. Though by no means so important a poet as he is a novelist, he is a genuine poet, the only significant poet of the symbolist age who was not a symbolist. His verse up to 1907 is contained in three separate volumes, of which the second, 1903–6, contains probably his best poems, including the powerful and haunting *Sapsán*, a poem of wild Bashkiria, and memorable evocations of the Mohammedan East. After 1907 he discontinued the practice of publishing his verse separately and composed most of his books of prose and verse.

Much of Búnin's prose is more "poetical" and more subjective than his verse. Purely lyrical compositions in prose are to be found in every one of his books. This lyrical style was the first aspect of his prose that attracted general attention to his individuality. In his first volumes (1892–1902) they were certainly the most interesting item; the rest consisted of realistically sentimental stories of the conventional type, or of attempts to emulate Chékhov in the representation of the disintegrating "pinpricks" of life (*The Schoolmaster*). The lyrical stories went back to the tradition of Chékhov (*The Steppe*), of Turgénev (*Forest and Steppe*), and of Goncharóv (*Oblómov's Dream*), but Búnin accentuated still further the lyrical element, eliminated all narrative skeleton, and at the same time studiously avoided (except in certain attempts tainted with "modernism") the diction of lyrical prose. His lyrical effects were produced by the poetry of *things*, not of rhythms or words. The most notable of these lyrical poems in prose is *Antónov Apples* (1900), where the smell of a special kind of apples leads him from association to association to reconstruct a poetical picture of the dying life of his class, the middle gentry of central Russia. The tradition of Goncharóv, with his epical manner of painting stagnant life, is especially alive in the lyrical "stories" of Búnin (one of them even bears the title *A Dream of Oblómov's Grandson*). In later years the same lyrical manner was transferred to other subjects than dying central Russia, and, for instance, his impressions of Palestine (1908) were written in the same restrained, subdued, and lyrical "minor key."

The Village, which appeared in 1910, presented Búnin under a new aspect. It is one of the sternest, darkest, and bitterest books in Russian literature. It is a "social" novel, and its subject is the poverty, darkness, and barbarity of Russian life. There is almost no development in time; it is almost static like a picture; but, for all that, the construction is masterly, and the gradual filling up of the canvas in a deliberately planned succession of strokes produces an impression of inevitable and conscious power. In the center of the "poem" stand the two brothers Krásov, Tíkhon and Kuzmá. Tíkhon is a successful shopkeeper; Kuzmá is unsuccessful in business and a "seeker after truth." The first part is written from Tíkhon's, the second from Kuzmá's, standpoint. Both are ultimately "undone," coming to the conclusion that all their life has been a failure. The background is the central Russian village— poor, savage, stupid, brutal, lacking in every moral foundation. Górky, in his indictment of the Russian peasant, speaks of Búnin as of the only writer who dared say the truth about the *muzhík* without idealizing him.

The Village, in spite of its great powerfulness, is hardly a perfect work of art: it is too long and loose and contains too much definitively "publicistic" matter; like Górky's, the personages of *The Village* talk and meditate at excessive length. But in his next work Búnin overcame this defect. This next work, *Sukhodól*, is one of the greatest masterpieces of modern Russian prose and, more than anything else, bears the impress of Búnin's original genius. As in *The Village*, Búnin carries to the utmost the unnarrative ("imperfective," as Miss Harrison has called it) tendency of the Russian novel and constructs his story athwart all temporal order. It is a perfect work of art, quite *sui generis*, and of which no European literature has a counterpart. It is the story of the "fall of the house" of Khruschëv, of the gradual undoing of a family of squires, told from the point of view of a female servant. Short and concentrated, and at the same time elastic and ample, it has all the "density" and tightness of poetry, though it never for a moment abandons the calm and level diction of realistic prose. *Sukhodól* is, as it were, a counterpart to *The Village*, and in both "poems" the theme is the cultural poverty, "rootlessness," emptiness, and savagery of Russian life. The same theme is repeated in a series of stories written between 1908 and 1914, many of which stand on the same high level, though hardly any one reaches the absolute perfection of *Sukhodól*. *A Goodly Life* (1912), to take one example, is the story told in the first person by a heartless (and naïvely self-righteous in her heartlessness) woman of peasant origin who succeeds in life after being the cause of the ruin of her son and the death of the rich young man who loved her. The story is remarkable, among other things, for its language—it is an exact reproduction of the dialect of a petty townswoman of Élets, with all the phonetic and grammatical peculiarities carefully reproduced. It is remarkable that even in reproducing dialect Búnin succeeds in remaining "classical," in keeping the words subordinate to the whole. This manner is the opposite of Leskóv's, who is always playing with his language and whose words always protrude to the point of beggaring the story. It is interesting to compare the two writers in the examples of *A Goodly Life* and Leskóv's sketch of a somewhat similar character, *The Amazon*. It is like the difference of the same Jesuit style in the hands of a Frenchman and in those of a Mexican. *A Goodly Life* is Búnin's only story told in dialect from beginning to end, but the speech of the Élets peasants, reproduced with equal precision and equally "unprotruding," reappears in the dialogue of all his rural stories (especially in *A Night Conversation*). Apart from the use of dialect, Búnin's language is "classical," sober, concrete. Its only expressive means is the exact notation of things; it is objective because its effect depends entirely on the "objects" spoken of. Búnin is probably the only modern Russian writer whose language would have been admired by the "classics," by Turgénev and Goncharóv.

It is almost an inevitable consequence of this "dependence on object" that when Búnin leaves the familiar and domestic realities of the Élets district and sets his stories in Ceylon or in Palestine, or even in Odessa, his style loses much of its vigor and aptness. In his exotic stories he is often inadequate, and especially when he is poetical the beauty of his poetry is apt to become mere tinsel. To keep free from this inadequateness when dealing with a foreign (or even with a Russian urban) subject, Búnin must mercilessly keep down his lyrical proclivities. He must be bald and terse at the hazard of becoming cheap. He has achieved this baldness and terseness in a few stories, one of which is considered by most of his (especially foreign) readers his indubitable masterpiece—*The Gentleman from San Francisco* (1915).

This remarkable story is well known in English translations. It belongs to the progeny of *Iván Ilyích*, and its "message" is quite in keeping with the teaching of Tolstóy: the vanity of civilization and the presence of death the only reality. But no direct influence of Tolstóy can be traced in Búnin's story, as it can in the best of Andréyev's. It is not a work of analysis, for Búnin is no analyst and no psychologist. It is a "thing of beauty," a solid "object"; it has the consistency and hardness of a steel bar. It is a masterpiece of artistic economy and austere, "Doric" expression. Like the two rural "poems" *The Village* and *Sukhodól, The Gentleman from San Francisco* has also its accompanying constellation of foreign and urban stories told in bald outline and with austere matter-of-factness. Among the best are *Kazimír Stanislávovich* (1915) and *Thieves' Ears* (1916), a powerful study of criminal perversity.

Of the more lyrical exotic and urban stories, the most notable are *The Dreams of Chang* (1916) and *Brothers* (1914). In both of them Búnin's lyrical poetry, torn away from its native soil, loses much of its vitality, and is often unconvincing and conventional. His language also loses its color and becomes "international." Still, *Brothers* is a powerful work. It is the story of a Singhalese jinrikisha man of Colombo and his English fare. It avoids the pitfall of sentimentality in a masterly way.

In 1933 Búnin was awarded a Nobel Prize, and he has continued to produce and develop in emigration. In addition to several collections of short stories and verse, among which *Dark Alleys* (1943) has received particular praise, he has written a short novel of early love (*Mítya's Love*, 1924–5) and begun a longer work of autobiographical fiction (*The Life of Arséniev*).

ANDRÉYEV

When Górky's popularity began to diminish, the first place in the public favor passed to Leoníd Andréyev (1871–1919). This process began before the Revolution of 1905. Soon after that date the Revolutionary school of fiction was finally superseded by a new school that may be called the metaphysical or the pessimistic school. These writers were in the height of their fame in the years immediately following the defeat of the First Revolution (1907–11), and the sociological historians of Russian literature have always tried to explain the whole movement by political disillusionment. In the success of the movement with the public, the political motive was certainly important, but the movement itself began earlier, and much of Andréyev's best and most characteristic work was written before 1905.

Old-fashioned critics and readers of the older generation of the orthodox radical (and, still more, of the conservative) school were scarcely able to distinguish between Andréyev and the symbolists. Both were to them equally detestable malformations. In reality there is very little in common between the two beyond the common tendency away from accepted standards and a decided inclination towards the grandiose and the ultimate. Both the symbolists and Andréyev are always somewhat stiltedly serious and solemn and distinctly lack a sense of humor. But the differences are far more important. The symbolists were united by a high degree of conscientious craftsmanship; Andréyev dealt in ready-made clichés and was simply no craftsman. Secondly, the symbolists were men of superior culture and played a principal part in the great cultural renaissance of the Russian intelligentsia; Andréyev, on the contrary, lacked culture as much as he despised it. At last—and this is the most important point—the symbolists stood on a foundation of a realistic (in the mediæval sense of the word) metaphysics, and even if they were pessimists of life, they were optimists of death—that is to say, mystics. Blok, alone of them, knew that absolute emptiness which brings him near Andréyev; but Blok's emptiness comes from a sense of exclusion from a superior and real Presence, not from a consciousness of universal void. Andréyev and Artsybáshev proceeded from a scientific agnosticism and were strangers to all mystical optimism—theirs was an allround and absolute pessimism—a pessimism of death as well as of life. It may be said, in short (with a degree of simplification), that while the symbolists proceed from Dostoyévsky, Andréyev proceeds from Tolstóy. The negation of culture and the intense consciousness of the elemental realities of life—death and sex—are the essence of Tolstoyism, and they reappear in the philosophy of Andréyev and of Artsybáshev. As for the purely literary influence of Tolstóy over these two writers, it can hardly be exaggerated.

Andréyev's family belonged to the small provincial intelligentsia. His father died early and the Andréyevs lived in poverty, but Leoníd received the usual middle-class education at the Gymnasium of Orël and in due time (1891) went to the University of Petersburg. At the end of his first term he attempted suicide for disappointed love, went home, and spent the next few years in idleness. Like practically all Russian intelligentsia young men who were not absorbed by Revolutionary ideas, Andréyev had no genuine interest in life. His life was only an effort somehow to fill up the void of his soul. This usually led to drunkenness, for such men needed some sort of intoxication to keep them running. So it was in the case of Andréyev. He was by no means gloomy or solitary; he had many friends and was rather gay and sociable than otherwise. But his gaiety was artificial and fictitious, and at the bottom of it was a vague, undirected restlessness. A characteristic episode of Andréyev's youth was his lying down between the rails under a train, which passed over him without injuring him. He liked to play with terror, and in later life Edgar Allan Poe's tales were his favorite reading. In 1893 Andréyev went again to the university, this time in Moscow, and in due time took his degree in law and was admitted to the bar (1897). But before that he had already begun his literary career. His first printed works were reports from the law courts and short stories printed in the Orël papers. His legal practice did not last long, for he was soon received into the literary press, and in 1898 his stories began to attract the attention of critics and fellow writers. One of the first men to encourage him was Górky. The two contracted a friendship that lasted till after 1905. By 1900 the distinctly Andréyev note appears, and in 1901 he published *Once Upon a Time There Lived . . . (Zhíli-býli)*, which remains one of his best stories. He was greeted as the rising hope of the new realism and the worthy younger brother of Górky. These were the happiest years of Andréyev's life. He had just been happily married; he was surrounded by admiring friends, largely young novelists who looked up to him as to a *maître;* his fame was growing; he was gaining money. And it was at the height of this happiness that he finally found the note of hopeless despair which is peculiarly his.

In 1902 appeared two stories, *The Abyss* and *In the Fog*, in which sexual subjects were treated with more than ordinary realism and audacity. In spite of the obvious earnestness, almost moralism, of the two stories, they were received with an angry uproar in the conservative and old-fashioned radical press, and the Countess S. A. Tolstóy wrote an indignant letter to the papers, protesting against such dirt in literature. She must have recognized in *In the Fog* traces of her husband's influence. After that Andréyev became the most debated author in Russia, and a large section of the press treated him with more than usual lack of courtesy. But his success with the public only grew, and from 1902 to at least 1908 every new story by him was a literary event and brought him new fame and new money. He became rich. In 1906 he lost his first wife, and though he married again, he never regained his early happiness, and gloom and emptiness became dominant forces in his life as well as in his work. He lived in Kuokkala, in Finland, where he had built a pretentious house in "modern style." His dress was as pretentious as his house. He required constant intoxication to keep going. He never ceased drinking, but the principal form this need for stimulants took was a constant succession of fads to which he gave himself away for short periods of time with pathetic wholeheartedness—now he was a sailor, now a painter; everything he did he did in grand style; he was as fond of bigness in life as he was in literature. His way of working was in bearing with all his style; he worked by fits and starts, dictating for whole nights at a time and finishing his stories and plays in extraordinarily short spaces. Then for months he would remain idle. When he dictated, the words poured out of his mouth in an uninterrupted flow of monotonous rhythmical prose with such speed that his typist had considerable trouble in keeping pace with him.

After 1908 Andréyev's popularity began to wane. He had now against him not only the old generation, but also a more dangerous enemy in the form of the young literary schools, who never regarded him as anything but a literary bubble. His talent also declined. After *The Seven That Were Hanged* (1908), he wrote nothing that can be compared with his best work. By 1914 he was a little more than the ghost of his literary self. The first World War woke him to new life. It was a new stimulant. He plunged head over heels into patriotism and anti-Germanism. He began writing frankly propaganda books, and in 1916 accepted the editorship of a newly founded large pro-war daily. In 1917 he naturally took up a decidedly anti-Bolshevík attitude, and during the Civil War he contributed freely to anti-Bolshevík propaganda. His last work was a passionate appeal, entitled *S O S*, to the Allies to save Russia from Bolshevík tyranny. He died at Kuokkala to the sounds of the Red guns of Petrograd holding back the last offensive of the White Army.

The personality of Leoníd Andréyev has already become the

theme of numerous memoirs. The most interesting are those by Górky and Chukóvsky.

Andréyev began as a naïve and unpretending, rather sentimental realist in the old "philanthropic" tradition in the manner of Korolénko, rather than of Górky, and it was by stories of this kind that he first attracted attention. But before long he developed a style of his own—or, to be more precise, two styles, neither of which was quite his own. One of these two styles, and by far the better, was learned from Tolstóy's problem stories, *The Death of Iván Ilyích* and *The Kreutzer Sonata*. The other is a "modernist" concoction of reminiscences from Poe, Maeterlinck, German, Polish, and Scandinavian modernists. The first of these two manners is sober and discreet; the second is shrill, rhetorical, and, to our present taste, ineffective and unpalatable. But it was a novelty in Russian literature, and as Andréyev's subjects were intelligible and interesting to the general reader, it had its moment of tremendous success. These two styles may almost seem to belong to two different writers, but the "message" conveyed by both is the same. It is a message of thorough nihilism and negation—human life, society, morals, culture, are all lies—the only reality is death and annihilation, and the only feelings that express human understanding of the truth are "madness and horror"—the opening words of *The Red Laugh*. Whether this is expressed with rhetorical emphasis or with soberly concentrated force, the substance is the same. It is the necessary outcome of all the history of the intelligentsia: the moment the *"intelligént"* ceased to be inspired by Revolutionary faith, the universe became to him a meaningless and terrible void.

If Andréyev had left unwritten the greater part of his works and we knew only his three best stories, we should think more highly of him as a writer, and his place as a classic would be less in jeopardy. The three stories I allude to are *Once Upon a Time There Lived* . . . (1901), *In the Fog* (1902), and *The Governor* (1906). They are all in the "Tolstoyan" manner. The first and the last proceed from *The Death of Iván Ilyích;* the second from *The Kreutzer Sonata*. The manner of Tolstóy is assimilated thoroughly and at the same time creatively. In both stories the growth of death in the consciousness of the man to die is traced with a strong and steady hand. It is all the more effective because the author never raises the tone of his voice and carefully avoids emphasis.

The Governor ends on a note of disinterested submission to the inevitable that is very distant from the religious rebirth in *The
Death of Iván Ilyích*. *In the Fog* is the powerful and cruel story of a
young boy who discovers the results of his early sexual relations,
and ends with the murder of a prostitute and suicide. The story,
though denounced on its appearance as pornography, is really
quite as moral and "cautionary" as Tolstóy's *Sonata*. It is full of
genuine tragedy, and the conversation between the boy and the
father, who lectures him on the danger of early sexual relations
without knowing of his son's illness, is a fine piece of dramatic
irony. Andréyev, though incapable of genuine humor, had an unmistakable gift of irony. A fair example of this irony may be seen
in his sketch *Christians*, in which a prostitute refuses to take the
oath in a law court on the ground that she cannot consider herself
a Christian. The dialogue, which verges on the grotesquely impossible, ridicules the judges and officers of law in the true Tolstoyan spirit.

But long before *The Governor* was written, Andréyev had already committed misconduct with the siren of modernism. *The
Wall*, his first metaphysical story in the rhetorical "modern"
style, was written as early as 1901. This was followed by a succession of "metaphysical" problem stories, most of which are in
the same intensely rhetorical style. At first Andréyev kept to the
familiar molds of realism, but later he preferred conventional
settings, which became predominant beginning with *The Red
Laugh*, (1904). Vanity of vanities; the meaninglessness, falseness,
hollowness of all human conventions and creations; the relativity
of moral standards; the voidness of all earthly desires; the insuperable isolation of man from man, are the subject of all these
stories, and above them the one great reality—death. Only two
stories of this period stand out for their merits—both of them have
Revolutionaries for their heroes—*Darkness* (1907) and *The Seven
That Were Hanged* (1908). In *Darkness* a tracked terrorist seeks
refuge in a brothel. The prostitute who receives him is offended by
his chastity and flings in his face the very Andreyevian question:
"What right have you to be good if I am bad?" *Darkness* offended
the left, and Andréyev, to exculpate himself from the charge of
disrespect for the terrorists, wrote *The Seven That Were Hanged*.
This is the story, from the sentence to the execution, of five terrorists and two common murderers who were sentenced to death.

Though it deals with Andréyev's favorite theme of death, its principal subject is not the horror of death, but the heroism and purity of the terrorists. In this respect it stands apart from the rest of Andréyev's work. It also stands apart from what he wrote about the same time for the elegant simplicity and reserve with which it is written. It is characteristic of the atmosphere of Russian public life that though Andréyev was quite non-political, he is firmly convinced of the sanctity of the terrorists. Even the prostitute has no doubt that the acme of goodness is to be a political assassin. *The Seven That Were Hanged* is as devout as anything in the Acts of the Martyrs. After 1908 Andréyev wrote more plays than stories. His last and longest novel, *Sáshka Zhegulëv* (1912), appeared when he was on the wane, and attracted comparatively little attention.

Andréyev wrote his first drama (*Towards the Stars*) in 1906, and after that date about a dozen other plays, some of which became very famous, but none of which is comparable to the best of his stories. These plays are of two kinds: realistic plays of Russian life in which he continued the tradition of Chékhov and Górky, bringing it still lower down and finally stultifying it; and symbolical dramas in a conventional setting. Of the latter group, *The Life of Man* (1907) and *He Who Gets Slapped* (1914) had a considerable success. In all of them he studiously avoids every suspicion of real life and live color. They are the distant descendants, through various, mainly Teutonic intermediaries, of the mystery plays of Byron. They are written in an intensely stilted, rhetorical, "international" prose, and their coloring is gaudily black and red, without any shades. *The Life of Man* is, after all, the best, for it does produce a certain cumulative effect by the monotonous chant of the unreal personages. Still, it is impossible to reread it. As for the philosophy of these plays, it is always the same—death and nonentity, and the vanity and falsity of everything human. In his last plays, both of the realistic and of the symbolical type, there is a notable growth of the element of melodrama. This makes them more theatrical and actable. A characteristic example of this later manner of Andréyev's is *He Who Gets Slapped*, which was turned into a movie drama in America. The combination it offers of tantalizingly obscure symbolism, of allegorically interpreted farce, and of the most orthodox sentimental melodrama is precisely the combination that must make it a "paramount picture" of the would-be high-brow type. Andréyev also tried his hand at "humorous" plays (*The Beautiful Sabine Women*, and so forth), but his heavy, joyless, and stilted fun is even worse than his gloomy rhetoric.

Andréyev as a writer (with the exception of the few stories mentioned above) is almost dead. The Andréyev feeling of the emptiness of the world has been (happily enough) lost by us, so we can appreciate him only in so far as he infects us æsthetically. But his rhetorical style is a mass of clichés; his words have no individual life—they are melted together into formless masses of verbal concrete. "Andréyev says 'boo' and I am not afraid," was Tolstóy's appreciation of one of his early stories, and though our taste may be different from Tolstóy's, we shall never again be frightened by the great majority of Andréyev's writings. Andréyev was a genuine and sincere writer. But sincerity counts for very little unless it has at its service the power of inevitable expression, that is to say, superior craftsmanship. Andréyev was a dilettante of form who had great pretensions and no tact. He will remain in the history of Russian civilization as a very interesting and representative figure—the most representative man of a dark and tragic phase in the evolution of the intelligentsia: when, losing faith in its naïve Revolutionary optimism, it suddenly found itself in the universal void—naked men, solitary and empty, on a meaningless earth under a cold and empty sky. This stage has most certainly been passed, and if we ever return to the experience that produced it, we shall have to find some new expression for our feelings, for Andréyev does not make us afraid. All this refers to that Andréyev who, intoxicated by success and self-importance, and unguided by culture and taste, embarked on the dark seas of modernism. The other Andréyev, who was a modest and intelligent follower of the great example of Tolstóy and who wrote *Once Upon a Time There Lived* . . . , *In the Fog*, and *The Governor*, has his secure, if modest, place in the pantheon of Russian authors.

ARTSYBÁSHEV

Soon after the First Revolution, Andréyev's popularity was almost eclipsed by the great vogue of the author of *Sánin*, Michael Petróvich Artsybáshev (1878–1927). In 1904 he had attracted attention and roused hopes by *The Death of Lande*, the story of a life of quest followed by a tragically meaningless death. In 1905–6 he pleased the radical public by a series of stories of the Revolution. But the Revolution was defeated, the intoxication passed, and a wave of disillusionment in public ideals swept the intelligentsia. Personal enjoyment and freedom from morality became the order of the day, and sexual license, often on a definitely pathological foundation, spread like an epidemic. This epidemic was both reflected and further favored by Artsybáshev's famous novel *Sánin*, which appeared in 1907. Its success was instant and tremendous. The old-fashioned critics cried out against its immorality, and the modernists pointed out the absence in it of all literary merit. But it was a sensation and everyone had to read it. It became for a few years the Bible of every schoolboy and schoolgirl in Russia. It would be wrong to suppose that Artsybáshev consciously sought either to corrupt schoolgirls or to gain money by pandering to animal instincts—Russian literature has never been openly meretricious; and he had from the very beginning shown symptoms of that Andreyevian nihilism which was the brand mark of the generation. Still, the effect was certainly serious, and the author of *Sánin* cannot be exculpated from having contributed to the moral deterioration of Russian society, especially of provincial schoolgirls. The didactic character of Russian literature (or at least the didactic spirit in which it had always been approached) was the cause of the strangely serious reception given to *Sánin*—it was read, not as light literature, but as a revelation and a doctrine. The book is indeed didactic; it is a heavy, professorial sermon on the text: Be true to yourselves and follow your natural inclinations. Artsybáshev's preaching proceeds directly from Tolstóy—only it is Tolstóy the other way round, and Tolstóy without genius. But the common ground is unmistakable—it is contempt for human conventions and culture, and the negation of all but the primitive realities. As literature, *Sánin* is very mediocre. It is long, tedious, overloaded with "philosophical" conversations. Artsybáshev avoids the modernist pitfalls of Andréyev, but his psychology is puerile—it can all be reduced to one pattern, borrowed from Tolstóy; he (or she) thought he wished this and that, but in reality he only wished quite another thing—that is, to quell his sexual desire, which is the only human reality.

The other reality of Artsybáshev's world is death; and to

death is devoted his second big novel, *At the Brink* (1911–12). It
is also heavily didactic—its subject is an epidemic of suicides that
destroyed all the intellectual elite of a provincial town. All Artsybáshev's stories, long or short, are stories with a purpose, and the
purpose is always to show the inanity of human life, the unreality
of artificial civilization, and the reality of only two things—sex and
death. After *At the Brink*, Artsybáshev devoted himself to the
stage. His plays are also purpose plays, and it is precisely owing to
the organizing force of the "purpose" that they have, unlike most
Russian plays, a genuine dramatic skeleton. They are quite actable
and, with good actors, have had deserved successes.

The Bolshevíks treated Artsybáshev very harshly. They included *Sánin* and other works in their index of forbidden books,
and finally expelled him from Russia (in 1923). At present no one
regards him as a significant writer but only as a curious and, on
the whole, regrettable episode in the history of Russian literature.

SERGÉYEV-TSÉNSKY

Sergéy Nikoláyevich Sergéyev-Tsénsky (1876–1945) never attained to those giddy heights of popularity which were the lot of
Andréyev and Artsybáshev, but now, when Andréyev's fame has
faded and Artsybáshev's gone, he emerges a much more significant
figure. He began his literary career in 1904. His stories soon attracted general attention and were warmly welcomed by many
critics but generally censured for an exclusive exuberance and
elaboration of style. His most important works of this early period
are *The Forest Quagmire* (1907), *Babáyev* (1907), *The Sadness of
the Fields* (1909), and *Movements* (1910). In 1914 there appeared
The Oblique Eléna, which was unexpectedly free from all his previous exuberance. Then he became silent for many years. During
all this time he lived in the Crimea, writing *Transfiguration*, a
novel of extraordinary vastness written as a history of the Russian
intelligentsia mentality from before the first World War to after
the Revolution. The first part of this novel appeared in 1923, and
Górky pronounced it the greatest Russian book since the beginning
of the century.

Sergéyev-Tsénsky's early work acquired a reputation for
exaggerated exuberance and elaboration of style. It is loaded with

imagery, comparisons—often farfetched—and bold metaphor. Alone of all his literary group, he had a feeling for words—for the actual verbal texture of his writings. His early style vibrates with expressiveness and life. It is "ornamental" prose very much akin to that cultivated by the disciples of Rémizov and Bély; but his starting point is different, and there is no actual connection between him and that school. One of the most striking merits of his early work is the wonderful vividness of the speech of his characters. He freely uses dialect and broken language and slang—and uses it with knowledge and precision. The conversation of Antón Antónovich, a Russianized Austrian Pole, the hero of *Movements*, is a masterpiece of exact notation and at the same time of phonetic effectiveness; the exuberant and unconquerable energy of the self-made man vibrates in every syllable and intonation of it. Tsénsky is equally precise in everything: he knows everything he writes about; he revels in technical terms—for instance, in *The Sadness of the Fields*, he makes his characters indulge in long technical conversations about the house they are building, and, an extraordinary thing, these conversations are never boring, so intensely alive are they. He is also one of the few writers who know and feel the geography of Russia and the individuality of its parts. In *The Oblique Eléna* (the strange title is the name of a coalshaft in the Donéts district) his style suddenly settles down, and he seems of set purpose to avoid all distracting ornament—a heroic development in an author with such personal style. In his post-Revolutionary *Professor's Narrative* (1924) he continues to shun all imagery and ornament, but revives his art of making you hear his characters speaking: the story is a narrative within a narrative, and the contained narrative is told by a Red Army officer in a language as characteristic and alive as Antón Antónovich's in *Movements*.

Apart from his style, Sergéyev-Tsénsky starts out in the same school as Andréyev and Artsybáshev—his principal themes are death, the tyranny of fate, the insuperable solitude of man, morbid psychological states, and the lure of crime. *The Forest Quagmire* (one of his most elaborately written works) is the story of a peasant girl who becomes an idiot subsequent to a violent fit of terror in the haunted wood and, after an irresponsible life, dies a tragic and hideous death. *The Sadness of the Fields* is the life of a woman whose children all die before their birth and who lives in constant terror of the mysterious forces of destruction in her womb. *Babáyev* is about a young, neurasthenic officer, morbidly attracted by the desire of crime, who finds an outlet to it (and ultimately his own death) in his work during the suppression of the Revolution. It is noteworthy that Tsénsky succeeds in making the politically attractive subject quite unpolitical. *Movements* is the undoing of a man; the energetic and exuberant Antón Antónovich, by a succession of strokes of fate, is brought to disgrace (he is convicted of arson), indifference, and death. The last chapters of the novel belong to the great family of *Iván Ilyích*. There is a note of noble and manly resignation in them, which grows in *The Oblique Eléna* (the history of how an engineer decided to commit suicide and how and why he did not) into a more active acceptance of life. The same return from an "everlasting no" to an "everlasting yea" seems to be the subject of *Transfiguration. The Professor's Narrative*, however, is outside this development: it is a steady objective study of the making of a murderer, of a man who can coolly and simply kill another man. The story is told to the Professor by the murderer himself (a Red Army commander, formerly an officer of the Imperial Army) with a directness and simplicity that makes one's flesh creep. It is a masterpiece of straightforward and concentrated narrative.[3]

FEUILLETONISTS AND HUMORISTS

A notable feature of Russian literary life at the end of the nineteenth and beginning of the twentieth century was the growth of the daily press. The large publishers did all they could to raise the literary standards of their publications. Some went as far as to give much place to genuine literature (especially the Cadet paper *Rech* in 1906–17), but a special style of journalese semi-literature was also developed that found its home in Suvórin's *Nóvoye vrémya* and in the capitalistic and liberal *Rússkoye slóvo*. This semi-lit-

[3] Sergéyev-Tsénsky more than fulfilled the promise that Mírsky found in him, becoming one of the acknowledged masters of Soviet literature. In both short stories and novels he was particularly successful in celebrating the heroism and endurance of the Russian people throughout their history. His *Ordeal of Sevastópol* (1939), a three-volume epic of the Crimean War, and *The Brusílov Breakthrough* (1942–3), a part of the *Transfiguration* series, concerned with the first World War, are the best-known of these later works.—Editor

erature was printed, as is the custom in French dailies, in the lower half of the middle pages, which is known by the French name *feuilleton*. The most brilliant and popular of the writers of these *feuilletons* was V. Doroshévich, who worked on the *Rússkoye slóvo*. He evolved a peculiar staccato style that was imitated by countless good, bad, and mediocre feuilletonists. Tolstóy at one time (about 1900) expressed the opinion that of living writers Doroshévich was second only to Chékhov.

The "days of freedom" of 1905–6 brought a great harvest of satirical journals, which, however, were very short-lived, being very soon suppressed by the government. But a result of their appearance was to refresh the stale atmosphere of the old humorous papers and give birth to a humorous paper of a somewhat more literary type—the *Satyricon*. This paper flourished from 1906 to 1917 and harbored a whole school of humorists. Of these writers of short stories, the most noteworthy are Téffy (pseudonym of Mme N. A. Buchínsky, sister of the poetess Lókhvitsky) and Arkády Avérchenko. Téffy combines the good old traditions of Russian literary humor. Her humor is delicate and founded on the careful choice of suggestive detail. There is nothing crude or coarse in her; she is a disciple of Chékhov. Avérchenko, on the other hand, is a pupil of the Anglo-American school of comic writing. His stories are full of crude buffoonery and extravagantly funny situations. He is as international and plebeian as Téffy is refined and Russian.

The *Satyricon* also had its poets, of whom the most celebrated is Sásha Chërny (pseudonym of A. Glíkberg). He wrote very creditable satirical verse and was the only unpoetical poet of any worth during the rule of symbolism. His example had a certain effect on the development of Mayakóvsky, who was also for a short time (1915–16) a contributor to the *Satyricon*.

Another notable humorist was the feuilletonist of the *Nóvoye vrémya*, Yúry Belyáyev. His style is a somewhat affected mixture of sentimental poetry and whimsical humor. His sentimentally comic vaudevilles of old Petersburg had a considerable success. His best-known book is *The Misses Schneider* (1912), the scandalous and pathetic story of two young girls, of a respectable family, gone wrong.

CHAPTER 4

The New Movements of the Nineties

I N SPITE of the great difference between the two parties of intelligentsia radicalism—the old populists and the new Marxists—they had in common certain immovable tenets, among which were agnosticism and the subordination of all human values to the ends of social progress and political revolution. Among the conservative and Slavophil sections of the educated classes, the supremacy of political and social over all other values was also the rule, and Christian orthodoxy was valued as a justification of political theories rather than for its own sake. Between atheism and progress, on the one hand, and religion and political reaction, on the other, the alliance was complete. To dissolve these alliances, and to undermine the supremacy of political over cultural and individual values, was the task of the generation of intellectuals who came of age in the last decade of the nineteenth century. The first of these two developments culminated in the theories of the Christian liberals who edited the *Landmarks* (1909) and in the various forms of mystical revolutionism of Merezhkóvsky to the socialist messianism of Ivánov-Razúmnik. All these movements, however, retain the other salient feature of the old intelligentsia-ism: they tend to identify (perhaps a little less crudely than their predecessors) moral good with public utility, with a marked predominance of the latter over the former.

But simultaneously with the growth of this new "civic" idealism, a more subversive attack was launched against the very foundations of radical intelligentsia-ism and of civic morality. Æstheticism substituted beauty for duty, and individualism emancipated the individual from all social obligations. The two tendencies, which went hand in hand, proved a great civilizing force and changed the whole face of Russian civilization between 1900 and 1910, bringing about the great renascence of Russian art and poetry that marked that decade. In literature the principal creative expression of the new movement is the poetry of the symbolists, but before we come to them, it is necessary to give an account of the new movements outside the domain of strictly imaginative literature.

The various currents of thought that combined to change the face of Russian culture and to overthrow the exclusive rule of the old intelligentsia outlook have so little in common that no general definition is possible, unless it be some anodyne and inexpressive adjective, such as "modern" or "new." Yet it is evident that they belong to one historical stratum, and that together they form one movement of revolt against the agnostic idealism of the old intelligentsia, and of intellectual and cultural expansion. Perhaps the Marxists are not far from the truth in their explanation of the facts; the new movements, according to them, were the symptoms of a social transformation, of the birth of a bourgeoisie, of an educated class with a place in civilized life.

What distinguishes these writers from the other literary groups of the time, from the Marxists, for instance, and from the Górky-Andréyev "school," is a distinctly superior cultural level. The Marxists and the Górky-Andréyev realists, however great may have been their personal (for instance, Górky's) superiority to the average man and even to the superior man, remained on the *cultural* level of the average Russian *"intelligént"* of about 1890. The æsthetes, the mystics, and the religious philosophers, whatever their personal value, worked for the enrichment and greater complexity of Russian culture. At the risk of scaring some of my prospective American readers from the whole lot of them, I will sum it up in one word by saying that they were all "high-brows."

In accordance with the general plan of this book, I am not going to give any detailed analysis of their *ideas*, but shall treat their work as literature. Consequently I shall give most of this chapter to men who are either, like Rózanov and Shestóv, not only great thinkers, but also great writers, or, like Merezhkóvsky, who, though intrinsically belonging to the second order, played a principal part in the literary evolution of the times. On the contrary, a writer like Berdyáyev, who deserves a prominent place in the history of Russian thought, will receive little more than a brief notice.

The "sources" of the new movements are as various as their currents. They are partly of Russian and partly of foreign origin. Of Russian writers, the greatest influence was exercised by Dostoyévsky—in both his aspects, as Christian and individualist—and by Soloviëv. Of foreign influences, the greatest was that of Nietzsche. The name of Nietzsche might well open the chapter, for the first symptom of a new movement to be noticed by the press and public was the appearance of Nietzscheism. Afterward Nietzscheism took all the forms possible in Russian literature, from the zoological immoralism of *Sánin* to the mythopoetic theories of Vyacheslav Ivánov. In the beginning, Nietzsche was first of all a powerful emancipator from the fetters of "civic duty." In this aspect he appears for the first time in *By the Light of Conscience*, by Mínsky (1890). Mínsky, who has already been mentioned in a preceding chapter as a "civic" poet, was regarded in the nineties as a principal leader of the new movement together with Volýnsky and Merezhkóvsky. But his work is intrinsically insignificant and demands little attention. Not much more remarkable is A. Volýnsky (pseudonym of A. L. Flékser), a critic who attacked the accepted radical authority in the name of a rather vague philosophical idealism. This required courage, and Volýnsky got some severe blows in the fight. Mikhaylóvsky proposed to "expel him from literature," and for many years he was under the boycott of the "civic" press. So, though his work is unimportant, he must be gratefully remembered as a "martyr" in the cause of emancipation. But the principal work of emancipation centered in Diághilev and his magazine *Mir iskússtva* and Merezhkóvsky.

THE ÆSTHETIC REVIVAL

The æsthetic revival is one of the most important aspects of the great revolt. In poetry it became one of the constituent elements of the symbolist movement, but its purest expression is found in art—especially in painting—and in art criticism. Appreciation of art and beauty was not, of course, an entirely new thing in Russian society. In the early days of intelligentsia radicalism, when it had not yet severed the ties that attached it to German idealism and

French romanticism, the good, the true, and the beautiful had been an inseparable trinity. By the end of the century this trinity was still dragging on a precarious and hectic existence, and we have seen that the eighties had witnessed a sort of half-hearted and timid revival of artistic values. But, after all, beauty was always the Cinderella of the family and was strictly subjected to her two elder sisters, nowhere more severely than in the idealist philosophy of Soloviëv. Taste was deplorably low and narrow. There was among the intelligentsia no active feeling for form, no artistic culture. There was a small number of æsthetically civilized people, but these were hopelessly conservative. They were watertight to every novel impression and capable only of chewing the old cud of idealist æstheticism.

The æsthetic pioneers of the nineties, on the contrary, were both genuinely cultured and frankly Revolutionary. They had two tasks to fulfill—to re-establish a direct contact with old art, and to promote and encourage *modern* art. In literature these tasks fell to the lot of the symbolists—in the plastic arts, to that of the brilliant group of painters and connoisseurs who are now known by the name of *Mir-iskússtva* men. *Mir iskússtva* (*The World of Art*), an art periodical founded in 1898 by Sergéy Pávlovich Diághilev (Dyágilev), became for several years the center of the new movement. It was devoted primarily to art, to the revival of Russian eighteenth-century painting and architecture, to the propaganda of modern French painting, to the popularizing of such Russian artists as Vrúbel, Sómov, Levitán, Sérov. But it also generously opened its columns to such independent critics as Rózanov and Shestóv. Until the symbolists founded their own organ in 1904, *Mir iskússtva* was not merely the only art magazine in Russia, but also the only literary magazine of the new movement. The civilizing work of Diághilev and his friends cannot be overestimated. We may have lost all taste for such a favorite of theirs as Aubrey Beardsley, but it is only owing to them and their successors that we have rediscovered our own pre-naturalist painters, classical architects, and our wonderful pre-Petrine art. It is owing to them that Russians know anything at all about the history of art and are capable of seeing anything in Florence or in Venice, in Velázquez or in Poussin. In 1890, the sole function of art in Russia was to "express ideas"; in 1915, Russian society was æsthetically one of the most cultivated and experienced in Europe.

Of the men to whom we owe all this, the principal names are, besides that of Diághilev himself, Alexander Benois, Ígor Grabár, and P. P. Murátov. Grabár, who organized the rediscovery of Russian art, is not important as a writer; Murátov, who belongs to a younger generation, quite apart from his importance in the revival of artistic culture, is one of the most brilliant essayists of modern Russian literature.

Alexander Nikoláyevich Benois (in Russian, Benuá) was born in Petersburg of a family of French extraction that has produced several artists of note. He is himself one of the most gifted and exquisite painters of the *Mir iskússtva* school, and his place of birth and his extraction are abundantly reflected in his writings. He is the greatest European of modern Russia, the best expression of the Western and Latin spirit. He was also the principal influence in reviving the cult of the northern metropolis and in rediscovering its architectural beauty, so long concealed by generations of artistic barbarity. His knowledge of Western art was enormous. He was saturated with the spirit of the seventeenth and eighteenth centuries. Long before the famous Florentine Exhibition of seicento painting, he had discovered the neglected charm of the great *barócco* painters of Italy. But he was never blind to Russian art, and in his work, as in that of the *Mir-iskússtva* men in general, Westernism and Slavophilism were more than ever the two heads of a single-hearted Janus. His essays, chiefly dealing with art criticism, reveal a very personal literary temperament. One of the best prose writers of his generation, he admirably adapts his style to the subtleties and refinements of his judgment. It is an easy, colloquial, man-of-the-world prose, equally removed from the pedantry of the scholar and from the slipshodness of the journalist. His principal work is the *History of Painting* (begun in 1911 and, owing to difficulties of printing, left unfinished in 1917); it is a work of more than local importance and deserves to be translated into every civilized language. For it combines the charm of a personal and eminently readable manner with an extraordinary wealth of first-hand information and acute critical judgment. Benois is not only a painter and an art critic—he is also an important figure in the history of the Russian stage as the author of several ballets, for which he both painted the decorations and wrote the scenarios. The most important of these is *Petrouchka*, the music of which, by Stravínsky, has made it widely known. The idea belongs to Benois, and once more he revealed in it his great love for his native town of Petersburg in all its aspects, classical and popular.

MEREZHKÓVSKY

The principal figure of the "modern" movement in literature during its first stages was Dmítry Sergéyevich Merezhkóvsky (1865–1941). Born in Petersburg, he studied at the University and began his literary career very early. As early as 1883, verse over his signature began to appear in the liberal magazines, and before long he was universally recognized as the most promising of the younger "civic" poets. When Nádson died (1887), Merezhkóvsky became his lawful successor. His early verse (collected in book form in 1888) is not strikingly above the level of its day, which was a very low one, but it shows a greater carefulness for form and diction; it is tidier and more elegant than that of his contemporaries. His reputation as the most promising poet of the younger generation was further enhanced by his narrative poem *Véra* (1890), written in a style that is the distant descendant of Byron's *Don Juan* but had been sentimentalized and idealized out of recognition by two generations of Russian poets. It is a story of self-disbelieving love, and it ends on a vaguely religious note. It was admirably adapted to suit the taste of the time and had a greater success than any narrative poem had had for several decades. About the same time Merezhkóvsky married Zinaída Híppius, a young poetess of outstanding talent, who later became one of the principal poets and critics of the symbolist movement.

New ideas were in the air, and the first indication had appeared in 1890 in the shape of Mínsky's "Nietzschean" book *By the Light of Conscience*. Merezhkóvsky soon followed suit and abandoned the colors of civic idealism. In 1893 he published a collection of essays, *On the Causes of the Present Decline and the New Currents of Contemporary Russian Literature*, and a book of poems under the aggressive and modern title *Symbols*. Together with his wife, with Mínsky, and with Volýnsky, he became one of the staff of the *Northern Messenger*, which came forth as the champion of "new ideas." These "new ideas" were on the whole a rather vague revolt against the positivism and utilitarianism of orthodox radi-

calism. In *Symbols* and *On the Causes*, Merezhkóvsky is as vague
as Volýnsky, but soon his "new ideas" began to take definite shape
and to form themselves into a religion of Greek antiquity. Henceforward he developed that taste for antithetic thinking which
finished by ruining both himself and his style. This antithetic
tendency found its first striking expression in his conception of
Christ and Antichrist, a trilogy of historical novels, the first of
which, *Julian the Apostate*, or *The Death of the Gods*, appeared in
1896. It was followed in 1901 by *Leonardo da Vinci*, or *The Gods
Resurrected*, and in 1905 by *Peter and Alexis*. The last of these belongs to already another period of Merezhkóvsky's evolution, but
the first two are characteristic of that stage of his activity which
was parallel to the Westernizing action of Diághilev and Benois.
Julian and *Leonardo* are animated by a pagan "Hellenic" feeling,
and the same spirit animates all he wrote between 1894 and 1900.
This includes a series of *Italian Novellas;* translations of *Daphnis
and Chloë* and the Greek tragic poets; and *Eternal Companions*
(1896), a collection of essays on the Acropolis, *Daphnis and Chloë*,
Marcus Aurelius, Montaigne, Flaubert, Ibsen, and Púshkin. All
these writings are centered in one idea—the "polar" opposition of
the Greek conception of the sanctity of the flesh, and of the Christian conception of the sanctity of the spirit, and the necessity of
uniting them in one supreme synthesis. This central antithesis dominates a number of minor antitheses (such as the Nietzschean antithesis of Apollo and Dionysos), so that the general impression of
his work as a whole is one of significant contrasts and relations. The
identity of opposites and the synthesis of contrasts dominate all
this world of interconnected poles. Every idea is a "pole," an
"abyss" and a "mystery." "Mystery," "polar," and "synthesis"
are his favorite words. Οὐρανὸς ἄνω, οὐρανὸς κάτω is his favorite
maxim, and its symbol the starry sky reflected in the sea. This
new world of his, with its mysterious connecting strings and
mutually reflected poles, attracted the tastes of a public that had
been for generations fed on the small beer of idealistically colored
positivism. Merezhkóvsky's popularity became very great among
the advanced and the young, and for about a decade he was the
central figure of the whole "modern" movement. At present all
this symbolism seems to us rather puerile and shallow, lacking in
those qualities which make the work of the genuine symbolists
more than a mere checkerboard of interesting straight lines. He

has neither the subtlety and saturated culturedness of Ivánov, nor
the intense personal earnestness of Blok, nor the immaterial Ariel-
like quality of Bély. His style also lacks charm. Even more obviously than his philosophy, Merezhkóvsky's prose is nothing more
than a network of mechanical antitheses. But in spite of this, all
his work is historically important and was for its time beneficent.
It introduced to the Russian reader a whole unknown world of
cultural values; it made familiar and significant to him figures and
epochs that had been only names in textbooks; it gave a life to
objects and buildings, to all the material side of bygone civilizations, which is loaded with such portentous symbolism in Merezhkóvsky's novels. This shallow symbolism is dead, but it has done
good educational service. After Merezhkóvsky, Florence and
Athens became something more than mere names to the Russian
intellectual, and if they are now living entities he owes it very
largely to the sophistications of *Julian* and *Leonardo*.

In 1901 Merezhkóvsky began publishing (in monthly instalments in *Mir iskússtva*) his most important work, *Tolstóy and
Dostoyévsky*. The first two of its three parts—*Life*, *Writings*, and
Religion—are the most intelligent and readable thing he ever
wrote. His interpretation of the personalities of Tolstóy and
Dostoyévsky dominated Russian literature for many years. Like
all his conceptions, it is a more or less cleverly constructed antithesis, which is developed in the most thoroughgoing way to explain and bring into order the minutest details of the life, work, and
religion of the two great writers. Tolstóy, in Merezhkóvsky's interpretation, is the great pagan and pantheist, the "seer of the
flesh" (*taynovídets plóti*)—a half truth there was some merit in
discovering in 1900. Dostoyévsky is the great Christian, "the seer
of the spirit" (*taynovídets dúkha*)—another half truth it was less
difficult to discover. The book may still be read with interest and
profit, but the simple-minded reader who is uninitiated into the
mazes of Merezhkóvsky's mentality will either be repelled by its
geometrical seesaw of contrasts or fall too easily into the carefully
woven nets of his sophistry. *Tolstóy and Dostoyévsky* marks the
transition of Merezhkóvsky from West to East—from Europe to
Russia, from the Greek to the Christian ideal. The "great pagan"
Tolstóy is consistently belittled before the "great Christian"
Dostoyévsky, and the messianic mission of Russia is everywhere

emphasized. *Peter and Alexis* (the third part of *Christ and Antichrist*), written immediately after *Tolstóy and Dostoyévsky* and published in 1905, is a further vindication of the "Russian" and "Christian" cause against the Western and pagan spirit of "Antichrist" embodied in Peter the Great.

In 1903 "the Merezhkóvskys" (a term that includes, besides him and his wife, their friend D. V. Filosófov) became the center of the "religious-philosophical" movement. They founded the excellent monthly review *Nóvy put* (*The New Way*), which opened its columns to the symbolists and to all the new movements (Blok and Bély made their first appearance in it), and they became the soul of the "religious-philosophical meetings," the primary aim of which was to bring together the cultured part of the Orthodox clergy and the religious part of the intelligentsia. These meetings attracted great interest and considerable attendance. Questions of the greatest religious and philosophical importance were discussed there, and they contributed greatly to that change of atmosphere in Russian intellectual life which is the subject of the present chapter.

At this time the Merezhkóvskys were at the height of their Slavophilism and Orthodoxy—for a moment even inclined towards a religious acceptance of autocracy. But the current of Revolution carried them to the left, and in 1905 they took a definitely Revolutionary attitude. After the failure of the Revolution they emigrated to Paris, where they published in French a violent collection of pamphlets, *Le Tzar et la Révolution.*

Merezhkóvsky's importance began to decline. His accession to Revolutionary doctrines did not give him much influence among the Revolutionaries—and Russian radicalism, even in so far as it has become mystical, has been little affected by his verbal constructions. One of the few men who came under the influence of the Merezhkóvskys was the terrorist Sávinkov, in whose sensational "confession," *The Pale Horse*, unmistakable traces were discerned, not of Merezhkóvsky's, but of Mme Merezhkóvsky's influence.

In 1914 the Merezhkóvskys, together with the majority of Russian radicals, adopted an anti-war attitude, but did not join the extreme *défaitistes*, and in 1917 assumed an attitude of decided opposition to Lénin and Bolshevism. After the Bolshevík *coup d'état* they still continued to lay all their hopes on the Constituent Assembly, and only after the dispersion of that assembly did they lose all hope in the triumph of "religious" Revolution. During 1918 and 1919 they lived in Petersburg, where Mme Merezhkóvsky published a book of violently anti-Bolshevík verse (those were days of lenient or inefficient censorship) and wrote her *Petersburg Diary.* Towards the end of 1919 the Merezhkóvskys succeeded in escaping from Soviet Russia and came at first to Warsaw, where they joined hands with Sávinkov and supported that notorious adventurer in his policy of fighting the Bolshevíks in alliance with Poland. However, they soon were disgusted with the treacherous duplicity of the Poles and retired to Paris, where they published *The Reign of Antichrist,* one of the most violent (and hysterical) books written against Bolshevism. There Merezhkóvsky devoted himself to Egyptian studies and, besides a series of "aphorisms," wrote a novel of Egyptian life, *The Birth of the Gods, or Tutankh-amen in Crete,* all of which are even more unreadable than his previous writings.

There is no need to deal in any detail with Merezhkóvsky's numerous books of "philosophical" prose published after *Tolstóy and Dostoyévsky* (*Gógol and the Devil, The Prophet of the Russian Revolution, Not Peace but a Sword, Sick Russia,* essays on Lérmontov, on Tyútchev and Nekrásov, and so on). In them he retains, and even exaggerates, the fundamental characteristic of his style— an immoderate love of antithesis. But whereas his early works are written in a reasonable and "tidy" manner, from about 1905 he developed a sort of verbal hysteria that has made all he wrote after that date utterly unreadable. Every one of his books and essays is a seesaw of mechanical antithesis sustained from beginning to end in the shrillest of hysterical falsettos. This style developed when he grew conscious of himself as a great philosopher and prophet, and its appearance is roughly simultaneous with the time his teaching took its final form. This teaching styles itself Third Testament Christianity. It insists on the imminence of a new revelation and on the approach of a new religious era. But his mysticism is not concretely personal like Soloviëv's; it represents the universe as a system of variously interconnected ideas reflected in individual and material symbols. His Christ is an abstraction, not a person. His religion is not based on personal religious experience, but on the speculations of his symmetry-loving brain. Judged by religious standards, his writings are mere literature. Judged by literary standards, they are bad literature.

Merezhkóvsky's fame outside Russia is mainly based on his novels. The first of these, *The Death of the Gods (Julian the Apostate*, 1896), is also the best. Not that it is in any sense a great novel, or even a novel at all in any true sense of the word. It is entirely lacking in creative power. But it is a good work of popularization, an excellent "home university" book that has probably interested more Russian readers in antiquity than any other single book ever did. The same may be said of *Leonardo da Vinci*, but this time with some reservation. In *Julian* the material is kept in hand and the "encyclopædia" side is not allowed to grow beyond all measure; *Leonardo* is already in danger of being stifled by quotations from sources and by the historical bric-a-brac, which is there only because Merezhkóvsky happens to know it. Besides, both these novels are disfigured by the artificiality of the ideas that preside over them, which are of his ordinary crudely antithetic kind. Both *Julian* and *Leonardo* are inferior to Bryúsov's *Fire Angel*. Merezhkóvsky's novels on Russian subjects (*Peter and Alexis, Alexander I, December the Fourteenth*), as well as his plays *Paul I* and *The Romanticists*, are on a much lower level of literary merit. They are formless masses of raw (sometimes badly understood, always wrongly interpreted) material, written from beginning to end in an intolerable hysterical falsetto, and saturated *ad nauseam* with his artificial, homuncular "religious" ideas. Merezhkóvsky is a victim of ideas. If he had never tried to have any ideas, he might have developed into a good novelist for boys, for even in his worst and latest novels, there is always a page or two that reveals him as a creditable and vivid describer of events. Thus, in the dreary *December the Fourteenth*, the scene in which a mutinous battalion of the guards rush down the street with bayonets lowered, its officers brandishing their swords, breathless with running and Revolutionary excitement, might have been quite in its place in a less sophisticated narrative.

To sum up, Merezhkóvsky's place in literary history is very considerable, for he was the representative man of a very important movement for more than a decade (1893–1905). But as a writer, he scarcely survives, and the first part of *Tolstóy and Dostoyévsky* remains his only work that will still be read in the next generation.

RÓZANOV

The name of Merezhkóvsky is usually associated with those of Rózanov and Shestóv. But beyond the fact that they were contemporaries, that they also wrote on questions of "religious philosophy," and that some of their most remarkable works take the form of commentaries on Dostoyévsky, there is practically nothing in common between Merezhkóvsky and these two writers. Though neither Rózanov nor Shestóv ever played such a central part in the literary movement as Merezhkóvsky did, they are much more important figures in the history of Russian literature, not only for the significance and genuineness of their religious ideas, but also as *writers* of the first order and of exceptional originality.

Vasíly Vasílievich Rózanov (1856–1919) was born in Vetlúga and he spent most of his early life in the capital of that province. He came of a poor middle-class family and received the usual middle-class education at a gymnasium, whence he went to the University of Moscow to study history. He was for many years a teacher of history and geography in various provincial secondary schools, but he never took any interest in his subjects and he had no pedagogic vocation. About 1880 he married Apollinária Súslov, a woman of about forty, who had been, in her youth, in intimate relations with Dostoyévsky. The marriage proved singularly unhappy. Apollinária was a cold and proud, "infernal" woman, with unknown depths of cruelty and sensuality, which seem to have been a revelation to Dostoyévsky (it was immediately after his journey with her that he wrote *Memoirs from Underground*). She lived with Rózanov some three years and then left him for another. They retained for each other a lifelong hatred. Apollinária refused to grant him a divorce. Several years after the rupture, Rózanov met, in Élets, Varvára Rúdnev, who became his unofficial wife. He could not marry her because of his first wife's intractability, and this largely explains his bitterness in all his writings on the question of divorce. This second, "unofficial" marriage was as happy as his first was unhappy.

In 1886 Rózanov published a book *On Understanding*, which he later described as "a continuous polemic against the University of Moscow," that is, against positivism and official agnosticism. It had no success, but it attracted the attention of Strákhov, who began a correspondence with Rózanov, introduced him into the conservative literary press, and finally arranged him an official appointment in Petersburg. This, however, did not much help Rózanov, and he remained in very straitened circumstances until the time he was invited by Suvórin (1899) to write for the *Nóvoye vrémya*, the only conservative paper that could pay its contributors well. Rózanov's early writings lack the wonderful originality of his developed style, but some of them are of great importance. Foremost among them is *The Legend of the Grand Inquisitor* (1890), a commentary on the episode in *The Brothers Karamázov*. It is the first of that long succession of Dostoyevskian commentaries (continued by Shestóv and Merezhkóvsky) which form such an important feature of modern Russian literature. It was the first attempt to delve deep into the mind of Dostoyévsky and to discover the mainsprings of his individuality. The fact that Rózanov, through his first wife, had "first-hand" knowledge of certain hidden aspects of Dostoyévsky is of particular importance. It is interesting in this connection to note that Rózanov lays great stress on the *Memoirs from Underground* as the central point in the work of Dostoyévsky. He feels with wonderful acuteness, as no one before him had done, Dostoyévsky's passionate and morbid striving towards absolute freedom, including the freedom of not desiring happiness. Among other things, the book contains a wonderful chapter on Gógol; Rózanov was the first to discover a thing that today seems a truism—that Gógol was not a realist and that Russian literature in its entirety is not a continuation but a reaction against Gógol. *The Legend* would suffice to make Rózanov a great writer, but the mature Rózanov has other qualities of a still higher order.

In the nineties Rózanov lived in Petersburg, in active intellectual intercourse with a few men who could lend him an understanding ear. This circle included all there was of independent conservative thought in Russia. It included I. F. Románov, who wrote under the pseudonym of Rtsy, and Fëdor Shperk, a philosopher who died young and whom Rózanov always recognized as the greatest man of genius he ever met. Shperk and Rtsy, according to Rózanov's own opinion, had an important influence on the formation of his style. Towards the end of the nineties Rózanov came into contact with the modernists, but though they gave him more unstinted recognition than any other party, he never became very intimate with them. In his writings Rózanov always had one curious defect, especially when he wrote on subjects that did not very deeply affect him—a certain lack of inhibition that made him go to lengths of paradox he did not seriously mean and that exasperated the more conventional. This cost him a biting and witty attack from Soloviëv, who nicknamed him Porfíry Golovlëv—the name of the hypocrite in Saltykóv's *Golovlëv Family*, who had the same lack of inhibition in his interminable and nauseously unctuous speeches. Another disagreeable incident for Rózanov was Mikhaylóvsky's proposal to "expel him from literature" for an insufficiently respectful article on Tolstóy.

In 1899 Rózanov became a permanent contributor to the *Nóvoye vrémya*, and this at last gave him a comfortable income. Suvórin gave him a free hand to write whatever he liked and as often as he liked, so long as he was brief and did not take up too much space in one number. This freedom and this obligation were largely active in developing Rózanov's peculiar fragmentary and seemingly formless mode of expression. About this time Rózanov's interest became concentrated on questions of marriage, divorce, and family life. He waged a determined campaign against the abnormal state of family life in Russia and in Christendom in general. He saw in the existence of illegitimate children the shame of Christianity. A child, he thought, should become legitimate by its very birth. He also dwelt with bitterness on the abnormal state of things conditioned by the difficulty of obtaining a divorce.[1] All this criticism converges in an attack on Christianity as an essentially ascetic religion that in its heart considers every sexual relation an abomination and only halfheartedly gives its blessing to marriages. At the same time he was irresistibly attracted by it, and especially by what he called its "dark rays"—those less apparent but really more fundamental features without which Christianity is not itself. The essential thing in Christianity, according to Rózanov, is sadness and tears, a concentration on death and "after death," and a renunciation of the world. A merry Christian, he said, was a contradiction in terms. To the religion of Christ he opposed the religion of God the Father, which he thought was the natural religion, the religion of growth and generation. This primitive naturalistic religion he found in the Old Testament, in the

---

[1] His writings on the question were collected in *The Family Problem in Russia* (two volumes, 1903).

sexual piety of mediæval Judaism, and in the religion of the
ancient Egyptians. His ideas on the philosophy of Christianity and
of his own "natural" (in fact phallic) religion are contained in a
series of books—*In the Realm of Riddle and Mystery* (two volumes,
1901), *In the Shade of Church Walls* (1906), *The Russian Church*
(1906), *The Dark Face* (*A Metaphysic of Christianity*, 1911), and
Moonlight Men (1913). His meditations on Egyptian religion appeared as a series of pamphlets during the last years of his life
(*From Oriental Motives*). In politics Rózanov remained a conservative. And though at bottom he was completely non-political, there
were reasons for his being so. As a profoundly mystical and religious mind, he was repulsed by the agnosticism of the radicals.
As an exceptionally independent thinker, he hated their obligatory
sameness. As an immoralist, he despised their drab moral respectability. He was also a born Slavophil—mankind existed for him
only in so far as it was Russian (or Jewish, but his attitude to the
Jews was ambiguous)—and the cosmopolitanism of the intelligentsia revolted him as much as did their agnosticism. Besides, for
many years anything like recognition and support came to him
only from the right—from Strákhov, and from Suvórin, afterwards
from the decadents. The radicals ceased to consider him a despicable reactionary only after 1905. The events of 1905, however,
somewhat disconcerted Rózanov, and for a time he was attracted
by the Revolution, most of all by the buoyant youth of its young
people. He even wrote a book (*When the Authorities Were Away*)
full of praise of the Revolutionary movement. At the same time,
however, he continued writing in his usual conservative spirit. At
one time he wrote conservative articles in the *Nóvoye vrémya* over
his full name, and radical articles in the progressive *Rússkoye
slóvo* over the pseudonym V. Varvárin. He did not regard this
inconsistency as anything outrageous. Politics were to him a very
minor business that could not be brought *sub speciem æternitatis.*
What interested him in both parties was only the various individualities that went to form them—their "taste," their "flavor,"
their "atmosphere." This point of view was not shared by the
majority of the republic of letters, and Rózanov was charged with
moral insanity by Peter Strúve and again threatened with boycott.

   Meanwhile the genius of Rózanov had reached its full maturity and found its characteristic form of expression. In 1912
Solitary Thoughts, Printed Almost Privately (*Uyedinënnoye, pochtí*

na pravákh rúkopisi) appeared. The book is described in the British
Museum catalogue as consisting of "maxims and short essays."
But these terms give no idea of the extraordinary originality of its
form. The little fragments ring with the sound of a live voice, for
they are constructed, not along the lines of conventional grammar,
but with the freedom and variety of intonation of living speech;
the voice often falls to a hardly audible, interrupted whisper. But
at times in its unconventional and unfettered freedom it attains
real eloquence and a powerful emotional rhythm. This book was
followed by *Fallen Leaves* (1913) and *Fallen Leaves, a Second
Basketful* (1915), which are a continuation of the same manner.
The capricious and, as he called it, "anti-Gutenberg" nature of
Rózanov finds a curious expression in the fact that, apart from
these books, his most remarkable utterances are to be found where
one would least expect them—for instance, in footnotes to other
people's letters. Thus, one of his greatest books is his edition of
Strákhov's letters (*Literary Exiles*, 1913) to himself; the footnotes
contain passages of unsurpassed genius and originality.

The Revolution of 1917 was a cruel blow to Rózanov. At first
he felt the passing enthusiasm he had felt in 1905, but soon he fell
into a state of nervous anxiety that lasted till his death. He left
Petersburg and settled at the Trinity Monastery near Moscow. He
continued writing, but under the new conditions he could make no
money out of his books. His last work, *The Apocalypse of the Russian Revolution*, appeared in little pamphlets in a very small number of copies and has become extremely rare.

His last two years were spent in poverty and misery. On his
deathbed he became finally reconciled with Christ, and he died
comforted by the sacraments. So his words (in *Fallen Leaves*) came
true: "But of course when I die I shall die *in the Church*, of course
I need the Church *incomparably more than I do literature* (don't
need that at all), and *our clergy, after all, are dearer to me than all*
[classes]."

The principal thing in Rózanov was his naturalistic religion
of sex and procreation. It was primarily a religion of marriage and
the family. It was strictly monogamous, and the child's part in it
is at least as great as the wife's. Rózanov was saturated with a
profound piety for the associations of the Russian Church—with
its services, its holy images, its poetry, and its clergy. He had an
infinitely sympathetic insight into the very essence of Christianity

and of its essentially ascetic and puritan ideal. But at the bottom of his heart was a religion that included both Christianity and natural religion. It was the primary element of religion—the feeling of a common life with the universe—a *religio*, a *pietas*. Christianity attracted him as a religion and at the same time repelled him as the enemy of another religion—the religion of life. What is particularly original in Rózanov, and what makes him so much akin to Dostoyévsky, is his peculiar attitude to morality. He was a profound immoralist, and at the same time he valued above all things sympathy, pity, and kindness. Moral good existed for him only in the form of natural, spontaneous, indestructible *kindness*. He had no use for systems, as he had no use for logic. He was altogether intuitive, and for depth of intuition he has no equals among the writers of the world, not even Dostoyévsky. This gift is displayed in every page of his writings, but most of all where he speaks of religion and of living personalities. The human personality was to him a supreme value—the only thing on a level with religion—and the pages he devotes to the characters of living persons are inimitable. As fair examples of his intuition and style, I may mention two passages (they are too long to quote): the last three pages of *A World of Things Indistinct and Undecided*, where he speaks of the difference in the Church's attitude to the six New Testament sacraments and the only old sacrament—marriage; and the passage on Vladímir Soloviëv (from the point of view of style, one of the greatest achievements in Russian prose since Avvakúm), characteristically contained in a footnote to one of Strákhov's letters.

Rózanov's style is, more than any other style, untranslatable. In it, the *intonation* is what matters. He uses various typographical devices to bring it out—quotation marks and brackets—but the effect is lost in another language: so rich is it in emotional shades and overtones, so saturated with the spirit of Russia, and so peculiarly Russian are the intonations. Nor is it, perhaps, after all very desirable (from the Russian patriot's point of view) to make propaganda for him among foreigners. There are people who hate—actively hate—Rózanov and who think him abominable and disgusting. Strictly Orthodox priests are united in this feeling with men of a very different orthodoxy, like Trótsky. Rózanov is the antipode of classicism, of discipline, of everything that is line and will. His genius is feminine—it is naked intuition without a trace of "architecture" in it. It is the apotheosis of "natural man," the negation of effort and of discipline. André Suarès has said of Dostoyévsky that he presented "the scandal of nakedness," but Dostoyévsky is quite decently draped in comparison with Rózanov. And the nakedness of Rózanov is not always beautiful. For all that, Rózanov was the greatest writer of his generation. The Russian genius cannot be gauged without taking him into account, and whatever way they turn out, we must take the responsibility for our great men.

SHESTÓV

Shestóv (1866–1938) has some points in common with Rózanov. Both are irrationalists and immoralists. Both value the human personality above all ideas and systems. Both found their starting point in Dostoyévsky, and later on a kindred spirit in the Old Testament. Both are mystics—but Rózanov is a biological mystic, a mystic of the flesh. Shestóv is a pure spiritualist. Rózanov is an irrationalist in practice as well as in theory: he is no logician, and the only arguments he is capable of are emotional and "intuitive" arguments. Shestóv fights reason with her own arms—in his confutation of logic he proves himself a consummate logician. Rózanov is deeply rooted in the Russian and "Slavophil" soil, and even in Judaism, what attracts him is its soil, its procreative roots. Shestóv has no roots in any soil: his thought is international, or rather supranational, and in this respect more akin to Tolstóy than to Dostoyévsky. The real name of Leo Shestóv is Leo Isaákovich Schwartzmann. He was born in Kíev of a family of wealthy Jewish merchants, studied for the bar, and was attracted to philosophy and literature only rather late in life. In his first book, *Shakspere and His Critic Brandes* (1898), he attacked the positivism and rationalism of the greatly overrated Danish critic in the name of a rather vague idealism that found its hero in the character of Brutus. The book reveals some of Shestóv's best literary qualities, but it stands apart from his later work in its attitude to idealism. For war against idealism in all its forms is the principal object of all Shestóv's later books, beginning with *The Good in the Teaching of Tolstóy and of Nietzsche* (1900) and *Dostoyévsky and Nietzsche: The Philosophy of Tragedy* (1901). These two books form the introduction to Shestóv's work and contain the whole force of his destructive criticism. They were followed by a book of fragmentary maxims, *The Apotheosis of Soillessness* (English translation: *All Things Are Possible*, 1905), and by a series of essays on individual writers (Ibsen, Chékhov, Berdyáyev). Then for many years Shestóv was silent; he lived abroad, studying the history of philosophy and mysticism. His next work, *Potestas Clavium* (1916), ushers in a new stage of his work in which, without in any way changing the main point of his outlook, he passes from modern individualists to the accepted religious leaders and mystics of the past—Luther, St. Augustine, Plotinus, St. Paul, and the Bible—and discovers in them the same truth he had found in Nietzsche and Dostoyévsky. In 1917 Shestóv (to the great disappointment of some of his admirers, who thought that his destructive spirit would sympathize with the destructive work of the Bolshevíks) assumed a distinctly anti-Bolshevík position. He left Russia and settled in Paris, where he remained until his death. His later work includes studies of Pascal, Kierkegaard, and Leóntiev.

Shestóv is a man of one idea, and in all his books he says the same thing over and over again. The keynote of all his writings is found in the closing lines of *Tolstóy and Nietzsche:* "Good—we now know it from the experience of Nietzsche—is not God. 'Woe to those who live and know no love better than pity.' Nietzsche has shown us the way. We must seek for that which is *above* pity, *above* Good. We must seek for God." The identification of good and reason with God has ever since Socrates been the foundation stone of our civilization. To confute this identification is the object of Shestóv. He opposes to it the religious experience of the great mystics, revealed to him by Nietzsche and Dostoyévsky, and afterwards confirmed by Pascal, by St. Paul, by Plotinus, and in the Old Testament—that God, the supreme and only value, transcends the human standards of morality and logic, and the seeking of this irrational and immoral God is the only thing worth doing. With particular relish Shestóv quotes the most paradoxical and pointed statements of this doctrine which he finds in Tertullian and in Luther and in other authoritative writers, and insists on the identity of experience of all the great mystics and on the essential incompatibility of their "Biblical" mentality with the Greek mentality. To transcend and reject morality and logic is the only

way to approach God. And this is attained only in those moments
of insurmountable crisis—of ultimate tragedy—which make a man
dead to life. Only when he is thus dead does he become alive to the
real reality—God. "The philosophy of tragedy," which reveals to
man the real entity, is the only philosophy Shestóv has anything
to do with. For the idealistic speculations of the accepted masters
of philosophy, from Socrates and the Stoics to Spinoza and Kant,
he has nothing but contempt and sarcasm. To a superficial observer Shestóv has all the appearance of a nihilist and a skeptic.
And this is to a certain extent true, for though the inner kernel of
his philosophy is profoundly religious and pious, it has—and can
have—no practical bearing. The symbolist's mentality is entirely
alien to him—the things of this world are an inferior reality, which
has no relation to the one real reality. They are indifferent, *adi-
aphora*, and religious standards can in no way be brought down to
measure them. Truth, to Shestóv, is a mathematical point of no
dimensions, which can have no action in the external world. The
external world is as it may be and remains unaffected by it. As
soon as Shestóv has to do with the world of ordinary experiences,
with the conduct of men and the facts of history, his religious
immoralism and irrationalism become inapplicable and unnecessary, and he falls back on the most ordinary common sense. It was
from the point of view of common sense that he condemned Bolshevism, not from that of his religion. But it must be granted that
Shestóv's method of writing on philosophical and religious subjects
forged a weapon that is most suitably used in the service of common sense; his style is the best and finest and aptest polemical
style ever used in Russian. Of the many readers of Shestóv, only a
minority are in tune with his central idea; the majority like in him
the great ironist, the master of sarcasm and argument. Though
Socrates and the moralist Tolstóy (as distinguished from Tolstóy
the mystic of *Memoirs of a Madman* and *Master and Man*) are his
worst enemies and have suffered more than anyone else from his
destructive criticism, as a writer and a dialectician he proceeds
from Socrates and Tolstóy more than from anyone else. He uses
the arms of logic and reason with admirable skill to the undoing of
logic and reason. His prose is at the opposite pole to Rózanov's; it
is the tidiest, the most elegant, the most concentrated—in short,
the most classical prose—in the whole of modern Russian literature.

OTHER "RELIGIOUS PHILOSOPHERS"

Whether we consider them as thinkers or as writers, Rózanov and Shestóv are intrinsically the most important figures of the "religious-philosophical" movement of 1900–10. But the main line of development was little affected by their influence. It proceeds from Vladímir Soloviëv. His friends the brothers Troubetzkóy, Prince Serge (1856–1905) and Prince Eugene (1862–1920), continued his tradition of political liberalism that was free from messianic nationalism and rooted in a Catholic Christianity firmly based in philosophical idealism. Eugene Troubetzkóy was a brilliant political pamphleteer, and his writings may be regarded as the "voice of conscience" guiding Russian political life.

The most remarkable "religious philosophers" who tried to Christianize politics were two men who began their career in the nineties as Marxists and, by a gradual evolution, ultimately came to a more or less strict Orthodoxy. These were Sergéy Nikoláyevich Bulgákov (1871–1944) and Nikoláy Alexándrovich Berdyáyev (1874–1948). This evolution from socialism to Orthodoxy and national liberalism is typical of a great number of Russian intellectuals between 1900 and 1910. In its more political aspect it appears in the writings of Peter Strúve. Bulgákov and Berdyáyev belong to the history of ideas rather than to that of literature. They are not powerful literary personalities. They are largely responsible (especially Berdyáyev) for the heavy and pedantic philosophical jargon that is now used by most modern writers on religious and philosophical subjects and that is so different from the examples of Tolstóy, Shestóv, Rózanov, even of Soloviëv.

A more solitary and curious figure is Paul Florénsky. His reputation as a writer and a philosopher is founded on *The Pillar and Foundation of Truth* (1913), which, as the subtitle says, is an *Essay towards an Orthodox Theodicy*. His thought is extraordinarily subtle and sophisticated: he delights in accepting the most unmodern interpretations and fulminates against heresy with the fire of a mediæval schoolman. And yet the moment he gives free rein to his own speculative thought, it becomes apparent that the core of his thought is quite unorthodox. The doctrine of St. Sophia, the feminine hypostasis of the Deity, is dearer to him than the truly orthodox dogmas of the Church. Under the rich splendor of his style, erudition, and dialectic, there is unmistakably apparent a soul full of strife, pride, and boundless spiritual desire. The most memorable passages in his book are those in which he describes the racking torments of doubt, which he identifies with the torments of hell. Florénsky is, after all, an æsthete for whom the orthodox dogma is a beautiful intellectual world, full of adventure and danger. His style is precious and ornate, and the whole book is strangely reminiscent of certain English writings of the seventeenth century, with their precious and ornate diction, their rigid and hard scholasticism, and the constant feeling of unknown forces of intellectual passion burning under the austere and repelling surface.

Though a return to orthodoxy was the ultimate form of the intellectual evolution of the early twentieth century, not all the "seekers after God" reached it. Some of them stopped at various intermediate stages on the march away from agnosticism and positivism. Of these, one of the most significant is Michael Ósipovich Gershenzón (1869–1925), a Jew, whose biographical and historical studies have contributed so much to our acquaintance with the Russian idealists of the thirties and the forties of the nineteenth century. His metaphysics is closely akin to that of the symbolists: it is a mysticism of impersonal forces that he has associated with the dynamic philosophy of Heraclitus the Dark. In his *Wisdom of Púshkin* (1919) he reveals both a wonderfully acute insight into certain details of Pushkinian problems and an equally remarkable lack of sympathy with the essential core of the great poet's personality. Gershenzón was one of those Russian intellectuals who welcomed the Communist Revolution as a great devastating storm that would free the modern soul from the oppressive scales of excessive culture and knowledge, and open the way towards a "naked man on the naked earth." This new Rousseauist nihilism of Gershenzón found a poignantly sincere expression in his part of that remarkable dialogue of letters in which he took part in 1920 with Vyacheslác Ivánov when the two were lying in a nursing home near Moscow.

The *Landmarks* AND AFTER

In 1909 a group of liberal intellectuals published a book entitled *The Landmarks*, containing essays by seven authors. It included, among others, contributions by Bulgákov, Berdyáyev, Gershenzón, and Peter Strúve. The book was an indictment of the whole spirit of the Russian intelligentsia: the intelligentsia was denounced as anti-religious, anti-philosophical, anti-statesmanlike, and anti-national. *The Landmarks* laid the foundation of a new national liberalism that rapidly spread among the more cultured strata of the intelligentsia and contributed a great deal towards the kindling of a patriotic war spirit in 1914 and towards the success of the White Army movement in 1918. The philosophical side of the movement is best reflected in the work of Bulgákov and Berdyáyev; its political aspect found its principal reflection in Peter Strúve, for more than twenty years a central figure in the evolution of the intelligentsia mind. A leader, in the nineties, of "legal" Marxism, and, in 1903–4, of Revolutionary liberalism, he became, after 1905, the head of that section of the liberal intelligentsia which was primarily patriotic and Russian and tended towards an acceptance of the imperialism that had been the tradition of Imperial Russia since Peter the Great, rejecting at the same time the decadent and exclusive nationalism of the successors of Alexander II. After 1917 he became the principal political brain of anti-Bolshevism and the most significant political writer among the *émigrés*. Saturated with a deep feeling and profound understanding of Russian history, he is a most brilliant political writer, and his short articles are sometimes masterpieces of concentrated thought and direct expression. When party feeling grows less acute, he will be recognized as one of the classics of Russian political thought and political literature.

Strúve's influence on political and historical thought has been great. Of the writers who proceed from him, I will mention only Dmítry Vasílievich Bóldyrev, a writer of very great promise who died in 1920 in Siberia in a Bolshevík prison. Those who knew him considered him a man of exceptional moral and spiritual purity. He was a philosopher by training, and his *opus magnum* was to have been a work on psychology. It remained unfinished. As a writer he is remembered almost exclusively for the few articles he published in 1917 in Strúve's *Russian Freedom* and directed against the *défaitisme* of the socialists. In them he reveals a quite exceptional polemical gift and a literary temperament of great originality. His pungent, racy, pointed, and vivid style places him in the very front rank of Russian prose writers.

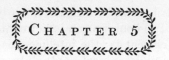

CHAPTER 5

The Symbolists

THE complex and many-sided movement of ideas described in the preceding chapter is closely connected with the movement in imaginative literature known as symbolism. Russian symbolism is part of the general cultural upheaval that changed the face of Russian civilization between 1890 and 1910. It was at once an æsthetic and a mystical movement: it raised the level of poetical craftsmanship, and it was united by a mystical attitude towards the world, which is expressed in the very name of symbolism. The name was, of course, borrowed from the French school of that name, but the importance of French influence must not be exaggerated. Only very few of the Russian symbolists had any considerable first-hand acquaintance with the work of their French godfathers, and Edgar Allan Poe had certainly a wider and deeper influence than any single French poet. But the principal difference between French and Russian symbolism was that while, for the French, symbolism was merely a new form of poetical expression, the Russians made it also a philosophy. They actually saw the universe as a system of symbols. Everything was significant to them, not only by itself, but as the reflection of something else. Baudelaire's famous sonnet *Correspondances* (in which the words *"des forêts de symboles"* occur) was used as the completest expression of this metaphysical attitude, and the line *"les parfums, les couleurs et les sons se répondent"* became a favorite slogan. Another favorite text were two lines from the last scene of *Faust:*

> *Alles Vergängliche*
> *Ist nur ein Gleichnis.*

430

This vision of the world as "a forest of symbols" is an essential feature in the work of every Russian symbolist and gives the whole school a distinctly metaphysical and mystic character. The only difference between the individual poets is the importance they attached to this mystical philosophy; to some, like Bryúsov, symbolism was primarily a form of art, and "the forest of symbols" was only the material of which to build. But others, and among them the most original and characteristic poets of the school— Ivánov, Blok, and Bély—wanted to make symbolism, above all, a metaphysical and mystical philosophy, and poetry subservient to the higher ends of "theurgy." This difference of interpretation became especially acute about 1910 and was one of the causes that led to the dissolution of the unity of the school.

There is much variety in the style of the individual symbolists, but they have also much in common. First of all, they are always intensely serious and solemn. Whatever the subject matter of the Russian symbolist, he always treats it *sub specie æternitatis*. The poet appears before the profane as the priest of an esoteric cult. All his life is ritualized. In Sologúb and in Blok this ritual solemnity is relieved by a keen and bitter feeling of "metaphysical irony," but only in Bély does it give way to a genuine and irrepressible gift of humor. Solemnity produces a partiality for "big" words; "mystery" and "abyss," familiar to us already in Merezhkóvsky, are among the most common in the symbolist vocabulary. Another feature common to all the symbolist poets is the great stress laid on the emotional value of mere sounds. Like Mallarmé, they tried to bring the art of poetry nearer to the twin art of music. In their writings the logical value of words is partly obliterated, and words—especially epithets—are used not so much for their exact meaning as for the emotional value of their form and sound: they cease to be signs, and become, to use the phrase of a Russian critic, "phonetic gestures." This partial subordination of sense to sound, together with the symbolical use of words, which gives every word and image so many meanings, combined to produce the general impression of obscurity that for a long time the general public considered the inevitable characteristic of "decadent" poetry.

In its initial stages symbolism was distinctly Western, for its principal task of raising the standards of poetical workmanship and of introducing new forms of poetical expression was most easily achieved by learning from foreign example. This "foreign" strain forever remained one of the constituent elements of symbolism, but it had also a "Slavophil" soul. And the general trend of its evolution was from foreign models back to national tradition. Dostoyévsky was a principal influence in this evolution: the symbolists had a full share in the general Dostoyevskianism of the time. Almost every symbolist was more or less powerfully affected by the individualism and tragic conception of life of the great novelist. But, apart from this, the symbolists played the same part in the "rediscovery" and revaluation of Russian literature as Diághilev and Benois in that of Russian art. They revived the work of many forgotten—or half-forgotten—or undervalued writers, but they also introduced fresh blood into the understanding of the national classics. They freed them from the accumulated varnish of textbook criticism and intelligentsia commonplace, and though they sometimes obscured them by the lacquer of their own mystical interpretation, they did splendid work in presenting the past of Russian literature in a new and fresh aspect.

Apart from everything else, in spite of their limitations and mannerisms, the symbolists combined great talent with conscious craftsmanship, and this makes their place so big in Russian literary history. One may dislike their style, but one cannot fail to recognize that they revived Russian poetry from a hopeless state of prostration and that their age was a second Golden Age of verse inferior only to the first Golden Age of Russian poetry—the age of Púshkin.

The first faint symptoms of the new movement appeared about 1890 in the work of the men who had begun as common-and-garden "civic" poets—Mínsky and Merezhkóvsky. But apart from a greater interest in metaphysical problems, a taste for metaphor, and (in the case of Merezhkóvsky) a slightly higher level of technique, this poetry differs little from the general run of the "eighties" poets and has little intrinsic value. The real beginners were Balmónt and Bryúsov, who were for many years the battering-rams of the new movement against the skull of the Philistine, and when the battle was won, they were recognized by the same Philistine as the greatest poets of their age. They both made their first appearance in the same year—Balmónt's *Under Northern Skies*, and *The Russian Symbolists*, a miscellany containing the first poems of Bryúsov, both appeared in 1894, the last year of Alexander III's reign.

BALMÓNT

Constantine Dmítrievich Balmónt (1867–1943) was born on his father's estate not far from Ivánovo-Voznesénsk, the "Russian Manchester." He was expelled from school on political grounds, and again when he went to Moscow University. But he succeeded in taking a degree at the College of Law at Yarosláv. There he printed in 1890 an insignificant book of verses, but his literary career began in earnest with the publication of *Under Northern Skies*. In the nineties Balmónt was considered the most promising of "decadent" poets and was given a good reception by those magazines which piqued themselves on being reasonably modern. He continued publishing books of poetry, of which *Buildings on Fire* (1900) and *Let Us Be as the Sun* (1903) contain his best poems. After that a precipitous decline of his talent began, and the volumes that appeared after 1905 are worthless. In the nineties he had forgotten his schoolboyish Revolutionism and was notorious (like the other symbolists) for his "uncivic" attitude, but in 1905 he joined the S. D. Party and published *Songs of an Avenger*, a collection of remarkably crude and violent party verse. In 1917, however, he took a firmly anti-Bolshevík position and eventually migrated. Even before the Revolution he had traveled much and seen many exotic countries, including Mexico and the South Sea islands.

Balmónt's work is voluminous, but by far the greater part of it may be swept aside as quite worthless. This includes all his original verse after 1905, most of his numerous translations (the complete metrical version of Shelley is especially bad; on the contrary, his translations of Edgar Allan Poe are quite acceptable), and all his prose without exception, which is the most insipid, turgid, and meaningless prose in the language. In so far as a place is reserved for him in the pantheon of genuine poets, he will be remembered for the six books of verse published from 1894 to 1904. Even in these books he is very uneven, for though he had at that time a genuine gift of song, he was always incapable of *working* at his verse; he could only sing like a bird in the bush. But he had a keen sense of form, and his poetry is pre-eminently formal; sound and tune are the most important things in his verse. In the nineties and early 1900's he struck the ear of the public with a richness of rhythm and vocal design that seemed even excessive, disconcerting, and, to the stancher of the radical puritans, wicked. This pageant of sound was a new thing in Russian poetry; its elements are borrowed (without any slavish imitation) from Edgar Allan Poe and from the Shelley who wrote *The Cloud*, *The Indian Serenade*, and *To Night*. Only Balmónt is less precise and mathematical than Poe, and infinitely less subtle than Shelley. These achievements went to his head, and *Let Us Be as the Sun* is full of assertions of this kind: "Who is equal to me in the power of song? No one!" and: "I am the refinement of Russian speech." These immodesties are not entirely unfounded, for in this peculiar quality of song Balmónt has no rival among Russian poets. But of refinement there is precisely very little in his verse. It is curiously devoid of the "finer touch" and of the finer shades. He has a sufficiently wide scale of emotion to express, from the brave fortissimo of the most characteristic poems of the last-named book to the sweet, subdued undertone of *Wayside Grasses* or *Belladonna*, but in every single case the expression is simple, monotonous, all in one note. Another serious shortcoming that he shares with Bryúsov, and that is explained by the necessarily Western character of his poetry, is his complete lack of feeling for the Russian language. His verse has a foreign appearance and, even at its best, sounds like a translation.

BRYÚSOV

Valéry Yákovlevich Bryúsov (1873–1924) was born in a merchant family. He received a good education, and in later life, by studious reading and constant work, he became perhaps the most widely informed man of his generation. In 1894, together with A. L. Miropólsky, he published *Russian Symbolists*, which had the success of a scandal. This and the books that followed it were for a whole decade the favorite laughingstock of the whole press. Bryúsov's name became the synonym of a literary mountebank, and while other symbolists, like Balmónt, Sologúb, and Híppius, were more or less welcome guests in the literary press, Bryúsov was forbidden its doors until at least 1905. Bryúsov hardly answered to his first reputation: far from being the mountebank he was imagined to be, he is one of the most solemn and dead-serious figures in the whole of Russian literature. But his early poetry was so unlike the usual run of Russian magazine verse that the blockheads of criticism could account for it only as insolent tomfoolery. In reality it is only a rather youthful, immature imitation of the French poets of the day. For many years every new book by Bryúsov was received with indignation or ridicule. But Bryúsov persevered. His style matured. His following grew. By 1903 he was the recognized head of a numerous and energetic literary school; by 1906 his school had won its struggle; symbolism was recognized as the whole of Russian poetry, and Bryúsov as the first Russian poet. *Stephanos*, which appeared in 1906 at the height of the Revolutionary excitement, was greeted with enthusiasm by the same critics who had ridiculed his early work. The date of its success is perhaps the most significant in the history of the symbolist march toward supremacy.

In 1900 Bryúsov became the *de facto* head of a publishing business which united the forces of the new movement. In 1904 it started a review, *Vesý* (*The Scales*), which lasted till 1909 and was without doubt the most civilized and European publication of its time. From 1900 to 1906 Bryúsov was the head of a compact and vigorous party on its march to success; after 1906 his position became even more influential. But his talents began to decline. *All My Melodies* (1909) marked no progress as compared with *Stephanos;* the books that followed betrayed a steady and accelerating decline. From the nineties on, Bryúsov worked with wonderful energy in the most various literary fields. In point of volume, his original poetry is only a small part of his whole output—he translated poetry with signal success; he wrote prose stories and plays; he reviewed almost every book of new verse; he edited classics; he worked in the archives, preparing material for the lives of Púshkin, Tyútchev, and others; he read enormously and was all the time the *de facto* editor of a magazine. At the same time he was by no means an ascetic—his abundant love poetry has a solid foundation in fact, and he explored the "artificial paradises" of opium and cocaine. This never impaired his working capacity. A fair example of this is his work on Armenian poetry; in 1915 a committee of Armenian patriots asked Bryúsov to edit a selection from the Armenian poets in Russian. In less than a year he learned the language, read all there was to read of books on the subject, and did the greater part of the translations for the enormous quarto volume *Armenian Poetry*, which appeared in 1916. The book is a wonderful monument of human industry and the best there is of its kind.

Bryúsov was always essentially unpolitical. His attitude to politics was purely æsthetic. It is well expressed in his lines (written in 1905): "Beautiful in the splendor of his power is the Oriental King Assarhaddon, and beautiful the ocean of a people's wrath beating to pieces a tottering throne. But hateful—are half-measures."

Till 1917 he took no part in politics, but after the Bolshevík triumph he became a Communist. This adhesion was caused not by any political conviction, but rather, on the contrary, by the lack in him of those political and moral inhibitions which prevented more "civic-minded" men from taking that step. Another reason may have been the feeling that he had lost touch with the times, that he was no longer a leader, and the hope once more to become advanced and modern by joining the most advanced of political parties. Again, the Revolution of 1917 answered very well to his æsthetic ideal of an "ocean of a people's wrath," and he distinctly sympathized with the mechanical schemes of Lénin.

He received at first a sinecure, then a more responsible post at the head of the censorship, but failed in the long run to adapt himself to the orthodox Communists and was replaced by a more trustworthy party man (the novelist Serafimóvich). He also failed to gain the recognition of the "left front" of poets whose favor he had courted ever since the first appearance of futurism. His last years were lonely, and he suffered acutely from being out of the movement. His only consolation was his work with the young proletarian poets, to whom he gave regular instruction in the art of poetry. He died in 1924, only fifty-one years old, but having outlived by about fifteen years the high-water mark of his fame.

Bryúsov's poetry shares with Balmónt's a general "foreign" air, the result of a more intimate connection with French and Latin than with Russian poetical tradition. It has also in common with Balmónt's a certain lack of refinement, of the "finer touch" and the finer shades. At its best it is gorgeous—all gold and purple; at its worst, gaudy. Like that of most Russian symbolists, it is continuously solemn and hieratic, and big words are his stock material. In his early poetry (1894–6) he tried to naturalize in Russia the "singing" accent of Verlaine and the early French symbolists, and to revive and modernize the "melodies" of Fet. But, on the whole, Bryúsov is not a "musical" poet, though, like all the Russian symbolists, he often uses his words as emotional gestures rather than as signs with a precise meaning. Though his verse is saturated with the culture of ages, Bryúsov is not a "philosophical" or thinking poet. At one time, under the influence of Iván Konevskóy, he devoted himself to writing metaphysical poetry; some of it makes excellent rhetoric, but there is very little philosophy in it, only a succession of pathetic exclamations and juxtapositions. Bryúsov's diction is terser and more compact than Balmónt's, and at times he achieves excellent feats of poetical compression and expressiveness, but it lacks precision, and his words, often splendid, are never "curiously felicitious." His favorite subjects are meditations on the past and future of humanity, the representation of carnal love as a mystical ritual, and—in a favorite catchword of twenty years ago—the "mysticism of every day," that is to say, evocations of the modern big towns as a forest of mysteries and symbols. His best work is contained in *Urbi et Orbi* (1903) and *Stephanos* (1906). The latter includes *Eternal Truth of Idols*, a series of magnificent variations of the eternal subjects of the Greek fable. Such poems as *Achilles at the Altar* (awaiting his fatal betrothal with Polyxene), *Orpheus and Eurydice*, and *Theseus to Ariadne* are the best achievement of the "classical" aspect of Russian symbolism, which aimed at hieratic majesty and symbolical pregnancy.

Bryúsov's prose is, on the whole, of a piece with his verse: it is solemn, hieratic, and academic. Its subjects are the same—pictures of the past and future, and the mysterious "abysses" of love, very often in its most perverse and abnormal aspects. Like his verse, it has a distinctly "translated" air. Bryúsov felt this and often modeled it according to some definite foreign model of the past ages. One of his best short stories, *In an Underground Prison*, is in the style of a *novella* of the Italian Renaissance. His best novel, *The Fire Angel* (1907), is the narrative of a German mercenary of the age of Luther. This device helped to save his prose from the dangers of "poeticalness" and of impressionism. On the whole, it is straightforward, manly, and free from mannerisms. The subject matter and the construction of his stories were much influenced by Edgar Allan Poe. Both the detailed and documented presentation of the future of civilization in *The Republic of the Southern Cross* and the cold-blooded study of pathological states of mind in a story like *Now That I Am Again Awake* bear the unmistakable impress of the great American. There is coldness and cruelty in all Bryúsov's prose—no sympathy, no pity, only a cold flame of sensual exaltation and a desire to penetrate into the farthest recesses of human perversity. But Bryúsov is no psychologist, and his visions of sensuality and of cruelty are only pageants of loud color. His principal work in prose is *The Fire Angel*, which is perhaps the best Russian novel on a foreign subject. The story is concerned with witchcraft and the trial of a witch. Dr. Faustus and Agrippa of Nettesheim appear. It is saturated with a genuine feeling for the epoch, and is as full of erudition as any of Merezhkóvsky's novels; but it is free from that writer's puerile sophistications, and as a narrative it is incomparably better. In fact it is a very good and ably constructed romance. The *Lanzknecht's* leisurely manner of narrating the thrilling and mysterious events of which he was a witness only adds to the tension of the reader's interest. Bryúsov's second novel, *The Altar of Victory* (1913), a romance of fourth-century Rome, marks a definite decline: the book is long and tedious and lacks every creative element.

METAPHYSICAL POETS

Bryúsov and Balmónt were the Westernizers—the miniature "Peter the Greats"—of Russian symbolism. Their work is not philosophical or intimate; it is loud and rhetorical. Both these poets sought to find a new language for the expression of "great poetry." Both of them were æsthetes, and their ideal of beauty was sufficiently near to the popular idea for them eventually to become popular poets. Other poets appeared who may be called the Slavophils of symbolism. For them the principal thing was not to make things of beauty, but to grasp the meaning of things. They did not seek for striking and eloquent expression, but tried to make their language adequate to their often complicated and abstruse ideas. They may be termed metaphysical poets.

Such was Iván Konevskóy (pseudonym of I. I. Oræus, 1877–1901), a young man of extraordinary promise and powerful personal attraction who was drowned at twenty-four while bathing in a river. He was a mystical pantheist, with a passionate desire to grasp and comprehend the universe in all its multiplicity. He was on the way towards creating a vigorous and terse manner of expression that would be adequate to all the complexity of his ideas. He said that "poetry must be a bit *rugged.*" His is decidedly so, but it is the ruggedness of Michelangelo struggling with the resistant marble. He had a wonderfully keen sense of the value of Russian words, which appeared to him in their naked aspects, stripped of their literary associations. In this respect he was a precursor of Khlébnikov. There are no banality and no cheap prettiness in his poetry. His best poems are powerful evocations of Nature—of the forest, of rain, of waterfalls, and of wind.

Another remarkable man of the period was Alexander Mik-háylovich Dobrolyúbov. Born in 1876, he appeared in the modernist coterie of the nineties, producing the impression of a madman on most people, of a saint on a few. He published two little pamphlets of verse and disappeared. He went "into the people," where he became the founder of a mystical and anarchist sect. He became so completely assimilated to the peasants that when he came to Yásnaya Polyána, Tolstóy, after a two hours' talk with him, was firmly convinced he had been talking to a genuine peasant and refused to believe that he was a "decadent" poet. His early poetry is aggressively original and obscure, but it is the obscurity of a man struggling to express new and unexpressed feelings in a new form, like Konevskóy's. Dobrolyúbov's poetry is singularly free from banality, and his *From the Book Invisible*, published by Bryúsov in 1905, consists of fragmentary notations in prose of his spititual states, especially of his communion with nature. The prose is interspersed with poems of extraordinary freshness and originality—mystical, Biblical, and nature hymns that proceed to a certain extent from the hymns of Russian Protestant sects but have in them the nervous throb of life of an intensely personal poet.

The most remarkable of these early metaphysical symbolists is Zinaída Híppius (1869–1945). Like Konevskóy and Dobrolyúbov, she avoids rhetoric and prettiness. She considers her matter more important than her manner, and she works at her form only to make it more flexible and adequate to the expression of her ideas. She is a Slavophil also, inasmuch as she proceeds not from any

French example, but from the Russian traditions—from Baratýn-sky, Tyútchev, and Dostoyévsky. The wife of D. S. Merezhkóvsky, she is a more original and significant writer than her somewhat overrated husband. Her activity was almost as many-sided as his; she wrote short stories and longer novels, plays, critical and political articles—and poetry. The most salient feature in all her writings is intellectual power and wit, things rare in a woman. In fact there is very little that is feminine in Mme Híppius, except a tendency to be oversubtle and a certain willfulness—the capriciousness of a brilliant and spoiled coquette. This last quality gives a peculiarly piquant flavor to her work, which is, on the whole, intense and serious. Like Dostoyévsky, she "feels ideas" as living entities, and all her literary life is a life "among ideas." Her imaginative prose is voluminous—but inferior in quality to her verse. It consists of several volumes of short stories, two longer novels, and one or two plays. All these are with a "purpose"—to give expression to some idea or to some subtle psychological observation. The ideas are the real characters in her stories, but she does not possess Dostoyévsky's power of giving them an individual and complete existence. Her characters are abstractions. Her most ambitious works, the two novels *The Devil's Doll* (1911) and *Román-Tsarévich* (1914), are weak offshoots of a great trunk—Dostoyévsky's *Possessed;* they are mystical studies in political psychology. A fair example of her manner may be had in her play *The Green Ring* (1914), which is available in English.

Her poetry is much more important. Some of it is also abstract and merely intellectual. But from the very beginning she made her verse a wonderfully refined and well-tempered instrument for the expression of her thought. She went on refining it and making it more obedient to every twist and turn of her subtle musings. Like Dostoyévsky's people, she oscillates between the two poles of spirituality and earthliness—between burning faith and apathetic skepticism—and it cannot be denied that her skeptical and nihilistic moods found more memorable expression than her moments of faith. She has an intensely acute feeling of the "stickiness," of the slime and ooze, of everyday life, and she feels her most intimate self in thrall to it. Paul Selver has translated what is perhaps her most characteristic poem in this order of ideas (*Psyche*). In *Crime and Punishment*, Svidrigáylov wonders if eternity is not but a "Russian bath-house with cobwebs in every corner." Mme Hippius took up the idea, and perhaps her best poems are variations of this theme. She has created for them a sort of quaint mythology, of filthy, "sticky," and quite morbidly attractive little demons.

In 1905 Zinaída Híppius, like her husband, became an ardent Revolutionary, and after that time she wrote much political verse, which is certainly the best of its kind—unrhetorical, unexpected, fresh, and often biting. She excels in sarcasm: a splendid example is *Petrográd*, a satire on the renaming of St. Petersburg. In 1917, like Merezhkóvsky, she took a violently anti-Bolshevík attitude. Her later political verse is often as good as the earlier, but in her later prose writings she does not show up very attractively. Her *Petersburg Diary*, describing life in 1918–19, is inspired by spiteful hatred rather than by noble indignation. However, her prose must not be judged by such examples. She is a brilliant literary critic, the master of a wonderfully flexible, expressive, and unconventional style (her critiques appeared over the signature of Antón Kráyny—Anton Extremist). Her judgment is swift and sure, and her sarcasm had a glorious time when she dealt with the swollen reputations of the early years of the century. Her criticism is frankly subjective, almost capricious, and is more valuable for its manner than its matter.

SOLOGÚB

All the writers hitherto mentioned in this chapter came from civilized upper-middle-class families of one of the two capitals. But the greatest and most refined poet of the first generation of symbolists rose from the lower orders, and his strange genius grew under the most unpropitious circumstances. Fëdor Sologúb (1863–1927), whose real name was Fëdor Kuzmích Tetérnikov, was born in Petersburg. His father was a shoemaker, and when he died, his mother became a domestic servant. With the help of her employer, Sologúb received a comparatively good education at a "teachers' institute." On terminating his studies, he got an appointment as schoolmaster in a small out-of-the-way provincial town. In time he was made district inspector of elementary schools, and at last, in the nineties, was transferred to Petersburg. Only after the great success of his famous novel *Mélky bes* was he able to leave his peda-

gogical work and rely on his literary income. Like the other symbolists, he was fundamentally unpolitical, and though in 1905 he
took up a distinctly Revolutionary attitude, he remained coldly
aloof in 1917 and after.

He began writing early in the eighties, but until about ten
years later, he did not come into contact with the world of letters.
His first books appeared in 1896, when he published three at
once—a volume of verse, a volume of short stories, and a novel,
Bad Dreams, at which he had worked for more than ten years. His
next book of verse and next book of short stories did not appear
until 1904. His great novel *Mélky bes*, at which he had worked
from 1892 to 1902, could not find a publisher for several years. It
began appearing in installments in a magazine in 1905, but the
magazine went out of existence. Only in 1907 was it at last published in book form, when it met with an enormous success.
Mélky bes brought Sologúb universal recognition and an all-
Russian reputation. But his later work, in which he gave freer
rein to his idiosyncrasies, did not meet with the same success, and
after 1910 people began to discern in him signs of diminishing
power. *The Created Legend* (1908–12), a remarkable and strangely
original book, met with an indifferent reception. *The Charmer of
Snakes* (1921), another novel, is decidedly weak, but his poetry
remained on the same high level, though its relative monotony
will hardly satisfy the lover of novelties and sensations.

Two aspects of Sologúb's work must be distinguished, for they
are not necessarily inseparable, nor do they seem to be interde-
pendent: his Manichæan idealism, and the peculiar "complex"
that is the result of a perverse and long-suppressed libido. There
can be no doubt that many of his writings, especially in his later
period, have no other *raison d'être* than to satisfy, by exteriorization, this "complex." It is not for the literary historian, but rather
for the specially trained psychoanlayst, to study it in detail. Delight in cruelty and in the humiliation of beauty is among its
prominent features. A minor but ever recurrent detail is the
"obsession" of *bare feet*. A heroine who walks barefoot is like his
sign manual in almost every one of Sologúb's novels and short
stories. His Manichæan philosophy, on the contrary, is purely
idealistic in the Platonic sense of the word. There is a world of
good—which is that of unity, calm, and beauty—and a world of
evil—which is that of diversity, desire, and vulgarity. This world

of ours is a creation of evil. Only inside oneself can one find the
other world of unity and calm. To free oneself from the evil
fetters of matter and to become a self-satisfied deity is the aim of
man. But man projects into the outer world his dreams of heaven
—and this produces the essential "romantic" irony of life. Sologúb
symbolizes this irony in two names borrowed from *Don Quixote*—
Dulcinea and Aldonsa. What we believe to be the ideal Dulcinea
turns out in fact to be the vulgar Aldonsa. Matter and desire are
the main expression of evil, and the only incarnation of the higher
world of ideals in real life is beauty—the ideal beauty of the nude
human figure. This is the meeting point of Sologúb's idealism and
his sensuality. His attitude towards fleshly beauty is always twofold—it is at once Platonically ideal and perversely sensual. The
flavor of Sologúb's sensuality is so repellent to many readers that
it becomes an insurmountable obstacle to the enjoyment of his
work. But even apart from this perversity, his philosophy itself
inclines towards a nihilism akin to Satanism. Peace and beauty
become identified with death; and the sun, the source of all life
and activity, becomes the symbol of the evil power. And in his
attitude to our existing religion—he takes a course opposite to that
of his mediæval predecessors the Albigenses—he identifies God
with the evil creator of the evil world, and Satan becomes the king
of the cool and calm realm of beauty and death.

Sologúb's poetry developed along different lines from that of
the other symbolists. His vocabulary, his diction, and his images
are closely akin to those of the eclectic poetry of the "Victorians."
His meters are simple and ordinary, but refined to the utmost
degree of perfection. His vocabulary is almost as small as Racine's,
but he uses it with almost equal precision and felicity. He is a
symbolist in that his words are symbols—with a double meaning—
and are used in their secondary, not in their ordinary, sense. But
the completeness of his philosophy allows him to use them with
an exactness that is almost classical. This, however, refers only to
that part of his poetry which reflects his ideal heaven or his
yearning for it. There is another series of poems that are, like his
Inferno, dark and cruel evocations of the evil diversity of the world;
and in them his language becomes cruder and richer and more
racy. This *Inferno* includes a curious cycle of poems, *Masks of
Other Existences*—reminiscences of the various forms his soul has
assumed in its previous incarnations. One of these is the lament of

a dog whining at the moon; it is certainly one of his best and most original poems. As for his idealistic lyrics, which are, after all, his greatest achievement, it is useless, unless one is a master of English verse, to attempt any translation of them. Their beauty is classical; it depends on the imponderables of rhythm and meaning. As in all classic poetry, the poet's silences are as important as his words; that which is left unsaid, as that which is said. It is the most refined and most delicate of all modern Russian poetry.

Although his verse is the most perfect and rarest flower of Sologúb's genius, his fame at home, and certainly abroad, is based on his novels rather than on his poetry. The first of these, *Bad Dreams*, is autobiographical and lyrical. The hero, Lógin, a schoolmaster in an out-of-the-way provincial town, has the same perverse obsessions and the same ideal visions as haunt Sologúb's own poetry. The novel is the history of a man capable of reaching the ideal, but who is in the thick of a world of vulgarity, cruelty, selfishness, stupidity, and lewdness. Russian provincial society is portrayed with incisive cruelty—a cruelty reminiscent of Gógol. But it is not realism in the good old Russian sense of the word, for it is all meant as a symbol of more than Russian vastness. Sologúb's second novel, *Mélky bes* (the English rendering of the name, *The Little Demon*, is inadequate; the French title, *Le Démon mesquin*, is better), is the most famous of all his writings, and it may be recognized as the most perfect Russian novel since the death of Dostoyévsky. Like *Bad Dreams*, it is apparently realistic but internally symbolical. It transcends realism, not because Sologúb introduces the mysterious demon *Nedotýkomka*, which, after all, may be explained away as a hallucination of Peredónov's, but because his aim is to paint not the life of a Russian provincial town, but life—the evil creation of God—as a whole. The satirical drawing is admirable—a touch more grotesque, and consequently more poetical, than in the earlier novel; but the town is only a microcosm of all life. The novel has two planes: the life of Peredónov, the incarnation of the joyless evils of life; and the idyllic loves of the boy Sásha Pýlnikov and Lyudmíla Rutílova. These two are the emanation of beauty, but their beauty is not pure—it has been polluted by the evil touch of life. The Sásha and Lyudmíla episode has a subtle sensual flavor, and is introduced, not only for its symbolical and constructive value, but also to answer the demands of the poets's libido. Peredónov has become a famous figure—in fact the most famous and memorable character of Russian fiction since *The Brothers Karamázov*—and his name is now a word of the literary language. It stands for the incarnation of sullen evil, which knows no joy and resents others' knowing it—one of the most terrible figures ever created by a poet. He lives in constant hatred and believes that all live in constant hatred of him. He loves to inflict cruelty and to dash to the ground the joys of others. He finally succumbs to a mania of persecution and commits murder in a state of insanity.

Sologúb's third novel, *The Created Legend* (more exactly, *The Legend in Process of Creation*), is his longest. It consists of three parts, each of which is a self-contained novel. In the first part the scene is laid in Russia in 1905. The hero is Triródov, a Satanist after the heart of Sologúb. He is also a Revolutionary, though only a contemplative one. Sologúb's own political attitude was then strongly Revolutionary, and it is natural that, with his philosophy, the existing order of things—the forces of reaction and conservatism—should appear as the fullest expression of evil life. The volume is full of scenes of horror and cruelty in the suppression of the Revolutionary movement; hence its title, *Drops of Blood*. Triródov is the ideal man who has nearest approached the serenity of death, and sheds around himself a cool and calm atmosphere, symbolized in his colony of "quiet boys"—a weird vision of Sologúb's perverse imagination. In the second and third parts the scene is shifted to the Kingdom of the United Islands, an imaginary volcanic group in the Mediterranean. These volumes have a powerful and subtle, if suspicious, charm. Unlike most Russian novels, they may be read for the interest of the story. It is a very complicated story of love and political intrigue. It is all dominated by the ever present danger, the volcano; and in the third part the eruption occurs. The story is symbolical but, as I have said, contains quite sufficient charm apart from its symbolism. The trilogy ends by the Republic of the United Islands electing Triródov their king!

Sologúb's short stories are a link between his poetry and his novels. Some of them are shorter sketches in the style of *Bad Dreams* and *Mélky bes*. Others, especially after 1905, are frankly fantastic and symbolical. In these more than anywhere else Sologúb gave free reign to his morbid sensual demands. *The Dear Page* and, of those stories which have been translated into English, *The Lady in Fetters* are typical examples of this kind. *The Miracle of the Boy Linus*, a Revolutionary story in a conventional poetical setting, is one of the most beautiful pieces of modern Russian prose. In general, Sologúb's prose is beautiful: limpid, clear, balanced, poetical, but with a keen sense of measure. In his later writings it is marred by certain irritating mannerisms. Apart from his other prose writings stand his *Political Fables* (1905), admirable both for the scathing point of their satire and for their remarkably elaborate popular language, rich in verbal effects (as all popular speech is) and reminiscent of the grotesque manner of Leskóv.

His plays are not on a level with his other writings. *The Sting of Death* and *The Gift of the Wise Bees* are academic pageants symbolizing the concepts of his philosophy. They are less genuine than his poetry and constantly fall into the category of falsely beautiful. More interesting is *Vánka the Butler and the Page Jehan*, an amusing piece of irony. The familiar history of the young servant who seduces the lady of the house is developed in two parallel variations—in mediæval France and in Muscovite Russia. It is a satire on Russian civilization, with its crudeness and poverty of forms, and is at the same time a symbol of the essential sameness of the evil diversity of life all over the world and throughout the ages.

ÁNNENSKY

Still older than Sologúb, still more eccentric to the general movement, and still later to be recognized was Innokénty Fëdorovich Ánnensky. Born in Omsk, he was the son of an important official and was educated at Petersburg. He took a degree in classics at the University of St. Petersburg and was invited to prepare for a chair. But he found himself incapable of concentrating on his thesis and instead became a teacher of ancient languages. He rose to be head master of the Gymnasium of Tsárskoye Seló, and afterward Director of Schools—that is, an official who has the supervision of the secondary schools of a large district. He was an eminent classical scholar and contributed articles and reviews to the philological reviews. He devoted himself to a complete Russian version of Euripides. In 1894 he published *Bacchæ*, and in time the rest. It

was not for nothing that he chose Euripides—the most journalistic
and least religious of the tragic poets. Ánnensky's mind was
eminently unclassical, and he did his best to modernize and
vulgarize the Greek poet. But all this would give him but a small
place in Russian literature were it not for his poetry. In 1904 he
published a book of lyrics (half of which was occupied by translations from French poets and from Horace) entitled *Quiet Songs* and
under the whimsical pseudonym of *Nik. T. O.* (read: *Niktó*—
nobody). He means it to be an allusion to the Polyphemus episode
in the *Odyssey*. This farfetched and elaborate allusion is typical of
Ánnensky. *Quiet Songs* passed unnoticed, even by the symbolists.
Poetry over his name continued to appear from time to time in the
magazines, and he brought out two books of critical essays, which
are remarkable both for the subtlety and penetration of his criticism and for the perverse pretensions of his style. In 1909 a few
people began to realize that Ánnensky was an uncommonly original and interesting poet. He was "taken up" by the Petersburg
symbolists and introduced to their poetical circles, where he at once
became a central figure. He was on his way to becoming a principal
influence in literature when he suddenly died of heart failure. He
had prepared for the press a second book of verse—*The Cypress
Chest*—which was published in 1910 and recognized in the inner
circle of Russian poets as a classic.

Ánnensky's poetry is in many ways different from that of all
his contemporaries. It is not metaphysical, but purely emotional—
or rather, perhaps, nervous. He had no Russian masters. In so far
as he had any masters at all, they were Baudelaire, Verlaine, and
Mallarmé. But on the whole his lyrical gift is remarkably original.
It is a rare case of a very late development. Nor did he at once
attain to perfection. *Quiet Songs* is distinctly immature (although
written at forty-eight). But in *The Cypress Chest* the majority of
the poems are flawlessly perfect jewels. Ánnensky is a symbolist,
in so far as his poetry is based on a system of "correspondences."
But they are purely emotional correspondences. His poems are
developed in two interconnected planes—the human soul and the
outer world; each of them is an elaborate parallel between a state
of mind and the external world. Ánnensky is akin to Chékhov, for
his material is also the pinpricks and infinitesimals of life. His
poetry is essentially human, and its appeal would be universal, for
it deals with the common stuff of humanity. His poems are con-

structed with disconcerting and baffling subtleness and precision. They are compressed and laconic—much of the structure has been pulled away, and only the essential points remain for the reader to reverse the process and grasp the unity of the poem. Few readers, however, feel themselves capable of the creative effort required. But the work is worth the while. Those who have mastered him usually prefer him to all other poets. For he is unique and always fresh. The extent of his poetry is small, his two books do not contain more than a hundred lyrics all told, and most of them are not over twenty lines long. This makes it comparatively easy to study. It must be added that Ánnensky's diction is studiously common and trivial. It is the unbeautiful language of every day— but his poetical alchemy transforms the ugly dross of vulgarity into the purest poetical gold.

Ánnensky's tragedies written in imitation of Euripides are not on the level of his lyrics. The most interesting is the posthumous *Thamiras Cytharede*. The subject is the Apollonian myth of the proud harpist who challenged the god to a contest in music and expiated his arrogance by the loss of his eyes. There is much poignant poetry in the tragedy, but it is eminently unclassical. Still less classical are his most curious translations from Horace. Altogether, considering his lifelong connection with the ancients, Ánnensky is quite disconcertingly free from any kinship with antiquity.

VYACHESLÁV IVÁNOV

The marriage of Russian symbolism and Greek tradition took place in the work of another scholar-poet, Vyacheslác Ivánovich Ivánov. He was born in Moscow in 1866, the son of a minor civil servant. He studied the classics and ancient history, partly under the guidance of Mommsen, and published a thesis on the tax-farming companies of ancient Rome. For a long time he lived abroad, away from any contact with Russian literary life. The only modern writers who influenced him were Nietzsche and Soloviëv. But he lived in the closest intimacy with the great poets of antiquity— with Dante and Goethe, and with the mystics and philosophers of all times. He was especially attracted by the mystic religions of Greece, and later (1903–4) he published an important study on the religion of Dionysos. He began writing verse early, but it remained unpublished for years, and he was free to develop a style entirely his own—hieratic and archaic, rich in expressive diction and majestic harmony, and quite unlike the poetry of his contemporaries. In 1903 he published a book of poems entitled *Pilot Stars*, the fruit of this isolated development. In spite of the unfamiliar appearance of his work, the symbolists at once discerned in Ivánov one of themselves and recognized him as a great poet. He entered the symbolist circles and even came under the influence of Merezhkóvsky, but on the whole he gave more than he received. His towering scholarship and powerful personal magnetism soon made him a master and a leader. In 1905, like the other symbolists, he did homage to the Revolution, and, in common with the young poet and Revolutionary George Chulkóv, he became the prophet of a new Revolutionary philosophy, which received the name of mystical anarchism. It preached the "non-acceptance of the world"[1] and the revolt against all external conditions, towards a complete freedom of the spirit. This mystical anarchism proved ephemeral, but the ascendancy of Ivánov over the modernist circles of Petersburg became unquestioned and lasted for six or seven years. Ivánov became the master of the Petersburg symbolists as opposed to those of Moscow led by Bryúsov. The essence of Ivánov's creed was that art was a mystical religious activity, an aspect of the complete syncretic human activity, and was to be dominated by mystical values and judged by religious standards. But his religion was syncretic and included all the religions of the world. The identification of Christ and Dionysos was one of its characteristic tenets. All was one—Christianity and paganism; sanctity and Luciferian pride; ascetic purity and sexual ecstasy—and all was religious and holy. The Muscovites opposed Ivánov, partly because, like Bryúsov, they wanted to preserve the autonomy of art against religion and philosophy; and partly because, like Bély, they desired a better-defined and less-inclusive religion that would not be seeking for the "synthesis of good and evil, of Christ and Lucifer." From 1905 to 1911 Ivánov remained the uncrowned king of Petersburg poets. His flat on the sixth floor of a house overlooking the Dúma building and the Taurida Park was known as the "Tower." Every Wednesday all poetic and

[1] The phrase alludes to the words of Iván Karamázov: "I accept God but I do not accept His world."

modern Petersburg met there, and the more intimate adepts stayed there, in mystical conversation and literary readings, till eight or nine on Thursday morning. In 1907 Ivánov lost his wife (known in literature as Lydia Zinóvieva-Annibál), but this did not break up the "Wednesdays." Only in 1912 did a succession of grievous incidents lead to Ivánov's estrangement from his most intimate friends. He left the "Tower" and went abroad; when he returned, he did not settle in Petersburg, but in Moscow. At the same time the disintegration of symbolism as a literary school brought an end to the intellectual hegemony of Ivánov, and he was henceforward "one of the many." The period of the "Tower" was the golden age of Ivánov's poetical work, which is contained in *Cor Ardens* (two volumes, 1911). The Second Revolution did not kindle Ivánov to the same enthusiasm as the first. He lived in and near Moscow, experiencing, like almost all Russian intellectuals, terrible hardships and privation, cold and hunger. In 1920 he wrote the beautiful *Winter Sonnets* and, together with Gershenzón, the *Correspondence between Two Corners*, both of which are among the most important monuments of the time. In 1921 he was appointed Professor of Greek in the State University of Azerbaiján, in Bakú, where for three years he lectured to young Tatars on Homer and Æschylus. In 1924 he left the Soviet Union on a mission to Italy, where he remained.

Shestóv, who was a master of pointed epigram, gave Ivánov the nickname of Vyacheslác the Magnificent, and "magnificent" is the best adjective one can think of for his style. In his first book there was still a certain primitivism, a "ruggedness," which gave it a freshness that is absent from his mature work. But *Cor Ardens* is the high-water mark of the ornate style in Russian poetry. His verse is saturated with beauty and expressiveness; it is all aglow with jewels and precious metals; it is like a rich Byzantine garment. "Byzantine" and "Alexandrian" are two very suitable epithets for his poetry, for it is full of the product of past ages, very scholarly, conscious, and quite unspontaneous. Ivánov is the nearest approach in Russian poetry to the conscious and studied splendors of Milton. In his verse every image, every word, every sound, every cadence, is part of one admirably planned whole. His language is archaic, and he likes to introduce Greek idioms. This is in the great tradition of ecclesiastic Russian and adds powerfully to the majesty of his numbers. Most of his poems are metaphysical; he also wrote many love lyrics and political poems, but love and politics are always treated *sub specie æternitatis*. His poetry is of course difficult, and hardly accessible to the man in the street, but, for those who can move in his sphere of ideas, there is in his heady and spiced wine an attractively troubling flavor. In his magnificence and his scholarship is hidden the sting of a refined and ecstatic sensuality—the sting of Astarte, rather than that of Dionysos. His poetry may be exclusive, Alexandrian, derivative (in so far as our culture is derivative), but that it is genuine, perhaps great poetry, there can be no doubt. The only objection that can be advanced against it is that it is too much of a good thing. Somewhat apart from the rest of his work stand *The Winter Sonnets* (1920); they are simpler, more human, less metaphysical. Their subject is the survival of the undying intellectual flame in the presence of elemental enemies—cold and starvation. Like so many symbolists, Ivánov was also a translator, and his versions of Pindar, Sappho, Alcæus, Novalis, and especially of the *Agamemnon*, are among the greatest achievements of Russian translated verse.

Ivánov's prose is as magnificent as his verse—it is the most elaborate and majestic ornate prose in the language. His earlier essays are contained in two volumes—*By the Stars* (1905) and *Furrows and Boundaries* (1916). In them he develops the same ideas as in his poetry. He believed that our times were capable of reviving the mythological creation of religious ages. He discovered in Dostoyévsky a great creator of myths, and he believed that the modern theater might become religious and choric like the Dionysian theater of Athens. His most remarkable prose work is the dialogue of letters he carried on with Gershenzón when the two philosophers lay convalescent in two corners of the same hospital ward in the worst days of Bolshevík destruction (*A Correspondence between Two Corners*, 1920). In it Gershenzón aspires, Rousseau-like, after a new and complete liberty, after a naked man on a new earth, free from the yoke of centuries of culture. Ivánov takes up the defense of cultural values, and speaks with pointed force and noble enthusiasm for the great past of human achievement against his nihilistic opponent. The six letters that form his part of the dialogue are a noble and proud defense of culture, all the more impressive from the circumstances in which they were written.

VOLÓSHIN

Maximilian Alexándrovich Volóshin (1877–1932) might almost be counted among the minor poets were it not for his poems on the Revolution, but these are so interesting as to require more than a mere mention. Born in South Russia, he traveled much in Central Asia and on the Mediterranean, and lived for many years in Paris, where he studied painting. Later he settled down at Koktebel, near Theodosia, in southeastern Crimea. In 1906–10 he was one of the intimates of the "Tower." In his early work Volóshin was a typical Westernizer. He translated French writers, introducing to the Russian public such men as Barbey d'Aurevilly, Henri de Régnier, Paul de Saint-Victor, and Paul Claudel. His poetry is somewhat metallic and coldly splendid. It is like a brilliant pageant of jewels or stained glass—one of his longest poems is on the stained glass of the cathedral of Rouen. He was strongly affected by Catholic mysticism, by the occult sciences, by Ægean and archaic Greece, and by the Mediterranean landscape. Among his best poems are splendid evocations of the Greek summer, full of the aroma of dry lavender, and *Cimmerian Darkness*, a cycle of sonnets on the Crimean winter. The Revolution called from him a series of remarkable "historical" poems on the destinies of Russia. Their burden is the conception of "Holy Russia," the country of pure Christian mysticism, oppressed by the State, which, according to Volóshin, is an alien growth in Russia—1917 was an elemental effort of Russia to free herself from its outlandish fetters. "Holy Russia" (in the poem of the same name) refused to be a princess in the tsar's chamber, she wanted to be free, so she lent her ear to evil advice, "delivered herself to the robber and to the felon, set fire to her farms and crops, destroyed her ancient abode, and went out into the world humiliated and a beggar, and the slave of the vilest slave. But," says Volóshin, "shall I dare cast a stone at thee? . . . Shall I not go on my knees before thee in the mire? blessing the trace of thy bare foot, thou wretched, homeless, drunken Russia—thou fool in Christ?" In another poem (*Transubstantiation*) he draws a picture of Rome in the sixth century, when the last flicker of Imperial Rome went out, and Papal Rome, "a new Rome, was born, great and primitive like the elements. Thus the grain of wheat, that it may grow, must dissolve. Dissolve, Russia, and come to new life as the Kingdom of the Spirit!"

Thus the most Western and cosmopolitan of Russian poets constructed a theory of super-Slavophil quietism. Volóshin's teaching is that all Russians should make peace and forgive each other. If they refuse to do so, he does it for them. *Poems of Terror* (1924) is a denunciation of the Civil War in this spirit of reconciliation. In spite of the burning actuality of these poems, one cannot fail to discern that, after all, they are as cold and academic as his early ones. Russia and Revolution, Christ and Lucifer, the Church and the International, are to him purely æsthetic entities absorbingly interesting in their combinations and as significant as the stained glass of Rouen or the myth of Atlantis, but in no way connected with practical and immediate issues. It is not surprising that he soon disappeared from the Soviet literary scene.

BLOK

The greatest of all symbolists was Alexander Alexándrovich Blok (1880–1921). His work is at once typical of the whole school—for no one carried further the realistic mysticism of Russian symbolism—and peculiar—for he has a definite air of kinship with the great poets of the romantic age. His poetry is more spontaneous and inspired than that of his contemporaries. His very appearance was that of a poet. There was in him the innate majesty of a fallen angel. Very handsome, he was a splendid specimen of what it became the fashion to call the Nordic race. He was the meeting point of several lines of traditions—he was both very Russian and very European. And to emphasize the fact, he was of mixed descent.

His father's family came over with Peter III from Holstein in the eighteenth century, but his father, Professor of Public Law at the University of Warsaw, was already more than half Russian by blood and an extreme Slavophil in his ideas. He was a self-tormented egoist, very attractive, but impossible to live with. His first wife, the poet's mother, separated from him immediately after the birth of their son, and they were subsequently divorced. Both remarried. The poet's mother was the daughter of Professor Bekétov, an eminent scientist and for many years Rector of the University of St. Petersburg.

After his parents' separation Blok remained with his mother, seeing his father only at rare intervals. In the Bekétov family, life was cultivated and idyllic. Winters were spent in the university; summers at Shakhmátovo, a little estate near Moscow. The Bekétovs mixed with the intellectual elite of the country, including the family of the great chemist Mendeléyev (whose daughter Blok married in 1903) and that of M. S. Soloviëv, the famous writer's brother and "better self."

In 1898 Blok went to the University, where he passed from the faculty of law to that of philology and took his degree only in 1906, when he had become a well-known poet. He began writing verse very early. By 1900 he was already an original poet, both in style and substance. His poetry at first remained unpublished. In 1903 a few poems of his appeared in the Merezhkóvskys' review, *The New Way*. In 1904 they appeared in book form as *Verses about the Beautiful Lady*. Blok always insisted that his poetry can be really understood and appreciated only by those who are in sympathy with his mystical experience. This assertion is especially true in regard to his first book. Unless one understands the mystical "setting," one is apt to take it for mere verbal music. To be understood, it must be interpreted. This, however, is no very difficult task with the help of Blok's own article *On the Present State of Russian Symbolism* (1910), a very important self-revelation, and of Bély's detailed commentary in his remarkable *Recollections of Blok*. The *Verses about the Beautiful Lady* is the history of a mystical "love affair" with a person whom Blok identified with the subject of Soloviëv's *Three Meetings*—Sophia, the Divine Wisdom, a feminine hypostasis of the Deity. Blok's mystical friends and he himself always insisted that these *Verses* are the most important part of his work, and though the ordinary poetry reader may be inclined to prefer the mighty numbers of the third volume, they are certainly very interesting and biographically important. Despite the influence of Soloviëv (in the matter) and Zinaída Híppius (in metrical form), they are quite original, and their style is strangely mature for a young man in his early twenties. The principal feature of this poetry is its complete freedom from everything sensual or concrete. It is a nebula of words, and affects the uninitiated as mere verbal melody. It answers better than any other poetry to Verlaine's rule "*de la musique avant toute chose.*" Nothing can be "*plus vague et plus soluble dans l'air*" than this poetry. Later, in his play *The Stranger*, Blok makes a poet (obviously a parody of himself) read out his verse to a waiter, and the waiter's verdict is: "Incomprehensible, but exceedingly refined, sir." Apart from the few initiated, the attitude of Blok's early admirers was much the same as the waiter's. The subsequent popularity of his early poetry (forming the first volume of the collected poems) was precisely due to a craze for poetry that would be as pure and as free of meaning as music.

Blok's poetry was at first appreciated only by the few. The critics either left it unnoticed or treated it with the ridicule and indignation that were the common lot of the symbolists. The public began to read it only much later. But the inner literary circles at once realized the importance of the new poet. Bryúsov and the Merezhkóvskys gave him a warm reception. The younger symbolists went still further. Two young Muscovites, Andréy Bély and Sergéy, the son of M. S. Soloviëv, discovered in him a message akin to their own spiritual experiences, and Blok became to them a prophet and seer, almost the founder of a new religion. These young mystics awaited, with fervent and strangely realistic faith, the coming of a new religious revelation, and Blok's ethereal poetry seemed to them the Annunciation of this new era. In his *Recollections* Bély has described the tense atmosphere in which the young Blok, himself, and Sergéy Soloviëv moved in the years 1903–4.

But this did not last. *Verses about the Beautiful Lady* was still on the press when a change came over Blok's visionary world. "The beautiful lady" refused herself to her lover. The world became empty to him, and the heavens clouded in darkness. Repelled by his mystical mistress, he turned towards the earth. This change made Blok certainly more unhappy and probably a worse man than he had been, but a greater poet. Only now his poetry begins to acquire human interest and becomes comprehensible to others than the elect few. It becomes more earthly, but at first his earth is not a material earth. His heaven-bred style succeeds in dematerializing the world of common experience; his world of 1904–6 is a drapery of fata morganas thrown over the more real but invisible heaven. His immaterial and purely musical style was admirably suited to evoke the mists and mirages of Petersburg, the illusionary city that had haunted the imagination of Gógol, Grigóriev, and Dostoyévsky. This romantic Petersburg, the dream city arising in the unreal misty atmosphere of the North on the uncertain quagmire of the Nevá delta, now becomes the background of Blok's poetry. "The beautiful lady" is replaced by the stranger (or strange woman), an immaterial but passionately present obsession that haunts the second volume of the collected verse (1904–8).

To the same period belongs a series of exquisite poems in which, for once, Blok displays an unexpected gift of homely and whimsical humor. The series is entitled, in a phrase from *Macbeth*, "*The Earth's Bubbles.*" It is about the homely and mischievous spirits that live in the woods and fields. Few poems have won more popular feeling for Blok than *The Little Priest of the Bogs*, a mysterious, impish, and good-natured creation of his fancy, who, standing finger-high amid the mounds,

> *prays, lifting his hat,*
> *for the reed that bends,*
> *for the ailing paw of a frog*
> *and for the Pope of Rome.*

Like most of the symbolists, Blok welcomed the Revolution of 1905. He joined the mystical anarchists. On one occasion he even carried a red flag. The defeat of the Revolution added to his despair and pessimism and emphasized the growing gloom of his soul. His poetry becomes, once and for all, the expression of that "fatal emptiness" (of which he speaks in a poem of 1912) which was familiar to many men of his generation. This "emptiness" has much in common with Andréyev's. The difference is that Blok was a greater genius and a man of greater culture—and that he *had* known a state of mystical bliss of which Andréyev could have no suspicion. An impotent desire to return into the radiant presence from which he had been expelled and a bitter resentment of the way he had been treated by "the beautiful lady" form the subject of his "lyrical dramas" written in 1906–7—*Balagánchik* (*The Puppet Show*) and *The Stranger*, which are among his earliest and most charming masterpieces. *Balagánchik*, a "pierrotic" comedy, was produced in 1907 and had a fairly long run. On those who saw it, *Balagánchik* produced an unforgettable impression. It contains much of Blok's very best lyrical matter, but it is in essence a satire, a parody, and a piece of grim blasphemy. It is a parody on Blok's own mystical experience and a satire on his mystical hopes and aspirations. His friends Bély and S. Soloviëv took it as an insult,

not only to themselves, but to their common faith in Sophia the
Divine Wisdom. This led to an estrangement, and the next period
passed for Blok in grim solitude. The lyrical charm and capricious
symbolism of *Balagánchik* may obscure from most readers its
terrible pessimism, but it is in essence one of the most blasphemous
and gloomiest things ever written by the poet.

The Stranger is a dreamy and romantic visionary drama developing the subject of the poem of the same name. It has less
lyrical charm than *Balagánchik*, but it shows at its best Blok's
ironic and grotesque realism, which only serves to enhance the
visionary romanticism of the main theme. Public houses henceforward become the frequent setting of Blok's poetry. It becomes
full of wine, women, and gypsy song, and all this against a background of passionate despair and hopeless yearning after the ir-
retrievably lost vision. Only at rare moments is he seized and
carried away from his slough of despond by the whirlwind of
earthly passion. Such a whirlwind is reflected in *The Snow Mask*,
an ecstatic lyrical fugue written in the first days of the year 1907.

Blok's genius reached its maturity about 1908. The lyrics
written between that date and 1916 are contained in the third
volume of his collected poems, which is, together with *The Twelve*,
certainly the greatest body of poetry written by a Russian poet
since the middle of the last century. He was a man neither of
great brains nor of great moral strength. Nor was he really a great
craftsman. His art is passive and involuntary. He is a recorder of
poetical experience rather than a builder of poetical edifices. What
makes him great is the greatness of the poetical spirit that fills
him, coming, as it were from other worlds. He has himself described
his creative process (in *The Artist*, 1913) as a purely passive process
very much akin to mystical ecstasy as it is described by the great
Spanish and German mystics. The ecstasy is preceded by a state
of boredom and prostration; then comes the unutterable bliss of a
wind from other spheres, to which the poet abandons himself,
will-lessly and obediently. But the rapture is interfered with by
"creative reason," which forces into the fetters of form the "light-
winged, benevolent, free bird" of inspiration; and when the work
of art is ready, it is dead to the poet, who subsides into his previous
state of empty boredom.

In the third volume Blok's style pulsates with a more intense
and nervous life than in his earlier work. It is more tense and full-

blooded. But, as in his earlier work, it depends to such an extent on the "imponderables" of diction, sound, and association that all translation is hopeless. The more purely lyrical poems can be read only in the original. But another group of poems, more ironical and consequently more realistic, are less completely untranslatable. Of one of them I will attempt a prose version:

Danse Macabre

How hard it is for a corpse among living men
To pretend to be alive and passionate!
But he must, he must squeeze himself into society,
Dissimulating, in the interests of advancement, the rattle of
*   his bones.*

The living are asleep. The dead man gets up from his grave,
And goes to the bank, to the courts of justice, to the senate;
The whiter the night, the blacker his feelings,
And the pens creak triumphantly.

All the day the dead man works at a memorandum.
Office time is over. And lo!
Wagging his hind parts, he whispers
An obscene anecdote into the ears of a senator.

Evening. A drizzling rain has covered with dirt
The passers-by, the houses, and all the other rubbish.
But the dead man—towards other obscenities
He is whirled away in a rickety taxi.

Into a crowded and columned ball-room
He hastens. He wears a well-made evening suit.
He is greeted with a graceful smile
By the hostess who is a fool and her husband who is another.

He is worn out by a day of official boredom.
But the rattle of his bones is covered by the music.
He gives hearty shakes to friendly hands,
Alive, alive, he must pretend to be.

Only at a distant column his eyes will meet with those
Of his companion—like him, she is dead.

Behind their conventional small talk
You hear the real words:

"Weary friend, I feel strange in this ball-room."
"Weary friend, the grave is cold."
"'Tis midnight."—"Yes, but you have not yet engaged
N. N. for a waltz. She is in love with you."

And over there N. N. is passionately waiting
For him, for him, with all her blood ablaze.
Her face, maidenly beautiful,
Displays the idiotic ecstasy of live love.

He whispers to her insignificant things,
Words that are charming to the living,
And he looks, how rosy her shoulders are,
How her head has inclined to her shoulder.

With more than human malice he pours out to her
The witty poison of ordinary society malice.
"How clever he is! How in love with me!"
In her ears, an uncanny, strange noise.
—It is bones rattling against bones.

The gloom and despair expressed here are characteristic of most of Blok's poetry after 1907. Yet for a while, and intermittently, Blok seems to have discovered a ray of hope that was to replace "the beautiful lady"; this was his love for Russia. It was a strange love, intensely aware of all that was base and vile in the beloved one, and yet reaching sometimes to veritable paroxysms of passion. The image of Russia identified itself in his mind with the Stranger and with the passionate and ambiguous women of Dostoyévsky, Nastásiya Filípovna (*The Idiot*) and Grúshenka (*The Brothers Karamázov*). Another symbol and mystical counterpart of Russia became the snowstorm and the blizzard, which in *The Snow Mask* had been a symbol of the cold and scorching storms of carnal passion, and which form the background of *The Twelve*. This Russian wind of passion is again associated with the songs of the gypsy choruses of Petersburg and Moscow. Many great writers (including Derzhávin, Tolstóy, and Leskóv) had understood before

Blok the lure and glamour of the gypsy chorus. There was in the middle of the nineteenth century a man of great but abortive genius, Apollón Grigóriev, who was, more than anyone, full of this gypsy poetry. He wrote several extraordinary songs that have been appropriated by the gypsies though they have forgotten his name. Blok practically discovered Grigóriev as a poet (as a critic he had always been well known) and "took him up." He edited a collected edition of Grigóriev's poems and wrote a preface that is one of his few prose articles which are worthy of the great poet, and in which he pays noble tribute to his forgotten predecessor.

Blok's love of Russia expressed itself in an acute sensibility for the destinies of his country, which sometimes verges on a genuine gift of prophecy. In this respect the lyrical fugue *The Field of Kulikóvo* (1908) is especially remarkable: it is full of dark and ominous presentiments of the great catastrophes of 1914 and 1917. Another remarkable poem (written in August 1914) gives the full extent of Blok's strange and irrational love of his country. It begins:

> *To sin shamelessly and uninterruptedly,*
> *To lose count of days and nights,*
> *And with a head heavy with drunkenness*
> *To insinuate oneself into God's temple.*

Then, accumulating detail on detail, he draws a picture of the most repulsive and degraded Russian character possible, and suddenly winds up:

> *Yes, and even in this form, my Russia,*
> *You are dearer to me than all the world.*

Apart from the lyrics contained in the third volume stand two longer works of the same period: the narrative poem *Retaliation* and the lyrical tragedy *The Rose and the Cross*. *Retaliation* was begun in 1910 under the influence of his father's death. It was planned to include three cantos, but only the first was completed. It is realistic in style and attempts to approach the methods of Púshkin and Lérmontov. It is the story of his father and himself, and Blok intended to make it a work of vast significance, illustrating the law of heredity and the consecutive stages of the disintegration of the old regime in Russia. He was unable to master his task, and the poem as a whole is not a success. But it contains many vigorous and beautiful passages. The beginning of the second canto reveals an unexpected gift of comprehensive historical vision; it is an excellent synthesis of Russia under Alexander III that might almost be quoted in every textbook of Russian history.

The Rose and the Cross (1913) is more conventional and less immediately striking than anything Blok ever wrote. The scene is laid in Languedoc in the thirteenth century. The play is very well constructed, and the lyrical quality of the poetry is on Blok's highest level. It is haunted from beginning to end, as by a leitmotiv, by the burden of a mysterious song sung by the Breton minstrel Gaëtan:

> *Joy, oh joy, that is suffering!*
> *Pain of unspeakable wounds!*

The final scene is perhaps his greatest achievement in pathetic irony.

Blok's attitude to the first World War, like the attitude of a large part of the advanced intelligentsia, was one of passive pacifism. When his turn came to go to the front, he exhausted all the means in his power to escape mobilization and succeeded in avoiding military service by joining a civilian "building detachment" engaged in fortifying the rear. The moment he heard of the fall of the monarchy, he deserted his post and returned to Petersburg. He was soon appointed Secretary to the Extraordinary Examining Committee, which was to investigate the actions of the ministers of the old regime that led to the Revolution.

During the Revolutionary years Blok came under the influence of the left S.R.'s and of their spokesman, the "Scythian" Ivánov-Razúmnik, who had evolved a sort of mystical revolutionary messianism, laying great stress on the revolutionary mission of Russia and on the fundamental difference of Socialist Russia from the bourgeois West. The left S.R.'s joined hands with the Bolshevíks and took an active part in overthrowing the provisional government. So Blok found himself on the Bolshevík side, together with his friend Bély, but against the great majority of his former friends, including the Merezhkóvskys. Blok's Bolshevism was not an orthodox Marxian Communism, but it was not by chance that he became a Bolshevík. The Bolshevík Revolution, with all its horrors and all its anarchy, was welcome to him as the manifestation of what he identified with the soul of Russia—the soul of the blizzard. This conception of the Bolshevík Revolution found expression in his greatest poem, *The Twelve*. The twelve are twelve Red guardsmen patrolling the streets of Petrográd in the winter of 1917–18, bullying the bourgeois, and settling, with the bullet, their quarrels among themselves for their girls. The figure twelve turns out to be symbolic of the twelve apostles, and in the end the figure of Christ appears, showing the way, against their will, to the twelve Red soldiers. This is a homage to Ivánov-Razúmnik's muddle-headed Revolutionary mysticism, and a testimony to the essentially irreligious character of Blok's own mysticism. Those familiar with the whole of Blok's poetry will know that the name of Christ did not mean to him what it does to a Christian —it is a poetical symbol with its own existence and its own associations, very different from those of the Gospels as well as from those of Church tradition. Any interpretation of "Christ" in *The Twelve* that did not take into account the whole of Blok's poetry would be meaningless. I do not have the space to discuss this problem here, but it is not its intellectual symbolism that makes *The Twelve* what it is—a great poem. The important thing is not what it signifies, but what it is. Blok's musical genius reaches its highest summit in it. From the point of view of rhythmical construction, it is a "miracle of rare device." The musical effect is based on dissonances. Blok introduces the rhythm and the diction of the vulgar and coarse *chastúshka* (factory song) and draws from them effects of unutterable vastness and majesty. The poem is built with wonderful precision. It develops with a tremendous swing, passing from one rhythmical form to another and fusing its dissonances into a superior harmony. In spite of its crude realism and its diction bordering on slang, one is tempted to compare it with such masterpieces of lyrical construction as *Kubla Khan* or the first part of *Faust*. The poem, on the face of it, is untranslatable, and to translate it well might seem an impossible miracle. This miracle, however, has been wrought, by Wolfgang Gröger, whose German version is almost on the level of the original.

In the same month as *The Twelve* (January 1918), Blok wrote *The Scythians*, a piece of intensely rhetorical invective against the Western nations for their not wanting to join in the peace proposed by the Bolshevíks. It is a powerful piece of eloquence but can hardly be called very intelligent, and is on an entirely inferior level as compared with *The Twelve*.

This was Blok's last poem. The new government, which valued
its few intellectual allies, gave Blok a lot to do, and for three years
he was hard at work at various civilizing and translating schemes
under the control of Górky and Lunachársky. His enthusiasm for
the Revolution fell after *The Twelve*, and he subsided into a state
of passive gloom, unbrightened even by the wind of inspiration.
He tried to resume work on *Retaliation*, but nothing came of it. He
was dreadfully tired—and empty. Unlike most writers, he did not
suffer from hunger or cold, for the Bolshevíks looked after him, but
he was a dead man long before he died. This impression is the
leitmotiv of all accounts of Blok during this period. *The Twelve*
had made him more widely famous than he had been before, but
the left literary schools in the last years of his life were united in
depreciating him. His death became a signal for his recognition
as a national poet of the first magnitude. There can be no doubt
that Blok is a great poet. But great though he is, he is also most
certainly an unhealthy and morbid poet, the greatest and most
typical of a generation whose best sons were stricken with despair
and incapable of overcoming their pessimism except by losing
themselves in a dangerous and ambiguous mysticism or by in-
toxicating themselves in a passionate whirlwind.

BÉLY

If Blok was the greatest of the symbolists, certainly the most
original and influential was Bély. Unlike Blok, whose nearest
affinities are in the past with the great romanticists, Bély is all
turned towards the future, and, of all the symbolists, he has most
in common with the futurists. The example of his prose especially
revolutionized the style of Russian prose writing. Bély is a more
complex figure than Blok—or even than any other symbolist; in
this respect he can easily vie with the most complex and disconcerting figures in Russian literature, Gógol and Vladímir Soloviëv,
both of whom had their say in his making. He is, on the one hand,
the most extreme and typical expression of the symbolist mentality;
no one carried farther the will to reduce the world to a system of
"correspondences," and no one took these "correspondences" more
concretely and more realistically; but this very concreteness of his
immaterial symbols brings him back to a realism quite outside the

common run of symbolist expression. His hold on the finer shades of reality—on the most expressive, significant, suggestive, and at once elusive detail—is so great and so original that it evokes the unexpected comparison with that realist of realists, Tolstóy. And yet Bély's world is an immaterial world of ideas into which this reality of ours is only projected like a whirlwind of phantasms. This immaterial world of symbols and abstractions appears as a pageant of color and fire; and in spite of the earnest intensity of his spiritual life, it strikes one rather as a metaphysical "show," splendid and amusing, but not dead earnest. The sense of tragedy is curiously absent from Bély, and in this again he is in bold contrast to Blok. His world is rather an elfland—beyond good and evil; in it Bély moves like a Puck or an Ariel—but an undisciplined and erratic Ariel. All this makes some people regard him as a seer and a prophet; others, as a sort of mystical mountebank. Whatever he is, he is strikingly different from all the symbolists by his complete lack of hieratic solemnity. Sometimes he is comic against his will, but on the whole he has most audaciously fused his comic appearance with his mysticism and utilized it with surprising originality. He is perhaps the greatest Russian humorist since Gógol, and to the general reader this is his most important and attractive aspect. But it is a humor that disconcerts at first and is very unlike anything else in the world. It took the Russian public some twenty years to learn to appreciate it, and it will hardly take the uninitiated foreigner by storm. But those who have tasted of it will always recognize it as (in the strict sense of the word) unique— one of the choicest and rarest gifts of the great gods.

Like many of his contemporaries, Andréy Bély (1880–1934) became famous under a pseudonym that finally replaced his inherited name (Borís Nikoláyevich Bugáyev) even in life. He was born in Moscow in the same year as Blok. His father (who appears in his son's writings as Professor Letáyev) was an eminent mathematician and Dean of the Faculty of Science at the University of Moscow. His son inherited a keen interest in the more abstruse mathematical problems. He studied at the private gymnasium of L. I. Polivánov, one of the best Russian educators of his day, who infected him with a profound interest in the Russian poets. At the house of M. S. Soloviëv, Bély used to meet Vladímir Soloviëv and early became an adept in his mystical teachings. The years immediately preceding and following the beginning of the new cen-

tury were for Bély and his precocious friend Sergéy Soloviëv an
era of ecstatic apocalyptic expectations. They believed, with the
most realistic concreteness, that the first years of the new century
would bring a new revelation—that of the Feminine Hypostasis,
Sophia—and that her coming would transform and transfigure
the whole of life. These expectations were enhanced by the news
of Blok's visions and poetry. At the same time Bély studied at
the University of Moscow, where he remained eight years, taking
degrees in philosophy and mathematics. Despite his brilliant ca-
pacities he was looked at askance by the professors for his "decadent" writings—some of them even refused to shake hands with
him at his father's funeral! The first of these "decadent" writings
appeared in 1902 under the disconcerting title *Symphony (Second,
Dramatic)*. A few exceptionally sensitive critics (M. S. Soloviëv,
Bryúsov, and the Merezhkóvskys) at once recognized in it something quite new and of unusual promise. It is almost a mature
work and presents a full idea of Bély's humor and his wonderful
gift of writing musically organized prose. But the critics treated it
and the works that followed with indignation and scorn, and for
several years Bély replaced Bryúsov (who was beginning to be
recognized) as stock target for all assaults on the "decadents." He
was reviled as an insolent clown whose antics desecrated the sacred
precincts of literature. The critics' attitude was natural and pardonable—in nearly all Bély's writings there is an unmistakable
element of foolery. The *Second Symphony* was followed by the
First (Northern, Heroic, 1904), the *Third (The Return*, 1905), and
the *Fourth (The Cup of Snowstorms*, 1908), and by a volume of
verse *(Gold in Azure*, 1904), all of which met with the same reception.

In 1905 Bély (one has to repeat this detail in the life of each
of the symbolists) was carried away by the wave of Revolution,
which he tried to unite with his Solovievian mysticism. But the
reaction that followed produced in Bély, as in Blok, a depression
and loss of faith in his mystical ideas. This depression appears in
two books of verse published in 1909: the realistic *Ashes*, where he
took up the traditions of Nekrásov, and *The Urn*, in which he
related his wanderings in the abstract wilderness of neo-Kantian
metaphysics. Bély's despair and depression have not the grim and
tragic bitterness of Blok's, and the reader cannot help taking him
somewhat less seriously, all the more since Bély's humorous gam-

bols are always there to divert him. All this time Bély wrote voluminously, in prose, brilliant but fantastic and impressionist critiques, in which he interpreted writers from the point of view of his mystical symbolism; and expositions of his metaphysical theories. He was highly valued by the symbolists but hardly known to the general public. In 1909 he published his first novel, *The Silver Dove.* This remarkable work, soon to have such an enormous influence on Russian prose, at first passed almost unnoticed. In 1910 he read a series of papers before the Poetry "Academy" of Petersburg on Russian prosody, from which one may date the very existence of Russian prosody as a branch of real knowledge.

In 1911 he married a girl who bore the poetical name of Ásya Turgénev, and the next year the young couple made the acquaintance of the notorious German "anthroposophist" Rudolf Steiner. Steiner's "anthroposophy" is a crudely elaborate, concrete, and detailed expression of the symbolist mentality, which regards the human microcosm as a parallel in every detail to the greater universal macrocosm. The Bélys fell under Steiner's spell and for four years lived in his magical establishment at Dornach, near Bâle ("Goetheaneum"). They took part in the construction of the Johanneum, which was all to be done by adepts without the intervention of profane workmen. In this period Bély published his second novel, *Petersburg* (1913), and wrote *Kótik Letáyev,* which appeared in 1917. When war broke out, he assumed a pacifist attitude. In 1916 he had to return to Russia to be mobilized, but the Revolution saved him from military service. Like Blok, he came under the influence of Ivánov-Razúmnik and his "Scythian" Revolutionary messianism; and in his (very weak) poem *Christ Is Risen* (1918) he identified Bolshevism with Christianity even more emphatically than Blok did.

Like Blok, Bély soon lost his faith in this identity, but, unlike Blok, he did not fall into a gloomy prostration. On the contrary, precisely in the worst years of Bolshevism (1918–21) he developed a feverish activity inspired with a faith in the great mystic renascence of Russia that was growing up in spite of the Bolshevíks. Russia, he thought, was developing before his eyes a new "culture of eternity" that was to displace the obsolete "humanist" civilization of Europe. Indeed, during these terrible years of starvation, destitution, and terror, there was in Russia a remarkable flowering of mystical and spiritualist creation. Bély became the center of this fermentation. He founded the *Volfila* (*Free Philosophical Association*), where the most burning problems of mystical metaphysics in their practical aspect were discussed with freedom, sincerity, and originality. He edited *The Dreamers' Journal* (1919–22), a non-periodical miscellany that contains almost all the best works published during these worst years. He gave lessons in poetry to the proletarian poets and lectured with enormous energy almost every day. In this period he wrote, besides much minor work, a series of important works: *The Memoirs of a Crank*, *The Crime of Nicholas Letáyev* (a continuation of *Kótik Letáyev*), a long poem entitled *The First Meeting*, and *Recollections of Blok*. He was, with Blok and Górky (who were as good as dead, for they wrote nothing), the biggest figure in Russian literature and far more influential than they. When, in 1922, there came the revival of the book trade, one of the first things done by the publishers was to reprint most of his work. In the same year he went to Berlin, where he became as central a figure among the *émigrés littérateurs* as he had been in Russia. But his ecstatic and peaceless mind did not permit him to remain abroad. In 1923 he returned to Russia, where he remained until his death.

One usually thinks of Andréy Bély as primarily a poet, and this is, on the whole, true; but his writings in verse are less in volume and significance than his prose. In verse he is almost always making experiments, and no one did more to open up the hidden possibilities of Russian verse, especially of its more conventional forms. His poetry does not have the accent of majesty and passionate intensity of Blok's. It is most easily and naturally assimilated if one takes it altogether as word play. His first book is full of Teutonic reminiscences (in subject more than in form). Nietzsche with the symbols of Zarathustra, and Boecklin with his centaurs, are present on many pages, but already here we have the first fruit of his humorous naturalism. *Ashes*, his most realistic book, is also the most earnest in tone, though it contains some of his best comical writing (*The Parson's Daughter and the Seminarist*). But the dominant note is one of grim and cynical despair.

The Urn (written after *Ashes*) is a most curious collection of pessimistic and whimsically ironical meditations on the non-existence of the world of realities revealed by Kant's philosophy. *After the Parting* (1922), a book of lyrics, is frankly a collection of verbal and rhythmical exercises. But his one longer poem, *The First Meeting* (1921), is a charming work. Like Soloviëv's *Three Meetings*, it is a mixture of grave and gay—a mixture that is curiously inseparable in Bély. A large part of it will again seem, to the uninitiated, nothing better than verbal and phonetic play. It must be joyfully accepted as such, and as such it is most exhilarating. But the realistic part of the poem is better than that. It contains some of his best humorous painting—the portraits of the Soloviëvs and the description of a big symphony concert in Moscow about 1900 are masterpieces of verbal expressiveness, delicate realism, and delightful humor. This poem is most closely connected with his prose works, and, like them, it is all based on a very elaborate system of musical construction, with leitmotivs, "correspondences," and "cross references."

In the preface to *The Dramatic Symphony*, Bély says: "This work has three senses: a musical sense, a satirical sense, and besides, a philosophical-symbolical sense." The same may be said of all his prose, except that the second meaning is not always strictly satirical—"realistic" would be more comprehensive. The philosophical meaning is what Bély probably thinks the most important, but for the reader the first way of enjoying his prose is not to take the philosophy too seriously and not to rack his brains in trying to discover the meaning. This would be useless, especially as regards the later "anthroposophic" work, the philosophy of which cannot be understood without a prolonged initiation at Dornach. But Bély's prose loses nothing from his philosophical symbols' being taken as merely ornamental. His prose is "ornamental prose"—an expression that later became a technical term. In this ornamental prose the symbols (and sound symbols) he uses to express his metaphysics are by no means the worst ornament. "Ornamental" is not the same as "ornate" prose. It is not necessarily marked by conventionally uplifted diction, as Sir Thomas Browne's or Vyacheslàv Ivànov's. On the contrary, it may be crudely realistic or even aggressively coarse (some of the younger "ornamentalists" went much farther in this respect than any naturalist ever dared to). The essential is that it keeps the reader's attention to every small detail: to the words, to their sounds, and to the rhythm. It is the opposite of Tolstóy's or Stendhal's analytical prose. It is the declaration of independence of the smaller unit. Western masters of "ornamental" prose are Rabelais, Lamb,

Carlyle. The greatest Russian ornamentalist was Gógol, whose work Bély discusses in the important *Mastery of Gógol* (1932). Ornamental prose has a decided tendency to escape the control of the larger unit, to destroy the wholeness of a work. This tendency is fully developed in almost every one of Bély's followers. But in Bély's own work it is counterbalanced by the musical architecture of the whole. This musical architecture is expressed in the very name of the *Symphonies*, and it is attained by a most elaborate system of leitmotivs and "cross references," crescendos and diminuendos, and parallel developments of independent but (by their symbolism) connected themes. However, the centrifugal tendencies of the style usually have the better of the centripetal forces of musical construction, and, with the possible exception of *The Silver Dove*, Bély's *Symphonies* and novels are but imperfect wholes. They cannot compare in this respect with the supreme unity of *The Twelve*. The *Symphonies* (especially *The Dramatic*) contain much that is excellent, chiefly of the satirical order, but they cannot be recommended to the inexperienced beginner. The best approach is either through *Recollections of Alexander Blok* or *The Silver Dove*.

The Silver Dove is somewhat less wildly original than his other works. It is closely modeled on the great example of Gógol. It cannot be called an imitative work, for it requires a powerful originality to learn from Gógol without failing piteously. Bély is probably the only Russian writer who has succeeded in doing so. The novel is written in splendid, sustainedly beautiful prose, and this prose is the first thing that strikes the reader. It is not so much Bély, however, as Gógol reflected in Bély, but it is always on Gógol's highest level, which is seldom the case with Gógol himself. *The Silver Dove* is somewhat alone also in being the one of Bély's novels that has the most human interest in it, where the tragedy is infectious and not merely puckishly ornamental. The scene is a rural district of central Russia. The hero is an intellectual who has drunk deep of the choicest fruit of European and ancient culture but remains unsatisfied and desires to find a new truth. He joins a set of peasants belonging to the mystical and orgiastic sect of the White Doves. He feels himself sucked in by their sensual mysticism, and though he knows moments of ecstatic bliss, he feels himself again attracted by the pure image of his forsaken "Western" love. He tries to escape but is murdered by the mystics, who fear the revelations he may make, once escaped from their spell. The novel contains much more narrative interest than most Russian novels do. The characters are vivid—like Gógol's, characterized largely by their physical features; the dialogue is alive and expressive. But what is perhaps especially wonderful is the evocations of nature, full of intense suggestiveness and pregnant poetry. The feeling of the monotonous and endless expanse of the Russian plain pervades the book. All this, together with the splendidly ornamental style, makes *The Silver Dove* one of the works of Russian literature most full of the most various riches.

Petersburg, like *The Silver Dove*, is also a novel on the philosophy of Russian history. In *The Silver Dove* the theme is the opposition between East and West; in *Petersburg*, their coincidence. Russian nihilism, in its two forms—the formalism of the Petersburg bureaucracy and the rationalism of the Revolutionaries—is represented as the meeting point of the devastating rationalism of the West with the destructive forces of the "Mongol" steppe. The two Ableúkhovs—the bureaucrat father and the Terrorist son—are of Tatar origin. *Petersburg* is connected with Dostoyévsky as much as *The Silver Dove* is with Gógol, but not with the whole of Dostoyévsky; only *The Double*, the most "ornamental" and Gogolian of all Dostoyévsky's writings, is reflected in Bély's novel. Its style is unlike that of its predecessor; it is not so rich, and it is, like *The Double*, tuned to a dominating note of madness. The book reads like a nightmare, and it is not always easy to realize exactly what is going on. It has a great power of obsession, and, like *The Silver Dove*, the narrative is thrilling. The story centers on an infernal machine that is due to explode in twenty-four hours, and the reader is kept in suspense by the detailed and many-sided account of these twenty-four hours and the hero's decisions and counter-decisions.

Kótik Letáyev is Bély's most original work. It is the story of his infancy and begins with his recollections of life in his mother's womb. It is built on a system of parallel lines: the one developed in the real life of the child, the other in the "spheres." It is certainly a work of genius, although the detail is disconcerting and the anthroposophical interpretation of the child's impressions as a repetition of the older experience of the race is not always convincing. The main thread of the story (if story it be) is the gradual formation of the child's idea of the external world. This process is expressed with the aid of two terms that may be rendered as "swarm" and "form" (*roy i stroy*). It is the crystallization of chaotic and infinite "swarms" into strictly circumscribed and orderly "forms." The development is symbolically enhanced by the fact that the child's father is an eminent mathematician, a master of "forms." But to the anthroposophist Bély, the boundless "swarms" are the truer and more significant reality. The continuation—*The Crime of Nicholas Letáyev*—is much less abstrusely symbolical and may easily be read by the uninitiated. It is unfolded in a real world: it is the story of the rivalry of his parents—his mathematical father and his elegant and frivolous mother—over his education. Here Bély is in his best form as a subtle and penetrating realist, and his humor (though the symbolism never ceases) reaches its most delightful expression. *The Memoirs of a Crank*, though splendidly ornamental, are better left unread by those not initiated in the mysteries of anthroposophy. But the *Recollections of Alexander Blok* (1922) are easy and simple reading. The musical construction is absent, and Bély obviously concentrates on the exact notation of fact. The style is also less ornamental, sometimes even rather untidy (which is never the case in his other works). The two or three chapters devoted to the anthroposophical interpretation of Blok's poetry should be skipped. The remaining chapters are a mine of the most interesting and unexpected information on the history of Russian symbolism, but, above all, they are delightful reading. Though he always looked up to Blok as to a superior being, Bély analyzes him with wonderful insight and penetration. The account of their mystical association in 1903–4 is extraordinarily vivid and convincing, so skillfully does he succeed in restoring the atmosphere of these connections. But perhaps the best thing in the whole *Recollections* is the portraits of the secondary personages, which are painted with all the wealth of intuition, suggestiveness, and humor of which Bély is capable. The figure of Merezhkóvsky is especially a masterpiece of the first order, and the tasseled slippers that Bély introduces as his leitmotiv will probably go down to posterity as the immortal badge of their wearer.[2]

---

[2] Three more volumes of memoirs followed the *Recollections*—*On the Border of Two Centuries* (1929), *The Beginning of a Century* (1932), and *Between Two Revolutions* (1933). To the last period also belong *Moscow* and *Masks*, two novels of a projected tetralogy on Russian life before, during, and after the Revolution.—Editor

MINOR SYMBOLISTS

One of the principal effects of the symbolist movement was to multiply a hundredfold the number of poets and to raise in an almost equal degree the average level of their workmanship and their social position in the estimation of the public and the publishers. After about 1905 the newcomers in Russian poetry were all more or less pupils of the symbolists, and all except the illiterate succeeded in writing verse of a technical standard that was inaccessible except to the greatest about the year 1890. The influence of symbolism went in several main directions—there were: the metaphysical and mystical school; the school of rhythm and verbal pageantry; the academic school, which imitated the mature style of Bryúsov; the "orgiastic" school, which aimed at the emancipation from the fetters of form towards a spontaneous expression of the "elemental" soul; the school of glorified vice; [3] and the school of sheer technical acrobatism.

The older metaphysical poetry of the early symbolists may be exemplified by the austere and unsensational poems of Jurgis Baltrusháitis, a Lithuanian who was a diligent translator of the Scandinavians and of D'Annunzio (we owe to him also an excellent version of Byron's *Vision of Judgment*). Sergéy Soloviëv, the precocious and brilliant mystic, turned out in his poetry to be nothing but a very accomplished disciple of Bryúsov's academic manner. Despite his mysticism and genuine Orthodoxy, his poetry is antique in the most heathen sense of the word. His life of his famous uncle, Vladímir, is, on the other hand, one of the most charming biographies in the language.

What the public liked in the symbolists was their verbal splendor and caressing melodies. This pageantry of the symbolists is best vulgarized in the poetry of Téffy (pseudonym of Mme N. A. Buchínsky, also well known for her humorous short stories); and the Balmontian intoxication with melodious rhythms, in the poetry of Victor Hoffman, who may be taken as the "typical minor" symbolist—with his sentimental prettiness and wistfulness, and his paraphernalia, so vulgarized afterward, of beautiful ladies and devoted pages. More promise than in any one of these poets was thought to be discerned in the exhilarating early verse

[3] I remember a dialogue between two young poets about 1907: "How I love the word *razvrát* (debauch)!" "I prefer the thing."

of Sergéy Gorodétsky. In his first book, *Yar* (roughly, "vital sap" —1907), he displayed a wonderful gift of rhythm and a curious power of creating a self-invented—quasi-Russian—mythology. But his subsequent books proved how little breath there was in him, and he degenerated rapidly into an easy and insignificant rhymester. *Yar*, however, remains as the most interesting monument of its time, when mystical anarchism was in the air, when Vyacheslav Ivánov believed in the possibility of a new mythological age, and when the belief was abroad that the vital forces of man's elemental nature were to burst the fetters of civilization and of the world order.

A curious and isolated figure is that of Count Vasíly Alekséyevich Komaróvsky, who was almost all his life on the border of insanity and crossed it more than once. This familiarity with madness gives a distinctive flavor to his very exiguous writings. His poetry, most of which is contained in his only book, *The First Stage* (1913), is exceedingly original, at once whimsical and ornate. There is in it a feeling of a terrible abyss over which he most lightheartedly weaves the sunlit spider webs of his splendid diction and erratic humor. Probably no poet ever succeeded in giving his verse that absolutely indefinable touch of unique personality so well as Komaróvsky did. Still more unique and indescribable is his prose, in which his whimsical willfulness runs riot, and the malicious and unaccountable twinkle in his eye is suggestive of the more than human freedom of a being that is supremely free from the laws of causation. There is nothing like Komaróvsky's prose that I know of in any language, but one must be singularly free from pedantry and open to unexpected enjoyments to appreciate it. Komaróvsky had connections with symbolism, especially with Ánnensky and Henri de Régnier, but he was not a symbolist— because he was not an "ist" of any kind.

"STYLIZATORS"

An important aspect of the Russian æsthetic revival—of which symbolism was but the most important literary expression—was a revival of interest in the artistic production of the past, both national and foreign. It often took the form, both in painting and in poetry, of consciously imitating the manner of old artists and

old writers. This kind of creative pastiche is known in Russian
literary jargon by the name of "stylization." In literature it
affected principally the domain of prose. The symbolists had no
fixed idea as to what sort of prose they wanted to write, and each
of them went his own way; so that while there is a symbolist school
of poetry, there is no symbolist school of prose. While some symbolists solved the problem by subjecting prose to rules derived
from poetry (Balmónt, Sologúb, Bély), and others indulged in a
free impressionism (Híppius), others again, not relying on themselves, sought for the guidance of some external authority and
came to imitate the prose of past ages. Such was the case of
Bryúsov, whose best prose is always a "stylization." The method
was not confined to prose, and many minor poets of the period
devoted themselves more or less entirely to pastiches, attaining
sometimes a great delicacy in this art. Such, for instance, is Yúry
Verkhóvsky, a great authority on the age of Púshkin and a skillful
pasticheur of its poets. But the greatest name in this connection is
Michael Alekséyevich Kuzmín, who, though a member of the
symbolist set (and for several years an inmate of the "Tower"),
as a writer stands apart from the symbolist school. He is a pure
æsthete. His favorite periods in the past are the Alexandrian age,
the early Byzantine times, and the eighteenth century. On the
other hand, he is firmly grounded in the Russian religious tradition and has a peculiar sense of sympathy for the Old Believers.
There is a distinct religious strain in his work, but it is not like
that of the symbolists—it is not metaphysical, but devotional
and ritual. This religious element is inseparable in him from a
refined and perverse sensuality. The two make a piquant blend
that is not to the taste of all. His poetry is different from that of
the symbolists in that it is more concrete and less solemn. The
feeling he expresses in it is almost invariably love. His craftsmanship is very high, and his verses are often exquisite. His first
poetical sequence, *Songs of Alexandria* (1906), is also his best. It
was inspired by the example of Pierre Louÿs's *Chansons de Bilitis*,
but there can be no doubt that the Russian poet's reconstructions
of Alexandrian love songs are far more delicate, refined, and suggestive. These songs were followed by the whimsically exquisite
"eighteenth-century" pastoral *The Seasons of Love* (1907), in
which his wonderful, almost acrobatic skill in handling rhyme is at
its best. (The music to the pastoral is also by Kuzmín.) His later

poetry consists partly of rather tedious allegorical love poems in the style of Petrarch's *Trionfi*, partly of exquisitely frivolous evocations of "the charming trifles" of life, in which he has no equal. In prose he vindicates the ideal of "beautiful clarity," inspiring himself by the example of the late Greek romancers, the Lives of the Saints, the Italian *novella*, and the French novel of the eighteenth century. His style is affected and advisedly Frenchified. Its charm lies in its piquant and perverse flavor, for though he writes novels of pure adventure, he is curiously lacking in the power to tell a story. His stories of modern life are indifferently constructed and seldom interesting. But what is admirable in them is the dialogue, which goes even farther than Tolstóy's in reproducing the actual accents and freedom of spoken language. He has also written scenarios for ballets, operettas, and plays. They are usually mischievous and frivolous, and their principal charm lies in the rhymed passages. The most exquisite of all is *The Comedy of St. Alexis*, an early work (1907) that is especially typical of his manner of treating sacred things and that contains some of his best songs.

KHODASÉVICH

The poets born after 1880 contributed little or nothing to the genuine achievement of symbolism. An exception is the case of Vladisláv Khodasévich (in Polish, Wladýslaw Chodasiéwicz, 1886–1939). Though in his technique he is almost free from symbolist influences, the general spirit of his poetry is much more akin to symbolism than to that of the younger school, for, alone of the younger poets, he is a mystic. His first book appeared in 1908, but he won general recognition only after the publication of his later, post-Revolutionary books, *The Way of the Grain* (1920) and *The Heavy Lyre* (1923), which are full of mature and confident art. Khodasévich is a mystical spiritualist, but in the expression of his intuitions he is an ironist. His poetry is the expression of the ironic and tragic contradiction between the freedom of the immortal soul and its thralldom to matter and necessity. This eternal theme is expressed in his verse with a neatness and elegance rather reminiscent of the wit of an older age. Wit, in fact, is the principal characteristic of Khodasévich's poetry, and his mystical poems regularly end with a pointed epigram. This manner is very effective and goes home to the most unpoetical reader. He sprang into popularity in 1919–20, when, under the influence of their superhuman suffering, the Russian intellectuals were more than usually open to the lure of mystic moods. But in spite of his mystical faith, he is a classicist, and his style is a skillful revival of the forms and fashions of the Golden Age of Púshkin.

RÉMIZOV

The symbolists, victorious in poetry, did not at first succeed in finding a new style in prose. Their efforts in this direction remained disconnected and ineffective. Up to about 1910 imaginative prose was dominated by the writers of the Górky-Andréyev school, but in the long run the influence of symbolism, and of writers connected with symbolism, made itself felt. Bély's novels, his part in introducing ornamental prose, and the characteristics of his own prose have already been discussed in connection with the rest of his work. Rémizov's action was in the same direction—towards more elaborate and conscious craftsmanship in the choice and arrangement of words—but with a difference. Bély's prose is rhythmical and "symphonic"; Rémizov's is primarily colloquial. The essence of his manner, which had been the manner of Leskóv, is expressed by the term *skaz*, which means the reproduction in written prose of the intonations of spoken language, with a particular eye for the individualization of the supposed narrator.

Alexéy Mikháylovich Rémizov is a pure Muscovite. He was born in 1877, in Taganka, in the "East End" of Moscow. His ancestors were wealthy merchants, but his parents had fallen out with the family and were reduced to rather straitened circumstances. So Rémizov grew up in comparative poverty, and his early experiences were chiefly of the street life in the industrial quarter of the metropolis. This life is reflected in the sordid nightmares of his first novel, *The Pond*. He received, however, the usual middle-class education at a secondary school and became a student of Moscow University. He began writing very early (his first works are dated 1896), but he was not published till 1902. Meanwhile, in 1897, for a trivial circumstance, he was expelled from the University and banished into the provinces, at first to the comparatively civilized town of Pénza, afterward to the remote Ust-Sysólsk, then again to the larger center of Vólogda. These ancient and out-of-the-way little towns are the background of some of his most characteristic stories—*The Clock, Stratilátov, The Fifth Pestilence*. In Vólogda he married Serafíma Dovgiéllo, an eminent student of palæography, whose name appears in the dedication of all his books. In 1904 he was released from police surveillance and allowed to choose his home. He settled in Petersburg, where he remained till 1921. His works had, since 1902, begun to appear in the publications of the modernists. His first book was published in 1907. For a long time his works had very few readers, and even the modernists looked upon him with mild wonder and were not always willing to lend him their columns. But in the inner circles of literature Rémizov became an exceptionally popular figure. His whimsical and mischievous humor led him to imagine a whole organization of which he was the Chancellor—the Great and Free House of Apes. Most eminent Russian writers and publishers received charters granting them some dignity in the House of Apes, written in a beautiful seventeenth-century cursive hand and signed, *propria cauda*, by Asýka, King of Apes. Among the first officers of the order were the Chancellor's intimate friends, the philosophers Rózanov and Shestóv. His rooms were a menagerie of all manner of toy animals and goblins, and many of his writings have them for their heroes. Gradually, especially after *Stratilátov*, which became known even before it was published, Rémizov became the head of a new school of fiction, and by the beginning of the first World War the literary press was full of imitations of this and similar stories. Príshvin, A. N. Tolstóy, and Zamyátin were the first in date to take up his lead. In 1916, when the selfish and shortsighted policy of the Entente insisted on Russia's mobilizing more men than she could arm, Rémizov was also mobilized, but, after a hospital test, liberated on grounds of illness. After he left the University, Rémizov never took any part in politics, but his writings during the war, in 1917 and the years following, are remarkable for their extraordinary sensitiveness to the life of the nation. The atmosphere of Petersburg during those tragic years of 1914–21 is nowhere so convincingly present as in such books of Rémizov's as *Mára, The Chronicle of 1917*, and *The Noises of the Town*. Nor did he take sides in and after 1917. *The Lament for the Ruin of Russia*, written in August-September 1917, though "political" in the best and broadest Greek sense of the word, is quite outside party politics. After living in Petersburg through the worst years of famine and cold, Rémizov, whose health was seriously jeopardized by all these privations, was at length allowed by the Soviet Government to leave Russia. At the end of 1921 he came first to Berlin; then, in 1923, to Paris, where he remained.

Rémizov's work is one of the most varied in the whole of Russian literature—to such an extent that few of his admirers can embrace the whole of it in their admiration. Those who value the "underground" Dostoyevskianism of *The Pond* will find little interest in the studied naïveté of *On a Field Azure;* those who like the lyrical eloquence of the mystery plays or of *The Lament for the Ruin of Russia* will be disgusted by such privately printed uncensored tales as *Tsar Dadón.* To get hold of the essence of Rémizov's personality, or to realize the unifying principle of his work, is the most difficult and baffling of tasks, so elusive and many-sided is he. He is the greatest of humorists, and at the same time he shows now and again a curious lack of humor that induces one to classify him with the most hieratic of symbolists. With this literary school his relations are unmistakable. He belongs to the same stratum in the history of Russian civilization. But there is more in him than mere symbolism, and what marks him off from all the rest of his contemporaries is that he is firmly rooted in the traditional Russian soil. All the Russian tradition—from the mythology of pagan times through all the Russianized forms of Byzantine Christianity to Gógol, Dostoyévsky, and Leskóv—has been absorbed and assimilated by Rémizov. His case, by the way, is one of those which refute the superficial idea of Russia as mainly a peasant country. All the most original and "Russian" of Russian writers—Gógol, Grigóriev, Dostoyévsky, Leskóv—neither belonged to nor knew the Russian peasantry. The same with Rémizov: he lived in the East End of Moscow, in Petersburg, in provincial towns big and little, but never more than a day or two in the country.

Rémizov is very largely a man of books and papers; it is not for nothing that he married a palæographer. No one in Russia has spoken of books with such sincere affection; in no one's mouth does the word *knízhnik* ("bookman," "lover of books") sound so caressing and laudatory as in Rémizov's. A large proportion of his writings is adaptations of folklore matter or of ancient legends.

One of his books, *Russia in Writ*, is a running commentary on certain ancient manuscripts in his possession. He is a very laborious writer—and in more senses than one. Not only is his work at his style as elaborate and patient as was Charles Lamb's (with whom he has certain points of resemblance), but his actual handwriting is a most elaborate and skillful revival of the cursive writing of the seventeenth century.

Rémizov's work may be divided into what we may conveniently call his prose and his poetry. In actual meter there is practically nothing, but the difference of diction and artistic object between his stories and, say, *The Lament for the Ruin*, justifies us in speaking of his poetry and in distinguishing it from his prose. Both intrinsically and historically, his prose is more important than his poetry. It is his prose that exercised such a profound influence on the younger generation of writers. In spite of its great variety, it is unified by one purpose—which is to de-Latinize and de-Frenchify the Russian literary language and to restore to it its natural Russian raciness. Russian literary prose, since the beginning of letters in the eleventh century down to the existent forms of journalese, has never been free from foreign grammatical influence. The Greek influence of the Slavonic translations of Church books, the Latin influence of the schools in the seventeenth and eighteenth centuries, the French influence paramount since Karamzín and Púshkin, all lie in thick layers on the Russian literary language of today and make it so very different from the spoken Russian of the people and from the pre-schoolmaster Russian of the upper classes. The difference lies principally in the syntax, and even writers who, like Tolstóy, were studiously colloquial in their diction could never go without a Latinized and Frenchified syntax. Only Rózanov, in his "anti-Gutenberg" prose, tried to create a more "spoken" form of written Russian. Rémizov has gone farther in this direction. His prose reproduces the syntax and intonation of spoken language—and of the spoken language in its least literary and most native forms. He has a keen sense for words—for individual words and for grammatical composition. His prose, often very studious and elaborate, is always new and never falls into clichés. He taught the Russian writer to value his words—to think of them as of independent beings and not to use them as mere signs or as parts of ready-made verbal groups. He often goes too far in this direction: he cannot resist the temptation to use a good old word he has chanced on in some old document or to coin a new one to suit his needs. His action on the language is largely parallel to that of the futurists, who also applied themselves to linguistic creation (Khlébnikov) and de-Latinizing the language.

Rémizov's prose works consist of novels and stories of contemporary Russian life; of legends taken from the *Prologue* or from the Apocrypha; of folk tales and fairy tales; of dreams; of memoirs and diaries; and of commentaries on old documents. He is not a storyteller in the true sense of the word, and his influence over younger writers greatly contributed to the disintegration of the narrative form. In his early stories the lyrical element is considerable. They are almost always concerned with the grotesque and the unusual, with a touch of Dostoyevskian psychological weirdness. A typical example is *Princess Mýmra* (1908), one of the latest and best in the series, which tells of the cruel disillusionment of a schoolboy who fell platonically in love with a harlot. A Dostoyevskian atmosphere of intense shame and humiliation dominates the story. Other early stories deal with the fantastic—with the familiar devils and goblins of Russian popular fancy, whom Rémizov usually speaks of with a semi-humorous twinkle in the eye, but who, for all that, are sometimes very seriously mischievous. The largest works of his early period are *The Clock* (written 1904; published 1908), a story of provincial life, which is only an imperfect sketch in comparison with those that followed; and *The Pond* (1902–5; published 1907), a novel of Moscow, in which he drew on the impressions of his childhood. There is still a lot of the untidy, poetical *moderne* in *The Pond*, which recalls the disagreeable manner of certain Polish and German novelists; but it produces a very powerful impression. The Dostoyevskian intensity of pain, of compassion with another's pain, and of morbid attention to pain wherever it is to be found, reaches in *The Pond* its most quintessential expression. The book is almost one uninterrupted paroxysm of pain and racking compassion. The filth and cruelty of life are portrayed with a ruthless realism that struck with horror even those who were accustomed to Górky and Andréyev. The same theme is taken up in *The Sisters of the Cross* (1910), where the squalid misery of the inhabitants of a large block of buildings in Petersburg—"Búrkov's house"—grows into a symbol of the world of misery. The principal theme of the book is the cruelty of fate to those "unanswering," defenseless, always unlucky and unsuccessful beings who come into the world to be the playthings of cruelty and treachery.

In 1909 Rémizov wrote *The Story of Iván Semënovich Stratilátov* (at first called *The Unhushable Tambourine*). In the way of formal fiction, it is his masterpiece. It is a story of provincial life centered in the character of the clerk Stratilátov, one of the most striking and extraordinary creations in the whole picture gallery of Russian fiction. Like most of Rémizov's characters, he is an underworld character, but with such peculiar touches as are quite out of the line of Dostoyévsky. The story is a masterpiece of construction, though the plan of it is not strictly narrative. Rémizov, alone of all Russian writers, is capable of these weird, uncanny effects, quite free from anything apparently terrible or uncanny, but which convey the unmistakable impression of the presence of minor devils. *The Fifth Pestilence* (1912) is also a provincial story. It is more piercingly human and less weird: it is the story of a scrupulously honest but cold and inhuman—and consequently intensely unpopular—examining magistrate against a background of provincial sloth, filth, and spite. The hated man is gradually forced to commit a glaring and unpardonable judicial blunder, and Rémizov's poetic justice makes his ruin come as an expiation of his cold and inhuman integrity. To the same period belongs *Petushók* (1911), the piercingly tragic story of a little boy killed by a chance shot during the suppression of the Revolution. It became one of the most influential of Rémizov's stories owing to the great richness of its "ornamentally" colloquial style.

In his later stories Rémizov's style becomes more chaste and less exuberant, always remaining as racy and as careful. The war years are reflected in *Mára (Fata Morgana,* 1917), which includes *The Teapot*, an extraordinarily delicate story of pity and sensitiveness. It is constructed with Chekhovian art and belongs to a long series of stories of pity—characteristic of Russian realism—to which belong Gógol's *Greatcoat* and Turgénev's *Mumú*. The Revolution and Bolshevík Petersburg are reflected in *The Noises of the Town* (1921), which also contains many lyrical pieces and legends. Somewhat apart from the rest of Rémizov's fiction stands *On a Field Azure*, which he began in 1910 and which appeared in 1922, with continuations at later dates. It is the story of a girl, Ólya, first at home in the country, then at school, and in the university, where she becomes an S.R. The story is one of his best: all the more so as he refrains in it from all the exuberance and originality of his style but keeps its essential characteristic—the purity of colloquial diction. It is remarkable for the subtly produced atmosphere—thin and delicate—of the old-world country home and for the charming drawing of the heroine's character. But it is not a novel—rather a series of anecdotes and glimpses of life.

In time Rémizov grew always more willing to abandon the hard-and-fast limits of fiction and to adopt freer forms. The most notable of these ventures are *The Chronicle of 1917*, a remarkably free and unjournalistic diary of his impressions during the Revolution, and *Rózanov's Letters* (1923), a worthy tribute to the memory of that remarkable man who was his intimate friend, but a book written by a Russian for Russians, and one that will appear wildly unintelligible to the foreigner. The same tendency towards less formal expression appears in *Russia in Writ*, a book of commented documents, chiefly of the early eighteenth century. In all these and in other fragmentary memoirs, Rémizov remains the wonderful stylist he is; nowhere does his mischievous and whimsical humor appear more freely and strangely. This twinkle in the eye, which is at times merely playful but at times becomes unexpectedly uncanny, is perhaps the ultimate and truest expression of Rémizov's personality. It reappears in his *Dreams*, which are accounts of real, genuine, and quite ordinary dreams such as one sees every night, but they are revived with all their peculiar logic, so simply intelligible to the sleeping man and so wildly strange to him when he is awake. Introduced into *The Chronicle of 1917*, they give it that unique and peculiarly Remizovian touch which is so inimitable.

As dreams have a logic of their own, so also do folk tales—and one that is very different from ours. This wonderful assimilation of the "fairy-tale" logic is the principal charm of Rémizov's numerous and varied *skázki* (a word customarily but not quite exactly rendered by the English "fairy tale." The German *Märchen* is a more exact equivalent). Some of these tales are his own and are connected with Ólya of *On a Field Azure*. They are perhaps the most delightful of all, so strangely and so convincingly alive are the hares, the bears, and the mice that inhabit them; so uncannily homely the goblins and devils; and so infectious their genuine dream logic. These fairy tales form a volume entitled *Tales of the Monkey King Asýka*. The same qualities, but without the same childlike atmosphere, reappear in *Tales of the Russian People*, which are founded on genuine folk tales but become delightfully new in the hands of Rémizov. The same style is reproduced in *St. Nicholas's Parables*, but these are more seriously meant and have a definitely religious object. The popular conception of the benevolent saint and miracle worker Nicholas as a help in every work, who will even help to cheat and steal, and will always intercede before God for the poor man, is particularly near to Rémizov's heart. These *Parables* are a link between the fairy tales and the legends. Some of the legends, especially those contained in *Travá-Muravá*, are merely humorous, complicated stories of adventures and wonders, in the style of the Greek romance—stories in which the absurdities of the narrative are brought out with affectionate emphasis. Such a story as *Apollo of Tyre* is a delightful example in this manner and a masterpiece of racy Russian.[4] Other legends are more rhetorical and ornate and have a more definite religious message. This religious message is very much akin to Rózanov's cult of kindness. Rémizov dwells on the well-known legend of the Virgin's visit to hell, where she was so moved by the sufferings of the damned that she wished to share them; and she finally obtained from God a release of all the damned souls from hell for forty days every year. This legend, of Byzantine origin, became especially popular in Russia, and Rémizov sees in it the fundamental religious conception of the Russian people—the religion of pure charity and compassion. Most of Rémizov's legends are from old Slavonic books, canonical or apocryphal, and ultimately of Byzantine origin, but he does not shun other sources. Some of his legends are of Western origin, and he has made adaptations from the folklore of various primitive nations.

Rémizov's legends are the connecting link between his prose and his poetry. If *Apollo of Tyre* is in his purest colloquial manner, the legends of the early *Limonar* (1907) are written in an elevated Slavonic style with a lyrical coloring. His "poetry" (with few exceptions, in rhythmical prose) is almost as various as his "prose." It includes the charming prose lyrics that, together with the Asýka tales, originally formed the book *Posolon* and its sequel *To the Ocean Sea*. It includes also some of the best pages of *The Noises of the Town*, inspired by the life of Petersburg in 1918–21, such as the

---

[4] *Apollo of Tyre* is a descendant of the same Greek romance of which Shakspere's *Pericles* is the best-known English version.

wonderful *Fences*, a lyric of spring after the "bestial" winter of 1919–20—walking in a suburb of Petersburg as the last fences are being taken down for fuel, he suddenly sees a vista opened on the infinite sea. Many of his prose lyrics are full of pathos and rhetoric, but the rhetoric is redeemed by the exquisite workmanship of words and by the poignancy of the emotion. Such is the *Lament for the Ruin of Russia*, full of passionate love and passionate suffering for his country.

But, on the whole, Rémizov's poetry is "secondary," derivative; it is a "bookman's" poetry, which would not have been written without the ancient poetry contained in old books, canonical and apocryphal. This derivativeness is also apparent in his mystery plays, which are also founded on apocryphal and popular plays. Those who love Rémizov the humorist will find little to their liking in *The Devil's Comedy*, in *George the Brave*, or in *Judas, Prince of Iscariot*. The plays are ritual and hieratic, saturated with ancient lore and symbolism. Even *King Maximilian* (1918), based on the amusing and absurd popular play of that name, is made into a mystery with profound symbols. Here more than anywhere is Rémizov a contemporary of the symbolists. The influence of his poetry and of his mystery plays was as small as that of his prose style and of his provincial stories was great. The principal difference between Rémizov and his followers is the difference between the generation born before and after (roughly) 1885—the older generation, in its greatest expression, is mystical and symbolical; the younger one is not. Rémizov the craftsman, linguist, and realist had a numerous following—the poet and mystic remained barren of influence.

CHAPTER 6

Poetry after 1910

GUMILËV AND THE POETS' GUILD

THE poetic generation born after 1885 continued the Revolutionary and cultural work of the symbolists—but ceased to be symbolists. About 1910 the symbolist school began to disintegrate, and in the course of the next few years rival schools came into existence, of which the two most important are the acmeists and the futurists. Acmeism (the rather ridiculous word was suggested with a satirical intention by a hostile symbolist and defiantly accepted by the new school) had its center in Petersburg. It was started in 1912 by Gorodétsky and Gumilëv as a reaction against the symbolist attitude. They refused to regard things as mere signs of other things. "We want to admire a rose," they said, "because it is beautiful, not because it is a symbol of mystical purity." They wanted to see the world with fresh and unprejudiced eyes as "Adam saw it at the dawn of creation." Their doctrine was a new realism, but a realism particularly alive to the concrete individuality of things. They tried to avoid the pitfalls of æstheticism and proclaimed as their masters (a queer set) Villon, Rabelais, Shakspere, and Théophile Gautier. Visual vividness, emotional intensity, and verbal freshness were the qualities they demanded of a poet. But they also wanted to make poetry more of a craft, and the poet not a priest but a craftsman. The foundation of the Guild of Poets was an expression of this tendency. The symbolists, who had wanted to make poetry a religious activity ("theurgy"), resented this development and remained (especially Blok) distinctly hostile to Gumilëv and his Guild.

Of the two founders of the new school, Gorodétsky has been mentioned elsewhere. By 1912 he had already outlived his talent.

He requires no further mention in this connection (except that after writing some exceedingly chauvinistic war verse in 1914, he became a Communist in 1918, and, immediately after the execution of Gumilëv by the Bolshevíks, wrote of him in a tone of the most servile vilification). Nikoláy Stepánovich Gumilëv, apart from his historical importance, is a true poet. Born in 1886 at Tsárskoye Seló, he studied at Paris and Petersburg. His first book, published in Paris, was kindly reviewed by Bryúsov, whose influence is very apparent in it as well as in the books that followed. In 1910 Gumilëv married Anna Akhmátova, who divorced him in 1918. In 1911 he traveled in Abyssinia and Gallaland, where he returned once more before 1914. He retained a peculiar affection for equatorial Africa. In 1912 he founded the Guild of Poets, whose publications had at first little success. In 1914 he was the only Russian author to enlist as a soldier (in the cavalry). He was twice awarded the St. George's Cross, and in 1915 obtained a commission. In 1917 he was detailed to the Russian contingent in Macedonia, but the Bolshevík Revolution found him in Paris. In 1918 he returned to Russia, largely from a spirit of adventure and love of danger. "I have hunted lions," he said, "and I don't believe the Bolshevíks are much more dangerous." For three years he lived in or near Petersburg, taking part in the big translation enterprises initiated by Górky, teaching the art of verse to younger poets, and writing his best poems. In 1921 he was arrested on the (apparently false) charge of conspiring against the Soviet Government and, after several months of imprisonment, was shot by order of the Cheká. He was in the full maturity of his talent; his last book was his best and was full of further promise.

Gumilëv's verse is most unlike the common run of Russian poetry: it is gorgeous, exotic, and fantastic; it is consistently in the major key and dominated by a note that is rare in Russian literature—the love of adventure and manly romance. His early book *Pearls* (1910), which is full of exotic splendors, sometimes in doubtful taste, contains *The Captains*, a poem in praise of the great sailors and adventurers of the high seas; with characteristic romanticism, it ends with an evocation of the Flying Dutchman. His war poetry is curiously free from all "political" feeling—the ends of the war are what interests him least. A new religious strain is present in these war poems that is rather different from the mysticism of the symbolists—it is a boyish and unquestioning faith, full of a spirit of joyful sacrifice. *The Tent* (1921), written in Bolshevík Petersburg, is a sort of poetical geography of Africa, his favorite continent. The most impressive poem contained in it— *The Equatorial Forest*—is the story of a French explorer among the gorillas and cannibals in the malaria-haunted forest of central Africa. His best books are *The Pyre* (1918) and *The Pillar of Fire* (1921). In them his verse acquires an emotional tenseness and earnestness that are absent from his early work. It contains such an interesting manifesto as *My Readers*, in which he prides himself on giving them a poetical diet that is not debilitating or relaxing and that helps them to play the man and be calm in the face of death. In another poem he expresses his wish to die a violent death and "not in my bed, before my lawyer and my doctor." His poetry becomes at times intensely nervous, as in the strange and haunting *Stray Tramcar*, but more often it attains to a manly majesty and earnestness, as in the remarkable dialogue of himself with his soul and his body—where the body ends its soliloquy with the noble words:

> But for all which I have taken, or yet desire,
> For all my sorrows, and joys, and follies,
> As it befits a man, I will pay
> By irrevocable and final death.

The last poem in the book, *Star-Terror*, is a strangely weird and convincing account of how primæval man first dared to look in the face of the stars. When he died, he was working on another poem of primæval times, *The Dragon*, a curiously original and fantastic cosmogony, of which only the first canto was completed.

The poets of the Guild, on the whole, are imitators of Gumilëv or of that precursor of theirs, Kuzmín. Though they write agreeably and efficiently, they need not detain us—their work is "school work." They are memorable rather as the principal figures of that gay and frivolous *vie de Bohème* which was such a prominent feature of *tout Pétersbourg* in 1913–16 and which had its center in the famous artistic cabaret of the Prowling Dog. But two poets connected with the Guild, Anna Akhmátova and Ósip Mándelstam, are figures of greater importance.

ANNA AKHMÁTOVA

The greatest name connected with acmeism and the Poets' Guild is that of Anna Akhmátova. This is the pseudonym (but one that has practically replaced the real name) of Anna Andréyevna Gorénko. She was born in Kíev in 1889. In 1910 she was married to Gumilëv. Her verse had been first published in Gumilëv's Paris miscellany in 1907; in 1912 her first book, *Evening*, appeared with a preface by Kuzmín, and attracted little attention outside the literary elite. But her second book, *Beads* (1914), had an unprecedented success. It made her at once famous, and went into more editions than any other book of verse of the new school. *The White Flock* appeared in 1917, and *Anno Domini* in 1922. After her divorce from Gumilëv she married V. K. Shiléyko, a brilliant Assyriologist, but a few years later they were separated. She remained in the Soviet Union after the Revolution, living in Leningrad.

Akhmátova's success is due to the personal and autobiographical character of her poetry: it is frankly "sentimental" in the sense that it is all about sentiment; and the sentiment is interpreted not in terms of symbolism or mysticism, but in simple and intelligible human language. Her main subject is love. It is always exceedingly actual, not only in sentiment, but in treatment. Her poems are realistic and vividly concrete: they are easily visualized. They always have a definite background—Petersburg, Tsárskoye Seló, a village in the Province of Tver. Many of them may be described as dramatic lyrics (a term not irrelevantly evocative of Browning—*Meeting at Night* and *Parting at Morning* might have been written by Akhmátova). The chief feature of these short pieces (they have seldom more than twelve, and never more than twenty, lines) is their great compactness. The technical perfection of her verse cannot be conveyed in a translation, but her manner of constructing her lyrics may be seen, for instance, from the following version by Mrs. Duddington: [1]

> *True tenderness is not to be mistaken*
> *For any other thing—and it's quiet.*
> *It is no use carefully wrapping*
> *My breast and shoulders in furs.*

[1] *Adelphi*, November 1923.

> *And it is no use your talking*
> *So humbly about first love.*
> *How well I know that staring,*
> *That greedy look in your eyes!*

I will venture to give my own version of another "dramatic lyric" in a somewhat different tone:

> *Ever since St. Agrafena's day,*
> *He keeps a crimson shawl,*
> *He is silent, but rejoices like King David,*
> *In his frosty cell the walls are white*
> *And no one talks to him.*
> *I will come and stand on his threshold;*
> *I will say, give me back my shawl.*

Both these quotations are specimens of her "first manner," which made her popularity and which predominates in *Beads* and in a large part of *The White Flock*. But in this latter book a new style makes its appearance. It dates from the poignant and prophetic poems bearing the suggestive title *July 1914*. It is an austerer and sterner style, and its subject matter is tragic—the ordeal her country entered on after the beginning of the war. The easy and graceful meters of her early verse are now replaced by the stern and solemn heroic stanza and similar measures. At moments her voice reaches a rude and somber majesty that makes one think of Dante. Without ceasing to be feminine in feeling, it becomes "manly" and "virile." This new style gradually ousts her early manner, and in *Anno Domini* it even invades her love lyrics and becomes the dominant note of her work. Her "civic" poetry can scarcely be termed political. It is above the medley of parties and is rather religious and prophetic. One feels in her voice the authority of one who has the power to judge and at once a heart that feels with more than common intensity.

The advanced schools of poetry soon came to consider Akhmátova old-fashioned and "reactionary," but there can be little doubt that her place is safe in the pantheon of posterity, among the small number of genuine poets.[2]

[2] After almost twenty years of virtual silence, Akhmátova began, in 1940, to appear more and more frequently in the Leningrad literary press. She was enjoying unusual success until the literary purge of 1946, when her poetry was authoritatively declared to be empty and alien to the Soviet people.—Editor

MÁNDELSTAM

Ósip Mándelstam (1892–1945), a Jew by birth who became a Mennonite, is one of the least prolific of poets. His two little books, *The Stone* (1913) and *Tristia* (1922), together contain less than a hundred short poems. Mándelstam is a man saturated with culture. He has an extensive knowledge of Russian, French, and Latin poetry, and most of his poetry is on literary and artistic subjects. Dickens, Ossian, Bach, Notre Dame, St. Sophia, Homer's catalogue of ships, Racine's *Phèdre*, a Lutheran burial, are among his characteristic subjects. All this is not introduced merely for decorative purposes, after the manner of Bryúsov, nor treated as symbols of some *Ens Realius*, as they would have been by Ivánov, but with genuine historical and critical penetration as individual phenomena with a well-defined place in the current of history. Mándelstam's diction attains sometimes to a splendid "Latin" sonority that is unrivaled by any Russian poet since Lomonósov. But what is essential in his poetry (however interesting his historical views may be) is his *form* and his manner of laying stress on it and making it felt. He achieves this by using words of various contradictory associations: magnificent and obsolete archaisms and words of everyday occurrence hardly naturalized in poetry. His syntax especially is curiously mixed—rhetorical periods tussle with purely colloquial turns of phrase. And the construction of his poems is also such as to accentuate the difficulty, the ruggedness of his form: it is a broken line that changes its direction at every turn of the stanza. His flashes of majestic eloquence sound especially grand in this bizarre and unexpected setting. His eloquence is magnificent, and, based as it is on diction and rhythm, it defies translation. But, apart from all else, Mándelstam is a most interesting thinker; and his prose essays contain perhaps the most remarkable, unprejudiced, and independent things that have ever been said on modern Russian civilization and on the art of poetry.[3]

SEVERYÁNIN

Symbolism was an aristocratic poetry, which appealed, all said and done, only to the elect. Akhmátova's poetry is more universally

[3] Mándelstam remained in the Soviet Union, but his subsequent work, very small in volume, was never accepted as forming any real contribution to Soviet literature. His *Egyptian Stamp*, a remarkable volume of imaginative and recollective prose, appeared in 1928.—Editor

interesting, but if it does not require any intellectual preparation, at least it demands from its reader a finer sensibility than that of the average newspaper-reader and picture-goer. But the picture-goer and newspaper-reader aspired to have his own poetry, and the great widening of poetical taste allowed by the symbolists permitted the inclusion within the pale of poetry of much that was not allowed by "Victorians." The moment came when vulgarity claimed a place on Parnassus and issued its declaration of rights in the verse of Ígor Severyánin (pseudonym of I. V. Lótarev, 1887–1942).

Severyánin called himself a futurist (ego-futurist), but he has little in common with the creative movement of Russian futurism. His poetry is an idealization of the aspirations of the average townsman, who dreams of cars, champagne, elegant restaurants, smart women, and fine perfumes. His originality was that he had the boldness to present all this in its naked naïveté and to give the philosophy of a hairdresser's assistant the gait of an almost Nietzschean individualism. He had a genuine gift of song and a considerable rhythmical inventiveness, and it was no wonder that his verse struck the jaded palates of the great men of symbolism. Sologúb, the most refined of them, wrote an enthusiastic preface to Severyánin's *Thunder-Seething Cup* (1913), and Bryúsov thought him the best promise in Russian poetry. All poetical Russia was for a moment dazzled and intoxicated by the richness of Severyánin's rhythms. The boom soon passed, and Severyánin passed out of the limelight. But he had meanwhile conquered the masses, and for several years his books sold all over Russia better than those of any other poet. With genuine futurism he has nothing in common. His claim to being a futurist was based on his love of such modern things as cars and palace hotels, and on his profuse coining of new words—most of which were in complete disharmony with the genius of the language. At first Severyánin's catchword of ego-futurism collected round him a group of young poets, but the better sort very soon abandoned his leadership and joined the camps of acmeism or genuine futurism.

FEMININE POETRY

Many poetesses flourished and met with more or less general recognition about the time Anna Akhmátova commanded the admiration of the reader. These poetesses, represented by such names as Marietta Shaginyán (later to achieve prominence as a Soviet prose writer) and Marie Morávsky, all had very much in common: they were "sentimental," and between them they monopolized emotional poetry. On a much higher level of creative poetic achievement, and entirely free from the doubtful amenities of "ladyish" poetry, is the remarkably original and fresh poetical talent of Marína Tsvetáyeva (maiden name of Marína Efrón, born in Moscow, emigrated in 1922). Her development was independent of all schools and guilds but is representative of a general tendency to escape from the fetters of "themes" and "ideas" into a free land of forms.

Her first book appeared in 1911. It was too obviously the work of a schoolgirl, but it seemed to promise something better. During the Revolutionary years she published nothing, but the verse she wrote between 1916 and 1920 was circulated in manuscript in Moscow, and when, after the revival of the book trade, she almost simultaneously published several new books of verse, it came as a revelation. She at once became one of the major lights of the poetic firmament. She evidently writes with great facility, and this sometimes reflects on the level of her work; much of it is second-rate and slovenly. But she is always original, and her voice can be mistaken for no one else's. For rhythmical swing she has few equals. She is especially a master of staccato rhythms, which give the impression of hearing the sound of hoofs of a galloping horse. Her poetry is all fire, enthusiasm, and passion; but it is not sentimental, nor even in the true sense emotional. It "infects," not by what it expresses, but by the sheer force of its motion. This force is quite spontaneous, for she is not a great craftsman and the level of her work varies greatly. At her worst she is painfully pretentious (as in her prose) and obscure. But there is nothing more exhilarating than some of her short poems—simple, direct, full of breath. She is intensely Russian (though without a trace of mysticism or religion), and her poetry constantly re-echoes with the sounds of the people's songs. Her long poem *The King-Maiden* (1922) is in this respect a true marvel. Except Blok in *The Twelve*, no one has achieved anything of the sort with the aid of Russian songs; it is a wonderful fugue on a popular theme, and, unlike the greater poet's poem, it is free from every trace of mysticism.

"peasant poets" and imaginists

In 1912, when symbolism was disintegrating and the young schools seemed to offer little promise, and even such leviathans as Sologúb and Bryúsov recommended Ígor Severyánin as the great poet of tomorrow, the attention of the poetry-reading public was attracted by a little book of verse that bore the name of Nicholas Klyúyev. It showed evident traces of symbolist influence, but it was still more full of the genuine lore and imagery of the people. It was fresh and racy—of the north Russian soil. Klyúyev (1885–1937) turned out to be a peasant from Lake Onéga. The Onéga country has preserved and developed, better than any other district, the ancient treasures of folk poetry, of artistic handicraft, of wooden architecture, and of ancient ritual. His poetry was animated by a cult of the people. It united an ancient religious tradition with a mystical Revolutionism. In 1917, when Ivánov-Razúmnik preached his Scythian theories, and Blok and Bély were among his followers, it was natural that Klyúyev, the poet of mystical "populism" and Revolutionism, should be extolled to the skies by these Scythians. For a moment, together with the younger peasant poet Esénin, he seemed one of the largest lights of Russian poetry. His poetry is the expression of a peculiar religion that accepts all the symbolism and ritual of the people's faith, but rejects its religious substance; Christianity is replaced by a cult of the people, and the images of Christian saints become holy, for those who worship them, not for what they represent. Klyúyev's poetry is overloaded with ornament, with bold and gaudy metaphor and symbolism. Despite his peasant origin he is saturated with tradition and overloaded with ages of culture almost more than any other poet. He tried to give a mystical interpretation to the Bolshevík Revolution and to identify it with the ancient religious movements of the Russian people. One of his most characteristic poems is *Lénin,* where he discovers in the Communist leader a kinship with the religious leaders of the Old Believers' schism!

The second peasant poet brought forward by the Scythians is Sergéy Esénin (1895–1925). He is a product of south Great Russia (Ryazán), which has not the ancient and archaic civilization of the north, and where the peasant had always a tendency to be semi-

nomadic with no firm roots in the soil. The Scythian Revolutionism
of Esénin was of a different kind from Klyúyev's: he had no interest
in religious symbolism and ritual; his mysticism was skin-deep, and
the quasi-blasphemous poems he wrote in 1917–18 were nothing
more than his contribution to a fashion that raged among the belated symbolists of the day. These poems, which seemed such
profound revelations to the good Ivánov-Razúmnik (and, later
on, to a few good European critics also), are in point of fact the
sheerest and most shamefaced nonsense. Fortunately for Esénin
his reputation does not stand and fall with these poems. He is a
genuine poet and has a rare gift of song. He is genuinely akin to
the spirit of the Russian folk song, though he does not adopt its
meters. This blend of wistful melancholy and insolent daredeviltry
is characteristic of the central Russian; it is present in the Russian
folk song, and in Esénin it manifests itself both in the pensive
sweetness of his elegies and in the aggressive coarseness of his
Confession of a Hooligan. There is no genuine mystical or religious
background in Esénin but a certain gay and careless nihilism that
any moment may turn into a sentimental wistfulness under the
influence of love, drink, or recollection. There is no vigor in Esénin;
if Klyúyev is a rural Byzantine or Alexandrian, Esénin is a sort of
peasant Turgénev who sees the disappearance of all the beauty
that is dear to him, laments it, but submits to the inevitable. His
short lyrics are often very beautiful, though in the long run monotonous. All their charm lies in the sweetness of their melody,
and his "tragedy" *Pugachëv* (1922), is not a tragedy at all but
merely a succession of (often exquisite) lyrics put into the mouths
of a famous rebel and of his companions and enemies.

After the Revolution, Esénin tried to play up to his reputation
of the "hooligan poet." He was the principal figure of the poetical
cafés that flourished in Moscow in 1918–20, and in 1922 he acquired a world-wide notoriety by his ephemeral marriage with
Isadora Duncan. In his exploits he was backed by some other poets,
who called themselves the imaginists [4] and were a very prominent
and noisy feature of literary life in Moscow. During the worst
days of Bolshevík tyranny, when book publishing had become impossible, the imaginists were a living reminder of undying freedom;

[4] The imaginists should not be thought of as the Russian counterpart of the American imagists, who have rather more in common with the acmeists than with the
imaginists.

they were the only independent group that were not afraid to make themselves noticed by the authorities, and they were wonderfully skilled in getting their slender little collections and manifestoes printed by fair means or foul. As poets, these imaginists are not of very great importance, and the names of Shershenévich, Márienhof, and the "Circassian" Kúsikov are not likely to survive. The theory of imaginism was that the principal thing in poetry is "imagery," and their poetry (as well as much of Esénin's) is an agglomeration of "images" of the most farfetched and exaggerated description. A principal point of their practice was not to distinguish between "pure" and "impure," but to introduce the coarsest and crudest images in the immediate neighborhood of the pathetic and sublime. Some of the imaginists were merely "hooligans," but in others a tragic "crack" (*nadrýv*, to use Dostoyévsky's word) is clearly present. They had a morbid craving for dirt, humiliation, and suffering, like the "man from underground." The most "Dostoyevskian" of these poets is Ryúrik Ivněv, who, despite the hysterical substance of his inspiration, sometimes succeeded in giving it a memorable and pointed expression, especially in certain poems on the tragic fate of Russia that are unexpectedly reminiscent of Akhmátova's.

THE RISE OF FUTURISM

Russian symbolism traced its tradition to a foreign source but ultimately developed along national lines. Russian futurism has nothing in common with the Italian futurist movement except the name itself and its most general associations. It is one of the most purely domestic developments of modern Russian literature. If one were obliged to point out any Western movement most like the first stages of Russian futurism, it would be the French dada movement, which, however, belongs to a later date. In its further stages, Russian futurism became very many-sided, and there is little in common between such poets as Khlébnikov, Mayakóvsky, and Pasternák beyond a general will to escape from the poetic conventions of the past age and to air the poetic vocabulary.

As a whole the work of the futurists may be summed up as follows: they *continued* the symbolists' work of revolutionizing and transforming metrical forms and of discovering new possibilities for Russian prosody; they fought against the symbolist idea of the mystical essence of poetry, replacing the conception of the poet as priest and seer by that of the poet as workman and artisan; they worked to destroy all the poetic canons of the past by divorcing poetry from what is traditionally considered poetic, from every kind of conventional and ideal beauty; and they worked at constructing a new language that would be free from the emotional associations of current poetical diction.

Russian futurism dates from 1910, when Khlébnikov's now famous etymological poem appeared, which was nothing but a series of fresh-coined derivatives from one word *smekh* (laughter). From 1911 to 1914 the futurists did their best to *épater le bourgeois* in their aggressively unconventional publications, in their public conferences, and even in their personal appearance (for instance, they painted pictures on their faces). They were treated like lunatics or insolent hooligans, but their principles and their work soon impressed themselves on their fellow poets, and they soon became the most vigorous literary group in the country. There can be no doubt that this revolutionary work in rejuvenating the methods of the craft and exploding the mystical solemnities of symbolism was bracing and invigorating to Russian poetry, which was showing dangerous symptoms of anæmia caused by a too spiritual and fleshless diet.

All those rejected by "bourgeois" literature found hospitality with the futurists. Many of these hangers-on were merely insignificant and ambitious poetasters, but the memory was preserved of at least one genuinely interesting writer—Eléna Guró (died young in 1910). Her delicate and sensitive free verse and beautifully light prose had passed quite unnoticed by the symbolists. Her two books, *The Hurdy-gurdy* (1909) and *The Little Camels of the Sky* (1912), are a wonderland of delicate and unexpected expression of the thinnest tissue of experience. They will certainly be "discovered" someday, and their author will be restored to the place to which she is entitled.

The founder of Russian futurism was Victor (or, as he renamed himself, Velemír) Khlébnikov (1885–1922), who died in extreme poverty when his friends were at the height of their popularity and official favor. He is an exceedingly curious and original figure. Unlike the other futurists, he was a kind of mystic, or rather he had the mystically realistic mentality of primitive

man. But his mysticism was one of *things* and words, not of ideas
and symbols. In life he was strangely superstitious, and in his
poetry he is rather a conjurer playing with the language than what
we understand by the word "poet." Words and forms had for him
an existence of their own, and his work in life was to create a new
world of words. He had a deep, primary feeling for the nature of
the Russian language. He is a Slavophil, but a pre-Christian, almost pre-pagan Slavophil. His Russia is free from all the scales of
Christian and European civilization, a Russia that has been
"scratched down to the Tatar." His vision of the primitive world
was not the pageant of Gumilëv's mythology, nor the virtuous
simplicity of Rousseau; what he was after was not natural man,
but magical man. All things were only a material for him to build
up a new world of words. This world of words is doubtless a creation of genius, but it is obviously not for the general public. He
is not, and probably never will be, read except by poets and
philologists, though an anthology *ad usum profanorum* might be
selected from his works that would present him more attractively
and accessibly than he chose to do himself. The poets have found
him an inexhaustible mine of good example and useful doctrine.
His work is also of great interest to the philologist, for he was a
lord of language. He knew its hidden possibilities and forced it to
reveal them. His work is a microcosm reflecting on an enormously
magnified scale the creative processes of the whole life history of
the language.

Khlébnikov in his creative linguistics was true to the genuine
spirit of the Russian language; his method is the same as that
used by the language itself—analogy. Another futurist, Kruchënykh, endeavored to create an entirely new language, or even to
use a new language, created *ad hoc*, for every new poem. This
movement led to little good, for Kruchënykh himself and most of
his followers had no feeling for the phonetic soul of Russian, and
their *written* inventions are, more often than not, simply unpro-
nounceable. But when this "trans-sense" (*zaúmny*) language is
used in sympathy with the phonetic soul of the language, it produces rather amusing and interesting effects. The essential thing
needed to make it come alive is a good delivery, which, adding to
the "trans-sense" words the perfectly sensible intonation, gives the
illusion of listening to "Russian as it might have been." The
"trans-sense" movement certainly contributed to the "de-Italian-

ization" of Russian poetry and favored a return to the rougher and ruder phonetic harmonies of the language.

A more eclectic group of futurists, instead of trying to create a new language or of going back to the primal roots of the old, tried to learn new methods from the old writers, especially those of the Golden Age (1820–30)—especially Yazýkov, who was a futurist *avant la lettre*—and of the eighteenth century. They continued the metrical researches of Andréy Bély, but their task, like that of the futurists, was to find fresh forms and new strength. These scholarly futurists have much in common with Mándelstam, and from their ranks came the remarkable poetry of Pasternák.

MAYAKÓVSKY

Vladímir Vladímirovich Mayakóvsky (1894–1930) was born in Transcaucasia. In 1908 he joined the Bolshevík Party; in 1911 he came in contact with the beginning futurists and began writing verse. He was hardly distinguished at first from the other futurists, but gradually he began to emerge as something essentially different from the rest. His poetry was not intended for the studio, but for the street; it was free from "trans-sense," it was full of human interest, and it was frankly rhetorical—but in a very new and unexpected way. When, in 1916, his poems appeared in book form, under the characteristic title *As Simple as Mooing*, they met with a considerable success. In 1917 Mayakóvsky shared the triumph of his party and became something like an official Bolshevík poet. Much of his poetry written in 1918–21 is direct political propaganda (*Mystery-Bouffe, 150,000,000*) or satires written more or less to order, and he contributed both drawings and verse to many propaganda posters of those years. As the futurists lost favor, Mayakóvsky's star also declined, but he is now canonized in the Soviet Union as the great poet of the October Revolution.

Mayakóvsky's poetry is extraordinarily unlike that of the symbolists: he recognized, as the only poet who at all influenced him (except the futurists), the satirist Sásha Chërny, the only man who wrote "unpoetical" verse during the reign of symbolism. In prosody, Mayakóvsky is a continuer of the symbolists; but the destruction of the classical syllabism of Russian verse, which with them was only one of many tendencies, becomes a fully developed system with Mayakóvsky. His versification is based on the number of stress accents (which in Russian is equivalent to the number of words) in a line and completely disregards all unstressed syllables. His rhyming system is also a development of symbolist tendencies, but here again Mayakóvsky has made a coherent system of what was only a tendency with the symbolists: the principal stress is laid on the consonants preceding and following the rhyming vowel; the quality and even the number of vowels that come after the stress is indifferent. He revels in long rhymes composed of more than one word and in punning rhymes—his whole method of rhyming would vividly remind the English reader of Browning: "ranunculus" and *"Tommy-make-room-for-your-uncle-us"* would be a good equivalent of the more conservative type of Mayakovskian rhyme. Mayakóvsky's new versification has had a very wide influence on Russian poetry, but it has not succeeded in superseding the old syllabic system, which is, after all, much more various and full of resource than his.

Mayakóvsky's poetry is very loud, very unrefined, and stands absolutely outside the distinction between "good" and "bad" taste. He uses the diction of every day in its cruder forms, deforming it to suit his needs in a direction opposite to that of the older poetical tradition. His language is free from "trans-sense" elements; but, considered as a literary language, it is a new dialect —a dialect that is entirely his own creation. For the way he puts to use the elements of spoken language makes them sound quite different from the usual. The harmony of his verse, with its heavy emphatic beat and its rude "unmusical" choice of sound, is like the music of a drum or a saxophone. There is a certain affinity between Mayakóvsky and Vachel Lindsay. But, apart from the difference of spirit animating the two poets, Lindsay's poetry is essentially musical, intended to be sung in chorus. Mayakóvsky's cannot be sung at all; it is declamatory, rhetorical—the verse of an open-air orator. Judged by only "Victorian" standards, his verse is simply not poetry at all; and judged by symbolist standards, it is no better. But it is largely owing to our symbolist education, which has widened to such an extent our poetical sensibility, that we are capable of appreciating this rowdy and noisy rhetoric. Mayakóvsky's appeal is direct and simple; his subjects can interest the most uncultured, while the high originality of his craftsmanship makes him a paramount figure in the eyes of the professional poet.

Mayakóvsky's favorite method of expression comprises (besides purely verbal effects based on the use of "unpoetical diction") metaphor and hyperbole. Both his metaphors and his hyperboles are developed in a realistic way, recalling to a certain extent the *concetti* of the seventeenth century. He indulges in what his commentators call the "realization of metaphor," which is a powerful way of giving life to worn-out clichés: if he introduces the hackneyed metaphor of his heart burning with love, he heightens it by developing a whole realistic picture of a fire, with firemen in helmets and top boots, infesting the burning heart. If he symbolizes the Russian people in the colossal figure of the *muzhík* Iván, the champion of Communism, he describes in detail how he wades the Atlantic to fight in single combat the champion of capitalism, Woodrow Wilson. The inspiration of Mayakóvsky's poetry is materialistic and realistic—this is his principal ground in common with atheistic Communism. His credo is expressed best of all in four lines of the prologue to *Mystery-Bouffe:*

> *We are fed up with heavenly candies,*
> *Give us real rye-bread to feed on!*
> *We are fed up with cardboard passions,*
> *Give us a live wife to live with!*

Though "Mayakóvsky," who is the hero of most of Mayakóvsky's early poems, may be interpreted as a synthetic impersonation, he is more naturally taken as the actual man, and in his political poems the pathos is Revolutionary, to be sure, and atheistic, but it is only superficially dyed in socialist colors. Mayakóvsky is not a humorist; in his satires he inveighs instead of ridiculing. He is an orator, and even his crudities and coarseness serve the ends of serious poetry. This is one of his most original features.

Mayakóvsky's principal works are his longer poems. Those written before 1917 are mainly egotistic in inspiration. There is a distinct decadent and neurasthenic element at the bottom of their loud clamor. The most remarkable of these poems are *Man*, an atheistic apotheosis of self, and *The Cloud in Trousers*, a "sentimental" poem with definite Revolutionary "premonitions." *War and Peace* is already a social poem. All these were written in 1915–

16. In 1917–18 he wrote the brilliant, exhilarating, and witty *Mystery-Bouffe*, an Aristophanesque satire of the bourgeois world defeated by the proletarians. In 1920 he wrote *150,000,000* (the figure represents the number of inhabitants in Russia), an invective against the "blockade" of Soviet Russia by the bourgeois West. After 1921 he wrote satires of internal Soviet disorders, but he also returned to egotistic poetry, most of which is on the subject of love. The lyrical poem *I Love* (1922)—free from excessive crudities, but constructed throughout on a system of elaborate *concetti*—is perhaps the most immediately attractive of his poems for the general poetry reader.[5]

PASTERNÁK

Borís Leonídovich Pasternák (born 1890) began publishing in 1913 in the *Centrifuga*, an association of "moderate," scholarly futurists. For several years he was little more than one of a great number of more or less promising poets, and his only book published before 1917 attracted little attention. In 1917 he wrote that wonderful series of lyrics which forms the book *My Sister Life*. It was not published at the time, but was circulated in manuscript, and Pasternák gradually became the universal master and exemplar. Imitations of his style began to appear in print before his book was published, and very few poets escaped his influence. Not only futurists like Aséyev, but poets of very different schools, like Mándelstam and Tsvetáyeva, were affected by it, and even Bryúsov's last verse is a conscientiously studious imitation of Pasternák. The book appeared in print only in 1922. It was followed by a second volume, *Themes and Variations* (1923), which, though not always on the same level as the first, at times even achieves greater things. His stories in prose are written in an equally original and interesting style. The public, unlike the poets, remained more or less cold to Pasternák because of his excessive difficultness.

It is very tempting to compare Pasternák with Donne: like Donne's—though not so long—Pasternák's poetry remained un-

[5] In 1930, harassed by private troubles and by enemies in anti-futurist literary camps, Mayakóvsky put an end to his own life. The principal works of his last period include one of his best long poems, *Vladímir Ilyích Lénin* (1924) and two satirical prose plays, *The Bedbug* (1928) and *The Bathhouse* (1930), both of which were banned by the authorities.—Editor

published and unknown except to poets; like Donne, he is a "poet's poet" whose influence on fellow craftsmen is far greater than his popularity with the reader. Passing to less external characteristics, Pasternák resembles Donne in his combination of great emotional intensity with highly developed poetical "wit"; like Donne's, one of his principal novelties is the introduction of technical and "vulgar" imagery in place of stock poetical diction; and, like Donne's, his verse consciously aims at avoiding the easy mellifluousness of the preceding period and at destroying the "Italianate" sweetness of poetic language.[6] In this respect, however, Pasternák is only one of the futurists.

Two things especially strike the reader in Pasternák: the great intensity of his poetical passions, which has led to comparisons with Lérmontov; and the extraordinary analytical acuteness of his vision combined with a deliberate freshness in expressing it. Pasternák's landscapes and still lifes are perhaps his most remarkable achievements. They give the impression of seeing the world for the first time; at first they seem ludicrously farfetched, but the oftener one rereads them, the more one realizes the almost mathematical precision and exactness of his imagery. For instance, he conveys thus the idea of the very familiar Russian sight of a road so polished by cart wheels that it reflects the stars by night: "And you cannot cross the road without treading on the whole universe." This is romantic in spirit. And here is a typical prosaic simile from a poem on spring: "The air is blue like the bundle of wash which a convalescent takes with him from the hospital."

Pasternák's rhythms are also remarkable; nowhere does he attain such force as in the wonderful series of lyrics (*Themes and Variations*) *The Quarrel*, on the subject of his final quarrel with his mistress. For emotional and rhythmical force, these nine lyrics have no rivals in modern Russian poetry. This emotional element makes Pasternák very different from the other futurists, with whom he has in common only the will to re-form poetical diction. The difference is emphasized by his non-political attitude and by the absence of "trans-sense." His obscurity, very real to a superficial reader, comes from the novelty of his way of seeing and noting what he sees, but needs no key to it—nothing more than

---

[6] I must add, however, that any direct influence of Donne on Pasternák is exceedingly improbable. There is only a general similarity of tendencies, and no coincidence of detail.

attention. If Pasternák proceeds from any master, it is, above all, Ánnensky, who was obscure in somewhat the same way. But Ánnensky was decadent and morbid to the core; Pasternák is quite free from all morbidity—his poetry is bracing and all in the major key.

The few prose stories he has written are remarkable for the same courage of seeing for himself; the first strange impression produced by this disintegration of the world along new lines gradually changes into an acceptance of this new world, or rather of this new way of reducing its multiplicity to intelligible forms. *The Childhood of Lüvers*, written in 1918, is a masterpiece of acute observation. It has drawn from critics comparisons with Marcel Proust, but it is as concise and concentrated as the work of the French novelist is vast and ample.[7]

[7] Pasternák has continued to develop his special poetic gifts in remarkable independence of current fashions. Besides several volumes of original verse, he has produced many translations from Georgian, German, French, and English poets, including excellent versions of *Hamlet, Othello, Romeo and Juliet*, and *Antony and Cleopatra*. The English reader now has at his disposal a volume of translations from Pasternák's prose, edited with a very good introduction by Stefan Schimanski (Lindsay Drummond Ltd., London, 1945). Mr. J. M. Cohen has translated a volume of *Selected Poems* for the same publisher.—Editor

EDITOR'S POSTSCRIPT

(To Paul McGeorge)

When Mayakóvsky committed suicide in 1930, Mírsky was to compare his death with Púshkin's as marking the end of an era in Russian literature.[1] "The objective meaning of his death," wrote Mírsky, "is clear—it is a recognition of the fact that the new Soviet culture does not need the individualistic literature that has its roots in pre-Revolutionary society. . . . [Mayakóvsky] showed his old spirit only in order to kill it. His suicide was the act of an individualist and at the same time a deathblow to individualism. [By it] he buried pre-proletarian literature forever."

Whatever qualifications one might wish to add to Mírsky's statement—and he himself added some at the time he made it—few would dispute that the late twenties and early thirties do mark a most important boundary in the history of Russian literature. Mírsky interpreted the change primarily as the fall of bourgeois individualism, and indeed, what surprises us most as we now look back on the writing of the preceding Civil War and NEP periods is the relatively independent tone, not only of individual writers, but particularly of literary schools and groups jostling against each other in an ill-fated struggle for recognition and favor.

The field was for a time open to almost all, for the morning after the Revolution found few of the established writers on the Bolshevík side. Most of them had gone, or were soon to go, into emigration,[2] and when, in November 1917, the party invited the

---

[1] See Mírsky's "*Dve smérti*: 1837–1930," in *Smert Vladímira Mayakóvskogo* (Berlin, 1931).

[2] The subject of *émigré* literature, covering not only the later periods of writers who had already made their reputations in Russia, but also the work of men like Aldánov (pseudonym of M. A. Landau) and Sírin (pseudonym of V. V. Nabókov) who have done all or most of their writing abroad, deserves separate study, especially as a chapter in the general history of Western contacts with Russia. Berdyáyev's works assume particular importance in this respect.

leading writers and artists of Petrograd to a meeting at the Smólny Institute, only a handful of people (including Blok, Mayakóvsky, and the theatrical producer Méyerhold) chose to attend. The general disorganization of society and the physical and moral sufferings of those early days were thus described by Mírsky:

> . . . the drastic enforcement of absolute State monopoly, coupled with wholesale political (and economic) terrorism, and the complete breakdown of the railways, made life in the towns of Soviet Russia, especially in Petersburg. something so unspeakably terrible that any description of the actual facts arouses natural disbelief— so impossible does it seem that any human being may have lived through three or four years of such unrelieved horror. It is not my task to record the sufferings of the bourgeois of Petersburg (Moscow being the seat of Government and situated nearer to the corn-producing provinces, the conditions there were a shade better). The writers suffered comparatively less, owing largely to the various "enlightening" contrivances of Górky, but even they had to live for months at a time on $\frac{1}{8}$ pound of bread a day—and even this was not always forthcoming. Most of them passed the winters of 1918–1919 and 1919–1920 without getting out of their fur coats, for the shortage of fuel was even more serious than the shortage of food. These conditions of literary life in Petersburg in 1918–1920 are vividly evoked in Victor Shklóvsky's *Sentimental Journey*. Writing could bring no money, because in the course of 1918 all the private publishing business died out and the State Press practically monopolized all the printing industry. To keep alive, writers had to work at translations for Górky's *World Literature* enterprise, or in the theatres, or to lecture in various extension schemes. Even for this they got only insignificant increases of their rations. Books bearing the dates 1919 and 1920, especially if not issued by the State Press (*Gosizdát*), are exceedingly rare, and in the future will probably be of special interest to collectors. If literary publication did not quite cease, it was due partly to a

few enlightened profiteers, partly to the extraordinary inventiveness of certain young authors who contrived to get hold of stocks of paper and have their books printed for nothing (the Imaginists were particularly good at this), partly to the State Press's publishing certain works of literary propaganda (Mayakóvsky). As for the Terror, the literary world suffered comparatively little from it: of course all the writers who were not Communists passed a few months in prison, but Gumilév was the only writer of note to be officially executed. A certain number of less prominent authors and university professors were killed in a less formal way in the provinces, or died in prison.

In spite of all these conditions, literary life did not cease. In Petersburg independent literary life centred round Bély's *Volfila* and similar groups, and assumed a pronouncedly mystical colouring. In Moscow it was much noisier and less dignified, and its principal centres were the poetical cafés, where Futurists and Imaginists read their verse and fought out their literary battles. The characteristic features of these years all over Russia were the aggressive and noisy prominence of Left literary groups; an almost morbidly exaggerated interest in the theatre coupled with an absolute disregard for the public (all the theatres lived on government grants and could thus dispense with the public's approval); an overwhelming predominance of verse over prose; and an extraordinary abundance of literary "studios," where young men were formally taught the rudiments of their art by eminent masters of the craft. The most notable of these studios were the one in Petersburg where Gumilév taught the art of poetry and Zamyátin the art of prose, and the officially supported studio of Proletarian poets in Moscow conducted by Bryúsov.[3]

To Mírsky's account should be added a word of gratitude for the Revolutionary government's interest and activity (under the particular influence of Lunachársky, Commissar of Education) in

---

[3] *Contemporary Russian Literature* (New York: Alfred A. Knopf, Inc., 1926), pp. 248–50. The quotation is from "Interchapter II: The Second Revolution," which has been omitted from this edition.

preserving monuments of the pre-Revolutionary cultural heritage. On this point Mírsky occasionally failed to distinguish between the attitude of the party and that of certain groups, especially the futurists, whose Revolutionary enthusiasm reached the point of rejecting all "bourgeois" art and literature in the name of a still unborn proletarian culture.

It is, of course, not surprising that this early, "café" period of Soviet literature should have been dominated by such extreme groups, who were almost the only literary friends of the Revolutionary government during the trying months of civil war. What is more interesting is the reserved and cautious attitude of the government and party towards their strange allies. Lunachársky's special concern for the "cultural heritage," which has already been mentioned, contrasts sharply with the strident nihilism of the futurists, who, already in their 1912 manifesto (*A Slap in the Face of Public Taste*), had solemnly dumped overboard "from the steamship of modernity" Púshkin, Dostoyévsky, Tolstóy, "and others, and others." Lénin was frank enough to declare himself a barbarian and confess that he did not understand Mayakóvsky (whose *Left March* he was forced to endure on public occasions as frequently as Truman has had to hear the *Missouri Waltz*) while he did understand and enjoy the poetry of Púshkin and Nekrásov. But there was more in Lénin's attitude than mere conservatism of literary taste or disapproval of the modernists' obscurities and strange effects. If a certain robust Philistinism has been a constant feature of the "official line" in art, it still does not explain the seriousness with which party leaders treated the theories of the contending literary schools.

For one thing, Lénin's realistic appreciation of the problems created by mass illiteracy made him distrustful of those who promised to effect a cultural revolution in Russia overnight. In addition, he feared the pretensions to hegemony of cultural groups that might easily become incubators of political heresy. These were the days when inexperience of the modern totalitarian state made it possible to conceive of autonomous organizations within its borders. The Proletkúlt, one of the leading contenders for power, even advanced the claim to being the "culture-creative class organization of the proletariat," on an equal level with the party as its political organization and the trade unions as its economic organization. And the Proletkúlt's chief theoretician was none other than Bogdánov, against whose philosophy Lénin had waged an all-out attack before the Revolution! Small wonder that Lénin, when he read in *Izvéstiya* that Lunachársky was supporting the Proletkúlt's demands, acted quickly and decisively to quash this neo-trinitarianism.

Lénin's violent reaction resulted in a decree of the Central Committee of the party (published December 1, 1920), one of the first important documents in the history of party policy towards literary and cultural workers. By it the Proletkúlt and its associated organizations were unequivocally placed under the supervision of the Commissariat of Education. Their leaders were informed that the "independence" of the Proletkúlt, appropriate and desirable under the Kérensky regime, could serve under altered circumstances only as a cover for "Machism" [4] in philosophy and futurism in art, both opposed to the genuine cultural interests of the proletariat. Notice was also served that the party, which up to then had been prevented by the military situation from devoting sufficient time to cultural affairs, would henceforth pay much closer attention to questions of popular education in general and to the Proletkúlts in particular.

This decree turned out to be only the beginning of a long campaign waged by the party against all attempts of particular groups to achieve autonomy in cultural matters. The subsequent history of literary politics in the Soviet Union is a stormy one until the State finally succeeds in containing all writers and literary groups within a single framework—its own. The details of the struggle cannot occupy us here. The most important fact that emerges is the relative consistency of the party line (despite several deviations, both apparent and real), which was eventually to reverse the situation of 1917 and secure the direct allegiance and political orthodoxy of *all* the intellectuals who might speak to the nation and to the world.

The Civil War period, under the conditions described above by Mírsky, witnessed a brief triumph of the spoken over the written word in literature, of poetry over prose. But neither the futurists, nor their offshoot the constructivists,[5] nor the poets of

---

[4] The philosophy of Ernst Mach strongly influenced Bogdánov's views, and the heresy of "Machism" has been repeatedly attacked by the Marxists.

[5] The leading constructivist was Iliá Selvínsky (born 1899). Loosely associated in the same "school" were Eduard Bagrítsky (1895–1934) and Vera Ínber (born 1893).

the Proletkúlt and its various progeny were able to hold the positions won by Esénin and Mayakóvsky. Soviet poetry has ever since fallen behind prose, although it may boast of Borís Pasternák, who easily ranks among the greatest lyric poets of this century.

With the introduction of the New Economic Policy, in 1921, not only were material conditions for publishing improved, but opportunities for non-Communist writers increased. Of special significance were the famous Serapion brothers, who declined to answer the insistent question of the times: "Are you with us or against us?" and declared themselves only for Serapion the Anchorite, on whose day in February 1921 they had formed their circle.[6] Prose soon replaced poetry as the commanding medium of expression, and the typical writers of the time turned to themes of the Revolution and the Civil War. In general it may be said that Soviet literature has been most successful in works of heroic proportions (mere size is not of first importance here, but rather the scale of conception), where bright colors, bold strokes, and strong, sharp outlines appear to best advantage; and some of the universally acknowledged classics of Soviet literature come from this early crop of Revolutionary fiction. Vsévolod Ivánov's *Partisans* (1922) and *Armored Train No. 14–69* (1922), Dmítry Fúrmanov's *Chapáyev* (1923), and Alexander Serafimóvich's *Iron Flood* (1924), all written by actual participants in the Civil War, deserve special mention here, along with Isaac Bábel's colorful tales of Budënny's cavalry in Poland, collected in *Konármiya* (*Red Cavalry*, 1926). Borís Pilnyák's *Naked Year* (1922), which enjoyed a sensational success at the time of its appearance, stands somewhat apart from the rest, both by its curious form and by its half-mystical interpretation of the Revolution as the rising of an "elemental" Russia against foreign masters. Other works on similar topics, like Leoníd Leónov's *Badgers* (1924), M. A. Bulgákov's *White Guard* (1925; dramatized in the following year as *The Days of the Turbíns*), and Alexander Fadéyev's *Rout* (1927), display—each in its own, quite different, way—a special interest in the psychological complexities

---

[6] From this circle, which dissolved itself in 1924, were graduated such well-known Soviet writers as the humorist Michael Zóschenko (born 1895); the novelists V. A. Kavérin (born 1902), Nicholas Nikítin (born 1897), Vsévolod Ivánov (born 1895), and Cónstantine Fédin (born 1892); and one of the leading Soviet poets, Nicholas Tíkhonov (born 1896). The members of the group were committed to no single style or program, but their work showed the influence of Eugene Zamyátin (1884–1937), a brilliant writer of "ornamental" prose, who emigrated in 1931.

of the subject. As the tumult of war died down, Soviet writers were to return again and again to the problems created by the Revolution for those who lived through it and had to make their peace with it. The masterpiece of Soviet fiction on this theme is, of course, Mikhaíl Shólokhov's *The Silent Don*, which was begun as early as 1926 (the first volume appeared in 1928) and was not completed until fourteen years later.

Despite continued grumblings from self-appointed custodians of proletarian purity in art, the relaxed atmosphere of the NEP had produced good results in literature. In 1925 a resolution of the Central Committee, noting that anti-proletarian and anti-Revolutionary elements among the "fellow travelers" had been reduced to insignificance, insisted on tactful treatment of non-proletarian and non-Communist "specialists" of literary technique, recommending that the party support free competition of various literary schools and stating categorically that no legalized monopoly over publication could be granted to any group. The resolution was meant to put an end to intra-party controversy and was clearly directed against the pretensions of a group called the Onguardists (from the name of their review—*Na postú* "on guard"). This group, which claimed proletarian orthodoxy for itself alone, differed from the Proletkúlt in claiming the right to act *under* the party's direction, not independently of it, but displayed the same intransigence towards the fellow travelers and others outside its own clique. It had been opposed by such critics as Bukhárin, Lunachársky, Rádek, and Trótsky, and the 1925 resolution, greeted as a charter of literary liberties, represented a temporary victory for this moderate party.

The triumph of the moderationists was unfortunately short-lived. With the institution of the first Five-Year Plan, the Onguardists returned to the attack, and RAPP (Russian Association of Proletarian Writers), under the leadership of the notorious Leopold Áverbakh, secured a virtual dictatorship over literary production—precisely what had been denied only a few years before. The policy of RAPP was carried out under the old, extreme-left slogan of the "social command." Writers were "commanded" or "challenged" in the spirit of socialist competition to perform assigned tasks. "Shock-brigades" of fiction writers, dramatists, and poets, as well as journalists, were sent to factories, collective farms, mines, and timberlands to report on individual

successes of the Five-Year Plan. Some enthusiasts even foresaw
the day when all literary production would fall in step with modern
industrial techniques, being planned and carried out on strict
assembly-line principles.

A few years later Áverbakh and his associates were to be
"unmasked" as Trotskyite wreckers, but they held the reins long
enough to steer Soviet literature into a sharp decline, and it has
since come to be generally recognized that most of the "Five-Year
Plan" writing is pretty poor stuff indeed. The style for it had been
set as early as 1924 by Gladkóv's novel *Cement*, which had dealt
with the reopening of a cement factory after the Civil War, and
which had been hailed on its appearance as marking a new turn
in world literature. Though inferior (at least from the Western
reader's point of view) to many less-publicized works of Soviet
fiction, it is by no means uninteresting and stands far above the
general level of its many imitations. Mission successfully accomplished by featureless, but superhumanly energetic, heroes in the
face of unbelievable natural obstacles and equally unbelievable
wrecker-villains—such is the common theme of these almost uni-
formly unreadable melodramas. Valentine Katáyev's *Time Forward!* (1932) is perhaps the most original novel of the lot,[7] while
Pogódin's *Tempo* (1930) and Kirshón's *Bread* (1930) are typical
plays of the same vintage, dealing respectively with the problems
of a tractor factory and of a collective farm.

An honorable exception from these general criticisms must be
made for Shólokhov's contribution to Five-Year-Plan literature,
Virgin Soil Upturned (1932–3), an original, serious, and unstereo-
typed treatment of collectivization among the Don Cossacks.
Except for *Virgin Soil Upturned*, the more interesting novels to
come from the literary Five-Year Plan, like Pilnyák's *The Volga
Falls to the Caspian Sea* (1930) and Leónov's *Sot* (1930), hold our
interest precisely for reasons that secured them only a cool reception from Soviet criticism—the greater complexity of their texture
and the development of psychological questions raised by Soviet
reconstruction.

By the time Soviet letters had been reduced to an unparalleled
low level through the "social command" and the sheer terrorism

---

[7] But his fantastic satire *The Embezzlers* (1927) and his delightful farce *Squaring
the Circle* (1929) are likely to find more readers. Katáyev's younger brother Eugene
(1903–42) is the "Petróv" of the famous pair of humorists "Ilf and Petróv."

exercised by Áverbakh's group, Maxím Górky had returned to Russia to take up permanent residence there, and it is doubtless under his influence that the conditions of literary production were eventually improved. On April 23, 1932, came the Central Committee's decree liquidating RAPP and creating a single union of Soviet writers, which both Communists and non-party-members were invited to join. At a great literary congress held in 1934, the need to improve the standards of literature was stressed, and relatively free discussion was encouraged of the problems facing Soviet writers. The stenographic report of this congress, which includes speeches by practically everyone of any importance in Soviet letters at the time, is of inestimable value to the student.

Since 1932 the general organization of Soviet literature has remained unaltered, and all writers are pledged to work together in harmony under the approved slogan of "Socialist Realism." Fortunately, this official style for all writing published in the Soviet Union has never been unambiguously defined, and, although certain works (like Shólokhov's *The Silent Don* and A. N. Tolstóy's *The Road to Calvary* and the unfinished *Peter I*) have been especially acclaimed as triumphs of socialist realism, there is still room for disagreement concerning its essentials. A few points, however, are eminently clear. For one thing, socialist realism is strictly opposed to the heresy of "formalism," by which Soviet critics tend to designate any obtrusive experimentation in literary technique. Socialist realism is also frequently contrasted with pre-Revolutionary, "bourgeois," critical realism, whose chief task was (and still is, in capitalist countries) to expose the abuses of a corrupt system. For although more or less room, depending on the expediencies of the moment, is left for "self-criticism," [8] the satirist must preserve a fundamental optimism if he is not to be called to accounts as a calumniator of the Soviet people. He must take pride in the frank tendentiousness, the open partisanship or "party-ness" (*partíynost*) of whatever he writes, and in times of particular stress the demands of *partíynost* will be especially heavy.

As the threat of war increased, party policy steered in the

---

[8] Under this heading has been included such contemporary satire as that of Valentine Katáyev, Ilf and Petróv, and Zóschenko (but the works of the last-named writer—or "pseudo writer," as he is now called—were declared "alien to Soviet literature" by the Central Committee in 1946). During the last war Alexander Korneychúk's play *The Front* (1942), criticizing inefficient Red Army officers of the older generation, was accepted as legitimate self-criticism.

direction of affirming the continuity of the national traditions, and
the increased output of historical fiction and drama is the most
notable single feature of the literature of the late thirties. The new
line was made clear in the usual way when, in 1936, no less a person
than the unofficial poet laureate of the Revolution, Demián Bédny
(pseudonym of Efím Pridvórov, 1883–1945), was publicly censured
for having disregarded it in his play *Heroes* (*Bogatyrí*). The play
was officially declared to represent an unfounded aspersion on the
heroes of the Russian *bylíny*, the chief of whom "represent in
the popular imagination the bearers of the historic features of the
Russian people," and it was removed from the boards as "alien to
Soviet art." This is the period that saw the triumph of heroic
nationalism in the works of A. N. Tolstóy (1882–1945) and S. N.
Sergéyev-Tsénsky, as well as the glorification of such national
heroes as Alexander Névsky, Dmítry Donskóy, Iván the Terrible,
Generalissimo Suvórov, Field Marshal Kutúzov, and military
leaders of even more recent history by a host of Soviet novelists
and playwrights.[9]

When war came, most of the leading Soviet authors turned
from their peacetime work to the job of reporting on the military
or industrial fronts. Tíkhonov, speaking to the Union of Soviet
Writers in May 1945, was able to state that some three hundred
writers had been decorated for their war services and that a hundred
and forty had died on the field of battle. The novels, plays, poems,
and sketches that appeared during the war mark only the beginning of what will undoubtedly be a "patriotic war" period of
Soviet letters. Soviet literary periodicals continue to devote the
major portion of their space to various facets of the great subject,
while critics are still heard to complain that the most important
side—the psychology of the Soviet hero—has not, in general, received satisfactory treatment. Here it may be suggested that a
long Soviet critical tradition of distrust towards "psychologism,"
combined with a tendency to interpret individual character creations schematically and in too generalized a manner, has borne
and continues to bear unwelcome fruit. It is hardly surprising that
the average writer prefers to sketch his hero in broad outline rather

[9] Earlier Soviet historical fiction, when it was not centered on the October Revo-
lution, was especially successful in fictional literary biographies. In this class Yúry
Tynyánov's novels about Küchelbecker (*Kyúkhlya,* 1925), Griboyédov (*Smert
Vazír-Mukhtára,* 1929), and *Púshkin* (1936) are easily the best.

than be charged with harboring a morbid interest in individual psychology, or—worse—with introducing some trait unbecoming to a hero of Soviet society. Meanwhile, in war literature, as in the literature of the Five-Year Plan, the "leather jackets," as A. N. Tolstóy called these faceless heroes, continue to multiply.

At the end of the war, during the short era of good feeling among the Allies, it was natural for foreign observers to hope for improved international literary relations and a corresponding decrease in the cultural isolationism that had been an unhappy feature of Soviet literature since the first Five-Year Plan. There is good reason to believe that this hope was shared by many writers within the Soviet Union as well, but it was soon crushed. On August 14, 1946, the Central Committee issued a decree specifically directed against the Leningrad literary reviews *Star* and *Leningrád* for publishing works "alien to Soviet literature," but also laying down the general cultural line for the period of postwar reconstruction. This decree, with its exegesis by Zhdánov, who was put in charge of carrying out reforms, and the much-publicized purges in both the arts and the sciences, all express a common reaction against Western trends within Soviet culture and a renewed emphasis on the didactic role of art, with its special obligation of inculcating the ideals of Soviet patriotism. "Groveling imitation" of the West—whether in literary style or in genetics—is everywhere berated, and Soviet literature seems condemned, for a time at least, to a routine of government-issue edification such as dried up its springs in the late twenties and early thirties. The bad effects of this shortsighted policy are already being felt, and when the minor, latter-day Averbakhs of the new reformation are eventually "unmasked," they will have much to answer for.

In the unfamiliar atmosphere of government edicts on cultural matters, literary purges, public confessions and penance of erring writers, and the hothouse aroma of much orthodox Marxist criticism, the outsider, on his first acquaintance with Soviet literature, runs the risk of seeing only its novelties and failing to notice its many points of contact with pre-Revolutionary Russian culture. But if he is observant, he will soon be reminded that this literature was not brought forth in a vacuum, and that it still draws nourishment from native sources. Soviet literary historians (who, incidentally, have added greatly to our knowledge about pre-Revolutionary Russian literature) rightly affirm the continuity of the

Russian tradition into present-day writing. This is not to say, of course, that all the elements of that tradition have survived with equal vigor (something hardly to be expected in any case), and even some of the best legacies of nineteenth-century Russia will no doubt long be treasured abroad more highly than at home (so, paradoxically, the mature Dostoyévsky and his spiritual progeny). Nor is it to say that Soviet literature is simply a continuation of Russian literature. As the expression, however muffled at times it may be, of a new and different society, it is necessarily something much more than that. But if there was ever a time when a deracinated, cosmopolitan culture might have been expected to flourish on Soviet Russian soil, that time has passed, and the student of Soviet literature, like the student of Soviet history, will find that his subject begins long before 1917.

Short English Bibliography

1. General Works

MAURICE BARING: *Landmarks in Russian Literature* (New York, 1910)

——: *An Outline of Russian Literature* (New York, 1914)

ALEXANDER BRUECKNER: *A Literary History of Russia* (London, 1908)

H. W. L. DANA: *Drama in Wartime Russia* (New York, 1943)

——: *Handbook on Soviet Drama* (New York, 1938)

MAX EASTMAN: *Artists in Uniform; a study of literature and bureaucratism* (New York, 1934)

JOSEPH FREEMAN, J. KUNITZ, L. LOZOWICK: *Voices of October; art and literature in Soviet Russia* (New York, 1930)

N. K. GUDZY: *History of Early Russian Literature* (New York, 1949)

I. F. HAPGOOD: *The Epic Songs of Russia* (New York, 1886)

RICHARD HARE: *Russian Literature from Pushkin to the Present Day* (London, 1947)

NORRIS HOUGHTON: *Moscow Rehearsals; an account of methods of production in the Soviet theatre* (New York, 1936)

NADINE JARINTZOV: *Russian Poets and Poems* (New York, 1917)

A. S. KAUN: *Soviet Poets and Poetry* (Berkeley, 1943)

P. A. KROPOTKIN: *Russian Literature* (New York, 1905) (later published as *Ideals and Realities in Russian Literature*)

JANKO LAVRIN: *An Introduction to the Russian Novel* (London, 1942)

——: *Russian Literature* (London, 1927)

KURT LONDON: *The Seven Soviet Arts* (London, 1937)

J. T. G. MACLEOD: *Actors Across the Volga: a study of the 19th century Russian theatres and of Soviet theatres in war* (London, 1946)

——: *The New Soviet Theatre* (London, 1943)

P. A. MARKOV: *The Soviet Theatre* (London, 1934)

T. G. MASARYK: *The Spirit of Russia; studies in history, literature and philosophy* (New York, 1919)

P. N. MILIUKOV: *Outlines of Russian Culture* (edited by Michael Karpovich) (Philadelphia, 1942)

D. S. MIRSKY: *Contemporary Russian Literature, 1881–1925* (New York, 1926)

——: *A History of Russian Literature from the Earliest Times to the Death of Dostoyevsky (1881)* (New York, 1927)

——: *Modern Russian Literature* (London, 1925)

HELEN MUCHNIC: *An Introduction to Russian Literature* (New York, 1947)

R. H. NEWMARCH: *Poetry and Progress in Russia* (New York, 1907)

M. J. OLGIN: *A Guide to Russian Literature (1820–1917)* (New York, 1920)

S. M. PERSKY: *Contemporary Russian Novelists* (Boston, 1913)

W. L. PHELPS: *Essays on Russian Novelists* (New York, 1911)

GEORGE REAVEY: *Soviet Literature To-day* (London, 1946)

H. G. SCOTT, EDITOR: *Problems of Soviet Literature; reports and speeches at the first Soviet writers' congress* (New York, 1935)

E. J. SIMMONS: *An Outline of Modern Russian Literature (1880–1940)* (Ithaca, 1943)

IVAR SPECTOR: *The Golden Age of Russian Literature* (Caldwell, Idaho, 1943)
GLEB STRUVE: *25 Years of Soviet Russian Literature (1918–1943)* (London, 1944)
LEON TROTSKY: *Literature and Revolution* (New York, 1925)
MELCHIOR DE VOGÜÉ: *The Russian Novel* (London, 1913)
KAZIMIERZ WALISZEWSKI: *A History of Russian Literature* (New York, 1900)
LEO WIENER: *The Contemporary Drama of Russia* (Boston, 1924)

2. Anthologies

(entered under names of editors and translators)

ALEXANDER BAKSHY: *Soviet Scene; six plays of Russian life* (New Haven, 1946)
BEN BLAKE: *Four Soviet Plays* (New York, 1937)
JOHN BOWRING: *Specimens of the Russian Poets* (2 volumes) (London, 1821, 1823)
C. M. BOWRA: *A Book of Russian Verse* (London, 1943)
——: *A Second Book of Russian Verse* (London, 1948)
JOHN COURNOS: *Short Stories out of Soviet Russia* (New York, 1929)
——: *A Treasury of Russian Life and Humor* (New York, 1943)
C. F. COXWELL: *Russian Poems* (London, 1929)
H. W. L. DANA: *Seven Soviet Plays* (New York, 1946)
BABETTE DEUTSCH, A. YARMOLINSKY: *Russian Poetry* (New York, 1930)
ELIZAVETA FEN: *Modern Russian Stories* (London, 1943)
——: *Soviet Stories of the Last Decade* (London, 1945)
J. FINEBERG: *Heroic Leningrad; documents, sketches and stories* (Moscow, 1945)
A. FLORES: *Literature and Marxism; a controversy of Soviet critics* (New York, 1938)
L. S. FRIEDLAND, J. R. PIROSHNIKOFF: *Flying Osip; stories of new Russia* (London, 1925)
STEPHEN GRAHAM: *Great Russian Short Stories* (New York, 1929)
M. GRINDEA: *Soviet Literature, Art, Music* (London, 1942)
B. G. GUERNEY: *The Portable Russian Reader* (New York, 1947)
——: *A Treasury of Russian Literature* (New York, 1943)
S. KONOVALOV: *Bonfire; stories out of Soviet Russia* (London, 1932)
JOSHUA KUNITZ: *Russian Literature since the Revolution* (New York, 1948)
JANKO LAVRIN: *A First Series of Representative Russian Stories, Pushkin to Gorky* (London, 1946)
EUGENE LYONS: *Six Soviet Plays* (Boston, 1934)
IVOR MONTAGUE, H. MARSHALL: *Soviet Short Stories* (London, 1942)
G. R. NOYES: *Masterpieces of the Russian Drama* (New York, 1933)
G. Z. PATRICK: *Popular Poetry in Soviet Russia* (Berkeley, 1929)
GEORGE REAVEY, M. SLONIM: *Soviet Literature; an anthology* (New York, 1934)
J. J. ROBBINS: *Azure Cities; stories of new Russia* (New York, 1929)
JOHN RODKER: *Soviet Anthology* (London, 1943)
P. SELVER: *Modern Russian Poetry* (New York, 1917)
GERARD SHELLEY: *Modern Poems from Russia* (London, 1942)
MARK VAN DOREN: *The Night of the Summer Solstice, and other stories of the Russian war* (New York, 1943)
LEO WIENER: *Anthology of Russian Literature from the Earliest Period to the Present Time* (2 volumes) (New York, 1902–3)
AVRAHM YARMOLINSKY: *A Treasury of Russian Verse* (New York, 1949)

Index

i

A NOTE ON THE TYPE
IN WHICH THIS BOOK IS SET

The text of this book was set on the Monotype in Scotch, a typeface that has been in continuous service for more than one hundred years. It is usually considered that the style of "modern face" followed in our present-day cuttings of Scotch was developed in the foundry of Alexander Wilson and Sons of Glasgow early in the nineteenth century. The new Wilson patterns were made to meet the requirements of the new fashion in printing that had been set going at the beginning of the century by the "modern" types of Didot in France and of Bodoni in Italy. It is to be observed that the modern *in these matters is a modernity of* A.D. *1800, not of today.*

The book was composed, printed, and bound by Kingsport Press, Inc., Kingsport, Tennessee.